Lecture Notes in Artificial Intelligence   3658

Edited by J. G. Carbonell and J. Siekmann

Subseries of Lecture Notes in Computer Science

Václav Matoušek   Pavel Mautner
Tomáš Pavelka (Eds.)

Text, Speech and Dialogue

8th International Conference, TSD 2005
Karlovy Vary, Czech Republic, September 12-15, 2005
Proceedings

 Springer

Series Editors

Jaime G. Carbonell, Carnegie Mellon University, Pittsburgh, PA, USA
Jörg Siekmann, University of Saarland, Saarbrücken, Germany

Volume Editors

Václav Matoušek
Pavel Mautner
Tomáš Pavelka
University of West Bohemia in Pilsen
Department of Computer Science
Univerzitni 8, 30614 Plzen, Czech Republic
E-mail: {matousek,mautner,tpavelka}@kiv.zcu.cz

Library of Congress Control Number: 2005931927

CR Subject Classification (1998): I.2.7, I.2, H.3, H.4, I.7

ISSN   0302-9743
ISBN-10   3-540-28789-2 Springer Berlin Heidelberg New York
ISBN-13   978-3-540-28789-6 Springer Berlin Heidelberg New York

Springer is a part of Springer Science+Business Media

springeronline.com

© Springer-Verlag Berlin Heidelberg 2005
Printed in Germany

Typesetting: Camera-ready by author, data conversion by Olgun Computergrafik
Printed on acid-free paper   SPIN: 11551874   06/3142   5 4 3 2 1 0

Preface

The International Conference TSD 2005, the 8h event in the series on Text, Speech, and Dialogue, which originated in 1998, presented state-of-the-art technology and recent achievements in the field of natural language processing. It declared its intent to be an interdisciplinary forum, intertwining research in speech and language processing with its applications in everyday practice. We feel that the mixture of different approaches and applications offered a great opportunity to get acquainted with the current activities in all aspects of language communication and to witness the amazing vitality of researchers from developing countries too. The financial support of the ISCA (International Speech Communication Association) enabled the wide attendance of researchers from all active regions of the world.

This year's conference was partially oriented towards multi-modal human-computer interaction (HCI), which can be seen as the most attractive topic of HCI at the present time. In this way, we are involved in a rich complex of communicative activity, facial expressions, hand gestures, direction of gaze, to name but the most obvious ones. The interpretation of each user utterance depends on the context, prosody, facial expressions (e.g. brows raised, brows and gaze both raised) and gestures. Hearers have to adapt to the speaker (e.g. maintaining the theme of the conversation, smiling etc.). Research into the interaction of these channels is however limited, often focusing on the interaction between a pair of channels. Six significant scientific results achieved in this area in the USA, Japan, Switzerland, Germany, The Netherlands, and the Czech Republic were presented by keynote speakers in special plenary sessions. Further, approx. 35 % of all submitted papers and their presentations were oriented towards multi-modal interaction as well.

This volume contains a collection of all the papers presented at the international conference organized by the Faculty of Applied Sciences of the University of West Bohemia in Pilsen in collaboration with the Faculty of Informatics, Masaryk University in Brno, and held in the world-famous spa town Karlovy Vary (West Bohemia, Czech Republic), September 12–16, 2005. Theoretical and more general contributions were presented in common (plenary) sessions. Problem oriented sessions as well as panel discussions then brought together the specialists in limited problem areas with the aim of exchanging the knowledge and skills resulting from research projects of all kinds. Each of the submitted papers was thoroughly reviewed by three members of the conference reviewing team consisting of more than 40 top specialists in the conference topic areas. A total of 52 accepted papers out of 134 submitted, altogether contributed by 131 authors and co-authors, were selected for presentation at the conference by the program committee and then included in this book.

We would like to gratefully thank the invited speakers and the authors of the papers for their valuable contributions and the ISCA for its financial support. Last but not least, we would like to express our gratitude to the authors for providing their papers on time, to the members of the conference reviewing team and program committee for their careful reviews and paper selection, to the editors for their hard work in preparing this volume, and to the members of the local organizing committee for their enthusiasm in organizing the conference.

June 2005   Václav Matoušek

Organization

TSD 2005 was organized by the Faculty of Applied Sciences, University of West Bohemia in Plzeň (Pilsen), in cooperation with the Faculty of Informatics, Masaryk University in Brno, Czech Republic. The conference Web–page is located at URL:

http://www.kiv.zcu.cz/events/tsd2005/.

Program Committee

Frederick Jelinek (USA), *general chair*
Hynek Heřmanský (Switzerland), *executive chair*
Eneko Agirre (Spain)
Geneviève Baudoin (France)
Jan Černocký (Czech Republic)
Attila Ferencz (Romania)
Alexander Gelbukh (Mexico)
Eva Hajičová (Czech Republic)
Jaroslava Hlaváčová (Czech Republic)
Eduard Hovy (USA)
Ivan Kopeček (Czech Republic)
Steven Krauwer (The Netherlands)
Ramesh Krishnamurthy (UK)
Cvetana Krstev (Serbia)
Václav Matoušek (Czech Republic)
Chafic Mokbel (Lebanon)
Elmar Nöth (Germany)
Karel Oliva (Austria)
Karel Pala (Czech Republic)
Nikola Pavešić, (Slovenia)
Vladimír Petkevič (Czech Republic)
Fabio Pianesi (Italy)
Josef Psutka (Czech Republic)
James Pustejovsky (USA)
Léon J. M. Rothkrantz (The Netherlands)
Ernst Günter Schukat-Talamazzini (Germany)
Pavel Skrelin (Russia)
Pavel Smrž (Czech Republic)
Taras Vintsiuk (Ukraine)
Yorick Wilks (UK)
Victor Zacharov (Russia)

Local Organizing Committee

Václav Matoušek *(chair)*, David Andrš, Milan Beránek, Kamil Ekštein, Jana Hesová, Svatava Kindlová, Jana Klečková, Miloslav Konopík, Jana Krutišová, Tomáš Maršálek, Pavel Mautner, Michal Merta, Roman Mouček, Helena Ptáčková *(secretary)*, Tomáš Pavelka, Pavel Slavík

Supported by: International Speech Communication Association (ISCA)

About Karlovy Vary

Karlovy Vary (Carlsbad) is the largest and best-known spa in the Czech Republic. The town is located not far from the Czech-German border. The distance between Karlovy Vary and Prague, the Czech capital, is 125 km. The altitude of the town is 370 m above sea level and surrounding hills reach up to 644 m. The climate is foothills. The town has 55,000 inhabitants. The architecture and the design of this spa city are closely connected with the function of this city of springs. The city or, more precisely, the city's spa centre, which is the most attractive part from the visitors' point of view, is situated around the meandering Teplá River. The river has been cutting through the hilly landscape full of forests and other vegetation since ancient times.

The oldest records of the settlement of this area go back roughly to the mid-14th century, when the valley around Hot Spring began to be settled on a continuous basis. The written history of the spa city began on 14 August 1370 when Charles IV granted the existing settlement freedoms and rights enjoyed by the nearby royal city of Loket at that time. The privileged status of Karlovy Vary as a spa is shown by a great number of granted privileges confirmed by the Bohemian rulers on an ongoing basis until 1858. The Karlovy Vary spa consisted in particular of baths from the Middle Ages until the late 16th century. Drinking the waters started to gain ground at the suggestion of the doctor Václav Payer who published his first expert book on the Karlovy Vary spa treatment in Leipzig in 1522. In his book, he recommended thermal water drinking besides taking baths. The local doctors Michael Reudenius and Johann Stephan Strobelberger became other enthusiastic promoters of drinking the waters in Karlovy Vary after 1600.

The initial Gothic and Renaissance town, later bearing the imprint of the Baroque style, was seriously damaged by two large fires in 1604 and 1759. The following stage of development, placed in the time period from the beginning to the first half of the 19th century, was overridden by the period of urban and architectural development of the settlement that followed afterwards. The buildings in the Classicist, Empire, Rococo or Biedermaier styles that were outdated or not corresponding to the new spirit of the time were gradually cleared to make space for the developments that already had the parameters required for existence in a by now world-famous spa. This period falls into the last third of the 19th century and continues into the beginning of the 20th century. Buildings, structures, parks, forest trails and other amenities of the urban environment that were coming into existence in this span of time give the face to the modern Karlovy Vary, as well. For this reason, the city spa centre is admired for the unity but not uniformity of its style and architecture. Uniformity is eliminated as the architecture of the city is imbued with the spirit of historicism, eclecticism and Art Nouveau.

Karlovy Vary is a city of colonnades. The best-known colonnade, which every spa visitor is sure to see, is the Hot Spring Colonnade. Over the time of the city's existence, it has changed its appearance several times. The original wooden garden-house over Hot Spring itself and the wooden troughs across the Teplá river distributing the thermal water to separate houses in Tržiště vanished long ago. The fine and delicate colonnade in the Empire style has disappeared as well. Also the imposing colonnade of cast iron was removed thanks to the second world war. The present colonnade conforms to the time when it was erected. The glass body of the massive colonnade of today, much too robust and not really matching the delicate environment of the spa, is awaiting a general renovation that is to take place shortly. It should convert the colonnade into a temple of health, corresponding to the local atmosphere. The Mill Colonnade should be declared as paramount to all of the others in the city. None other than Josef Zítek, the renowned architect of the Neo-Renaissance style, is its author. It is a structure featuring the main three-bay hall spatially zoned with Corinthian columns bearing the panel ceiling of the main terrace. Roughly in the middle, the hall is widened with a semicircle niche serving as an orchestra pit. The central parts of the colonnade are emphasized by Zítek's pavilion, partly used as a spa café. The terrace over the pavilion and the terrace referred to above are floodlit and used as a spa promenade. Another colonnade, so inseparable from the local colour of Karlovy Vary, is the Market Colonnade. It was constructed in 1883 in place of the former town hall. Immediately after the erection, the colonnade was extended to form a street frontage with small shops designed in a similar style. Both of the structures are linked, constructed of wood, and their architectural impression is clearly that of a spa.

Karlovy Vary can be proud of its extraordinary rich cultural tradition. It is caused in particular by centuries-old visits to the spa city. Every visitor, not only the famous ones, has been an asset and valuable testimonial for Karlovy Vary. That is why the inhabitants of Karlovy Vary have always respected their guests very much and have tried to make their spa stay pleasant in every way possible. The spa society meeting in Karlovy Vary has been gaining in international character since the early 18th century. Besides the aristocracy, the European cultured elite have liked to stay close to the Thermal Spring. Visits of celebrities are a traditional speciality of Karlovy Vary and have had a great impact on and have enriched the city's history. Karlovy Vary has been popular in particular among celebrities from the worlds of music, literature and poetry. Making a list of famous guests of Karlovy Vary according to their popularity at the Thermal Spring, we should place Johann Wolfgang Goethe, a German poet, first, and the Russian czar Peter the Great undoubtedly second. Both of the men went down in the cultural history of Karlovy Vary in a very significant manner. Their stay in the most famous Czech spa is commemorated by dozens of memorial plaques, monuments, books, stories and legends.

Karlovy Vary has not only its spa centre, but also surrounding satellite quarters gradually affiliated to the original historical centre. Similar to other towns in the country, these districts provide housing for most of the population in a more or less successful way. Also, manufacturing facilities and services are concentrated there. Moser glass and Karlovarská Becherovka (38 % alcohol, 10 % sugar, known as "the 13th spring"), are the traditional specialties of Karlovy Vary. The Karlovy Vary International Film Festival annually presents more than 200 category A films from the whole world. The last, the 40th International Film Festival, was organized July 1–9, 2005 and attended by many world-famous film stars.

Table of Contents

Speech

Dialogue

Language Modeling Experiments with Random Forests

Frederick Jelinek

Johns Hopkins University, Center for Language and Speech Processing
309 Barton Hall, 3400 N. Charles St., Baltimore, MD 21218
jelinek@clsp.jhu.edu

Abstract. L. Breiman recently introduced the concept of random forests (randomly constructed collection of decision trees) for classification. We have modified the method for regression and applied it to language modeling for speech recognition. Random forests achieve excellent results in both perplexity and error rate. They can be regarded as a language model in HMM form and have interesting properties that achieve very robust smoothing.

V. Matoušek et al. (Eds.): TSD 2005, LNAI 3658, p. 1, 2005.

The Role of Speech
in Multimodal Human-Computer Interaction
(Towards Reliable Rejection of Non-keyword Input)

Hynek Hermansky, Petr Fousek, and Mikko Lehtonen

IDIAP Research Institute, Martigny, Switzerland
{hermansky,fousek,mlehton}@idiap.ch

Abstract. Natural audio-visual interface between human user and machine requires understanding of user's audio-visual commands. This does not necessarily
require full speech and image recognition. It does require, just as the interaction
with any working animal does, that the machine is capable of reacting to certain particular sounds and/or gestures while ignoring the rest. Towards this end,
we are working on sound identification and classification approaches that would
ignore most of the acoustic input and react only to a particular sound (keyword).

1 Introduction

Daily experience suggests that not all words in the conversation, but only a few important ones, need to be accurately recognized for satisfactory speech communication
among human beings. The important key-words are more likely to be rare-occurring
high-information-valued words. Human listeners can identify such words in the conversation and possibly devote extra effort to their decoding. On the other hand, in a typical
automatic speech recognition (ASR) system, acoustics of frequent words are likely to
be better estimated in the training phase and language model is also likely to substitute
rare words by frequent ones. As a consequence, important rare words are less likely
to be well recognized. Keyword spotting by-passes this problem by attempting to find
and recognize only certain words in the utterance while ignoring the rest. Doing this in
a confident way would open new possibilities in human-computer interaction.

2 Proposed Approach

Since keyword spotting is relatively younger than ASR, it is not clear if the LVCSR-
based keyword spotting approaches are a consequence of a simple inertia in engineering
where any new problem is seen in the terms of the old one, or the optimal strategy. In
this work we study an alternative approach where the goal is to find the target sounds
from an acoustic stream while ignoring the rest.

Towards this goal, we propose hierarchical processing where first equally-spaced
posterior probabilities of phoneme classes are derived from the signal, followed by
estimation of the probability of the given keyword from the sequence of phoneme posteriors.

V. Matoušek et al. (Eds.): TSD 2005, LNAI 3658, pp. 2–8, 2005.

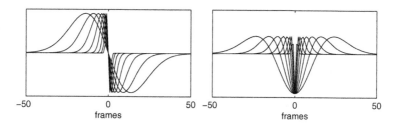

Fig. 1. Normalized impulse responses of the two sampled and truncated Gaussian derivatives for $\sigma = 8 - 130$ ms.

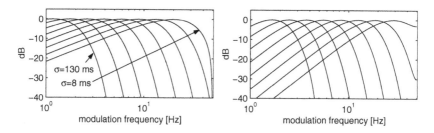

Fig. 2. Normalized frequency responses of first two sampled and truncated Gaussian derivatives for $\sigma = 8 - 130$ ms.

3   Steps of Hierarchical Processing

3.1   From Acoustic Stream to Phoneme Posteriors

The first step derives estimates of phoneme posteriors at 10 ms steps (100 Hz sampling rate) from the speech data. This is accomplished as follows: First a critical-band spectral analysis (auditory spectral analysis step from PLP technique [1] is carried out and a bank of 2-D bandpass filters with varying temporal and spectral resolutions is applied to the resulting critical-band spectrogram. We implemented the 2-D filtering by first processing a trajectory of each critical band with temporal filters and subsequently applied frequency filters to the result. By filtering temporal trajectory of each critical band with a bank of fixed length low-pass FIR filters representing Gaussian functions of several different widths (determined by standard deviation σ) and by subsequently computing first and second differentials of the smoothed trajectories we would obtain a set of modified spectra at every time step. The same filter-bank is applied to all bands.

In the implementation, we use directly the discrete versions of the first and second analytic derivatives of a Gaussian function as impulse responses. Filters with low σ values yield finer temporal resolution, high σ filters cover wider temporal context and yield smoother trajectories. All temporal filters are zero-phase FIR filters, i.e. they are centered around the frame being processed. Length of all filters is fixed at 101 frames, corresponding to roughly 1000 ms of signal, thus introducing a processing delay of 500 ms. First and second derivatives of Gaussian function have zero-mean by the definition. By using such impulse responses we gain an implicit mean normalization of

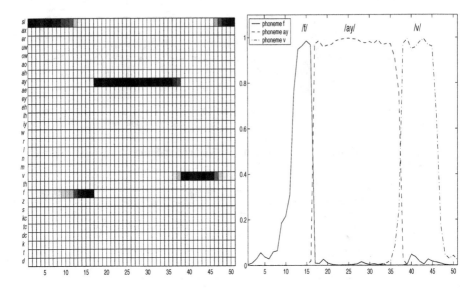

Fig. 3. Left: Posteriogram of the word *five* followed by silence. Right: Trajectories of phoneme probability estimates.

the features within a temporal region proportional to the σ value, which infers robustness to linear distortions. Since we use discrete impulse responses with a length fixed at 101 samples, we approximate real Gaussian derivatives with certain error, which increases towards both extremes of σ, thus limiting the possible σ values to a range of approximately 6–130 ms. In our experiments we use eight logarithmically spaced impulse responses in a σ range 8–130 ms. These responses representing the first and the second Gaussian derivatives are shown in the left and right parts of Fig. 1, respectively. Related frequency responses are illustrated in Fig. 2.

Temporal filtering of 15 critical band trajectories with a bank of 2×8 filters (two derivatives of the Gaussian at eight different standard deviations) results in 16 modified auditory spectra at every 10 ms step, containing overall $15 \times 2 \times 8 = 240$ features.

Subsequently we implement the full 2-D filtering by applying frequency filters to the modified auditory spectra. The first frequency derivative is approximated by a 3-tap FIR filter with impulse response {-1.0; 0.0; 1.0}, introducing three-bands frequency context. This time-invariant filter is applied across frequency to each of the 16 modified auditory spectra. Since derivatives for the first and last critical bands are not defined, we obtain $(15 - 2) \times 16 = 208$ features.

Final feature vector is formed by concatenating the 240 features from temporal filtering with the 208 features from the full 2-D filtering, thus yielding 448 features. This feature vector is fed to an MLP neural net classifier (TANDEM probability estimator [2]), which is trained to give an estimate of phoneme posterior probabilities at every 10 ms step (phoneme posteriogram). An example of such phoneme posteriogram for the word "five" is shown in Fig. 3. The keyword is in this case easy to spot because the phoneme segments are well classified in the posteriogram. However, this is not always

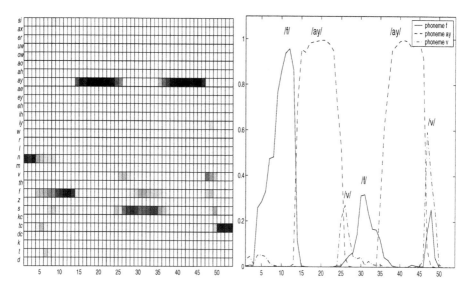

Fig. 4. Left: Posteriogram of a sequence *five five* with classification errors and weak posteriors. Right: Trajectories of phoneme probability estimates.

the case. Fig. 4 illustrates a more difficult case for the same word, where the speech rate is higher and there are classification errors. More details of the technique can be found in [3].

3.2   From Phoneme Posteriors to Words

Multiple input, two-node output MLP is used for mapping of relatively long (1010 ms) span of the posteriogram to a posterior probability of a given key-word being within this time span.

Thus, the input to the MLP is a 2929-dimensional vector (29 phoneme posteriors at 100 Hz frame rate). The MLP is trained on the training part of the OGI Digits database (about 1.3 hours of speech), containing 11 digits from zero to nine (including "oh").

In the operation, the input phoneme posteriogram of the unknown utterance is converted to the key-word posteriogram by sliding the 1010 ms window frame-by-frame over the phoneme posteriogram. A typical keyword posteriogram is shown in Fig. 5.

Even though (as illustrated in the figure) to human eye the frame-based posterior estimates usually clearly indicate the presence of the underlying word, the step from the frame-based estimates to word-level estimates is very important. It involves nontrivial operation of information rate reduction (carried sub-consciously by human visual perception while studying the posteriogram) where the equally sampled estimates at the 100 Hz sampling rate are to be reduced to non-equally sampled estimates of word probabilities. In the conventional (HMM-based) system, this is accomplished by searching for an appropriate underlying sequence of hidden states.

We have opted for more direct communication-oriented approach where we postulated existence of a matched filter for temporal trajectories of word posteriors, with

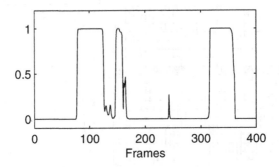

Fig. 5. An example of key-word posteriogram.

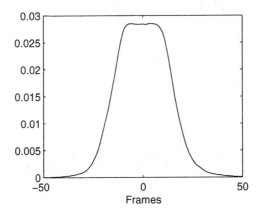

Fig. 6. Impulse response of the key-word matched filter.

impulse response derived by averaging 1 s long segments of trajectories of the respective words, aligned at the word centers. In deriving these averages, we need to deal with cases where the window contains more than one key-word. In the current work, these segments were not included in computing the average.

Resulting filter is shown in Fig. 6, and an example of the filtered posteriogram is illustrated in Fig. 7.

In the next step, local maxima (peaks) for each filtered trajectory were found. The values in the peaks were taken as estimates of probability that the center of the given word is aligned with the center of the impulse response of the respective matched filter and retained, all other data were discarded. An example of such a peak can be seen in Fig. 7.

The whole technique is schematically illustrated in Fig. 8.

4   Results

As a test we have processed about 104 minutes of speech data containing fluent pronunciation of digit strings (OGI Numbers [4]). Among 12389 digits, there were 1532

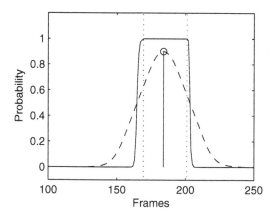

Fig. 7. Raw time trajectory of key-word posterior probability (solid line), filtered trajectory (dashed line) and estimated location of the key-word (circle). Region between dotted lines represents

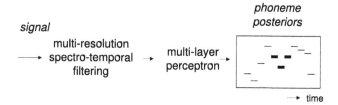

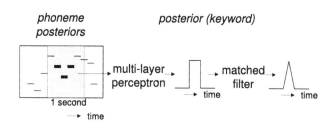

Fig. 8. Schematic diagram of the proposed technique.

"one"s. 1339 (87.4%) of these were correctly identified, and there were 19 (1.2%) false alarms and 193 (12.6%) misses. Most of misses are caused by smearing short drops in probability due to filtering (as discussed below) that may indicate a succession of several target words. Not counting these errors, the overall detection rate would be 93.4%.

5   Summary and Discussion

Hierarchical classification of relatively long chunks of speech signal has been applied to spotting a target word in speech stream. This hierarchical procedure estimates posterior probabilities of phonemes from multi-resolution speech representation obtained by time-frequency filtering of critical-band spectral energy, followed by the estimation of probability of occurrence of the targeted word in the neighborhood of the current time instant. A simple deletion of the speech signal for the instants where the trajectory is below certain threshold allows for retention of most of the targeted speech.

In order to uniquely identify the presence of the underlying target word, a simple procedure is introduced in which the time trajectory of key-word probability is filtered by a box-car shaped matched filter, representing mean length of the key-word and above-threshold peak of this trajectory indicate occurrence of the key-word. The filtering eliminates most of spurious short peaks, thus allowing for simple counting the identified key-words but it also often eliminates short drops in the probability due to several successive key-words which are then counted only as one word.

Result reported in this paper is very preliminary and should be taken only as an indication of feasibility of the proposed approach. Similar approach can be also applied to spotting of phonemes [5] and then digits could be represented as sequences of phonemes. Currently, such an approach yields yet significantly higher word-spotting detection rates.

The presented technique is very straightforward, involves neither any time-warping nor any searches, and can be implemented on-line with a relatively short algorithmic delay. It offers simple but interesting alternative to most of the current speech recognition approaches with a potential for further evolution.

References

1. Hermansky, H.: Perceptual linear predictive (PLP) analysis of speech, J. Acoust. Soc. Am., Vol. 87, No. 4, April 1990.
2. Hermansky, H., Ellis, D.P.W.E., Sharma, S.: Connectionist Feature Extraction for Conventional HMM Systems, Proc. of ICASSP 00, Istanbul, Turkey, 2000.
3. Hermansky, H., Fousek, P.: Multiresolution RASTA filtering for TANDEM-based ASR, Proc. of Interspeech 2005, Lisbon, Portugal, September 2005.
4. Cole, R.A., Noel, M., Lander, T., Durham, T.: New Telephone Speech Corpora at CSLU, In Proc. of Eurospeech '95, pp. 821–824, Madrid, Spain, 1995.
5. Lehtonen, M., Fousek, P., Hermansky, H.: Hierarchical Approach for Spotting Keywords, IDIAP Research Report, 2005.

Why Is the Recognition of Spontaneous Speech so Hard?

Sadaoki Furui, Masanobu Nakamura, Tomohisa Ichiba, and Koji Iwano

Tokyo Institute of Technology, Department of Computer Science
2-12-1 Ookayama, Meguro-ku, Tokyo, 152-8552 Japan
{furui,masa,tichiba,iwano}@furui.cs.titech.ac.jp
http://www.furui.cs.titech.ac.jp

Abstract. Although speech, derived from reading texts, and similar types of speech, e.g. that from reading newspapers or that from news broadcast, can be recognized with high accuracy, recognition accuracy drastically decreases for spontaneous speech. This is due to the fact that spontaneous speech and read speech are significantly different acoustically as well as linguistically. This paper reports analysis and recognition of spontaneous speech using a large-scale spontaneous speech database "Corpus of Spontaneous Japanese (CSJ)". Recognition results in this experiment show that recognition accuracy significantly increases as a function of the size of acoustic as well as language model training data and the improvement levels off at approximately 7M words of training data. This means that acoustic and linguistic variation of spontaneous speech is so large that we need a very large corpus in order to encompass the variations. Spectral analysis using various styles of utterances in the CSJ shows that the spectral distribution/difference of phonemes is significantly reduced in spontaneous speech compared to read speech. Experimental results also show that there is a strong correlation between mean spectral distance between phonemes and phoneme recognition accuracy. This indicates that spectral reduction is one major reason for the decrease of recognition accuracy of spontaneous speech.

1 Introduction

State-of-the-art speech recognition technology can achieve high recognition accuracies for read texts or limited domain spoken interactions. However, the accuracy is still rather poor for spontaneous speech, which is not as well structured acoustically and linguistically as read speech [1, 2]. Spontaneous speech includes filled pauses, repairs, hesitations, repetitions, partial words, and disfluencies. It is quite interesting to note that, although speech is almost always spontaneous, until recently speech recognition research has focused primarily on recognizing read speech. Spontaneous speech recognition as a specific research field has only recently emerged about 10 years ago within the wider field of automatic speech recognition (e.g. [3–7]). Effectively broadening the application of speech recognition depends crucially on raising recognition performance for spontaneous speech.

In order to increase recognition performance for spontaneous speech, it is necessary to build acoustic and language models specific to spontaneous speech. Our knowledge of the structure of spontaneous speech is currently insufficient to achieve necessary breakthroughs. Although spontaneous speech phenomena are quite common in human

V. Matoušek et al. (Eds.): TSD 2005, LNAI 3658, pp. 9–22, 2005.

communication and may increase in human machine discourse as people become more comfortable conversing with machines, analysis and modeling of spontaneous speech are only in the initial stages. It is widely well known that spectral distribution of continuously spoken vowels or syllables is much smaller than that of isolated spoken vowels or syllables, which is sometimes called spectral reduction. Similar reduction has also been observed for spontaneous speech in comparison with read speech (e.g. [8, 9]). However, as of yet no research has been conducted using a large spontaneous database nor on the relationships between the spectral reduction and spontaneous speech recognition performance.

The next section in this paper overviews our spontaneous speech project focusing on the large-scale Japanese spontaneous speech corpus, and reports results of speech recognition experiments using the spontaneous speech corpus, including several analyses on speech recognition errors. Then, the paper reports investigations on spectral reduction using cepstral features that are widely used in speech recognition, based on the spontaneous speech corpus. In the following section, the difference of distances between each pair of phonemes in spontaneous speech and that in read speech is analyzed, and the relationship between the phoneme distances and phoneme recognition performance in various speaking styles is investigated.

2   "Spontaneous Speech: Corpus and Processing Technology" Project

2.1   Overview of the Project

A 5-year Science and Technology Agency Priority Program entitled "Spontaneous Speech: Corpus and Processing Technology" was conducted in Japan from 1999 to 2004 [1], and accomplished the following three major objectives.

1. A large-scale spontaneous speech corpus, Corpus of Spontaneous Japanese (CSJ), consisting of roughly 7M words (morphemes) with a total speech length of 650 hours has been built [10, 11].
2. Acoustic and language modeling for spontaneous speech recognition and understanding using linguistic as well as para-linguistic information in speech was investigated [2].
3. Spontaneous speech recognition and summarization technology was investigated.

2.2   Corpus of Spontaneous Japanese (CSJ)

Mainly recorded in the Corpus of Spontaneous Japanese (CSJ) are monologues such as academic presentations (AP) and extemporaneous presentations (EP) as shown in Table 1. AP contains live recordings of academic presentations in nine different academic societies covering the fields of engineering, social science and humanities. EP is studio recordings of paid layman speakers' speech on everyday topics like "the most delightful memory of my life" presented in front of a small audience and in a relatively relaxed atmosphere. Therefore, the speaking style in EP is more informal than

Table 1. Contents of the CSJ

Type of speech	# speakers	# files	Monologue/ Dialogue	Spontaneous/ Read	Hours
Academic presentations (AP)	838	1006	Monolog	Spont.	299.5
Extemporaneous presentations (EP)	580	1715	Monolog	Spont.	327.5
Interview on AP	*(10)	10	Dialog	Spont.	2.1
Interview on EP	*(16)	16	Dialog	Spont.	3.4
Task oriented dialogue	*(16)	16	Dialog	Spont.	3.1
Free dialogue	*(16)	16	Dialog	Spont.	3.6
Reading text	*(244)	491	Dialog	Read	14.1
Reading transcriptions	*(16)	16	Monolog	Read	5.5
*Counted as the speakers of AP or EP				Total hours	658.8

in AP. Presentations reading text have been excluded from AP and EP. The EP recordings provide a more balanced representation of age and gender than the AP. The CSJ also includes a smaller database of dialogue speech for the purpose of comparison with monologue speech. The dialogue speech is composed of an interview, a task oriented dialogue, and a free dialogue. The "reading text" in the table indicates the speech reading novels including dialogues, and the "reading transcriptions" indicates the speech reading transcriptions of APs or EPs by the same speaker. The recordings were manually given orthographic and phonetic transcription. Spontaneous speech-specific phenomena, such as filled pauses, word fragments, reduced articulation or mispronunciation, and non-speech events like laughter and coughing were also carefully tagged. The "reading text" speech is not used in the analysis in this paper.

One-tenth of the utterances, hereafter referred to as the Core, were tagged manually and used for training a morphological analysis and part-of-speech (POS) tagging program [12] for automatically analyzing all of the 650-hour utterances. The Core consists of 70 APs, 107 EPs, 18 dialogues and 6 read speech files (speakers). They were also tagged with para-linguistic/intonation information, dependency-structure, discourse structure, and summarization. For intonation labeling of spontaneous speech, the traditional J_ToBI method [13] was extended to X_JToBI [14], in which inventories of tonal events as well as break indices were considerably enriched.

Figure 1 shows mean values of the ratio of disfluencies, specifically filled pauses (F), word fragments (D), and reduced articulation or mispronunciation (W), to the total number of words included in AP, EP, dialogues (interviews, task oriented dialogues and free dialogues), and utterances reading the transcription of AP (read transcription speech), respectively. These results show that approximately one-tenth of the words are disfluencies in the spontaneous speech in the CSJ, and there is no significant difference among the overall ratios of disfluencies in terms of AP, EP or dialogues. It is also observed that the ratio of F is significantly higher than that of D and W. The read transcription speech still include disfluencies, since they are reading transcriptions of a subset of AP.

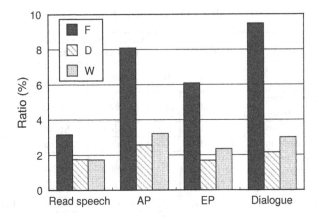

Fig. 1. Ratios of filled pauses (F), word fragments (D), and reduced articulation or mispronunciation (W) in AP, EP, dialogue, and read transcription speech

3   Progress Made and Difficulties Encountered in Spontaneous Speech Recognition

3.1   Test Sets for Technology Evaluation

In order to evaluate the spontaneous speech recognition technology, three test sets of presentations have been constructed from the CSJ so that they well represent the whole corpus with respect to various factors of spontaneous speech [15]. The analysis by Shinozaki et al. [16] (see Section 3.3) concluded that speaking rate (SR), out-of-vocabulary (OOV) rate (OR) and repair rate (RR) were three major speaker attributes highly correlated with accuracy. Other factors mainly depended on one or more of these three. For example, word perplexity (PP) was also highly correlated with the accuracy, but if its correlation with the OR was removed, we found actually that the correlation between PP and accuracy was significantly reduced. However, OR is intrinsically dependent on vocabulary and is thus variable when the lexicon is modified. On the other hand, the difference of PPs among speech data is generally more stable, even when the language model is revised. Therefore, we decided to take into account PP instead of OR, in combination with SR and RR, in the test-set selection.

Since the speaking styles and vocabularies of AP and EP are significantly different, we set up respective test sets. In addition, considering the fact that most of the AP presentations were given by male speakers, we set up two sets for the academic category: a male-only set and a gender-balanced set. Thus, we have three test sets, each of which consists of 10 speakers: male speakers AP, gender-balanced AP, and gender-balanced EP. The remaining AP as well as EP presentations, excluding those having overlap with the test sets in terms of speakers, were set up as training data (510 hours, 6.84 M words). The utterances were digitized by 16 kHz and converted into a sequence of feature vectors consisting of MFCC (Mel-frequency cepstrum coefficients), ΔMFCC and Δlog-energy features, using a 25 ms-length window shifted every 10 ms. Benchmark

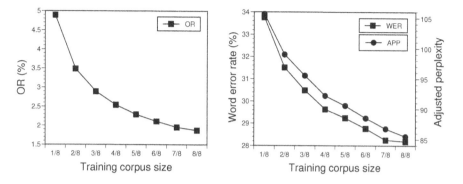

Fig. 2. Word error rate (WER), adjusted test-set perplexity (APP) and out-of-vocabulary (OOV) rate (OR) as a function of the size of language model training data

results of speech recognition using these three test sets have also been presented in our previous paper [15].

3.2 Effectiveness of Corpora

By constructing acoustic and language models using the CSJ, recognition errors for spontaneous presentation were reduced to roughly half compared to models constructed using read speech and written text [1, 3]. Increasing the size of training data for acoustic and language models has decreased the recognition error rate (WER: word error rate) as shown in Figures 2 and 3 [17]. They show the results averaged over the three test sets. Figure 2 indicates WER, adjusted test-set perplexity (APP) [18] and OOV rate (OR), as a function of the size of language model training data with the condition that the acoustic model is constructed using the whole training data set (510 hours). The adjusted perplexity was used, since it normalizes the effect of the reduction of OOV rate on the perplexity according to the increase of training data size. On the other hand, Figure 3 shows WER as a function of the size of acoustic model training data, when the language model is made using the whole training data set (6.84M words).

By increasing the language model training data size from 1/8 (0.86M words) to 8/8 (6.84M words), the WER, the perplexity and the OOV are relatively reduced by 17%, 19%, and 62%, respectively. By increasing the acoustic model training data from 1/8 (64 hours) to 8/8 (509 hours), the WER is reduced by 6.3%. The best WER of 25.3%, obtained by using the whole training data set for both acoustic and language modeling, shown at the extreme right condition in Figure 3, is 2.9% lower in the absolute value than that shown in Figure 2. This is because the former experiment of Figure 3 combined $\Delta\Delta$MFCC and $\Delta\Delta$log-energy with the three features of MFCC, ΔMFCC and Δlog-energy which were used in the experiment of Figure 2. All these results show that WER is significantly reduced by an increase of the size of training data and almost saturated by using the whole data set. This strongly confirms that the size of the CSJ is meaningful in modeling spontaneous presentation speech using the standard model training strategies.

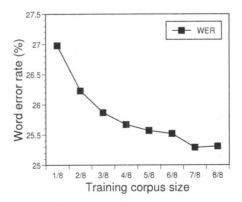

Fig. 3. WER as a function of the size of acoustic model training data

3.3   Analysis of Spontaneous Speech Recognition Errors

Individual differences in spontaneous presentation speech recognition performances have been analyzed using 10 minutes from presentations given by 51 male speakers, for a total of 510 minutes [16]. Seven kinds of speaker attributes were considered in the analysis. They were word accuracy (Acc), averaged acoustic frame likelihood (AL), speaking rate (SR), word perplexity (PP), out of vocabulary rate (OR), filled pause rate (FR) and repair rate (RR). The speaking rate, defined as the number of phonemes per second, and the averaged acoustic frame likelihood were calculated using the results of forced alignment of the reference tri-phone labels after removing pause periods. The word perplexity was calculated using trigrams, in which prediction of out-of-vocabulary (OOV) words was not included. The filled pause rate and the repair rate were the number of filled pauses and repairs divided by the number of words, respectively.

Analysis results indicate that the attributes exhibiting a real correlation with the accuracy are speaking rate, OOV rate, and repair rate. Although other attributes also have correlation with the accuracy, the correlation is actually caused through these more fundamentally influential attributes.

The following equation has been obtained as a result of a linear regression model of the word accuracy with the six presentation attributes.

$$Acc = 0.12AL - 0.88SR - 0.020PP - 2.2OR + 0.32FR - 3.0RR + 95 \,. \quad (1)$$

In the equation, the regression coefficient for the repair rate is -3.0 and the coefficient for the OOV rate is -2.2. This means that a 1% increase of the repair rate or the OOV rate corresponds respectively to a 3.0% or 2.2% decrease of word accuracy. This is probably because a single recognition error caused by a repair or an OOV word triggers secondary errors due to linguistic constraints. The determination coefficient of the multiple linear regression is 0.48, which is significant at a 1% level. This means that roughly half of the variance of the word accuracy can be explained by the model.

Table 2. Japanese phonemes

Vowel	/a,i,u,e,o,a:,i:,u:,e:,o:/
Consonant	/w,y,r,p,t,k,b,d,g,j,ts,ch, z,s,sh,h,f,N,N:,m,n/

4 Spectral Space Reduction in Spontaneous Speech and Its Effects on Speech Recognition Performances

4.1 Spectral Analysis of Spontaneous Speech

Results of recognition experiments using the spontaneous presentations in the CSJ clearly show that spontaneous speech and read speech are acoustically different. In order to clarify the acoustical differences, spectral characteristics of spontaneous speech have been analyzed in comparison with that of read speech [19]. Utterances with various speaking styles (speaking types) in the CSJ, such as AP, EP, utterances reading the transcription of AP (read transcription speech), and dialogues, were used in the analysis. The dialogue utterances consisted of interviews on AP, interviews on EP, task dialogues, and free dialogues. In order to avoid the effect of individual differences, utterances in different styles by the same five male and five female speakers were compared. Since not only the speakers but also the text were identical for the reading of the transcribed speech and the original AP utterances, very precise comparative analysis could be performed.

These utterances were segmented by silences with durations of 400 ms or longer. If the length of the segmented unit was shorter than 1 sec, it was merged with the succeeding unit. The segmented utterances are hereafter called "utterance units".

The whole set of 31 Japanese phonemes, consisting of 10 vowels and 21 consonants, are listed in Table 2. The mean and variance of MFCC vectors for each phoneme in various speaking styles were calculated to analyze the spectral characteristics of spontaneous speech as follows.

1. 39-dimensional feature vectors, consisting of 12-dimensional MFCC, log-energy, and their first and second derivatives, were extracted from utterances using a 25 ms-length window shifted every 10 ms. The CMS (cepstral mean subtraction) is applied to each utterance unit.
2. A mono-phone HMM with a single Gaussian mixture was trained using utterances of every combination of phonemes, speakers, and utterance styles. Every HMM had a left-to-right topology with three self-loops.
3. The mean and variance vectors of the 12-dimensional MFCC at the second state of the HMM were extracted for each phoneme and used for the analysis.

4.2 Projection into the PCA Space

Table 3 shows the total number of phoneme samples used in this experiment for each speaker and each speaking style. Each presentation has a duration of 10 minutes in average. Figure 4 shows examples of the distribution of mean MFCC vectors of all the

16   Sadaoki Furui et al.

Table 3. Total number of phoneme samples for each speaker and each speaking style

	Speaker ID	Read speech	AP	EP	Dialogue
Male	M1	7,420	7,371	5,213	9,915
	M2	10,768	10,815	6,000	14,489
	M3	12,118	12,211	8,525	17,616
	M4	23,154	23,208	8,615	19,892
	M5	8,598	8,651	11,518	29,862
Female	F1	12,162	12,071	10,119	25,428
	F2	7,843	7,757	7,206	20,141
	F3	11,383	11,360	4,837	17,044
	F4	8,111	8,038	8,232	20,999
	F5	17,797	17,848	9,598	22,083

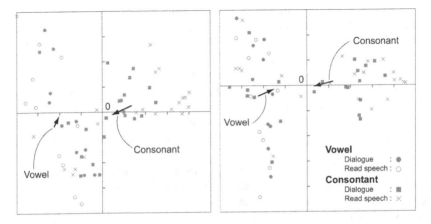

Fig. 4. Examples of distributions of mean MFCC vectors of all the phonemes projected into the 2-dimensional PCA space for dialogue and read speech by two speakers. The arrows indicate the deviations of vowel and consonant centers from the read speech to the dialogue speech

vowels and consonants, projected into 2-dimensional vector spaces constructed by the Principal Component Analysis (PCA), for the dialogue and read speech by two speakers (left: F5, and right: M5), respectively. These speakers were selected since their voices have relatively large perceptual differences between the two speaking styles. In the figure, x and y axes indicate the first and the second PCA vectors, respectively. The two arrows in each figure indicate deviations of vowel and consonant centers from the read speech to the dialogue speech.

The results clearly show that the distribution of mean MFCC vectors of dialogue speech is closer to the center of the distribution of all the phonemes than the distribution of read speech. In other words, the size of spectral space for the phonemes in spontaneous speech is smaller compared to that of read speech.

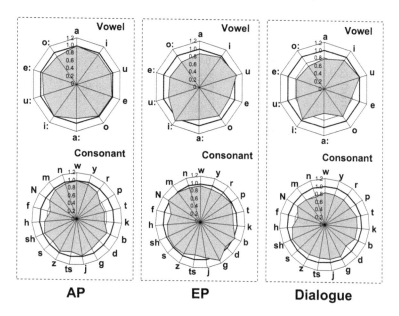

Fig. 5. The reduction ratio of the vector norm between each phoneme and the phoneme center in the spontaneous speech to that in the read speech

4.3   Reduction Ratio of the Distribution of Phonemes

In order to quantitatively analyze the reduction of the distribution of phonemes, Euclidean norms/distances between the mean vector of each phoneme and the center of the distribution of all phonemes, that is the vector averaged over all the phonemes, were calculated, and the ratio of the distance for spontaneous speech (presentations and dialogues) to that of read speech was calculated for each phoneme as follows.

$$red_p(X) = \frac{\|\boldsymbol{\mu}_p(X) - \mathrm{Av}[\boldsymbol{\mu}_p(X)]\|}{\|\boldsymbol{\mu}_p(R) - \mathrm{Av}[\boldsymbol{\mu}_p(R)]\|} \, . \tag{2}$$

Here $\boldsymbol{\mu}_p(X)$ is the mean vector of a phoneme p uttered with a speaking style X, $\boldsymbol{\mu}_p(R)$ is the mean vector of a phoneme p of read speech, and Av indicates the averaged value.

Results using the mean MFCC vector of the second state of the HMM with a single Gaussian mixture as the mean vector for each phoneme are shown in Figure 5.

The figure shows the reduction ratios $red_p(X)$ averaged over all the speakers, separately for AP, EP, and dialogues. /N:/ and /ch/, which rarely occurred in the utterances listed in Table 3, were not used in this analysis. The condition of $red_p(X) = 1$ is indicated by a thick line. The dialogues include interviews on AP and EP, task dialogues, and free dialogues. Results in the figure show the reduction of the MFCC space for almost all the phonemes in the three speaking styles, and this is most significant in dialogue utterances.

Figure 6 shows mean reduction ratios for vowels and consonants, respectively, for each speaking style. These results show that the reduction of the distribution of phone-

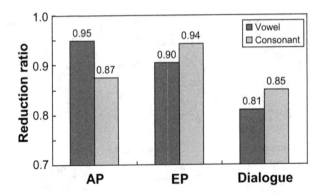

Fig. 6. Mean reduction ratios of vowels and consonants for each speaking style

mes in the MFCC domain in comparison with that of read speech is observed for all the speaking styles, and most significantly for dialogue speech.

4.4   Reduction of Distances Between Phonemes

In the previous section, the reduction of MFCC space was measured by the ratio of the distance between each phoneme and the phoneme center in spontaneous speech to that in read speech. In this section, the reduction of cepstral distance between each phoneme pair is measured. The Euclidean distance using the mean MFCC vector of each phoneme and the Mahalanobis distance, which takes into account the variances, were measured. The definition of Mahalanobis distance $D_{ij}(X)$ between phoneme i and j spoken with a speaking style X can be written as follows.

$$D_{ij}(X) = \sqrt{\frac{K\sum_{k=1}^{K}(\mu_{ik}(X) - \mu_{jk}(X))^2}{\sum_{k=1}^{K}\sigma_{ik}^2(X) + \sum_{k=1}^{K}\sigma_{jk}^2(X)}}. \tag{3}$$

Where, K is the dimension of an MFCC vector ($K = 12$). $\mu_{ik}(X)$ and $\sigma_{ik}^2(X)$ are the kth dimensional elements of the mean and the variance vector of MFCC for phoneme i uttered with a speaking style X. In the case of the Euclidean distance between phonemes i and j, the denominator in the above formula (3) is set to a constant value.

   Five males and five females were randomly selected from the CSJ for this experiment. The total number of phoneme samples for each speaking style was 45,242 (read speech), 80,095 (AP), 55,102 (EP), or 56,583 (dialogues). The read speech set in the CSJ includes various kinds of "reading transcriptions" and "reading novels including dialogues". The dialogue set includes variation of "interview" and "free dialogue". Therefore, speech materials of read speech and dialogues for this experiment were selected so as to represent as many variations of speaking styles as possible. Speech materials

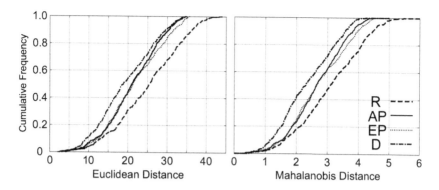

Fig. 7. Distribution of distances between phonemes

of AP and EP were randomly selected from the test-set data of CSJ designed for speech recognition experiments.

Figure 7 shows the cumulative frequency of distances between phonemes for each speaking style. The left-hand side of the figure shows the case using the Euclidean distance, whereas the right-hand side shows the case using the Mahalanobis distance. The x axis indicates the Euclidean or the Mahalanobis distance, and the y axis indicates the cumulative frequency. These results clearly show that the distances between phonemes decrease as the spontaneity of the utterances increases (D $\gg$ EP > AP $\gg$ R). The Wilcoxon's rank order test with a significance level of p-value ≤ 0.01 shows that the distributions of each speaking style are statistically different from each other, except between AP and EP.

4.5 Relationship Between Phoneme Distances and Phoneme Recognition Performance

Differences of the size of distribution of between-phoneme distances are expected to be related to the phoneme recognition performance for various speaking styles. This section investigates the relationship between the between-phoneme distances and the phoneme recognition accuracy using utterances by many speakers. Mono-phone HMMs with a single Gaussian mixture for phoneme recognition were trained for each speaking style, using utterances by 100 males and 100 females for AP and 150 males and 150 females for EP. These speakers were randomly selected from the CSJ, and the total number of phoneme samples were approximately two million for AP and EP, respectively. A 38-dimensional feature vector was used as the acoustic feature. The same data as used in Section 4.4 were used for the evaluation experiment. A phoneme network with di-phone probabilities was used as a language model for recognition. The insertion penalty was optimized for each speaking style.

Figure 8 shows the relationship between the mean phoneme distance and the phoneme recognition accuracy. The left-hand side of the figure shows the case using Euclidean distance and the right-hand side shows the case using Mahalanobis distance as the distance between phonemes for each speaking style. Correlation coefficients be-

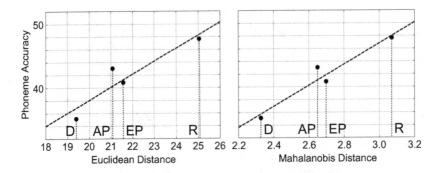

Fig. 8. Relationship between phoneme distances and phoneme recognition accuracy

tween the mean phoneme distance and the phoneme recognition accuracy are 0.93 in the case using Euclidean distance and 0.97 in the case using Mahalanobis distance. The lines in Figure 8 indicate the regression over the four points. These results clearly show a strong correlation between mean phoneme distance and phoneme accuracy. This means that the phoneme recognition accuracy can be estimated by the mean phoneme distance. That is, the reduction of the Euclidean distances between phonemes is a major factor contributing to the degradation of spontaneous speech recognition accuracy. It can also be concluded that the relationship between the phoneme distance and the phoneme recognition accuracy becomes slightly more significant if the variances of phoneme spectra are also taken into account.

5   Conclusion

In order to increase recognition accuracy for spontaneous speech, it is necessary to build acoustic and language models using spontaneous speech corpora. It was found through our recognition experiments for spontaneous academic presentations (AP) in the Corpus of Spontaneous Japanese (CSJ), that recognition accuracy increases as the training data size increases even up to 510 hours or 6.84M words for both acoustic and language model training. This indicates that spontaneous speech is so variable that it needs a huge corpus to encompass the variations. However, it is impossible to collect a huge corpus for every new application. Therefore, it is important to clarify general features of spontaneous speech and establish a mechanism for adapting a task-independent model to a specific task using task-specific features [3, 20–22].

By comparing spontaneous speech and speech reading a transcription of the spontaneous speech, it was clarified that spectral distribution of spontaneous speech is significantly reduced compared to that of read speech. Although this was true for all the spontaneous speech analyzed in this paper, that is, academic presentations (AP), extemporaneous presentations (EP), and dialogues, the reduction was most significant for dialogues, which are obviously more spontaneous than the other styles. It has also been found that the more spontaneous the speech, the smaller the distances between phonemes become, and that there is a high correlation between the mean phoneme distance and the phoneme recognition accuracy. In summary, spontaneous speech can be characterized by the reduction of spectral space in comparison with that of read speech, and this is one of the major factors contributing to the decrease in recognition accuracy.

Our future research includes analysis over wider range of spontaneous speech using utterances other than those included in the CSJ. Broadening speech recognition applications depends crucially on raising the recognition performance of spontaneous speech. Although we have clarified spectral reduction and its effects on spontaneous speech recognition, it is not yet clear how we can use these results for improving recognition performances. Creating methods for adapting acoustic models to spontaneous speech based on the results obtained in this research is one of our future targets.

This paper has focused on acoustic properties of spontaneous speech. Since there exist significant differences in linguistic characteristics between spontaneous speech and read speech, our future research includes investigating linguistic characteristics of spontaneous speech and their effects on speech recognition performances. How to incorporate filled pauses, repairs, hesitations, repetitions, partial words, and disfluencies still poses a big challenge.

The large-scale spontaneous speech corpus, CSJ, used in the experiments reported in this paper, will be stored with XML format in a large-scale database system developed by the 21st Century COE (Center of Excellence) program "Framework for Systematization and Application of Large-scale Knowledge Resources" at Tokyo Institute of Technology so that the general population can easily access and use it for research purposes [23]. We hope international collaboration in building large-scale spontaneous speech corpora as well as analysis and modeling of spontaneous speech based on the corpora will advance the progress of speech recognition technology.

Acknowledgements

This research was supported by the Science and Technology Agency Priority Program "Spontaneous Speech: Corpus and Processing Technology" and the 21st Century COE Program "Framework for Systematization and Application of Large-scale Knowledge Resources".

References

1. Furui, S.: Recent advances in spontaneous speech recognition and understanding. Proc. IEEE Workshop on SSPR, Tokyo (2003) 1–6
2. Furui, S.: Toward spontaneous speech recognition and understanding. In: Chou, W. and Juang, B.-H. (eds.): Pattern Recognition in Speech and Language Processing, CRC Press, New York (2003) 191–227
3. Shinozaki, T., Hori, C. and Furui, S.: Towards automatic transcription of spontaneous presentations. Proc. Eurospeech, Aalborg, Denmark (2001) 491–494
4. Sankar, A., Gadde, V. R. R., Stolcke, A. and Weng, F.: Improved modeling and efficiency for automatic transcription of broadcast news. Speech Communication, vol.37 (2002) 133–158
5. Gauvain, J.-L. and Lamel, L.: Large vocabulary speech recognition based on statistical methods. In: Chou, W. and Juang, B.-H. (eds.): Pattern Recognition in Speech and Language Processing, CRC Press, New York (2003) 149–189

6. Evermann, G. et al.: Development of the 2003 CU-HTK conversational telephone speech transcription system. Proc. IEEE ICASSP, Montreal (2004) I-249–252

7. Schwartz, R. et al.: Speech recognition in multiple languages and domains: the 2003 BBN/LIMSI EARS system. Proc. IEEE ICASSP, Montreal (2004) III-753–756

8. van Son, R.J.J.H. and Pols, L.C.W.: An acoustic description of consonant reduction. Speech Communication, vol.28, no.2 (1999) 125–140

9. Duez, D.: On spontaneous French speech: aspects of the reduction and contextual assimilation of voiced stops. J. Phonetics, vol.23 (1995) 407–427

10. Maekawa, K.: Corpus of Spontaneous Japanese: Its design and evaluation. Proc. IEEE Workshop on SSPR, Tokyo (2003) 7–12

11. Maekawa, K., Kikuchi, H. and Tsukahara, W.: Corpus of spontaneous Japanese: design, annotation and XML representation. Proc. International Symposium on Large-scale Knowledge Resources, Tokyo (2004) 19–24

12. Uchimoto, K., Nobata, C., Yamada, A., Sekine, S. and Isahara, H.: Morphological analysis of the Corpus of Spontaneous Japanese. Proc. IEEE Workshop on Spontaneous Speech Processing and Recognition, Tokyo (2003) 159–162

13. Venditti, J.: Japanese ToBI labeling guidelines. OSU Working Papers in Linguistics, vol.50 (1997) 127–162

14. Maekawa, K., Kikuchi, H., Igarashi, Y. and Venditti, J.: X-JToBI: an extended J-ToBI for spontaneous speech. Proc. ICSLP, Denver, CO (2002) 1545–1548

15. Kawahara, T., Nanjo, H., Shinozaki, T. and Furui, S.: Benchmark test for speech recognition using the corpus of spontaneous Japanese. Proc. IEEE Workshop on Spontaneous Speech Processing and Recognition, Tokyo (2003) 135–138

16. Shinozaki, T. and Furui, S.: Analysis on individual differences in automatic transcription of spontaneous presentations. Proc. IEEE ICASSP, Orlando (2002), I-729–732

17. Ichiba, T., Iwano, K. and Furui, S.: Relationships between training data size and recognition accuracy in spontaneous speech recognition. Proc. Acoustical Society of Japan Fall Meeting (2004) 2-1-9 (in Japanese)

18. Ueberla, J.: Analysing a simple language model – some general conclusion for language models for speech recognition. Computer Speech & Language, vol.8, no.2 (1994) 153–176

19. Nakamura, M., Iwano, K. and Furui, S.: Comparison of acoustic characteristics between spontaneous speech and reading speech in Japanese. Proc. Acoustical Society of Japan Fall Meeting (2004), 2-P-25 (in Japanese)

20. Lussier, L., Whittaker, E. W. D. and Furui, S.: Combinations of language model adaptation methods applied to spontaneous speech. Proc. Third Spontaneous Speech Science & Technology Workshop, Tokyo (2004), 73–78

21. Nanjo, H. and Kawahara, T.: Unsupervised language model adaptation for lecture speech recognition. Proc. IEEE Workshop on Spontaneous Speech Processing and Recognition, Tokyo (2003) 75–78

22. Shinozaki, T. and Furui, S.: Spontaneous speech recognition using a massively parallel decoder. Proc. Interspeech-ICSLP, Jeju, Korea, vol.3 (2004) 1705–1708

23. Furui, S.: Overview of the 21st century COE program "Framework for Systematization and Application of Large-scale Knowledge Resources". Proc. International Symposium on Large-scale Knowledge Resources, Tokyo (2004) 1–8

On the Acoustic Components
in Multimedia Presentations

Klaus Fellbaum and Bettina Ketzmerick

Brandenburg University of Technology Cottbus, Germany
fellbaum@tu-cottbus.de

Abstract. This paper describes some of our activities in the area of elearning with a special focus on the speech (or more general: on the acoustic) component. We found out that in many (probably the most) electronic tutorials the main emphasis is on the visual presentation with partly excellent 3D video and graphical material, but the acoustic components are more or less primitive ones or forgotten. That's why we made several investigations on how speech, music, sounds, noise etc. can enrich and improve the elearning material, above all when these components are used with their synergy and completion to the visual components in the sense of a real multimedia presentation.

1 Introduction

It is well known that a *multimedia* presentation can remarkably support the understanding and learning process. An area which makes extended use of this technique are teleteaching and telelearning programs designed for school and university classes. During the last years we have been involved in several teleteaching projects which were financially supported by the German government. The aim of the projects was twofold: an extended investigation and the development of multimedia learning tools and the establishment of a mobile computer infrastructure enabling the students to get access to many information sources like teaching programs, chatrooms and course books. ('Notebook University'). An extended summary of the results can be found in [1].

After an in-depth evaluation of multimedia courses, existing so far in the internet or as commercial programs, we made a surprising discovery. The authors of the teleteaching material have focused their efforts mainly (and very often exclusively) on the *visual* presentation. We found excellent 3D animations and video sequences but there were only very few examples which satisfactorily took care of the *acoustic* presentation, more precisely, of acoustic dialogue components. In some cases there were verbal (spoken) explanations or comments but (surprisingly again) the speakers usually were untrained speakers (either the producers of the courses themselves or the next-door neighbour who happened to find time to speak the text).

Based on these experiences we decided to put the accent of our investigations on the acoustic components, above all:
- the role of speech in teleteaching programs,
- the synergy of speech to other media (graphics, images, video sequences),
- the suitability of speakers for different teaching contents (explanations, questions, comments etc.),

V. Matoušek et al. (Eds.): TSD 2005, LNAI 3658, pp. 23–32, 2005.

- the quality requirements (for both, the professionalism of the speaker and the technical quality),
- the use of non-voice acoustic components (tones, sounds etc.),
- the use of speech in the human-computer dialogue including speech recognition and synthesis and
- the use of speech recognition for the control of multimedia devices during the course presentation (on/off switching of audio and video devices or light, acoustic control of the pc/laptop power point presentation etc.).

In the next sections we will report about some of our results, but before that we will present some basic definitions in the area of multimedia and characteristics of different media.

2   General Comments on the Subject 'Medium'

The term *medium* is used in different ways, we partly find inconsistent definitions. For an in-depth description of multimedia definitions and multimedia technology the book of *Steinmetz* [2] can be recommended. In our opinion it is the best to define a medium according to the *human perception* and the *time dependence*. *Visual* media are text, hypertext, graphics, pictures and video. *Auditive* media are speech, sounds, noise and music.

A very important distinction feature is the time dependence. For example, a text is a static (or time-independent) medium and speech is fluent (or time dependent). We will show in the next sections that the time dependence has a crucial importance for the presentation of contents.

The term *multimedia* implies the presence of several, minimally two, media. Usually and more precisely, minimally one medium must be time independent and another time dependent. In addition, multimedia means a computer-based production, manipulation, presentation, storage and communication of the information [2]. At least, multimedia contains the ability of *interactivity*, which means, the user can communicate with the multimedia system and the system responds. All these characteristics play important roles in the design and use of electronic teaching systems.

Another term is *multimodal*. It means the way how presented information has an effect on several sensory organs.

Finally, the term *multicodality* is used. It characterises that for a presentation of information several symbol systems or codes are applied. For example, a presentation might be a sequence of letters, an image, a pictogram or a spoken sequence and so on.

It must be emphasised that multimedia per se does not yet imply an added value. The key point is how the different media are acting together, how they complete each other and how they produce synergy; the optimal mixture generates the value.

As a matter of fact, it is quite impossible to define general rules how to optimally use and mix media. However, some advices for a multimedia presentation are given here:

- None of the media must cover the complete information (this would, for example, happen when a lecturer would read out a text which is presented on a viewgraph) because then the other media would be unnecessary.

- Electronic media persuade an author to overfeed the audience with multimodality (in terms of animations sounds etc.); this is more confusing than helpful. On the other hand, if multimedia aids are available, the audience expects their application (and will be unsatisfied when the lecturer does not make use of them).
- The human storage capacity and the attention are restricted which is quite obvious when we think of fluent media like speech or a video. We will come back to that later.
- A skilled multimedia presentation might put the illusion into somebody's mind that even difficult facts are simple. Difficulties might be covered with attractive animations. But, as a matter of fact, a difficult subject remains difficult, independent on the multimedia efforts.

3   The Medium 'Speech'

It is well known that speech plays a key role in communication [3]. The reasons for that are as follows:
- Speech is perceived directly and immediately. It is human's most important and natural form of communication.
- It has high information capacity; also very complex contents can be expressed by speech.
- It has an individual character.
- It reaches also a distracted or unattended partner.
- It only requires very simple input and output devices (microphone, loudspeaker, headphone).

There are, however, also some problems or disadvantages with speech:
- Speech has a fluent, non-documenting character.
- The memory for spoken information is very restricted, that means, speech sequences must not be too long.
- The speech flow dictates the perception speed.
- Speech might disturb uninvolved persons; problems can occur with confidential information.
- A later change or completion of a word vocabulary is difficult (exception: when speech synthesis is used).

As explained later in more detail, speech in a teaching program mostly serves as a complementary, explaining or enriching medium. Speech has a special value as interaction medium, for example if we think of a teaching program with exercises based on speech input (speech recognition) and a spoken system reaction (speech replay or speech synthesis).

4   Speech Input and Speech Dialogue Systems

Concerning speech input, especially speech recognition, which can be either used for answering questions, to control the teaching program ('stop', 'next question', 'repeat', 'what's the correct answer?' and so on) or to control presentation devices (beamer, audio and video recorder and so on) during a lecture, the demands on a correct recognition are rather high; an unsatisfactory recognition rate would immediately result in acceptance problems.

Fortunately we only need relatively simple forms of recognition. A program control consists of a restricted set of commands and if the system controls the speech dialogue (which usually is the case in a tutorial program) then the questions, formulated by the system, can be designed in a way that it only leaves a restricted set of spoken alternatives to the user [3].

When we think of an advanced speech dialogue system, for example a telephone-based enquiry system or a tutorial system which allows a freely spoken dialogue and, in addition, a web access, the demands on the speech recognition and synthesis components are highly increased. It is important to state that input and output have narrow links to each other and a dialogue is by far more than the sum of both. The dialogue manager plays a key role in the system, and its design, comfort and 'intelligence' is the main factor for the user's acceptance of the whole application [4]. Fig. 1 shows such a dialogue system.

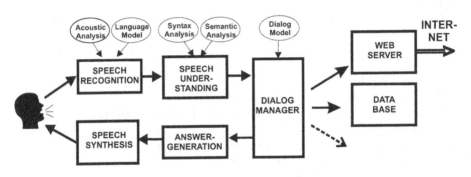

Fig. 1. Speech dialogue components for an intelligent user interface [5].

In complex applications, the dialogue manager performs a *user modeling* with which trained and untrained users or – in our case – users with or without previous knowledge can be distinguished and the dialogue is flexibly adapted to the individual dialogue step, the user's reaction and the requirements of the tutorial task.

5   Speech Output

Concerning speech output, it is very important to keep in mind that the perception speed is given and the user has to follow in real-time. If the listener wants to have some selected parts repeated which means to jump back in the text, the problem arises that it is nearly impossible to find the exact beginning of the desired speech sequence.

In comparison, the situation is totally different when we use a text as input. Text is a *static* or *time-independent* medium. The reader can perceive a text at will, maybe once or several times, that means he or she can decide the perception speed. There is no problem to jump in a text back and forth or to get an overview of a whole text page.

These fundamental differences between speech and text require a careful attention when we design a multimedia tutorial.

We will now come back to details for a speech presentation and we want to list some important requirements (some more details are presented in several conference papers [6] – [10]):

- The user expects a high speech quality. Speech with telephone bandwidth (300-3400 Hz) is unacceptable; it should be wideband speech of 8 kHz or more bandwidth.
- A trained speaker is expected. Any dialects, hesitations, slips of the tongue, syntactic or semantic incorrect expressions are intolerable. If these things happen, even the best visual animation does not compensate it and the complete presentation will be unacceptable.
- Speakers (even trained speakers) are sometimes not suited for a certain speech contribution. The problem is that the suitability cannot be justified from a purely factual point of view; it is more an emotional matter and has to be investigated by listening tests using different types of content (descriptions, questions, tests, comments etc.) and different types of speakers (male/female, deep and high voices, clear and aspirated voices etc. [11]).
- In some cases it is advantageous not to restrict on one voice, this could be boring. The use of various voices is an efficient help to structure speech information because one can distribute voices to different contents. One voice might act as commentator, another as presenter of examples or exercises. It is, however, important to keep this distribution fixed for the whole lecture, otherwise it would cause confusion.
- As mentioned before, the capacity of the human short time memory is restricted. The listener cannot keep many details in his or her mind. The best is to present important items visually (for example as statements or definitions) and to comment and complete them verbally. Simultaneously presented visual and acoustic information is perceived twice which increases the learning effect. It must be emphasised that this does not mean to repeat the text message word by word. Speech should embed the text statements which might be only key words or fragments, speech puts the right stress on the words, it interprets the meaning and supports the understanding. We will come back to this aspect later.

6   Example of a Multimodal Tutorial: Model of the Human Speech Production

We developed in the framework of a research project, funded by the German Ministry of Education and Science, among others an elearning module (tutorial) about electronic speech processing [12]. This subject has two advantages for our discussion: it explains in detail the production and analysis of speech and it investigates the application of it from the didactical point of view.

We will give now an example which demonstrates the use of the speech component. It is based on the explanation how the human speech production works and how it can serve as an example for a technical realisation. The system is based on the well-known synthesis part of an LPC vocoder (Fig. 2).

The general idea is to create the graphic step by step. Each of the steps is accompanied by a verbal comment. In addition, a part of the graphic is marked by a coloured

Introduction (verbally)
Human speech production, Distinction of two
sequential steps (excitation and articulation),
functions of the lungs, voiced and unvoiced
sounds, ...

Continuation
The vocal cords are replaced by a tone generator
which is marked by a circle, the tone frequency is
called fundamental frequency, ...

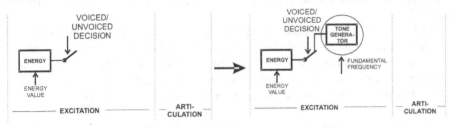

and so on...

The complete speech machine
This is the complete system. If all parameters are set,
the system can produce natural speech...

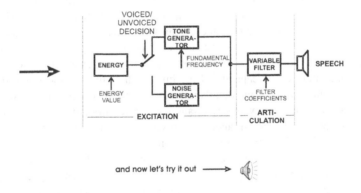

and now let's try it out ➔ 🔊

Fig. 2. The sequential presentation of a speech machine.

circle (see second graphic in Fig. 2) and the spoken explanation directly refers to such
a detail (for example ... "the excitation is performed by a tone generator; see the red
circle"...). It is quite obvious that the combination of an increased completion and
a showing or *deixis* act has more value and information than the description of the final
graphic (third graphic in fig. 2). A similar effect is possible by a spoken comment and
a simultaneous flashing or the change of a colour (e.g. from black to red).

It must be mentioned here that the *synchronism* between the figurative and the verbal
description is of crucial importance. For a practical implementation, this might cause
difficulties, but with some experience in Java and Flash programming, it can be handled.

Our vocoder example obviously still has another advantage: when the user clicks on
the loudspeaker symbol of the graphic, the system really speaks.

In an advanced version of the program, parameters like the fundamental frequency
can be changed and this effect is audible. Fig. 3 shows a screenshot of the demonstration

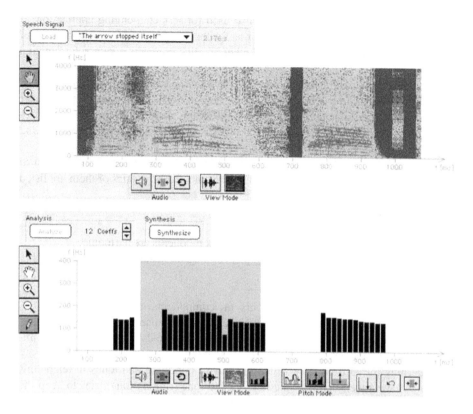

Fig. 3. Demonstration program of our speaking machine (screenshot). The upper part shows the spectrogram of a spoken sentence and the bars in the lower part represent the fundamental frequency.

part of the program. For more information, the reader is referred to [12]; a complete version of the system can be found on our website [13].

7 Non-speech Acoustic Information; Tones, Music and Noise

As a matter of fact, acoustic information (be it speech or non-speech) is extensively used in movies or tv performances. However, if we consider elearning modules or animations, the situation is different. As mentioned earlier, producers of this modules or animations have their main focus on the visual presentation. But when we think, for example, of a 3D animation of buildings then we find excellent, quasi-realistic scenarios. Sometimes the user can enter buildings, can use the stairs and open doors, but what's missing mostly are environment sounds, the echo of the steps, the sounds of people going around, door clapping and so on. The main reason for the renunciation of sounds is the enormous expenditure to produce natural sounds. To be as realistic as possible does not only mean a high sound quality but also a spatial presentation (stereo, or better, artificial-head sounds) which can be as expensive as the visual production.

Non-speech acoustic information is also used for less challenging applications if we think, for example, of action games or as feedback information or confirmation of manual operations like using a keyboard where a click confirms a keystroke function etc.

An interesting detail regarding sounds is the phenomenon of *good sounds* and *bad sounds*. The terms *good* and *bad* characterise the emotional impression of the listener and they can be used metaphorically for a right/wrong answer of a question or a correct/incorrect operation of a system input. Other examples are ringing tones (*good tones*) and busy tones (*bad tones*) in telephony.

Many ergonomic and psychological investigations have been made in the past to find objective criteria for good and bad sounds. Some characteristics of them are listed here:

Good sound:
- low frequency,
- if the sound consists of a frequency mix, the components are harmonic,
- if the sound consists of an impulse sequence: long impulses and long pauses.

Bad sound:
- high frequency,
- if the sound consists of a frequency mix, the components are disharmonic,
- if the sound consists of an impulse sequence: short impulses and short pauses.

Fig. 4 (after *Noe*) shows the areas of good and bad sounds. Parameters are the impulse duration and the pause duration.

Concerning the last example which deals with good and bad tones in telephony, these tones have a well-defined function. A good tone (ringing tone) tries to keep the user on line while a bad tone asks to finis h the activity and to disconnect the telephone line (in order to get it free for other subscribers). If we think of a computer program, a bad tone normally signals that the user has made a mal operation or malfunction.

Another interesting application for tones can be found with a telephone answering machine. This machine usually starts with an introducing text and ends it up with a single *beep*. This beep has two functions. Firstly it signals the end of the introduction. Without the beep the user would be uncertain if the end of the text has been reached or if something follows. Secondly the beep requests the user to speak. This example of the beep use demonstrates very well that even a simple (not to say a trivial) procedure or technical realisation is of great benefit. As a matter of fact, also this example can be extended to many other applications, for example to elearning programs. In general, the beep procedure is an efficient method in a man-machine dialogue (enquiry systems, training systems and so on), but also in a man-man dialogue in the case of a half-duplex connection, in which the partners have to switch between speaking and listening. The switch function between these two communication directions is combined with a beep production which clearly marks the transition between the speaking directions.

We will not go into details with other types of acoustic components. Music obviously serves as trailer ('trademark' of a broadcast station, of a special program or simply as a break for relaxes) and noise or noise-like sounds are used to model a realistic acoustic environment, as mentioned before.

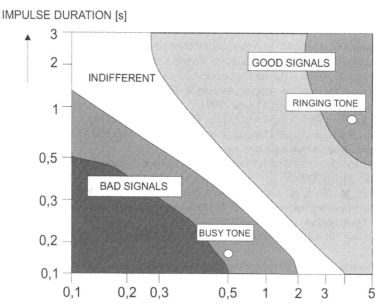

Fig. 4. Areas of good and bad signals.

8 Conclusions

In our paper we have tried to give a summary of our experiences we could collect during several research projects in the area of elearning programs. The focus was on the acoustic components in multimedia presentations because we found out that these components, and among these the speech information, leaves much to desire.

An in-depth investigation of the medium speech produced interesting facts and identified many sources of errors. Some really self-evident items are often simply forgotten, among others (and as mentioned before) a sufficient speech quality and the fact that long sequences of speech overburdens the human short-term memory and finally (and most seriously) that the key point of a good learning program is the *right mix* of media, this mix with its various synergy effects guarantees the best possible way of learning.

Finally, it would be an error to believe that elearning is just a continuation or extension of the 'classical' natural (face-to-face) learning. Electronic forms of learning (elearning) have their own rules and what we need are new learning theories [14].

It is true when learning experts regret that the multimedia technology has grown much faster than our understanding of human learning procedures under multimedia conditions. In this area much more work has to be done.

References

1. Fellbaum, K.; Göcks, M.: eLearning an der Hochschule. Shaker Verlag Aachen (2004)
2. Steinmetz, R.: Multimedia-Technologie. Springer Verlag Berlin (2000)
3. Fellbaum, K.: Human-Human Communication and Human-Computer Interaction by Voice. Lecture on the Seminar "Human Aspects of Telecommunications for Disabled and Older People". Donostia (Spain), 11 June 1999
4. Fellbaum, K.: Speech Input and Output Technology-State of the Art and Selected Applications. 8th International Conference on Applications of Natural Language to Information Systems, June 2003, Burg, Germany.
5. Kunzmann, S.: Applied speech processing technologies-our journey. The ELRA Newsletter, January-March 2000.
6. Eichner, M.; Wolf, M.: Untersuchungen zum Einsatz von Sprachtechnologien in der Lernumgebung eines Internet-basierten Studienganges. In: Hoffmann (Hrsg.): Studientexte zur Sprachkommunikation 24, Dresden 2002.
7. Hoffmann, R.; u.a.: An Interactive Course on Speech Synthesis. Proc. MATISSE, London (1999)
8. Ketzmerick, B.: Zum Einsatz akustischer Komponenten im e-Learning-Modul "Elektronische Sprachsignalverarbeitung". In: Hoffmann (Hrsg.): Studientexte zur Sprachkommunikation 24, Dresden 2002.
9. Fellbaum, K; Ketzmerick, B.: Über die Rolle der Audio-Komponente bei der Multimedia-Kommunikation. In: Hoffmann (Hrsg.): Studientexte zur Sprachkommunikation 24, Dresden 2002
10. Fellbaum, K; Ketzmerick, B.: Audio-Komponenten beim E-Learning - eine erste Bestandsaufnahme. In: Kroschel, K. (Hrsg.): Studientexte zur Sprachkommunikation 26, Karlsruhe 2003
11. Ketzmerick, B.: Stimmklang und Sprechtempo als charakteristisches Merkmal von Stimmen. In: Hess, W.; Stöber, K. (Hrsg.): Studientexte zur Sprachkommunikation 22, Bonn 2001
12. Fellbaum, K., Richter, J.: Human Speech Production Based on a Linear Predictive Vocoder - An Interactive Tutorial. Proc. MATISSE, London, 1999.
13. www.kt.tu-cottbus.de/speech-analysis/
14. Dittler, U.: E-Lerning. Oldenbourg Wissenschaftsverlag. München (2003).

Fusing Data Streams
in Continuous Audio-Visual Speech Recognition

Leon J.M. Rothkrantz, Jacek C. Wojdeł, and Pascal Wiggers

Man–Machine Interaction Group
Delft University of Technology
Mekelweg 4, 2628 CD Delft, The Netherlands
{l.j.m.rothkrantz,p.wiggers}@ewi.tudelft.nl
j.c.wojdel@tnw.tudelft.nl

Abstract. Speech recognition still lacks robustness when faced with changing noise characteristics. Automatic lip reading on the other hand is not affected by acoustic noise and can therefore provide the speech recognizer with valuable additional information, especially since the visual modality contains information that is complementary to information in the audio channel. In this paper we present a novel way of processing the video signal for lip reading and a post-processing data transformation that can be used alongside it. The presented Lip Geometry Estimation (LGE) is compared with other geometry- and image intensity-based techniques typically deployed for this task. A large vocabulary continuous audio-visual speech recognizer for Dutch using this method has been implemented. We show that a combined system improves upon audio-only recognition in the presence of noise.

1 Introduction

Over the past decade large vocabulary continuous speech recognition has reached impressive levels of performance. Recognition rates of systems having vocabulary sizes as large as 64K words lie well over 90% [1]. However, such results are typically found on clean, read speech that has been recorded under controlled laboratory conditions. When faced with more realistic situations where recognizers, among other things, have to deal with channel and environmental noise as well as with background speech the performance rapidly deteriorates.

These problems can be attacked using noise filtering methods in a preprocessing step as well as techniques to adapt the speech models to the new environmental conditions for example using maximum likelihood linear regression [2]. Although useful by themselves these methods have their limitations, especially when being confronted with highly dynamic conditions or background speech. For example, noise filtering using spectral subtraction [3] might result in loss of information under such circumstances. To make speech recognition systems truly robust additional information sources that do not suffer from acoustic noise should be employed on top of these techniques.

Human speech recognition provides some suggestions on where to find such information. It is for example well known that humans use the visual modality when

V. Matoušek et al. (Eds.): TSD 2005, LNAI 3658, pp. 33–44, 2005.

processing speech, in particular by registering mouth movements [4, 5]. A fact best illustrated by the McGurk effect [6] that shows that most people perceive the sound /da/ when watching a video sequence of someone uttering /ba/ while hearing /ga/.

Several authors have shown that automatic lip reading in itself is feasible for tasks such as speech/non-speech detection, digit recognition and even isolated word recognition [8–10, 16, 18]. What makes lip reading really interesting however, aside from obviously not being affected by noise, is that the information it provides is mostly complementary to the information captured by the acoustic processing stages of speech recognition. Whereas speech recognition techniques are particularly good at detecting voicing and to a lesser extend the manner of speech, lip-reading focuses on the place of articulation, since the articulators involved are completely or partially visible. As an example think of the phonemes /s/ and /f/, acoustically these are very similar, both are unvoiced fricatives, but the lip movements made to produce these sounds are rather different.

In this paper we present a new method for processing the video signal, which we call lip geometry estimation (LGE). This method is conceptually a middle road between purely geometrical models of the lips and image intensity-based representations. First, an overview of different processing techniques is given in Section 2. Section 3 continues with an in-depth description of LGE. Section 4 discusses the relationship between different lip-reading techniques, showing that different geometric models capture more or less the same information. Building upon this discussion section 4.1 introduces a projection to a person independent feature space. Finally, section 5 presents a system for continuous audio-visual speech recognition that employs LGE.

2   Lip Reading Techniques

Obviously, the first task in lip reading is locating the lips in a video image, possibly preceded by locating the face. Both tasks can be accomplished using image processing techniques like template matching or edge detection [9]. Subsequently, a number of steps are performed on the raw image to obtain a representation that captures the essential information from which features for classification can then be extracted.

Many methods [14, 15] work directly on the raw image. These typically use a fixed resolution window on the mouth region and treat the intensity values of the pixels in this window as an extracted data vector. The drawback of such approaches is that they produce very large vectors. Therefore, often transformations to smaller spaces that optimize some statistical property of the data are used, like PCA or DTC [14, 15]. These can be followed by transformations that optimize class separability, like LDA and a data rotation using MLLT, which is particularly useful when recognition is to be performed with hidden Markov models that usually assume independent features. Feature mean normalization, where the mean of the features is subtracted from the features on a per utterance basis might also be in order, as this is a well-known technique to temper person dependency to some extent [7].

Apart from the vector length pure intensity based approaches suffer from a strong dependency on illumination conditions and the fact that most person dependent features such as skin tone are retained, while geometric dependencies are discarded.

At the other end of the spectrum live methods that do away with the actual image, but try to track a number of characteristic points in the face [9, 16]. The relative positions of these points then provide the features. This allows for enormous data reduction and complete independence of illumination conditions. The difficulty with this technique is finding and tracking these points; a task that itself is very sensitive to illumination conditions. Optical flow analysis [11] deals with this by not using any prior knowledge of the shape of the lips at all. Instead it finds the distribution of apparent velocities of movements of bright patterns in the image.

Alternatively, the point tracking approach can be taken a step further by creating complete geometric models of the lips and match those upon the image [12, 17]. These predefined shapes can range from simple parabolas to complex three-dimensional models of the lips. This allows for more robust tracking as they can deal with small local distortions that might be devastating for a point tracker or an intensity based method.

Combinations of these methods also exist [12, 17]. For example a contour can be used to estimate the size and rotation of the mouth. Subsequently transformations of pixels inside this mouth region can be used to obtain features [13].

3   Lip Geometry Estimation

In this section we will describe step by step a feature extraction method called Lip Geometry Estimation (LGE). The presented technique is unique because it does not rely on any a-priori geometrical lip model. At the same time it differs from totally unstructured approaches of raw image extraction by the fact that it retains the notion of the lip geometry as the observable. An overview of the signal processing steps described in this section is depicted in 1.

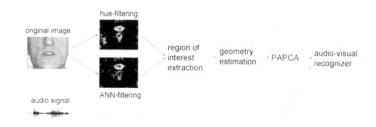

Fig. 1. Signal processing pipeline for audio-visual speech recognition based on LGE

3.1   Lip-Selective Image Filtering

As the first step in video processing, we have to locate the mouth in the image. Fortunately, in a video containing only the face, the lips have a distinct coloring that allows us to find them with a simple lip-selective filter rather than with complicated object recognition techniques. In our current research we use several different filters depending on the illumination conditions and the quality of the recorded video sequences.

Hue-Based Filtering. This is probably the simplest way of performing lip-selective filtering. It was first proposed in [12] and incorporates a parabolic shaped filter on the hue component of a given pixel that cuts off the colors that fall outside a given interval:

$$F_{hue}(h) = \begin{cases} 1 - (h - h_0)^2/w^2 & \text{if } |h - h_0| \leq w; \\ 0 & \text{if } |h - h_0| > w. \end{cases} \tag{1}$$

The filter is defined by the center of the interval h_0 and its half width w. In order to select the lips in the image, the value of h_0 must be around 0 (red color) and w about 0.25. We also may use the hue-based filter in combination with the similarly shaped parabolic value filter if the difference between the hue components of the face and lips is not sufficient for robust lip detection. Using a product of those two filters, one can for example remove the noise of the dark or bright background, where the hue values behave rather randomly. Parameters of both hue and value based filters can be set automatically by optimizing the filter's separation of color histograms prepared for the lip region and the rest of the face.

Filtering with ANNs. A hue-based filter is very simple and computationally very effective. Unfortunately, during our experiments we found that in many cases, if the illumination of the face is not perfect, the hue component itself is not sufficient for proper lip selection. Instead of putting additional constraints on the filtered color, we decided to use a black-box approach. We trained a simple feed-forward neural network and used it as a filter. The network that was used has only 5 neurons in a hidden layer and one output neuron. It was fed with the RGB values from a pixel in the image. The small size of the network allows for on-line training, so that we could use different networks for different video sequences as long as the first frame in the video sequence was prepared with the target outputs for the network.

3.2   Region of Interest

Even with optimal filtering of the mouth, in some cases the filtered image contains unwanted artifacts. In order to reduce the impact of such occurrences, we extract a region of interest (ROI) from the whole image, by using vertical and horizontal signatures. Each signature is a vector containing sums of the pixel values for a specific row or column of the image. The boundaries of the ROI can be found by looking for raising and falling edges in each of the vectors. Even if the artifacts are big enough to appear on the image signatures, their influence can be removed by assuming temporal consistency of the ROI boundaries between consecutive frames. Only the part of the filtered image that falls within the ROI is further processed.

3.3   Feature Vectors Extraction

The extracted ROI is normalized and treated as a bivariate distribution $I(X,Y)$. The mean of this distribution $[EX, EY]$ approximates accurately and in a stable way the center of the mouth. Using this value, we transform the image into polar coordinates:

$$J(a,r) = I\big(EX + r\cos(a), EY + r\sin(a)\big) \tag{2}$$

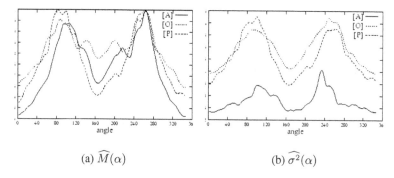

(a) $\widehat{M}(\alpha)$ (b) $\widehat{\sigma^2}(\alpha)$

Fig. 2. Average values of $\widehat{M}(\alpha)$ and $\widehat{\sigma^2}(\alpha)$ for specific visemes

and we concentrate on the conditional distributions $J(a = \alpha, r)$. We therefore define the following functions of mean and variance values for any angle α:

$$M(\alpha) = \frac{\int_r J(\alpha, r) \cdot r\, dr}{\int_r J(\alpha, r)\, dr} \tag{3}$$

$$\sigma^2(\alpha) = \frac{\int_r J(\alpha, r) \cdot (r - M(\alpha))^2\, dr}{\int_r J(\alpha, r)\, dr}. \tag{4}$$

As the image is discrete rather that continuous, all of the values are obtained from summation rather than integration, so we only operate on estimations of those values, namely $\widehat{M}(\alpha)$ and $\widehat{\sigma^2}(\alpha)$. The value of $\widehat{M}(\alpha)$ for a specific angle relates directly to the distance of the lips from the center of the mouth in a given direction. Therefore, a vector constructed from those values for a number of angles describes the shape of the mouth on a given image. Such shape profiles were gathered from a video sequence of spoken Dutch. Viseme groups were created. Fig. 2(a) shows three profiles for visemes [A], [o u O y Y 2: 9:] and [p b m]. In order to obtain scale independence, the vectors were scaled so that all their values fit in the $\langle 0, 1 \rangle$ interval. It can be seen that the [O] viseme can be distinguished from the others by its relatively high $\widehat{M}$ value in the middle. There is however no feasible way of distinguishing between [A] and [p b m] visemes. The lip shapes that correspond to those visemes are completely different (mouth closed versus mouth opened), but scaling of feature vectors removes all of those differences. As the values of $\widehat{M}$ alone are not sufficient for extracting useful data from the video sequence, we use additional information about the variance of conditional distributions ($\widehat{\sigma^2}$). Those values are also scaled in order to obtain size independence, but the scaling factor is directly determined by the values of $\widehat{M}$ rather than $\widehat{\sigma^2}$. These values capture the fact that the lips of a wide-stretched mouth, appear thinner than those of a closed mouth when related to the overall size of the mouth. As an example, the [A] viseme clearly shows much lower $\widehat{\sigma^2}$ values than the other visemes (see Fig. 2(b)). The last stage of feature vector extraction is sub-sampling of the $\widehat{M}$ and $\widehat{\sigma^2}$ functions into vectors that can be further processed. Obviously, the chosen sampling rate is a compromise between accuracy and processing efficiency. After some experiments with the data we chose to use the 18-dimensional vectors for both $\widehat{M}$ and $\widehat{\sigma^2}$ [18].

3.4 Intensity Features Extraction

The features discussed up to now concentrate on the shape of the lips, but the sounds that are being spoken also depend on the position of the teeth and most of all on the position of the tongue. Unfortunately, these are often not visible. However, the part of the teeth that is visible can easily be found, using an intensity filter, since they are much brighter than the rest of the face.

The tongue on the other hand is hard to detect as it has almost the same color as the lips, but it is straightforward to find the part of the mouth cavity that is not obscured by the tongue as it usually is much darker that the rest of the face. We use stepwise linear shaped filters for identifying the teeth and the mouth cavity, given by:

$$f_{\text{teeth}}(v) = \begin{cases} 0 & \text{for } 0 \leq v \leq t_{\text{teeth}}; \\ \eta(v - t_{\text{teeth}}) & \text{for } t_{\text{teeth}} < v \leq 1. \end{cases} \tag{5}$$

$$f_{\text{cav}}(v) = \begin{cases} 0 & \text{for } t_{\text{cav}} \leq v \leq 1; \\ \gamma(t_{\text{cav}} - v) & \text{for } 0 \leq v < t_{\text{cav}}. \end{cases} \tag{6}$$

With threshold values $t_{\text{teeth}}, t_{\text{cav}} \in \mathbb{R}$. The slope steepness factor $\eta = (1 - t_{\text{teeth}})^{-1}$ is calculated so that the resulting filter produces values in the $[0, 1]$ interval; γ is calculated in the same way. The resulting images are once again interpreted as distributions and a number of quantitative values is extracted from them: the total area of the highlighted region and the position of the center of gravity relative to the center of the mouth:

$$p_\phi = \sum_{x,y} I_\phi(x, y) \tag{7}$$

$$X_\phi = \frac{1}{p_\phi} \sum_{x,y} x I_\phi(x, y) - X_{\text{center}} \tag{8}$$

$$Y_\phi = \frac{1}{p_\phi} \sum_{x,y} y I_\phi(x, y) - Y_{\text{center}} \tag{9}$$

where $\phi \in \{teeth, cav\}$. Fig. 3 shows an example of changes in p_{teeth} and p_{cav} during the pronunciation of the Dutch number sequence *zes, acht* (six, eight). It can be well seen how the visibility of the teeth dominates during the pronunciation of the word *zes* (["zEs]) and how the increase of the p_{cav} at the end of the sequence relates to the phoneme [A] in *acht* ["Axt] being spoken later.

4   Relations Between Models

In a post processing stage, the features obtained by any of the above described feature extraction techniques can be transformed using Principal Component Analysis (PCA).

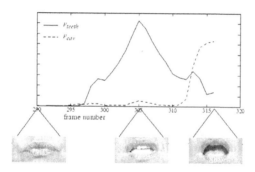

Fig. 3. Changes in two intensity features

Table 1. Correlation between 1st PCs of different tracking techniques

	RI	PT	MBT	LGE
Raw Image	1.00000			
Point Tracking	0.73325	1.00000		
Model-Based Tracking	0.69635	0.98266	1.00000	
LGE	0.65130	0.92246	0.93243	1.00000

The rationale behind this kind of linear transformation is that it allows for grading the newly obtained features according to their contribution to the overall variation in the dataset. It is also very common that the main Principal Components (PCs) relate to some properties of the data that can be intuitively named. For example, in the dataset obtained from tracking the points on the mouth contour, the first PC can be described as the degree of openness of the mouth. The second PC represents the degree to which the mouth is stretched. Surprisingly, this observation holds independently of the feature extraction method and can even be found in three-dimensional tracking [20].

To investigate this effect we implemented several different systems, one that works directly on the extracted ROI, the LGE system described above as well as a point- and a model-based tracker. The color-based point tracker tracks 10 points on the mouth contours. The points are located on different ascending or descending edges of the color filtered image of the ROI. The outer contour of the mouth is described by the mouth corners and the points laying on the mouth contour at $\frac{3}{8}$, $\frac{1}{2}$ and $\frac{5}{8}$ of the mouth width. On the inner mouth contour, two points laying exactly at $\frac{1}{2}$ of the mouth width are tracked. The model-based tracker comprises four parabolas that approximate the inner and outer contours of the lips. The model is constrained with respect to possible configurations, so that the inner contour is limited to the positions within the outer contour and some degree of symmetry is preserved with respect to the vertical axis.

Table 1 summarizes the correlations between the first PC from the different lip tracking techniques. The correlation between the data based on the geometric properties of the lips does not fall below 0.9, which means that there is no significant difference between those methods. The raw-data extraction path is totally different from the geometric one and therefore the correlation between its first component and the others is significantly lower; just above 0.65.

If lip reading techniques do indeed capture the desired information it should be possible to find a relationship with the speech audio signal since both have a common cause. To test this hypothesis we looked at the mutual information of the audio and video streams. If those signals are somehow related, we may expect that the mutual information measure will peak when they are in sync and be negligible when they are far out of sync. The results of such a calculation where the start of the video stream is shifted from 4 seconds before the start of the audio stream (100 frames) to 4 seconds after the start of the audio stream are presented in Fig. 4. In order to simplify the calculations we assumed that both signals have a Gaussian nature. It can clearly be seen that there is a relevant amount of information that is shared between the two modalities and that this information is at least to some extent preserved in the stream of features extracted from the visual data.

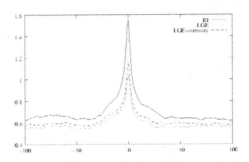

Fig. 4. Mutual information for audio and video features

4.1   Person Independent Feature Space

Even though data extraction techniques capture the proper and relevant information from the incoming signal, they cannot always guarantee that for different subjects the dynamic ranges will be preserved. However, as argued above experiments show that the first few principal components, independent of a person's lip shape, consistently match with the same descriptive labels referring to the physical changes of the mouth shape. This suggests that we may acquire a more useful and reliable projection of the data set by applying PCA on a per person basis.

There are some potential issues that have to be considered when performing a Person Adaptive PCA (PAPCA). Firstly, a suitable projection matrix should be constructed within a short period of time without requiring a large set of recordings from each subject. Our experiments show that in case of LGE, the projection stabilizes within about 30 seconds of speech data. That is, 30 seconds of speech data usually covers a whole range of possible mouth shapes. The other caveat in performing PAPCA is that although the directions of the components reflect the information in the data set, their orientation is purely coincidental. There is no guarantee that the PCs will not flip to opposite orientation. This can be remedied in different ways. It is possible for example to build a recognizer in such a way that it is invariant of the sign of the feature vector components. Although this solution is very simple, it influences negatively the number of

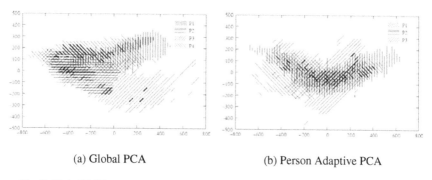

(a) Global PCA   (b) Person Adaptive PCA

Fig. 5. Global PCA versus Person Adaptive PCA for LGE features of different persons

classes in the input that can be distinguished by the recognizer. Another solution would be to put specific constraints on the projection matrix based on our knowledge of possible mouth movements; this is the one we chose to implement. The third relatively simple problem that remains is that the dynamic ranges of the shape changes may be different for different people. Fortunately, this can be fixed relatively easy by using the variance in each of the PCs to scale the data appropriately. The results of projecting data from three different subjects using the adapted transformations is depicted in 5(b). All of the gathered data sets display the same U-shape structure, which relates to the fact that in normal speech the mouth is a bit narrowed when it is closed or fully open, and when it is maximally stretched it is usually also half opened. Moreover, the distribution overlap for all subjects remains above 0.8.

5   Bimodal Speech Recognition

In this section we will describe our continuous speech processing system augmented with lip reading capabilities, which was developed for the purpose of testing the LGE technique in this context. In the literature, one can find encouraging results with early integration schemes when applied to limited vocabulary recognition [21]. We decided therefore to start with the earlier developed speech recognizer and to extend it with lip reading capabilities by using a state synchronous multi-stream HMM architecture [19]. Because recognition rates are already pretty high for a baseline auditory-only speech recognizer, we cannot really expect much further improvement from introducing of the visual modality or fine-tuning of the integration strategies. What is much more interesting is whether the lip reading-capable system would show an improvement over our baseline speech recognizer in noisy conditions. As can be seen in Fig. 6, our bimodal speech recognizer did not perform significantly different from the baseline system if the signal to noise ratio (SNR) was above 8dB. However at lower SNR values, lip reading appeared to help the speech recognition significantly. The improvement can be seen as a perceptual noise reduction by on average 1.4dB for the SNRs below 8dB. The results depicted in Fig. 6 show that the benefits of lip reading for speech recognition depend on the level of acoustic noise in the incoming data. We decided to investigate which part of the recognizer is most affected by noise, and where lip reading might help even

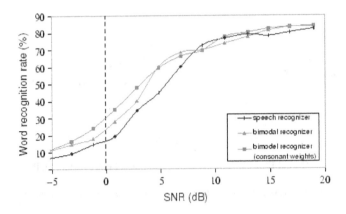

Fig. 6. Recognition performance of three different speech recognizers for different SNR levels

more. It turned out that the recognition of consonants suffers most from the presence of noise. At the same time, the lip reading part of the system seemed to perform especially well on consonants. Concluding, we can improve the performance of our system by varying the stream weights for consonants depending on the SNR level. The results of such experiments are also depicted in Fig. 6. The effective noise reduction is on average 2.5dB, more than 1dB better than the noise reduction of the fixed weight system. The disadvantage of this approach is that the noise level must be known beforehand in order to adjust the weights accordingly. In typical situations such information is not available during speech processing. There are however methods for estimating the weighting coefficients based on different measures of the incoming signal [22].

6   Conclusions

The quest for the most accurate and robust processing model for lip tracking is still on. Many researchers strive to achieve the perfect processing pipeline with hopes to overcome the problems inherent in lip reading. It is our opinion that this noble quest may not be that relevant to lip reading recognition results as generally assumed. Entirely different methods extract essentially the same amount of information from the video signal. This is a very important result for the lip reading community. The developers of lip reading systems may now start to concentrate on the recognition models themselves and assume that they will be able to plug in any mouth tracking method that appears to be the most robust at a later point in time. The LGE method developed by us and used in several experiments up to now appears to be very competitive with other approaches with some strong points on in its favor. The previously mentioned equivalence of different geometry-based methods suggests that the results from our current and previous experiments also apply to other processing models. Finally, the PAPCA based on the variability of the normal speech data provides a good base for a feature space that is person independent. It satisfies several conditions that need to be met before it can be used in a lip reading application. First of all, the projection can be established on the basis of a relatively small amount of calibration data. Second, it allows us to remove the inter-person differences from the extracted features. And last but certainly not least it provides us with a relatively good separation of the phoneme/viseme distributions.

References

1. Young, S.: Large vocabulary continuous speech recognition: A review. In Proceedings of the IEEE Workshop on Automatic Speech Recognition and Understanding, pages 3–28, Snowbird, Utah, December 1995. IEEE.
2. Fujimoto, M., Ariki, Y.: Noise Robust Speech Recognition by Integration of MLLR Adaptation and Feature Extraction for Noise Reduced Speech, IPSJ SIGNotes Spoken Language Processing No.039.
3. Boll, S.F.: Suppression of acoustic noise in speech using spectral subtraction, IEEE Trans. Acoust. Speech Signal Process. ASSP–27 (1979) pp. 113-120.
4. Sumby, W.H., Pollack, I.: Visual contribution to speech intelligibility in noise. Journal of the Acoustical Society of America, 26:212–215, 1954.
5. Benoit, K.S., Mohamadi, C.: Audio-visual intelligibility of French speech in noise. Journal of Speech and Hearing Research, 37:1195–1203, 1994.
6. McGurk, H., MacDonald, J.: Hearing lips and seeing voices, Nature, vol. 264, pp. 746–748, 1976.
7. Potamianos, G., Neti, C., Gravier, G., Garg, A., Senior, A.W.: Recent advances in the Automatic Recognition of Audiovisual , Proceedings of the IEEE, Vol. 91, No. 9, September 2003.
8. Chen, T.: Audio-Visual speech processing. IEEE Signal Processing Magazine, pages 9-21, January 2001.
9. Luettin, J., Thacker, N.A., Beet, S.W.: Speechreading using shape and intensity information, in Proceedings of ICSLP'96, 1996, pp. 44–47.
10. Stork, S.W., Hennecke, M.E. (Eds.): Speechreading by Humans and Machines, ser. NATO ASI Series, Series F: Computer and Systems Sciences. Berlin: Springer Verlag, 1996.
11. Tamura S., Iwano K., Furui, S.: Multi-Modal Speech Recognition Using Optical-Flow Analysis for Lip Images, J. VLSI Signal Process. Syst., volume 36, no. 2–3, 117–124, 2004, Kluwer Academic Publishers
12. Coianiz, T., Torresani, L., Caprile, B.: 2D deformable models for visual speech analysis. In D.G. Stork and M.E. Hennecke, ed. Speechreading by Humans and Machines. NATO ASI Series, Series F: Computer and Systems Sciences. Springer Verlag, Berlin, 1996.
13. Nefian, A.V., Liang, L., Pi, X., Liu, X., Murphy, K.: Dynamic Bayesian Networks for Audio-Visual Speech Recognition, EURASIP Journal on Applied Signal Processing 2002:11, 1–15.
14. Neti, C., Potamianos, G., Luettin, J., Matthews, I., Glotin, H., Vergyri, D.: Large-vocabulary audio-visual speech recognition: A summary of the Johns Hopkins Summer 2000 Workshop, in Proc. Works. Multimedia Signal Processing, Cannes, France, 2001, pp. 619–624.
15. Krone, G., Talle, B., Wichert, A., Palm, G.: Neural architectures for sensorfusion in speech recognition, in Proc. Europ. Tut. Works. Audio-Visual Speech Processing, Rhodes, Greece, 1997, pp. 57–60.
16. Goecke, R., Millar, J., Zelinsky, A., Robert-Ribes, J.: Automatic extraction of lip feature points. In proceedings of the Australian Conference on Robotics and Automation ACRA 2000, pages 31-36, Melbourne, Australia, September 2000.
17. Massaro, D.W., Stork, D.G.: Speech recognition and sensory integration, American Scientist, 86:236–244, 1998.

18. Wojdel, J.C., Rothkrantz, L.J.M.: Using Aerial and Geometric Features in Automatic Lipreading, in Proc. Eurospeech 2001, Scandinavia, September 2001.
19. Wiggers, P., Wojdel, J.C., Rothkrantz, L.J.M.: Medium vocabulary continuous audio-visual speech recognition, in Proceedings of ICSLP 2002, Denver CO, USA: ISCA, September 2002, pp. 1921-1924.
20. Kshirsagar, S., Mangnenat-Thalman, N.: Viseme space for realistic speech animation. In: Massaro et al. (2001), pp. 30-35.
21. Potamianos, G., Neti, C.: Automatic speechreading of impaired speech. In: Massaro et al (2001), pp. 177–182.
22. Lucey, S., Sridharan, S., Chandran, V.: A link between cepstral shrinking and the weighted product rule in audio-visual speech recognition. In proceedings of ICSL 2002. ISCA, Denver CO, USA.

Speech Based User Interface
for Users with Special Needs

Pavel Slavík, Vladislav Němec, and Adam J. Sporka

Czech Technical University in Prague, Faculty of Electrical Engineering
Department of Computer Science and Engineering
Karlovo náměstí 13, 12135 Praha 2, Czech Republic

Abstract. The number of people using computers is permanently increasing in last years. Not all potential users have all capabilities that allow them to use computers without obstacles. This is especially true for handicapped and elderly users. For this class of users a special approach for design and implementation of user interfaces is needed. The missing capabilities of these users must be substituted by capabilities that these users have. In most of cases the use of sounds and speech offers a natural solution to this problem. In the paper the outline of problems related to special user interfaces will be discussed. In further the examples of application of user interfaces using special forms of speech and related acoustic communication will be given.

1 Introduction

Along with the continuous "wide-spreading" of the modern technologies, including personal computers, multimedia and the internet, requirements on the quality of human-machine interaction keep emerging. Although these requirements are partly induced by new technologies and types of applications user has to interact with, quite large set of requirements originates in specific needs of the users. The growing segment of population that works with computers imposes another large class of requirements for design and implementation of user interfaces.

In this paper, we focus on interfaces for users with various special needs—especially users with various forms of impairment limiting their abilities to perceive information in one or more modalities, or to control an application. During our experiments, special forms of speech and related acoustic communication used for providing information to the user or as a control mechanism were examined and investigated.

2 Obstacles in UI Induced by Impairments

Basic schema of human-machine interaction introduces the view of a dialogue held between these two communication partners. This scenario implies the existence of two communication channels: One channel that allows the user to receive information from the system (input channel) and another channel making possible to control the system (control channel). Particular impairment on the user's side limits somehow the use of one or both of these channels. In this section, we will describe various forms of such limitation. In further text, we will concentrate on the investigation of user interfaces for

V. Matoušek et al. (Eds.): TSD 2005, LNAI 3658, pp. 45–55, 2005.

the visually impaired users (the input channel impairment) and motor impaired users (the control channel impairment) in which case the speech and sound control will be our preferable means of control.

The assistive techniques and technologies are based on mapping of modalities or controls. On one side there are modalities and controls that certain groups of users are unable to use, while on the other side there are modalities and controls that are usable by this group. The assistive technologies map the modalities that *have to* be used (e.g. screen with text containing important information for a visually impaired user) onto those that *can* be used (e.g. speech synthesis).

2.1   Limitations of User's Input Channel

Limitations in input channel are the reason of the user's impairment of sensation. Depending on the degree of the impairment, the reception of information is limited or impossible through the impaired senses.

Visual Impairments. Apart from the ocular motor problems and other impairments (such as color blindness, photophobia etc.), there are two main categories of visual impairment in the general population that significantly influence user interface needs:

- Total loss of sight. Users in this category are unable to read and perceive graphic or other visual information. The blindness also often changes the understanding of the human environment itself and states new paradigms for cognition and thinking.
- The partial sight allows use the visual modality with some restrictions or modifications — for example, screen magnifiers, attention attractors etc. However, the users in this category can of course use the solutions for the users with no sight as well.

The assistive technologies for the visually impaired users are often based on adaptation of the graphic user interface to acoustic or haptic modality. The acoustic modality may carry the information either via speech synthesis or non-verbal audio (auditory icons [5] and earcons [1]). The haptic modality [16] may be also used to convey textual information (Braille line), however using haptic mouse devices, force feedback joysticks, or special hardware such as Phantom [13] enables the user also to perceive spatial relations between the elements of the user interface.

Other Impairments. For sake of completeness, we will now briefly mention hearing and cognitive disabilities that also significantly limit the ability to receive information, however in this article we do not provide their detailed discussion of them.

Hearing impairments cause difficulties of reception of information through the sound. According to [6] the surrounding sound can be divided into the following levels: *social* (e.g. human talk or music), *warning* (informing about important events or danger), and *primitive* (ambient sound). When adapting a system, which uses the acoustic modality, we do not necessarily have to provide an access to the ambient level of sound to users with the hearing impairments as it does not carry any information important for the function of the system. For two other classes, the solution is either:

- to change the interaction mechanism to avoid the sound warning or eliminate the necessity of informing the user of such situations, or

– to map the acoustic modality onto a different modality the user is able to perceive (for example, the visual modality may be used to deliver the information either through the synthesis of sign language, or written text).

Cognitive difficulties cover wide area of various (mostly mental) impairments resulting in problems with information perception and understanding. This problem cannot be solved by previously mentioned information transformation—it requires introducing new concepts and interaction paradigms, because the problem does not lie in the selected presentation modality but in the understanding the task itself.

2.2 Limitations in Control Channel

The limitations of the control channel represent an opposite problem than the limitations of the input channel. While some users may have no problems receiving the external information, their ability of physical motion needed when operating a computer may be reduced by one of many forms of motor disabilities [21].

The primary goal of the assistive technologies for people with motor disabilities is to provide a transparent replacement of devices that can not be used due to the impairment. They may be divided into the following categories:

– *Computer vision based techniques.* They are based on monitoring of visible changes of posture (such as nose tip tracking [7]) or eye tracking [15].
– *Contact controllers.* E.g. muscle activity sensors, sip-and-puff controllers, or tongue joysticks.
– *Methods of processing of acoustic signal.* This category is represented by the speech recognition or currently emerging methods of non-speech audio control that make use of continuous monitoring of certain acoustic parameters of the sound produced by the user.

Another possible division of the control techniques is the discrete vs. continuous control. While the discrete methods are operated in a "query-response" manner (such as the speech recognition) and are therefore useful for issuing individual commands, the continuous methods (eye-tracking, non-speech audio, tongue joysticks, etc.) are more suitable for a real-time control of analogue values (such as coordinates of the mouse cursor pointer).

3 Our Research of Assistive Techniques

In this section we present research activities of our department focused on reducing the barriers between applications and users with specific needs. According to classification introduced in section 2 we will present the systems and experiments divided into two groups depending on the type of the interaction communication channel (input or control).

3.1 Information Presentation

The information presentation is performed through the input channel. We have focused our activities on the providing access to information for the visually impaired users.

Speech-Based Navigation in Virtual Environment. In this area we have performed several experiments with the goal to test the possibility of creation a full-featured virtual 3D environment browser allowing visually impaired users to walk through scenes and inspect them. The complex test system provides several means of information delivery concerning navigation and surrounding environment.

Our virtual navigation system, as described in [11], is based on enhanced geometrical description of 3D scene comprising textual description of all objects and their relations (see Fig. 1). Avatar (representation of the user in virtual environment) can move freely in a virtual scene and get the information about the surrounding environment using special queries. By means of information acquired this way the user can make flexible decisions about their next move.

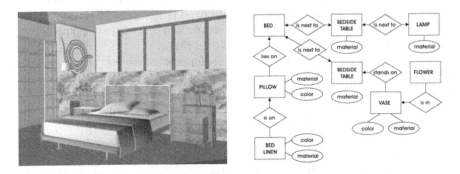

Fig. 1. The example of the 3D scene and part of its functional description.

The navigation and queries are controlled by mouse gestures [14] and all feedback from system is realized as textual information that is converted to speech using a commonly available text-to-speech system. The queries allow to inspect object properties, relations, avatar's neighborhood etc.—for example "what are all wooden objects in the room?", "which is the nearest object?" or "what is to the right from my current position?"

Later on, we have enhanced this type of navigation with simulated cane tapping. The cane is used by the visually impaired people to gain additional information on the surrounding environment. As the cane collides with the floor, walls and other objects in vicinity, the collisions generate sound depending on the features of the objects. The sounds are also subject to the reverberation of the environment. From its timbre and length, the visually impaired people receive information on the size of the environment.

By simulation of cane tapping in virtual environment, it is possible to make a virtual walk through the scene. We have implemented such an extension to our 3D environment browser. We have employed a simple method of sound bank (database of sound samples indexed by appropriate materials) and methods of spatial audio [4] using common 3D sound acceleration hardware [2].

Another extension to our 3D environment browser we have built is the "obstacle radar". Also this concept allows the users to explore interactively the vicinity of their avatar. The sonar provides sonification of the surrounding obstacles in the scene (see

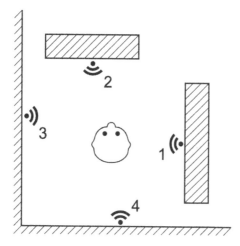

Fig. 2. Principle of sonar. The numbers denote the order in which the virtual sources produce sounds.

Fig. 2) in a similar way like in [18]. When activated, every obstacle visible from the position of avatar becomes a virtual sound source and produces a short beep.

To distinguish the type of the obstacle, during basic experiments we have assigned different sound stimuli to walls, doors and other obstacles. To ease the localization, we have selected a compound synthesized signal, as suggested in [9]. To enhance the information, the beep of each door is followed by the name of room on the other side of the door recited by the text-to-speech, properly spatialized to match its spatial relation to the avatar.

In more complex use-case the speech providing description of an obstacle is used for all objects—as we have implemented for door. The textual description transformed to speech is also used for all obstacles user collides with.

All these concepts were successfully tested in pilot version of the navigation system. The experiments proved the validity of our navigation concept and the usability of the solution ([10], [11].) Users were able to navigate in virtual scene, create mental model concerning the topology of objects in scene, materials of the objects and floor, size of individual rooms in virtual apartment etc. The system was also extended to integrate low cost haptic devices [12].

Tangible Newspaper. In this section, a prototype of a system based on tracking of user's index finger and use of the text-to-speech synthesis is described. In this system, the process of scanning a newspaper by eyes is mapped onto the motion of the finger. The current position of finger specifies the area of interest while the speech synthesis substitutes the process of reading of text in the area of interest.

While presentation of text by means of various techniques, such as the text-to-speech synthesis or Braille line, is a well-established discipline, relatively small amount of attention has been paid to the presentation of layout of the printed material to the visually impaired. In certain kinds of documents, such as the newspapers or stationery prints, the layout of a document brings its reader important contextual information that allows to evaluate the importance of different parts of the document (e.g. the headline story usually placed on the upper half of the cover page being more important than other news located on a different position of the same page.) Though this information may be presented explicitly (textual description of context, or non-speech audio), certain amount of perception of authenticity could be gained if the visually impaired readers were able to "touch" the layout of the page by themselves.

We have elaborated this idea in the prototype of our system Tangible Newspaper [19] that allows the blind users to explore the layout of the document rather than its actual content. The document is placed on a desk in the view of a camera placed above it. The tip of user's index finger is tracked by means of algorithms of the computer vision. As the user moves the finger over the document, the layout of its logical units (articles) is revealed by means of a sonification of their boundaries and the speech synthesis. Fig. 3 shows the schema of the system.

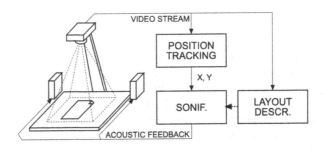

Fig. 3. Conceptual Overview of the Tangible Newspaper.

From the initial user study as described in [19], we were able to conclude that the users were capable to explore the spatial relations and positioning of the polygonal regions within the presented documents.

3.2 Acoustic Methods of User Interface Control

In our research of alternative control methods in the human-computer interaction we have focused mainly on the use of the sound as the primary control channel for users with reduced or no ability of use the conventional devices, such as keyboards or mice.

Non-speech Acoustic Control of Mouse Pointer. Though the eye tracking may be successfully used to emulate the mouse device, certain limitations (such as high cost of the device or users physical challenges) may prevent the users from using it. Among the low-cost alternatives, the acoustic control is one of the easiest to implement and deploy. Acoustic methods of mouse control usually involve the use of the speech recognition. Through a set of voice commands, the user may control the positioning of the mouse pointer on the screen and control the operation of the mouse buttons.

However, severe motor impairments are frequently accompanied by speech disorder. It is not unusual that the acoustic manifestations of such people are limited only to humming or hissing which render the speech recognition techniques unusable for them. Having this in mind, we have developed a system that maps the movement of the mouse device onto special melodic patterns, as shown in Fig. 4. Only horizontal motion, vertical motion, or clicking may be performed at a time. The system is based on measurement of basic frequency of voice and tracking its changes over time.

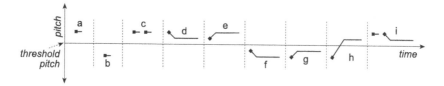

Fig. 4. Examples of control tones. a—left button click, b—right button click, c—double click, d—motion down, e—motion up, f—motion to the left, g—motion to the right, h—fast motion, i—drag and drop.

The usability tests we have performed have shown that this method of mouse control may fully substitute the mouse device in common operations such as web page browsing [17] and may be used by people in all age groups [18].

Non-speech Acoustic Control of Keyboard Emulation. A similar motivation and approach have been employed to implement the non-speech acoustic operated keyboard emulation. Different keys are mapped on unique acoustic patterns produced by the user. We have identified the following two mappings. Both make use of the tracking of the basic voice frequency of humming.

The *pitch-to-address* mapping method is based on definition of an address space in which each key is assigned a unique address. Fig. 5 shows an example of address space $4 \times 4 \times 4$, four lines, each containing four blocks, of which each contains four keys. An address is specified as a sequence of its coordinates A1, A2, and A3. The value of each coordinate is given by humming a tone whose frequency belongs to certain interval. During the operation, for the users reference, they are being shown the onscreen table of characters, and a visual feedback of progress of entering the key addresses.

The principle of the *pattern-to-key* mapping method is to recognize the acoustic gestures, short melodic patterns, composed of individual tone primitives. They may be considered a certain extension of the well-known Morse Code. Each key is assigned a unique acoustic gesture. By producing an acoustic gesture, appropriate keystroke is emulated. The gestures are composed of the following tone primitives: low tone _, high tone ¯, raising tone /, and falling tone \. Also for this method, the users may use the onscreen reference and visual feedback. The set of gestures of as shown in Table 1.

From the initial usability experiment we have performed it was clear that the users were able to use the system to enter the text.

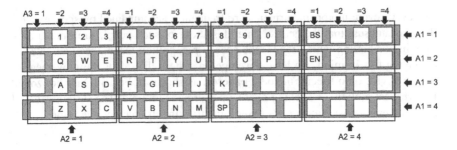

Fig. 5. Pitch-to-address mapping address space; SP...space, EN...enter, BS...back space; E.g. to emulate a keystroke of key 'R', coordinates A1, A2, and A3 must be 2, 2, and 1.

Table 1. Pattern-to-mapping method.

key	gesture	key	gesture	key	gesture	key	gesture
A	//	K	V_	U	V	4	__V
B	_V	L	_	V	\/	5	‾‾/
C	/‾	M	‾/	W	\/\/	6	‾‾\
D	‾∧	N	‾\	X	/\	7	‾‾∧
E	_	O	∧	Y	V‾	8	‾‾V
F	/_	P	_∧	Z	\‾/	9	‾‾
G	∧_	Q	/_\	0	___	Space	_
H	\\	R	_\	1	__/	Back.	__
I	\	S	/\/	2	__\	Enter	_/
J	‾V	T	/	3	__∧		

Acoustic Control of Games. A special type of applications is represented by computer games whose primary purpose is to entertain and amuse their users (players). As the segment of population affected by the gaming industry continuously grows, it becomes important to take into account also the players with specific needs.

While the principles of the user interface of many turn-taking games (such as chess or checkers) or strategic simulators (e.g. SimCity) do not differ from the user interface of other common desktop applications, the situation is different for games played in "real time", such as different.

E.g. in Tetris [20], the users ability to quickly issue a control command is critical, while the amount of possible commands is fairly limited to elementary operations such as "shift the brick sideways", "rotate the brick", and so on. When designing the acoustic control for the motor impaired people, it is useful to map these individual commands directly onto acoustic patterns rather than trying to emulate another control device (such as keyboard) by means of which Tetris is usually controlled on a standard PC.

In our current research, we compare the efficiency of speech and non-speech control of some of the classic game genres with Tetris as one of our use cases (Fig. 6). While most speech recognizers wait for the users to finish their utterance, and only then they

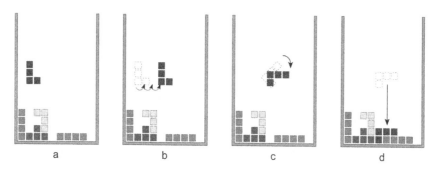

Fig. 6. A sequence of board configurations of the Tetris game. a → b: a brick moved three steps to the right; b → c: the brick turned clockwise; c → d: the brick dropped.

initiate the recognition, the non-speech audio may be processed and interpreted on-the-fly as users produce it. A game may be therefore more responsive when controlled by means of the non-speech audio. A comparison between the speech and non-speech control is shown in Tab. 2. It shows the elements of control used to steer a brick on the game board as shown in figure 6.

Table 2. Comparison of speech and non-speech acoustic control of tetris.

Step	Speech recognition	Non-speech control
a → b	"right", "right", "right"	Raising tone; kept until the brick moves three steps to the right
b → c	"clockwise"	Short flat tone
c → d	"drop"	Long flat tone

The evaluation of above mentioned control method is a work in progress, however results of a preliminary study are encouraging. Most users participating in a demonstration stated that they found these methods of control of the game natural and amusing. A performance study to compare the efficiency of speech vs. non-speech control is an immediate follow-up.

4 Conclusion

In this paper, we have described and illustrated problems that the users with various forms of impairments are facing in their practice using computer systems and interacting with common applications. We have shown that using a suitable mapping of one kind of information onto another it is possible to minimize the impact of impairment on the user's performance.

The mapping concepts were successfully tested in various applications implementing audible user interfaces for information access and control. The concept of virtual environment browser for visually impaired users (based on speech and spatial sound) and the tangible newspaper application were described in part discussing the information providing, several concepts of controlling mouse pointer and keyboard using sound were introduced in part discussing audible application control. All these concepts and systems summarize the general thought of the mapping of modalities according to user specific needs.

Our future work is focused on the development of the methodology for extensive usability evaluations of the above methods and systems. Particularly, user and usability tests of various non-speech control techniques and their comparison to existing assistive devices will be performed.

References

1. Blattner, M., Sumikawa, D., Greenberg, R.: Earcons and icons: their structure and common design principles. Human Computer Interaction vol. 4 (1989) 11–44
2. EAX – Redefining the Audio Experience. Available at: http://www.soundblaster.com/eax/ (May 2005)
3. Franklin, K. M., Roberts, J. C. : Pie Chart Sonification. In: Proceedings of the Seventh International Conference on Information Visualization: 4–9. IEEE, London (2003)
4. Funkhouser, T., Jot, J.-M., Tsingos, N.: Sounds Good to Me!. Computational Sound for Graphics, Virtual Reality, and Interactive Systems. SIGGRAPH 2002 Course Notes, ACM (2002)
5. Gaver, W.: Auditory icons: Using sound in computer interfaces. Human-Computer Interaction, 2. Lawrence Erlbaum Associates, Inc (1986) 167–177
6. Gilkey, R. H., Weisenberger, J. M.: The sense of presence for the suddenly deafened adult. Presence: Teleoperators and Virtual Environments, 4 (1995) 357–363
7. Gorodnichy, D. O., Malik, S., Roth, G.: Nouse – 'Use Your Nose as a Mouse' – a New Technology for Hands-free Games and Interfaces. In: Proceedings of International Conference on Vision Interface VI'2002 (2002) 354–361
8. Hämäläinen, P., Höyseniemi, J.: A Computer Vision and Hearing Based User Interface for a Computer Game for Children. In: Universal Access, Theoretical Perspectives, Practice, and Experience, LCNS 2615. Springer-Verlag Berlin, Heidelberg (2003) 299–318
9. Kurniawan, S. H., Sporka, A., Němec, V., Slavík, P.: Design and Evaluation of Computer-Simulated Spatial Sound. In Proceedings of the 2nd Cambridge Workshop on Universal Access and Assistive Technology. University of Cambridge Press, Cambridge, UK (2004) 137–146
10. Nemec, V., Mikovec Z., Slavik P.: Adaptive Navigation of Visually Impaired Users in Virtual Environment on the World Wide Web. In: Universal Access: Theoretical Perspectives, Practice, and Experience, 7th ERCIM International Workshop on User Interfaces for All, Paris, France, October 24–25, 2002, Revised Papers. LNCS 2615, Springer (2003) 68–79
11. Nemec, V., Sporka, A., Slavik, P.: Interaction of Visually Impaired Users in Virtual Environment with Spatial Sound Enhancement. In: Universal Access in HCI: Inclusive Design in the Information Society. Mahwah, New Jersey : Lawrence Erlbaum Associates, Publishers (2003) 1310–1314
12. Nemec, V., Sporka, A., Slavik, P.: Haptic and Spatial Audio Based Navigation of Visually Impaired Users in Virtual Environment Using Low Cost Devices. In: User-Centred Interaction Paradigms for Universal Access in the Information Society. Berlin: Springer (2004) 452–459.

13. PHANTOM Overview, on-line product presentation.
http://www.sensable.com/products/phantom_ghost/phantom.asp (May 2005)
14. Raskin, J.: The Humane Interface. Addison-Wesley (2000)
15. Sibert, L. E., Jacob, R. J. K.: Evaluation of Eye Gaze Interaction. In: Proceedings of CHI 2000 Conference on Human Factors in Computing Systems. ACM Press, The Hague, The Netherlands. (2000) 281–288
16. Sjöström, C.: Using Haptics in Computer Interfaces for Blind People. In: Proceedings of the Conference on Human Factors in Computing Systems (CHI2001), ACM Press, Seattle, USA (2001)
17. Sporka, A. J., Kurniawan, S. H., Slavik, P.: Whistling User Interface (U3I). In: User-Centred Interaction Paradigms for Universal Access in the Information Society. Berlin: Springer (2004) 472–478
18. Sporka, A. J., Kurniawan, S. H., Slavik, P., Mahud, M.: Tonal Control of Mouse Cursor (U3I): A Usability Study with The Elderly. To appear in proceedings of HCI International 2005, Las Vegas, Nevada (2005)
19. Sporka, A. J., Nemec, V., Slavik, P.: Tangible Newspaper for the Visually Impaired Users. In: Proceedings of CHI 2005. New York: ACM Press (2005) 1809–1812
20. Tetris. Entry in Wikipedia, the free encyclopedia. Available at:
http://en.wikipedia.org/wiki/Tetris (May 2005)
21. WebAIM: Motor Disabilities. http://www.webaim.org/techniques/motor (May 2005)

Automatic Construction of a Valency Lexicon of Czech Adjectives*

Drahomíra "Johanka" Doležalová

Institute of Formal and Applied Linguistics, Faculty of Mathematics and Physics
Charles University, Malostranské nám. 25, CZ-118 00, Praha 1 – Malá Strana, Czech Republic
johanka@ucw.cz

Abstract. This paper describes conversion of a surface valency lexicon of Czech verbs to a surface valency lexicon of adjectives that can be derived from these verbs and that use their (possibly modified) valency frames. After preparing the necessary data by hand, the conversion can be fully automatic and every change of the source lexicon can be automatically reflected in the destination lexicon. We have successfully converted the verb valency lexicon "Brief" with about 15,000 verbs to a valency lexicon of about 27,000 deverbal adjectives. The paper also describes some interesting peculiarities in the process of creating passive adjectives and their valency frames.

1 Introduction

Our work was performed as part of a rule-based morphological disambiguation project [5]. Disambiguation rules written manually by linguists often use surface valency information, which is represented by lists of verbs or adjectives having obligatory/facultative/impossible valency of some kind. Using these lists, the grammatical rules can, for example, remove accusative tags from all words in a sentence in case accusative valency is impossible for any word in the sentence.

We started with extracting necessary valency lists from corpora (ČNK, [1]), but then we decided to try to generate the lists automatically from a verb valency lexicon. We have chosen "Brief" [3], which was the largest surface verb valency lexicon available (about 15,000 verbs).

After successfully generating all necessary valency lists of verbs we needed also valency lists of deverbal adjectives, so we have developed a software tool for automatic conversion of Brief to a surface valency lexicon of adjectives derived from the verbs included in Brief (keeping the same format). (In fact, there exists no valency lexicon of Czech adjectives that would be comparable to the size of Brief, which, however, comprises only verbs.) Our lexicon includes about 27,000 adjectives with their surface valency frames. This paper describes the types of adjectives included in the lexicon, the process of conversion and the difficulties we had to deal with.

---

* The work described is funded by the *MŠMT* project No. LC536

V. Matoušek et al. (Eds.): TSD 2005, LNAI 3658, pp. 56–60, 2005.

2   Converting Verbs to Deverbal Adjectives

There are six types of deverbal adjectives, cf. [4], three of them use valency frames of the original verb – processual adjectives, resultative active adjectives and passive adjectives.

- *processual adjectives* are derived from imperfective verbs and they are used to modify the original subject (*psát – píšící* (*to write – writing*)). They have the same valency frames as the original verb;
- *resultative active adjectives* are derived from perfective verbs and they are also used to modify the original subject (*dokončit – dokončivší* (*to finish – finished* (*with something*))). They have also the same valency frames as the original verb;
- *passive adjectives* are derived from almost all the verbs having an object (typically expressed by accusative valency) and they are used to modify this object (*psát – psaný* (*written*), *dokončit – dokončený* ((*to be*) *finished*)). They take over valency frames including object position, but without this position itself.

To build the lexicon, we need to have all the adjectives of these three types with links to their original verbs (because of the valency frames). There are three ways of obtaining this data:

1. generating the adjectives from the verbs automatically (using our own paradigms)
2. using information about the derivation from a morphological lexicon
3. deriving the adjectives by hand.

We considered the automatic generation of the adjectives to be complicated (because of irregularities) and therefore for the first version of the lexicon we have combined the methods 2 and 3. We have tried to use information about the derivation from a morphological lexicon [2] and we have obtained about 85 % adjectives (the regular ones) with the necessary links to their original verbs, cf. [7]. The irregularly derived adjectives can also be obtained from the morphological lexicon, but without links, so we have derived them by hand (about 4,000 adjectives derived from 3,200 verbs). We had a feedback from ČNK [1] and from the verb valency lexicon concerning the missing adjectives – every verb must "produce" at least one processual or resultative active adjective and if the verb has an object (typically represented by accusative valency), it must have at least one passive adjective.

For the next version of the lexicon we have developed about 90 derivational paradigms (every paradigm specifies a suffix of a verb which is to be removed and suffixes of all three types of deverbal adjectives) and semi-automatically assigned them to the verbs. Indeed, this work could not be done without the first version of the lexicon – the paradigms are based mostly on this data.

If we don't want to overgenerate, we also need to know the aspect of every verb (because processual adjectives are derived only from imperfective verbs, likewise resultative active adjectives are derived only from perfective verbs). We have obtained this information from two morphological lexicons [2] [6] and then we made necessary comparisons and manual corrections.

Both [2] and [6] have a system of derivational paradigms for deverbal adjectives, but our system is more sophisticated and covers more boundary types of deverbal adjectives. Only 15 out of 15,000 verbs in Brief do not fit any of the paradigms and we keep them as exceptions (these derivations are "absolutely irregular": *být (to be) – jsoucí, housti (to play violin) – hudoucí, hudený* etc.).

3   Converting Valency Frames

Having the list of deverbal adjectives with links to their original verbs, the conversion of valency frames looks trivial (and for the most part of the lexicon it really is trivial).

Example 1. The valency of the verb *dokumentovat (to document)* which is both perfective and imperfective and the derived adjectives.
The valency of the verb in the "brief" format:

```
dokumentovat <v>hTc4,hTc4-hTc6r{na},hTc4-hTc7
```

The same entry in the verbose format:

```
dokumentovat
= co                    # what (acc)
= co & na čem           # what (acc) & on what (loc)
= co & čím              # what (acc) & by what (inst)
```

The derivational paradigm for this verb:

```
dokumentovat o -ovat -ující -ovavší -ovaný
```

The derived adjectives in the brief format[1]:

```
dokumentovaný <a>aOtY <o>dokumentovat <v>,hTc6r{na},hTc7
dokumentovavší <a>aDtM <o>dokumentovat <v>hTc4,hTc4-hTc6r{na},hTc4-hTc7
dokumentující <a>aNtG <o>dokumentovat <v>hTc4,hTc4-hTc6r{na},hTc4-hTc7
```

The same entry in the verbose format:

```
dokumentovaný          # passive adjective
= ; prázdná valence    # void valency frame
= na čem               # on what (loc)
= čím                  # by what (inst)
dokumentovavší         # resultative active adjective
= co                   # what (acc)
= co & na čem          # what (acc) & on what (loc)
= co & čím             # what (acc) & by what (inst)
dokumentující          # processual adjective
= co                   # what (acc)
= co & na čem          # what (acc) & on what (loc)
= co & čím             # what (acc) & by what (inst)
```

The derivation is performed by a Perl script. The script uses the verb valency lexicon and our additional data about all these verbs (derivational paradigm and aspect). Every time any of the data sources is changed, one can run the script and build a new lexicon. The script can also report some inconsistencies in the data (typos, missing verbs etc.).

---

[1] In the entries of passive adjectives the passive actor in the instrumental case is the default and therefore omitted. The instrumental valency mentioned in the frame means that the adjective has one more complementation in the instrumental case.

4 Peculiarities and Problems

After the application of the trivial algorithm mentioned above, many passive adjectives found in ČNK were not listed in our lexicon. This way we have found some peculiarities or exceptions in the derivation process.

Some verbs have an object in a case different from accusative (genitive, dative, instrumental), and a few (not all!) of them also form a passive adjective modifying the original object. For example: *ublížit komu – ublížený (to hurt someone (dat) – hurt)*, *opovrhovat kým – opovrhovaný (to despise someone (inst) – despised)*, *dotázat se koho – dotázaný (to ask someone (gen) – asked)* unlike its synonymous counterpart *zeptat se koho – *zeptaný*.

Another type of exception consists in that some perfective verbs describing the process affecting not an object in any case but the subject also form a passive adjective modifying the original subject behaving as an object. For example: *zemřít – zemřelý (to die – died)*, *vyrůst – vyrostlý (to grow up – grown)*, *zmrznout – zmrzlý (to freeze – frozen)*, *narodit se – narozený (to be born – born)*, *vydařit se – vydařený (to be successful – successful)*.

We have listed and included about 400 exceptions of this kind in the lexicon. Exceptions of the second type take over the whole valency information of the original verb, exceptions of the first type behave as common passive adjectives (taking over all the frames including an object without the object), and the program must only replace accusative by the case relevant for the verb. We also added a void valency frame to all these adjectives.

Example 2. The valency of the verb *opovrhovat* and derived adjectives.

```
opovrhovat <v>hPTc7
opovrhující <a>aNtG <o>opovrhovat <v>hPTc7
opovrhovaný <a>aVtY <o>opovrhovat <v>,

opovrhovat
= kým|čím              # sb (inst)
opovrhující           # processual adjective
= kým|čím              # sb (inst)
opovrhovaný           # passive adjective
= ; prázdná valence    # void valency frame
```

Example 3. The valency of the verb *narodit se* and derived adjectives.

```
narodit se <v>,hPTc7,hPc3
narodivší se <a>aDtM <o>narodit se <v>,hPTc7,hPc3
narozený <a>aDtY <o>narodit se <v>,hPTc7,hPc3

narodit se
= ; prázdná valence    # void valency frame
= kým|čím              # (as) sb (inst)
= komu                 # to sb (dat)
narodivší se           # resultative active adjective
```

```
= ; prázdná valence      # void valency frame
= kým|čím                # (as) sb (inst)
= komu                   # to sb (dat)
narozený                 # passive adjective
= ; prázdná valence      # void valency frame
= kým|čím                # (as) sb (inst)
= komu                   # to sb (dat)
```

5   Conclusion

We have compiled a surface valency lexicon including nearly all adjectives that can be
derived from verbs included in the verb valency lexicon Brief. Our lexicon uses almost
the same format, so it can be automatically processed using the tools developed for
Brief. Everyone who uses (and possibly modifies) Brief can make his own copy of our
lexicon corresponding with his version of Brief. Every automatic tool using Brief can
be easily modified in order to use our lexicon, which was verified in the rule-based
morphological disambiguation project where both lexicons are very useful. During the
comprehensive testing of the whole disambiguation system it was also verified that the
lexicon contains no significant errors.

References

1. Czech National Corpus. Faculty of Arts, Charles University. http://ucnk.ff.cuni.cz.
2. Hajič, J.: Disambiguation of Rich Inflection (Computational Morphology of Czech). Vol. 1.
   Karolinum Charles University Press Prague (2004)
3. Horák, A.: Verb Valency and Semantic Classification of Verbs. In: Proceedings of Text, Speech
   and Dialogue Brno (1998) 61–66
4. Karlík, P., Nekula, M., Rusínová, Z. et al. (eds.): Příruční mluvnice češtiny. Brno (1995)
5. Oliva, K., Hnátková, M., Petkevič, V., Květoň, P.: The Linguistic Basis of a Rule-Based Tagger
   of Czech. In: Proceedings of Text, Speech and Dialogue Brno (2000) 3–8
6. Sedláček, R.: Morphemic Analyser for Czech. PhD. thesis FI MU Brno (2004)
7. Spousta, M.: Automatické přiřazení tvaroslovných vzorů v češtině. Master thesis MFF UK
   Praha (2005)
```
```

WebTranscribe – An Extensible Web-Based Speech Annotation Framework

Christoph Draxler

Institut für Phonetik und Sprachliche Kommunikation (IPSK)
Universität München

Abstract. WebTranscribe is a platform independent and extensible web-based annotation framework for speech research and spoken language technology. The framework consists of an annotation editor front-end running as a Java Web Start application on a client computer, and a DBMS on a server. The framework implements a "select – annotate – save" annotation workflow.

The annotation capabilities are determined by annotation editors, implemented as plug-ins to the general framework. An annotation configuration generally consists of an editor, editing buttons, a signal display and a quality assessment panel. A configuration file determines which plug-ins to use for a given annotation project.

WebTranscribe has been used in numerous projects at BAS and has reached a mature state now. The software is freely available [19].

1 Introduction

The annotation of spoken language is a time-consuming and expensive task that requires skilled annotators or experts in the domain.

In speech processing, large corpora (thousands of speakers with a few hundred spoken items each in speech recognition (e.g. SpeechDat [12], etc.), or less than ten speakers with thousands of items for speech synthesis corpora (BITS [11], ESP [5])) need to be annotated under tight time and budget constraints, often on only one or a few annotation levels, e.g. orthography and phoneme level, etc. In speech research, relatively small speech corpora, e.g. from field or articulatory recordings (e.g. electro-magnetic articulatory or speech disorder recordings etc.), are annotated in great detail on as many annotation levels as possible, e.g. orthographic, phonetic, phonemic, sensor data interpretations, etc.

A web-based annotation system can provide significant advantages over classical platform dependent annotation systems with only local data access. For the annotation of large corpora, work can be performed by many annotators in parallel on any standard computer with a modern browser. For the annotation of highly specialized corpora, there may be only a few experts world-wide. They can work collaboratively on a corpus regardless of their geographic location and without the need of maintaining potentially inconsistent copies of a corpus under development.

Although the need for systems to support collaborative annotation was recognized quite early [13], and tools and models have been proposed [15], most of the current annotation editors do not support distributed or collaborative annotation (cf. 2.2).

V. Matoušek et al. (Eds.): TSD 2005, LNAI 3658, pp. 61–68, 2005.

The BAS (Bavarian Archive for Speech Signals) at the Phonetics Institute (IPSK) of Munich University has long advocated the use of web-based annotation procedures (see e.g. [8]). However, only recently have technologies become available that allow a truly platform independent and configurable implementation of such a system. Earlier attempts, such as WWWTranscribe, lacked a graphical signal display, or, like WWWSig-Transcribe [9], were hampered by platform- or browser-dependencies of Java applets. With WebTranscribe, these limitations have been overcome.

2   Architecture

2.1   Client/Server Architecture

In a client/server architecture, the server provides controlled access to resources held in the local file system or in database systems, and it runs the application software necessary to provide the service (often called "business logic"). The client is responsible for the input and output of data.

Modern desktop and laptops have sufficient processing power for complex applications, e.g. signal processing, statistical computations, graphical rendering, or document processing. Many applications can thus be shifted from the server to be performed on the client, reducing the workload on the server and minimizing data transfer.

2.2   Annotation Workflow

In general, the annotation workflow consists of the following main steps: select a data item to annotate, create a new or edit a given annotation, save the annotation text and select the next data item. Between these steps, auxiliary tasks are performed: render the data item to a given output medium, consult additional resources to relate the current annotation to existing annotations, and perform formal consistency checks on the validation text. Optionally, format conversions may be necessary.

The software traditionally used for the annotation of speech signals is a single-user desktop application. Resources are stored locally, often in a proprietary format. The exchange of data is possible by using the import and export functions; however, this may not preserve all the information, and it is a manual and thus error-prone process.

Praat [3], CHILDES [16], or Transcriber [1] are annotation editors of this type. They do not support collaborative or distributed annotations of speech data. EMU [7] and TableTrans [15] allow storing annotation data in a DBMS on a server as an option, but this is not the default. Furthermore, they are not platform-independent and they rely on access to the DBMS via dedicated protocols or database-specific communication ports.

In a web-based annotation workflow, signal and annotation data is stored on the server, along with shared resources such as lexicons, treebanks, other annotations, manuals, documents and application software. Resources can, but need not be shared across different projects.

The annotation is performed on the client. The annotator logs in on a remote client and opens a connection to the annotation server. The data to be annotated is either requested via a search form, or is provided automatically by the server. The annotator edits the annotation; for this annotation additional resources may be consulted. When the annotation is done, the client performs a formal consistency check and any auxiliary computation. After that, the data is transmitted to the server for storage.

A web-based workflow with client-side processing has a number of significant advantages:

– the formal correctness of the annotation data can be checked before it is entered into the database,
– network traffic between client and server is minimized because only valid data is transmitted, and
– computationally heavy processing is moved from the server to the client.

Additionally, once the annotation data is saved on the server, it immediately becomes available to other annotators in the same project (or even in other projects). This is especially important for shared resources, e.g. updates to lexicons or project statistics.

3 Implementation

WebTranscribe is a web-based framework for the annotation of speech signals. It stores signal files and annotations in a DBMS on a web server, implements an automatic or user-specified selection of signals to be annotated, features an extensible plug-in architecture for annotation editors, and provides an efficient transfer of data between server and client.

WebTranscribe is implemented in Java 1.4 as a Java Web Start application and uses certificates for authentification. The server is a standard open source Apache Tomcat web server.

3.1 Configuration

WebTranscribe must be configured for a specific annotation procedure. The configuration file is an XML-formatted text file, which is installed together with the application bundle on the server. Many different configurations can co-exist on a single server, and they can share resources.

This configuration links the DBMS on the server with the annotation editor, lists the plug-ins to use for the annotation task, and defines the access privileges for the shared resources.

3.2 Annotation Editor

An annotation editor provides support for an annotation task. It features a signal display, a text pane for the annotation text, and editing buttons that automate often-needed steps in the annotation. For time-dependent annotations, the annotation editor links signal segments to the annotation text, for multi-level annotations the editor keeps track of the dependencies between the different annotation levels.

Editing buttons and keyboard shortcuts enter marker symbols into the annotation or perform simple processing tasks such as case conversion, conversion from digits, numbers, date, time and currency expressions to explicit text, etc. This not only speeds up the annotation, it also improves its consistency.

A formal consistency check is performed when the annotation is done. This ensures that only valid data is transferred to the server, minimizing network traffic.

3.3   Transcription Objects

The basic data structure of WebTranscribe is the *transcription object*. Transcription objects implement the exchange of data between the server and the client, and they are used internally by the annotation editor. A transcription object contains a reference to the signal, segmentation information, an identifier, the original contents of the annotation, e.g. the prompt or an automatically created raw transcript, the final annotation text, an assessment of the signal quality, an identifier for the transcriber, and timestamps.

A transcription object is created by the annotation editor. Initially it contains only an identifier of the current annotation project. The transcription object is sent to the server where it receives a link to the signal file, any existing annotation data, and a time-stamp. The transcription object is returned to the client where the annotation is edited. Once the annotation is done and has been checked, it is copied to the transcription object together with administrative data. The transcription object is then transmitted to the server where it is stored in the DBMS.

3.4   Server Components

The server is responsible for storing the signal and annotation data. It keeps track of which signals are currently being processed and which annotations have been saved to the database. It operates in two modes for the selection of signals: in the automatic mode, the next signal not yet processed is sent to the client, in the manual mode it returns the signal corresponding to the search criteria specified by the client, e.g. through a query form.

In WebTranscribe, the server side of the application consists of a database access and a session management module.

4   Use in Projects

WebTranscribe has successfully been used in several projects at the BAS and IPSK. The DBMS and the server software were the same in all projects, only the annotation editor plug-in had to be customized to the requirements of the project. Generally, this customization is performed by subclassing a generic annotation editor class.

4.1   Touareg

In December and January 2004/2005 the IPSK recorded 30 British native speakers in a VW Touareg car for Siemens. The vocabulary consisted of roughly 450 UK city names which had to be read and spelled under different driving conditions. The recordings were made with 4 microphones using the SpeechDat-Car recording platform.

The annotation was orthographic with noise and signal truncation markers plus the pronunciation if the utterance deviated from the canonic pronunciation as given in the lexicon. The formal consistency check performed a lexical and syntactical analysis of the annotation text and provided detailed error messages to the transcriber. An annotation could only be saved to the database if a signal fragment had been selected, the annotation text was formally correct, and the signal quality had been assessed.

The WebTranscribe framework was configured with the standard waveform signal display, a project specific annotation editor with editing buttons for phoneme symbols, text transformations e.g. converting from "W O O D B R I D G E" to "W double O D B R I D G E", insertion of noise markers and for resetting the annotation editor (see Fig. 1).

4.2 SmartWeb

SmartWeb is a German research project that aims to provide multimodal access to the WWW via mobile handheld devices [20]. The data collection for SmartWeb is carried out by the IPSK in Munich. In the SmartWeb recordings, speakers connect to the SmartWeb server and start a structured dialog. In this dialog, they are given scenario-specific instructions and asked to formulate queries and requests to the server. Speech is recorded in high-bandwidth by the handheld device, and via the UMTS or GSM network on the server.

The annotations to perform are a) segmenting the dialog into turns, b) a basic orthographic transcript, and c) a sophisticated annotation with a large set of markers, e.g. to denote noise or overlaps. These markers may be singleton markers or extend over several annotation tokens.

The annotation editor for SmartWeb consists of a signal display and two separate editors. The first editor is for the basic orthographic transcript, the second one for the detailed annotation. This second editor features editing buttons for copying the basic transcript, and to enter marker symbols into the text (see Fig. 1).

The formal consistency checking tests the lexical and syntactical correctness of the annotation.

4.3 Ph@ttSessionz

In Ph@ttSessionz, a database of regional speech variants of approx. 1000 adolescent speakers is collected in high bandwith quality in schools all over Germany [18]. For the actual recordings, the SpeechRecorder software is used [10].

The material recorded is a superset of the RVG [4] and the German SpeechDat database. It contains application-oriented vocabulary, i. e. digits, numbers, date and time expressions and phonetically rich sentences, but also non-scripted speech, e.g. answers to questions such as "How would you ask the directory service for the telephone number of your school", or "Tell us a funny story".

Test recordings have been performed successfully in two Bavarian schools, and production recordings have started in April 2005. Currently, parallel recordings can be performed in five different locations. These locations receive the recording equipment from IPSK and return it as soon as their recordings are done.

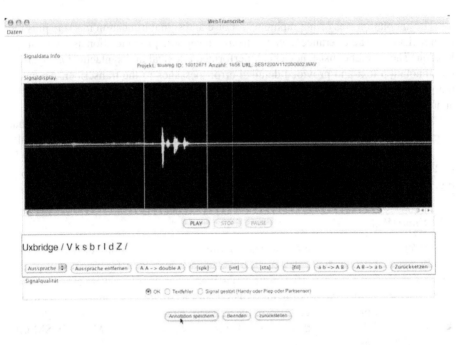

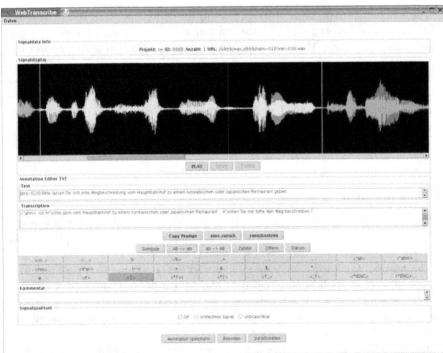

Fig. 1. WebTranscribe for Touareg and SmartWeb annotations. The editor panels are customized to the functionality required by the respective annotation systems and formats.

For Ph@ttSessionz, the annotation editor of WebTranscribe will consist of a display of the signal waveform, editing buttons for the conversion of numbers to string expressions and for the insertion of noise markers, including truncated signals and speech repairs.

5   Conclusion and Outlook

The concept of a web-based workflow has been successfully implemented at the BAS for several years now, beginning with the early large scale SpeechDat recordings and the subsequent annotations. WebTranscribe is now a stable framework for the annotation of speech data. Currently, the main limitations are the small number of available signal displays and annotation editors, and the focus on time-aligned signal annotation. The first limitation is a chicken-and-egg problem, and it can be overcome by not only implementing annotation editors, but by sharing them in the community. To foster the development of annotation plug-ins, the software is freely available via the BAS website [19].

For modelling the dependencies between different annotation levels, various approaches have been proposed, e.g. annotation graphs [2], ATLAS [14], the EMU database descriptions [6] or the BAS Partitur format [17]. We are currently exploring the feasibility of incorporating such a model into WebTranscribe.

Acknowledgements

Parts of this work have been supported by the German Federal Ministry of Education and Research grant no.01IVB01 (BITS). The author would like to thank S. Leonardi, M. Vitusevych, K. Jänsch and H. Mögele for their contributions to WebTranscribe.

References

1. Barras, C., Geoffrois, E., Wu, Z., Liberman, M.: Transcriber: development and use of a tool for assisting speech corpora production. Speech Communication **33** (2001)
2. Bird, S., Liberman, M.: A Formal Framework for Linguistic Annotation. Speech Communication, 33 (1,2) (2001) 23–60
3. Boersma, P., Weenink, D.: Praat, a system for doing phonetics by computer. Technical Report Technical Report 132, Institute of Phonetic Sciences of the University of Amsterdam (1996)
4. Burger, S., Schiel, F.: RVG 1 – A Database for Regional Variants of Contemporary German. In: Proc. of the 1st Intl. Conf. on Language Resources and Evaluation, Granada (1998) 1083–1087
5. Campbell, N.: Speech & expression: the value of a longitudinal corpus. In: Proceedings of LREC. (2004)
6. Cassidy, S., Harrington, J.: Emu: an enhanced speech data management system. In: Proceedings of SST'96, Adelaide (1996)
7. Cassidy, S., Harrington, J.: Multi-level annotation in the emu speech database management system. Speech Communication (2001) 61–77
8. Draxler, C.: WWWTranscribe – a Modular Transcription System Based on the World Wide Web. In: Proc. of Eurospeech, Rhodes (1997)

9. Draxler, C.: WWWSigTranscribe – a Java Extension of the WWWTranscribe Toolbox. In: Proceedings of LREC, Granada (1998)
10. Draxler, C., Jänsch, K.: Speechrecorder – a universal platform independent multi-channel audiorecording software. In: Proceedings. of 4th Intl. Conference on Language Resources and Evaluation, Lisbon (2004)
11. Ellbogen, T., Schiel, F., Steffen, A.: The BITS speech synthesis corpus for german. In: Proceedings of LREC 2004, Lisbon (2004)
12. Höge, H., Draxler, C., van den Heuvel, H., Johansen, F., Sanders, E., Tropf, H.: Speech-Dat Multilingual Speech Databases for Teleservices: Across the Finish Line. In: Proc. of Eurospeech 99, Budapest (1999)
13. Huckvale, M., Brookes, D., Dworkin, L., Johnson, M., Pearce, D., Whitaker, L.: The SPAR speech filing system. In: Proc. of European Conference on Speech Technology, Edinburgh (1987)
14. Laprun, C., Fiscus, J., Garofolo, J., Pajot, S.: Recent improvements to the ATLAS architecture. Technical report, National Institute for Standards and Technology (2003)
15. Ma, X., Lee, H., Bird, S., Maeda, K.: Models and tools for collaborative annotation. In: Proceedings of LREC, Gran Canaria (2002)
16. MacWhinney, B.: The CHILDES system. American Journal of Speech-Language Pathology **5** (1996) 5–14
17. Schiel, F., Burger, S., Geumann, A., Weilhammer, K.: The Partitur Format at BAS. FIPKM report #35, Institut für Phonetik und Sprachliche Kommunikation, Universität München (1997)
18. Steffen, A., Draxler, C., Baumann, A., Schmidt, S.: Ph@ttSessionz: Aufbau einer Datenbank mit Jugendsprache. In: Proceedings of DAGA 2005. (2005)
19. WebTranscribe software. (http://www.phonetik.uni-muenchen.de/bas/software/)
20. Wahlster, W.: Smartweb: Mobile applications of the semantic web. Informatik (2004)

Learning Syntactic Patterns Using Boosting and Other Classifier Combination Schemas

András Hócza, László Felföldi, and András Kocsor

University of Szeged Department of Informatics
6720 Szeged, Árpád tér 2
{hocza,lfelfold,kocsor}@inf.u-szeged.hu
http://www.inf.u-szeged.hu

Abstract. This paper presents a method for the syntactic parsing of Hungarian natural language texts using a machine learning approach. This method learns tree patterns with various phrase types described by regular expressions from an annotated corpus. The PGS algorithm, an improved version of the RGLearn method, is developed and applied as a classifier in classifier combination schemas. Experiments show that classifier combinations, especially the Boosting algorithm, can effectively improve the recognition accuracy of the syntactic parser.

1 Introduction

Syntactic parsing is the process of determining whether sequences of words can be grouped together. Syntactic parsing is an important part of the field of natural language processing and it is useful for supporting a number of large-scale applications including information extraction, information retrieval, named entity identification, and a variety of text mining applications.

Hungarian language is customarily defined as an agglutinative, free word order language with a rich morphology. These properties make its full analysis difficult compared to Indo-European languages. Unambiguous marks for the automatic recognition of phrase boundaries do not exist. For example, the right bound of noun phrases could be the nouns as a head, but there is a possibility of replacing noun phrase heads with its modifiers. Determining the left bound of noun phrases is harder than the head, as it could be a determinant element. However, due to the possibility of a recursive insertion, it is so not easy to decide which determinant and head belong together.

This paper introduces the PGS (Pattern Generalization and Specialization) algorithm, an improved version of the RGLearn algorithm [4], for learning syntactic tree patterns, and it describes how one can improve the performance of this learner by applying classifier combination schemas. Classifier combinations aggregate the results of many classifiers, overcoming the possible local weakness of the individual inducers, producing a more robust recognition. After comparing them to related works the results look fairly promising.

This paper is organized as follows. Section 2 summarizes the related works on the topic of syntactic parsing. Section 3 presents the method used for learning grammar from an annotated corpus. Section 4 then gives a short introduction to classifier com-

V. Matoušek et al. (Eds.): TSD 2005, LNAI 3658, pp. 69–76, 2005.

bination techniques. The proposed methods are tested in Section 5. After, conclusions and suggestions for future study are given in the last section.

2   Related Works

Several authors published results of syntactic parsing especially made for English. Generally the performance is measured with three scores: precision, recall and an $F_{\beta=1}$ rate which is equal to 2*precision*recall/(precision*recall). The latter rate has been used as the target for optimization. Ramshaw and Marcus [7], for instance, built a chunker by applying transformation-based learning ($F_{\beta=1}$=92.0). They applied their method to two segments of the Penn Treebank [6] and these are still being used as benchmark data sets. Tjong Kim Sang and Veenstra [8] introduced cascaded chunking ($F_{\beta=1}$=92.37). The novel approaches attain good accuracies using a system combination. Tjong Kim Sang [9] utilized a combination of five classifiers for syntactic parsing ($F_{\beta=1}$=93.26).

Up till now there is no good-quality syntactic parser available for the Hungarian language. Benchmark data sets for correctly comparing results on Hungarian do not exist yet either. The HuMorESK syntactic parser [5] developed by MorphoLogic Ltd uses attribute grammar, assigning feature structures to symbols. The grammar part employed in the parser was made by linguistic experts. Another report on the ongoing work of a Hungarian noun phrase recognition parser [10] is based on an idea of Abney's [1] using a cascaded regular grammar and it has been tested on a short text of annotated sentences ($F_{\beta=1}$=58.78). The idea of using cascaded grammars seems beneficial, this technique being used in all Hungarian parser developments. A noun phrase recognition parser [4] is applied machine learning methods to produce grammar of noun phrase tree patterns from annotated corpus ($F_{\beta=1}$=83.11).

3   Learning Tree Patterns

In this section the learning task of syntactic tree patterns will be described which contains the preprocessing of training data, generalization and specialization of tree patterns. An improved version of RGLearn [4] named PGS (Patten Generalization and Specialization) was used as a tree pattern learner. The novelty of PGS is the use of λ parameters which have an influence on the quality of learned tree patterns. The pattern unification method and the search method for best patterns have also been modified.

3.1   Preprocessing of Training Data

The initial step for generating training data is to collect syntactic tree patterns from an annotated training corpus. The complete syntax tree of sentence must be divided into separate trees and a cascade tree building rules to prepare the parser to reconstruct it. In parsing, using of context free grammar has a lot of advantages, but the conditions of pattern usage may completely disappear. Some structural information can be salvaged if tree patterns are used. To generate cascaded grammar, linguistic experts have defined the following processing levels for the Hungarian language:

- Short tree patterns of noun, adjective, adverb and pronoun phrases.
- Recursive complex patterns of noun, adjective, adverb and pronoun phrases.
- Recursive patterns of verb phrases.
- Recursive patterns of sub-sentences.

3.2 Generalization of Tree Patterns

Using the collected tree patterns the syntactic parser is able to reconstruct the tree structure of training sentences. But, in order to perform the syntactic parsing of an unknown text to a fair accuracy, the collected tree patterns must be generalized. Generalization means that the lexical attributes of each tag are neglected except for the POS codes. In this phase the learning problem is transformed into a classification problem. Namely, which set of lexical attributes would supply the best result for the decision problem of tree pattern matching, i.e a given tree structure covers a given example or not. To support the learner, positive and negative examples are collected from a training set for each tree type. The example in Figure 1 shows the complete tree pattern learning process.

3.3 Specialization of Tree Patterns

Negative examples are the bad classifications of generalized tree pattern and they must be eliminated. Therefore specialization selects each possible lexical attribute from positive examples making new tree patterns and tries to find the best tree patterns with unification.

Sentence parts (examples):
1: ... $(_{NP}Tf(_{ADJP}Afp-sn)_{ADJP}Np-sn)_{NP}$ ...
2: ... $(_{NP}Tf(_{NP}Afp-pn)_{NP}Nc-pa---s3)_{NP}$ ...
3: ... $(_{NP}(_{NP}Ti(_{NP}Afs-sn)_{NP})_{NP}(_{NP}Nc-s2)_{NP}$ ...
4: ... $(_{NP}Tf(_{ADJP}Afp-sn)_{ADJP}Nc-sn)_{NP}$ ...
5: ... $(_{NP}Tf(_{ADJP}Afp-sn)_{ADJP}(_{ADJP}Afp-sn)_{ADJP})_{NP}$ ...

Generalized pattern (one of four possible): $(_{NP}T*(_{ADJP}A*)_{ADJP}N*)_{NP}$
Coverage: positive {1,4}, negative {2,3}, uncovered {5}
Specialized pattern: $(_{NP}T*(_{ADJP}A*)_{ADJP}N???n)_{NP}$
Coverage: positive {1,4}, negative {}, uncovered {2,3,5}

In the lexical codes each letter is a lexical attribute, the first one being the part of speech. Notations:
$T*$: determiner, $A*$: adjective, $N*$: noun, $N???n$: noun with a lexical attribute,
$?$: a letter of any kind, $*$: one or more letters of any kind,
$(_X,)_X$: beginning and ending of phrase X, NP: noun phrase, $ADJP$: adjective phrase.

Fig. 1. A tree pattern learning example.

The initial step of specialization generates all possible new tree patterns extending generalized tree patterns with exactly one attribute from the covered positive examples.

The next steps of specialization extends the set of tree patterns with all possible new tree patterns by a combination of each pair of tree patterns. The combination of two tree patterns means the union of their lexical attributes. To avoid the exponential growth of a tree pattern set weak tree patterns are excluded by applying error statistics on positive and negative examples. Here the following score of a given tree pattern is used as the target for maximization:

$$\text{score} = \lambda_1 *(pos\text{-}neg)/pos + \lambda_2 *(pos\text{-}neg)/(pos+neg)$$

where *pos* is the number of covered positive examples, *neg* is the number of covered negative examples and $\lambda_1 + \lambda_2 = 1$.

Fruitful unifications dramatically decrease the negative coverage, resulting positive coverage almost in the same time. The score maximization runs parallel on every positive example. A new tree pattern is stored only if a covered positive example exists where the score of new tree pattern is greater than the previous maximum value. Specialization stops when the current step did not improve any maximum value.

Appropriate setting of λ factors in linear combination can provide the optimal tree pattern set. A greater λ_1 may result in tree patterns with high coverage, while a greater λ_2 may result high accuracy but there is a possibility of low tree patterns appearing with a low coverage.

4   Classifier Combinations

Classifier Combinations are effective tools for machine learning and can improve the classification performance of standalone learners. A combination aggregates the results of many classifiers, overcoming the possible local weakness of the individual inducers, producing a more robust recognition. A fair number of combination schemas have been proposed in the literature [12], these schemas differing from each other in their architecture, the characteristics of the combiner, and the selection of the individual classifiers. From a combination viewpoint, classifiers can be categorized into the following types:

- abstract: the classifier yields only the most probable class label
- ranking: it generates a list of class labels in order of their probability
- confidence: the scores for each class are available

In the following we will assume that the classifiers are capable of generating information of the confidence type.

4.1   Combination Schemas

Let x denote a pattern, and $(\omega_1, \dots, \omega_n)$ the set of possible class labels. The parameters p_i^j will represent the output of the i-th classifier for the j-th class. Furthermore, let $\mathcal{L}(x)$ denote the correct class labelling for each training sample $x \in S$, and $\mathcal{C}_i$ refer to a function that maps the pattern x to the class label assigned by the i-th classifier:

$$\mathcal{C}_i(x) = \omega_k, \quad k = \underset{j}{\arg\max}\, p_i^j(x). \tag{1}$$

The combined class probabilities $\hat{p}^j$ are calculated from the corresponding values of classifiers p_i^j according to combination rules described later. The class label $\hat{\mathcal{C}}(x)$ selected by the combiner is the one with the largest probability:

$$\hat{\mathcal{C}}(x) = \omega_k, \quad k = \underset{j}{\operatorname{argmax}} \hat{p}^j(x). \tag{2}$$

There are numerous combination rules mentioned in the literature. The traditional combination methods are listed here:

Sum Rule:

$$\hat{p}^j(x) = \sum_{i=1}^{N} p_i^j(x) \tag{3}$$

Product Rule:

$$\hat{p}^j(x) = \prod_{i=1}^{N} p_i^j(x) \tag{4}$$

Max Rule:

$$\hat{p}^j(x) = \max_{i=1}^{N} p_i^j(x) \tag{5}$$

Min Rule:

$$\hat{p}^j(x) = \min_{i=1}^{N} p_i^j(x) \tag{6}$$

Borda Count:

$$\hat{p}^j(x) = \sum_{i=1}^{N} \sum_{\substack{k=1 \\ p_i^k(x) \leq p_i^j(x)}}^{n} 1 \tag{7}$$

4.2 Boosting

Boosting[13] was introduced by Shapire as a method for improving the performance of a weak learning algorithm. The algorithm generates a set of classifiers by applying bootstrapping on the original training data set and it makes a decision based on their votes. AdaBoost changes the weights of the training instances provided as input for each inducer based on classifiers that were previously built. The final decision is made using a weighted voting schema for each classifier, whose weights depend on the performance of the training set used to build it.

Algorithm 1 *Adaboost M1 algorithm*

> **Require:** Training Set S of size m, Inducer $\mathcal{I}$
> **Ensure:** Combined classifier C^*
> $S' = S$ with weights assigned to be $1/m$
>   **for** $i = 1 \ldots T$ **do**
> $S' = $ bootstrap sample from S
> $C_i = \mathcal{I}(S')$

$$\epsilon_i = \sum_{\substack{x_j \in S' \\ C_i(x_j) \neq \omega_j}} \text{weight of } x_j$$

if $\epsilon_i > 1/2$ **then** reinitialize sample weights
$\beta_i = \frac{\epsilon_i}{(1-\epsilon_i)}$
for all $x_j \in S'$ such $C_i(x_j) = \omega_j$ **do**
    weight of x_j = weight of $x_j \cdot \beta_i$
end for
normalize weights of instances to sum 1
end for

$$C^*(\mathbf{x}) = \operatorname*{argmax}_j \sum_{\substack{i \\ C_i(\mathbf{x}) = \omega_j}} \log \frac{1}{\beta_i}$$

end

The Adaboost algorithm requires a weak learning algorithm whose error is bounded by a constant strictly less than 1/2. In the case of multi-class classifications this condition might be difficult to guarantee, and various techniques should be applied to overcome this restriction.

5 Experiments

5.1 Evaluation Domain

In order to perform well and learn from the various *Natural Language Processing* tasks and achieve a sufficient standard of *Information Extraction*, an adequately large corpus had to be collected which serves as the training database. A relatively large corpus of texts of various types was collected, called the Szeged Corpus [2]. It has six topic areas of roughly 200 thousand words each, meaning a text database of some 1.2 million words. One of the domain is short business news items issued by the Hungarian News Agency[1].

Initially, corpus words were morpho-syntactically analysed and then manually POS tagged by linguistic experts. The Hungarian version of the internationally acknowledged MSD (Morpho-Syntactic Description) schema [3] was used for the encoding of the words. The MSD encoding schema can store morphological information about part-of-speech determined attributes on up to 17 positions. About 1800 different MSD labels are employed in the annotated corpus. The texts of the Szeged Corpus have been parsed, where annotators marked various type of phrase structures.

5.2 Evaluation Methods

The training and test datasets were converted from a subset of the business news domain of the Szeged Corpus. During the experiments we generated 50 learners by training the PGS algorithm on different training sets, these sets beeing created by randomly

---

[1] MTI, Magyar Távirati Iroda (http://www.mti.hu), "Eco" service.

drawing 4000 instances with replacement from the original training set. The λ_1 parameter of the PGS algorithm was selected for optimal performance on the original train dataset. According to the preliminary investigations the PGS algorithm attains its maximal recognition accuracy when λ_1 is set to 0.7, hence this setting was used during the combination experiments.

5.3   Results

The syntactic tree pattern recognition accuracy of the standalone classifier was 78.5 % on the business-news domain using 10-fold cross-validation. Based on their performance the combination schemas can be divided into 3 groups. The schemas Max, Min, and Prod have roughly the same performance: they cannot significantly improve the classification accuracy of the PGS learner. Borda Count and Sum rule can take advantage of combinations, and get an 82 % score on the test data-set. The best classification was obtained by using the Boosting algorithm, achieving an an accuracy of 86 %. Note that the Adaboost.M1 algorithm cannot reduce the training error rate to zero owing to the fact that the Boosting algorithm requires that the weighted error should be below 50%, and this condition is not always fulfilled.

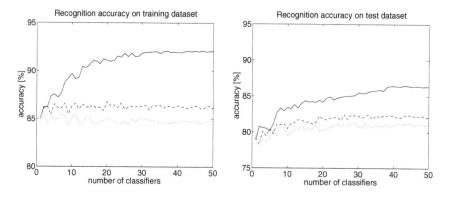

Fig. 2. Classification accuracy of the combination schemas on the training and testing datatset (solid: Boosting, dashed: Sum Rule, dotted: Max Rule).

Fig. 2 shows the classification performance for schemas Max, Sum, and Boosting. The graphs show the measured accuracy on the training and test datasets as a function of the number of the applied classifiers in the combination schema. Comparing these results with the performance of the standalone learner, we see that combinations can improve the classification accuracy by some 10%.

6   Summary and Future Work

In this paper, the authors presented a general machine learning method for syntactic parsing. A new learning method the PGS was introduced as an improved version of the RGLearn algorithm. The accuracy of tree pattern recognition was effectively improved using classifier combination schemas, the best performance being achieved by the Boosting algorithm.

In the future we plan to use the ontological information that can be the extension of a morpho-syntactic description. This system has been primarily applied to the business news domain so far, but we would like to process other Hungarian domains of the Szeged Corpus and to adapt the methods to parsing English texts as well.

References

1. Abney S. (1996) Partial Parsing via Finite-State Cascades, in Proceedings of ESSLLI'96 Robust Parsing Workshop, pp. 1-8.
2. Alexin, Z., Csirik, J., Gyimóthy, T., Bibok, K., Hatvani, Cs., Prószéky, G., Tihanyi, L.: Manually Annotated Hungarian Corpus, in Proceedings of the Research Note Sessions of the 10th Conference of the European Chapter of the Association for Computational Linguis-tics EACL03, Budapest, Hungary, 2003, pp. 53-56.
3. Erjavec, T., Monachini, M.: Specification and Notation for Lexicon Encoding, Copernicus project 106 "MULTEXT-EAST", Work Package WP1 - Task 1.1 Deliverable D1.1F,1997.
4. Hócza, A.: Noun Phrase Recognition with Tree Patterns, in Proceedings of the Acta Cyber-netica, Szeged, Hungary, 2004.
5. Kis, B., Naszódy, M., Prószéki, G.: Complex Hungarian syntactic parser system in Proceedings of the MSZNY 2003, Szeged, Hungary, 2003, pp. 145-151
6. Marcus, M.P., Santorini, B., Marcinkiewicz, M.A.: Building a large annotated corpus of English: the Penn Treebank, Association for Computational Linguistics, 1993.
7. Ramshaw, L.A., Marcus, M.P.: Text Chunking Using Transformational-Based Learning, in Proceedings of the Third ACL Workshop on Very Large Corpora, Association for Computational Linguistics, 1995.
8. Tjong Kim Sang, E.F., Veenstra, J.: Representing text chunks, in Proceedings of EACL '99, Association for Computational Linguistics, 1999.
9. Tjong Kim Sang, E.F.: Noun Phrase Recognition by System Combination, in Proceedings of the first conference on North American chapter of the Association for Computational Linguistics, Seattle,2000, pp. 50-55.
10. Váradi T.: Shallow Parsing of Hungarian Business News, in Proceedings of the Corpus Linguistics 2003 Conference, Lancaster,2003, pp. 845-851.
11. Duda, R.O., Hart, P.E., Stork, D.G.: Pattern Classification, John Wiley & Sons Inc., 2001.
12. Jain, A.K.: Statistical Pattern Recognition: A Review, IEEE Trans. Pattern Analysis and Machine Intelligence, Vol. 22. No. 1, January 2000.
13. Shapire, R.E.: The Strength of Weak Learnability, Machine Learnings, Vol. 5, pp. 197-227, 1990.
14. Vapnik, V.N.: Statistical Learning Theory, John Wiley & Sons Inc., 1998.

Text Classification with Tournament Methods

Louise Guthrie[1], Wei Liu[1], and Yunqing Xia[2]

[1] Department of Computer Science, University of Sheffield
211 Portobello Street, Sheffield, UK S1 4DP
{louise,w.liu}@dcs.shef.ac.uk
[2] Department of Systems Engineering and Engineering Management
The Chinese University of Hong Kong Shatin, Hong Kong
yqxia@se.cuhk.edu.hk

Abstract. This paper compares the effectiveness of n-way $(n > 2)$ classification using a probabilistic classifier to the use of multiple binary probabilistic classifiers. We describe the use of binary classifiers in both Round Robin and Elimination tournaments, and compare both tournament methods and n-way classification when determining the language of origin of speakers (both native and non-native English speakers) speaking English. We conducted hundreds of experiments by varying the number of categories as well as the categories themselves. In all experiments the tournament methods performed better than the n-way classifier, and of these tournament methods, on average, Round Robin performs slightly better than the Elimination tournament.

1 Introduction

We base this work on a probabilistic classifier which assumes that each category is modeled so that the probability of belonging to that category can be computed. When a new piece of text arrives, we compute the probability of that new text coming from each of the populations and classify it in the one that is most likely (Maximum Likelihood). The question we ask here is whether it is more effective to use a combination of binary classifiers to decide the results. We simulated round robin tournaments and single elimination tournaments (described in section 2) for the classification of email in [1] into user defined folders and showed the tournament methods performed better than n-way classification. In this paper we focus on a very different application domain: one to classify segments of speech (we worked from the human transcriptions) into the language of origin of the Speaker [2], and conducted a series of experiments where the number of categories and the particular categories in the experiment are varied. In all cases, the tournament methods perform better than the n-way classification and the results are consistent with or initial experiments on email classification.

2 Classification

Various approaches towards text classification have been developed in the past few years, ranging from traditional document classification algorithms to newer spam-detection techniques [3]. The most popular approaches to text classification are decision

V. Matoušek et al. (Eds.): TSD 2005, LNAI 3658, pp. 77–84, 2005.

trees like the popular C4.5 algorithm [4], Naïve Bayesian and related Bayesian learning methods [5, 6], clustering techniques such as the k-nearest neighbor algorithm [7] and boosting [8], support vector machines [9], neural networks [10], and statistical learning and induction methods [11]. Although a range of experiments have attempted to determine the best method for classification, this is not our purpose here. In this paper we use a simple probabilistic classifier (described below) and compare n-way classification to the use of multiple binary classifiers of the same type. This classification method is successfully employed in EU FASiL project to classify personal emails to predefined folders [12].This classifier has several advantages in that it is simple but mathematically defensible, it allows the computation in advance of the probability of correct classification, and eliminates the need for smoothing. The same question could be asked of any of the above classification algorithms.

2.1   An Overview of the n-Way Classification Scheme

In each problem we model the categories using a class based multinomial distribution [13], and use a maximum likelihood estimator to do the classification. An overview of the classification algorithm for n categories is defined below. All binary classifies used in our experiments follow the same algorithm where.

Initially, a class of "distinguishing words" W_i is identified from training data for each of the categories $C_i(i = 1 \ldots n)$. Intuitively, the class W_i consists of "words" that appear frequently in the category C_i, but infrequently in all classes C_j, where $j \neq i$.

We define a class W_{n+1} which consists of all "words" not in any of the W_i. In various experiments we allow "words" to represent a single word or bigram (2 adjacent words). The classes W_i are disjoint, and the parameters in the multinomial distribution correspond to the estimated probabilities that a given word or phrase belongs to one of the classes W_i which are estimated from the training data. This gives rise to a different multinomial distribution for each of the n categories, where each category (or population) is described by the distribution of its words or phrases in the distinguishing sets W_i ($i = 1 \ldots n$).

After each of the categories is modeled with the multinomial distribution defined above, a classifier is built which takes as input an unseen document, and uses a maximum likelihood estimator to decide for which population it is most likely to have come.

Although this is a Bayesian approach, where the experiment is the repeated selection of a "words" from a document, what is recorded is which of the W_i's the "word" belongs to. In [13], mathematical details are given of the scheme and the selection of the classes and it is shown that the classification scheme can be augmented to use the prior distribution of the classes if that is known. However, in the experiments below, we chose not to assume any knowledge of the distribution of the classes, so as to compare the classifiers under the strictest conditions.

[13] also shows that once the sets $W_i(i = 1 \ldots n + 1)$ are chosen, we can compute the probability of correct classification and that probability varies with the choice of the classes W_i. Our intuition was that it is more difficult to chose beneficial classes W_i when n is larger than 2, hence we looked at solving the problem of categorizing into n categories with repeated use of binary classifiers. We considered two methods of arranging the binary classifiers which have an analogy to round robin tournaments and single elimination tournaments.

3   The Tournaments

The tournament classification approaches below describe the process of classifying a document into one of n categories, using only binary classifiers. By adopting different rules to combine candidates, the classification task is broken down into a set of binary classifications.

3.1   An Elimination Tournament

In the Elimination Tournament (ET) method, the approach is similar to what is used in the Wimbledon Championship, where players compete against other players determined by the sortition before the game starts. After every match, one of the two players goes into the next round and the unlucky loser is eliminated.

In ET classification, a sortition will be setup before classification to generate the competition rules. The rules are then followed in the future classification, i.e. category elimination. The winner in the last round is then considered as the best category.

When implementing our ET algorithm, we keep a list of all categories (the native language of a set of English speakers in one of our applications). A document is classified as follows: Each time the document is compared against the first two categories taken out from the list with our binary classifier. And each time the "winner" category of these two will be added back to the original list (thus the loser of this run is eliminated and the list size is decreased by one). This process is repeated until only one category is left in the list. And the surviving category will be the category of that document. In other words, an elimination tournament of n categories will have total $n - 1$ comparisons before obtaining a final outcome. Nevertheless the elimination process can yield unfair competition if we simply add the winning category of a pair back to the head of the list, in which case if we have an odd number of categories, the last category will end up having been compared only once at the last comparison. Since our binary classifier is class symmetric (*i.e.* classifying between categories i and j is the same as classifying between j and i), we adapt the method by adding it to the tail of the list. In this case we give fair treatment to every category in our initial list.

3.2   A Round Robin Tournament

Instead of eliminating the losers, scores are assigned to every category in the Round Robin Tournament (RRT); therefore, every category will accumulate a total score after all the binary classification processes are finished. The one that has the highest score will be selected as the category for the input document. The scheme that forces every category to compete against all others before determining the best category for the input document follows the same rule as league championships. As an analogy, a category corresponds to a soccer team in the England Premiership, and the team who wins the cup then corresponds to the category that the input document most likely belongs to.

To carry out the RRT, a binary classification between every two categories is run with the binary classifier trained before classification. A competition table, which is exactly the same one as we see in the England Premiership, is maintained by the system to record the winners and losers, and the score table is then derived from the competition

Table 1. RRT scoring scheme

	Role		
Scheme	Winner	Looser	Level
S1	3	0	1
S2	1	-1	0

table by assigning the winner, loser or level teams with different scores. In our RRT experiments, we design the two scoring schemes described in Table 1. The scoring scheme S1 is exactly the same scoring scheme as England Premiership, while in scheme S2 a punishment score is assigned to the loser. An empirical study shows that S1 is more accurate in determining the best category and consequently we then applied the scoring scheme S1 in our experiments described in the section 4.

It is very likely that, under such scheme, a tie will occur in our final outcome, that is, two or more categories end up having the same score, and with fewer categories it becomes more likely. One straightforward but somehow naive approach will be the "random pick", which picks the designated category at random. In these experiments, however, we use an alternative approach, since further information is available. When a tie is found at the end of the round robin tournament, we pick out the categories that are tied and perform an additional tie-break operation: if it is a two-way tie, say, category i and category j, since we already have the binary classification result of $< i, j >$, the final category will simply be that of the winner of $< i, j >$. If there is a three-way tie or more, we will perform the n-way classifier on these tie categories and whichever survived will be the category of that particular document.

4 Experiments

Speakers with different language origins show different characteristics or habits in their wording while speaking. This gives rise to the possibility of constructing speech models for language origins in order to improve the quality of general speech recognition [14]. As the speech transcription is merely plain text and speaker's language origin can be recorded for every piece of text in the annotation period, text classification methods then can be applied to determine the speaker's language origin [2].

We have conducted substantial experiments on both tournament algorithms with unigrams and bi-grams on identifying the language of origin of a speaker. In this section we will describe our experimental procedure and the corpus. Finally, results will be presented and analyzed.

4.1 Data Set and Pre-processing

The original speech transcription comes from three sources: the International Computer Science Institute (ICSI) Meeting Corpus, the Trans-language English Database (TED), and the Michigan Corpus of Academic Spoken English (MICASE). We combined all the speech transcriptions according to language origins and save them in 33 files. Size of all files varies from 25 to 921721 words. All data is in English, but much of it is

Table 2. Selected language statistics

Language	Words	size(bytes)
English	921721	844871
German	126777	829917
Spanish	78348	499609
French	53551	435797
Dutch	21238	127039
Korean	18541	117267
Malayalam	14657	99674
Thai	10712	73749
Turkish	10613	62577
Hindi	8081	49796

spoken by non-native English speakers, and the language of origin of the speakers is known. In [2] a corpus was created that chose the ten languages of origin which have the richest data (Table 2) out of the total 33. The data was segmented into a collection of text pieces. Each piece of text is about 100 words[1].

4.2 Description of Experiments

The split-sample validation method is introduced in our experiment to manage the training and testing data. To be specific, we split the text collection into training/testing sets by random, using a 90%/10% split on each language.

In our experiments, we first produce all binary classifiers which combine every two language origins with our n-way classifier as the base classifier. After all the binary classifiers are generated, the test sets are then processed by them, and results are then recorded in each tournament classification.

To compare the tournament methods with traditional methods, we setup the baseline classification method to be n-way classification which is described in section 2. Both unigrams and bi-grams are used to compare the methods. In order to evaluate the performance and compare each approach, we considered the problem of classifying into n languages, where $n = 3, 4, 5$, and 10, and in each case we performed all possible combination of experiments for the 10 languages.

For example, when $n = 3$, we look at the classification of a document into one of 3 languages of origin, and since there are 120 ways to choose 3 things from 10 ($C(3, 10) = 120$), we ran 120 experiments for $n=3$. Similarly for $n=4$, we ran 210 experiments, for $n=5$, 252 experiments and one for $n=10$.

4.3 Evaluation Criteria and Results

We adopted accuracy measure to evaluate our algorithm. Accuracy is defined as: the documents correctly classified divided by the total documents in one classification

---

[1] However, we still maintain sentence integrity, in some cases the text will exceed 100 words.

process. It is more intuitive to use the contingency table to define accuracy as below: Therefore, the accuracy for the binary classification on category A and B will be $(x + y)/(x + i + j + y)$[11]. Similarly classification accuracy can be computed for more than two categories.

Table 3. Contingency table

	A is correct	B is correct
Classify as A	x	i
Classify as B	j	y

Because we performed various combinations, and each combination can have hundreds of comparisons, the average accuracy, defined in (1), is reported for every combination run.

$$\overline{Accuracy} = \frac{1}{C(n,m)} \sum_{i=1}^{C(n,m)} A_i \qquad (1)$$

where A_i denotes the accuracy of experiment i.

Experimental results using unigrams are presented in Table 4. Note that all accuracies in Table 4 and Table 5 represent average accuracy over that particular combination.

Table 4. Unigram accuracy

Language combinations	Train/ test doc	n-way	ET	RRT	RRT Improvement over n-way
3		0.783	0.805	0.804	2.627%
4	3217/351	0.685	0.737	0.737	7.620%
5		0.596	0.679	0.680	14.160%
10		0.356	0.501	0.504	41.600%

Table 5. Bi-gram accuracy

Language combinations	Train/ test doc	n-way	ET	RRT	RRT Improvement over n-way
3		0.794	0.797	0.798	0.516%
4	3217/351	0.719	0.739	0.740	2.975%
5		0.652	0.692	0.695	6.689%
10		0.416	0.550	0.556	33.562%

4.4 Discussion

From Table 4 we can see that as the number of language combination increased, the accuracy decreased as expected. Yet both tournament methods have out-performed the n-way classifier in each run. Also such improvement is proportional to the language combinations. In one extreme case where all ten languages are used for classification, the accuracy increased dramatically from 35.6% by n-way classifier to 50% by tournament algorithms, yielding over 40% improvement. Considering bi-grams we achieved similar results (Table 5), but with the bi-gram approach, overall accuracy is increased despite the method used. We believe this is true. Since a particular speaker tends to use different short phrases or combination of words according to their nationality, his/her nationality can be more accurately identified with bi-grams than with singular words.

Of the tournament methods, ET and RRT performed very close to each other; nevertheless RRT yielded slightly better overall accuracy.

5   Conclusion

The results described in this paper, together with our results in a previous paper [1], show that in two very different problem domains the tournament methods improve the results of n-way classification. This is encouraging since we know that binary classification is memory efficient and training is only concerned with two categories at a time. Thus a multi-class classification task that is too large to be run in memory can be reduced by means of binary classification.

Acknowledgement

We would like to thank Siddharth Sehgal at Univ.of Sheffield who kindly provided the transcribed speech corpora. We would also like to thank Dr Joe Guthrie for valuable suggestions on improving tournament tie breaking.

References

1. Xia, Y., Liu, W., Guthrie, L.: Email Categorization with Tournament Methods. Proc. of NLDB'2005, Alicante, Spain, 2005.
2. Sehgal, S.: Identification of Speaker Origin From Transcribed Speech Text. Thesis (MSc, supervisor Guthrie, L). University of Sheffield, UK, 2004.
3. Smadja, F., Tumblin, H.: Automatic Spam Detection as a Text Classification Task. Elron Software, 2003.
4. Quinlan, J.R.: Programs for Machine Learning. Morgan Kaufmann, San Mateo, 1993.
5. Lewis, D.: Naive Bayes at forty: The independence assumption in information retrieval. Proc. ECML-98, Chemnitz, 1998.
6. McCallum, A., Nigam, K.: A comparison of event models for naive bayes text classifi-cation. AAAI-98 Workshop on Text Categorization, 1998.
7. Androutsopoulos, I., Koutsias, J., Chandrinos, K.V., Paliouras, G., Spyropoulos, C.D.: An Evaluation of Naive Bayesian Anti-Spam Filtering. Proc. of the work-shop on Machine Learning in the New Information Age, 2000.
8. Carrerras, X., Marquez, L.: Boosting Trees for Anti-Spam Email Filtering. Proc. RANLP-2001, 2001.
9. Thorsten, J.: A Statistical Learning Model of Text Classification with Support Vector Machines. Proc. SIGIR-01, New Orleans. ACM Press, New York, 2001.
10. Wiener, E., Pederson, J.O., Weigend, A.S.: A neural network approach to topic spotting. Proc. SDAIR-95, Nevada, Las Vegas, 1995, pp. 317-332.

11. Yang, Y.: An evaluation of statistical approaches to text categorization. Journal IR., 1999, 1(1/2):67-88.
12. Xia, Y., Dalli, A., Wilks, Y., Guthrie, L.: FASiL Adaptive Email Categorization System. Proc. of CICLing-2005, LNCS 3406, pp. 723¨C734, Mexico City, Mexico, 2005.
13. Guthrie, L., Guthrie, J., Walker, E.: Document classification by machine: theory and practice. Proceedings of the 16th International Conference on Computational Linguis-tics (COLING 94), Kyoto, Japan, 1994, pp. 1059-1063.
14. Doddington G.: Speaker Recognition based on Idiolectal Differences between Speakers in Proc. Eurospeech 2001, vol. 4, pp. 2521-2524, Aalborg, Denmark, Sept. 3-7, 2001.

New Meta-grammar Constructs
in Czech Language Parser synt*

Aleš Horák and Vladimír Kadlec

Faculty of Informatics, Masaryk University Brno
Botanická 68a, 602 00 Brno, Czech Republic
{hales,xkadlec}@fi.muni.cz

Abstract. In this paper, we present and summarize the latest development of the Czech sentence parsing system synt. The presented system uses the meta-grammar formalism, which enables to define the grammar with a maintainable number of meta-rules. At the same time, these meta-rules are translated into rules for efficient and fast head driven chart parsing supplemented with evaluation of additional contextual constraints. The paper includes a comprehensive description of the meta-grammar constructs as well as actual running times of the system tested on corpus data.

1 Introduction

The development of a grammar for syntactic analysis of natural language texts is a tedious process which always tends to keep adding new rules for capturing uncovered language phenomena up to the moment, where the number of rules becomes hardly maintainable. Such "rule overload" is solved with several competing approaches ranging from stochastic parsing [1], through various automatic learning algorithms [2] to loosening the strictness of the analysis with a shallow parsing algorithm [3].

In the synt system approach, a deep syntactic representation of sentence is required, since the resulting analysis is used as an input for the Normal translation algorithm [4] producing a meaning representation of NL expressions with constructions of Transparent intensional logic. Therefore, we have decided to apply the meta-grammar concept with three consecutive grammar forms. The underlying analyzer is an augmented head driven parser based on a context-free backbone with interleaved evaluation of contextual constraints.

2 Description of the System

The meta-grammar concept in synt consists of three grammar forms denoted as G1, G2 and G3. Human experts work with the meta-grammar form, which encompasses high-level generative constructs reflecting the meta-level natural language phenomena

* This work has been partly supported by Czech Science Foundation under the project 201/05/2781 and by Grant Agency of the Academy of Sciences of CR under the project 1ET400300414.

V. Matoušek et al. (Eds.): TSD 2005, LNAI 3658, pp. 85–92, 2005.

like the word order constraints, and enable to describe the language with a maintainable number of rules. The meta-grammar serves as a base for the second grammar form which comes into existence by expanding the constructs. This grammar consists of context-free rules equipped with feature agreement tests and other contextual actions. The last phase of grammar induction lies in the transformation of the tests into standard rules of the expanded grammar with the actions remaining to guarantee the contextual requirements.

Meta-grammar (G1). The meta-grammar consists of global order constraints that safeguard the succession of given terminals, special flags that impose particular restrictions to given non-terminals and terminals on the right hand side (RHS) and of constructs used to generate combinations of rule elements. Some of these meta-grammar constructs have already been described in [5], in this paper we present a summary of all the constructs including the latest additions.

We use the arrow in the rule for specification of the *rule type* (->, -->, ==> or ===>). A little hint to the arrow form meaning can be expressed by 'the thicker and longer the arrow the more (complex) actions are to be done in the rule translation'. The smallest arrow (->) denotes an ordinary CFG transcription and the thick extra-long arrow (===>) inserts possible inter-segments between the RHS constituents, checks the correct order of enclitics and supplies several forms of the rule to make the verb phrase into a full sentence.

The *global constructs* (%enclitic, %order and %merge_actions) represent universal simple regulators, which are used to inhibit some combinations of terminals in rules, or which specify the actions that need some special treatment in the meta-grammar form translation.

The main *combining constructs* in the meta-grammar are order(), rhs() and first(), which are used for generating variants of assortments of given terminals and non-terminals.

```
/* budu se ptat - I will ask */
clause ===> order(VBU,R,VRI)
/* ktery ... - which ... */
relclause ===> first(relprongr) rhs(clause)
```

The order() construct generates all possible permutations of its components. The first() and rhs() constructs are employed to implant content of all the right hand sides of specified non-terminal to the rule. The rhs(N) construct generates the possible rewritings of the non-terminal N. The resulting terms are then subject to standard constraints, enclitic checking and inter-segment insertion. In some cases, one needs to force a certain constituent to be the first non-terminal on the RHS. The construct first(N) ensures that N is firmly tied to the beginning and can neither be preceded by an inter-segment nor any other construct.

There are several generative constructs for defining rule templates to simplify the creation and maintenance of the grammar. One group of such constructs is formed by a set of %list_* expressions, which automatically produce new rules for a list of the given non-terminals either simply concatenated or separated by comma and co-ordinative conjunctions.

A significant portion of the grammar is made up by the verb group rules (about 40 %). Therefore we have been seeking for an instrument that would catch frequent repetitive constructions in verb groups. The obtained addition is the %group keyword illustrated by the following example:

```
%group verbP={
  V:     verb_rule_schema($@,"(#1)")
         groupflag($1,"head"),
  VR R: verb_rule_schema($@,"(#1 #2)")
         groupflag($1,"head"),
}

/* ctu/ptam se - I am reading/I am asking */
clause ====> order(group(verbP), vi_list)
  verb_rule_schema($@,"#2")
  depends(getgroupflag($1,"head"), $2)
```

Here, the group verbP denotes two sets of non-terminals with the corresponding actions that are then substituted for the expression group(verbP) on the RHS of the clause non-terminal. In order to be able to refer to verb group members in the rules, where the group is used, any group term can be assigned a *flag* (any string). By that flag an outside action can refer to the term later with getgroupflag construct.

Many rules, e.g. those prescribing the structure of a clause, share the same rule template — they have the same requirements for inter-segments filling and the enclitics order checking as well as the RHS term combinations. To enable a global specification of such majority of rules, we provide a *rule template* mechanism, which defines a pattern of each such rule (the rule type and the RHS encapsulation with some generative construct).

Some grammatical phenomena occur very rarely in common texts. The best way to capture this sparseness is to train rule probabilities on a large data bank of derivation trees acquired from corpus sentences. Since preparation of such corpus of adequate size (at least tens of thousands of sentences) is a very expensive and tedious process, we have for now overcome this difficulty with defining *rule levels*. Every rule without level indication is of level 0. The higher the level, the less frequent the appropriate grammatical phenomenon is, according to the guidance of the grammarian. Rules of higher levels can be set on or off according to the chosen level of the whole grammar.

Apart from the common generative constructs, the meta-grammar comprises feature tagging actions that specify certain local aspects of the denoted (non-)terminal. One of these actions is the specification of the head-dependent relations in the rule — the head() and depends construct which allow to express the dependency links between rule terms.

The Second Grammar Form (G2). As we have mentioned earlier, several pre-defined grammatical tests and procedures are used in the description of context actions associated with each grammatical rule of the system. The pruning actions include:

- grammatical case test for particular words and noun groups
- agreement test of case in prepositional construction
- agreement test of number and gender for relative pronouns
- agreement test of case, number and gender for noun groups
- type checking of logical constructions

```
np -> adj_group np
    rule_schema($@, "lwtx(awtx(#1) and awtx(#2))")
    rule_schema($@, "lwtx([[awt(#1),#2],x])")
```

The contextual actions propagate_all and agree_*_and_propagate propagate all relevant grammatical information from the selected non-terminals on the RHS to the one on the left hand side of the rule.

The rule_schema action presents a prescription for building a logical construction out of the sub-constructions from the RHS. Each time a type checking mechanism is applied and only the type-correct combinations are passed through.

Expanded Grammar Form (G3). The feature agreement tests can be transformed into context-free rules. For instance in Czech, similar to other Slavic languages, we have 7 grammatical cases (nominative, genitive, dative, accusative, vocative, locative and instrumental), two numbers (singular and plural) and three genders (masculine, feminine and neuter), in which masculine exists in two forms — animate and inanimate. Thus, e.g., we get 56 possible variants for a full agreement between two constituents.

The number of rules naturally grows in the direction G1 < G2 < G3. The current numbers of rules in the three grammar forms are 253 in G1, 3091 in G2 and 11530 in G3, but the grammar is still being developed and enhanced.

3 Parser

We restrict our work to lexicalized grammars, where terminals can only appear in lexical rules in the form of $A \rightarrow w_i$. This restriction allows us to simplify the implementation and it also enables to separate a lexicon from the grammar. The parsing module of synt, the libkp library, provides an efficient implementation of standard parser tasks:

- syntactic analysis of sentences in natural language based on context-free grammars that can be large and highly ambiguous;
- efficient representation of derivation trees;
- pruning of the trees based on the application of contextual constraints;
- selecting n most probable trees based on computed probabilities of edge values (e.g. the frequency characteristics obtained from tree-banks);

The parsing process consists of several steps. Firstly, the packed shared forest [6] is produced by the standard CF parsing algorithm. Then the contextual constraints are applied. Finally, most probable trees are selected. The order of the last two steps can be reversed. We use this multi-pass approach, because all these functions are implemented as plug-ins that can be modified as needed or even substituted with other implementations. For example, we have compared four different parsing algorithms which use identical internal data structures (Earley's top-down and bottom-up chart parser [6],

Princeton WordNet: awaken:1, wake:5, waken:1, rouse:4, wake up:1
Definition: cause to become awake or conscious
FIMU Vallex: budit:1 impf. / vzbudit:1 pf. / probudit:1 pf.
frame: CAUSE $<$cause:4$>^{obl}_{col}$ VERB PAT $<$person:1$>^{obl}_{koho4}$
example: probudil mě hluk pf. / that noise awoke me
example: budí mě budík impf./ an alarm clock wakes me up

Fig. 1. An example of FIMU Vallex verb frame.

head-driven chart parser [7] and Tomita's GLR [8]. All these implementations produce the same structures, thus applying contextual constraints or selecting n best trees can be shared among them.

3.1 Evaluation of Contextual Constraints

The contextual constraints (or actions) defined in the meta-grammar can be divided into four groups:

1. rule-tied actions
2. agreement fulfillment constraints
3. post-processing actions
4. actions based on derivation tree

The rule-based probability estimations are solved on the first level by the rule-tied actions, which also serve as rule parameterization modifiers.

Agreement fulfillment constraints serve as chart pruning actions and they are used in generating the expanded grammar G3. The agreement fulfillment constraints represent the functional constraints, whose processing can be interleaved with that of phrasal constraints.

The post-processing actions are not triggered until the chart is already completed. Actions on this level are used mainly for computation of analysis probabilities for a particular input sentence and particular analysis. Some such computations (e.g. verb valency probability) demand exponential resources for computation over the whole chart structure. This problem is solved by splitting the calculation process into the pruning part (run on the level of post-processing actions) and the reordering part, that is postponed until the actions based on derivation tree.

The actions that do not need to work with the whole chart structure are run after the best or n most probable derivation trees are selected. These actions are used, for example, for determination of possible verb valencies within the input sentence, which can produce a new ordering of the selected trees, or for the logical analysis of the sentence.

The edge probability computations use information from several supporting resources, such as a tree-bank of testing sentences or a list of verb valencies. The latter one is currently the most promising resource, since we are working on an enhanced list of verb frames (FIMU Vallex), see [9], featuring syntactic dependencies of sentence constituents, their semantic roles and links to the corresponding Czech WordNet classes. An example of such verb frame is presented in the Figure 1. The list currently contains more than 3000 verbs which, when gathered in synonymic groups, share about 1700 verb frames.

3.2 Implementation

In the libkp library, every grammar rule has zero, one or more semantic actions. The actions are computed bottom-up serving the purpose of:
– computing a value used by another action on the higher level;
– throwing out incorrect derivation trees.

For example, the following grammar rule for genitive constructions in Czech has three semantic actions:

```
npnl -> np np +0.0784671532846715
   test_gen ( $$ $2 )
   prop_all ( $$ $1 )
   depends:1 ( $$ $1 $2 )
```

First line contains a grammar rule with its frequency obtained from a tree-bank. The contextual constraints are listed on the lines bellow it. The number 1 after the colon represents an internal classification of the action. We can turn an evaluation of actions with specified type on and off. The $$ parameter represents the return value. The $k parameter is a variable where we store a value of k-th nonterminal of the rule. Notice that the presented notation is not entered directly by users. It is generated automatically from the meta-grammar G1.

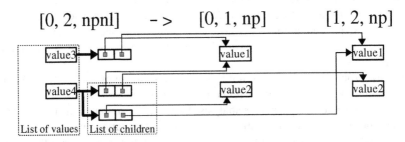

Fig. 2. Example of the forest of values.

The Representation of Values. It was shown that parsing is in general NP-complete if grammars are allowed to have agreement features [10]. The pruning constraints in libkp are weaker than general feature structures. A node in the derivation tree has only limited number of values, e.g. the number of values for noun groups in our system is at most 56.

During the run of the chart based parsing algorithm the results of the parsing process are stored in a packed shared forest of Earley's items [6]. To compute the values, we build a new forest of values instead of pruning original packed shared forest. The worst-case time complexity for one node in the forest of values is therefore 56^{δ}, where δ is the length of the longest right-hand side grammar rule. Notice that this complexity is independent on the number of words in input sentence.

The values in the forest of values are linked with Earley's items. An item contains a single linked list of its values. Each value holds a single linked list of its children. The child is one dimensional array of values. This array represents one combination of values that leads to the parent value. Notice that there can be more combinations of values that leads to the same value. The i-th cell of the array contains a reference to a value from i-th symbol on the RHS of the corresponding grammar rule. The i-th symbol has not to be used to compute the parent value. We use only reference to Earley's item from such unused cell.

The Figure 2 shows an example representing rule npnl -> np np and containing three Earley's items. Each item on the RHS of the rule contains two values, *value1* and *value2*. This gives us four possible combinations. The semantic action computes from combinations *value1* × *value2* and *value2* × *value1* the same value *value4*. The combination *value2* × *value2* was classified as incorrect (by the action), so it is not here.

3.3 Results

In the current stage of the meta-grammar development, synt has achieved an average of 92.08 % coverage on corpus sentences with about 84 % cases where the correct syntactic tree was present in the result. However, the process of determining the correct tree is still premature.

An average time of analysis of one sentence from the corpus data was 0.28 seconds[1]. More details of timing results can be found in the Table 1.

Table 1. Results of running the synt parser on 10.000 corpus sentences (run on Intel Xeon 2.2GHz).

#sentences	10000 sentences from DESAM corpus
#words	191034 words
Maximum sentence length	155 words
Minimum sentence length	2 words
Average sentences length	19.1 words
Time of CFG parsing	5 minutes 52 seconds
Time of evaluating constraints (actions)	38 minutes 32 seconds
Overall time with freeing memory	46 minutes 9 seconds
Average #words per second	68.97
Size of the log file	1.2 GiB
#accepted sentences	9208

4   Conclusions

The presented parsing system synt has already proven its abilities in analysis of running texts in both speed and coverage of various sentence types. With continuous devel-

---

[1] The average running time includes generation of log file messages.

opment of the grammar in order to obtain coverage of the necessary language phenomena, we obtain a quality general purpose system for deep syntactic analysis of natural language texts even for language with such extent of non-analytical features as the Czech language is.

The current development of the system lies mainly in probabilistic ordering of the obtained analyzes with the usage of language specific features such as augmented valency frames in FIMU Vallex.

References

1. Bod, R.: An efficient implementation of a new dop model. In: EACL 2003. (2003) 19–26
2. Collins, M., Duffy, N.: New ranking algorithms for parsing and tagging: Kernels over discrete structures, and the voted perceptron. In: ACL 2002. (2002) 263–270
3. van den Bosch, A., Buchholz, S.: Shallow parsing on the basis of words only: A case study. In: ACL 2002. (2002) 433–440
4. Horák, A.: The Normal Translation Algorithm in Transparent Intensional Logic for Czech. PhD thesis, Faculty of Informatics, Masaryk University, Brno (2002)
5. Smrž, P., Horák, A.: Large scale parsing of Czech. In: Proceedings of Efficiency in Large-Scale Parsing Systems Workshop, COLING'2000, Saarbrucken: Universitaet des Saarlandes (2000) 43–50
6. Earley, J.: An efficient context-free parsing algorithm. In: Communications of the ACM. Volume 13. (1970) 94–102
7. Kay, M.: Algorithm schemata and data structures in syntactic processing. In: Report CSL-80-12, Palo Alto, California, Xerox PARC (1989)
8. Tomita, M.: Efficient Parsing for Natural Languages: A Fast Algorithm for Practical Systems. Kluwer Academic Publishers, Boston, MA (1986)
9. Horák, A., Hlaváčeková, D.: Transformation of wordnet czech valency frames into augmented vallex-1.0 format. In: Proceedings of LTC 2005, Poznan, Poland (2005) accepted for publication.
10. Barton, G.E., Berwick, R.C., Ristad, E.S.: Computational complexity and natural language. MIT Press, Cambridge, Massachusetts (1987)

Anaphora in Czech: Large Data and Experiments with Automatic Anaphora Resolution

Lucie Kučová and Zdeněk Žabokrtský*

Institute of Formal and Applied Linguistics, Charles University (MFF)
Malostranské nám. 25, CZ-11800 Prague, Czech Republic
{kucova,zabokrtsky}@ufal.mff.cuni.cz
http://ufal.mff.cuni.cz

Abstract. The aim of this paper is two-fold. First, we want to present a part of the annotation scheme of the Prague Dependency Treebank 2.0 related to the annotation of coreference on the tectogrammatical layer of sentence representation (more than 45,000 textual and grammatical coreference links in almost 50,000 manually annotated Czech sentences). Second, we report a new pronoun resolution system developed and tested using the treebank data, the success rate of which is 60.4 %.

1 Introduction

Coreference (or co-reference) is usually understood as a symmetric and transitive relation between two expressions in the discourse which refer to the same entity. It is a means for maintaining language economy and discourse cohesion ([1]). Since the expressions are linearly ordered in the time of the discourse, the first expression is often called *antecedent*. Then the second expression (*anaphor*) is seen as 'referring back' to the antecedent. Such a relation is often called *anaphora*[1]. The process of determining the antecedent of an anaphor is called *anaphora resolution* (AR).

Needless to say that AR is a well-motivated NLP task, playing an important role e.g. in machine translation. However, although the problem of AR has attracted the attention of many researches all over the world since 1970s and many approaches have been developed (see [2]), there are only a few works dealing with this subject for Czech, especially in the field of large (corpus) data.

The present paper summarizes the results of studying the phenomenon of coreference in Czech within the context of the Prague Dependency Treebank 2.0 (PDT 2.0)[2]. PDT 2.0 is a collection of linguistically annotated data and documentation and is based on the theoretical framework of Functional Generative Description (FGD). The annotation scheme of the PDT 2.0 consists of three layers: morphological, analytical and tectogrammatical. Within this system, coreference is captured at the tectogrammatical layer of annotation.

---

* The research reported on in this paper has been supported by the grant of the Charles University in Prague 207-10/203329 and by the project 1ET101120503.

[1] Unfortunately, these terms tend to be used inconsistently in literature.

[2] PDT 2.0 is to be released soon by the Linguistic Data Consortium.

V. Matoušek et al. (Eds.): TSD 2005, LNAI 3658, pp. 93–98, 2005.

## 2	Theoretical Background

In FGD, the distinction between grammatical and textual coreference is drawn ([6]). One of the differences is that (individual subtypes of) grammatical coreference can occur only if certain local configurational requirements are fulfilled in the dependency tree (such as: if there is a relative pronoun node in a relative clause and the verbal head of the clause is governed by a nominal node, then the pronoun node and nominal node are coreferential), whereas textual coreference between two nodes does not imply any syntactic relation between the nodes in question or any other constraint on the shape of the dependency tree. Thus textual coreference easily crosses sentence boundaries.

Grammatical Coreference. In the PDT 2.0, grammatical coreference is annotated in the following situations (see a sample tree in Fig. 1)[3]: (i) relative pronouns in relative clauses, (ii) reflexive and reciprocity pronouns (usually coreferential with the subject of the clause), (iii) control (in the sense of [7]) – both for verbs and nouns of control.

Textual Coreference. For the time being, we concentrate on the case of textual coreference in which a demonstrative or an anaphoric pronoun (also in its zero form) are used[4]. The following types of textual coreference links are special (see a sample tree in Fig. 2)[5]:

- a link to a particular node if this node represents an antecedent of the anaphor or a link to the governing node of a subtree if the antecedent is represented by this node plus (some of) its dependents[6]: *Myslíte, že rozhodnutí NATO, zda se [ono] rozšíří, či nikoli, bude záviset na postoji Ruska?* (Do you think that the decision of NATO whether [**it**] will be enlarged or not will depend on the attitude of Russia?)
- a specifically marked link (segm) denoting that the referent is a whole segment of text, including also cases, when the antecedent is understood by inferencing from a broader co-text: *Potentáti v bance koupí za 10, prodají si za 15.(. . .) Odhaduji, že do 2 let budou schopni splatit bance dluh a třetím rokem už budou dělat na sebe. A na práci najmou jen schopné lidi. Kdo **to** pochopí, má náskok.* (The big shots buy in a bank for 10 and sell for 15. (. . .) I guess that within two years they will be able to pay back the debt to the bank and in the third year they will work for themselves. And they will hire only capable people, it will be in their best interest. Those who understand **this**, will have an advantage.)
- a specifically marked link (exoph) denoting that the referent is "out" of the co-text, it is known only from the situation: *Následuje dramatická pauza a pak již vchází **On** nebo **Ona**.* (Lit. (there) follows dramatic pause and then already enters **He** or **She**.)

---

[3] We only list the types of coreference in this paper; detailed linguistic description will be available in the documentation of the PDT 2.0.

[4] With the demonstrative pronoun, we consider only its use as a noun, not as an adjective; we do not include pronouns of the first and second persons.

[5] Besides the listed coreference types, there is one more situation where coreference occurs but is difficult to be identified and no mark is stored into the attributes for coreference representation. It is the case of nodes with tectogrammatical lemma #Unsp (unspecified); see [9]. Example: *Zmizení tohoto 700 kg těžkého přístroje hygienikům ohlásili (**Unsp**) 30. června letošního roku.* (Lit.: The disappearance of the medical instrument weighing 700 kg to hygienists[**they**] announced on June 30th this year.)

[6] This is also the way how a link to a clause or a sentence is being captured.

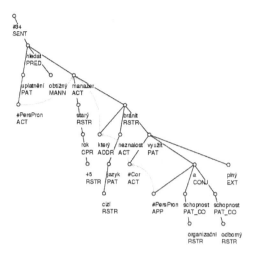

Fig. 1. Simplified PDT sample with various subtypes of grammatical coreference. The structure is simplified, only tectogrammatical lemmas, functors, and coreference links are depicted. The original sentence is '*Obtížněji hledají své uplatnění manažeři starší 45 let, kterým neznalost cizích jazyků brání plně využít své organizační a odborné schopnosti.*' (Lit.: More difficultly search their self-fulfillment manages older than 45 years, to which unknowledge of foreign languages hamper to use their organization and specialized abilities).

3   Annotated Data

Data Representation. When designing the data representation on coreference links, we took into account the fact that each tectogrammatical node is equipped with an identifier which is unique in the whole PDT. Thus the coreference link can be easily captured by storing the identifier of the antecedent node (or a sequence of identifiers, if there are more antecedents for the same anaphor) into a distinguished attribute of the anaphor node. We find this 'pointer' solution more transparent (and – from the programmer's point of view – much easier to cope with) than the solutions proposed in [3] or [4].

At present, there are three node attributes used for representing coreference: (i) coref_gram.rf – identifier or a list of identifiers of the antecedent(s) related via grammatical coreference; (ii) coref_text.rf – identifier or a list of identifiers of the antecedent(s) related via textual coreference; (iii) coref_special – values segm (segment) and exoph (exophora) standing for special types of textual coreference.

We used the tree editor TrEd developed by Petr Pajas as the main annotation interface[7]. More details concerning the annotation environment can be found in [8]. In this editor (as well as in Figures 1 and 2 in this paper), a coreference link is visualized as a non-tree arc pointing from the anaphor to its antecedent.

Quantitative Properties. PDT 2.0 contains 3,168 newspaper texts annotated at the tectogrammatical level. Altogether, they consist of 49,442 sentences with 833,357 tokens (summing word forms and punctuation marks). Coreference has been annotated

---

[7] http://ufal.mff.cuni.cz/~pajas

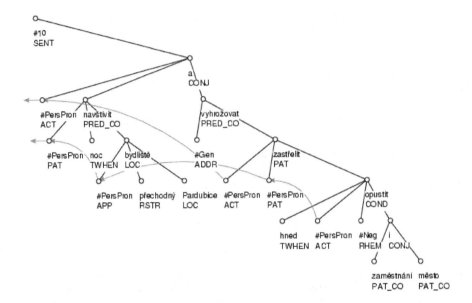

Fig. 2. Simplified PDT sample containing two textual coreference chains. The original sentence is *'Navštívil ji v noci v jejím přechodném bydlišti v Pardubicích a vyhrožoval, že ji zastřelí, pokud hned neopustí zaměstnání i město.'* (Lit.: [He] visited her in night in her temporary dwelling in Pardubice and threatened [her] that [he] will shoot her if [she] instantly does not leave her job and city.).

manually (disjunctively[8]) in all this data. After finishing the manual annotation and post-annotation checks and corrections, there are 23,266 links of grammatical coreference (dominating relative pronouns as the anaphor – 32 %) and 22,365[9] links of textual coreference (dominating personal and possessive pronouns as the anaphor – 83 %), plus 505 occurrences of **segm** and 120 occurrences of **exoph**.

4   Experiments and Evaluation of Automatic Anaphora Resolution

In [8] it was shown that it is easy to get close to 90 % precision when considering only grammatical coreference[10]. Obviously, textual coreference is more difficult to resolve

---

[8] Independent parallel annotation of the same sentences were performed only in the starting phase of the annotation, only as long as the annotation scheme stabilized and reasonable inter-annotator agreement was reached (see [8]).

[9] Similarity of the numbers of textual and grammatical coreference links is only a more or less random coincidence. If we would have annotated also e.g. bridging anaphora, the numbers would be much more different.

[10] This is not surprising, since in the case of grammatical coreference most of the information can be derived from the topology and basic attributes of the tree (supposing that we have access also to the annotation of morphological and analytical level of the sentence). However, it opens the question of redundancy (at least for certain types of grammatical coreference).

(there are almost no reliable clues as in the case of grammatical coreference). So far, we attempted to resolve only the textual coreference links 'starting' in nodes with tectogrammatical lemma #PersPron. This lemma stands for personal (and personal possessive) pronouns, be they expressed on the surface (i.e., present in the original sentence) or restored during the annotation of the tectogrammatical tree structure.

We use the following procedure (numbers in parentheses were measured on the training part of the PDT 2.0)[11]: For each detected anaphor (lemma #PersPron):

– First, an initial set of antecedent candidates is created: we used all nodes from the previous sentence and current sentence (roughly 3.2 % of correct answers disappear from the set of candidates in this step).

– Second, the set of candidates is gradually reduced using various filters: (1) candidates from the current sentence not preceding the anaphor are removed (next 6.2 % lost), (2) candidates which are not semantic nouns (nouns, pronouns and numeral with nominal nature, possessive pronouns, etc.), or at least conjunctions coordinating two or more semantic nouns, are removed (5.6 % lost), (3) candidates in subject position which are in the same clause as the anaphor are removed, since the anaphor would be probably expressed by a reflexive pronoun (0.7 % lost) (4) all candidates disagreeing with the anaphor in gender or number are removed (3.7 % lost), (5) candidates which are parent or grandparent of the anaphor (in the tree structure) are removed (0.6 % lost), (6) if both the node and its parent are in the set of candidates, then the child node is removed (1.6 % lost), (7) if there is a candidate with the same functor with anaphor, then all candidates having different functor are removed (3.4 % lost), (8) if there is a candidate in a subject position, then all candidates in different than subject positions are removed (2.4 % lost),

– Third, the candidate is chosen from the remaining set which is (linearly) the closest to the given anaphor (12.5 % lost).

When measuring the performance only on the evaluation-purpose part of the PDT 2.0 data (roughly 10 % of the whole), the final success rate (number of correctly resolved antecedents divided by the number of pronoun anaphors) is 60.4 %[12].

The whole system consists of roughly 200 lines of Perl code and was implemented using ntred[13] environment for accessing the PDT data. The question of speed is almost irrelevant: since the system is quite straightforward and fully deterministic, ntred running on ten networked computers needs less than one minute to resolve all #PersPron node in PDT.

5 Final Remarks

We understand coreference as an integral part of a dependency-based annotation of underlying sentence structure which prepares solid grounds for further linguistic investigations. It proved to be useful in the implemented AR system, which profits from the

---

[11] The procedure is based mostly on our experience with the data. However, it undoubtedly bears many similarities with other approaches ([2]).

[12] For instance, the results in pronoun resolution in English reported in [10] was also around 60 %.

[13] http://ufal.mff.cuni.cz/~pajas

existence of the tectogrammatical dependency tree (and also from the annotations on the two lower levels).

As for the results achieved by our AR system, to our knowledge there is no other system for Czech reaching comparable performance and verified on comparably large data.

References

1. Halliday M. A. K., Hasan, R.: Cohesion in English, Longman, London (1976)
2. Mitkov, R.: Anaphora resolution. Longman, London (2001)
3. Plátek, M., Sgall, J., Sgall, P.: A Dependency Base for a Linguistic Description. In: Sgall, P.(ed.): Contributions to Functional Syntax, Semantics and Language Comprehension. Academia, Prague (1984) 63-97
4. Hajičová, E., Panevová J., Sgall, P.: Coreference in Annotating a Large Corpus. In: Proceedings of LREC 2000, Vol. 1. Athens, Greece (2000) 497-500
5. Hajičová, E., Panevová, J., Sgall, P. Manuál pro tektogramatické značkování. Technical Report ÚFAL-TR-7 (1999)
6. Panevová, J.: Koreference gramatická nebo textová? In: Banys, W., Bednarczuk, L., Bogacki, K. (eds.): Etudes de linguistique romane et slave, Krakow (1991)
7. Panevová, J.: More Remarks on Control. In: Prague Linguistic Circle Papers, Benjamin Publ. House, Amsterdam – Philadelphia (1996) 101-120
8. Kučová L., Kolářová V., Pajas P., Žabokrtský Z., and Čulo O.: Anotování koreference v Pražském závislostním korpusu. Technical Report of the Center for Computational Linguistics, Charles University, Prague (2003)
9. Kučová L., Hajičová E. 2004), Coreferential Relations in the Prague Dependency Treebank. Presented at 5th Discourse Anaphora and Anaphor Resolution Colloquium, San Miguel, Azores (2004)
10. Barbu C., Mitkov, R.: Evaluation tool for rule-based anaphora resolution methods. In: Proceedings of ACL'01, Toulouse, France (2001) 34-41

Valency Lexicon of Czech Verbs VALLEX: Recent Experiments with Frame Disambiguation*

Markéta Lopatková, Ondřej Bojar, Jiří Semecký,
Václava Benešová, and Zdeněk Žabokrtský

Institute of Formal and Applied Linguistics
Faculty of Mathematics and Physics, Charles University, Prague
{lopatkova,bojar,semecky,benesova,zabokrtsky}@ufal.mff.cuni.cz

Abstract. VALLEX is a linguistically annotated lexicon aiming at a description of syntactic information which is supposed to be useful for NLP. The lexicon contains roughly 2500 manually annotated Czech verbs with over 6000 valency frames (summer 2005). In this paper we introduce VALLEX and describe an experiment where VALLEX frames were assigned to 10,000 corpus instances of 100 Czech verbs – the pairwise inter-annotator agreement reaches 75%. The part of the data where three human annotators agreed were used for an automatic word sense disambiguation task, in which we achieved the precision of 78.5%.

1 Introduction

A verb is traditionally considered to be the center of the sentence, and description of syntactic and syntactic-semantic behavior of verbs is a substantial task for linguists. Theoretical aspects of valency are challenging. Moreover, valency information stored in a lexicon (as valency properties are multifarious and cannot be described by general rules) belongs to the core information for any rule-based task of NLP (from lemmatization and morphological analysis through syntactic analysis to such complex tasks as e.g. machine translation).

There are tens of different theoretical approaches, tens of language resources and hundreds of publications related to the study of verbal valency in various natural languages. It goes far beyond the scope of this paper to give an exhaustive survey of all these enterprises – [1] gives a survey and a short characteristics of the most prominent projects.

The present paper is structured as follows: in Section 2 we summarize the basic properties of the lexicon VALLEX, in Section 3 we describe the human-annotated data where corpus occurrences of selected verbs are assigned to valency frames, in Section 4 we report the experiment with automatic frame assignment.

2 Valency Lexicon of Czech Verbs VALLEX

The VALency LEXicon of Czech verbs (VALLEX in the sequel) is a collection of linguistically annotated data and documentation, resulting from an attempt at formal

---

* The research reported in this paper has been partially supported by the grant of Grant Agency of Czech Republic No. 405/04/0243 and by the projects of Information Society No 1ET100300517 and 1ET101470416.

V. Matoušek et al. (Eds.): TSD 2005, LNAI 3658, pp. 99–106, 2005.

description of valency frames of Czech verbs. VALLEX version 1.0 was publicly released in autumn 2003[1]. VALLEX 1.0 contained roughly 1400 verbs with 4000 valency frames. At this moment, the latest version of VALLEX data contains roughly 2500 verbs with more than 6000 valency frames. All verb entries are created manually. Manual annotation and accent put on consistency of annotation are markedly time consuming and limit the speed of quantitative growth, but guarantees a significant rise of quality.

VALLEX is closely related to Prague Dependency Treebank (PDT)[2]. Both PDT and VALLEX are based on Functional Generative Description of Czech (FGD), being developed by Petr Sgall and his collaborators since the 1960s (see [3], valency theory within FGD esp. in [4]). Applying the principles of FGD to a huge amount of data means a great opportunity to verify and expand the theory, to refine the functional criteria set up. The modification of 'classical' FGD valency theory is used as the theoretical background in VALLEX 1.0 (see [5] for a detailed description of the framework).

On the topmost level, VALLEX[3] consists of **word entries** corresponding to complex units, verb lexemes (the VALLEX entries for the verbs *odpovídat* and *odpovídat se* is shown in Figure 1). The particular word entry is characterized by the **headword lemma**, i.e. the infinitive form of the respective verb (including the reflexive particle if it exists) and its **aspect** (perfective, imperfective or biaspectual). The tentative term **base lemma** denotes the infinitive of the verb, excluding the reflexive particle (i.e. the output of a morphological analysis).

Each word entry is composed of a non-empty sequence of **frame entries** relevant for the headword lemma. The frame entries (marked with subscripts in VALLEX) roughly correspond to individual senses of the headword lemma. The particular word entry is characterized by a **gloss** (i.e. verb or paraphrase roughly synonymous with the given frame/sense) and by **example(s)** (i.e. sentence fragment(s) containing the given verb used with the given valency frame). The core valency information is encoded in the **valency frame**.

Each valency frame consists of a set of **valency members / frame slots**, each corresponding to an (either required or specifically permitted) complementation of the given verb. The information on a particular valency member includes the following points:

– **'Functor'** expresses the type of relation between the verb and its complementation[4]. Complementations are divided into (i) inner participants / arguments (like Actor, Patient and Addressee for the verb *přinést*₁ [to bring], as in *někdo*.ACT *přinese někdo*.PAT *někomu*.ADDR [sbd brings st to sbd] or Actor, Patient and Effect for the verb *jmenovat*₃ [to nominate], as in *někdo*.ACT *jmenuje někoho*.PAT *něčím*.EFF

---

[1] http://ckl.mff.cuni.cz/zabokrtsky/vallex/1.0/

[2] However, VALLEX is not to be confused with a larger valency lexicon PDT-VALLEX created during the annotation of PDT, see [2]. PDT-VALLEX contains more verbs (5500 verbs), but only frames occurring in PDT (over 9000 frames), whereas in the more complex VALLEX the verbs are analyzed in all their meanings. In addition, richer information is assigned to particular valency frames.

[3] Detailed description can be found in [6].

[4] The complete list of functors used in VALLEX together with English examples can be found in [6].

odpovídat (imperfective)

[1] odpovídat$_1$ $\sim$ odvětit [answer; respond]
- frame: ACT$_1^{obl}$ ADDR$_3^{obl}$ PAT$_{na+4,4}^{opt}$ EFF$_{4,aby,ať,zda,že}^{obl}$ MANN^{typ}
- example: *odpovídal mu na jeho dotaz pravdu / že ...* [he responded to his question truthfully / that ...]
- asp.counterpart: odpovědět$_1$ pf.
- class: communication

[2] odpovídat$_2$ $\sim$ reagovat [react]
- frame: ACT$_1^{obl}$ PAT$_{na+4}^{obl}$ MEANS$_7^{typ}$
- example: *pokožka odpovídala na včelí bodnutí zarudnutím* [the skin reacted to a bee sting by turning red]
- asp.counterpart: odpovědět$_2$ pf.

[3] odpovídat$_3$ $\sim$ mít odpovědnost [be responsible]
- frame: ACT$_1^{obl}$ADDR$_3^{obl}$PAT$_{za+4}^{opt}$MEANS$_7^{typ}$
- example: *odpovídá za své děti; odpovídá za ztrátu svým majetkem* [she is responsible for her kids]

[4] odpovídat$_4$ $\sim$ být ve shodě [match]
- frame: ACT$_{1,že}^{obl}$PAT$_3^{obl}$REG$_7^{typ}$
- example: *řešení odpovídá svými vlastnostmi požadavkům* [the solution matches the requirements]

odpovídat se (imperfective)

[1] odpovídat se$_1$ $\sim$ být zodpovědný [be responsible]
- frame: ACT$_1^{obl}$ADDR$_3^{obl}$PAT$_{z+2}^{obl}$
- example: *odpovídá se ze ztrát* [he answers for the losses]

Fig. 1. VALLEX entries for the base lemma *odpovídat (answer, match).*

[sbd nominates sbd as sbd]) and (ii) free modifications (adjuncts) as Time, Location, Manner and Cause[5].
- Possible **morphemic form(s)** – each complementation can be expressed by a limited set of morphemic means (pure or prepositional cases, subordinated clauses or infinitive constructions are the most important); possible morphemic form(s) are specified either explicitly (as a list of forms attached to a particular slot) or implicitly[6].
- **'Type'** – the following types of complementations are distinguished: obligatory (in the deep (tectogrammatical) structure) and optional for inner participants ('obl' and 'opt'), and obligatory and typical ('typ') for free modifications.

In addition to this obligatory information, also optional attributes may appear in each frame: flag for idiom, list of aspectual counterpart(s), information on control, affiliation to a syntactic-semantic class:

---

[5] Here we are leaving aside a small group of complementations on the border-line between inner participants and free modifications, quasi-valency complementations, see [5].

[6] The set of possible forms is implied by the functor of the complementation, see [6].

- **Flag for idiom** – VALLEX describes primary or usual meanings of verbs, however some very frequent idiomatic frames[7] are included as well. They are marked by idiomatic flag and include lemmas of words in the phraseme.
- **Aspectual counterpart** – aspectual counterpart(s) need not be the same for all senses of the given verb; if they exist, they are listed in particular frame entries[8] (see figure 1).
- **Control** – if a verb has a complementation in an infinitive form (regardless its functor), the valency member of the head verb that would be the subject of this infinitive is marked.
- **Syntactic-semantic classes** – particular frame entries are tentatively sorted into classes. Constructed in a 'bottom-up way', these classes are based on deep analysis of mainly syntactic properties of verbs in their particular senses. For the time being, 24 big groups involving next to half of the verb frames have been established[9].

3   VALEVAL

VALEVAL[10] is a lexical sampling experiment with VALLEX 1.0 for which 109 base lemmas from VALLEX 1.0 were selected. For each lemma 100 random sample sentences were extracted from CNC. See [7] for more details and examples.

Three human annotators in parallel were asked to choose the most appropriate verb entry and the frame for the extracted sentence within a context of the three preceding sentences. The annotators had also an option to indicate that the particular sentence is not a valid example (e.g. due to a tagging error) of the annotated lemma at all or that they got completely confused by the given context. A valid answer indicates a verb entry and a frame entry index. Optionally, a remark that the corresponding frame was missing could have been given instead of the frame entry index. If the annotators were not able to decide on a single answer, they have been given the possibility of assigning more than one valid answer (labelled as 'Ambiguous annotations' in Table 1). Also, a special flag could be assigned to a valid answer to indicate that the annotator is not quite sure (labelled as 'Uncertain annotations').

3.1   Inter-annotator Agreement

Table 2 summarizes inter-annotator agreement (IAA) and Cohen's κ statistic [9] on the 10256 annotated sentences. The symbol Ø indicates plain average calculated over base lemmas, wØ stands for average weighted by frequency observed in CNC. Considering all the three parallel annotations, the exact match of answers reaches 61% (weighted)

---

[7] Idiomatic frame is tentatively characterized either by a substantial shift in meaning (with respect to the primary sense), or by a small and strictly limited set of possible lexical values in one of its complementations.

[8] Iterative verbs occur in entries of the corresponding non-iterative verbs, but they have no own word entries.

[9] However rough these classes are, they serve for controlling the consistency of annotation.

[10] Inspired by SENSEVAL ([8]), a word sense disambiguation task, VALEVAL aims at valency frame disambiguation.

Table 1. Annotated data size and overall statistics about the annotations.

Lemmas annotated	109
Sentences annotated	10256
Parallel annotators	3
Total annotations	30765 (100%)
Uncertain annotations	1045 (3.4%)
Ambiguous annotations	703 (2.3%)
Marked as invalid example	172 (0.6%)
Annotator got confused	90 (0.3%)
Marked as missing frame	1673 (5.4%)

or 67% (unweighted). If the 'uncertainty' flags are disregarded, we find out that the agreement rises to 66% or 70%, respectively. In other words, annotators agree on the most plausible answer, even if they are not quite sure. If only such sentences where none of the annotators doubted are taken into account, the exact match reaches 68% or 74% (this comprises 90.5% of the sentences).

The κ statistic compensates IAA for agreement by chance. The level of 0.5 to 0.6 we achieve is generally considered as a *moderate agreement*, while 0.6 to 0.8 represents *significant agreement*. This moderate agreement is not an unsatisfactory result compared to other results such as [10], who reports pairwise IAA for French verbs between 60% and 65% and κ of 0.41.

Table 2. Inter-annotator agreement and κ.

	Match of 3 Annotators				Average Pairwise Match			
	IAA [%]		κ		IAA [%]		κ	
	wØ	Ø	wØ	Ø	wØ	Ø	wØ	Ø
Exact	61.4	66.8	0.52	0.54	70.8	74.8	0.54	0.54
Ignoring Uncertainty	65.9	69.8	0.58	0.59	74.8	77.7	0.60	0.59
Where All Were Sure	68.2	73.7	0.58	0.62	76.7	80.9	0.61	0.64

Average pairwise IAA is provided to allow for a rough comparison with some cited results, although the specific circumstances are not always directly comparable. [11] achieve an IAA for Czech verbs of 45% to 64%. For Japanese verbs, IAA of 86.3% is achieved by [12]. [13] report IAA of 71% for Senseval-2 English verbs tagged with WordNet synsets. Grouping some senses together to form a more coarse grained sense inventory allowed the authors to improve the IAA to 82%.

4   Automatic Frame Disambiguation

4.1   Data Source: 'Golden VALEVAL'

VALLEX frames correspond to verb senses (meanings). From this perspective, performing word sense disambiguation (WSD) of Czech verbs means choosing the most

Table 3. Baselines for WSD on 8066 'Golden VALEVAL' sentences for 108 lemmas.

	wØ	Ø
Entropy	1.54	1.28
VALLEX frames per lemma	12.46	7.61
Seen frames per lemma	5.85	4.85
10-fold Baseline WSD Accuracy	59.79%	66.19%

appropriate frame. 'Golden VALEVAL' is a corpus suitable for evaluating frame disambiguation. It comprises 8066 VALEVAL sentences covering 108 base lemmas where there was exact agreement across the annotators or a single answer was selected in a postprocess annotation aimed at eliminating clear typing errors and misinterpretations.

The difficulty of the WSD task is apparent from Table 3 looking at the (weighted or unweighted average) number of available frames per base lemma and entropy. The number of frames per lemma is estimated both from the whole VALLEX ('VALLEX frames per lemma') as well as from the set of actually observed frames in the golden VALEVAL corpus ('Seen frames per lemma').

The baseline accuracy is achieved by choosing the most frequent frame for a given lemma. The baseline was estimated by a 10-fold cross-validation (the most frequent frame is learned from 9/10 of the data and the unseen 1/10 is used to estimate the accuracy, the average result from 10 runs of the estimation is reported).

For purposes of further experiments, Golden VALEVAL was automatically tagged, lemmatized and enriched with surface syntactic structures automatically assigned by the Czech version of the parser reported in [14]. After the exclusion of unparsed sentences, 6666 sentences remained for our task.

4.2 Method and Selected Features

For an automatic selection of the VALLEX frame to which a given verb occurrence belongs, we generated a vector of features for each occurrence. We evaluated the decision tree machine learning method available in C5 toolkit[11]. 10-fold cross-validation was used for evaluation.

We experimented with several features containing information about the context of the verb. The following list describes different groups of features:

- Morphological: purely morphological information about lemmas in a 5-word window centered around the verb. Czech positional morphological tags (used also in PDT) contain 15 categories and all of these were taken as individual features, counting 75 features altogether.
- Syntax-based: information gained from the dependency tree of the sentence, including mostly Boolean information about morphological and lexical characteristics of dependent words (e.g. presence of a noun or a nominative pronoun in a given case dependent on the verb, presence of a given preposition with a given case dependent on the verb).

---

[11] http://www.rulequest.com/see5-info.html

4.3   Results

Weighting the accuracy by the number of sentences in our training set (labelled as ∅ in Table 4), we gained 73.9% accuracy for morphological features and 78.5% accuracy for syntax-based features, respectively, compared to baseline 67.9% (baseline for the 6666 parsed sentences). Weighting the accuracy by the lemma frequency observed in the Czech National Corpus (labelled as w∅), the accuracy dropped to 67.1% for the morphological features and 70.8% for syntax-based features respectively, compared to baseline 63.3%.

Table 4. Accuracy of frame disambiguation.

	w∅	∅
Baseline	63.3%	67.9%
Morphological	67.1%	73.9%
Syntax-based	70.8%	78.5%

The syntax-based features alone led to better results, and even the combination of both of the types of features did not bring any improvement. This could happen because the morphological information is already included in the syntax-based features (as they contain information mainly about morphological characteristics of syntactically related words) and because the syntactic structure of the sentence depicts enough information to achieve the rate of disambiguation which can be obtained using this method.

5   Conclusions and Future Work

We have presented the current state of building valency lexicon of Czech verbs VALLEX. We have also described the VALEVAL experiment which allowed us to improve consistency of selected VALLEX entries and provided us with golden standard data for WSD task. The first results in WSD are reported.

In future we plan to extend VALLEX in both qualitative aspects (e.g. description of alternations and types of reflexivity) and quantitative aspects. We will continue the WSD experiments, we intend to incorporate features based on WordNet classes and animacy.

References

1. Žabokrtský, Z.: Valency Lexicon of Czech Verbs. PhD thesis, Faculty of Mathematics and Physics, Charles University in Prague (2005) in prep.
2. Hajič, J., Panevová, J., Urešová, Z., Bémová, A., Kolářová, V., Pajas, P.: PDT-VALLEX: Creating a Large-coverage Valency Lexicon for Treebank Annotation. In: Proceedings of The Second Workshop on Treebanks and Linguistic Theories. Volume 9 of Mathematical Modeling in Physics, Engineering and Cognitive Sciences., Vaxjo University Press (2003) 57–68

3. Sgall, P., Hajičová, E., Panevová, J.: The Meaning of the Sentence in Its Semantic and Pragmatic Aspects. D. Reidel Publishing Company, Dordrecht (1986)
4. Panevová, J.: Valency Frames and the Meaning of the Sentence. In Luelsdorff, P.L., ed.: The Prague School of Structural and Functional Linguistics, Amsterdam-Philadelphia, John Benjamins (1994) 223–243
5. Lopatková, M.: Valency in the Prague Dependency Treebank: Building the Valency Lexicon. Prague Bulletin of Mathematical Linguistics **79–80** (2003) 37–60
6. Žabokrtský, Z., Lopatková, M.: Valency Frames of Czech Verbs in VALLEX 1.0. In: Frontiers in Corpus Annotation. Proceedings of the Workshop of the HLT/NAACL Conference. (2004) 70–77
7. Bojar, O., Semecký, J., Benešová, V.: VALEVAL: Testing VALLEX Consistency and Experimenting with Word-Frame Disambiguation. Prague Bulletin of Mathematical Linguistics **83** (2005)
8. Edmonds, P.: Introduction to Senseval. ELRA Newsletter **7** (2002)
9. Carletta, J.: Assessing agreement on classification task: The kappa statistics. Computational Linguistics **22** (1996) 249–254
10. Véronis, J.: A study of polysemy judgements and inter-annotator agreement. In: Programme and advanced papers of the Senseval workshop, Herstmonceux Castle (England) (1998) 2–4
11. Hajič, J., Holub, M., Hučínová, M., Pavlík, M., Pecina, P., Straňák, P., Šidák, P.: Validating and Improving the Czech WordNet via Lexico-Semantic Annotation of the Prague Dependency Treebank. In: Proceedings of LREC 2004. (2004)
12. Shirai, K.: Construction of a Word Sense Tagged Corpus for SENSEVAL-2 Japanese Dictionary Task. In: Proceedings of LREC 2002. (2002) 605–608
13. Babko-Malaya, O., Palmer, M., Xue, N., Joshi, A., Kulick, S.: Proposition Bank II: Delving Deeper. In: Frontiers in Corpus Annotation. Proceedings of the Workshop of the HLT/NAACL Conference. (2004) 17–23
14. Charniak, E.: A Maximum-Entropy-Inspired Parser. In: Proceedings of NAACL-2000, Seattle, Washington, USA (2000) 132–139

AARLISS – An Algorithm for Anaphora Resolution in Long-Distance Inter Sentential Scenarios

Miroslav Martinovic, Anthony Curley, and John Gaskins

Computer Science Department, TCNJ, 2000 Pennington Road, Ewing, NJ, USA
{mmmartin,curley2,gaskins2}@tcnj.edu

Abstract. We present a novel approach for boosting the performance of pronominal anaphora resolution algorithms when search for antecedents has to span over a multi-sentential text passage. The approach is based on the identification of sentences which are "most semantically related" to the sentence with anaphora. The context sharing level between each possible referent sentence and the anaphoric sentence gets established utilizing an open-domain external knowledge base. Sentences with scores higher than a threshold level are considered the "most semantically related" and ranked accordingly. The qualified sentences accompanied with their context sharing scores represent a new, reduced in size, and a more semantically focused search space. Their respective scores are utilized as separate preference factors in a final phase of the resolution process - the antecedent selection. We pioneer three implementations for the algorithm with their corresponding evaluation data.

1 Motivation

Though a high proportion of pronominal anaphors (90%+) have their antecedents in the same or the preceding sentence, particular text genres are known to be much more prone to a long-distance pronominalization. Consequently, any open-domain NL application is expected to account for such cases. *"Amy, the ape ensnaring beauty will be played by **Naomi Watts** in 2005 Peter Jackson's new film King Kong. And, it's happening already - shaking, panic attacks, drooling. The thought of a year without a Peter Jackson film is traumatic for fans now accustomed to their yearly fix of Lord of the Rings. But with King Kong on the horizon, there is still hope. However, despite Jackson's enormous appeal to the audience, it is **her** freshness and youth that will at the end trademark the film."* For an open domain question answering system presented with the question *"What actress is expected to epitomize Peter Jackson's new movie 'King Kong'?"*, a successful resolution of the pronominal anaphora **her** will at the end make the difference between producing and missing the right answer. And, a successful search for its antecedent will have to span over five very long and complicated metaphorical sentences.

Question answering as well as other NL applications are expected to produce the requested information in a compact self-contained unit that can be readily digested by the user. While single sentence retrieval techniques represent a viable basis for this goal, their inability to handle inter sentential (and particularly long-distance) anaphora demonstrates a serious deficiency that needs to be managed.

V. Matoušek et al. (Eds.): TSD 2005, LNAI 3658, pp. 107–114, 2005.

The major base line models for anaphora resolution include linguistic syntactic/semantic approaches ([5], [6], [17], [22]), as well as corpus-based statistical ones ([2], [3], [7], [18], [19]). While a number of proposed anaphora resolution algorithms addresses the situation in which the anaphora referent is known to be in a body of text containing more than two sentences, they treat the multi-sentence text either as a bag of words or a bag of phrases with little or no emphasis on syntactic and even less on semantic structure of the sentence. Individual sentences are rarely recognized as relatively autonomous units of information.

Semantically unrelated sentences only very infrequently contain a detectable referent and should not be considered when searching for one. On the contrary, only semantically related ones should be further analyzed and the antecedent search space conveniently gets reduced to only a few sentences - a very important fact for long distance spans.

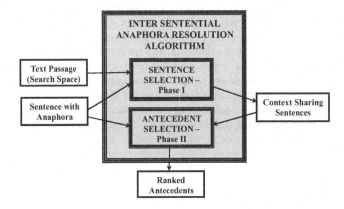

Fig. 1. General Overview of the Algorithm.

This approach, evidently tailored and suitable for long distance anaphora resolution blends seamlessly into the answer pinpointing phase of our question answering system. In there, a retrieved text passage that includes a sentence with the answer may also find the sentence to contain an essential anaphora. Consequently, the reference needs to be resolved and the found referent substituted for the anaphora into a final, comprehensible, one sentence answer.

2   Overall Architecture of AARLISS

AARLISS has been designed to process a body of plain text that includes sentences with possible referents, and the anaphoric sentence. The final result is a list of ranked anaphora antecedents. The resolution process comprises of two major phases: (i) sentence selection phase (SSP) and (ii) antecedent selection phase (ASP).

2.1   Sentence Selection in AARLISS

The sentence selection phase establishes whether and in what capacity a sentence from the text passage shares the context with the anaphoric sentence. An external knowl-

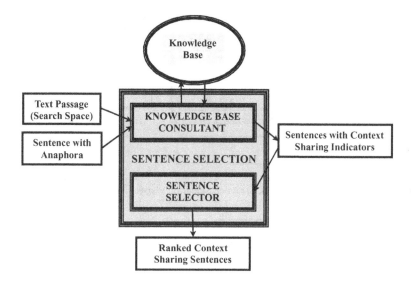

Fig. 2. Sentence Selection Phase.

edge base is consulted to assess the context sharing level and a numerical indicator is produced that reflects that.

All sentences first need to be preprocessed by the Knowledge Base Consultant module into a form that could be further analyzed. This module also interprets the context-describing information received from the knowledge base and calculates the context sharing indicators for each individual sentence. A simple ranking follows and only the sentences over the threshold are used for antecedent selection phase.

2.2 Antecedent Selection in AARLISS

The architecture for the antecedent phase is depicted in Figure 3. It examines the noun phrases for constraints in order to eliminate those that cannot possibly be antecedents for the given anaphora. The remaining phrases are then processed for preferences and ranked accordingly by its Chooser module. Our novel addition to this rather standard architecture is that the context sharing indicators weigh into the scoring procedure of the chooser and are combined with other preferences used. And, since they are a result of a semantic processing using a knowledge base, our algorithm can be characterized as a semantic, salience-based one.

3   Implementations

AARLISS has three implementations incremental with respect to the amount and sophistication level of tools used. Currently, its external knowledge base is the WordNet 2.0 lexical database ([9]). WordNet's public accessibility governed our choice despite our recognition of its shortcomings for the given context (as reported in [14] and [21]). Alternatively, we are experimenting with ResearchCyc KB system ([15]).

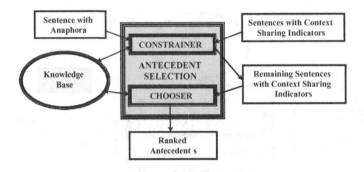

Fig. 3. Sentence Selection Phase.

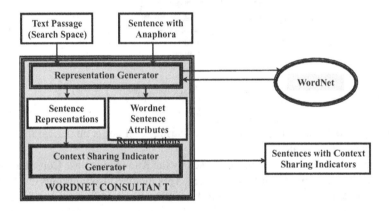

Fig. 4. Sentence Selection Phase Commonalities.

All three implementations tag (Implementations I and II) or parse (Implementation III) the sentences and then form representations from the main verb and (pro)nouns. The level of context sharing between two given sentences gets evaluated by analyzing how congruent their representations are. All implementations include shallow processing that disambiguates word senses within the representations. Figure 4 depicts the architecture commonalities while Figure 5 depicts implementation particulars of the WordNet (Knowledge Base) Consultant module.

Most essential differences between the three implementations are located in their sentence selection phase, the essential booster for inter sentential long-distance pronominal anaphora resolution. In Implementation I, each sentence gets reduced to its main verb and its related (pro)nouns. Thus, the representation "hurled/VBN: midst/NN, crowd/NN, fan/NN, bouquet/NN, stage/NN." is all that was saved from the sentence "In the midst of a completely jubilant crowd, a fan hurled a bouquet onto the stage storming it from beneath").

Subsequently, the verb component of each sentence is "semantically" compared with the verb component of the anaphoric sentence in order to determine the context sharing level. More precisely, WordNet synonyms, hypernyms, hyponyms, cause_to and coordinate terms are recorded for the main verb of each sentence. The ratio of shared words to the total number of words is calculated. The experiments we conducted using this method provided a convincing evidence of the veracity of the assumption that the more shared terms the corresponding sentences possess, the higher is the likelihood of the shared context between them.

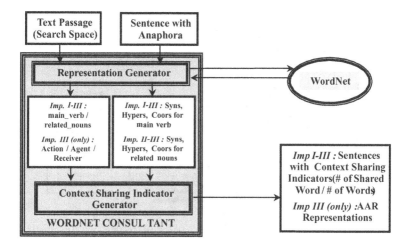

Fig. 5. WordNet Consultant Particulars.

In Implementation II, lists of WordNet synonyms, hypernyms, hyponyms and coordinate terms are recorded not only for sentences' main verbs, but also for all related nouns. In our previous example, in addition to terms for the main verb "hurl", synonyms, hypernyms, hyponyms and coordinate terms of related nouns ("midst", "crowd", "fan", "bouquet" and "stage") get included, as well. Here, we trade off the added run time for increases of the pool of available semantic knowledge.

On top of all the previous analysis, the Action/Agent/Receiver (AAR) Implementation III utilizes a simple shallow parsing in order to preserve a basic syntactic information and identify the agent (subject) causing the main verb action (predicate) together with its receiver (direct object). Other nouns in the representation are treated as indirect objects. Subsequently, the chooser module of the antecedent selection phase examines two kinds of paths in the WordNet usage. It first starts from a referent's sentence and follows all possible *synonym / hypernym / hyponym / cause_to / coordinate term* paths from its main verb. If any of them ends at the main verb of the anaphoric sentence or any of its synonyms, hypernyms, or hyponyms, it is taken to testify that the acting agent of the referent sentence *caused* something *to* the acting agent of the anaphoric sentence and the anaphora should resolve into the action receiver of the referent sentence (reverse syntactic/semantic parallelism case). Similarly, if a *synonym / hypernym / hyponym* path without a *cause_to* term leads to the main verb of the anaphora sentence or any of its synonyms, hypernyms, or hyponyms, it is interpreted to suggest a kind of direct syntactic/semantic parallelism and the anaphora is resolved into the action agent of the referent sentence. If none of the attempted paths leads to the main verb of the anaphora sentence, the implementation simply proceeds with further preference factors processing as before.

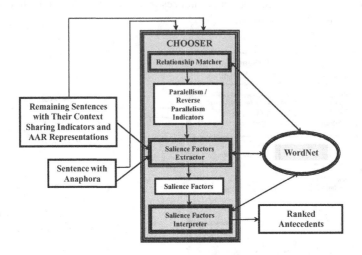

Fig. 6. Implementation III : Chooser Module of the Antecedent Selection Phase.

Following is an illustration of identifying reversed parallelism when attempting to determine the right antecedent for *"It"* of the anaphoric sentence *"**It** suffered only minor damage."* following the referent sentence *"The boat fired at **the ship**."*. The referent sentence gets processed first and produces the representation *fire(boat, ship,_)* where the action of *firing* taken by the agent *boat* affected the receiver *ship*. Rephrasing this to better fit our discovery process, the action of *firing* by the agent *boat caused to* the receiver *ship* to be *fired* at. Similarly, we have *suffer(it, damage, _)* for the anaphoric sentence. Next, WordNet provides us with *"shoot"* as one of the synonyms of the main verb *"fire"*, *"hurt"* as a hypernym for *"shoot"*, and finally *"suffer"* as a *cause to* term for *"hurt"*. Because *the boat* (the acting agent of *firing* (*shooting* and *hurting*)) was a *cause to* the receiver, *the ship* to be *fired* at, it was also a *cause to it* (the acting agent of the sentence *"It suffered only minor damage."*) to take its action (*suffer*). Finally, based on this reversed parallelism, *it* correctly resolves into *the ship*.

4   Evaluation Procedure, Results and Comparisons

The sentence collections used for testing were random domain-wise, and multi-sentential in order to test and challenge the abilities of our algorithm, AARLISS. We particularly scrutinized the system's novel sentence selector component. Its inclusion in AARLISS improved overall system's precision by 10.58%, from 63.1% to 73.68%. At the same time, the recall level fell only by 1.5%. The overall execution time increased by 12.95% while its antecedent selection phase got 5% faster because of its now reduced and more focused search space. This appears as a more than tolerable increase considering the precision benefits and negligent recall decrease. All of the sample text passages had between 2 and 6 sentences with a reasonably even distribution of the sentence lengths (25% for 2 sentence long passages, 25% for 3, 25% for 4, 15% for 5, and 10% for 6 sentence long passages).

Being open-domain, fully automated and functioning without any hand intervention either on text or the system itself, the precision of AARLISS (73.68%) compares very favorably with other known resolution algorithms ([1], [2], [4], [5], [6], [7], [9], [10], [11], [12], [13], [15], [20], [21]) whose precision reportedly falls between 60 and 70%. In addition, most of the reported algorithms deal mainly with intra sentential examples and frequently, performance reports on long distance inter sentential samples are absent.

Regarding the distribution of different term classes and their impact on accuracy of the AARLISS, synonyms were found for 36.8% of main verbs in tested sentences, hypernyms for 45%, hyponyms for 46%, cause_to for 38.2% and coordinate terms for 65%. Synonyms contributed in 85.7% of correctly resolved examples, hypernyms in 77.8%, hyponyms in 75.2%, cause_to terms in 70.1% and coordinate terms in 76%.

The fact that AARLISS appears to operate rather indifferently to the size of the text passage (+-2% change in success rate) fully corroborates the initial intuition that the method is naturally tailored for long distance, inter sentential scenarios.

The Action/Agent/Receiver implementation of AARLISS demonstrated further overall performance improvements of +3.9% in the antecedent selection phase.

5   Conclusions and Future Work

More testing, evaluation and experimentation with diverse text corpora and other Word-Net term classes is in progress and thus far corroborating our present results. Though AARLISS was developed for use in a QA system's answer pinpoint phase where the text size has already been reduced to a small and manageable quantity, its scalability and applicability in larger contexts will be further explored. In addition, the Action/Agent/Receiver implementation will be incorporated into the sentence selector module (presently, it is only in the antecedent selector module). Finally, we are looking into other available knowledge bases like ResearchCYC and experimenting with possibilities of their incorporation.

References

1. Bunescu, R. Associative Anaphora Resolution : A Web-Based Approach. In Procedings of the Workshop on the Computational Treatment of Anaphora. EACL 2003, 2003.
2. Dagan, I., Itai A. Automatic Processing of Large Corpora for the Resolution of Anaphora References. In Proceedings of COLING'90, 1990.
3. Grosz, B.J., Joshi, A.K., Weinstein, S. Centering: A Framework for Modeling the Local Coherence of Discourse. In Computational Linguistics, 21(2):203-225, 1995.
4. Hajicova, E., Kubon, V., Kubon, P. Stock of Shared Knowledge : A Tool for SolvinPronominal Anaphora. In Proceedings of the 15th International Conference on Computational Linguistics, 1:127-133, 1992.

5. Harabagiu, S., Moldovan, D. Enriching the WordNet Taxonomy with Contextual Knowledge Acquired from Text, In Natural Language Processing and Knowledge Representation: Language for Knowledge and Knowledge for Language, (Eds) S. Shapiro and L. Iwanska, AAAI/MIT Press, 1998.
6. Hobbs, J. Resolving Pronominal References. In Lingua 44:311-338, 1978.
7. Kennedy, C., Boguraev, B. Anaphora for Everyone : Pronominal Anaphora Resolution without a Parser. In Proceedings of the 13th Annual International Conference on Computational Linguistics (COLING'96), 1996.
8. Lapin, S., Leass, H.J. An Algorithm for Pronominal Anaphora Resolution. In Computational Linguistics, 20(4):535-561, 1994.
9. Miller, G. WordNet : A Lexical Database for English. In Communications of the ACM, 38(1):49-51, 1995.
10. Mitkov, R. Robust Pronoun Resolution with Limited Knowledge. In Proceedings of the 17th International Conference on Computational Linguistics (COLING'98) and 36th Annual Meeting of the Association for Computational Linguistics (ACL 1998), 869-875, 1998.
11. Morton, T.S. Using Correference in Question Answering. In Proceedings of the 8th Text Retrieval Conference (TREC-8), 1999.
12. Mitkov, R., Evans, R., Orasan, C. A New, Fully Automatic Version of Mitkov's Knowledge-Poor Pronoun Resolution Method. In Proceedings of the 3d International Conference on Intelligent Text Processing and Computational Linguistics (CICLing-2002), 2002.
13. Navarretta, C. Combining Information Structure and Centering-Based Models of Salience for Resolving Intersentential Pronominal Anaphora, In A. Branco, T. McEnery and R. Mitkov (eds.): DAARC 2002 - 4th Discourse Anaphora and Anaphora Resolution Colloquium, Edicoes Colibri, 135-140, 2002.
14. Poessio, M. Associative Descriptions and Salience : A Preliminary Investigation. In Proceedings of the Workshop on the Computational Treatment of Anaphora. 10th Confer-ence of the European Chapter of the ACL (EACL 2003), 2003.
15. Reed SL, Lenat D. Mapping Ontologies into Cyc. Proc of AAAI 2002.
16. Siddharthan, A. Resolving Pronouns Robustly : Plumbing the Depths of Shallowness. In Proceedings of the Workshop on the Computational Treatment of Anaphora. 10th Conference of the European Chapter of the ACL (EACL 2003), 2003.
17. idner, C.S. Towards a Computational Theory of Definite Anaphora Comprehension in English Discourse. Technical Report 537, MIT Artificial Intelligence Laboratory, 1976.
18. Soon, W.M., Ng, H.T., Lim, C.Y. A Machine Learning Approach to Coreference Resolution of Noun Phrases. In Computational Linguistics, 27(4):521-544, 2001.
19. Strube, M., Wolters, M. A Probabilistic Genre-Independent Model of Pronominalization. In Proceedings of the 1st Conference of the North American Chapter of the ACL, 18-25, 2000.
20. Vicedo, J.L., Ferrandez, A. Anaphora Resolution in Question Answering Systems. In Proceedings of the 38th Annual Meeting of the ACL (ACL2000), 2000.
21. Viera, R., Poessio, M. An Empirically-Based System for Processing Definite Descriptions. In Computational Linguistics,26(4):539-593, 2000.
22. Webber, B.L. A Formal Approach to Discourse Anaphora. Garland Publishing, London, 1999.

Detection and Correction of Malapropisms in Spanish by Means of Internet Search*

Igor A. Bolshakov[1], Sofia N. Galicia-Haro[2], and Alexander Gelbukh[1]

[1] Center for Computing Research (CIC), National Polytechnic Institute (IPN), Mexico
igor@cic.ipn.mx, gelbukh@gelbukh.com
www.Gelbukh.com
[2] Faculty of Sciences, National Autonomous University of Mexico (UNAM), Mexico
sngh@fciencias.unam.mx

Abstract. Malapropisms are real-word errors that lead to syntactically correct but semantically implausible text. We report an experiment on detection and correction of Spanish malapropisms. Malapropos words semantically destroy collocations (syntactically connected word pairs) they are in. Thus we detect possible malapropisms as words that do not form semantically plausible collocations with neighboring words. As correction candidates, we select words similar to the suspected one but forming plausible collocations with neighboring words. To judge semantic plausibility of a collocation, we use Google statistics of occurrences of the word combination and of the two words taken apart. Since collocation components can be separated by other words in a sentence, Google statistics is gathered for the most probable distance between them. The statistics is recalculated to a specially defined Semantic Compatibility Index (SCI). Heuristic rules are proposed to signal malapropisms when SCI values are lower than a predetermined threshold and to retain a few highly SCI-ranked correction candidates. Our experiments gave promising results.

1 Introduction

Malapropism is a type of semantic error that replaces one content word by another existing word similar in sound or letters but semantically incompatible with the context and thus destroying text cohesion, e.g., Spanish *mañana sopeada* 'overridden morning' for the intended *mañana soleada* 'sunny morning.' Two interconnected tasks arise: (1) detecting erroneous words and (2) suggesting candidates for their correction.

Hirst & St-Onge [5] proposed detecting suspected malapropisms as words not related to any word in the context and selecting correction candidates as words similar to the suspected ones but related to the words in the context; if such a possible correction is found then the suspected word is signaled to the user along with the proposed correction. As a particular measure of relatedness between words, they used the distance in WordNet graph. In particular, this distance is determined through paradigmatic relations (synonyms, hyponyms, hyperonyms), mainly between nouns. The syntactic links between words are ignored. The matched words are usually in different sentences or even paragraphs.

---

* Work done under partial support of Mexican Government (CONACyT, SNI, CGEPI-IPN).

V. Matoušek et al. (Eds.): TSD 2005, LNAI 3658, pp. 115–122, 2005.

Bolshakov & Gelbukh [1] observed that malapropos words destroy collocations the original word was in, where by a collocation we mean a combination of two syntactically linked (maybe through an auxiliary word such as a preposition) and semantically compatible content words. The resulting word combinations usually retain their syntactic type but lose their sense, as in the example above. Thus, the general idea in [1] is similar to [5], but the anomaly detection is based on syntactico-semantic links between content words. A much smaller context–only one sentence–is needed for error detection, and words of all four open POSs–nouns, verbs, adjective, and adverbs–are considered as collocation components (collocatives). To test whether a content word pair is a collocation, three types of linguistic resources were considered: a precompiled collocation dictionary, a large corpus, or a Web search engine. However the experiment described in [1] was limited.

This paper extends [1] by intensive experimentation with Google as a resource for testing Spanish collocations (for English, the results would be even much more statistically significant). The Web is widely considered now as a huge (but noisy) linguistic resource [3], [4]. To use it for malapropism detection and correction, we had to revise the earlier algorithm and to develop new threshold-based procedures. Especially important was to investigate collocations of various syntactical types with collocatives either sequentially adjacent (forming bigrams, which are sufficiently explored [3]) or distant from each other (such collocations are insufficiently explored [8]; they are considered in dependency grammar approaches [7]).

The rest of the paper is organized as follows. In Section 2 we give a classification of syntactical types for collocations frequent in Spanish and demonstrate that some collocations can have rather distant collocatives. In Section 3, we explore frequencies of collocative co-occurrences in relation with the distance between them and discuss what part of the co-occurrences are real collocations. In Section 4, we present a method of malapropism detection and correction using a Semantic Compatibility Index (SCI) as a numeric measure for semantic compatibility of collocatives. In Section 5, we give details on our test collection. In Section 6 we describe our experiments. We dispose the collocatives of 125 rather common Spanish collocations at the most probable distances, convert them to malapropisms, and then gather word combinations for potential correction by replacing one component of the suspected malapropos collocation by its paronyms (e.g., similar words [2]).We use Google statistics to obtain SCI values. Finally, in Section 7 we give conclusions and discuss future work.

2   Collocations in Their Adjacent and Disjoint Forms

We consider syntactico-semantic links between collocatives as in dependency grammars [7]. Each sentence can be syntactically represented as a dependency tree with directed links 'head → its dependent' between tree nodes labeled by words of the sentence. Going along these links in the direction of the arrows from one content node through any functional nodes down to another content node, we obtain a labeled substructure corresponding to a word combination. If this is a meaningful text, we call such word combination a *collocation*. Such a definition of collocations ignores their frequencies and idiomaticity.

Table 1. Frequent types and structures of Spanish collocations

Type	Code	Depend. subtree	Example	%
Modified → Modifier	1.1	Adj ← N	*vago presentimiento*	2
	1.2	N → Adj	*mañana soleada*	20
	1.3	Adv ← Adj	*moralmente inferior*	1
	1.4	Adj → Adv	*libre forzosamente*	1
	1.5	V → Adv	*salir botando*	3
	1.6	V → Pr → N	*junta con (las) manos*	5
	1.7	N → Pr → N	*hijos de familia*	6
	1.8	Adv → Adv	*mirando fijamente*	2
	1.9	Adv → Pr → Adj	*negando en rotundo*	3
Noun → Noun Complement	2.1	N → Pr → N	*mechón de canas*	6
	2.2	N → Pr → V	*goma de mascar*	1
Noun → Noun Attribute	3.1	N → N	*rey mago*	1
Verb → Noun Complement	4.1	V → N	*afilar navajas*	17
	4.2	V → Pr → N	*tener en mente*	9
Verb → Verbal Complement	5.1	V → Pr → V	*trata de cambiar*	1
	5.2	V → V	*piensa escribir*	1
Verb → Adjective Complement	6.1	V → Adj	*era liso*	3
	6.2	V → Pr → Adj	*duda de todo*	1
Verb Predicate → Subject	7.1	N ← V	*colección crece*	1
	7.2	V → N	*existe gente*	1
Adjective → Noun Complement	8.1	Adj → Pr → N	*lleno de tierra*	3
Adverb → Noun Complement	9.1	Adv → N	*pateando puertas*	1
	9.2	Adv → Pr → N	*junto con (su) familia*	1
Coordinated Pair	10.1	N → Cc → N	*ida y vuelta*	4
	10.2	Adj → Cc → Adj	*sano y salvo*	2
	10.3	V → Cc → V	*va y viene*	2
	10.4	Adv → Cc → Adv	*rápidamente y bien*	1
			Total:	100

The most frequent types of Spanish collocations (as dependency sub-trees [7]) are given in Table 1. The types and subtypes are determined by POS of collocatives and their order in texts; V stands for verb, N for noun, Adj for adjective or participle, Adv for adverb, Pr for preposition. Usually dependency links reflect subordination between words (1.1 to 9.2). However, there exist coordinate dependency with collocatives of the same POS linked through the coordinating conjunction Cc (10.1 to 10.4).

Though adjacent in the dependency tree, collocatives can be distant in linear word order. The possible distances depend on the collocation type and specific collocatives. E.g., 3.1-collocatives are usually adjacent, whereas the 4.1-collocation *dejar cargo* 'to leave position' can contain intermediate context of 0 to 3 or even more words:

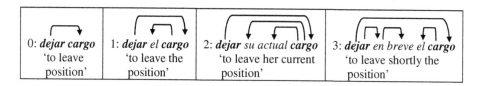

0: *dejar cargo* 'to leave position'	1: *dejar el cargo* 'to leave the position'	2: *dejar su actual cargo* 'to leave her current position'	3: *dejar en breve el cargo* 'to leave shortly the position'

3   The Most Probable Distance Between Collocatives

A specific (malapropos or not) collocation encountered in a text has a specific distance between collocatives. However, to explore collocations in a general manner, we have to consider each collocative pair in its most probable distance. Before determining the most probable distances between specific collocatives by means of the Web, it is necessary to clarify correspondences between the Web frequencies of collocative co-occurrences and occurrences of real collocations potentially formed by them. Google statistics of co-occurrences of any two strings with any N intermediate words can be gathered by queries in quotation marks containing these strings separated with N asterisks, e.g., "dejar * * cargo" for $N = 2$. So we intended to compare frequencies of the two kinds of events in the following way.

We took at random ten different commonly used collocations in their arbitrary textual form (maybe inflected) with unknown length of intermediate context. Co-occurrence frequencies for each collocative pair were evaluated with 0 to 5 intermediate asterisks. We cannot determine automatically whether counted co-occurrences are real collocations or merely random coincidences of words, possibly from different sentences. To evaluate the true portion (TP) of collocations in the automatically counted amounts, we looked through the first hundred snippets with co-occurrences for various lengths of intermediate context and manually analyzing their syntax. Multiplying the Google statistics (GS) by TP values, we obtained approximate collocation statistics (CS), see Table 2.

Table 2. Statistics of co-occurrences and collocations

Collocation	Statistics	Number of intermediate words					
		0	1	2	3	4	5
dejar ... cargo 'leave ... position'	GS	301	17600	735	973	846	737
	TP	0.93	0.99	0.63	0.54	0.11	0.09
	CS	280	17424	463	525	93	66
tentar ... suerte 'have ... luck'	GS	516	1230	2160	239	70	33
	TP	1.00	1.00	0.98	0.85	0.83	0.49
	CS	516	1230	2117	203	58	16
tener ... mente 'have ... mind'	GS	22400	1220	93	97	68	120
	TP	1.00	0.99	0.06	0.05	0.10	0.07
	CS	22400	1208	6	5	61	8
cortarse ... venas 'cut ... sales'	GS	3	5500	47	7	321	9
	TP	1.00	1.00	0.79	0.86	1.00	1.00
	CS	3	5500	37	6	321	9
fijar ... fecha 'define ... date'	GS	4720	13400	1320	693	1350	2320
	TP	0.89	0.77	0.38	0.28	0.23	0.24
	CS	4201	10318	502	194	311	557

One can see that within 0 to 5 intermediate words, GS has one or more local maxima, whereas the first local maximum of CS is at 0 to 2 and in all cases is unique, coinciding with the first local maximum of GS. So we can believe Google statistics in that the most probable distance between collocatives of real collocations corresponds to the first local maximum of GS. The majority of collocative co-occurrences counted by the Web at the distances 0 to 3 are real collocations, whereas at greater distances they are mostly coincidences of words without direct syntactic relation. This does not mean that collocations cannot be more distant, but the Web is not suited for collocation testing at greater distances, in contrast with collocation databases.

4   Algorithm for Malapropism Detection and Correction

The main idea of our algorithm is to look through all pairs of content words W_i within a sentence, testing each pair on syntactic and semantic compatibility. If the pair is syntactically combinable but semantically incompatible, a malapropism is suspected. Then all primary candidates for correction are tested on semantic compatibility with the context. The list of secondary candidates is ranked and only the best ones are kept:

---

for all content words W_i and W_j in sentence such that $j < i$ **repeat**
  if SyntCombinable(W_j, W_i) **& not** SemCompatible(W_j, W_i) **then**
    ListOfPairs = $\varnothing$
    for each paronymy dictionary
      for all paronyms P of the left collocative W_j **repeat**
        if SemAdmissible(P, W_i) **then** InsertToListOfPairs(P, W_i)
      for all paronyms P of the right collocative W_i **repeat**
        if SemAdmissible(W_j, P) **then** InsertToListOfPairs(W_j, P)
Filter(ListOfPairs), LetUserTest(ListOfPairs)

Here, Boolean function **SyntCombinable**(V, W) determines if the word pair (V, W) forms a syntactically correct word combination. It implements a partial dependency parser searching for a conceivable dependency chain with V and W at the extremes that includes their intermediate context, see Table 1.

Boolean functions **SemCompatible**(V, W) and **SemAdmissible**(V, W) both check if the pair (V, W) is semantically compatible. The procedure **Filter**$(ListOfPairs)$ selects the best candidates. These three procedures heavily depend on the available resources for collocation testing.

When the resource is a text corpus, **SemCompatible**(V, W) determines the number $N(V, W)$ of co-occurrences of V and W within a limited distance one from another in the whole corpus. If $N(V, W) = 0$, it returns False. Otherwise, for a definite decision it is necessary to syntactically analyze each co-occurrence, which is considered impractical in a large corpus. In the case of ambiguity of whether the co-occurrences are real collocations or mere coincidences in a text span, only statistical criteria are applicable. According to one criterion, the pair is compatible if the relative frequency $N(V, W)/S$ (empirical probability) of the co-occurrence is greater than the product of relative frequencies $N(V)/S$ and $N(W)/S$ of V and W taken apart (S is the corpus size). Using logarithms, we have the following rule for compatibility of a pair:

$$\mathrm{MII}(V, W) \equiv \ln(N(V, W)) + \ln(S) - \ln(N(V) \times N(W)) > 0,$$

where $\mathrm{MII}(V, W)$ is the mutual information index [6].

In the Web searchers, only a statistical approach is possible. Search engines automatically deliver statistics about the queried words and word combinations measured in numbers of pages. We can re-conceptualize MII with all Ns as numbers of relevant pages and S as the page total managed by the searcher. However, now N/S are not the empirical probabilities (but presumably values monotonically connected with them).

To heuristically estimate the collocative pair compatibility, we propose a Semantic Compatibility Index (SCI) value similar to MII:

$$\mathrm{SCI}(N, M) \equiv \begin{cases} \ln N(V, W) - \frac{1}{2}(\ln N(V) + \ln N(W)) + \ln P & \text{if } N(V, W) > 0, \\ NEG & \text{if } N(V, W) = 0 \end{cases}$$

where NEG is a negative constant symbolizing $-\infty$; P is a positive constant to be chosen experimentally. An advantage of SCI as compared to MII is that the total number of pages is not needed to be known. Because of the factor 1, SCI does not depend on monotonic or oscillating variations of the statistics of the search engine, just as MII.

SemCompatible returns $False$ and thus signals the pair (V_m, W_m) as a malapropism if $\mathrm{SCI}(V_m, W_m) < 0$, whereas **SemAdmissible** returns $True$ and admits the primary candidate (V, W) as a secondary one if the SCI values for the candidate and the malapropism conform to the following threshold rule:

$$\mathrm{SCI}(V, W) > \mathrm{SCI}(V_m, W_m) > NEG \text{ or } \mathrm{SCI}(V_m, W_m) = NEG \text{ and } \mathrm{SCI}(V, W) > Q,$$

where Q, $NEG < Q < 0$, is a constant to be chosen experimentally.

Filter procedure operates on a whole group of secondary candidates, ranking them by SCI values. The chosen candidates are all n those with positive SCI; if $n = 1$ then one more with a negative SCI value is admitted, or two more if $n = 0$.

5   An Experimental Set of Malapropisms

When a malapropism is detected in text, it is not initially known which collocative is erroneous. We try to correct both, but only one combination corresponds to the intended collocation; we call it *true correction*. Sometimes an error transforms one collocation to another semantically plausible collocation, which happens rarer and contradicts the extra-collocational context, e.g., *nueva ola* 'new wave' changed to *nueva ala* 'new wing.' We call such errors quasi-malapropisms. Their detection (if possible) usually permits to restore the intended word.

We have collected our experimental set in the following way. We took at random 125 valid collocations, most of them commonly used. Collocatives in each collocation were then separated to their most probable distance in the way described in Section 3. The number of intermediate asterisks in the search pattern was determined for the whole group. Then one collocative in each pair was changed to another real word of the same POS through an elementary editing operation, thus forming a malapropism. To simulate the detection and correction phase, other editing operations were then applied to the both components of the resulting test malapropism, each change giving a correction candidate. Each resulting word combination was included in the set.

Collocation statistics		Word statistics		Collocation statistics		Word statistics	
mañana sopeada (1.2)	0	*mañana*	3180000	*rey vago* (3.1)	10	*rey*	6330000
		sopeada	99			*vago*	652000
macana sopeada	0	*macana*	173000	*bey vago*	0	*bey*	1670000
mañana soleada	3710	*soleada*	48100	*ley vago*	1	*ley*	11800000
mañana topeada	0	*topeada*	117	*reg vago*	0	*reg*	17600000
mañana copeada	0	*copeada*	15	*reo vago*	7	*reo*	1360000
mañana hopeada	0	*hopeada*	4	*rey lago*	198	*lago*	4280000
mañana jopeada	0	*jopeada*	26	**rey mago**	8320	*mago*	705000
				rey pago	88	*pago*	5160000
ora liso (6.1)	7	*ora*	13100000	*rey vaho*	0	*vaho*	28800
		liso	382000	*rey vaso*	4	*vaso*	882000
ara liso	0	*ara*	4160000	*rey vado*	2	*vado*	659000
era liso	922	*era*	37700000				
osa liso	0	*osa*	3810000				
ova liso	0	*ova*	1880000				
ora luso	1	*luso*	579000				
ora laso	1	*laso*	144000				
ora leso	2	*leso*	247000				

Fig. 1. Several malapropisms and their primary candidates with Google statistics

The set (Fig. 2) thus consists of groups with headlines containing malapropisms with their collocation subtype codes (cf. Table 1). The changed word is underlined. The true correction is marked in bold. In total, the set includes 977 correction candidates, i.e. 7.82 primary candidates per error. The number of quasi-malapropisms is 8.

6 An Experiment with Google and Its Results

The initial groups of the experimental set supplied with statistics are given in Fig. 2. As many as 71 (56.8%) malapropisms and 662 (67.7%) primary candidates were not met in Google. However we keep hope that further elaboration of the statistics and threshold procedures could give much better results.

To obtain all negative SCI values for all true malapropisms, we took $P = 3500$. The value $NEG \approx -9$ is taken lower than SCI values for all events met. The value $Q = -7.5$ is adjusted so that all candidates with non-zero occurrences have SCI values greater then this threshold. The distribution of SCI values rounded to the nearest integers for malapropisms and their true corrections is shown in Fig. 3. The peak for malapropisms is reached at -4, while for their true corrections it is between 2 and 3.

Malapropism	Type	SCI	Strength	Candidates	SCI
mañana sopeada	1.2	−9.00	true	*mañana soleada*	1.98
ora liso	6.1	−4.27	true	*era liso*	−0.32
rey vago	3.1	−4.06	true	*rey mago*	2.62
				rey lago	−2.02
pelado venial	1.2	−9.00	true	*pecado venial*	2.67
				pelado genial	−3.06
hombre mosco	1.2	−5.31	true	*hombre hosco*	0.71
				hombre tosco	−0.19
comida sola	1.2	−3.18	quasi	*comida sosa*	−1.34

Fig. 2. Several malapropisms and best candidates with their SCI values

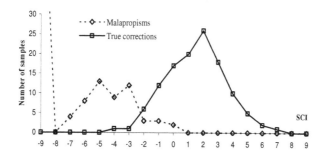

Fig. 3. Distribution of SCI for malapropisms and their true corrections

Though none of the eight quasi-malapropisms was taken into account while selecting the constant P, our algorithm detected all of them: their SCI values are too low to be admitted as collocations by our algorithm. That is, the algorithm detected all unintended real word errors (in our experimental set).

SemAdmissible function leaves 207 secondary candidates of 977 primary ones (decrease by 4.72), while **Filter** procedure reduces them to 175 best candidates (total decrease is 5.58). Thus the lists of the best candidates contain on an average 1.4 entries, cf. several groups with SCI values and decision qualifications in Fig. 4. Among the best candidates always were true corrections, and only four of them were not first-ranked. The most commonly used collocations among primary candidates always enter into the selected list, as true corrections or not.

Hence the results of our experiment are very promising. SCI proved to be an excellent measure for detecting malapropisms and selecting the best correction candidates.

7   Conclusions

A method for detection and correction of malapropisms is proposed. It is based on Google occurrence statistics recalculated as a novel numeric Semantic Compatibility Index for syntactically linked words (collocatives). The experiment was conducted on a test set of 117 malapropisms and 8 so-called quasi-malapropisms (collocations existing in language but used erroneously in a given context). All 125 errors were detected and for all of them their intended correction candidates entered highly ranked into the lists of best correction candidates selected by the algorithm.

References

1. Bolshakov, I.A., Gelbukh, A.: On Detection of Malapropisms by Multistage Collocation Testing. In: NLDB´2003, GI-Edition, LNI, V. P-29, Bonn, 2003, p. 28-41.
2. Bolshakov, I.A., Gelbukh, A.: Paronyms for Accelerated Correction of Semantic Errors. International Journal on Information Theories and Applications, Vol.10, 2003, pp. 11-19.
3. Keller, F., Lapata, M.: Using the Web to Obtain Frequencies for Unseen Bigram. Computational linguistics, V. 29, No. 3, 2003, p. 459-484.
4. Kilgarriff, A., Grefenstette, G.: Introduction to the Special Issue on the Web as Corpus. Computational linguistics, V. 29, No. 3, 2003, p. 333-347.
5. Hirst, G., St-Onge, D.: Lexical Chains as Representation of Context for Detection and Corrections of Malapropisms. In: C. Fellbaum (ed.) WordNet: An Electronic Lexical Database. MIT Press, 1998, p. 305-332.
6. Manning, Ch., Schütze, H.: Foundations of Statistical Natural Language Processing. MIT Press, 1999.
7. Mel'čuk, I.: Dependency Syntax: Theory and Practice. SONY Press, NY, 1988.
8. Wermter, J., Hahn, U.: Collocation Extraction Based on Modifiability Statistics. Proc. COLING'2004, Geneva, Switzerland, August 2004, p. 980-986.

The Szeged Treebank

Dóra Csendes[1], János Csirik[1], Tibor Gyimóthy[1], and András Kocsor[2]

[1] Department of Informatics, University of Szeged
H-6720 Szeged, Árpád tér 2., Hungary
{dcsendes,csirik,gyimi}@inf.u-szeged.hu
[2] MTA-SZTE Research Group on Artificial Intelligence
H-6720 Szeged, Aradi vértanúk tere 1., Hungary
{kocsor}@inf.u-szeged.hu

Abstract. The major aim of the Szeged Treebank project was to create a high-quality database of syntactic structures for Hungarian that can serve as a golden standard to further research in linguistics and computational language processing. The treebank currently contains full syntactic parsing of about 82,000 sentences, which is the result of accurate manual annotation. Current paper describes the linguistic theory as well as the actual method used in the annotation process. In addition, the application of the treebank for the training of automated syntactic parsers is also presented.

1 Introduction

The availability of accurately annotated data is becoming an increasingly important factor in the developments of Computational Linguistics. To support that, linguists and developers of natural language processing systems design different annotation schemes and tools which allow for adding as much linguistic information to texts as possible. Inspired by the research results of the Penn Treebank and several other treebank projects, our research group set out to create a golden standard treebank for Hungarian, containing reliable syntactic annotation of texts. Project work contained the selection and adjustment of the theory used for syntactic analysis, the design of the annotation methodology, the adaptation of the available tag-sets to Hungarian, automated pre-processing, manual validation and correction, and experiments with machine learning methods for automated parsing. The current paper presents an overview of the Szeged Treebank initiative and its results to date.

The treebank currently contains detailed syntactic analysis of approx. 82,000 sentences (1.2 million words) based on a generative grammar approach. Annotated files are available in XML format using the TEI DTD P2[1] scheme. Ideally, the treebank should contain samples of all the syntactic structures of the language, therefore, it serves as a reference for future corpus and treebank developments, grammar extraction and other linguistic research. It also serves as a reliable test suite for different NLP applications, as well as a basis for the development of computational methods for both shallow and deep syntactic parsing, and information extraction. Well-defined methods or elaborate

---

[1] The TEI DTD description is available at the following website: http://www.tei-c.org

V. Matoušek et al. (Eds.): TSD 2005, LNAI 3658, pp. 123–131, 2005.

theoretical foundations for the automated syntactic analysis of Hungarian texts were lacking at the start of the project. For this reason, novelty of the project work lies in the design of a practical approach for syntactic annotation of natural language sentences.

The current paper is structured as follows. After commenting on related treebank initiatives for other languages, we continue to introduce the backgrounds of the project and the theory designed for the syntactic annotation of texts. In section 4, we describe the used tag-set and the annotation process in some detail, while in section 5 we discuss results achieved by machine learning algorithms for automated syntactic parsing of texts. We close the paper with some words about current and future works.

2 Related Works

Treebanks typically contain morphological, morpho-syntactic, syntactic and sometimes even semantic information about a language, therefore, they are a valuable source of further research in the fields of theoretical linguistic and computational language processing. Treebanks – especially if manually annotated – greatly help the development of effective syntactic parsers and other automated tools used for the analysis of natural language. Because of their efficient applicability in computational linguistics, numerous treebank projects have been initiated over the past ten years.

One of the most notable of all, the Penn Treebank project [12] produced skeletal parses on top of an initial POS tagging showing rough syntactic and semantic information on about 2.5 million words of American English. Syntactic parsing of the texts included the annotation of predicate-argument structures.

Another prominent treebank proposition is the Prague Dependency Treebank (PDT) [7] for Czech. The project's theoretical background is a dependency-based syntax handling the sentence structure as concentrated around the verb and its valency, but also containing the dimension of coordination. Texts are annotated on the morphological, syntactic and the tectogrammatical (linguistic meaning) levels, therefore, the nodes of the dependency tree are labelled by symbols containing information about all three of these levels. An attempt to incorporate information on discourse structure (topic-focus opposition) has also been initiated by researchers of the PDT project.

Several other projects for Slavic languages follow the PDT approach. The Slovene Dependency Treebank (in progress), for example, aims to add syntactic annotation to the available morphologically annotated TELRI corpus using analytic tree structures. In the Dependency Treebank for Russian [3], the syntactic data are also expressed in the dependency formalism, but the inventory of syntactic functional relations is considerably richer than in the PDT. With its unique approach of HPSG-based annotation, the BulTreeBank [14] is an exception. It contains detailed syntactic structure for 1 million words in a graph-form following the HPSG scheme which allows for a consistent description of linguistic facts on every linguistic level, incl. phonetic, morphological, syntactic, semantic and discourse.

The TIGER Treebank [5] is a more recent initiative for German language. Its first version contains 35,000 syntactically annotated sentences from the Frankfurter Rundschau newspaper, but the project intends to build the largest and most exhaustively annotated natural language resource for German. In its encoding, the TIGER Treebank uses a hybrid combination of dependency grammar and phrase structure grammar. The Turin University Treebank (TUT) [10] built for Italian combines the dependency approach with the predicate-argument structure paradigm of the PennTreebank project and is characterized by a rich grammatical relations system.

Some treebank annotation schemes aim at theory-independent interpretation, like the ones applied in the Spanish Treebank [16] or the French Treebank [1]. Treebank projects are also initiated for several other languages, such as Swedish [13], Japanese (the Hinoki Treebank) [4], Turkish [2], Arabic [11], just to mention a few.

3 Preliminaries and Theoretical Guidelines

3.1 Szeged Corpus as the Predecessor

The Szeged Treebank project was preceded by an extensive, four-year-long work aimed at the creation of a golden standard corpus for Hungarian language. The resulting Szeged Corpus is a manually annotated natural language database comprising 1.2 million word entries (with 145,000 different word forms) and an additional 225,000 punctuation marks [6]. With this, it is the largest manually processed Hungarian textual database that serves as a reference material for corpus linguistic research and applications for the language. It is a thematically representative database containing texts from six different genres, namely: fiction, newspaper articles, computation-related scientific texts, short essays of 14-16-year-old students, legal texts, and short business news.

Language processing of the Szeged Corpus includes morphological analysis, POS tagging and shallow syntactic parsing. Shallow parsing went as far as marking bottom-level NP structures, and clause annotation. Machine learning methods for POS tagging [9] and shallow parsing [8] have been trained on the corpus with considerable success. High accuracy results (over 97% per word accuracy) for POS tagging are especially notable, considering the fact that (i) the richness of Hungarian morphology poses a considerable challenge to automated methods, and that (ii) due to the applied encoding scheme, the ratio of ambiguous words are almost 50%.

3.2 Theoretical Background, Methodology and New Approaches

Since no syntactic annotation schemes were available for Hungarian, the major challenge of the Szeged Treebank project was to adapt the theoretical foundations of Hungarian syntax to a more practical syntactic annotation methodology. When designing the methodology, researchers aimed to:
– demonstrate the varieties of Hungarian syntactic patterns exhaustively;
– stay in correlation with the newest linguistic theories[2];
– create an annotation scheme that can be used extensively in later research activities and in computer assisted practical solutions.

---

[2] References: É. Kiss K., Kiefer F., Siptár J.: *Új magyar nyelvtan*, Osiris Kiadó, Bp., 1999.; Alberti G., Medve A.: *Generatív grammatikai gyakorlókönyv I-II.*, Janus/Books, Bp., 2002.; Kiefer F., ed.: *Strukturális magyar nyelvtan I. Mondattan*, Akadémiai Kiadó, Bp., 1992.

Research results showed that the most promising theoretical frame for the definition
of the annotation scheme would be generative syntax in combination with certain dependency formalism, (the latter being considered more suitable for languages with free
word order). Our approach resembles dependency-based syntax to the extent in which
it handles the sentence structure as concentrated around the verb and its argument structure, but it does not assign syntactic types to each sentence component relation. However, the proposed structure does contain information as to which components of the
sentence are syntactically linked, and describes each node of the tree with complex
labels. These labels contain morphological and syntactic description of the sentence
components in the form of attributes.

In building a syntactic tree, the initial step is the (re)creation of the deep sentence
structure. In a deep structure of a Hungarian sentence, it is always the verb that stands
in the first position and it is followed by its arguments. Since Hungarian has a relatively
free word order, arguments of the verb can move anywhere in the sentence occupying
so-called functional positions. Naturally, by moving certain arguments, the meaning of
the sentence is likely to change accordingly. Arguments that moved somewhere else,
leave traces in their original position, which are indexed to their newly occupied position (see Figure 1., i, j, k elements). When applying this theory to the Szeged Treebank's
XML format, we decided not to keep the traces in the treebank, instead, we added a new
NODE label within the verb phrase and described the given argument with attributes.
The resulting syntactic trees do not appear in the form of a tree, but as bracketed XML
structures, (however, the transformation into a tree is always possible). The first figure
(Fig. 1) shows the original tree with the argument traces, while the second one (Fig. 2)
illustrates our XML representation of the same sentence.

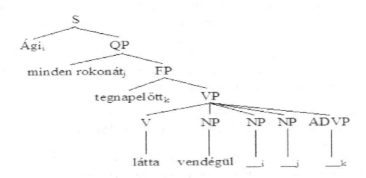

Fig. 1. A syntactic tree example.

The features of the defined treebank annotation formalism allows for the description
of particular linguistic structures and phenomena occurring in Hungarian. It organises
the represented information in different layers, keeping them separate to facilitate the
selection of data during a number of large-scale NLP applications incl. information
extraction, phrase identification in information retrieval, named entity recognition, machine translation, and a variety of text-mining operations.

```
<CP id="file.1.1">
  <NP id="file.1.2"> Ági </NP>
  <NP id="file.1.3">
    <ADJP> minden </ADJP>
    rokonát
  < /NP>
  <ADVP id="file.1.4"> tegnapelőtt </ADVP>
  <V_ id="file.1.5">
    <V0> látta </V0>
    <CHILDREN>
      <NODE idref="file.1.2" type="NP" role="NOM">   </NODE>
      <NODE idref="file.1.3" type="NP" role="ACC">   </NODE>
      <NODE idref="file.1.4" type="ADVP" role="TLOCY">   </NODE>
      <NODE idref="file.1.6" type="NP" role="ESS">   </NODE>
    < /CHILDREN>
  < /V_>
  <NP id="file.1.6"> vendégül </NP>
  <c> . </c>
< /CP>
```

Fig. 2. An XML representation.

4   Annotation of the Szeged Treebank

Similarly to the majority of annotation projects, the Szeged Treebank also follows the Penn Treebank approach, which distinguishes an automatic annotation step followed by manual validation and correction.

4.1   The Set of Syntactic Tags

The tag-set used in the project shows correlation with many other internationally accepted syntactic tag-sets. The list of tags is as follows:
- ADJP: adjectival phrases
- ADVP: adverbial phrases, adverbial adjectives, postpositional personal pronouns
- c: punctuation mark
- C0: conjunctions
- CP: clauses (also for marking sentences)
- INF_: infinitives (INF0, CHILDREN, NODE)
- NEG: negation
- NP: noun phrases (groups with noun or predicative adjective or inflected personal pronouns as head)
- PA_: adverbial participles (PA0, CHILDREN, NODE)
- PP: postpositional phrases
- PREVERB: preverbs
- V_: verb (V0, CHILDREN, NODE)
- XP: any circumstantial or parenthetic clause that is not a direct part of the sentence

Attributes of a node may contain information about the node's type (e.g., NP, ADVP, etc.), and its morpho-semantic role in the sentence (e.g., nominative, instrumental, inessive, terminative, locative, etc.) also to be seen in Figure 2.

4.2 Pre-processing of Texts

Pre-processing of the texts was conducted in two steps. Initially, the full structure of NPs was marked. Since Hungarian is a highly inflectional language, the grammatical role of a certain syntactic unit is typically defined by the inflection of its head. Due to the fact that it is mostly NPs that occur as heads of a syntactic unit, it can be said that the grammatical structure of Hungarian sentences are determined by inflected nominal structures, therefore, it was crucial to mark NPs in the first phase. Automatic pre-parsing of the sentences was completed with the help of the CLaRK[3] program, in which syntactic rules have been defined by Hungarian linguistic experts for the recognition of NPs. The basic mechanism of CLaRK for linguistic processing of text corpora is a cascaded regular grammar processor. The manually defined NP annotation rules heavily rely on the use of such regular expressions that, in turn, define increasingly complex NP structures. Initially, base NPs containing noun heads are identified. Following that, more complex NP structures are defined based on the coordination and/or merge of possessive NPs and NPs with heads other than nouns. Rules can be applied to the same piece of text recursively. A remarkable ∼70% accuracy was already achieved in the pre-parsing phase, due to the efficient definition of expert rules. For the pre-parsing of all other structures (ADJP, ADVP, etc.), we developed our own tool, which applies manually defined simple grammatical rules for the automated pre-annotation of sentences.

4.3 Manual Validation of Syntactic Trees

Manual validation and correction of the syntactic structures and their attributes was performed by a group of linguist especially trained for this task. They used a locally developed editor for the task and worked 24 person-months on the project.

Considering the annotation of the inner structure of NPs, certain difficulties have to be highlighted. Firstly, it should be noted that marking the boundaries (beginning and ending) of NPs is a problematic matter, the reason for which is the possible replacement of a noun head of the NP with its modifiers. Another problematic area is the left recursive insertion of progressive and perfect participles that often bring several adjuncts (sometimes long embedded clauses) into the NP. To avoid problems deriving from such peculiarities of Hungarian language, carefully defined rules were laid down for the manual correction of NPs. Due to the lack of space, we will not describe the manual validation of other syntactic constituents in detail, but it has to be noted that it proved to be much more straight-forward than that of the NPs. As a result of the annotation, we receive the detailed structure of the syntactic tree and the functional description of every node.

---

[3] The CLaRK system was developed by Kiril Simov at the Bulgarian Academy of Sciences in the framework of the BulTreeBank project (http://www.bultreebank.org).

Table 1. NP recognition results.

Categories of recognition	Precision	Recall	Fβ=1
Complete NP structures	81.28%	87.43%	84.24%
Boundaries (first and last elements) of NP structures	88.31%	92.08%	90.15%
NP structures (depth<=2)	86.02%	89.72%	87.83%
NP structures (depth>2)	74.71%	78.19%	76.41%

5 Training and Testing Machine Learning Algorithms for Full Syntactic Parsing

Textual data is often used for the training of different machine learning methods in order that they can solve problems occurring in the field of Computational Linguistics. While there are several methods that use text in its raw, unanalysed form (cv. unsupervised training), more accurate results can be obtained by using annotated corpora for the training.

Research groups studying the structure of Hungarian sentences have made a great effort to produce a consistent and extensive syntax rule system, yet these are not or just partially adapted to practical, computer related purposes so far. This implied that there is a strong need for a technology that would be able to divide a Hungarian sentence into syntactical segments, recognize their structure, and based on this recognition, would assign an annotated tree representation to each sentence. The main goal, therefore, was to develop a generally applicable syntactic parser for Hungarian based on the Szeged Treebank annotations. Different learning methods have been studied, such as rule-based, numeric and logic algorithms. Taking into consideration the specific features of Hungarian language, it was found that logic methods can be best applied to our puroses, therefore a parser was developed based on this founding.

For training and testing the parsers, we used a set of 9600 sentences (thematically selected from the business news domain) divided into 10 sections for ten-fold cross validation. The input of the parsers was morphologically analysed text and the output was bracketed syntactically analysed sentences. Parsing rules were retrieved from the annotated Szeged Corpus and were combined with manually defined ones.

5.1 NP Recognition

The table below shows average results of the ten-fold cross validation test performed by the developed parser for the recognition of NPs.

5.2 Full Syntactic Parsing

In the case of full syntactic parsing, we aimed at the recognition of shorter multi-level tree structures, incl. ADJPs, ADVPs, PAs, etc. The training resulted in ~1500 different tree patterns where the leaves contain detailed morphological and morpho-semantic information about the component. Test results for full parsing of short trees can be seen in the following table.

Table 2. Recognition results for full syntactic structures.

	Classification			Tree pattern recognition					
	Yes	No	Accuracy	Etalon	Predict	Correct	Precision	Recall	Fβ=1
A0	12688	2411	84,03%	5978	5648	4341	76,86%	72,62%	74,68%
A1	11788	2704	81,34%	6291	5595	4350	77,75%	69,15%	73,20%
A2	12476	2619	82,65%	6390	5733	4486	78,25%	70,20%	74,01%
A3	11835	2471	82,73%	6097	5419	4326	79,83%	70,95%	75,13%
A4	11031	1607	87,28%	5347	5286	4398	83,20%	82,25%	82,72%
A5	11740	1585	88,11%	5577	5553	4677	84,22%	83,86%	84,04%
A6	11404	1622	87,55%	5488	5440	4562	83,86%	83,13%	83,49%
A7	11624	1596	87,93%	5640	5489	4656	84,82%	82,55%	83,67%
A8	12052	2079	85,29%	5989	5739	4676	81,48%	78,08%	79,74%
A9	12499	2811	81,64%	6691	5755	4593	79,81%	68,64%	73,81%
Average			*84,85%*				*81,01%*	*76,14%*	*78,45%*

A0 to A9 are the ten sections of the treebank that were selected for the training of the parser. Columns 'Yes' and 'No' show whether the parser's guess about a certain structure was correct or not (i.e., whether it recognises a structure as a syntactic one, and if yes, what kind). 'Accuracy' measures were calculated from these results. The 'Etalon' column presents the number of manually marked syntactic structures, thus, the golden standard. The 'Predict' column shows the number of structures that were identified by the parser, while the 'Correct' column shows the number of correctly identified structures.

Results of Table 2. are only preliminary ones, and can be considered as base-line results in syntactic parsing of Hungarian sentences. It must be admitted that better results are already available for other languages (cf. results of the Link, NLTK, Stanford Parser, Apple Pie parsers), but due to the fact that this is a fresh initiative for Hungarian, and that the number of tree patterns is much higher than for other languages, results can be considered promising. Further improvements in this field are the nearest future plan of the group.

6   Current and Future Works

As a first step, we intend to improve the results of automated syntactic parsing both on the shallow and the detailed levels. With sufficiently reliable parsers, we will be able to create larger databases, and improve our information extraction (IE) system as well. Current results are already implemented in the IE system, and preliminary tests indicate that results are better than that achieved with shallow parsing, therefore, there is a good chance for further improvement. To support IE from another perspective, some of our current work aims at building general top-level and detailed domain specific ontologies for Hungarian. As a continuation of the Szeged Treebank project, we intend to enrich the texts with detailed semantic information in the future. Using the results of previous and future projects, we aim at developing a fully automated method for the extensive analysis and processing of Hungarian sentences on all levels.

References

1. Abeillé, A., Clément, L., Toussenel, F.: Building a Treebank for French in A. Abeillé (ed) Treebank:. Building and Using Parsed Corpora, Kluwer Academic Publishers, pp 165-187 (2003)
2. Atalay, N.B., Oflazer, K., Say, B.: The Annotation Process in the Turkish Treebank in Proceedings of the EACL'03 Workshop on Linguistically Interpreted Corpora (LINC), Budapest, Hungary (2003)
3. Boguslavsky, I., Grigorieva, S., Grigoriev, N., Kreidlin, L., and Frid, N.: Dependency treebank for Russian: concepts, tools, types of information in Proceedings of COLING-2000, Saarbrücken, Germany (2000)
4. Bond, F., Sanae F., Chikara H., Kaname K., Shigeko N., Nichols, E., Akira O., Takaaki T., Shigeaki A.: The Hinoki Treebank: A Treebank for Text Understanding in Proceedings of the IJCNLP 2004, Hainan Island, China and in LNCS vol. 3248 (2004)
5. Brants, S., Dipper, S., Hansen, S., Lezius, W. and Smith, G.: The TIGER Treebank in Proceedings of the Workshop on Treebanks and Linguistic Theories (TLT 2002), Sozopol, Bulgaria (2002)
6. Csendes, D., Csirik, J., Gyimóthy, T.: The Szeged Corpus: A POS tagged and Syntactically Annotated Hungarian Natural Language Corpus in Proceedings of TSD 2004, Brno, Czech Republic and LNAI vol. 3206 (2004)
7. Hajic, J.: Building a Syntactically Annotated Corpus: The Prague Dependency Treebank in Issues of Valency and Meaning, pp. 106-132, Charles University Press, Prague (1999)
8. Hócza, A., Iván, Sz.: Learning and recognizing noun phrases in Proceedings of the Hungarian Computational Linguistics Conference (MSZNY 2003), pp. 72-79, Szeged, Hungary (2003)
9. Kuba, A., Csirik, J., Hócza, A.: POS tagging of Hungarian with combined statistical and rule-based methods in Proceedings of TSD 2004, Brno, Czech Republic and LNAI vol. 3206 (2004)
10. Lesmo, L., Lombardo, V., Bosco, C.: Treebank Development: the TUT Approach in Proceedings of ICON 2002, Mumbay, India (2002)
11. Maamouri, M., Bies, A., Buckwalter, T., Mekki, W.: The Penn Arabic Treebank: Building a Large-Scale Annotated Arabic Corpus in Proceedings of the NEMLAR International Conference on Arabic Language Resources and Tools, Cairo, Egypt, (2004)
12. Marcus, M., Santorini, B., Marcinkiewicz, M.: Building a large annotated corpus of English: the Penn Treebank in Computational Linguistics, vol. 19 (1993)
13. Nivre, J.: What kinds of trees grow in Swedish soil? A comparison of four annotation schemes for Swedish in Proceedings of the Workshop on Treebanks and Linguistic Theories (TLT 2002), Sozopol, Bulgaria (2002)
14. Osenova, P., Simov, K.: BTB-TR05: BulTreeBank Stylebook, BulTreeBank Project Technical Report š 05 (2004)
15. Simov, K., Simov, A., Kouylekov, M., Ivanova, K., Grigorov, I., Ganev, H.: *Development of Corpora within the CLaRK System: The BulTreeBank Project Experience* in Proceedings of the Demo Sessions of EACL'03, pp. 243-246, Budapest, Hungary (2003)
16. Torruella, M.C., Antonín, M.: Design Principles for a Spanish Treebank in Proceedings of The Workshop on Treebanks and Linguistic Theories (TLT2002), Sozopol, Bulgaria (2002)

Automatic Lemmatizer Construction
with Focus on OOV Words Lemmatization*

Jakub Kanis and Luděk Müller

University of West Bohemia, Department of Cybernetics
Univerzitní 8, 306 14 Plzeň, Czech Republic
{jkanis,muller}@kky.zcu.cz

Abstract. This paper deals with the automatic construction of a lemmatizer from a Full Form - Lemma (FFL) training dictionary and with lemmatization of new, in the FFL dictionary unseen, i.e. out-of-vocabulary (OOV) words. Three methods of lemmatization of three kinds of OOV words (missing full forms, unknown words, and compound words) are introduced. These methods were tested on Czech test data. The best result (recall: 99.3 % and precision: 75.1 %) has been achieved by a combination of these methods. The lexicon-free lemmatizer based on the method of lemmatization of unknown words (lemmatization patterns method) is introduced too.

1 Introduction

A lemmatizer (which associates group of words with the same stem with one basic word form, base or lemma) or a stemmer (which associates group of words with their stem) is used in various kinds of natural language applications like information retrieval systems (IR systems) [1], TTS systems [2], word sense disambiguation, text classification [1], and translation (we intend to use a lemmatizer for translation from the Czech language to Sign Supported Czech and to the Czech Sign Language). However, a usage of a lemmatizer yields mixed results. For example, there are works dealing with IR systems where the usage of a lemmatizer leads to better performance of IR [4] on one hand and on the other hand there are works reporting no influence on the IR results [3]. In addition, Krovetz [3] has concluded that accurate stemming of English can improve performance of the IR system and Monz [4] has confirmed this conclusion. Thus, the accuracy or more exactly the recall (because generally it is possible to assign more than one lemma to one word) is an important issue of a lemmatizer. In this paper we introduce the automatic language independent construction of a high accurate lemmatizer. First, we describe the lemmatizer construction from a Full Form - Lemma (FFL) dictionary. We describe two methods for the lemmatization of full word forms which are not in the FFL dictionary but their lemma is present in the FFL dictionary. Then we introduce the method for lemmatization of unknown words, i.e. words whose neither full form nor lemma is in the FFL dictionary. In the next section we describe the experiments with the lemmatizer for several languages and show how the well made lemmatization of out-of-vocabulary (OOV) words can improve the lemmatization of a test data. The last section summarizes this paper.

---

* Support for this work was provided by GA AS Czech Republic, project No. 1ET101470416.

V. Matoušek et al. (Eds.): TSD 2005, LNAI 3658, pp. 132–139, 2005.

2 Construction of Lemmatizer

2.1 Lemmatizer

There are two main processes used for derivation of new words in a language: the inflectional and the derivative process. The words are derived from the same morphological class (for example the form CLEARED and CLEARS of the verb CLEAR) in the inflectional process while in the derivative process are derived from other morphological classes (CLEARLY). The creation of a new word can be reached by applying a set of derivation rules in the both processes. The rules provide adding or stripping prefixes (prefix rule) and suffixes (suffix rule) to derive a new word form. From this point of view, the lemmatization can be regarded as the inverse operation to the inflectional and derivative processes. Thus, we can obtain lemmatization rules via the inversion of the given derivation rules [2]. Alternatively, we can induce them simply from the FFL dictionary (see Section 2.2). The lemmatization rules induction is advantageous when derivation rules are given because the inducted rules and a lexicon of lemmas are error free contrary to the manually created ones which can contain some errors. The usual error is a mismatch between a derivation rule condition and the string that had to be stripped. We will compare the lemmatization rules generated trough the inversion of the handcrafted derivation rules and the lemmatisation rules induced from the FFL dictionary automatically in the experiment results section. The FFL dictionary was created by a morphological generator from the derivation rules. The generator produces the full word forms from the corresponding lemmas contained in the lexicon.

The set of derivation rules is a set of if-then rules (for example, a simple derivation rule is: if a word ends by E, then strip E and add ION, i.e. in the symbolic form: $E > -E, ION$). The set of rules should cover all morphology events of the given language. The completeness of the lexicon strongly influences the successfulness of the lemmatization because a proper basic form (lemma) can be found only if it is included in the lexicon [2]. Unfortunately, there are a lot of OOV words in real natural language processing applications which should be also lemmatized. In addition, if the FFL dictionary is used for the lemmatization rules induction, there still can be some full forms of a word in the test corpora which are not in the dictionary. Therefore, in the next sections we describe two different methods for lemmatization of full forms which are missing in the FFL dictionary, and present a method for lemmatization of additional OOV words.

2.2 Induction of Lemmatization Rules from FFL Training Dictionary

The FFL dictionary consists of pairs: [full word form, lemma]. The induction of lemmatization rules is based on searching for the longest common substring of the full form and the lemma. We are looking for lemmatization rules in the form if-then rules described in the previous section. The algorithm of searching the longest common substring is based on dynamic programming. The detailed description of the algorithm is given in [5].

The form of the derived lemmatization rules depends on a position of the longest common substring in the full form and the lemma. The longest common substring can be at the beginning, in the middle, or at the end of the full form and the lemma. For example, if we have a pair of strings BAC and ADE, where A, B, C, D, and E are their substrings (each substring is a sequence of characters, e.g. $A = a_1....a_n$), then we can derive two lemmatization rules, which transform the full form BAC into the lemma ADE. The first one is the prefix rule $B > -B$ and the second one is the suffix rule $C > -C, DE$. The substring B before and the substring C after the longest common substring A represents the condition of the prefix and the suffix rule, respectively.

We suppose that no more than two rules are applied to the lemma during the derivation process: the suffix and/or the prefix rule. To illustrate all possible forms of lemmatization rules, we show a table (Table 1) of pairs: [full word form, lemma] for all combinations of positions of the longest common substring A in the pair of strings and the lemmatization rules derived from them.

Table 1. All possible forms of lemmatization rules used in the inductive process

Full Form	Lemma	Prefix Rule	Suffix Rule	Alternative Rules	
ABC	ADE		BC > -BC, DE		
ABC	DAE	A > D	BC > -BC, E	. > D	
ABC	DEA	A > DE	BC > -BC	. > DE	
BAC	ADE	B > -B	C > -C, DE		
BAC	DAE	B > -B, D	C > -C, E		
BAC	DEA	B > -D, DE	C > -C		
BCA	ADE	BC > -BC	a_n > DE		. > DE
BCA	DAE	BC > -BC, D	a_n > E		. > E
BCA	DEA	BC > -BC, DE			

There are general lemmatization rule forms in the third and the fourth column, which we use in the inductive process of lemmatization rules. In the second, third, seventh and eighth rows there are also alternative rules in the last two columns (the dot in the rule means an arbitrary string). These alternative rules were derived in the same way as the rules in the example above (BAC and ADE). Because there are no substrings before (row 2 and 3) or after (row 7 and 8) the common substring A, the derived lemmatization rules are stripped-only rules (see [2]) and therefore, they have to be replaced by other no stripped-only rules. The condition of a new prefix rule is the whole common substring A and the condition of a new suffix rule is the last character a_n of substring A. If there is no common substring then a rule which substitutes the full form for its lemma is created. For example, the pair of words JE and ON creates the rule: $JE > -JE, ON$. The absence of common substring is caused by the presence of irregular words in the language, i.e. words with the irregular inflectional and derivative process. Every induced rule has its identification code (*rule id* or *rule index*). Every lemma together with a set of ids of lemmatization rules which has been induced from this lemma (called "*lemma applicable rules*"), i.e. a sort list of the rule ids, is stored in the lemma lexicon [2].

2.3   Lemmatization of Missing Full Forms

When we want to construct the lemmatizer from the FFL dictionary, we have to cope with the following problem. The problem is the absence of some full forms in the FFL dictionary, especially if we have the FFL dictionary which has not been created by the morphological generator.

Generalization of Lemma Lexicon (GLL). This method works with the lemma lexicon, which has been build in the inductive process of lemmatization rules. A lemma lexicon entry is a lemma with its "lemma applicable rules". Suppose that for some lemma and its relevant full forms the lemma lexicon contains only the information on rules which are used during the lemmatization of these full forms. This information is checked in the lemmatization process and thus the situation that the relevant full form is missing causes that this missing full form cannot be lemmatized. To provide the lemmatization of the missing relevant full forms, we need to add the ids of rules which lemmatize these missing forms to the lexicon. This problem can be viewed as a problem of automatic finding "lemma applicable rules" patterns or as lemma clustering based on the "lemma applicable rules". We assume that there are some lemmas with their all relevant full forms in the FFL dictionary which can be served as the patterns. Once we have the patterns, we assign them to the lemmas in the lexicon and create a new lemma lexicon consequently.

To find the patterns, we create a co-occurrence matrix A of dimension n x n, where n is the number of lemmatization rules. The rule ids denote row and column indexes of A; the matrix element a_{ij} comprises the information on how many times the rule i together with the rule j has been seen in the list of the rule ids. Now we go trough all the lemmas in the lexicon and count how many times the rule i together with the rule j has occurred in the lemma list of the rule ids. The rows in the matrix are treated as searched patterns, i.e. if we see the rule i in a lemma list we enrich this list by adding the indexes of all columns (the rules) whose elements of the i-th row are positive. This enrichment brings a higher recall but a lower precision. A better way is to enrich the list by the column indexes which score is higher than some threshold. We used the threshold equal to one and obtained increasing in the recall by 2.58% but decreasing in the precision by 5.6% for our development data (for more detail see section 3). Because this method decreases the precision we develop another method: Hierarchical Lemmatization without Rule Permission Check.

Hierarchical Lemmatization Without Rule Permission Check (HLWRPC). The first problem of the previous method is that the enriched lexicon is used on all lemmatized words. The second one is that finding the right patterns which do not drop the precision is a very difficult task. We should make some changes in the lemmatization process to cope with these two problems. First, we try to use the lemmatization algorithm described into [2] on the investigated word. If it finds some lemma then this lemma is considered as the result otherwise the investigated word is the missing full form. In this case, we use a new lemmatization algorithm without the rule permission check, i.e. if we find some lemma in the lemma lexicon then we do not check if the lemmatization rules used during this lemmatization process are "lemma applicable rules". In this way, the lemma lexicon is totally generalized without the negative influences on a precision and a recall. This method increases the recall by 2.7% and the precision by 0.1% for development data (details are given in Section 3).

2.4 Lemmatization of OOV Words

The OOV words are words which are not in the FFL dictionary and therefore, we cannot lemmatize them by the lemmatization algorithm [2]. There are three types of the OOV words. The first type is the situation when the full form is missing in the FFL dictionary but its lemma is in the FFL dictionary. The lemmatization of the missing full forms has been described in the previous section. The second type is a word whose neither full form nor lemma is in the lexicon. This word is called an unknown word. The last type is a compound word whose partial word has its lemma in the lexicon. For lemmatization of compound words we use the same lemmatization algorithm (without rule permission check) as the one for the missing full forms. The difference is that we do not lemmatize the compound word directly. First, we remove some characters from the beginning of the compound word and subsequently the rest is lemmatized by the lemmatization algorithm without rule permission check. The question is: What is the minimal length of the rest which still can represent some full form? We provide several experiments and chose the length of six characters as the minimal length of the rest.

A set of *"word applicable rules"* (rules which condition is true for the given word) can be assigned to every word. One set can be assigned to several different words and hence it can be considered as the lemmatization pattern. In order to create the lemmatization patterns we go trough a whole FFL dictionary and for every pair [full form, lemma] we find "word applicable rules" (the lemmatization pattern). This lemmatization pattern together with the ids of winning rules and a *count of winnings* of every winning rule is saved to the pattern table. The winning rule is every rule which converts the full form to the lemma (if the full form is the same as the lemma then the winning rule is the empty rule but it is taken into account too). If the pattern already exists then we increase the score of the winning rules only. The winning rules are sorted by their count of winnings. We use two pattern tables - the prefix pattern table (word applicable prefix rules only) and the suffix pattern table (word applicable suffix rules only) specially. When we lemmatize the unknown word, we try to apply all the lemmatization rules and the applicable rules create prefix and suffix pattern. Then we find these patterns in the relevant table and apply the winning rules which have the highest count of winnings on the unknown word.

3   Experiments and Results

Two data sources have been used for the experiments, the Prague Dependency Treebank (PDT 1.0) and dictionaries and rule files from the Ispell [7]. The PDT 1.0 is a corpus of annotated Czech texts having three-level structure [6]: morphological, analytical, and tectogrammatical. For the construction and evaluation of the lemmatizer we have used only training, development, and test data from the morphological level. The data from the PDT 1.0 represent the FFL dictionary (PDT 1.0 FFL dictionary) with missing full forms. Ispell dictionary and rules file represent FFL dictionary (Ispell FFL dictionary) without missing full forms. The Ispell FFL dictionary is created by the morphological generator from the ispell dictionary and the derivation rules file. The Ispell FFL dictionary is used to compare the lemmatization rules acquired via inversion of manually handcrafted derivation rules with the lemmatization rules induced from a FFL dictionary. We have chosen the Ispell dictionaries and rules files for the Czech, English, and

Finnish language because these languages represent three basic types of language: inflective, analytical, and agglutinative language, respectively.

The lemmatizer output should be all lemmas from which the lemmatized word can be derived. This is a multiple output thus we have to count a recall (R) and a precision (P). The recall is computed as the number of the right lemmatized words to the number of all lemmatized words ratio. The word is lemmatized correctly when there is its reference lemma in the lemmatizer output. The reference lemma is the unambiguous lemma which is assigned to the given word by a human expert. The precision is computed as the ratio of the number of the right lemmatized words to the number of all lemmas generated by the lemmatizer for all correct lemmatized words.

We have created two lemmatizers to compare the inversion and the induced lemmatization rules, the first one (Lem_LM) is based on language morphology (lemmatization rules acquired via the inversion of manually handcrafted derivation rules) [2] and the second one (Lem_FFL) is induced from the Ispell FFL dictionary. We have used the Ispell FFL dictionary also for the comparison of the recall and the precision of these two lemmatizers. The results are shown in Table 2.

Table 2. The comparison of the lemmatizers

Language	Czech					English					Finnish				
	R [%]	P [%]	N. of errors	N. of prefix rules	N. of suffix rules	R [%]	P [%]	N. of errors	N. of prefix rules	N. of suffix rules	R [%]	P [%]	N. of errors	N. of prefix rules	N. of suffix rules
Lem_LM	99.99	94.85	280	13	2533	96.56	95.23	4 750	3	43	99.62	94.27	19765	6	18612
Lem_FFL	100	95.63	0	52	1619	100	95.04	0	3	33	100	94.27	0	14	11271

We lemmatize the training data (Ispell FFL dictionary created by the morphological generator), so the recall should be 100 %. However, it is valid for the Lem_FFL only because there are errors in the ispell rules files [2]. The Lem_FFL (recall 100 %) can cope with these errors.

The methods for the lemmatization of missing full forms, unknown, and compound words have been tested on the development and test morphological data from the PDT 1.0. The results are given in Table 3.

Table 3. The results of the methods for the lemmatization of OOV words

Method	Morphological development data			Morphological test data		
	R [%]	P [%]	# of errors	R [%]	P [%]	# of errors
Lem_FFL	95.06	76.42	5212	95.41	76.74	4736
Lem_FFL_Gen_Dic	97.64	70.8	2492	X	X	X
Lem_FFL_Hierar	97.8	76.53	2356	X	X	X
Lem_FFL_Compound	95.82	76.1	4411	X	X	X
Lem_FFL_Unknown	98.6	76.14	1481	X	X	X
Lem_FFL_Hierar_Cmd_Unk	99.31	74.59	726	99.3	75.1	712

In the first row the result for lemmatizer (Lem_FFL) trained on the PDT 1.0 FFL dictionary is given. In the next rows the results of the methods for the lemmatization missing full forms (GLL – Lem_FFL_Gen_Dic; HLWRPC – Lem_FFL_Hierar), compound (Lem_FFL_Compound), and unknown (Lem_FFL_Unknown) words used with

Lem_FFL lemmatizer are shown. The best result, which has been achieved by a combination of the methods, is in the last row.

The presented method for the lemmatization of the unknown words can lemmatize every word and works without a lemma lexicon. It can be used like a lexicon-free lemmatizer also. This lemmatizer has been tested on the ispell FFL dictionaries and on the development data from the PDT 1.0. The results are presented in Table 4.

Table 4. The lemmatizer based on the lemmatization of the unknown words only

	Ispell FFL dictionaries			PDT 1.0 – morphological development data	
	Czech	English	Finnish	All development data	Lemmas not seen in training data
Lem_WR	R: 84.86 % P: 68.89 %	R: 79.6 % P: 96.94 %	R: 71.91 % P: 98.08 %	R: 76.44% P: 78.41%	R: 82.01 % P: 82.37 %
Lem_All	R: 100 % P: 8.16 %	R: 100 % P: 48.89 %	R: 100 % P: 31.98 %	R: 99.85 % P: 10.32 %	R: 98.59 % P: 9.36 %
Lemmatization patterns					
# of prefix patterns	51	3	14	192	
# of suffix patterns	1241	33	8522	2177	

In the first row is the method (Lem_WR) which applies the winning lemmatization rules, with the highest count of winnings, of a relevant pattern on the lemmatized word. The second method (Lem_All) applies all winning lemmatization rules (independently on the count of winnings) of the relevant pattern.

4   Conclusions

We have introduced the method for the automatic construction of the lemmatizer from the FFL dictionary and the methods for lemmatization of three types of the OOV words (missing full forms, unknown (missing lemmas), and compound words). The methods have been evaluated on different types of data and the best result achieved on the test data had recall 99.3 % and precision 75.1 %. The baseline experiment was carried out with the lemmatizer induced from the PDT 1.0 FFL dictionary without applying any methods of lemmatization of OOV words. The baseline method achieved recall 95.41 % and precision 76.74 % (see Table 3). We have shown that the induction of the lemmatizer from a FFL dictionary is useful in case when a lemma lexicon and derivation rules are at disposal (see Table 2). The method for the lemmatization of the unknown words can be used as a lexicon-free lemmatizer (see Table 4).

References

1. Gaustad, T.: Linguistic knowledge and word sense disambiguation. Groningen Dissertations in Linguistics, (2004), ISSN 0928-0030
2. Kanis J., Müller L.: Using the lemmatization technique for phonetic transcription in text-to-speech system, In Text, speech and dialogue. Berlin: Springer, (2004). s. 355-361.ISBN 3-540-23049-1.

3. Krovetz, R.: Viewing morphology as an inference process. In Horfhage,R., Rasmussen,E., and Willett, P., editors, Proceedings of the 16th Annual International ACM SIGIR Conference on Research and Development in Information Retrieval, pages 191-203, Pittsburgh (1993).
4. Monz, C.: From document retrieval to question answering. PhD thesis, Institute for Logic, Language and Computation, University of Amsterdam, Amsterdam (2003).
5. Daniel Hirschberg's page: http://www.ics.uci.edu/ dan/class/161/notes/6/Dynamic.html
6. Böhmová, A., Hajič, J., Hajičová, E., Hladká, B.: The Prague Dependency Treebank: Three-Level annotation scenario. -In: A. Abeillé, editor, Treebanks: Building and using syntactically annotated corpora. Kluwer Academic Publishers (2001).
7. Ispell dictionaries and rules files: http://fmg-www.cs.ucla.edu/geoff/ispell-dictionaries.html

Modeling Syntax of Free Word-Order Languages: Dependency Analysis by Reduction*

Markéta Lopatková[1], Martin Plátek[2], and Vladislav Kuboň[1]

[1] ÚFAL MFF UK, Praha
{lopatkova,vk}@ufal.mff.cuni.cz
[2] KTIML MFF UK, Praha
martin.platek@mff.cuni.cz

Abstract. This paper explains the principles of dependency analysis by reduction and its correspondence to the notions of dependency and dependency tree. The explanation is illustrated by examples from Czech, a language with a relatively high degree of word-order freedom. The paper sums up the basic features of methods of dependency syntax. The method serves as a basis for the verification (and explanation) of the adequacy of formal and computational models of those methods.

1 Introduction – Analysis by Reduction

It is common to describe the syntactic structure of sentences of English or other fixed word-order languages by phrase structure grammars. The description of the syntactic structure of Latin, Italian, German, Arabic, Czech, Russian or some other languages is more often based on approaches which are generally called dependency based. Both approaches are based on stepwise simplification of individual sentences, on the so-called analysis by reduction. However, the basic principles of the phrase-structure and dependency based analysis by reduction are substantially different. The phrase-structure based analysis (of fixed word-order languages) can be naturally modeled by the bottom-up analysis using phrase structure (Chomskian) grammars. This paper should help the reader to recognize that it is necessary to model the dependency analysis by reduction of languages with a high degree of word-order freedom differently. We try to explain explicitly the common basis of the methods for obtaining dependencies, presented in [3, 4, 7].

Unlike the artificial (programming) languages, the natural languages allow for an ambiguous interpretation. Instead of a complete formal grammar (of an artificial language), for natural languages we have at our disposal the ability of sentence analysis – we learn it at school, it is described by means of implicit rules in grammars of a given language.

The grammar textbooks are based on the presupposition that a human understands the meaning of a particular sentence before he starts to analyze it (let us cite from the 'Textbook of sentence analysis' (see [10]):"A correct analysis of a sentence is not

---

* This paper is a result of the project supported by the grant No. 1ET100300517. We would like to thank an anonymous reviewer for his valuable comments and recommendations.

V. Matoušek et al. (Eds.): TSD 2005, LNAI 3658, pp. 140–147, 2005.

possible without a precise understanding of that sentence, ... "). An automatic syntactic analysis (according to a formal grammar), on the other hand, neither does presuppose the sentence understanding, nor has it at its disposal. On the contrary, it is one of the first phases of the computational modeling of a sentence meaning.

What is actually the relationship between the sentence analysis and the analysis by reduction? In simple words, the sentence analysis is based on a more elementary ability to perform the analysis by reduction, i.e. to simplify gradually the analyzed sentences. The following simplified example illustrates the methodology of the dependency analysis by reduction.

Example 1. The sentence *'Studenti dělali těžkou zkoušku.' [Lit.: Students passed difficult exam.]* can be simplified (while preserving its syntactical correctness) in two ways (see also the scheme in Fig. 1) – by the deletion of the word form *studenti* or by the deletion of the word form *těžkou* (but not by the deletion of the word form *zkoušku* – the sentence *'*Studenti dělali těžkou.'* is not acceptable in a neutral context). In the second step we can remove the word form *těžkou* (in the first branch of the analysis) or the word form *studenti*, or even the word form *zkoušku* (in the second branch). In the last step we can delete the word form *zkoušku* (in the first branch), or the word form *studenti*.

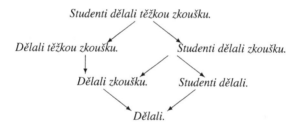

Fig. 1. The DAR scheme for the sentence *'The students passed a difficult exam.'*

The DAR scheme is closely related to a dependency tree, Fig. 2 shows the dependency tree for the sentence *Studenti dělali těžkou zkoušku.*

(i) A particular word depends on (modifies) another word from the sentence if it is possible to remove this modifying word (while the correctness of the sentence is preserved).

(ii) Two words can be removed stepwise in an arbitrary order if and only if they are mutually independent.

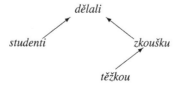

Fig. 2. The dependency tree for the sentence *'Studenti dělali těžkou zkoušku.'*

This example illustrates the way how we can obtain an information about dependencies (relationships between modified and modifying words in a sentence) using DAR. Let us stress the following fact: if taking correct Czech sentences with permuted word order, e.g. *'Těžkou zkoušku studenti dělali.'* or *'Těžkou dělali studenti zkoušku.'*, we get totally analogical reduction scheme as for the original sentence (the deleted words are identical in all steps of the reduction). This indicates that the dependency analysis by reduction allows to examine dependencies and word order independently. In other words, it provides a method for studying the degree of independence of the relationship between modified and modifying words in a sentence on its word order.

In this paper we concentrate on the description of rules for a dependency analysis by reduction of Czech, a language with a relatively high degree of word-order freedom, and on clarification of the relation between a dependency analysis by reduction and dependency sentence analysis.

The main reason for studying the analysis by reduction is the endeavor to gain a clear idea about its formal and computational modeling. Note that a formal model of analysis by reduction, restarting automata, is already intensively studied (see e.g. [3, 6]).

2   Dependency Analysis by Reduction

The **dependency analysis by reduction (DAR)** is based on stepwise simplification of a sentence – each step of DAR is represented by exactly one **reduction operation** which may be executed in two ways:

(i) by deleting at least one word of the input sentence, or

(ii) by replacing an (in general discontinuous) substring of a sentence by a shorter substring.

The possibility to apply certain reduction is restricted by the necessity to preserve some (at least the first one) of the following **DAR principles**:

(a) preservation of syntactical correctness of the sentence;

(b) preservation of lemmas and sets of morphological categories characterizing word forms that are not affected by the reduction operation;

(c) preservation of the meanings of words in the sentence (represented e.g. by valency frame[1], or by a suitable equivalent in some other language);

(d) preservation of the independence of the meaning of the sentence (the sentence has independent meaning if it does not necessarily invoke any further questions when uttered separately)[2].

With respect to a concrete task (e.g. for grammar checking) it is possible to relax these DAR principles; those which are not relaxed are then called **valid DAR principles** (e.g. in the example 1 we have relaxed the principle of preservation of the independence of sentence meaning).

If it is possible to apply a certain reduction in a certain step of DAR (preserving all valid principles), we talk about **admissible reduction**. By the application of all admis-

---

[1] The valency frame describes syntactic-semantic properties of a word, see e.g. [5].

[2] A sentence with independent meaning consists of a verb, all its semantically 'obligatory' modifications and (recursively) their 'obligatory' modifications, see [7].

sible reductions it is possible to get all **admissible simplifications** of a sentence being reduced.

We are going to use the term **DAR scheme (reduction scheme)** of a sentence of a given language for an oriented graph, whose nodes represent all admissible simplifications of a given sentence (including the original sentence) and whose edges correspond to all admissible reductions that can be always applied to a starting node of the edge and whose result is the admissible simplification of a sentence in its final node.

Example 2. The reduction scheme of the sentence '*Studenti dělali těžkou zkoušku.*' in Fig 1 illustrates the reductions of the type (i) – we delete at least one word of the input sentence in every step of the DAR whereas the possibility of branching captures the non-deterministic nature of the DAR. The reduction of the type (ii) is illustrated by possible simplification of the sentence *Kursem prošlo patnáct studentů. [Lit.: Course completed fifteen students.].* Its reduction scheme is presented in Fig 3 (again, the principle (d) of the preservation of independence of meaning is relaxed).

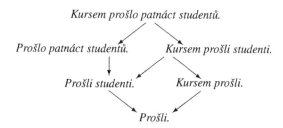

Fig. 3. The reduction scheme for the sentence '*Kursem prošlo patnáct studentů.*'

3   The Structure of Reduction and a Dependency Tree

The DAR scheme allows to introduce and classify various types of relationships. On the basis of these relationships we can define a structure of a sentence reduction.

Let us have a language L, a sentence $v \in L$, $v = v_1 v_2 ... v_m$, where $v_1, v_2, ..., v_m$ are the words, and a DAR scheme of the sentence v. We will say that the words v_i $i \in N, N \subseteq \{1, 2, ...m\}$ constitute a **reduction component**, if all words v_i are always removed at the same moment (i.e. in the DAR scheme all words v_i are removed in one step, which corresponds to a single edge in the scheme). We will say that the word v_i is **dependent (in the reduction)** on the word v_j, if the word v_i is deleted earlier than v_j in all branches of the DAR; the word v_j will be called a **governing (in the reduction)** word.

We will say that the words v_i and v_j are **independent on each other (with regard to the reduction)**, if they can be deleted in an arbitrary order (i.e. there is a DAR branch in which the word v_i is deleted earlier than the word v_j, and there is a DAR branch in which the word v_j is deleted earlier than the word v_i).

Based on the terms of dependency and component in the reduction we can define a reduction structure of a sentence, as it is illustrated in the following example.

Example 3. The reduction scheme of the sentence *'Studenti dělali těžkou zkoušku.'* *[Lit.: Students passed difficult exam.]* which preserves all DAR principles (including the principle (d) preservation of the independence of the meaning of the sentence) can be found on Fig. 4 – the verb *dělat* has two 'obligatory' modifications corresponding to a subject and a direct object, the noun *studenti* does not have obligatory modifications, therefore the sentence with independent meaning has a form *'Studenti dělali zkoušku.'* *[Lit.: Students passed exam.]*

Studenti dělali těžkou zkoušku.

↓

Studenti dělali zkoušku.

Fig. 4. The DAR scheme for the sentence *'Studenti dělali těžkou zkoušku.'* when applying the principle of preservation the independence of the sentence meaning.

The **reduction structure** can be captured by a diagram in which the nodes represent individual words from the sentence, the horizontal edges connect a reduction component (an edge always connects two neighboring words of a reduction component). The oblique edges reflect reduction dependencies; they are considered to be oriented from the dependent word (or from the whole reduction component) towards the governing word (or, again, towards the whole reduction component, if it is governing that particular word (component)). The linear order of nodes (left to right) captures the word-order (the order of words in the sentence). Fig. 5 shows the reduction structure representing the sentence *Studenti dělali těžkou zkoušku.*

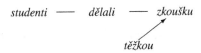

Fig. 5. The reduction structure for the sentence *'Studenti dělali těžkou zkoušku.'*

Traditionally, the structure of a (Czech) sentence is described by a dependency tree. Such a description is transparent and proper for sentences not complicated by coordinations, ellipses and by some marginal phenomena. The **dependency tree** is a structure that is a finite tree in the sense of a graph theory, and it has a root into which all paths are directed and whose nodes are totally (linearly left-to-right) ordered. The nodes represent the occurrences of word forms used in the sentence, the edges represent the relationship between a governing and a governed word (unit) in the sentence.

The only thing left to describe is how to get a dependency tree from a reduction structure. Reduction dependencies are easy, the respective edges characterize the relationship between the modifying and the modified word, the order of words in the sentence is preserved.

For reduction components it is necessary to find out which word from a given component will be considered as governing and which one will be dependent. For this purpose it is necessary to introduce additional rules for individual linguistic phenomena, which are studied in more detail in the following section.

4   Reduction Relationships in a Natural Language

The formal typology of dependencies introduced in the previous section corresponds to a traditional linguistic classification – in this section we will try to describe this correspondence in more detail.

Let us suppose that the reader is familiar with basic linguistic notions such as subordination[3] (relation between modified sentence member and its modifying sentence member), complementation of verb/noun/adjective/adverb, inner participant (argument) and free modification (adjunct), obligatory and optional complementation. Description of these terms can be found e.g. in [9], [7] and [5].

Dependencies (in DAR) allow to model directly the optional free modifications – here it is possible to replace the whole pair by a modified word, a 'head' of the construction (without loosing the independence of meaning, the principle (d) of DAR). Thus we can capture the relationships like *těžká zkouška, jde pomalu, jde domů, přichází včas [Lit.: difficult exam, (she) walks slowly, (he) goes home, (he) comes in time]*. The governing word (in the reduction) corresponds to the modified word in the sentence, the dependent word (in the reduction) corresponds to the word which modifies it (see Fig. 6).

It remains to determine the governing and dependent member in those cases in which the modified or modifying member of this dependency consist of the whole reduction component, rather than of a single word.

(i) If the modifying member consists of the reduction component, then the dependent member is the governing word of this component (the remaining members of the component constitute a subtree with a root in this governing word).

(ii) If the modified sentence member consists of the reduction component, then the whole construction in general has ambiguous meaning (interesting examples for Czech can be found in [2]).

Fig. 6. Dependencies in DAR model free modifications.

Reduction components allow for modeling more complex relationships between word occurrences. These are either (a) morpho-syntactic relationships, or (b) syntactically-semantic relationships.

---

[3] The term of 'subordination' describes the language relationship, while the term of 'dependency' is reserved here for formal structures, by means of which language relationships are modeled.

(a) Reduction components describe so-called **formemes**, the units corresponding to individual sentence members – these are especially prepositional groups (as *na stole, vzhledem k okolnostem [Lit.: on table, with respect to circumstances]*) or complex verb forms (*přijel jsem, tiskne se [Lit.: (I) did arrive, (it) is being printed]*).

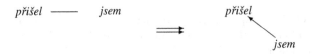

Fig. 7. A possible transformation of formemes into a dependency subtree.

In traditional linguistics each formeme constitutes one node of the diagram, or dependency tree describing syntactic structure of the sentence, see e.g. [10] or [9]. In these theories only the meaningful words (especially meaningful verbs, nouns, adjectives and adverbs) are represented by independent nodes. However, for many practically oriented tasks (e.g. grammar-checking, building of a syntactically annotated corpus) it is appropriate to represent each word of a sentence by its own node. In order to preserve the traditional data type of the dependency tree it is necessary to specify additional rules on the basis of which even the reduction components can be transformed into subtrees, i.e. it is necessary to specify which word from the formeme will be considered governing and which one will be dependent. Such rules are usually of a technical nature and they can differ in individual projects (Fig. 7 shows the solution adopted in [1]).

(b) The second type of relationships modeled by reduction components are syntactically-semantic relationships. These are especially **valency relationships** – the relationships of a verb, noun, adjective or adverb and its obligatory valency complementation(s) (as e.g.*studenti dělali zkoušku, Petr dal Pavlovi dárek, začátek přednášky [Lit.: students passed exam, Petr gave Pavel gift, beginning (of) lecture]*). These constructions cannot be replaced by a single word, the 'head' of the construction, without loosing the independence of meaning, DAR principle (d).

Traditional linguistics captures the valency relationships using dependency tree (see [9] and [10]). The theoretical criterion for the determination of modified and modifying sentence member, the principle of analogy in the layer of word classes is discussed in [9] – the verb is considered as a modified word (as an analogy to verbs without obligatory complementations), the verb complementations are the modifying words; similarly for nouns, adjectives, adverbs and their complementations. This principle of analogy is also adopted for determining the governing word during the transformation of reduction structure to a dependency tree: the verb is considered as a governing word, the verb complementations are its dependent words; similarly for nouns, adjectives, adverbs.

Let us note that the analogy principle can be simply substituted by a relaxation of the condition (d) preserving the independence of meaning of DAR.

Concluding Remarks

The DAR allows to formulate the relationship of basic syntactic phenomena: a dependency and a word order. This approach is indispensable especially for modeling

Fig. 8. The transformation of valency relationships into a dependency subtree.

the syntactic structure of languages with a free word-order, where the dependency and word-order are very loosely related and where they are also related in a different manner from language to language (let us compare this situation with English, where the dependencies are determined (mainly) by a very strict word-order).

The paper shows that the dependencies can be derived from two different, not overlapping, simply observable and language independent phenomena: from the reduction dependency and from reduction components. It also points out that the (Czech) traditional linguistic taxonomy of language phenomena corresponds to this division. We have mentioned the formal model of analysis by reduction, restarting automata. We have thus outlined one important step how to pass the observations about dependencies from traditional linguistics into the formal terms suitable for computer linguistics.

References

1. Hajič, J.: Building a Syntactically Annotated Corpus: The Prague Dependency Treebank. In: Issues of Valency and Meaning. Studies in Honour of Jarmila Panevová (ed. Hajičová, E.), Karolinum, Prague, pp. 106-132 (1998)
2. Holan, T., Kuboò, V., Oliva, K., Plátek, M.: On Complexity of Word Order. In: Les grammaires de dépendance - Traitement automatique des langues (TAL), Vol. 41, No. 1 (q.ed. Kahane, S.), pp. 273-300 (2000)
3. Jančar, P, Mráz, F., Plátek, M., Vogel, J.: On Monotonic Automata with a Restart Operation. Journal of Automata, Languages and Combinatorics, Vol. 4, No. 4, pp. 287-311 (1999)
4. Kunze, J.: Abhängigkeitsgrammatik. Volume XII of Studia Grammatica, Akademie Verlag, Berlin (1975)
5. Lopatková, M.: Valency in the Prague Dependency Treebank: Building the Valency Lexicon. In: PBML 79-80, pp. 37-59 (2003)
6. Otto, F.: Restarting Automata and their Relations to the Chomsky Hierarchy. In: Developments in Language Theory, Proceedings of DLT'2003 (eds. Esik, Z., Fülöp, Z.), LNCS 2710, Springer, Berlin (2003)
7. Panevová, J.: Formy a funkce ve stavbě české věty. Academia, Praha (1980)
8. Plátek, M., Lopatková, M., Oliva, K.: Restarting Automata: Motivations and Applications. In: Proceedings of the workshop "Petrinetze" (ed. Holzer, M.), Technische Universität München, pp. 90-96 (2003)
9. Sgall, P., Hajičová, E., Panevová, J.: The Meaning of the Sentence in Its Semantic and Pragmatic Aspects (ed. Mey, J.), Dordrecht:Reidel and Prague:Academia (1986)
10. Šmilauer, V.: Učebnice větného rozboru. Skripta FF UK, SPN, Praha (1958)

Morphological Meanings
in the Prague Dependency Treebank 2.0

Magda Razímová and Zdeněk Žabokrtský*

Institute of Formal and Applied Linguistics, Charles University (MFF)
Malostranské nám. 25, CZ-11800 Prague, Czech Republic
{razimova,zabokrtsky}@ufal.mff.cuni.cz
http://ufal.mff.cuni.cz

Abstract. In this paper we report our work on the system of grammatemes (mostly semantically-oriented counterparts of morphological categories such as number, degree of comparison, or tense), the concept of which was introduced in Functional Generative Description, and is now further elaborated in the context of Prague Dependency Treebank 2.0. We present also a new hierarchical typology of tectogrammatical nodes.

1 Introduction

Human language, as an extremely complex system, has to be described in a modular way. Many linguistic theories attempt to reach the modularity by decomposing language description into a set of levels, usually linearly ordered along an abstraction axis (from text/sound to semantics/pragmatics). One of the common features of such approaches is that word forms occurring in the original surface expression are substituted (for the sake of higher abstraction) with their lemmas at the higher level(s). Obviously, the inflectional information contained in the word forms is not present in the lemmas. Some information is 'lost' deliberately and without any harm, since it is only imposed by government (such as case for nouns) or agreement (congruent categories such as person for verbs or gender for adjectives). However, the other part of the inflectional information (such as number for nouns, degree for adjectives or tense for verbs) is semantically indispensable and must be represented by some means, otherwise the sentence representation becomes deficient (naturally, the representations of sentence pairs such as '*Peter met his youngest brother*' and '*Peter meets his young brothers*' must not be identical at any level of abstraction). On the tectogrammatical level (TL for short) of Functional Generative Description (FGD, [8], [9]), which we use as the theoretical basis of our work, this means is called grammatemes[1].

---

* We would like to thank professor Jarmila Panevová for an extensive linguistic advice. The research reported in this paper has been supported by the projects 1ET101120503, GA-UK 352/2005 and GAČR 201/05/H014.

[1] Just for curiosity: almost the same term 'grammemes' is used for the same notion in the Meaning-Text Theory ([3]), although to a large extent the two approaches were created independently.

V. Matoušek et al. (Eds.): TSD 2005, LNAI 3658, pp. 148–155, 2005.

The theoretical framework of FGD has been implemented in the Prague Dependency Treebank 2.0 project (PDT, [4]), which aims at complex annotation of large amount of Czech newspaper texts[2]. Although grammatemes are present in the FGD for decades, in the context of PDT they were paid for a long time a considerably less attention, compared e.g. to valency, topic-focus articulation or coreference. However, in our opinion grammatemes will play a crucial role in NLP applications of FGD and PDT (e.g., machine translation is impossible without realizing the differences in the above pair of example sentences). That is why we decided to further elaborate the system of grammatemes and to implement it in the PDT 2.0 data. This paper outlines the results of almost two years of the work on this topic.

2   Tectogrammatical Nodes and Hierarchy of Their Types

2.1   Node Structure

At the TL of PDT, a sentence is represented as a tectogrammatical tree structure, which consists of nodes and edges[3]. Only autosemantic words have 'their own' nodes at the TL, while functional words (such as prepositions, subordinating conjunctions or auxiliary verbs) do not. Tectogrammatical node itself is a complex data structure: each node can be viewed as a set of attribute-value pairs. The attributes capture (besides others)[4] the following information:

- Attribute t-lemma contains the lexical value of the node, represented by a sequence of graphemes, or an 'artificial' t-lemma, containing a special string. The lexical value of the node mostly corresponds to the morphological lemma of the word represented by the node. The artificial t-lemma appears as a t-lemma of a restored node (that has no counterpart in the surface sentence structure, e. g. node with t-lemma #Gen), or it corresponds to a punctuation mark (present in the surface structure; e. g. node with t-lemma #Comma) or to a personal pronoun, no matter whether it is expressed on the surface or not (t-lemma #PersPron). In special cases the t-lemma can be composed of more elements (e.g. the t-lemma of a reflexive verb consists of the verbal infinitive and the reflexive element *se*: c.f. *dohodnout_se* in Fig. 3).
- Attribute functor mostly expresses the dependency relation (deep-syntactic function) between a node and its parent (thus it should be viewed as associated with the edge between the node in question and its parent rather than with the node itself).
- Attribute subfunctor specifies the dependency relation in a more detail.
- There is a set of coreference attributes, capturing the relation between two nodes which refer to the same entity.
- Attribute tfa serves for the representation of topic-focus articulation of the sentence according to its information structure.

---

[2] PDT 2.0 will be publicly released soon by Linguistic Data Consortium.

[3] Edges will not be further discussed in this paper, since they represent relations between nodes, whereas grammatemes belong always only to one node. However, suggested classification of nodes has interesting consequences for the classification of edges.

[4] Full documentation of all tectogrammatical attributes will be available in the documentation of PDT 2.0.

- There is a set of grammateme[5] attributes. Grammatemes are mostly tectogrammatical counterparts of morphological categories (but some of them describe the derivation information).
- Attribute nodetype and sempos specify the type of the node.

The last two attributes serve for node typing, which is necessary if we want to explicitly condition the presence or absence of other attributes (not only grammatemes) in the node in question (for instance, tense should never be present with rhematizer nodes)[6]. The proposed hierarchy (sketched in Fig. 1) consists of two levels. The top branching renders fundamental differences in node properties and behavior (Section 2.2), whereas the secondary branching (applicable only on complex nodes, Section 2.3) corresponds to the presence or absence of individual grammatemes (morphological meanings) in the node.

2.2 Division on the First Level – Node Types

Having studied various properties of tectogrammatical nodes, we suggest the following primary classification (in each node, it is captured in attribute nodetype):

- The **root** of the tectogrammatical tree (nodetype=root) is a technical node whose child is the governing node of the sentence structure.
- **Complex nodes** (nodetype=complex) represent autosemantic words on the TL (see Section 2.3 for detailed classification),
- **Atomic nodes** (nodetype=atom) represent words expressing the speaker's position, modal characteristics of the event, rhematizers etc.
- **Roots of coordination and apposition constructions** (nodetype=coap) contain the lemma of a coordinating conjunction or an artificial t-lemma substituting punctuation symbols (e.g. #Comma, #Colon).
- **Dependent nodes of foreign phrases** (nodetype=fphr) bear components of a phrase consisting of foreign words, not determined by Czech grammar; t-lemma of these nodes is identical with the surface (i.e., unlemmatized) form in the surface structure of the sentence.
- **Dependent nodes of phrasemes** (nodetype=dphr) create with their parent node one lexical unit with a meaning that does not follow from the meanings of the dependent node and of its parent.
- **Roots of foreign and identification phrases** (nodetype=list) bear one of the artificial t-lemmas #Forn or #Idph (regardless of the functor). The node with t-lemma #Forn is a parent of (above described) dependent nodes of foreign phrases which stand as children nodes of this Forn-node in the order corresponding to the order in the surface structure of the sentence. The node with the t-lemma #Idph plays the

---

[5] In this paper we return the term 'grammateme' as used e.g. in [7], thus we use it differently from [2], in which this term covered also subfunctors.

[6] Of course, the idea of formalizing the presence or absence of an attribute in a linguistic data structure by typing the structures is not new – typed feature structures play a central role in unification grammars for a long time. However, no formal typology of tectogrammatical nodes was ever elaborated in PDT (or even in FGD, although its usability was anticipated e.g. in [7]) before the presented work.

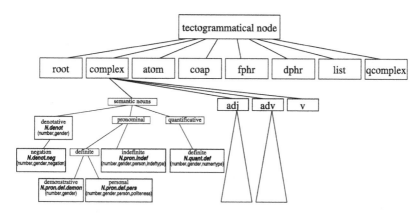

Fig. 1. Type hierarchy of tectogrammatical nodes.

role of the governing node of a structure having a function of name (e.g. a title of a book or movie).

- **Quasi-complex nodes** (nodetype=qcomplex) are mostly restored nodes filling empty (but obligatory) valency slots. These nodes receive a substitute t-lemma according to the character of the complementation they stand for, e.g. the quasi-complex node with the substitute t-lemma #Gen plays the role of an inner participant, which was deleted in the surface sentence structure because of its semantic generality.

2.3 Division on the Second Level – Semantic Parts of Speech

Complex nodes (nodetype=complex) are further divided into four basic groups, according to their semantic parts of speech. Semantic parts of speech belong to the TL and correspond to basic onomasiological categories of substance, quality, circumstance and event (see [1]). The semantic parts of speech are semantic nouns (N), semantic adjectives (Adj), semantic adverbs (Adv) and semantic verbs (V). In PDT 2.0, semantic nouns, adjectives and adverbs are further subclassified[7].

The appurtenance of a tectogrammatical node to the semantic part of speech is stored in the attribute **sempos**. The value of this attribute delimits the set of grammatemes that are relevant for the node belonging to the concrete part-of-speech group. The inner structure of semantic nouns is illustrated in the bottom left-hand part of Fig. 1.

The semantic parts of speech are not identical with the 'traditional' parts of speech (i.e. ten parts of speech in the Czech tradition). Traditional nouns, adjectives, adverbs and verbs belong mostly to the corresponding semantic parts of speech (but there are exceptions, mostly due to derivation; see below); traditional pronouns and numerals

---

[7] Semantic verbs require a different type of inner classification, which has not been developed yet. This is related to difficult theoretical questions, concerning e.g. the presence or absence of tense in an infinitival verbal expression synonymous with a (tensed) subordinate clause (mentioned also in [3]).

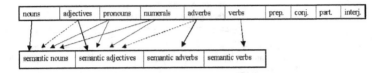

Fig. 2. Relations between traditional and semantic parts of speech. Arrows in bold indicate 'prototypical' relations, dotted arrows represent the classification following the derivation and thin arrows follow the distributing of pronouns and numerals into semantic parts of speech.

were distributed to semantic nouns or semantic adjectives according to their function in the tectogrammatical sentence structure, see Fig. 2[8].

Another reason for differentiating between traditional and semantic parts of speech is that certain derivation relations are distinguished on the TL (in the sense of Kurylowicz's syntactic derivation, see [5]), the occurrence of which results in a change of part of speech. At the TL, the derived word is represented by the t-lemma that it was derived from, and the semantic part of speech corresponds to the t-lemma rather than to the original word. We illustrate this on the example of possessive adjectives and deadjectival adverbs in the following paragraphs.

Possessive adjectives as denominative derivates are represented by the t-lemma of their base nouns; **sempos** of these (traditional) possesive adjectives is 'N' on the TL. E.g. in Fig. 3, the possessive adjective *Mečiarova* (Mečiar`s) is represented by the node with t-lemma *Mečiar* and functor APP (expressing the 'lost' semantic feature of appurtenance).

Deadjectival adverbs are represented by adjectives; their traditional part of speech is 'adverb', while **sempos** is 'Adj'. E.g. in Fig. 3, *rozumně* (rationally) is represented by the node with t-lemma *rozumný* (rational).

The following types of derivation concern only the traditional pronouns and numerals. A single t-lemma corresponding to the relative pronoun is chosen as the representant of all types of 'indefinite' pronouns (i.e. relative, interrogative, negative etc). E.g. in Fig. 3, the negative pronoun *nic* (nothing) is represented by the t-lemma *co* (something) (which is equal to the relative pronoun), the semantic feature lost from the t-lemma is represented by the value of the grammateme **indeftype** (in this case value **negat**).

In a similar way, all types of (definite as well as indefinite) numerals (i.e. basic, ordinal etc.) are represented by the t-lemma corresponding to the basic numeral. The semantic feature of the numeral is marked in the value of the grammateme **numertype**.

3   Grammatemes and Their Values

Grammatemes belong only to complex nodes. Most grammatemes are tectogrammatical counterparts of morphological categories. Some of them describe derivation information. The set of grammatemes which belong to a concrete complex node is delimited by the value of the attribute **sempos** of this node.

---

[8] Naturally, prepositions (which are not represented by a node on the TL) as well as conjunctions, particles and interjections (which belong to other node types than to the complex one) are not grouped into semantic parts of speech.

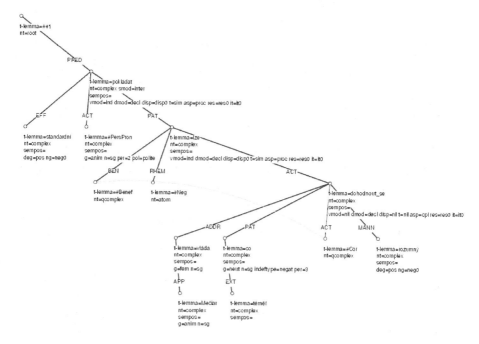

Fig. 3. Simplified tectogrammatical representation (only **t-lemma**, **functor**, **nodetype**, **sempos**, and grammatemes are depicted) of the sentence: *"Pokládáte za standardní, když se s Mečiarovou vládou nelze téměř na ničem rozumně dohodnout? "* (Do you find it standard if almost nothing can be agreed on with Mečiar`s government?).

There are 16 grammatemes in the PDT 2.0. We list them in the following paragraphs (the grouping is only tentative).

Grammatemes having their counterpart in a morphological category are the following: (1) **number** (singular, plural; N)[9]; (2) **gender** (masculine animate, masculine inanimate, feminine, neuter; N); (3) **person** (1, 2, 3; N); (4) grammateme of degree of comparison **degcmp** (positive, comparative, superlative, absolute comparative; Adj, Adv); (5) grammateme of verbal modality **verbmod** (indicative, imperative, conditional; V); (6) **aspect** (processual, complex; V); (7) **tense** (simultaneous, anterior, posterior; V).

Grammatemes containing derivation information are the following: (8) **numertype** (basic, set, kind, ord, frac; N, Adj); (9) **indeftype** (relat, indef1 to indef6, inter, negat, total1, total2; N, Adj, Adv); (10) **negation** (neg0, neg1; N, Adj, Adv).

Other grammatemes: (11) grammateme **politeness** (basic, polite; N); (12) grammateme of deontic modality **deontmod** (debitive, hortative, volitive, possibilitive, permissive, facultative, declarative; V); (13) grammateme of dispositional modality **dispmod** (disp0, disp1; V); (14) grammateme **resultative** (res0, res1; V); (15) grammateme **iterativeness** (it0, it1; V).

---

[9] There is the list of distinguished values in the parenthesis, together with the value of **sempos** which implies the presence of the given grammateme.

The grammateme of sentence modality (16) **sentmod** (enunciative, exclamatory, desiderative, imperative, interrogative) differs from the other grammatemes, since its presence is implied by the position of the node in the tree (sentence or direct speech roots and roots of parenthetical constructions) instead of by the value of **sempos**.

4   Implementation

The procedure for assigning grammatemes (and **nodetype** and **sempos**) to nodes of tectogrammatical trees was implemented in **ntred**[10] environment for accessing the PDT data. Besides almost 2000 lines of Perl code, we created a number of rules for grammateme assignment written in a text file using a special economic notation (roughly 2000 lines again), and numerous lexical resources (e.g. special-purpose list of verbs or adverbs). As we intensively used all information available also on the two 'lower' levels of the PDT (morphological and analytical), most of the annotation could have been done automatically with a highly satisfactory precision. We needed only around 5 man-months of human annotation for solving very specific issues.

For the lack of space, a detailed description of the whole procedure could not be included into this paper. Just to demonstrate that grammatemes are not just dummy copies of what was already present in the morphological tag of the node, we give two examples. (1) Deleted pronouns in subject positions (which must be restored at the TL) might inherit their gender and/or number from the agreement with the governing verb (possibly complex verbal form), or from an adjective (if the governor was copula), or from its antecedent (in the sense of textual coreference). (2) Future verbal tense in Czech can be realized using simple inflection (perfectives), or auxiliary verb (imperfectives), or prefixing (lexically limited).

The procedure was repeatedly tested on the PDT data, which was extremely important for debugging and further improvements of the procedure. Final version of the procedure was applied on all tectogrammatical data of the PDT: 3,168 newspaper texts containing 49,442 sentences with 833,357 tokens (word forms and punctuation marks). All these data, enriched with node classification and grammateme annotation, will be included in PDT 2.0 distribution.

5   Conclusions

We believe that two important goals have been achieved in the present prospect: (1) We suggested a formal classification of tectogrammatical nodes and described its the consequences on the system of grammatemes, and thus the tectogrammatical tree structures become formalizable e.g. by typed feature structures. (2) We implemented an automatic and highly-complex procedure for capturing the node classification, the system of grammatemes and derivations, and verified it on a large-scale data, namely on the whole tectogrammatical data of PDT 2.0. Thus the results of our work will be soon publicly available.

---

[10] http://ufal.mff.cuni.cz/~pajas

In the paper we do not compare our achievements with related work, since we are simply not aware of a comparably structured annotation on comparably large data in any other publicly available treebank.

In the near future, we plan to separate the grammatemes, which bear the derivational information ('derivemes', such as numertype) from the grammatemes having their direct counterpart in traditional morphological categories. The long-term aim is to describe further types of derivation: we should concentrate on productive types of derivation (diminutive formation, formation of feminine nouns etc.). The set of derivemes will be extended in this way. The next issue is the problem of subclassification of semantic verbs.

References

1. Dokulil, M.: Tvoření slov v češtině I. Praha, Academia (1962)
2. Hajičová, E., Panevová, J., Sgall, P. Manuál pro tektogramatické značkování. Technical Report ÚFAL-TR-7 (1999)
3. Kahane, S.: The Meaning-Text Theory. In: Dependency and Valency. An International Handbook of Contemporary Research (2003)
4. Hajičová E. et al: The Current Status of the Prague Dependency Treebank. Proceeings of the 4th Internation Conference Text, Speech and Dialogue, LNAI2166, Springer (2001)
5. Kurylowicz, J.: Dérivation lexicale et dérivation syntaxique. Bulletin de la Société de liguistique de Paris, 37, (1936)
6. Panevová J.: Formy a funkce ve stavbě české věty. Praha, Academia (1980)
7. Petkevič, V.: Underlying Structure of Sentence Based on Dependency: Formal description of sentence in the Functional Generative Description of Sentence, FF UK, Prague (1995)
8. Sgall, P.: Generativní popis jazyka a česká deklinace. Praha, Academia (1967)
9. Sgall, P., Hajičová, E., Panevová, J.: The Meaning of the Sentence in Its Semantic and Pragmatic Aspects. Praha, Academia (1986)

Automatic Acquisition of a Slovak Lexicon from a Raw Corpus*

Benoît Sagot

INRIA-Rocquencourt, Projet Atoll,
Domaine de Voluceau, Rocquencourt B.P. 105
78 153 Le Chesnay Cedex, France

Abstract. This paper presents an automatic methodology we used in an experiment to acquire a morphological lexicon for the Slovak language, and the lexicon we obtained. This methodology extends and refines approaches which have proven efficient, e.g., for the acquisition of French verbs or Croatian and Russian nouns, adjectives and verbs. It only relies on a raw corpus and on a morphological description of the language. The underlying idea is to build all possible lemmas that can explain all words found in the corpus, according to the morphological description, and to rank these hypothetical lemmas according to their likelihood given the corpus. Of course, hand-validation and iteration of the whole process is needed to achieve a high-quality lexicon, but the human involvement required is orders of magnitude lower than the cost of the fully manual development of such a resource. Moreover, this technique can be easily applied to other languages with a rich morphology that lack large-coverage lexical resources.

1 Introduction

Among the different resources that are needed for Natural Language Processing tasks, the lexicon plays a central role. It is for example a prerequisite to any wide-coverage parser. However, the development or enrichment of a large and precise lexicon, even restricted to morphological information, is a difficult task, in particular because of the huge amount of data that has to be collected. Therefore, most large-coverage morphological lexicons for NLP concern only a few languages, such as English. Moreover, these lexicons are usually the result of the careful work of human lexicographers who develop them manually over years, and for this reason they are often not freely available.

The aim of this paper is to show that this is not the only possible way to develop or enrich a morphological lexicon, and that this process can be automatized in such a way that the needed human labor is drastically reduced, at least for categories that have a rich morphology[1]. The only requirements are a raw corpus and a morphological description of the language. This makes it possible to build morphological lexicons in

---

* We would like to thank very warmly Katarína Maťašovičová, native speaker of Slovak, who has been our validator during the acquisition process described here.

[1] We do not consider here closed classes like prepositions, pronouns or numerals, because they can be easily described manually and/or because they don't have a rich morphology, if any.

V. Matoušek et al. (Eds.): TSD 2005, LNAI 3658, pp. 156–163, 2005.

relatively little time for languages that received less attention until now, for example because they are spoken by less people and/or because they are not supported by a large NLP community. We applied our methodology to Slovak language.

The idea of learning lexical information (with or without manual validation) is not new. It has been successfully applied, among other tasks, to terminology [1], collocations [2] or sub-categorization properties [3]. All assume the availability of a morphological lexicon. But to our knowledge, very few work has been published on automatic acquisition of morphological lexicons from raw corpus. Experiments have been conduced by Oliver and co-workers on Russian and Croatian [4, 5] to acquire or enlarge lexicons of verbs, nouns and adjectives. Independently, Clément, Sagot and Lang [6] have published the methodology they used to acquire a lexicon of French verbs. This paper is an extension of these methods for at least three reasons. First, we do not take into account only inflectional morphology, but also derivational morphology, which allows a better precision and recall as well as the acquisition of derivational relations in the lexicon. Second, we use a morphological description that is more powerful than the purely concatenative morphology used in previous works. Third, our algorithm relies on a very simple but rigorous probabilistic model[2].

The main idea is that the acquisition of the lexicon of a corpus in a given language can be achieved by the iteration of a three-step loop:

1. Given the morphological description of the language, build all possible lemmas that can possibly explain the inflected forms found in the corpus,
2. Rank these possible lemmas according to their likelihood given the corpus,
3. Validate manually best ranked lemmas.

In the remainder of this paper, we will describe these steps, our morphological description of Slovak and our current results, with an emphasis on step 2.

2   Slovak Morphology

Like most other Slavic languages, and contrary to English or French, Slovak is an inflected language. This means that nouns and adjectives (among others) are inflected according to their gender and number, but also their grammatical function or to the preposition that governs them (case). This inflection is mostly realized by changing the ending of the word according to its inflectional class (or paradigm), but the stem itself can be affected. The latter occurs in particular for some feminine and neuter nouns in their genitive plural form. For example, *žena* ("woman"), in which the stem is *žen-*, has the genitive plural form *žien*.

2.1   Slovak Language

The Slovak language is a Slavic (and therefore Indo-European) language that is the official language of the Slovak Republic. Its closest relative is the Czech language. Both languages coexisted during a long period within former Czecho-slovakia. For this reason, and because of the proximity of these languages, most Slovak understand Czech,

---

[2] This is already the case in [6], but the model presented here seems more convincing.

and people wishing to learn "the" language spoken in Czechoslovakia learned Czech. Consequences of this are for example that Slovak language is under-represented among language manuals[3], and that it received less attention than other Slavic languages such as Czech or Russian. The only big project concerning Slovak in computational linguistics is the Slovak National Corpus [7], which is a highly valuable resource. Because we think that having only one resource for a given language is not necessarily satisfying, we decided not to use this resource and the information it contains. However, we intend to compare our lexicon with this corpus in the near future.

2.2 Description of Slovak Morphology

As already mentioned in the introduction, automatic lexical acquisition of a morphological lexicon from a raw corpus strongly relies on morphological knowledge. Moreover, this knowledge has to be represented and used in a symmetrical way, in the sense that we want to be able to *inflect* lemmas (associated with an inflectional class) but also to *ambiguously un-inflect* forms found in the corpus into all possible lemmas that might explain them. Moreover, the morphological description of the language must be written by hand, and therefore in a reasonable format. It must also be exploited in a very efficient way, since we want to deal with big corpora, and therefore with a big amount of hypothetical lemmas.

Our description of the Slovak morphology[4], inspired among others from [8] and validated by a native speaker of the language, is represented by an XML file that contains three main kinds of objects, which will be described successively:

1. letters, and the classes they belong to,
2. fusion rules that model the interaction of the final letters of a stem and the initial letters of an ending,
3. inflectional classes.

The list of letters deserves no special comment. We associate with each of those letters a list of the phonetic classes of the phoneme they denote. We use six classes: consonants, soft consonants, non-soft consonants, vowels, long vowels (including diphtongs), short vowels.

The second kind of information we built about Slovak morphology is the interaction between the final letters of a stem and the initial letters of an ending. This is done through a set of fusion patterns which allow to model with a reasonable amount of inflectional classes phenomena that can be explained by standard classes, provided fusion patterns are used. Let us take an example. If a stem ending in t' like *kost'* ("bone") gets an ending beginning with i, as in our example the ending i of the locative singular, then the result is not -t'i- (here *kost'i) but -ti- (here *kosti). Therefore, we

---

[3] For example, and to our knowledge, Slovak is today the only official language of a European country for which no manual in French language is available.

[4] It is important to state here that this morphological description is not the main point of the paper. Any other morphological description, possibly better or more justified from a linguistic point of view, could be used. The only requirement is that this description must be able to give all inflected forms of a given lemma, as well as all possible lemmas having a given form in their inflectional paradigm.

can describe a pattern t′i → ti. Another example is the plural genitive *žien* of *žena* mentioned above: we decide that the ending is in this case -, and we add the following fusion pattern, where \c means "any letter of the class of consonants": e\c- → ie\c. We also defined the special operator $ that means "end of word", and the special class * that matches any letter. An example that uses these operators is the pair of patterns bec* → bc* and bc\$ → bec, which allows to model the alternance between the -bec form of some stems when they get an empty ending and the -bc form of the same stems when the ending is non-empty (e.g., *vrabec*, *vrabca*,...). Both patterns are needed since we need our morphological description to be usable in both directions: from a lemma to its forms, using the first rule, and from a form to its possible lemmas, using the second rule.

The third set of information we designed is the set of inflectional classes. For each class, we list its name, the ending that has to be removed from the lemma to get the stem, and (when needed) a regular expression that stems using this inflectional class have to match. To exemplify the latter point, we say that verbs in -at′/-iam/-ajú (like *merat* ′) have stems that must end with a soft consonant. Each inflectional class contains a set of inflected forms defined by their ending and a morphological tag, supplemented, if needed, by another regular expression that the stem must match. This allows to merge into one inflectional class two paradigms that differ only on a few forms in a way that can be predicted from the stem[5]. Classes also contains derived lemmas, defined by their ending and their inflection class. For example, the inflectional class of regular -at′ verbs have (for the moment) two possible derivations, namely the associated noun in -anie and the associated adjective in -aný.

3 Automatic Acquisition of the Lexicon

As mentioned in the introduction, we iterate a three-step loop as many times as wanted. The three steps are the generation and the inflection of all possible lemmas, the ranking of these possible lemmas, and a partial manual validation. Each step takes into account the information given by the manual validator during previous steps. We shall now describe these steps one after the other. The probabilistic model we developed that underlies step 2 is described in the corresponding paragraph.

3.1 Generation and Inflection of all Possible Lemmas

For our experiments, we use a relatively small corpus of 150,000 words representing 20,000 different words. This corpus includes texts produced by the European Union (including the project of Constitutional Treaty) and free-of-use articles found on Internet (both scientific and journalistic style are represented). The first step is to remove from the corpus all words that are present in a hand-crafted list of words belonging to closed classes (pronouns, some adverbs, prepositions, and so on).

---

[5] For example, we have only one inflectional class for regular -at′ verbs. The form-level regular expression checks if the last vowel of the stem is long or short, thus allowing to decide between the endings -ám, -áš,..., and the endings -am, -aš,.... Indeed, infinitive, participle and 3rd person plural endings are identical, as well as derived lemmas (see below).

After the extraction of the words of our corpus and their number of occurrences, we need to build all hypothetical lemmas that match the morphological description of Slovak language and have among their inflected form at least one word which is attested in the corpus. We then need to inflect these hypothetical lemmas to build all their inflected forms (we call "lemma" a canonical form with the name of its inflection class[6]). To achieve these goals, we developed a script that reads our morphological description and turns it into two programs. The first one can be seen as a non-deterministic morphological parser (or ambiguous lemmatizer), and the second one as an inflecter. In a few dozens of seconds, the first program generates 73,000 hypothetical lemmas out of the 20,000 different words of the corpus. These lemmas are then inflected by the second program in a few other dozens of seconds, thus generating more than 1,500,000 inflected forms, each one being associated with its lemma and a morphological tag.

3.2   Ranking Possible Lemmas

At this point, our goal is to rank the hypothetical lemmas we generated in such a way that the best ranked lemmas are (ideally) all correct, and the least ranked lemmas are all erroneous. Therefore, we need a way to model some kind of plausibility measure for each lemma. We have chosen to compute the likelihood of each lemma given the corpus. Since we do not have the required information to do so directly, we use a fix-point algorithm according to the following model.

We consider the following experiment: we choose at random in the corpus a token (i.e., one occurence of an inflected form, hereafter simply "form"). The probability to have chosen a given form f is $P(f) = occ(f)/n_{tot}$, where $occ(f)$ is the number of occurrences of f in the corpus and n_{tot} the total number of words, both known. Let us call $\mathcal{L}_f$ the set of all hypothetical lemmas that have f as one of their inflected forms. We denote by $P(l)$ the probability that the token we chose is an inflected form of l, and by $P(f|l)$ the probability to have chosen an occurrence of f given the fact that we have chosen an inflected form of the lemma l. We then have the following equality (for the first iteration of the fix-point algorithm, $P(l)$ is initialized to an arbitrary value P_0, typically 0.1):

$$P(f|l) = \frac{P(f) - \sum_{l' \in \mathcal{L}_f, l' \neq l} P(l')P(f|l')}{P(l)}.$$

The Bayes formula allows us then to compute the probability to have chosen an inflected form of the lemma l given the fact that we have chosen an occurrence of f, i.e., the probability for f to come from the lemma l:

$$P(l|f) = \frac{P(l)P(f|l)}{\sum_{l' \in \mathcal{L}_f} P(l')P(f|l')}.$$

This gives directly the probability that we have chosen a form f coming from l:

$$P(f \wedge l) = P(f)P(f|l).$$

---

[6] Hence, a same canonical form can come from several different lemmas, provided they do not belong to the same inflectional classes.

Let us define the probability $\Pi(l)$ (very different from $P(l)$) that l is a valid lemma[7]. We then introduce the *odd* of the lemma l, defined by

$$O_l = \frac{\Pi(l)}{1 - \Pi(l)}.$$

It is well known that the Bayes formula can be expressed as a formula on odds in the following way: learning a new information i (here, the fact that f is – or is not – attested in the corpus) multiplies the odd of the hypothesis "the lemma l is valid" by the odds ratio $OR_l(f)$ defined by:

$$OR_l(f) = \frac{P(i \text{ if } l \text{ is valid})}{P(i \text{ if } l \text{ is not valid})}.$$

This has to be done for each possible form of l, and not only its attested forms. If f is attested in the corpus, the previous formula becomes

$$OR_l(f) = \frac{\sum_{l \in \mathcal{L}_f} P(f \wedge l)}{\sum_{l' \in \mathcal{L}_f, l' \neq l} P(f \wedge l)}.$$

If it is not, we need to evaluate the probability of *not* finding the inflected form f given the corpus, both if l is and is not valid, since the odds ratio is the ratio between these two probabilities. But as can be easily seen, this ratio is equal to the probability of having not chosen the form f given the fact that we have chosen an inflected form of lemma l. To compute this, we use the probability that the chosen form ends with a given ending, given the inflection class of its lemma (this is done thanks to $P(f|l)$ and the related morphological information). For space reasons, we will not give the (simple) details of this computation.

Once having computed all odds ratios, we just need to assume that the original odd (knowing nothing about the corpus) of each lemma is $O_l^0 = 1$ (i.e., $\Pi^0(l) = 1/2$), except if it is an already validated lemma. We then have the odds of each lemma given the corpus by computing the product of O_l^0 by all odds ratios of the form $O_l(f)$, where f is an inflected form of l. These odds are in fact slightly modified, in order to take into account the presence of prefixes that are productive derivational morphology mechanisms. For example, the odds of lemmas `urobit'` and `robit'` (with their common inflectional class) are mutually augmented, in order to take into account the fact that they co-occur and the fact that `u-` is a valid prefix.

At this point, we can compute the probability $\Pi(l) = O_l/(1 + O_l)$ that l is valid. If we denote by $\mathcal{F}_l$ the set of all inflected forms of l, we can define the number of occurrences of l by $occ(l) = \sum_{f \in \mathcal{F}_l} occ(f).P(l|f)$. We then have a new way to compute $P(l)$, by saying that $P(l) = occ(l).\Pi(l)/n_{tot}$. The latter formula allows to iterate anew the whole computation, until convergence.

After the last iteration (in practice, we do 15 iterations), lemmas are ordered according to the probability that they are valid. Lemmas that have a probability equal to 1 are ordered according to $occ(l)$. When appropriate, we associate to lemmas their derived lemmas.

---

[7] Of course, if some lemmas have already been validated, e.g., if one starts from a non-empty lexicon, then $\Pi(l) = 1$ for all these lemmas.

3.3 Manual Validation

The manual validation process is performed on the ordered list of lemmas generated at the last step. The aim of this step is to classify the best-ranked lemmas in one of the following classes:

- valid lemmas, that are appended to the lexicon,
- erroneous lemmas generated by valid forms (i.e., by verbal, nominal or adjectival forms that have to be associated in the future to another lemma),
- erroneous lemmas generated by invalid forms (i.e., by forms that are either not verbal, nominal or adjectival, or that are misspelled; such forms have to be filtered out from the corpus during the next iteration of the complete process).

This manual validation step can be performed very quickly, and without any indepth linguistic knowledge. We asked a native speaker of Slovak, who has no scientific background in linguistics, to perform this task. The only preparation needed is to learn the names of the inflectional categories. Once several dozens or hundredths of lemmas are validated this way, the whole loop is started anew.

4   Results and Perspectives

Using this method, and after a few iterations of the whole loop (including 2 hours only of cumulated validation time), we have acquired, in a few hours only, a lexicon of Slovak language containing approximately 2,000 lemmas generating more than 50,000 inflected forms (i.e., 26,000 different tokens[8]). These forms cover 74% of the attested forms of the corpus that have not been ruled out manually (like prepositions, adverbs, particles, pronouns, and so on). By construction, the precision is 100% since our lexicon is manually validated[9].

While preliminary[10], these results are very promising, especially if the short validation time is taken into account. First, they show the feasibility of a process of automatic lexical acquisition, even on a relatively small corpus. This method only relies on the fact that Slovak has a rich morphology. Therefore, it can be applied easily to any language (or category in a language) for which one has a morphological module that can be used in both manners (from lemmas to forms and from forms to hypothetical lemmas). Second, they have led to a Slovak lexicon that will be made freely available on Internet in the near future, under a free-software license. While not yet wide-coverage, this lexicon is interesting for at least two reasons: it contains information on derivational morphology (prefixes, nominalizations and adjectivizations of verbs), and it contains real-life words found in the corpus that may be absent from standard dictionaries, as for example *korpusový*, adjectivization of *korpus* ("corpus").

---

[8] Indeed, a same token can be the inflected form of several lemmas, or more frequently several inflected forms of the same lemma but with different morphological tags.

[9] Figures given here concerns the current state of the lexicon. As said later on, we go on acquiring this lexicon, and these figures will be higher very soon.

[10] In particular, the corpus we used could be much bigger. This should be the case in our future work on this topic.

Of course, we are still going on in the validation process and iteration of the whole loop. We also want to increase the size of our corpus, both to raise the precision of the process and to acquire a more varied lexicon.

References

1. Daille, B.: Morphological rule induction for terminology acquisition. In: Proceedings of the 18th International Conference on Computational Linguistics (COLING 2000), Saarbrucken, Germany (2000) 215–221
2. Dunning, T.: Accurate methods for the statistics of surprise and coincidence. Computational Linguistics **19** (1993) 61–74
3. Briscoe, T., Carroll, J.: Automatic extraction of subcategorization from corpora. In: Proceedings of the Fifth Conference on Applied Natural Language Processing, Washington, DC (1997)
4. Oliver, A., Castellón, I., Màrquez, L.: Use of internet for augmenting coverage in a lexical acquisition system from raw corpora: application to russian. In: IESL Workshop of RANLP '03, Bulgaria, Borovets, Bulgaria (2003)
5. Oliver, A., Tadić, M.: Enlarging the croatian morphological lexicon by automatic lexical acquisition from raw corpora. In: Proceedings of LREC'04, Lisbon, Portugal (2004) 1259–1262
6. Clément, L., Sagot, B., Lang, B.: Morphology based automatic acquisition of large-coverage lexica. In: Proceedings of LREC'04, Lisbon, Portugal (2004) 1841–1844
7. Jazykovedný ústav Ľ. Štúra SAV: Slovenský národný korpus (Slovak National Corpus). URL: http://korpus.juls.savba.sk (2004)
8. Pečiar, Š. *and others*: Pravidlá Slovenského Pravopisu. Vydavateľstvo Slovenskej Akadémie Vied, Bratislava (1970)

Equilibrium Points of Single-Layered Neural Networks with Feedback and Applications in the Analysis of Text Documents

Alexander Shmelev and Vyacheslav Avdeychik

Bineuro, 195415, 53, Vernadskogo pr., Moscow, Russia
{a.shmelev,v.avdeychik}@bineuro.ru

Abstract. This report describes a technology of coding of the text documents used within the framework of a working breadboard model of meta-search system developed in "Bineuro" with context-dependent processing and with classification of search results. The technology of automatic analysis and coding of text documents is based on text corpus representation in the form of an associative semantic network. Code vectors are generated as the equilibrium points of neural network with feedback and with parallel dynamics, such as Hopfild network with an asymmetrical matrix of feedback. These code vectors can be used for tasks of ranging, automatic cluster analysis of documents and in many other tasks connected to automatic post processing of search results by the search engines on the Internet. As an example of application of code vectors we will consider below a task of classification of text documents.

1 Definitions and Theorems

The basic object of research submitted in this report is the equilibrium points of dynamic single-layered neural networks with feedbacks and parallel dynamics. The matrix of feedbacks is symmetric for classical Hopfild networks [1]. This restriction is absent for networks considered by us. The dynamics of a status of such a neural network can be described as follows. During each moment of time of discrete time series $t = 0, 1, 2, \ldots$ the output signals of neurons are multiplied on corresponding weight factors synapse connections, then are summarized and go to the inputs of neurons where constant external biases also enter as additional components. The received summary value will be transformed by means of activity functions of corresponding neurons which output values form a status vector of the neural network at the following time moment. We shall assume that neurons activity functions are continued.

Before we pass to studying statuses of equilibrium points of such neural networks we shall give some definitions and designations. Let $W = (w_{ij})$, $w_{ij} \in \mathbb{R}$ be a matrix of weights of feedbacks of a neural network. We do not assume that a matrix of weights W is symmetric.

Let $h_k : \mathbb{R} \to \mathbb{R}$, $k = 1, \ldots, n$ be a activity function of k-th neuron. The dynamics of a network is determined by the performance of sequence of iterations, at each the fixed entrance bias vector $x = (x_1, \ldots, x_n)$ not dependent on iteration number and also the weighed sum of output values of a network on previous iteration, where weighing occurs according to feedbacks and their weight values, enter on the network input

V. Matoušek et al. (Eds.): TSD 2005, LNAI 3658, pp. 164–170, 2005.

$$x_k^t = x_k + \sum_{i=1}^{n} w_{ik} y_i^{t-1}.$$ (1)

On an output of t-th iteration we obtain a vector $y^t = (y_1^t, \ldots, y_n^t)$, where

$$y_k^t = h_k \left(x_k^t \right) = h_k \left(x_k + \sum_{i=1}^{n} w_{ik} y_i^{t-1} \right).$$ (2)

Definition 1. *A map $H_x : \mathbb{R}^n \to \mathbb{R}^n$, where*

$$H_x (y) = \left(h_1 \left(x_1 + \sum_{i=1}^{n} w_{i1} y_i \right), \ldots, h_n \left(x_n + \sum_{i=1}^{n} w_{in} y_i \right) \right),$$ (3)

is called a transfer map corresponding to the input vector $x \in \mathbb{R}^n$.

Definition 2. *A vector $y = (y_1, \ldots, y_n)$ is called an equilibrium point of neural network corresponding to the input vector x, if the following equality is held*

$$H_x (y) = y.$$ (4)

Theorem 1. *If an activity function $h_k : \mathbb{R} \to \mathbb{R}$ is continued and bounded $\forall k = 1, \ldots, n$, than there exists at least one equilibrium point for every input vector $x = (x_1, \ldots, x_n)$. Besides, if an activity function $h_k : \mathbb{R} \to \mathbb{R}$ is smooth $\forall k = 1, \ldots, n$, than there exist odd number of equilibrium points for the input vector of a general position (i.e. the set of input vectors with even or infinity number of equilibrium points is the set of zero measure).*

Proof. Because the transfer map H_x is bounded, there exists a ball $B^n \subset \mathbb{R}^n$ with a radius large enough and the center in the origin of coordinates, that $H_x (B^n) \subset B^n$. Brouwer theorem guarantees existence of the fixed point of the transfer map $H_x : B^n \to B^n$, because H_x is continued.

In order to prove second conclusion of this theorem we consider two submanifolds in direct product $\mathbb{R}^n \times \mathbb{R}^n$:

1. $\Delta = \{(y, y) \mid y \in \mathbb{R}^n\}$ - graph of the identical map $id : \mathbb{R}^n \to \mathbb{R}^n$,
2. $\Gamma_x = \{(y, H_x (y)) \mid y \in \mathbb{R}^n\}$ - graph of the transfer map $H_x : \mathbb{R}^n \to \mathbb{R}^n$.

Sard theorem claims that by means of infinitesimally small deformation of the parameter x, a graph Γ_x of the map H_x may be reduced to general position with respect to the diagonal Δ. In case of general position the submanifolds Δ and Γ_x are transversally intersected in some set of points $\Delta \cap \Gamma_x$ without any limit points. As the transfer map H_x is bounded, the set $\Delta \cap \Gamma_x$ is finite for input vector x of general position, moreover, the submanifolds Δ and Γ_x are transversal for every point $y \in \Delta \cap \Gamma_x$. Hence, we may calculate the intersection index $\Gamma_x \circ \Delta$ as Lefschetz number $\Lambda (H_x)$ of the map H_x.

It is known that Lefschetz number is represented as the sum

$$\Lambda (H_x) = \sum_{y \in \Delta \cap \Gamma_x} sign (y),$$ (5)

where

$$sign\,(y) = \begin{cases} +1 \text{ when } \det\,(E - d_y H_x) > 0, \\ -1 \text{ when } \det\,(E - d_y H_x) < 0. \end{cases}$$

$(\det\,(E - d_y H_x) \neq 0$, because the submanifolds Δ and Γ_x are transversally intersected). Lefschetz number $\Lambda\,(H_x) = \pm 1$, since the transfer map H_x is homotopic to the constant map. We are designate as A a number of points $y \in \Delta \cap \Gamma_x$ with $sign\,(y) = +1$, and as B a number of points $y \in \Delta \cap \Gamma_x$ with $sign\,(y) = -1$. Then $\Lambda\,(H_x) = A - B = \pm 1$. Consequently, a total number of intersection points $\sharp\,(\Delta \cap \Gamma_x) = A + B = 2B \pm 1$ is odd number. $\square$

The following definition restricts the class of neural networks under consideration.

Definition 3. *The single-layered neural network with feedback weight matrix $W = (w_{ij})$ is called an associative semantic neural network if the following conditions occur:*

1. *w_{ij} is a weight of the connection from output of i-th neuron to input of j-th neuron;*
2. *$0 \leq w_{ij} \leq 1$, $\forall i, j = 1, \dots, n$, where n is a number of neurons;*
3. *$\sum_{j=1}^{n} w_{ij} \leq 1$, $\forall i = 1, \dots, n$.*

Theorem 2. *If a activity function $h_k : \mathbb{R} \to \mathbb{R}$, $\forall k = 1, \dots, n$ is contracting, then there exist the unique equilibrium point $y = (y_1, \dots, y_n)$ of associative semantic neural network for every input vector $x = (x_1, \dots, x_n)$. Moreover, the dependence $y = y\,(x)$ is continued (and smooth, if the activity functions $h_k : \mathbb{R} \to \mathbb{R}$ are smooth). The sequence $y^t = H_x\,(y^{t-1})$, converges to the equilibrium point $y\,(x)$, for every initial vector y^0, moreover, the degree of convergence is proportional to the degree of convergence of sequence r^n, for some $r \in (0, 1)$.*

Proof. The conclusions follow from Picard theorem on fixed point of contracting map. It is sufficient to prove that the transfer map H_x is contracted.

Let $r \in (0, 1)$ be such number, that the inequality $|h_k\,(u) - h_k\,(v)| \leq r|u - v|$ is held $\forall u, v \in \mathbb{R}$, $\forall k = 1, \dots, n$. And let $y, z \in \mathbb{R}^n$, where $y = (y_1, \dots, y_n)$, $y = (y_1, \dots, y_n)$. Then

$$d\,(H_x\,(y), H_x\,(z)) = \tag{6}$$

$$\sqrt{\sum_{k=1}^{n} \left(h_k \left(x_k + \sum_{i=1}^{n} w_{ik} y_i \right) - h_k \left(x_k + \sum_{i=1}^{n} w_{ik} z_i \right) \right)^2} \leq \tag{7}$$

$$r \sqrt{\sum_{k=1}^{n} \left(\left(x_k + \sum_{i=1}^{n} w_{ik} y_i \right) - \left(x_k + \sum_{i=1}^{n} w_{ik} z_i \right) \right)^2} = \tag{8}$$

$$r \sqrt{\sum_{k=1}^{n} \sum_{i=1}^{n} w_{ik}^2 \,(y_i - z_i)^2} = r \sqrt{\sum_{i=1}^{n} (y_i - z_i)^2 \sum_{k=1}^{n} w_{ik}^2} \leq \tag{9}$$

$$r \sqrt{\sum_{i=1}^{n} (y_i - z_i)^2 \sum_{k=1}^{n} w_{ik}} \leq r \sqrt{\sum_{i=1}^{n} (y_i - z_i)^2} = r d\,(y, z), \tag{10}$$

where $d(.,.)$ is Euclidian metrics in the space $\mathbb{R}^n$. Hence, $\exists r \in (0,1)$, that the inequality $d(H_x(y), H_x(z)) \leq rd(y,z)$ is held $\forall y, z \in \mathbb{R}^n$. And hence, the map H_x is contracted.   □

Example 1. If activity functions of neurons of associative semantic neural network are logistic

$$h(u) = \frac{1}{1 + e^{-u}} \tag{11}$$

then the number $r \in (0,1)$ we shall choose as $r = \frac{1}{2}$, because

$$0 \leq h'(u) \leq 1. \tag{12}$$

In this case the degree of convergence of sequence of output vectors to the equilibrium point have a degree $\frac{1}{2^n}$.

2   Generation Algorithm of Semantic Code Vectors for Text Documents

It will be shown below how to use the constructed associative semantic neural network for construction of vectors of text documents coding sense. From the point of view of semantics, such a network induces a semantic context within the framework of which (or in view of which) code vectors of text documents are generated. Besides the results of testing of the received code vectors will be submitted by the example of a task of text documents classification.

Let some corpus of text documents C is defined, and the dictionary of terms V representing some set of words and word-combinations is defined. The dictionary V can be constructed, for example, by selection and morphological analysis of the most significant words and word-combinations in the documents of the corpus C carrying the basic semantic loading (for example - nouns).

We compare (V, C) to the associative semantic network which is the oriented graph. We shall designate through $A = \{A_i \mid i = 1, \ldots, N\}$ set of nodes of a network, and through $\langle A_i, A_j \rangle$ - the oriented edge of a network with the beginning in node A_i and the ending in node A_j. The set of nodes of an associative semantic network bijectively corresponds to the set of elements of the dictionary V. In other words, each node of the graph corresponds to some term of the dictionary V. Further, in order to simplify we shall designate the node of the graph and the corresponding term by the same letter.

Weight value w_{ij} is compared to each oriented edge $\langle A_i, A_j \rangle$. There exists a set of ways of assignment of weights to edges of the associative semantic network. We shall consider the following two methods.

Method 1. Construction Under Sentences

If a couple of terms $\{A,B\}$ is included into one common sentence of some document of the document corpus, the nodes A and B are connected by edges $\langle A, B \rangle$ and $\langle B, A \rangle$. Let us designate:

– $\sharp A$ - number of entrances of the term A in all documents of the corpus;
– $\sharp\{A, B\}$ - number of joint entrances of the terms A and B in sentences of the document corpus.

Let us compare weight value $w_{ij} = \frac{\#\{A_i, B_j\}}{\#A_i}$ to the edge $\langle A_i, A_j \rangle$ and weight value $w_{ji} = \frac{\#\{A_i, B_j\}}{\#A_j}$ to the return edge $\langle A_j, A_i \rangle$. Weights w_{ij} satisfy to the following conditions: $0 \leq w_{ij} \leq 1, \sum_{j=1}^{n} w_{ij} \leq 1, \forall i, j = 1, \dots, n$. The weight w_{ij} can be interpreted as "densities" of joint entrances of terms A_i and A_j in sentences of document corpus under relation to all entrances of the term A_i in document corpus, or as a relative probability $P(\{A_i, A_j\} \mid A_i)$. We have $w_{ij} = w_{ji} = 0$ if terms A_i and A_j have no joint entrances in sentences of the corpus.

Method 2. Construction Under Window

We shall consider the nearest neighborhood (window) for each word in the document corpus. For example, we shall consider a window like

$$[(w_{n-2}, w_{n-1}), f_n, (w_{n+1}, w_{n+2})]. \tag{13}$$

Here f_n is the central element of a window, and the window radius is 2. For example, for a piece of the text *"this parrot is no more"* such a window will look like this: *[(this parrot) is (no more)]*.

We fix radius of the window. If a couple of terms $\{A, B\}$ is included into one common window of the document corpus, nodes A and B are connected by edges $\langle A, B \rangle$ and $\langle B, A \rangle$. We shall designate:

- $\#A$ - number of entrances of the term A in all documents of the corpus;
- $\#\{A, B\}$ - number of entrances of the term B into all windows with the central element A.

The rest is the same as in the first method.

The constructed oriented graph is called an associative semantic network for the given document corpus. This associative semantic network can be connected with the associative semantic neural network by the following construction. We compare node A_i of the semantic graph to the neuron i of a neural network. Target value of neuron i we shall submit on the input of neuron j with weight w_{ij}. As an activity function of neurons we shall choose, for example, the logistical map $h(u) = \frac{1}{1+e^{-u}}$. This neural network, obviously, satisfies to all conditions of theorem 2.

In order to construct a code vector of some text document D let us define the initial code vector of length N, where N is the number of nodes of an associative semantic network, and at the same time it's also the number of elements in the dictionary of terms. One of the way of definition of an initial vector means that i-th component of an initial vector is equal 1 if i-th term is included into the document D and 0 in otherwise. At definition of an initial vector it is possible to take into account also weights of terms in the document D, entering relative frequency of entrance of the given term in the document.

The initial code vector moves on an input of an associative semantic neural network as an entrance vector of biases and then the sequence of iterations which by the theorem 2 converges to some unique equilibrium point continuously dependent on an initial vector is carried out. The found equilibrium point C_D of an associative semantic neural network, by definition, is a semantic code vector of the document D.

Each component of the semantic code vector represents a numerical rating of semantic weight of a corresponding term in the given text. The components of a semantic code vector allow to estimate the relative contribution of various concepts to the common sense of the text.

If we analyze formation of a semantic code vector during consecutive iterations to an equilibrium point of a neural network it is visible, that on the first iteration on an output of a network we obtain a vector, which nonzero components bijectively correspond to the terms which are included in the text. If the text doesn't contain some terms then the corresponding component in this vector will be equal to zero. On the second iteration to nonzero components of the first iteration those components are added which correspond to the terms which are not included in the text, but have direct associative connections with terms included in the text. On the third iteration nonzero components are added which correspond to terms which have direct associative semantic connections with terms of previous iteration, etc.

Thus, after achieving of the equilibrium point, components of a code vector will represent distribution of the weights which take into account the semantic contribution of terms corresponding to them of the considered text document within the framework of a context determined of the document corpus C.

3 Semantic Code Vectors in a Task of Text Classification

To estimate the semantic code vectors of text documents numerical experiments on classification of sample of text documents have been carried out. As a measure of "quality" of coding the percent of correctly classified documents by means of the trained classifying neural network has been chosen.

In order to construct an associative semantic network, and also to carry out morphological analysis of words software product WordNet 2.0 has been used. Formation of weight values of semantic connections has been executed by a method of construction under sentences on the basis of the analysis of a collection of 37000 texts, novels and newspaper articles. The text collection takes about 50 MB. As an experimental sample of documents for testing semantic coding the collection of documents open in a free access in Internet [2] was used. This collection represents a set of electronic letters divided on subjects. Each letter concerns to one subject (class). We have 20 classes in this collection in all.

We have been created the separate neural network for each class, which should separate code vectors (corresponding to documents) belonging and not belonging to the given class. We have been used single-layered perceptron network with one binary neuron, carrying out linear division of classes for classification. We have been selected 20 documents from each class for testing from all set of documents. The semantic code vectors for all selected documents preliminary have been created and moved on an input of a network. An unit output corresponded to that the document belongs to the given class, and zero one - that does not belong. Each of 20 networks was trained during 5000 cycles on training sample. We have been analyzed network outputs on the vectors corresponding to training sample for a rating of code vectors. Results of experiment are shown in Table 1, where

$$Precision(class) = \frac{\text{number of documents refered to the class correctly}}{\text{total number of documents refered to the class}}, \quad (14)$$

Table 1. Precision and Recall of text classification

Class name	Precision	Recall	F1
ralt.atheism	1,00	1,00	1,00
comp.graphics	1,00	0,75	0,86
comp.os.ms-windows.misc	1,00	1,00	1,00
comp.sys.ibm.pc.hardware	1,00	0,45	0,62
comp.sys.mac.hardware	1,00	1,00	1,00
comp.windows.x	1,00	1,00	1,00
misc.forsale	1,00	1,00	1,00
rec.autos	1,00	0,75	0,86
rec.motorcycles	1,00	1,00	1,00
rec.sport.baseball	1,00	1,00	1,00
rec.sport.hockey	1,00	1,00	1,00
sci.crypt	1,00	1,00	1,00
sci.electronics	1,00	0,45	0,62
sci.med	1,00	1,00	1,00
sci.space	1,00	1,00	1,00
soc.religion.christian	1,00	1,00	1,00
talk.politics.guns	1,00	1,00	1,00
talk.politics.mideast	0,41	1,00	0,58
talk.politics.misc	1,00	1,00	1,00
talk.religion.misc	1,00	1,00	1,00
Average main	**0,97**	**0,92**	**0,93**

$$Recall(class) = \frac{\text{number of documents refered to the class correctly}}{\text{actual number of documents in the class}} \qquad (15)$$

$$F1(class) = \frac{2Recall(class)Precision(class)}{Recall(class) + Precision(class)} \qquad (16)$$

4   Conclusion

In this paper we presented a method of coding of the texts based on text corpus representation in the form of an associative semantic network. As our experimental results on text collection have shown, these codes are very effective in text classification from the point of view of recall and precision. Moreover, the complexity of an algorithm of code construction is enough low, because, as it has been shown, the degree of convergence to the equilibrium point of associative semantic network is proportional to the degree of convergence of geometric progression.

References

1. Luger, G.F.: Artificial intelligence. Structures and strategies for complex problem solving. Addison Wesley, 2002.
2. http://www-2.cs.cmu.edu/afs/cs.cmu.edu/project/theo-20/www/data/news20.tar.gz

A Syntax and Semantics Linking Algorithm for the Chinese Language*

Zhou Qiang and Dang Zhengfa

State Key Laboratory of Intelligent Technology and Systems
Dept. of Computer Science and Technology
Tsinghua University, Beijing 100084, P.R. China
zq-lxd@mail.tsinghua.edu.cn, dantifer@tsinghua.edu.cn

Abstract. Many statistics-based approaches have been proposed to label semantic roles automatically. For language lack of large-scale semantically annotated corpora, e.g. Chinese, these approaches do not work well. In this paper we proposed an unsupervised syntax and semantic linking algorithm, and make full use of current Chinese language resources to equip it with detailed linking knowledge. Therefore, the semantic role labeling task can be attributed to a data-driven application of the linking algorithm. Some preliminary experiment results demonstrate the ability of the linking algorithm for the automatic semantic role labeling on current Chinese treebank.

1 Introduction

Recent years have witnessed the growing interest in corpora with semantic annotation, especially on the predicate-argument structure and thematic role level. Some semantically-annotated corpus, such as FrameNet[1] and PropBank[6], have been manually built in English. More and more NLP applications, including information extraction, question answering and machine translation, are expecting the supports from semantic annotation of text corpora.

Realizing the importance of this task, many researchers have devoted themselves to the exploration of automatic semantic role labeling algorithms, including Gildea[5], Chen[2], Fleischman[4], Thompson[9] and Swier[8]. Most of them took semantic role labeling as a statistical classification task, and focused on the technical aspects of supervised learning models. In order to optimize the performance of the models, they need "new features", "more data", and "more sophisticated models" [12]. These supervised learning methods are limited by their reliance on the semantically-annotated corpus as training data, which are expensive to produce and may not be representative. To deal with these problems, Swier[8] developed a method of unsupervised semantic role labeling that avoids the need for expensive manual labeling of text, and enables the use of large and representative corpora.

As far as Chinese is concerned, things are quite different. We don't have large-scale semantically annotated corpus now, so we cannot use similar statistical methods

---

* This work was supported by the Chinese National Science Foundation (Grant No. 60173008). The authors thank three anonymous reviewers for their helpful comments and advices.

V. Matoušek et al. (Eds.): TSD 2005, LNAI 3658, pp. 171–178, 2005.

to label semantic roles automatically. To our knowledge, the only rule-based exploration for Chinese was done by Xue & Kulick [11]. They built a labeling tool to add semantic roles for Penn Chinese Treebank. The preliminary evaluations on 30 Chinese verbs demonstrated the feasibility to automatically label semantic roles by using some simple mapping rules.

In fact, the interface between syntax and semantics is also the hot spots in theoretical linguistics community. Many linguists proposed to divide the predicate-argument structure into two different descriptive layers: the syntactic argument layer and semantic argument layer, and tried to find some universal linking principles between these two layers so as to form a good solution for the syntax and semantics relation problem. Although for different goals, their research achievements can bring us some new views to reformat the current semantic role labeling task in computational linguistics community.

In the paper, we proposed a syntax and semantic linking algorithm to computationally simulate some useful research achievements obtained by theoretical linguists, and equipped the algorithm with detailed linking knowledge extracted from current large-scale Chinese treebank and semantic lexicons. Therefore, the semantic role labeling task can be attributed to a data-driven syntax to semantics linking procedure under the supporting of the linking algorithm and language resources. Some preliminary experimental results demonstrate the ability of the linking algorithm for the automatic semantic role labeling on current Chinese treebanks.

The structure of the paper is as follows. Section 2 gives the overview of the linking algorithm. Section 3 introduces some Chinese language resources used in the algorithm. Section 4 discusses our current semantic role labeling procedure. Section 5 gives some evaluation results. The final section 6 is the conclusion.

2   The Syntax and Semantics Linking Algorithm

Figure 1 shows the overall structure of the syntax and semantics linking algorithm, where the syntactic representation, linking rules and semantic representation form the kernel data-driven computational modules of the algorithm, and the treebank and semantic lexicons can provide the useful syntactic and semantic descriptive knowledge for linking procedure. They can be adjusted for different languages. So the architecture design guarantees the flexibility and portability of the linking algorithm for different language applications. For the purpose of syntax and semantics linking, we should firstly select the suitable syntactic and semantic representations. In respect of syntax, we adopted an optimal representation proposed by Van Valin *et al* [10] to reflect the following two universal distinctions that every language makes in clause level. One is the contrasts between predicating elements and non-predicating elements. The other is the contrasts between these noun phrases (NPs) and preposition phrases (PPs) that are arguments of the predicate and those that are not. Under this scheme, each clause is partitioned into *nucleus* predicates, their *core* arguments and the *periphery* parts. In respect of semantics, we adopted the commonly-used scheme of predicate-argument structure and thematic role representation, where key points are lexical decomposition, logical structure, and thematic roles.

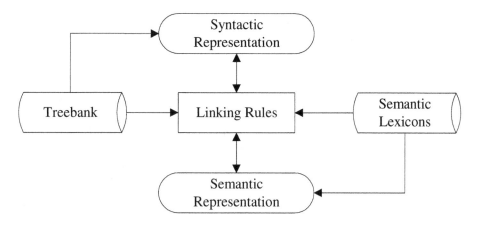

Fig. 1. Overview of the syntax and semantics linking algorithm

The implementation of the syntax and semantics linking is controlled by the linking rule module. We designed two types of linking rules: verb frame rules and preposition pattern rules.

A verb frame rule describes the core argument linking under the control of a predicate verb. It consists of several slots to describe the detailed information of syntactic arguments, semantic arguments and their linking relations. The linear priority arrangements of the predicate verb and slots in the frame show the special syntactic alternations in different languages. So they are language-dependent, and some language-specific resources can be used to equip the suitable knowledge.

A preposition phrase in a sentence has two types of semantic contributions. Firstly, as a special predicating element, a preposition can have its own arguments and form a logical structure similar with that of a verb. Secondly, as a periphery part in a clause, a preposition phrase can describe many other important situation elements of different events, such as time, location and so on. So a preposition pattern rule should reflect the above two kinds of linking knowledge.

In Chinese, there are some special prepositions only have one of the above functions in a clause, i.e. they can only introduce some special semantic roles in the sentence. Some typical examples are as follows:

– *Bei, Gei, Rang*: to introduce Agent and Theme.
– *Ba, Jiang*: to introduce Patient and Result.

These prepositions and their corresponding PPs are treated as special core arguments and they are given special descriptions in the verb frame rules.

3   Chinese Language Resources

After several years of research in Chinese NLP, we have accumulated many useful Chinese language resources, which can be used to equip the necessary Chinese knowledge in the linking algorithm. We will briefly introduce three main parts of them in the section.

(1) Tsinghua Chinese Treebank (TCT)

TCT is a large-scale syntactically-annotated Chinese corpus[14]. Its current version TCT(v1.0) contains about 1,000,000 Chinese words of texts drawn from a balanced collection of literary, journalistic, academic, and other documents published in 1990s. A characteristic of TCT is the usage of a new two-tagset annotation scheme for Chinese treebank[15]. Under this scheme, every Chinese sentence will be annotated with a complete parse tree, where each non-terminal constituent is assigned with two tags. One is the syntactic constituent tag, which describes its external functional relation with other constituents in the parse tree. The other is the grammatical relation tag, which describes the internal structural relation of its sub-components. They form an integrated information annotation for the syntactic constituent in a parse tree through top-down and bottom-up descriptions.

The detailed syntactic description information under this scheme provides us with flexible selections to automatically transform current phrase structure trees into other useful syntactic representations, such as dependency trees[3] and functional chunk sequences[16], where the contrasts between predicating elements and non-predicating elements and the explicit relations between possible syntactic arguments (NPs and PPs) and their predicates can be easily represented. We can use some simple heuristics to discriminate the real syntactic arguments or adjuncts (non-arguments) among them. Therefore, most typical syntactic templates with explicit syntactic arguments can be easily extracted and summarized to form the optimal syntactic representation for the Chinese language.

(2) Contemporary Chinese Predicate Verb Dictionary (CCPVDP)

CCPVD is a dictionary for the semantic role and frame knowledge of Chinese predicate verbs[7]. In the dictionary, each verb entry will be given the detailed descriptions of the semantic roles of its core arguments, their selectional restrictions and the corresponding syntactic constituents and grammatical functions. Its key characteristic lies in the provision of some basic or transformed role frames to describe syntactic alternations of different semantic arguments in Chinese real text sentences. The following is an example:

- Verb entry: *huode* (Obtain)
- Semantic role 1: Experiencer, its typical syntactic argument: np-SUB
- Semantic role 2: Theme, its typical syntactic argument: np-OBJ
- Basic role frame: Experiencer *huode* (Obtain) Theme

From it, we can extract such a verb frame rule: np-SUB *huode* np-OBJ → Experiencer *huode* Theme. It can build the direct linking relation between the subject and object constituents in the syntactic argument structure of a clause with the Experiencer and Theme roles of its semantic argument representation.

The current CCPVD version contains 5646 Chinese high-frequency verbs with 7575 different senses, which form 8389 basic semantic role frames and 5101 transformed frames. All the information was manually summarized by linguistic experts based on language performance examples extracted from large-scale Chinese corpus. They can provide important knowledge for verb frame rules in current linking algorithm.

(3) Contemporary Chinese Grammatical Knowledge Base (CCGKB) Apart from the above language resources, we also used some semantic knowledge extracted from

the CCGKB[13]. In the preposition bank of the CCGKB, the possible semantic role implementations of 94 high-frequency Chinese prepositions are given. They can provide basic knowledge for preposition pattern rules in current linking algorithm. Among them, 58 (62%) prepositions have one possible role explanation, 36 (34%) prepositions have two or more possible role explanations. So some detailed role disambiguation knowledge should be given for them in the corresponding preposition pattern rules. The following is an example: *yi*(by) NP → Manner, which means this PP can build the 'Manner' role relation between its prepositional object NP with the *nucleus* predicate in a clause.

4   Semantic Role Labeling in Chinese

Now, the semantic role labeling task can be attributed to such a computational problem: Firstly, transform the parse trees into the uniform syntactic representation. Secondly, link the syntax to semantics under the supporting of the linking algorithm. Thirdly, label the suitable thematic roles for different syntactic constituents, based on the role information described in the corresponding linking rules.

To make full use of our current language resources, we adopted the following processing strategies: (1) We selected the parse trees extracted from TCT as the input data of the labeling algorithm, where the correct syntactically-annotated sentences after manual proofreading can make us focus on the performance evaluation of the kernel parts of the linking algorithm; (2) We used the CCPVD and CCGKB to equip the main linking knowledge in verb frame rules and preposition pattern rules respectively; (3) We selected the general thematic roles that are commonly assumed in linguistic theory, including Agent, Patient, Theme, Time, etc. as the labeling target. They can be easily mapped from the semantic roles defined in CCPVD and CCGKB.

The detailed semantic role labeling procedure is as follows:

Firstly, we automatically transform the complete phrase structure trees annotated in TCT into dependency trees, where the relations between predicating elements and their possible syntactic arguments can be clearly represented. Then, we use some simple heuristics to discriminate the core arguments and peripheral adjuncts among them. In Chinese sentences, most NPs in the subject or object function positions can be treated as the core arguments, and most PPs in the adverbial function positions can be treated as the peripheral adjuncts. But some PPs among them with special prepositions, such as *Bei, Ba*, etc. should be treated as the core arguments. In the meantime, some complex Chinese verb structures, including multiple verb structures[1] and conjunction structures, should be separated into several simple verb frames. After the above approaches, we can get the suitable syntactic representation for further syntax to semantics linking.

Secondly, we search all possible relevant rules in the linking rule base by using the predicate verbs and prepositions as keywords. Then, we match the syntactic arguments with the suitable slots in verb frames and preposition patterns to find a best linking rule. To deal with some argument ellipsis phenomena in real text sentences, we also

---

[1] There are two or more infinitive verbs in a Chinese clause. For example, in the Chinese sentence: *"Ta qu tushuguan cha ziliao"*(He went to a library to look up some data.), there are two infinitive verbs: *"qu"* and *"cha"*, which describe two co-occurrence events.

propose some simple partially matching strategies. For example, we can use the complete verb frame rule: "np-SUB *Huode* np-OBJ" to match the subject ellipsis structure: "*Huode* np-OBJ" and the object ellipsis structure "np-SUB *Huode*" to get the suitable semantic role annotations for them.

Finally, all the referring expressions in the syntactic representation can be associated with the suitable argument variables in the semantic representation. So the thematic roles for them can be automatically labeled in the sentence.

Now, we can give some further explanations about the above labeling procedure through a detailed example.

We select such a TCT annotated sentence as the input of the semantic role labeling algorithm: [dj-ZW *Liuyisi*/nP [vp-ZZ [pp-JB *yi*/p [mp-DZ 9.9/m *miao*/q]] [vp-PO [vp-AD *huode*/v *le*/u] [np-DZ [mp-DZ 100/m *mi*/q] *jinpai*/n]]]] ./w^2 (Lewis won the gold medal in the 100-metre with a time of 9.9 second).

After transforming it into a dependency tree, we obtain the following functional chunk sequence of the sentence: [np-SUB *Liuyisi*/nP] [pp-ADV *yi*/p 9.9/m *miao*/q] [vp-PRED *huode*/v *le*/u] [np-OBJ 100/m *mi*/q *jinpai*/n]. They provide us with enough information to discriminate the nucleus predicate, core arguments and peripheral adjuncts in the sentence. Therefore, we can easily extract the following verb frame and preposition pattern structures:

– Verb frame: *Liuyisi*/nP(Lewis) *huode*/v(win) *jinpai*/n(gold medal);
– Preposition pattern: *yi*/p(by) *miao*/q(seconds);
    Then, after the syntax to semantic linking, we obtain the following semantic role labeling result: [PRED: *huode*, SUB-Experiencer: *Liuyisi*, ADV-Manner: 9.9 *miao*, OBJ-Theme: 100 *mi jinpai*]

5   Experiments and Discussions

To test the performance of the semantic role labeling algorithm, we stochastically selected several annotated sentences from TCT, automatically transformed them into dependency representation, and randomly extracted 1655 verb frames and 560 preposition patterns from them as the input data of the labeling algorithm. Then, we manually checked the automatic labeling results and classified them into the following three types: (1) Knowledge missing cases: We cannot find the suitable linking knowledge; (2) Correct labeling cases: All the slots in verb frames or preposition patterns must be assigned the correct semantic roles; (3) Error labeling cases: There are one or more labeling errors in the verb and preposition rules.

Table 1 summarized our results. Among about 15% cases of missing verbs, we find most of them are compound verbs. For example, *Jijin*(squeeze into) = *Ji*(squeeze) + *Jin*(into), whose logical structure can be represented as: Squeeze(x,y) CAUSE Into(x,y), where x and y can be related to different thematic roles of two predicates "Squeeze"

---

^{2} The part-of-speech and syntactic tags used in this sentence are as follows: nP–personal name, p–preposition, m–numeral, q–classifier, v–verb, u–particle, w–punctuation; , dj–simple sentence, vp–verb phrase, pp–preposition phrase, mp–numeral phrase, np–noun phrase; ZW–subject-predicate relation, ZZ–adverbial-head relation, JB–preposition-object relation, DZ–attribute-head relation, PO–predicate-object relation.

and "Into". It is a productive word-forming pattern in Chinese. How to integrate such a sense combination scheme into current linking algorithm is an important issue we must explore in the future research. Other missing cases are due to the usages of low-frequency verbs and prepositions in real-world Chinese texts. We hope to use some word clustering and machine learning techniques to automatically acquire the related linking knowledge for them.

Table 1. Semantic role labeling results in Chinese verb frames and preposition patterns

	Knowledge missing	Correct labeling	Error labeling
verb	239	1257	159
frames	14.44%	75.95%	9.61%
preposition	44	487	29
patterns	7.86%	86.96%	5.18%

Except the non-labeling cases due to the missing knowledge, the correct labeling rate for the semantic roles in verb frames and preposition patterns can reach 88.77% and 94.38% respectively. These results are encouraging on the condition of only using some simple linking rule matching strategies. They will provide us with a good start to develop an efficient semantic role labeling tool so as to support the construction of a large-scale semantically-annotated corpus on the basis of the current syntactically-annotated corpus TCT.

An error analysis makes clear two major issues that require further study: (1) Some thematic roles cannot be correctly linked based on current simple matching strategies, because different senses of a same verb may have different role frames. Some selectional restrictions for different role representations may be useful to deal with this problem. (2) Some semantic arguments may appear in different syntactic positions in a sentence due to some special pragmatic alternations. The current linking strategies cannot deal with these problems. To integrate some universal linking principles summarized by linguists into current linking procedure may be a good solution for them.

6   Conclusions

Automatic role labeling can assign suitable semantic explanation for each referring expression in a syntactically-annotated sentence. Due to the lack of large-scale semantically-annotated corpus for building a supervised learning model in Chinese, we have to explore a new way for automatic semantic role labeling. In the paper, we proposed a syntax and semantics linking algorithm, and made full use of current Chinese language resources to equip the useful knowledge in the algorithm. Therefore, the semantic role labeling task can be attributed to a detailed application of the algorithm to the treebank sentences. Some preliminary experimental results show that except the non-labeling cases, the correct labeling rate in verb frames and preposition patterns can reach 88.77% and 94.38% respectively, based on the correct parse tree annotations in TCT.

Although these results are promising, they are only a first step in demonstrating the potential of the linking algorithm. We need to explore more new techniques to improve the descriptive ability of the algorithm. Applying some unsupervised learning methods in current TCT sentences may be a good choice. We also hope to integrate current linking techniques into our syntactic Chinese parser to build a new parser to output the syntactic trees annotated with semantic roles.

References

1. Baker, C.F., Fillmore, C.J., Lowe, J.B.: The berkeley framenet project. In Proceedings of the COLING-ACL 98, Montreal, Canada, 1998.
2. Chen, J., Rambow, O.: Use of deep linguistic features for the recognition and labeling of semantic arguments. In Proc. of the Conf. on Empirical Methods in Natural Language Processing (EMNLP-03), Sapporo, Japan. 2003.
3. Zhengfa, D., Qiang, Z.: Automatically convert treebank from phase structure to dependency structure. Technical report 04-0501, NLP group, Dept. of Computer Science and Technology, Tsinghua University, 2004.
4. Fleischman, M., Kwon, N., Hovy, E.: Maximum entropy models for FrameNet classification. In Proceedings of EMNLP-03, Sapporo, Japan, 2003.
5. Gildea, D., Jurafsky, D.: Automatic labeling of semantic roles, Computational Linguistics, 23(3), 2002, pp. 245-288.
6. Kingsbury, P., Palmer, M.: From Treebank to PropBank. In Proc. of the 3rd International Conference on Language Resources and Evaluation (LREC-2002), Las Palmas, Spain, 2002.
7. Xingguang, L. et al.: Contemporary Chinese Predicate Verb Dictionary. Beijing Language and Culture University Press, 1994.
8. Swier, R.S., Stevenson, S.: Unsupervised Semantic Role Labelling, In Proc. of the Conference on Empirical Methods in Natural Language Processing (EMNLP 2004), Barcelona, Spain, 2004, pp. 95-102.
9. Thompson, C., Levy, R., Manning, C.: A generative model for FrameNet semantic role labeling. In Proc. of the Fourteenth European Conf. on Machine Learning (ECML-03), (2003).
10. Van Valin, R.D., Lapolla, R.J.: Syntax: structure, meaning and function. Cambridge University Press, 1997.
11. Nianwen, X., Kulick, Seth.: Automatic Predicate Argument Structure Analysis of the Penn Chinese Treebank. In Proc. of Machine Translation Summit IX, New Orleans, Louisiana, USA, 2003.
12. Nianwen, X., Palmer, M.: Calibrating Features for Semantic Role Labeling. In Proc. of the Conference on EMNLP-04, 2004.
13. Shiwen, Y., Xuefeng, Z., et al.: Contemporary Chinese Grammatical Knowledge Base (Second Edition). Tsinghua University Press, 2003.
14. Qiang, Z.: Build a Large-Scale Syntactically Annotated Chinese Corpus. In Proc. of 6th International Conference of Text, Speech and Dialogue (TSD2003), Czech Republic. Springer LNAI 2807, 2003, pp. 106-113.
15. Qiang, Z.: Annotation Scheme for Chinese Treebank. Journal of Chinese Information Processing, 18(4), 2004, pp. 1-8.
16. Qiang, Z., Drabek, E.F., Ren, F.: Annotating the functional chunks in Chinese sentences. In Proc.s of the Third International Conference on Language Resources and Evaluation (LREC2002), Las Palmas, Spain, 2000, pp. 731-738.

Fuzzy Information Retrieval
Indexed by Concept Identification

Bo-Yeong Kang, Dae-Won Kim, and Hae-Jung Kim

Information and Communications University
Munji-dong, Yuseong-gu, Daejeon, Korea
kby@icu.ac.kr

Abstract. To retrieve relevant information, indexing should be achieved using the concepts of the document that a writer intends to highlight. Moreover, the user involvement is increasingly required to extract relevant information from information sources. Therefore, in the present work we propose a fuzzy retrieval model indexed by concept identification: (1) a concept identification based indexing and (2) a novel fuzzy ranking model. The concept based indexing identifies index terms by considering the concepts of a document, and a novel fuzzy ranking model based on the user preference is presented, which is able to calculates the relevance ranking based on the user preference.

1 Introduction

The growth of the Internet has seen an explosion in the amount of information available, leading to the need for increasingly efficient methods for information retrieval. However, existing information retrieval systems have some limitations in terms of the indexing and relevance ranking of documents when searching and extracting information. To extract the semantically important terms, indexing should be based not only on the occurrences of terms in a document, but also on the content of the document. Despite this obvious need, most existing indexing and weighting algorithms analyze term occurrences without attempting to resolve the meaning of the document.

The other aspect of information retrieval considered here, the user involvement, is increasingly required to extract relevant information from information sources. In searching documents, the discrimination of relevant information from non-relevant information is often processed automatically by a retrieval system; users cannot give an accurate description for their information need, and thus the discrimination values of query terms cannot be calculated accurately. In spite that the user has an ability to reflect their preference for the information need in searching, conventional systems are limited to incorporate the user preference when calculating the rank of documents.

Taking the problems of existing methods into account, in this study we develop a fuzzy retrieval model indexed by concept identification that is indexed by conceptual approach and calculates the rank of documents based on the user preference. The proposed system is indexed by the concept identification method, which was presented by Kang et al. [3] and can achieve semantically important terms based on the concept. Using the index information generated by the concept identification method, a new fuzzy similarity measure of exploiting the user preference calculates the relevance ranking between a document and a query.

V. Matoušek et al. (Eds.): TSD 2005, LNAI 3658, pp. 179–186, 2005.

2 Previous Work

Many fuzzy ranking models, often referred to as the extended boolean models, have been showing their superior performance in handling the uncertainty involved in the retrieval process [1, 2]. Here, each document D is considered as a fuzzy set where w_{di} is the degree of membership of an index term t_i to the document D. A similar interpretation can arise for the query Q. Thus, the ranking is achieved by calculating a similarity between two fuzzy sets D and Q. The best-known ranking models are the MMM, PAICE, and P-NORM.

The Mixed Min and Max (MMM) model is one of the simplest models employing fuzzy set theory. In this model, a ranking between a document and a query of the form 'D and Q' is calculated through the intersection of the two sets. Similarly, a ranking of the form 'D or Q' is calculated through the union of the two sets. Thus, given a document D with index term weights $(w_{d1}, w_{d2}, \ldots, w_{dn})$ for terms $(t_1, t_2, \ldots, t_n)$, the document-query similarity in the MMM model is computed as:

$$S(D,Q) = c_1 \times \min(w_{d1}, w_{d2}, ..., w_{dn}) + c_2 \times \max(w_{d1}, w_{d2}, ..., w_{dn}) \quad (1)$$

where c_1 and c_2 are softness coefficients.

The PAICE model is a general extension to the MMM model. In comparison to the MMM model that considers only the minimum and maximum weights for the index terms, the PAICE model incorporates all of the term weights when calculating the similarity:

$$S(D,Q) = \sum_{i=1}^{n} r^{i-1} w_{di} / \sum_{i=1}^{n} r^{i-1} \quad (2)$$

where r is a constant coefficient and w_{di} is arranged in ascending order. When $n = 2$, the PAICE model shows the same behavior as the MMM model does.

The MMM and PAICE models do not provide a way of evaluating query weights. They consider only the document weights w_{di} in their similarities. In contrast, the P-NORM model reflects the query weight $(w_{q1}, w_{q2}, \ldots, w_{qn})$ for the query terms $(t_1, t_2, \ldots, t_n)$ in its similarity. The similarity for document-query relevance is calculated as:

$$S(D,Q) = 1 - \left(\frac{\sum_{i=1}^{n} (1 - w_{di})^p (w_{qi})^p}{\sum_{i=1}^{n} (w_{qi})^p} \right)^{1/p} \quad (3)$$

where p is a control coefficient ranged from 1 to ∞. In general, the P-NORM model has shown superior effectiveness to other fuzzy relevance ranking models.

3 Fuzzy Retrieval Model Indexed by Concept Identification

3.1 Motivation and Approach

As we show below, the conventional indexing and ranking approaches are limited in their ability to retrieve the best-matched documents to a given query. First, let us consider the computation of the index terms.

"**Dr. Kenny** has invented an **anesthetic machine**. This **device** controls the **rate** at which an **anesthetic** is pumped into the **blood**".

The important terms that could be topics of the text are 'anesthetic' and 'machine'. However, the TF weight of the term 'machine' is 1, which is the same as that of semantically unimportant terms such as 'rate' and 'blood'. If we look for lexical chains in the sample text that are groups of related lexical terms [4], we obtain the six chains: 'Dr.', 'Kenny', 'machine-device', 'anesthetic-anesthetic', 'rate', and 'blood'. In this scheme, the terms 'machine' and 'device' belong to the same chain because they are related by a hypernym relation, and the two 'anesthetic' terms are related by an identity relation. This approach correctly indicates that the focus terms of the text are 'anesthetic' and 'machine/device'.

In addition to the above problem in the conventional indexing of term frequency, conventional ranking models are also suffer from the following shortcoming in their approach to uncertainty. Let us suppose that we are given a vector of query Q with a fuzzy set of the term and its membership degree:

$$Q = \{(fuzzy, 0.8), (system, 0.7), (korea, 0.3), (author, 0.2)\} \qquad (4)$$

A document collection consists of four documents (D_1, D_2, D_3, D_4) in which each document is represented as a fuzzy set of the index term and its weight.

$$D_1 = \{(fuzzy, 0.8), (system, 0.7)\}$$
$$D_2 = \{(fuzzy, 0.2), (system, 0.2), (korea, 0.3), (author, 0.2)\}$$
$$D_3 = \{(korea, 0.7), (author, 0.8)\}$$
$$D_4 = \{(fuzzy, 0.8), (system, 0.7), (korea, 0.3), (author, 0.2)\}$$

Given a query Q and the document collection, we are wondering what is the best result of ranking? Intuitively, we know that D_4 is the most relevant document and D_3 is the least relevant. However, it is arguable to say which one of the two documents D_1 and D_2 has a higher rank. One can regard that the rank of D_1 is higher than that of D_2 because D_1 contains the index terms ('fuzzy' and 'system') showing high-matching similarities. We can also consider that D_2 is more relevant than D_1 because the number of matched terms in D_2 is larger than those in D_1. Such discrepancies arise because conventional ranking models are limited to resolve the uncertainty in a retrieval system.

To solve the addressed problems, we propose a fuzzy retrieval model indexed by concept identification: (1) an indexing based on concept identification and (2) a novel ranking model based on the user preference. The indexing method takes a concept identification based approach using lexical chains for extracting index terms and assigning weights to them. The key notion of the proposed ranking model is to develop a similarity measure between fuzzy sets in which users can assign their own preference to the decision of ranking.

3.2 Indexing Scheme by Concept Identification

In this section, we briefly introduce the concept identification-based indexing suggested by Kang et al. [3].

Concepts. In accordance with the accepted view in the linguistics literature that lexical chains provide a good representation of discourse structures and topicality of segments [4], here we take each lexical chain to represent a concept that expresses one aspect of the meaning of a document. Therefore, we define a concept as a weighted lexical chain using the following definition: The relation information that was considered on the grouping of lexical terms was supported automatically by the machine readable thesaurus, WordNet [7].

Definition 1. *Let* $T = \{t_1, t_2, \ldots, t_n\}$ *be the set of terms in a document, and* $R = \{identity, synonym, hypernym(hyponym), meronym\}$ *be the set of lexical relations. Let* $C = \{c_1, c_2, \ldots, c_m\}$ *be the set of concepts in a document. A concept* $c_i \in C$ *is composed of a set of* t_j *and* r_k, *where* $r_k \in R$, $t_j \in T$. *Each* c_i *and* t_j *have a weight score that represents their respective degrees of semantic importance within a document.*

Membership Degree of an Index Term to a Document. To quantify the importance degree of a term within a document, we exploit the link information of the term. We regard that the terms heavily related to neighboring terms are semantically more important than other terms. Therefore, based on term relations, we define the scoring function for each term in the concept.

Definition 2. *Let* $T = \{t_1, t_2, \ldots, t_l\}$ *be the set of terms in a concept. Let* $R = \{identity, synonym, hypernym(hyponym), meronym\}$ *be the set of lexical relations. Let* $\tau(r_k, t_j)$ *be the number of relations* $r_k \in R$ *that term* $t_j \in T$ *has with the other terms, and let* $\omega(r_k)$ *be the weight of relation* r_k. *Then the score* $\lambda(t_j)$ *of term* t_j *is defined as:*

$$\lambda(t_j) = \sum_{r_k \in R} \tau(r_k, t_j) \times \omega(r_k), \quad 1 \leq j \leq l. \tag{5}$$

We extract the terms in each concept as index terms, and regard the term scores assigned to those terms as the index weights that represent the semantic importance within the document.

Definition 3. *Let* $C = \{c_1, c_2, \ldots, c_n\}$ *be the set of representative concepts for a document. Let* $T = \{t_{i1}, t_{i2}, \ldots, t_{il}\}$ *be the set of terms in concept* $c_i \in C$. *Then, the index terms and their weights for the document are defined as*

$$I = \{(t_{ij}, \lambda(t_{ij})) \mid t_{ij} \in c_i, 1 \leq i \leq n, 1 \leq j \leq l\}. \tag{6}$$

The normalized weight of a semantic index term becomes the membership degree of the term to a document where it was involved.

3.3   Fuzzy Relevance Ranking Based on User Preference

Having established the index terms from given documents, a ranking model to calculate the similarity between a document and a query is required. We introduce a notion of user

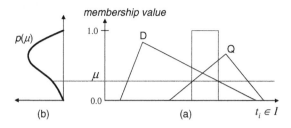

Fig. 1. Preference-based similarity computation: (a) overlap degree at μ between a document D and a query Q; (b) a membership preference function

preference, which can provide a more clear ranking result. In this study, each document is represented and regarded as a fuzzy set:

$$D = \{(t_i, \mu_D(t_i)) \mid (t_i, \lambda(t_i)) \in I, \mu_D(t_i) = \lambda(t_i)\} \tag{7}$$

where t_i is a term in the index set I and $\lambda(t_i)$ is a normalized term weight. $\mu_D(t_i)$ represents a measure of degree to which the document D is characterized by each index term t_i. Eq. 7 can be expressed in L. Zadeh's convenient notation as $D = \sum_{i=1}^{n} \mu_D(t_i)/t_i = \mu_D(t_1)/t_1 + \mu_D(t_2)/t_2 + \ldots + \mu_D(t_n)/t_n$.

A variety of similarity measures between fuzzy sets have been proposed [5, 6]. However, most of these measures have no mechanism to reflect the user preference. Thus we propose a novel similarity measure incorporating the user preference or intention. Firstly, the similarity measure computes the degree of overlap between a document and a query. For each document (D) and query (Q) represented in fuzzy set, we obtain the overlap value between two fuzzy sets at each membership degree (μ) before computing the total overlap. The overlap function $f(\mu)$ at a membership degree μ between D and Q is defined as:

$$f(\mu : D, Q) = \sum_{i=1}^{n} \delta(t_i, \mu : D, Q) \tag{8}$$

where

$$\delta(t_i, \mu : D, Q) = \begin{cases} 1.0 & \text{if } \mu_D(t_i) \geq \mu \text{ and } \mu_Q(t_i) \geq \mu \\ 0.0 & \text{otherwise} \end{cases} \tag{9}$$

$\delta(t_i, \mu : D, Q)$ determines whether two sets are overlapped at the membership degree μ for index term t_i. It returns an overlap value of 1.0 when the membership degrees of the two sets are both greater than μ; otherwise, it returns 0.0. Figure 1(a) depicts an overlap value $f(\mu)$ at membership degree μ between two fuzzy sets. The index terms $t_i \in I$, satisfying both $\mu_D(t_i) \geq \mu$ and $\mu_Q(t_i) \geq \mu$, are given a value 1.0 by Eq. 9. Based on this calculation, we derive the following definition of the similarity measure between a document and a query.

Definition 4. *Let D and Q be two fuzzy sets representing a document and a query, respectively. Let $f(\mu : D, Q)$ be an overlap function at a given membership degree*

μ between D and Q, and $p(\mu)$ be a membership preference function. Then, a similarity $S(D,Q)$ between D and Q is defined as

$$S(D,Q) = \sum_{\mu} f(\mu : D, Q)p(\mu) \qquad (10)$$

$S(D,Q)$ is obtained by summing $f(\mu : D,Q)$ over the whole range of membership degrees. A larger value of $S(D,Q)$ means that two sets D and Q are more similar to each other, indicating that D is more relevant to Q.

Here, $p(\mu)$ is a preference function of membership, which is determined by the user. When two ranking results that have different fuzzy sets yield the same degree of similarity, the preference function is able to discern the two ranking results by focusing on the higher range of membership degrees. When users search the Web for information, they tend to focus on the document with the terms of highest matching. Thus the relevance of the highest-matched document plays an important role in user satisfaction. In such cases, $p(\mu)$ is given a value in the range [0.7,1.0] when $\mu_D(t_i)$ is considered significant, i.e., $\mu_D(t_i) \geq 0.7$. Under this case, index terms with higher weights place greater emphasis on the calculation of the similarity between D and Q. Conversely, $p(\mu)$ is given a value in the range [0.0,0.3] when $\mu_D(t_i)$ is considered insignificant, i.e., $\mu_D(t_i) \leq 0.3$. Given the preference function $p(\mu)$ in Fig. 1(b), the similarity $S(D,Q)$ is obtained by summing the product of $f(\mu : D,Q)$ and $p(\mu)$ for all membership degrees.

Example 1. Consider the ranking problem in Section 3.1. For simplicity, let us suppose that $f(\mu, D, Q)$ is calculated at six μ values ($\mu = 0.0, 0.2, 0.4, 0.6, 0.8, 1.0$). Given that $p(\mu)$ is assigned a value of 1.0 if $\mu_D(t_i) \geq 0.6$ and 0.5 otherwise, the similarity $S(D_1, Q)$ is found to 6.0 by the following calculation:

$$S(D_1, Q) = \sum_{\mu} f(\mu : D_1, Q)p(\mu)$$
$$= f(0.0)p(0.0) + f(0.2)p(0.2) + f(0.4)p(0.4) + \ldots + f(1.0)p(1.0)$$
$$= 2 \times 0.5 + 2 \times 0.5 + 2 \times 0.5 + \ldots + 0 \times 1.0 = 6.0$$

Similarly, we find that $S(D_2, Q) = 4.0$, $S(D_3, Q) = 2.0$, and $S(D_4, Q) = 8.0$. Thus the ranking sequence is $D_4 \rightarrow D_1 \rightarrow D_2 \rightarrow D_3$. It is clear that D_4 is the most relevant to Q, and D_3 is the least relevant. Notably, by assigning greater preference on the terms of higher membership degrees, D_1 has a higher rank than D_2 even though the number of matched terms of D_1 is smaller than those of D_2. We see from this example that the proposed similarity measure can clarify the uncertainty in retrieval process by explicitly reflecting the user preference.

4   Experimental Results

To demonstrate the effectiveness of the proposed method, we conducted retrieval experiments in which the proposed ranking method was compared with the PAICE and P-NORM model in the two indexing settings of TF×IDF and concept based indexing.

The retrieval results were assessed using the precision and recall measures; precision is the ratio of the number of relevant documents retrieved over the total number of documents retrieved, and recall is the ratio of relevant documents retrieved over the total number of relevant documents.

The data set employed was the TREC-2 collection of 1990 Wall Street Journal (WSJ) documents, which comprises 21,705 documents; the built-in 40 queries were used for relevance judgement. The parameters used in the proposed indexing and ranking methods were set as follows: the weights $w(r_k)$ of the five relations used in the grouping of terms were set from 0.1 to 1.5 (identity highest and meronymy lowest) [7]; and the preference function $\rho(\mu)$ is given a value of 1.0 if $\mu_D(t_i) \geq 0.6$ and 0.1 otherwise. The parameters used for the PAICE and P-NORM models were set to $r = 1.0$ and $p = 2$.

Table 1. Comparison of the average precision and recall of each ranking model using TF×IDF index for Top 5 documents

Top N	Precision			Recall		
	PAICE	P-NORM	Proposed	PAICE	P-NORM	Proposed
Top 1	12.50	7.50	10.00	1.82	0.28	0.63
Top 2	10.00	8.75	10.00	2.40	0.71	1.05
Top 3	7.50	8.33	13.33	2.46	1.42	3.53
Top 4	7.50	11.25	11.88	2.82	5.89	3.94
Top 5	7.00	9.50	11.50	3.09	6.05	4.29
Avg.	8.90	9.07	11.34	2.52	2.87	2.69

Table 1 lists the search results of the three ranking models using TF×IDF index, average precision and recall from Top 1 to Top 5 documents. The search results show that the precision of the proposed model outperformed those of the PAICE and P-NORM models. The average precision of the PAICE and P-NORM models are 8.90% and 9.07%, respectively. We see that the average precision of the proposed ranking model for the top-ranked document (11.34%) is higher than those of the other two models. The average recall of the PAICE and P-NORM models are 2.52% and 2.87%, respectively. In this case, the proposed model gives an average recall of 2.69%.

Table 2 lists the average precision and recall of the three ranking models using the concept based index. It is observed that the proposed ranking model outperforms the PAICE and P-NORM models. The PAICE and P-NORM models give average precisions of 13.55% and 20.78% respectively. In contrast, the proposed model gives the higher average precision of 21.42% for the top-ranked documents. Moreover, it is clear that the concept based approach to indexing shows its superior performance to TF-based indexing on the proposed ranking model. The average precisions of the three ranking models were markedly improved by the concept identification based indexing.

5   Conclusion

In this paper, the limitations of conventional indexing and ranking methods are examined. Based on these considerations, a new fuzzy retrieval system incorporating the

Table 2. Comparison of the average precision and recall of each ranking model using concept identification based index for Top 5 documents

Top N	Precision			Recall		
	PAICE	P-NORM	Proposed	PAICE	P-NORM	Proposed
Top 1	20.00	22.50	20.00	3.33	1.29	0.97
Top 2	12.50	21.25	22.50	3.88	5.05	3.53
Top 3	12.50	20.00	23.33	4.96	5.82	7.41
Top 4	11.25	20.63	21.25	5.34	7.12	8.37
Top 5	11.50	19.50	20.00	5.99	8.13	9.07
Avg.	13.55	20.78	21.42	4.70	5.48	5.87

notion of conceptual indexing has been proposed for document retrieval. The proposed preference-based ranking provides more clear similarity calculation between a document and a query by allowing users to assign their preference or intention to the weights of terms.

References

1. Lee, J.H.: On the evaluation of Boolean operators in the extended boolean retrieval framework, Proceedings of the 17th SIGIR conference, 1994, pp. 182–190.
2. Baeza-Yates, R. et al.: Modern information retrieval, Addison-Wesley, 1999.
3. Kang, B., Kim, V., Lee, S.: Exploiting concept clusters for content-based information retrieval, Information Sciences, Volume 170, Issues 2-4, 2005, pp. 443–462.
4. Hirst, G., St-Onge, D.: Lexical chains as representations of context for the detection and correction of malapropisms, In: Christiane Fellbaum (editor), WordNet: An electronic lexical database, Cambridge, MA:The MIT Press, 1998.
5. Wang, W.J.: New similarity measures on fuzzy sets and on elements, Fuzzy Sets and Systems, Volume 85, 1997, pp. 305–309.
6. Fan, J., Xie, W.: Some notes on similarity measure and proximity measure, Fuzzy Sets and Systems, Volume 101, 1999, pp. 403–412.
7. This is available from Wordnet Online [http://www.cogsci.princeton.edu/ wn].

A Theme Allocation for a Sentence
Based on Head Driven Patterns

Bo-Yeong Kang and Sung-Hyon Myaeng

School of Engineering, Information and Communications University
119, Munji-ro, Yuseong-gu, Daejeon, 305-732, Republic of Korea
{kby,myaeng}@icu.ac.kr

Abstract. Since sentences are the basic propositional units of text, knowing their themes should help various tasks requiring the knowledge about the semantic content of text. In this paper, we examine the notion of sentence theme and propose an automatic scheme where head-driven patterns are used for theme assignment. We tested our scheme with sentences in encyclopedia articles and obtained a promising result of 98.96% in F-score for training data and 88.57% for testing data, which outperform the baseline.

1 Introduction

Words and phrases (terms) are the unit for many practical text-based information systems. For document retrieval, for example, the semantic content of text is often determined by the existence or absence of terms in a text unit such as a document or a paragraph. Even automatic summarization systems based on key sentence extraction mostly rely on key terms or clue terms.

While a careful manipulation of terms with a statistical model would give rise to a text-based system with relatively high performance, term mismatches often cause low recall. As a way to alleviate the need to handle term mismatches, some researchers attempted to deal with themes of documents [3–6]. In those approaches, however, the notion of theme has been dealt with vaguely and assumed to be extractable based on term frequency. Moreover, most of the past work on using themes was limited to determining the theme for a whole document.

Our interest in this work is on the theme of sentences, which can serve as the basis for the theme of larger units of text in general and is crucial for question answering and automatic summarization in particular. When a question answering system identifies candidate sentences that are likely to contain an answer, for example, the decision should be made based at a theme-level, rather than at a lexical level. The following example from the TREC-9 QA test collection shows the case.

Q: What is the name of the inventor of Silly Putty? (TREC-9 Question 811)
A: Silly Putty was a war baby. A *General Electric scientist* in New Haven, Conn., stumbled upon its formula while trying to make synthetic rubber during World War II.(In WSJ910222-0177)

V. Matoušek et al. (Eds.): TSD 2005, LNAI 3658, pp. 187–194, 2005.
© Springer-Verlag Berlin Heidelberg 2005

안코나-에서 태어-났-다. 로마대학교-에서   의학-을   배우-고,
Ancona-at bear-pst-dec. Rome University-in medicine-obj. study-and
동 대학   부속병원-의   정신병과조수-가   되-었-다.
Same Univ. hospital-of   psychiatrist-comp.   become-pst-dec
1898-년-부터   2-년-간   로마-의 국립 특수교육학교-에서 일한 다음
1898-year-from 2-years-for Rome-of Orthophrenic-school-in work after
로마대학교-에 재임학,   7-년-간   교육학-을   배-웠-다.
Rome Uni.   Reentrance, 7-years-for education-obj. learn-pst-dec.
1907-년   3-6-세-까지의 노동자 자녀들을 위한 유치원-을   열-어,
1907-year   3-6-year-old   laborer children for   kindergarten-obj. open-and,
이른바   몬테소리법(法)에 의한   교육을   실시하-였-다.
So-called   Montessori-method by   education-obj. do-pst-dec.

Fig. 1. An example from an encyclopedia article

It is clear that the relationship between the word *inventor* in the query and the phrase *stumble upon* in the candidate sentence plays the crucial role for a match to occur. At a lexical level, however, the relationship can be shown only through a series of categorical and morphological transformations:

Inventor[noun] → invent[verb] → stumble upon

which requires a machine-readable dictionary or a lexical database like WordNet [2] with a sophisticated handling of a syntactic category modification and morphological variation.

A solution we propose to this problem is to match on themes by automatically determining the theme of a sentence. Once the theme of the query is known (e.g. *invention*), sentences with the same or a related theme could be selected as candidates for answer extraction. In this paper, we describe a new method for automatically assigning a theme to individual sentences. Our work focuses on theme assignment for sentences based on head-driven patterns, especially in encyclopedia articles.

2   Theme Assignment Based on Head-Driven Patterns

2.1   Overview

A theme is a generalization of the life or world that a discourse explains or entails [1, 7]. The generalization aspect of a theme makes the discourse represented in a higher level abstraction. It can be done both at a surface level, replacing terms with other higher level terms like hypernyms, and at a content level, considering the intention, goal, and evaluation of the writer. In an expository text in which the main goal is to deliver facts, however, only the surface generalization is necessary to express a theme [7] without content-level generalization.

For instance, Figure 1 depicts a part of the body content for an article where the title word is *Maria Montessori* in an encyclopedia. The body text contains clauses like 안코나에서 태어났다, meaning somebody *was born at Ancona*, 로마대학교에서 의학을 배우고, meaning somebody *studied medicine in University of Rome*. Through an analysis for a predicate and its argument, we can generalize each clause into a discourse category such as 출생(birth) and 교육(education). It is this generalized discourse category of a clause that we treat as the theme of a sentence in this paper. Here, we take the these clauses that explain the topic for a comment, and defined the notion of a comment as follows:

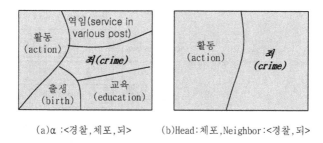

(a)α :<경찰,체포,되>   (b)Head:체포,Neighbor:<경찰,되>

Fig. 2. Theme category space

Definition 1 (Comment). *A comment* α *is a phrase that explains the topic of a sentence and defined as a list consisting of a verb(V), a predicative noun(P_N), and a peripheral noun(N):*

$$\alpha = < N, P\_N, V >$$

where N denotes a general noun or a named entity, V a verb including a functional verb, P_N a predicative noun that is extracted from the sentence when a functional verb such as 하(do) *is used in the sentence.*

For instance, from the phrase 하버드대학-에서 공부-하였-으며 (somebody did study at Harvard), we can extract the comment <하바드(Harvard), 공부(study), 하(do)> including the predicative noun 공부(study) in front of the function verb 하(do). The predicative noun is a term that indicates the noun 교육(education) in the description 교육-하-다(education-do), which is followed by the functional verb 하(do).

Definition 2 (Sentence theme). *A sentence theme is defined as a term T that the sentence is generalized to. It is generated by* < α, γ, Δ, Φ > *where* α *is a comment,* γ *the head-driven pattern reconfigured from* α, *and* Δ *a theme category used for the comment generalization. A theme mapping function,* Φ : γ → T, *maps a head-driven pattern* γ *into a theme category T* ∈ Δ.

Figure 2 illustrates two different methods to determine the theme using the comment <경찰(police), 체포(arrest),되(suffix for passive mode)>. Figure 2 (a) depicts the case where all possible theme categories are first generated from the three elements constituting the comment and given equal weights without a head. In the case of (b), the second element, 체포(arrest), is designated as the head and works as the only element that generates the possible theme categories. Other elements, 경찰(police) and 되(a suffix)), merely serve as neighbors to help determining the theme category between the two. By ruling out unimportant theme categories, the theme assignment task is expected to be more accurate.

Figure 3 depicts the schematic overview of the proposed method for sentence theme assignment. When applied to a sentence S, the proposed method first extracts the comment α and generates the head-driven patterns γ from the comment α. These head-driven patterns γ result from reconfiguration of the comment. Finally the theme mapping function φ assigns the theme T for a sentence S based on the head-driven patterns γ.

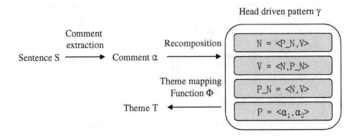

Fig. 3. Theme assignment procedure

Table 1. A part of the theme category set

Top level	Middle level
추상(abstraction)	이름(name)/관계(relation)..
행위(action)	기록(record)/연구(study)..
사건(event)	사망(death)/출생(birth)..
개체(entity)	작품(a piece of work)

Example 1. Let the first sentence in Figure 1, 안코나에서 태어났다, be the input sentence S. It says Maria Montessori was born in Ancona. S is processed to produce the comment α, $<$안코나(Ancona), null, 태어나(be born)$>$. From α, a head-driven pattern γ such as 안코나(Ancona) $=$ $<$null, 태어나(be born)$>$ or 태어나(be born) $=$ $<$안코나(Ancona), null$>$ is formed. Then the theme mapping function ϕ selects 출생(birth) as the theme T using the head-driven pattern, and finally the theme T is assigned to the sentence S.

2.2   Theme Category Set Construction

We assume that the important concept of a sentence will be embodied in the terms that are most frequently used in the text; hence, we construct the theme category set based on the terms with high term frequency (TF)(nouns and verbs). Having calculated the TF of nouns and verbs extracted from the encyclopedia domain, we select the terms occupying the upper 30% of the total TF values as the candidate terms for the category construction. Table 1 shows a part of the theme category set constructed from the person domain in the encyclopedia.

2.3   Theme Assignment

We conjecture that by emphasizing a particular element in a comment, this theme assignment task can be done more effectively. We enumerate four different types of head-driven patterns and evaluate them with experiments.

Table 2. Head-driven patterns derived from the sample comments

Ptn.	Head =	<Neighbor>	
1	하(do)	학교(school)	공부(study)
	죽(die)	전투(battle)	null
2	학교(school)	공부(study)	하(do)
	전투(battle)	null	죽(die)
3	공부(study)	학교(school)	하(do)
	null	전투(battle)	죽(die)
4	공부(study)	학교(school)	하(do)
	죽(die)	전투(battle)	null

Definition 3 (Head Driven Pattern). *A head-driven pattern is generated from a comment by selecting an element as the head and making the others neighbors dependent on it. Four different types of head-driven patterns are of our interest.*

$$(Pattern\ 1)\ V = < N, P\_N >$$
$$(Pattern\ 2)\ N = < V, P\_N >$$
$$(Pattern\ 3)\ P\_N = < N, V >$$
$$(Pattern\ 4)\ P = < c_1, c_2 >$$

In the head-driven pattern 4, P stands for a predicate generalized from the predicative noun or the verb, whichever exists in the comment. c_1 and c_2 are the remaining elements in the comment other than the one that serves as P. This can be seen as a combination of patterns 1, 2, and 3.

In the head-driven pattern 1, for example, the verb (V) is the head and the peripheral noun(N) and the predicative noun(P_N) are the neighbors. The theme of the head, V, is determined by the neighbors, N and P_N, and becomes the theme of the comment. The head-driven patterns 2 and 3 are used in the same way. In the case of the head-driven pattern 4, the predicate P is the head. Table 2 shows how the two comments $<$학교(school), 공부(study), 하(do)$>$ 와 $<$전투(battle), null, 죽(die)$>$ are converted into the four types of head-driven patterns.

Given a head-driven pattern generated from a comment, the next step is to select the most probable theme from each pattern. For each pattern, we define a theme mapping function that selects a theme. Below are the four mapping functions:

(Func. 1) Φ_1: $V = < N, P\_N > \rightarrow T$, where $N, V, P\_N \in \alpha$ and $T \in \Delta$
(Func. 2) Φ_2: $N = < V, P\_N > \rightarrow T$, where $N, V, P\_N \in \alpha$ and $T \in \Delta$
(Func. 3) Φ_3: $P\_N = < N, V > \rightarrow T$, where $N, V, P\_N \in \alpha$ and $T \in \Delta$
(Func. 4) Φ_4: $P = < c_1, c_2 > \rightarrow T$, where $P, c_1, c_2 \in \alpha$ and $T \in \Delta$

Each mapping function is currently implemented with a Naive Bayesian classifier. For example, given that a comment α represented as $< n_k, pn_k, v_k >$ and its head-driven pattern 1, $v_k = < n_k, pn_k >$, the theme of the head v_k must be chosen among the possible theme categories with the contextual information provided by the neighbor $< n_k, pn_k >$. The problem now becomes that of classifying the pattern into one of the

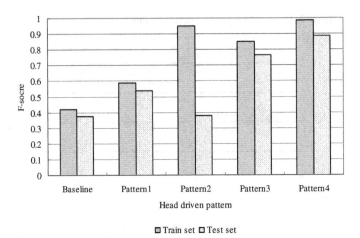

Fig. 4. Theme assignment result for each head driven pattern

theme categories or assigning a theme to the pattern generated from the comment. By directly applying the Bayesian classifier, we get:

$$T = argmax_{T_i \in \Delta} P(T_i|v_k) \tag{1}$$
$$= argmax_{T_i \in \Delta} \frac{P(v_k|T_i)P(T_i)}{P(v_k)}$$
$$= argmax_{T_i \in \Delta} \frac{P(n_k, pn_k|T_i)P(T_i)}{P(n_k, pn_k)}$$
$$= argmax_{T_i \in \Delta} P(n_k, pn_k|T_i)P(T_i)$$

As usual, the probabilities are estimated based on a training data. After the probability of a theme T_i of v_k is calculated for every i, the theme with the highest probability is chosen.

3   Experimental Results

The proposed method was applied to the 2,381 documents in the person domain of Dusan Dong-a Encyclopedia. After preprocessing 2,381 documents for named entity tagging, and morphological analysis, the system extracted 9,987 comments, which were divided into the train and test sets. We used precision, recall and F-score as measures for the theme assignment effectiveness.

3.1   Baseline

We used the method explained in Figure 2 (a) as the baseline since it considers all the theme categories obtainable from the elements in a comment without presupposing a head and neighbors, whereas the proposed method assumes that the head plays a crucial role in assigning a theme to a comment.

The theme assignment process of the baseline method is basically the same as Equation 1. When a comment is represented as $\alpha = < a_1, a_2, a_3 >$, $P(T_i|\alpha)$ and $P(a_1, a_2, a_3|T_i)P(T_i)$ are calculated for each theme T_i, and then the category T_i that has the highest value is assigned to the theme of the comment α.

The performance of the baseline method was evaluated by F-score micro average after conducting 5-fold cross validation on the extracted 9,987 comments. When the train set was used for both learning and testing, the performance was 41.9% in F-score whereas it decreased to 37.4% when the test set was used after learning on the train set.

Table 3. The performance improvement of the proposed method for the baseline

	Train set	Test set
Baseline	0.4192	0.3743
Pattern 1	0.5875(+40.12%)	0.5375(+43.60%)
Pattern 2	0.9491(+126.36%)	0.3802(+1.58%)
Pattern 3	0.8511(+102.98%)	0.7634(+103.95%)
Pattern 4	0.9886(+135.77%)	0.8857(+136.61%)

3.2 Theme Assignment Based on Sentence Patterns

We ran experiments for the four types of head-driven patterns and compared the results with that of the baseline. Figure 4 shows the result for the two cases, testing on the data identical to the train data and on the data different from it. All the scores are in micro averaged F-score with 5-fold cross validation.

It is clear that the head-driven pattern 4 gives the best result compared to the other head-driven patterns: the F-score is as high as 98.86% for the train set and 88.57% for the test set. Performance improvements over the baseline are shown in Table 3. The results show that while using either a verb alone or a predicative noun alone as a head (as in the pattern 1 and 3) helps the theme assignment process, compared to the baseline where no head is used, the idea of using both predicate nouns and verbs as a head, whenever possible, gives even more improvements. Nouns play a certain role as a head for determining a theme, but predicates seem to be far more important and affect more strongly on the theme of a sentence.

Our failure analysis on the baseline and the patterns 1 and 3 results revealed that many errors were made because a particular theme was favored and assigned disproportionately. As shown in Table 4, among the 1,044 errors (52.8% of the total number of comments) made for the baseline case, 778 (39.4% of the total number of comments) were due to the fact that a specific theme, 활동(activity), was assigned. A similar trend is also found in the case of the patterns 1 and 3 although the total percentage of errors for the pattern 3 is much less.

4 Conclusion

This paper presents a sentence theme assignment method utilizing the head-driven patterns that place an emphasis on a particular constituent of a sentence. Based on a series

Table 4. Analysis of errors for the test set

	Total error	Caused by specific assign.
Baseline	0.5282	0.3941
Pattern 1	0.4161	0.3692
Pattern 3	0.1913	0.1213

of experiments on 9,987 comments extracted from 2,381 documents in Dusan Dong-A Encyclopedia, we could see that the predicates (i.e. verbs and predicate nouns) in a sentence are strong indicators for determining the theme of a sentence. With the promising experimental result, we believe that the proposed theme assignment method opens new possibilities for various research fields such as text summarization, and discourse analysis.

References

1. Cunningham, J.W., Moore, D.M.: The Confused world of main idea, In J.F. Baumann.(ed.), Teaching main idea, N.Y.:IRA, 1986.
2. Fellbaum, C. et al.: WordNet:An eletroic lexical database, The MIT press:IRA, 1998.
3. Yang, Y.: An evaluation of statistical approaches to text categorization, Information retrieval, 1998.
4. Jeong,T.J., Jang,B.T.: Web Information search using reinforcement learning, In proceedings of the Korean information science society conference(KISS), 2001.
5. Park, K.R., Jang, E.J, Park, S.G.: Improved link analysis algorithm using document feature information, In KISS'03, 2003.
6. Lee, S.E., Hwang, I.J.: Summarizing relevant web pages based on semantic region, In KISS'03, 2003.
7. Seo, H.: A Study on the structure and theme-construction of Korean discourses, Ph.D dissertation, Seoul National University, 2002.

A Hybrid Approach to Statistical Language Modeling with Multilayer Perceptrons and Unigrams*

Fernando Blat, María José Castro, Salvador Tortajada, and Joan Andreu Sánchez

Departament de Sistemes Informàtics i Computació
Universitat Politècnica de València, E-46022 València, Spain
{fblat,mcastro,stortajada,jandreu}@dsic.upv.es

Abstract. In language engineering, language models are employed in order to improve system performance. These language models are usually N-gram models which are estimated from large text databases using the occurrence frequencies of these N-grams. An alternative to conventional frequency-based estimation of N-gram probabilities consists on using neural networks to this end. In this paper, an approach to language modeling with a hybrid language model is presented as a linear combination of a connectionist N-gram model, which is used to represent the global relations between certain linguistic categories, and a stochastic model of word distribution into such categories. The hybrid language model is tested on the corpus of the Wall Street journal processed in the Penn Treebank project.

1 Introduction

Language modeling is the attempt to characterize, capture and exploit regularities in natural language. In problems such as automatic speech recognition, machine translation, text classification or other pattern recognition tasks, it is useful to adequately restrict the possible or probable sequences of units which define the set of sentences (*language*) allowed in the application task. In general, the incorporation of a language model reduces the complexity of the system (it guides the search for the optimal response) and increases its success rate.

Under a statistical framework, a language model is used to assign to every possible word sequence W an estimation of the a priori probability of being the correct system response $\Pr(W) = \Pr(w_1 \ldots w_{|W|})$. Statistical language model are usually based on the prediction of each linguistic unit in the sequence given the preceding ones [1, 2]:

$$\Pr(w_1 \ldots w_{|W|}) = \Pr(w_1) \ldots \Pr(w_{|W|}|w_1 \ldots w_{|W|-1}) = \prod_{i=1}^{|W|} \Pr(w_i|h_i), \quad (1)$$

where $h_i = w_1 \ldots w_{i-1}$ denotes the *history* from which unit w_i has to be predicted. The number of parameters to estimate becomes intractable as the length of the sentence increases. N-gram models [1] are the most extended method to reduce this number

---

* This work has been supported by the Spanish CICYT under contract TIC2003-07158-C04-03.

V. Matoušek et al. (Eds.): TSD 2005, LNAI 3658, pp. 195–202, 2005.

approximating the probability of a word as if only the last $N-1$ words have influence, and taking into account that an approximation has been made, we can write

$$\Pr(w_1 \dots w_{|W|}) \approx \prod_{i=1}^{|W|} \Pr(w_i | w_{i-N+1} \dots w_{i-1}). \qquad (2)$$

The N-grams are simple and robust models, and they can adequately capture the local restrictions between words. The parameters of the model are learned from text using the occurrence frequencies of these N-grams, that is, subsequences of N word units. Deciding a value for N requires a trade-off between detail and reliability: larger values of N would provide more detailed models; however, more parameters implies that more training data is needed for the parameter values to be reliably estimated. Note that the number of parameters grows very fast (exponentially) with N (there are $|\Omega|^N$ N-grams, where Ω is the vocabulary) so typical values for N are two and three and these models cannot exploit long-term dependencies between linguistic units. In order to alleviate this problem, some techniques can be applied, such as smoothing or clustering techniques, class N-grams, integrated models, etc. (for a review, see [2]). We have worked in a different line to solve the above problem: connectionist language models.

The connectionist approach to language modeling is introduced in Section 2. Learning N-gram models with feed-forward neural networks is described in Section 3, along with some results and analysis of their performance in different tasks with the Penn Treebank corpus (Sections 4 and 5). Finally, we draw some conclusions and propose new directions in connectionist language modeling in Section 6.

2   Statistical Language Modeling with Neural Networks

A different approach to statistical language models based on N-grams consists on using neural networks. We will call "connectionist N-gram model" to a statistical language model which follows equation (2) and where the probabilities that appear in that expression are estimated with a neural network (a multilayer perceptron (MLP) [3, 4], for example). The model naturally fits under the probabilistic interpretation of the outputs of the neural networks: if a neural network is trained as a classifier, the outputs associated to each class are estimations of the posterior probabilities of the defined classes. The demonstration of this assertion can be found in a number of places, for example, in [4].

A first step in this direction was given in 1989 by Nakamura and Shikano [5] who empirically showed how MLPs can emulate N-gram model predictive capabilities with additional generalization features.

We have been working in connectionist language modeling since 1999 [6–9]. Our experimental work provided empirical evidence on MLP capability to emulate N-gram models on a small-vocabulary Spanish text corpus. Our results on bigrams and trigrams favorably compared connectionist models with conventional ones: in both the bigram and the trigram case, connectionist models achieved a lower test set perplexity. Specially the neural network for trigrams performed much better than the conventional trigram. Moreover, in the trigram case, the connectionist model implied a large reduction (more than 95%) in the number of free parameters over the conventional one. Similar conclusions were obtained by Xu and Rudnicky [10]. Their experimental results (with a moderate vocabulary size task and by using a single layer network) showed that the artificial neural network could learn a language model with a performance even better than standard N-gram models.

The work of Bengio et al. [11, 12] showed on two large text corpora that a neural probabilistic model very significantly improved on a state-of-the-art trigram model. Their model learnt simultaneously a distributed representation for each word of the vocabulary with the probability function for word sequences. Generalization was obtained because a sequence of words that had never seen before got high probability if it was made of words that were similar to words forming an already seen sentence. Other recent works of Schwenk et al. extended successfully the same approach to different large vocabulary continuous speech recognition tasks [13–15].

On the other hand, recurrent neural networks can also be applied directly to the connectionist statistical language modeling problem. One possibility would be to use Elman networks [16], where the activations at the first hidden layer may be fed back to the input layer using context units. The context units could be fully connected to the first hidden layer via the context weights. Elman style networks are multilayer networks with simple recurrences, that is, with back-connections whose weights are fixed to value one. These recurrences attempt to catch the dynamicity in parsing natural language and have the potential to learn temporal dependencies of unspecified length. This architecture might develop an internal temporal representation which encodes the number of previous linguistic units needed to predict the following one; that is, the hidden layer might be expected to encode a representation of the history in equation (1). Therefore, we could avoid the design decision to select the value of N, as the recurrent architecture would not need the histories to be previously categorized into equivalence classes.

In a recent work by Rodriguez [17], experiments with a simple recurrent network were reported. The recurrent network was trained on a large corpus in order to examine the ability of the network to learn bigrams, trigrams, etc., as a function of the size of the corpus. The author performed experiments with the Wall Street Journal database in order to make predictions of the next possible letter. Thus, a vocabulary of 28 symbols (letters from the English alphabet) was used. With enough training data and hidden units, the network was capable to learn 5 and 6-gram dependencies.

The advantages of the connectionist approach to language modeling are due to their automatic estimation (the same feature as with statistical language models), the lowest (in general) number of parameters of the obtained models and the automatic smoothing performed by the neural networks estimators. Estimation of connectionist N-gram models in ambitious tasks is needed in order to fulfill these advantages. This is not trivial: the larger the lexicon is, the larger the number of parameters the neural network needs. The problem becomes even harder when using recurrent neural networks. We think that the use of a distributed representation for each word of the vocabulary (as in [12]), along with its combination of a connectionist language model for the same task which uses categorized lexicon, can be a successful approach for tasks with large lexica. In this paper, we present an approach to the latter idea: a hybrid language model defined as a linear combination of a connectionist N-gram model, which is used to represent the global relations between certain linguistic categories, and a stochastic model of word distribution into such categories.

3   Hybrid Language Model with MLPs and Unigrams

In the statistical approach to language modeling with MLPs, the input layer is equivalent to the history of the N-gram and the output layer estimates the posterior probability of each word of the vocabulary. The input layer can be seen as a vector of bits where each unit represents a word in the vocabulary. This means that, as we use a local representation of the sample data, the number of input units must be $|\Omega|$ for a bigram model and $2|\Omega|$ for a trigram model. In the output layer there are $|\Omega|$ units, each one representing a word. The *softmax* activation function is used at the output layer in order to normalize the sum of the output units to one, thus corresponding the most likely word to the conditional probability $\Pr(w_i|w_{i-N+1}\ldots w_{i-1})$.

To solve the main problems derived from large vocabularies we proposed a stochastical model defined as a combination of a connectionist language model using an MLP for part-of-speech (POS) categories, LM_c, and a distribution model of words into such categories, LM_w [1]. This combination allows us to create a language model that treats with words.

The LM_c emulates a connectionist N-gram model $\Pr(c_i|c_{i-N+1}\ldots c_{i-1})$ as explained above with an MLP. In this case, input and output are POS categories: the input layer represents the history of the POStags, $c_{i-N+1}\ldots c_{i-1}$, and the output layer represents the conditional probability of each category:

$$\Pr(c_1\ldots c_{|W|}) \approx \prod_{i=1}^{|W|} \Pr(c_i|c_{i-N+1}\ldots c_{i-1}).\tag{3}$$

On the other hand, the distribution model LM_w only works with words. For each word w there is a POStag associated c. Each tag can be viewed as the category the words labeled belong to. So, the parameters of the word category distribution LM_w can be estimated as

$$\Pr(w|c) = \frac{N(w,c)}{\sum_{w'} N(w',c)},\tag{4}$$

where $N(w,c)$ is the number of times that the word w has been labeled with the POStag c. Note that a word can be associated to one or more categories.

We combined both expressions (3) and (4) as proposed in [18] to get the probability of a word w_i having a history of $w_{i-N+1}\ldots w_{i-1}$ and thus, equation (2) is converted to

$$\Pr(w_i|w_{i-N+1}\ldots w_{i-1}) = \sum_{c:w_i\in c} \Pr(w_i|c)\Pr(c|c_{i-N+1}\ldots c_{i-1}),\tag{5}$$

where the summation is defined over all possible categories c that a word belongs to.

4   Experiments with the Penn Treebank Corpus

The corpus used in the experiments was the part of the Wall Street Journal that had been processed in the Penn Treebank Project[2] [19]. This corpus consists on a set of

---

[1] Experiments are carried out with the Penn Treebank corpus, where each word of each sentence is labeled with a POStag.

[2] Release 2 of this data set can be obtained from the Linguistic Data Consortium with Catalog number LDC95T7.

English texts from the Wall Street Journal distributed in 25 directories. The total number number of words is about one million, being about 49,000 different. The whole corpus was automatically labeled with two different kinds of labeling: a POStag labeling and a syntactic labeling. The POStag labeling consists on a set of 45 different labels, and the syntactic labeling of 14 labels.

The corpus was divided in three sets: training, tuning and test. The main characteristics of these partitions are described in Table 1. In order to compare our language model with other models developed using this corpus, we processed the corpus taking into account the restrictions considered in other works [18, 20]. The considered restrictions were the following:

– training, tuning and test partitions were composed of directories 00-20, 21-22 and 23-24 respectively, as shown in Table 1;
– the vocabulary was composed of the 10,000 most frequent words appearing in the training;
– all capital letters were uncapitalized;
– all words that had the POStag CD (cardinal number) were replaced by a special symbol that did not appear in the training.

Table 1. Partitions from the Wall Street Journal corpus.

Data set	Directories	No. of sentences	No. of words
Training	00-20	42,075	1,004,073
Tuning	21-22	3,371	80,156
Test	23-24	3,762	89,537

We have developed a hybrid language model for this task following expression (5). The parameters of both models LM_c and LM_w were estimated from the training set sentences.

5   Evaluating the Language Models

The measure of the quality of a estimated language model M usually is the perplexity of a test set T defined as:

$$PP(T, M) = \frac{1}{\left(\prod_{i=1}^{|T|} \Pr_M(w_i | w_{i-N+1} \ldots w_{i-1}) \right)^{\frac{1}{|T|}}} . \tag{6}$$

Perplexity can be intuitively interpreted as the geometric mean of the branch-out factor of the language [2, 21]: a language with perplexity x has roughly the same difficulty as another language in which every word can be followed by x different words with equal probabilities. Thus, the lower the perplexity of a language model, the better the language model is.

5.1   Connectionist Language Model LM_c for the Categorized Corpus

Two different types of experiments were performed. We trained an MLP as an N-gram, for N equal to 2 and 3, with the POStags as vocabulary. In order to establish the optimum topology, we have done an exhaustive scanning using the tuning set for one and two hidden layers with a number of units varying from 2 to 128. The activation function for the hidden layer was the *logistic* function. With a bigram model the best topology was one hidden layer with 16 units, which means 1,567 parameters to calculate. In the trigram model the best topology had one hidden layer with 128 units, that is, 12,207 parameters.

The *back-propagation with momentum* algorithm [3], which is one of the most general methods for supervised training of MLPs, was used. Several scannings have been done in order to achieve the best values for the learning rate and the momentum term. The perplexity of the connectionist N-gram models for the POStagged sentences of the Penn Treebank corpus corpus are shown in Table 2, along with the perplexity of conventional N-grams estimated with the "CMU-Cambridge Statistical Language Modeling Toolkit (SLM) v2" [22].

Table 2. Test set perplexity of the language models for the POStagged Penn Treebank corpus.

Language Model	MLP-Bigram	MLP-Trigram	Bigram	Trigram
Test set perplexity	9.47	8.27	10.34	9.08

5.2 Hybrid Language Model with Connectionist N-Grams

To solve the main problems derived from large vocabularies we proposed a stochastical model defined as a combination of a connectionist language model using a MLP for categories (LM_c) and a distribution model of words into categories (LM_w) as explained in Section 3. This combination allows us to create a language model that treats with words.

When an unknown word (word not seen during the training process) appears in the test set, equation (4) is equal to zero. Then we apply a small ϵ over all categories in order to smooth the accumulated probability and equation (5) is converted to

$$\Pr(w_i|w_{i-N+1}\ldots w_{i-1}) = \sum_c \epsilon \Pr(c|c_{i-N+1}\ldots c_{i-1}),\qquad(7)$$

where the summation is defined over all categories c of the corpus. Table 3 shows the tuning set perplexity for various values of ϵ. Note that, in the tuning set, more than 5% of the words are unknown.

Finally, we have applied the hybrid language model to the test set of the Penn Treebank corpus (with the best values of ϵ for the tuning set) and the test set perplexity is shown in Table 4. We have also estimated a trigram model which uses words directly, using linear discounting as a smoothing technique [18]. The test set perplexity was 167.30.

6 Discussion and Conclusions

In this paper, we have combined a POStag connectionist N-gram model with a unigram model of words. The results for this hybrid language model (see Table 4) show that this new approach is feasible.

Table 3. Tuning set perplexity of the hybrid language model with different smoothing values ϵ.

ϵ	Bigram	Trigram
0.0001	301.55	255.16
0.00001	207.65	173.52
0.000001	200.49	167.14
0.0000001	200.13	166.84
0.00000001	200.12	166.85
0.000000001	200.12	166.86

Table 4. Test set perplexity for the language models for the Penn Treebank corpus.

Language Model	MLP-Bigram	MLP-Trigram
Test set perplexity	208.46	173.86

As we can see in Table 2, the behaviour of the connectionist model for the POStagged corpus, LM_c, offers better performance than the conventional class N-gram models. Thus, we think that a whole connectionist N-gram language model could give better performance than that obtained by the hybrid model. However, estimating a connectionist N-gram language model for this task presents a major problem: the size of the vocabulary. A distributed representation of the vocabulary (as in [12]) is needed.

Another way to improve the proposed hybrid model is to combine it with an N-gram model of words, as it is done in [18]. The idea is to use the N-gram model to capture the short-term dependencies among words (with a trigram, for example) that our hybrid model has not been able to (it only uses a unigram to capture this information).

Finally, a common problem in both conventional and connectionist N-gram models is the difficulty to model long-term dependencies. Recurrent neural networks as explained in Section 2 could be use to automatically solve this problem.

References

1. Bahl, L., Jelinek, F., Mercer, R.: A Maximum Likelihood Approach to Continuous Speech Recognition. IEEE Trans. on PAMI **5** (1983) 179–190
2. Jelinek, F.: Statistical Methods for Speech Recognition. MIT Press (1998)
3. Rumelhart, D., Hinton, G., Williams, R.: Learning internal representations by error propagation. In: PDP: Computational models of cognition and perception, I. MIT Press (1986)
4. Bishop, C.: Neural networks for pattern recognition. Oxford University Press (1995)
5. Nakamura, M., Shikano, K.: A study of English word category prediction based on neural networks. In: Proc. of the ICASSP, Glasgow (Scotland) (1989) 731–734
6. Castro, M., Casacuberta, F., Prat, F.: Towards connectionist language modeling. In: Proc. of the Symposium on Pattern Recognition and Image Analysis, Bilbao (Spain) (1999) 9–10
7. Castro, M., Prat, F., Casacuberta, F.: MLP emulation of N-gram models as a first step to connectionist language modeling. In: Proc. of the ICANN, Edinburgh (UK) (1999) 910–915
8. Castro, M.J., Polvoreda, V., Prat, F.: Connectionist N-gram Models by Using MLPs. In: Proc. of the NLPNN, Tokyo (Japan) (2001) 16–22
9. Castro, M.J., Prat, F.: New Directions in Connectionist Language Modeling. In: Computational Methods in Neural Modeling. Vol. 2686 of LNCS. Springer-Verlag (2003) 598–605

10. Xu, W., Rudnicky, A.: Can Artificial Neural Networks Learn Language Models? In: Proc. of the ICSLP, Beijing (China) (2000)
11. Bengio, Y., Ducharme, R., Vincent, P.: A Neural Probabilistic Language Model. In: Advances in NIPS. Volume 13., Morgan Kaufmann (2001) 932–938
12. Bengio, Y., Ducharme, R., Vincent, P., Jauvin, C.: A Neural Probabilistic Language Model. Journal of Machine Learning Research **3** (2003) 1137–1155
13. Schwenk, H., Gauvain, J.L.: Connectionist language modeling for large vocabulary continuous speech recognition. In: Proc. of the ICASSP, Orlando, Florida (USA) (2002) 765–768
14. Schwenk, H., Gauvain, J.L.: Using continuous space language models for conversational speech recognition. In: Work. on Spontaneous Speech Process. and Recog., Tokyo (2003)
15. Schwenk, H.: Efficient Training of Large Neural Networks for Language Modeling. In: Proc. of the IJCNN, Budapest (2004) 3059–3062
16. Elman, J.: Finding structure in time. Cognitive Science **14** (1990) 179–211
17. Rodriguez, P.: Comparing Simple Recurrent Networks and n-Grams in a Large Corpus. Journal of Applied Intelligence **19** (2003) 39–50
18. Benedí, J., Sánchez, J.: Estimation of stochastic context-free grammars and their use as language models. Computer Speech and Language (2005) In press.
19. Marcus, M.P., Santorini, B., Marcinkiewicz, M.A.: Building a Large Annotated Corpus of English: The Penn Treebank. Computational Linguistics **19** (1994) 313–330
20. Roark, B.: Probabilistic top-down parsing and language modeling. Computational Linguistics **27** (2001) 249–276
21. Rosenfeld, R.: Adaptative statistical language modeling: A maximum entropy approach. PhD thesis, Carnegie Mellon University (1994)
22. Clarkson, P., Rosenfeld, R.: Statistical Language Modeling using the CMU-Cambridge toolkit. In: Proc. of the Eurospeech, Rhodes (Greece) (1997) 2707–2711

Supervised and Unsupervised Speaker Adaptation in Large Vocabulary Continuous Speech Recognition of Czech*

Petr Cerva and Jan Nouza

SpeechLab, Technical University of Liberec
Halkova 6, 461 17, Liberec 1, Czech Republic
{petr.cerva,jan.nouza}@vslib.cz
http://itakura.kes.vslib.cz/kes/indexe.html

Abstract. This paper deals with the problem of efficient speaker adaptation in large vocabulary continuous speech recognition (LVCSR) systems. The main goal is to adapt acoustic models of speech and to increase the recognition accuracy of these systems in tasks, where only one user is expected (e.g. voice dictation) or where the speaking person can be identified automatically (e.g. broadcast news transcription). For this purpose, we propose several modifications of the well known MLLR (Maximum Likelihood Linear Regression) method and we combine them with the MAP (Maximum A Posteriori) method. The results from a series of experiments show that the error rate of our 300K-word Czech recogniser can be reduced by about 9.9 % when only 30 seconds of supervised data are used for adaptation or by about 9.6 % when unsupervised adaptation on the same data is performed. ...

1 Introduction

Speech recognition systems with large vocabulary have attracted much attention over the last years and the recent increase in computer power brings them much closer to users. For acoustic modelling, these systems use mainly continuous density hidden Markov models (CDHMMs) created in a process of a multi-style training. In this process, data recorded by various microphones in environments with different level of a background noise and by speakers with different speaking characteristics, age and gender, are used. After such training the systems can operate well under various conditions and can be used as speaker independent (SI).

However, in some practical tasks, like voice dictation or broadcast news transcription, the speaker is known a priori or he/she can be identified. In these applications, the speaker dependent (SD) systems could be used instead of the SI ones. It is well known that the SD models, trained only on data recorded by the given speaker perform better. On the other side, the amount of recordings required for the SD models (several hours of speech) is too big and not available in practice. Hence, another solution must be searched to increase the system performance for one speaker. The often used solution consists in the adaptation of the original SI system to that person. In this approach, the

---

* This work was supported by the Czech Grant Agency in project no. 102/05/0278.

V. Matoušek et al. (Eds.): TSD 2005, LNAI 3658, pp. 203–210, 2005.

speaker is asked to record significantly smaller amount of data (only several minutes). If a proper method is used, the speaker adapted (SA) system converges to the accuracy of the SD system. No wonder that efficient speaker adaptation techniques are object of intensive research [1]. In this paper we propose several modifications of the well-known MAP [2] and MLLR [3] adaptation methods applied both for supervised and unsupervised manner.

This paper is structured as follows: The next section is focused on the description of the basic principles used in speaker adaptation methods. In section 3 we propose several modifications of these methods and in section 4 we evaluate them in extensive experiments performed on a Czech speech database. The conclusion is summarised in the last section.

2   Basic Principles Used in Speaker Adaptation Methods

The following description focuses on the adaptation of Gaussian means of CDHMMs. In our previous work we showed that updating of Gaussian variances and/or mixture weights brought only small additional effect, which was claimed also by other authors [5] or [6].

2.1   Maximum A Posteriori (MAP) Method

The first method is based on the estimation of new SD parameters from the adaptation data. The updated parameters are then obtained as a linear interpolation (weighted sum) between the original SI and new SD parameters. This interpolation can be expressed for means of CDHMMs with Gaussian mixture state observation densities as

$$\boldsymbol{\mu}_{ik}^{SA} = \lambda_{ik}\boldsymbol{\mu}_{ik}^{SI} + (1 - \lambda_{ik})\boldsymbol{\mu}_{ik}^{SD} \tag{1}$$

where $\boldsymbol{\mu}_{ik}^{SI}$ is the mean vector of the k-th mixture component of state i of the given SI model, $\boldsymbol{\mu}_{ik}^{SA}$ is the adapted mean vector and $\boldsymbol{\mu}_{ik}^{SD}$ is the ML estimate of this vector computed from all adaptation data. Term λ_{ik} represents the weighting factor of the linear interpolation and is given by fraction

$$\lambda_{ik} = \frac{\tau_{ik}}{\tau_{ik} + \sum_{t=1}^{T} \zeta_t(i, k)} \tag{2}$$

The term τ_{ik} in 2 has the meaning of a free adaptation parameter while the term $\sum_{t=1}^{T} \zeta_t(i, k)$ represents the total occupation likelihood of the given mixture. The latter represents the amount of the data used for its adaptation. T is the number of feature vectors from adaptation data. The MAP estimate convergences to the SD model, which is theoretically the best for the given speaker, when the value of τ_{ik} decreases or when the amount of adaptation data increases. The major limitation of the MAP method consists in the fact that only the parameters of the models observed in the adaptation data can be adapted.

2.2   Maximum Likelihood Linear Regression (MLLR) Method

The MLLR method is based on linear transformation of SI parameters [3]. The main advantage of this method consists in increasing the adaptation speed, because one transformation can be used for several Gaussian components at once. It is applied to those Gaussians that are acoustically close and that share the same regression class. For each mean vector of regression class m, this transformation can be calculated according to

$$\boldsymbol{\mu}_{ik}^{SA} = \mathbf{W}_m \boldsymbol{\xi}_m^{SI} \tag{3}$$

where $\mathbf{W}_m$ is the transformation matrix calculated to maximize the likelihood of the adaptation data and $\boldsymbol{\xi}_m^{SI} = [1 \ \mu_m^{SI}(1) \ \mu_m^{SI}(2) \ ... \ \mu_m^{SI}(P)]^T$ is the extended vector of means of the SI model (with offset set to one). P is the length of feature vector.

3   Proposed Modifications of the Basic Methods

All the proposed modifications of the two above mentioned methods have been developed and implemented within our own speech processing platform that include tools for CDHMM training and testing.

3.1   MLLR with Static Regression Classes

The first proposed modification (denoted as MLLR1) is based on the assumption that the regression classes for MLLR can be formed manually by splitting all the acoustic models into several groups. After this splitting, each group should contain only the models that are close in the acoustic space.

In our case, all HMM models of Czech phonemes were classified into five groups according to the raw phonetic categories: vowels (a, á, o, ó...) , voiced (z, ž, v...) and unvoiced (s, š, f...) fricatives, voiced (b, d...) and unvoiced explosives (p, t...). The sixth group was made of the models belonging to noises (breath, ehm...) and the seventh group contained only the silence model.

3.2   MLLR with Regression Classes Formed into a Binary Tree

The second modification (named as MLLR2) is based on clustering all the acoustic models with the use of a binary regression tree. The main advantage of this approach consists in the fact that during the adaptation process the tree can be searched down from the root towards the leaves while calculating the transformations only for those nodes where sufficient amount of the adaptation data is available.

In preliminary experiments (not presented in this paper) we found that the clustering is more effective, when the first two nodes of the regression tree are created manually by splitting all the acoustic models into two groups: models of noises and models of phonemes.

3.3   Combination of MAP and MLLR

The advantages of both the MAP and MLLR can be effectively utilized by their combination. We tried to combine the MAP and the MLLR2 methods. The adaptation was then performed in two steps: the mean vectors of the SI models were transformed by the MLLR2 method at first and the transformed values were used as priors for the MAP based adaptation.

The benefit of this approach consists in the fact that also the models not seen in the adaptation data can be adapted while the parameters of the models with a lot of adaptation data can converge to the values of the SD model. Some other possibilities how to combine the MAP and the MLLR method can be found in [5] and [9].

3.4   Unsupervised Adaptation and Two Pass Recognition

Speaker adaptation can be performed in two basic modes: as a supervised or unsupervised process. In the former case the adaptation data are available before and their phonetic transcription can be prepared or at least checked by a human expert. In the unsupervised case, the data are not prepared and their text and phonetic transcription is obtained as the result of recognition. The recognition system must perform well at least on phonetic level.

In our research, we applied unsupervised adaptation also in a two-pass recognition scheme. In the first pass, we used well adapted SA models in the recognizer that created text and phonetic transcription for the test utterance. Then we performed unsupervised adaptation by the same method and finally we used the resulting twice adapted models in the second recognition pass. The experimental evaluation of this approach is given in section 4.3.

4   Experimental Evaluation

In all experiments described in this paper we used our own LVCSR system operating with the vocabulary containing the most frequent 312,490 Czech words. The language model of this system is based on smoothed bigrams estimated on a corpus compiled from about 2 GB of Czech (mainly newspaper) texts.

The system employs CDHMMs of 48 context independent phonemes [7] with 100 mixtures per state for acoustic modelling. The feature vector includes 39 MFCC parameters (13 static coefficients and their first and second derivatives) calculated from signal sampled at 16 kHz.

Each individual test consisted in the recognition of 1060 sentences (more than 15,000 words, with total length 2 hours) recorded by five different speakers. The recordings came either from FM radio or from a microphone connected to a PC. A varying amount of other recordings of these 5 people was used for adaptation.

4.1   Overall Comparison of Speaker Adaptation Methods in the Supervised Task

The first experiment (Fig. 1) was focused on the general comparison of the methods described in the previous section. We performed this experiment for all five speakers from the test database and we used a varying amount (from 0.5 to 15 minutes) of speaker specific data for model adaptation to each of them. The presented results were calculated as values averaged over all five speakers.

The recognition accuracy of the baseline SI system was 79.4 % and the system worked with our largest available vocabulary containing 312 thousands of the most frequent Czech words. Similar results (not presented in this paper) were also obtained for smaller vocabularies.

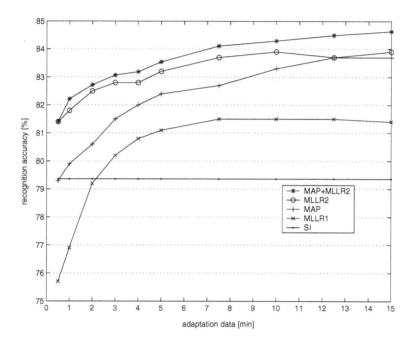

Fig. 1. Graph of overall results of speaker adaptation methods for different amount of used adaptation data in the supervised task. Recognition accuracy of the SI system was 79.4 %

The results of this experiment show that the MLLR2 method with the regression tree outperforms the MLLR1 method with static classes. It is because the parameters formed into the tree structure were transformed dynamically depending on the amount of the available data. For small amount of adaptation data, the MLLR1 method gives even worse results than the SI system.

The Word Error Rate (WER) can be reduced most effectively for all amounts of the adaptation data when the combination of MAP and MLLR2 is used. Similar results are presented for a system with a smaller vocabulary and English language in [5].

The MAP method appears as very ineffective for small amount of adaptation data, because the models not seen in the adaptation data remain unchanged. In [8], where the MAP technique was used for the adaptation of a system based on triphones, the effect was significantly lower, because much more models stayed non-adapted in this case. The improvement of the recognition accuracy becomes slow for all the used methods, when the amount of the adaptation data is larger than 10 minutes.

4.2 Comparison of Efficiency of Supervised and Unsupervised Speaker Adaptation

The aim of the second experiment (Table 1) was to investigate how much the performance of the speaker adaptation depends on the type of the used adaptation data. The presented measure denoted as WERR (Word Error Rate Reduction) represents the relative reduction of the WER compared to the baseline SI system. Regarding the results of the previous experiment, we used the combination of the MAP and MLLR2 for both supervised and unsupervised adaptation. We used the same set of the adaptation data as in the previous experiment.

In the unsupervised case, the text and phonetic transcription of the adaptation data were created using our LVCSR system. Because the training data were recognized by the SI system with 81.1 % success rate, approximately two words from the phonetic transcription of each adaptation sentence might be wrong. On the other side, the recogniser was able to detect noises (such as breaths, uhm, etc) better than a human.

Table 1. Comparison of MAP + MLLR2 adaptation in supervised and unsupervised tasks. The baseline recognition accuracy of the SI system was 79.4 %

adaptation data [min]	0.5	1	2	4	5	7.5	10	12.5	15
supervised adaptation based on combination of MAP and MLLR2									
accuracy [%]	81.4	82.2	82.7	83.2	83.5	84.1	84.3	84.5	84.6
WERR [%]	9.9	13.8	16.3	18.5	20.2	23.0	23.9	24.8	25.5
unsupervised adaptation based on combination of MAP and MLLR2									
accuracy [%]	81.3	81.4	82.2	83.03	83.3	83.5	83.6	83.8	83.0
WERR [%]	9.6	9.7	13.7	17.7	19.0	19.9	20.4	21.5	17.5

From the results of this experiment it is evident that although the recognition accuracy of the system created by unsupervised adaptation increases more slowly than the accuracy of the system based on the supervised adaptation, the difference between the two approaches is small and the unsupervised system performed suprisingly well.

The differences in accuracy are evident mainly for the bigger amounts of the adaptation data. For example, while the WERR of the system adapted on 10 minutes of the supervised data is 23.9 %, the WERR of the system created by the unsupervised adaptation on the same amount of data is 20.4 %.

4.3 Unsupervised Speaker Adaptation in a Two-Pass Recognition

The last experiment (Table 2) investigated the possibility of the combination of the supervised and unsupervised adaptation. We tried to increase the recognition accuracy of our recogniser by running the recognition process in two consecutive passes. We hoped that such approach could improve the recognition rate in such off-line tasks like, e.g. broadcast news transcription.

In the first pass, we used the SA models created by combining the MAP and the MLLR2 method and using 10 minutes of the training data for text and phonetic transcription of the testing data. Then we performed unsupervised adaptation by the same method on the testing data and finally, we used the twice adapted models in the second recognition pass. The recognition accuracy in the first pass (the baseline value for this experiment) was 84.29 %.

We tried to perform the unsupervised adaptation on different amount of the testing data. So we created one acoustic model for each sentence of each speaker. In other tests we did it for several sentences (using from 0.5 to 10 minutes of speech data) and finally we repeated it for all the sentences of each speaker.

Table 2. Results of two-pass recognition based on unsupervised adaptation on testing data. The recognition accuracy in the first pass (the baseline value) was 84.29 %

the length of unsupervised data [min]	one sentence	0.5	1	2	5	10	all sentences of each speaker
accuracy [%]	83.98	84.03	84.11	84.23	84.34	84.38	84.59
WERR [%]	-2.0	-1.7	-1.1	-0.4	0.3	0.6	1.9

The results summarised in Table 2 show that the recognition in the second pass (based on the unsupervised adaptation on the testing data) did not lead to additional improvement of the recognition accuracy. On contrary, the unsupervised adaptation on smaller amounts of testing data yielded even slightly worse accuracy than the baseline system adapted on 10 minutes of supervised data. When all the testing sentences of each speaker were used for unsupervised adaptation, the WERR value was the best, though the improvement was not significant.

Furthermore, it is clear that the computation time in this case is more than twice longer. It is because the data were recognized twice in the first and in the second pass and another time was consumed by the process of speaker adaptation.

5   Conclusion

The results obtained from most of the experiments demonstrated that speaker adaptation based on the combination of the MAP and MLLR2 methods leads to the best improvement of the recognition accuracy for one given speaker. For example, the recognition accuracy of the system adapted on only 30 seconds of annotated data increased from 79.4 % to 81.4 %. If 10 minutes of speech was used for the adaptation, the recognition rate improved by 5 % and reached 84.3 %.

The performance of the system created by unsupervised adaptation increased more slowly compared to the previous strategy, but the difference was rather low. For example, the accuracy of the systems adapted on 10 minutes of the supervised data was only 0.7 % higher than the accuracy of the system adapted on the same amount of unsupervised data. On the other side, our expectation that a two-pass recognition scheme based on unsupervised adaptation on the testing data could bring another improvement was not approved, at least not for smaller amount of adaptation data.

Recently, all the successfully running methods have been applied in the design of a system for automatic broadcast news transcription [4], where the employment of the acoustic models adapted to the key-speakers improved the overall transcription accuracy.

References

1. Woodland, P. C.: Speaker Adaptation: Techniques and Challenges. Proc. IEEE Workshop on Automatic Speech Recognition and Understanding, Keystone, 1999
2. Gauvain, J.L., Lee, C.H.: Maximum A Posteriori Estimation for Multivariate Gaussian Mixture Observations of Markov Chains. IEEE Trans. SAP, Vol. 2, pp. 291-298, 1994
3. Leggetter, C.J. and Woodland, P.C.: Flexible Speaker Adaptation Using Maximum Likelihood Linear Regression. Proc. ARPA Spoken Language Technology Workshop, pp. 104-109, 1995, Morgan Kaufmann
4. Nouza, J., Nejedlova, D., Zdansky, J., Kolorenc, J.: Very Large Vocabulary Speech Recognition System for Automatic Transcription of Czech Broadcast Programs. Proc. of Int. Conference on Spoken Language Processing (ISCLP'04), Jeju, October 2004
5. Huang X.D., Acero A., Hon H.W.: Spoken Language Processing. Prentice Hall 2001
6. Gales M.J.F. and Woodland P.C.: Mean and Variance Adaptation Within the MLLR Framework. Computer Speech and Language, Vol. 10, pp. 249-264, 1996
7. Nouza, J., Psutka, J., Uhlir, J.: Phonetic Alphabet for Speech Recognition of Czech. Radioengineering, vol.6, no.4, pp.16-20, Dec.1997
8. Zelezny, M.: Speaker adaptation in continuous speech recognition system of Czech. PhD thesis (in Czech). ZČU of Plzeň 2001
9. Chesta, C., Siohan, O., Lee, C.H.: Maximum a posteriori linear regression for hidden Markov model adaptation. In Proceedings of European Conference on Speech Communication and Technology, volume 1, pages 211-214, Budapest, Hungary, 1999

Modelling Lexical Stress

Rogier C. van Dalen, Pascal Wiggers, and Leon J.M. Rothkrantz

Man–Machine Interaction
Delft University of Technology
Mekelweg 4, 2628 CD Delft, The Netherlands
{r.c.vandalen,p.wiggers,l.j.m.rothkrantz}@ewi.tudelft.nl

Abstract. Human listeners use lexical stress for word segmentation and disambiguation. We look into using lexical stress for speech recognition by examining a Dutch-language corpus. We propose that different spectral features are needed for different phonemes and that, besides vowels, consonants should be taken into account.

1 Introduction

Prosody is an important part of the spoken message structure. The foundation of prosody of many languages is laid by *lexical stress* [1]. Higher prosodic levels attach to the words at stressed syllables [2].

Lexical stress is used by listeners to identify words. Though the orthography does not normally encode stress, English has minimal pairs like *súbject – subjéct, trústy – trustée*, and *désert – dessért*. Pairs like *thírty – thirtéen* or *digréss – tígress* differ very little except in the stress pattern.

Even though in English and Dutch stress is not on a fixed syllable of the word, all morphologically simplex words of Germanic origin and many others do start with a stressed syllable. Listeners use this for segmentation of speech into words [3]. English-hearing children appear to associate stressed syllables with word onsets at the age of seven months already [4].

Dutch listeners use the stress pattern to identify words before they have been fully heard as well. When hearing the beginning of a word *octo-*, Dutch listeners will decipher whether it is *octó-* or *ócto-* and reconstruct *octóber* or *óctopus* [5].

Garden-variety speech recognisers do not use lexical stress, useful though it may be. This paper will describe how lexical stress can be automatically detected. It will be determined what features correlate most strongly with lexical stress, considering benefits for speech recognition.

2 Related Work

There has been research on the acoustic correlates of lexical stress. Sluijter [6] in fundamental linguistic research on the acoustic properties of stress minimal pairs demonstrated that lexical stress in English and Dutch is signalled mostly through duration, formant frequencies, intensity, and *spectral tilt*. The latter is a feature that denotes the

V. Matoušek et al. (Eds.): TSD 2005, LNAI 3658, pp. 211–218, 2005.

energy in high frequency bands relative to the energy in low frequency bands. Van Kuijk [7] examined the acoustic properties of a larger corpus of Dutch telephone speech and found similar results: a combination of duration and spectral tilt was the best predictor for lexical stress.

Lexical stress has been used to generate a confidence metric [8]. Of those that have actually used lexical stress recognition in a speech recogniser [9–11], only Wang and Seneff [10] have been able to effect a performance gain. This is probably what the other authors are after as well; but how this is to be done is not discussed. Van den Heuvel [11] hopes "distinguishing stressed and unstressed vowel models may have a general impact on recognition results."

Notably, none of the previous approaches has taken into account the well-observed influence that stress has on consonants: stressed and unstressed consonants are realised differently [1] and stressed consonants have a longer duration [12]. Consonants are influenced by speaking style in the same ways as vowels are: duration, spectral tilt and formant frequencies (for consonants with a formant structure) [13]. This suggests similar effects can be found for lexical stress on consonants. The closest thing to a rationale for not regarding consonants in automatic lexical stress recognition is the claim that consonants do not carry lexical stress in [10]. This claim is not further motivated, and it will be demonstrated to be incorrect.

3 Model

3.1 Objectives

Since humans use lexical stress in processing speech, modelling it could help speech recogniser performance. We expect the following advantages from using lexical stress.

Phone model accuracy Current speech recognition systems have severe problems coping with speech that is pronounced much faster or slower than the speech it is trained on. Phonemes in unstressed syllables are less often realised canonically than those in stressed syllables. Therefore separating phone models into stressed and unstressed versions may increase predictive strength of the models, improving recognition. For example, unstressed vowels tend to become /ə/[1]. Because the range /ə/–/aː/ is split into into /ə/–/aː/–/ˈaː/, the phone models may become more accurate.

Word segmentation English hearers, when presented with a faint recording "conduct ascends uphill", will reconstruct words starting at stressed syllables, for example, "the doctor sends a pill" [3]. Humans use stress for segmentation; a speech recogniser could use this strategy too.

Word recognition Lexical stress signals differences between:
1. words with the same segmental content and different meanings (e.g. Du. *vóorko-men* 'happen' – *voorkómen* 'prevent');
2. words of different categories (e.g. En. *récord* – *recórd*);
3. similar words with different stress patterns (e.g. En. *portráy* – *pórtait*).

---

[1] In both Dutch and English.

3.2   Syllables

Lexical stress is specified for syllables as a whole. This poses a problem for speech recognisers, which typically use phonemes as units. Earlier approaches have circumvented this problem by using only vowels for stress detection. When consonants are included as well, their specification must match the vowels' in the same syllable. This can be done by using a consistently stress-marked lexicon: if it contains both /'s 'ʌ 'b d ʒ ɛ k t/ and /s ʌ b 'd 'ʒ 'ɛ 'k 't/, the recogniser would never hypothesise /s 'ʌ b 'd ʒ 'ɛ k 't/.

In the linguistic literature a difference is made between realisations in the coda and in the onset. For example, English /t/ is pronounced as [tʰ] in *táil*, but as [t] in *rétail* and *líght* [1]: /t/ is only aspirated in the onset of a stressed syllable.

3.3   Acoustic Representation

To integrate recognition in a speech recogniser, stressedness can be modelled one phoneme at a time. We look into acoustic correlates of lexical stress that can be fed into a speech recogniser, for example by including them in the feature vectors.

Fundamental Frequency Stress is typically thought to be connected to pitch. However, from linguistic literature [2] and literature on automatic stress recognition [14] it is expected that pitch is not straightforwardly correlated with lexical stress. Its acoustic correlate, the fundamental frequency, can straightforwardly be included in a speech recogniser's feature vector though.

Formants Unstressed phonemes can have more reduced realisations than their stressed counterparts; this is visible in the formant values. Standard MFCCs should be able to capture this difference. Note that MFCCs do not directly model formants, but frequency bands. Separating MFCC-based phone models into stressed and unstressed models, whose formant values are confined to a smaller area, will therefore increase MFCCs' ability to recognise the phonemes.

Spectrum The energy in a number of frequency bands can be extracted from the waveform to yield information about the spectral tilt.

Intensity Overall intensity is generally thought to be associated with lexical stress. However, [6] claims that what is often perceived as loudness variation may actually be spectral tilt: speaking effort would be the common cause.

Duration Lexical stress is generally found to be correlated with phoneme duration [6, 7, 12]. However, information about phoneme duration is not available during first-pass recognition. Standard HMMs can encode duration through transition probabilities, but this does not work well in recognition. A number of alternatives have been proposed though [15–18].

Derivatives In [10] it is found that fundamental frequency slope is a better predictor of stress than the raw fundamental frequency. Spectral features are measures for the effort with which phonemes are pronounced. The speaking effort is a continuous measure: it probably increases over the beginning of a stressed syllable and decreases over the end. We therefore expect that derivatives for spectral features also may be correlated with lexical stress, especially for consonants.

4   Experimental Set-Up

We bootstrapped a speech recogniser, made with HTK [19], from Wiggers' system [20] and did measurements on the Delft DUTAVSC corpus [21]. We used the stress marks from the CELEX lexicon. All phonemes in stressed syllables were marked as stressed, except for function words, which were marked as unstressed. All features were normalised over the whole of one utterance. The intensity measure was included in the feature vectors by HTK. For the energy in spectral bands we used the Linux program *sox* and Praat. [6] chooses spectral bands so that the formants least influence the results; we use the same bands: 0 – 0.5 kHz, 0.5 – 1 kHz, 1 – 2 kHz, and 2 – 4 kHz.

The fundamental frequency was extracted with Praat [22]. Where Praat did not find the fundamental frequency, it was linearly interpolated. This has a number of advantages over using an out-of-range value:

– It formalises the notion of the intonational tune in the linguistic literature [2, 23, 24], where it is pictured as a non-interrupted curve.
– From the linguistic literature, a pitch peak on or near the stressed syllable is expected. Through interpolation, even voiceless phonemes will include pitch information, so that a pitch peak at the onset or the coda of the syllable will be noticed.
– If Praat does not find voicing where there is, linear interpolation provides a reasonable workaround. This increases the algorithm's robustness.
– An out-of-range value, rather than giving the recogniser information about stress, would inject inappropriate information about apparent voicedness.

5   Results

The results were assembled by collecting feature vectors from phones that were segmented with forced alignment. The most discriminating features are candidates for inclusion in a speech recogniser that aims at recognising lexical stress. We did not find any significant results from the fundamental frequency data; duration and spectral features, however, do show much separation.

5.1   Duration

Similarly to [6, 7], we found that duration is in general a good indicator of stressedness. Stressed vowels are quite consistently longer than their unstressed counterparts (see Fig. 1(a)). Not all consonants are, as shown in Fig. 1(d): for stops the duration does not seem to differ at all, probably because stops' complete closure makes it difficult to produce lengthened ones sensibly: only the silence would be longer. Liquids consistently show a large difference, as exemplified by /l/ in Fig. 1(b), while fricatives are in between (Fig. 1(c)).

5.2   Spectral Tilt

We find that different spectral tilt features apply for different phonemes. For many phonemes stressedness correlates well with some spectral tilt measure. This may be

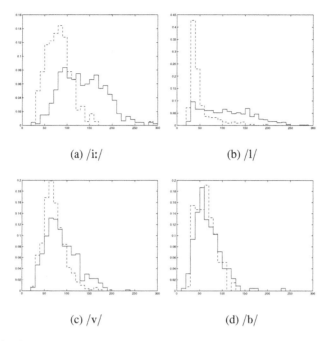

(a) /iː/   (b) /l/

(c) /v/   (d) /b/

Fig. 1. Distributions of durations of stressed (stroked lines) and unstressed (dashed lines) phonemes in ms.

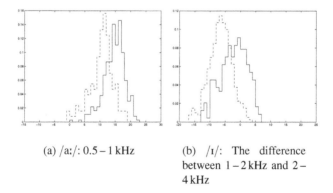

(a) /aː/: 0.5 – 1 kHz   (b) /ɪ/: The difference between 1 – 2 kHz and 2 – 4 kHz

Fig. 2. Distributions of spectral tilt features for stressed (stroked lines) and unstressed (dashed lines) vowels in ms.

why [6] found clear correlations on a limited set of phonemes, while [7] had troubles finding correlates with a limited set of features (two). Our results show much more difference than the latter found; this may also be due to the telephone speech they used being spectrally impoverished. Figure 2 shows how spectral features correlate with long vowels (as in Fig. 2(a)) and with short vowels (as in Fig. 2(b)).

Most interestingly, the features that work for vowels give similar results for consonants. Figures 3(a) and 3(b) shows how stressed and unstressed consonants differ in

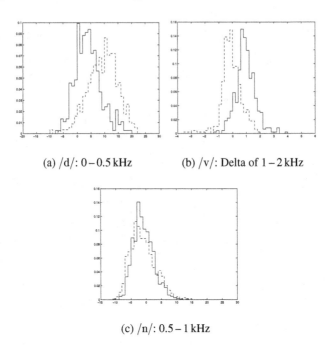

(a) /d/: 0 – 0.5 kHz   (b) /v/: Delta of 1 – 2 kHz

(c) /n/: 0.5 – 1 kHz

Fig. 3. Distributions of spectral tilt features for stressed (stroked lines) and unstressed (dashed lines) vowels in ms.

terms of spectrum. On the other hand, /n/ (Fig. 3(c)) does not show spectral disparity at all. We suspect two factors play a role here:

- The effect of speaking effort for fricatives and stops on the spectrum may be greater due to their friction-based realisation.
- From a perception perspective, stressed and unstressed /n/ already differ greatly in duration (similarly to Fig. 1(b)) so the difference in spectrum is not as vital for distinguishing the two.

6   Conclusion

This paper has described the importance and the feasibility of detecting lexical stress in speech. That stress works on the syllable level can be modelled effectively by adding stress marks to the phonemes in the lexical entries of a speech recogniser.

Lexical stress has been demonstrated to influence acoustically not only vowels, but also consonants. The same features that are canonically associated with stressed vowels (duration, spectral tilt, intensity) are correlates of stress for consonants. Various spectral tilt features apply to various phonemes. Using the duration of a phoneme while it is being recognised is not well possible with the Viterbi algorithm and standard HMMs. Another algorithm should be used if duration modelling is considered important.

Given the fact that many consonants will participate in the decision whether a syllable is stressed, we hope that implementing lexical stress recognition, even without extensive duration modelling, will improve general recognition performance on three accounts: general phone recognition, word segmentation and word recognition.

References

1. Ewen, C.J., van der Hulst, H.: The Phonological Structure of Words. Cambridge University Press (2001)
2. Ladd, D.R.: Intonational phonology. Number 79 in Cambridge Studies in Linguistics. Cambridge University Press, Cambridge (1996)
3. Harley, T.: The Psychology of Language: From Data to Theory. Psychology Press, Hove (2001)
4. Thiessen, E.D., Saffran, J.R.: When cues collide: Use of stress and statistical cues to word boundaries by 7- to 9-month-old infants. Developmental Psychology **39** (2003) 706–716
5. Cooper, N., Cutler, A., Wales, R.: Constraints of lexical stress on lexical acces in English: Evidence from native and non-native listeners. Language and Speech **45** (2002) 207–228
6. Sluijter, A.: Phonetic Correlates of Stress and Accent. PhD thesis, Leiden University (1995)
7. van Kuijk, D., Boves, L.: Acoustic characteristics of lexical stress in continuous telephone speech. Speech Communication **27** (1999) 95–111
8. Bouwman, A.G.G., Boves, L.: Using information on lexical stress for utterance verification. Proceedings of ITRW on Prosody in ASRU, Red Bank (2001) 29–34
9. van Kuijk, D., van den Heuvel, H., Boves, L.: Using lexical stress in continuous speech recognition for Dutch. Proceedings ICSLP IV (1996) 1736–1739
10. Wang, C., Seneff, S.: Lexical stress modeling for improved speech recognition of spontaneous telephone speech in the JUPITER domain (2001)
11. van den Heuvel, H., van Kuijk, D., Boves, L.: Modelling lexical stress in continuous speech recognition. Speech Communication **40** (2003) 335–350
12. Greenberg, S., Carvey, H., Hitchcock, L., Chang, S.: Temporal properties of spontaneous speech — a syllable-centric perspective. Journal of Phonetics **31** (2003) 465–485
13. van Son, R.J.J.H., Pols, L.C.W.: An acoustic profile of consonant reduction. Proceedings ICSLP **3** (1996) 1529–1532
14. Xie, H., Andreae, P., Zhang, M., Warren, P.: Detecting stress in spoken English using decision trees and support vector machines. In: Proceedings of the second workshop on Australasian information security, Data Mining and Web Intelligence, and Software Internationalisation, Australian Computer Society, Inc. (2004) 145–150
15. Wang, X.: Duration modelling in HMM-based speech recognition. PhD thesis, University of Amsterdam (1997)
16. Russell, M.J., Moore, R.K.: Explicit modelling of state occupancy in hidden Markov models for automatic speech recognition. Proceedings of ICASSP **10** (1985) 5–8
17. Ramesh, P., Wilpon, J.G.: Modeling state durations in hidden Markov models for automatic speech recognition. Proceedings of ICASSP **1** (1992) 381–384
18. Sitaram, R.N.V., Sreenivas, T.: Incorporating phonetic properties and hidden Markov models for speech recognition. Journal of the Acoustical Society of America **102** (1997) 1149–1158
19. Young, S., Evermann, G., Hain, T., Kershaw, D., Moore, G., Odell, J., Ollason, D., Povey, D., Valtchev, V., Woodland, P.: The HTK book (for HTK version 3.2.1) (2002)
20. Wiggers, P., Wojdel, J.C., Rothkrantz, L.J.: Development of a speech recognizer for the Dutch language. Proceedings of 7th annual scientific conference on web technology, new media, communications and telematics theory, methods, tools and applications (EUROMEDIA) (2002) 133–138

21. Wojdeł, J.C.: Automatic Lipreading in the Dutch Language. PhD thesis, Delft University of Technology, Delft (2003)
22. Boersma, P.: PRAAT, a system for doing phonetics by computer. Glot International **5** (2001) 341–345
23. Bolinger, D.: Intonation and its Parts. Edward Arnold, London (1986)
24. Bolinger, D.: Intonation and its Uses. PhD thesis, Stanford University (1989)

The Sound Database Formation for the Allophone-Based Model for English Concatenative Speech Synthesis

Karina Evgrafova

Department of Phonetics St-Petersburg State University
Universitetskaya emb. 11, Saint-Petersburg, Russia
karinaevgr@mail.ru

Abstract. The goal of this paper is to describe the development of the sound database for the allophone-based model for English concatenative speech synthesis. The procedure of the sound unit inventory construction is described and its main results are presented. At present moment the optimized sound units inventory of the allophonic database for English concatenative speech synthesis contains 1200 elements (1000 vowel allophones and 200 consonant allophones). The smoothness of junctions between the allophones shows high quality of the segmentation made. The decrease in the number of the database components in the result of optimization does not affect the quality of the resulting synthesized speech. At the level of segments it can be evaluated as fairly high in terms of both naturalness and intelligibility.

1 Introduction

The paper deals with the sound database formation for English concatenative speech synthesis.The main objectives of the concatenative speech synthesis and the peculiarities of an allophone-based model are described in literature [1], [7].

The fundamental principles of the English allophonic database formation have been already described by the author [2]. In the present paper, the procedure of the sound unit inventory construction for English allophonic database is described and its main results are presented.

The research has been carried out in three steps. In the first step, the acoustic material for the allophonic database was obtained. As a second step, the optimization of the allophonic base was performed. And, finally, perceptual tests were conducted to evaluate the quality of the allophonic inventory developed.

2 Sound Material Preparation

In creating the database of sound elements it is first necessary to obtain basic material, containing all segments required for the organization of a wordform. In the allophone-based model these segments are allophones, that is realizations of English phonemes in definite phonetic contexts. Descriptions of all combinatory and positional allophones of English phonemes can be found in literature [3], [4]. Taking into account these descriptions, a lexicon of 3300 words and phrases containing English allophones in specified

V. Matoušek et al. (Eds.): TSD 2005, LNAI 3658, pp. 219–225, 2005.

contexts was formed [2]. The lexicon was recorded from a female speaker. The recorded speech was digitized at F16KHz. In the following step, segmentation of the recorded speech was performed. Sound units corresponding to the realizations of allophones in the natural physical limits were extracted from the natural speech stream.

It should be noted that in the allophonic model the precise definition of the boundary between two neighboring allophones is of great importance [8]. The quality of the constructed allophone depends on how accurately the boundaries are determined. It is necessary for the allophone to preserve the information contained in transitions, which provides the naturalness of the concatenation. To achieve this aim all coarticulation rules must be taken into account [3].

Thus a lot of effort was invested in the definition of the physical boundaries between allophones during the segmentation process.

To evaluate the accuracy of the segmentation two types of tests were carried out [5].

1. An extracted from a word allophone was inserted into a word or a syllable having a similar phonetic context. (E.g. /i/ from *wick* was inserted into *wig* instead of /i/ from *wig*). If it led to perceptible change of acoustic properties of the word the right or the left boundary was shifted and the listening experiment was repeated. The physical boundaries of the allophone were set finally only after the needed perceptual effect was achieved.
2. By means of the EDS program (a program for digital treatment of speech signals developed at St.-Petersburg University of Telecommunications) the extracted allophones were combined into a sound file. After that the listening experiment was conducted to evaluate naturalness of the string synthesized. After testing all extracted allophones were saved in separate sound files.

To improve the quality of the synthesized speech certain consonant clusters were included into the database as one unit. It concerns the following clusters:

– plosive+fricative in a final position (ps, bz, ts, dz, ks, gz);
– plosive+lateral sonant /l/ (/tl, dl, pl, bl, kl, gl/);
– plosive+nasal sonant /n/, /m/, /ng/ (bn, pn, tn, dn etc.);
– plosive+ plosive/affricative (td, gd, kt, pt etc.).

Thus, as the result of segmentation, the allophonic database inventory was obtained. At that stage it contained about 3000 concatenation units. As it is well-known, any sound database must be compact. It is necessary to include all the units needed for quality during synthesis and at the same time to minimize the size of the inventory. Consequently, the optimal proportion between the number of the database elements and the quality of the synthesized speech should be found. This task was accomplished in the following step.

3 Optimization of the Base of Allophones

After the database of sound elements had been developed, there arose a possibility to reduce the number of the database elements. The previously defined set of all the theoretically *necessary* allophones was reduced by enlarging the classes of allophone contexts and looking for basic allophones which were still more tolerant to specific contexts.

As a result of numerous experiments, which were carried out under a thorough audio control, a *sufficient* set of fewer basic allophones was defined. The set included all the necessary *basic* allophones which could be used instead of certain combinatory allophones [7]. (E.g. in the course of listening experiments it was found out that vowel allophones with /u/ in the left-hand context are similar considerably to those having /w/ in the left. The choice was made in favour of the allophones following /w/ as the combination /w/+vowel is more frequent than /u/+vowel).

Thus the number of the left-hand contexts for vowels was reduced up to 11 classes and the right-hand contexts up to 9 classes. The consonant contexts are presented by the 5 right-hand and 10 left-hand classes.

The tables below show the results of the experiments (the definition of the phoneset used in the tables is in http://festival/lib/mrpa_phones.scm): Table 1 shows necessary vowel contexts, Table 2 – types of vowel left-hand contexts, Table 3 – types of vowel right-hand contexts, Table 4 – consonant contexts, Table 5 – left-hand contexts for consonants, Table 6 – right-hand contexts for consonants.

Another way to reduce the number of allophones in the database was used. All the allophones that are possible at word boundaries only were excluded from the database.

Table 1. Vowel contexts

	0	t	p	k	L	R	j	w	@
1	+	+	+	+	+	+	+	+	+
2	+	+	+	+	+	+	+	+	+
3	+	+	+	+	+	+	+	+	+
4	+	+	+	+	+	+	+	+	+
L	+	+	+	+	+	+	+	+	+
R	+	+	+	+	+	+	+	+	+
j	+	+	+	+	+	+	+	+	+
w	+	+	+	+	+	+	+	+	+
ng	+	+	+	+	+	+	+	+	+
@	+	+	+	+	+	+	+	+	+
0	+	+	+	+	+	+	+	+	+

Table 2. Types of vowel left-hand contexts

1	Forelingual /t, d, ch, jh, s, z, sh, zh, th, dh/
2	Backlingual /k,g/ and glottal /h/
3	Labials /p, b, f, v/
4	Nasals /m, n/
L	Consonant /l/
R	Consonant /r/
j	Consonant /y/ and vowels /i, ii, ai, oi, ei/
w	Consonant /w/ and vowels /uu, oo, ou, au/
ng	Consonant /ng/
@	Vowels /@, i@, u@, e@, @@, aa/
0	Absolute beginning

Table 3. Types of vowel right-hand contexts

1	Forelingual
2	Backlingual /k, g, ng/, glottal /h/
3	Labials /p, b, f, v/
4	Nasals /m, n/
L	Consonant /l/
R	Consonant /r/
j	Consonant /y/ and vowels /i, ii, i@/
w	Consonant /w/ and vowels /uu, oo, ou, au/
@	Vowels /@, e, uh, a, aa, @@, ei, e@, au, ai, ou/
0	Final position

Table 4. Consonant contexts

	0	i	a	o	t	f	th	r	n	L
0_c	+	+	+	+	+	+	+	+	+	+
s_c	+	+	+	+	+	+	+	+	+	
t_c	+	+	+	+	+	+	+	+	+	

Table 5. Left-hand consonant contexts

0_c	absolute beginning, after a vowel, after a consonant
s_c	following /s/ for /p, t, k/
t_c	following /p, t, s, h/ for /m/ /n/ /l/ /r/ /j/ /w/

Table 6. Right-hand consonant contexts

0	final position
i	preceding /i ii/ and /y/ for all consonants, except /y/
a	preceding the unrounded vowels /e, uh, a, @, @@, aa, ou, au, e@, i@, ai/
o	preceding the rounded vowels /o, oo, u, uu, u@, oi/ for all consonants, except /w, sh, zh, ch, jh, r/
t	preceding the plosives /p, b, t, d, k, g/ and affricatives /ch, jh/ for /p, b, t, d, k, g/
f	preceding the labio-dentals /f, v/ for /p, b, m, n/
th	preceding the dentals /th, dh / for /t, d/
r	preceding /r/ for /t, d, n/
n	preceding the nasals /n, m/ for /p, b, t, d, k, g/
L	preceding /l/ for /p, b, t, d, k, g/

A micro pause which appears between words as a result of this reduction does not affect the naturalness of the synthesized speech but at the same time improves its intelligibility. Thus it was possible to reduce the size of the allophonic database up to 1200 elements (1000 vowel allophones and 200 consonant allophones). As a result of the optimization, important theoretical and practical results were obtained. The conducted experiments showed that a number of vowels with different right-hand or left-hand contexts having different articulatory characteristics do not differ acoustically. Consequently, the number of basic allophones which are different from the acoustical point of view turned out to be significantly less than that of the traditionally defined articulatory allophones described in literature [3], [4].

4   Evaluation Tests and Their Results

The quality of the obtained allophonic database inventory was evaluated in perceptual tests. About 70 phrases containing 215 frequent allophones were synthesized. The main criteria of evaluation were the degree of naturalness and intelligibility. The tests showed the following results.

- At the level of segments the quality of the synthesized speech was evaluated as rather high in terms of both naturalness and intelligibility. The junctions between allophones proved to be absolutely imperceptible. This fact confirmed the accuracy of physical boundaries definition between the segments and also demonstrated that the database inventory was formed in a correct way (see Fig. 1 and Fig. 2 as in examples).
- At a prosodic level, however, the degree of naturalness was not evaluated as high. It mainly concerned phrases containing three and more words which sounded unnatural from the prosodic point of view. It can be explained by the fact that fundamental frequency of the units selected to build up a phrase to be synthesized is usually different from the one requested by the prosodic model of the phrase. This lack of coordination in formant and harmonic positions at the junction of sound units requires a special procedure of smoothing spectral parameters at the boundaries of allophones. The application of traditional spectral smoothing algorithms can result in distortion of individual characteristics of speaker's voice and in lowering of naturalness of synthesied speech [6]. To avoid it, the physical boundaries of allophones were chosen in such a way as to minimize spectral smoothing at the junction of formants and harmonics. Nevertheless at present moment the difference in formants and harmonics positions at certain allophone junctions still exists. Therefore the necessity for smoothing remains. Alternatively, techniques of prosody modifications can be incorporated to produce speech with the expected prosodic characteristics. These modifications, however, can degrade the output speech signal.

Thus the evaluation tests demonstrated fairly high quality of the synthesized speech at the level of segments. As to its prosodic characteristics, further work at their improvement is required.

5   Discussion

The present research was aimed at solving both theoretical and applied problems. Theoretically, it was necessary to consider the realization of each of English phonemes in all possible phonetic contexts in order to define a set of *basic*allophones that could be used instead of certain combinatory allophones. The obtained set of *basic* allophones includes only *acoustical* allophones, that is allophones different from the acoustical point of view. The sounds that have different right-hand or left-hand contexts and different articulatory characteristics but at the same time are identical acoustically were excluded

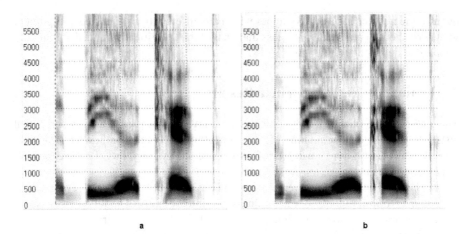

Fig. 1. *A beer keg*: a – natural, b – synthesized signals

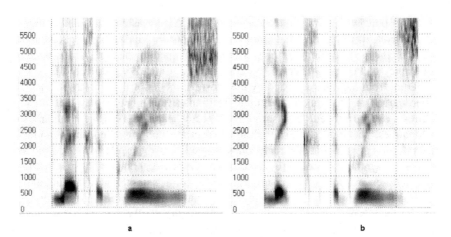

Fig. 2. *Nick agrees*: a – natural, b – synthesized signals

from the set of *basic acoustical* allophones. As the result, the set of *basic acoustical* allophones appeared to be 3 times less than the number of *articulatory* allophones of English phonemes. The obtained theoretical results were used in solving the following applied problem. The assumption that certain groups of phonemes have similar co-articulatory effects on neighboring segments has made it possible to reduce the number of units in the inventory of the constructed sound database without affecting the quality of the synthesized speech. Time required for the formation of the inventory based on the set of *basic acoustical* allophones was reduced significantly. Besides the reduction of the number of basic units makes it possible to reduce time and effort in including new voices into the synthesis system. It should be also noted, that the obtained knowledge about the types of consonants having similar effects on neighboring sounds can be also successfully used in suballophone set formation. For example, in suballophone-based system the vowel halves with /w/ in left context can be used for constructing vowel allophones having both /w/ and a rounded vowel in left context. And, finally, the reduced set of *basic acoustical* allophones has allowed to develop compact speech segment database for English concatenative synthesis. Although the current trend in concatenative speech synthesis is to use large databases of acoustic units, smaller optimized databases are needed in low-memory devices (e.g. mobile phones, pocket PCs, etc.).

6   Conclusion

At present moment the optimized sound unit inventory of the allophonic database for English concatenative speech synthesis contains 1200 elements (1000 vowel allophones and 200 consonant allophones). The smoothness of junctions between the allophones shows high quality of the segmentation made. The decrease in the number of the database components in the result of optimization does not affect the quality of the resulting synthesized speech. At the level of segments it can be evaluated as fairly high in terms of both naturalness and intelligibility.

References

1. Bondarko, L.V., Kuznetsov, V.I., Skrelin, P.A.: The Sound System of the Russian Language from the point of view of the objectives of Russian Speech Concatenative Synthesis. (In Russian.) In: Bulleten' foneticheskogo fonda russkogo jazyka, N 6. St-Petersburg-Bochum (1997)
2. Evgrafova, K.V.: The Principles of the English Allophonic Database Formation. (In Russian.) In: Foneticheskij litsej. St-Petersburg (2004) 23-36
3. Gimson, A.C.: An Introduction to the Pronunciation of English. London (1962)
4. O'Connor, J.D.: Phonetics. London (1977)
5. Shalonova, K.B.: The Acoustical Characteristics of the Transitions between Sounds. (In Russian.) St-Petersburg (1996)
6. Skrelin, P.A.: Concatenative Russian Speech Synthesis: Sound Database Formation Principles.In: Proc. of the SPECOM'97, Cluj-Napoka
7. Skrelin, P.A.: The Phonetic Aspects of Speech Technologies. (In Russian.) St-Petersburg (1999)
8. Skrelin, P.A.: The Segmentation and Transcription. St-Petersburg (1999)

Using Artificially Reverberated Training Data in Distant-Talking ASR*

Tino Haderlein[1], Elmar Nöth[1], Wolfgang Herbordt[2,**],
Walter Kellermann[2], and Heinrich Niemann[1]

[1] University of Erlangen-Nuremberg, Chair for Pattern Recognition
(Informatik 5), Martensstraße 3, 91058 Erlangen, Germany
Tino.Haderlein@informatik.uni-erlangen.de
http://www5.informatik.uni-erlangen.de
[2] University of Erlangen-Nuremberg
Chair of Multimedia Communications and Signal Processing
Cauerstraße 7, 91058 Erlangen, Germany

Abstract. Automatic Speech Recognition (ASR) in reverberant rooms can be improved by choosing training data from the same acoustical environment as the test data. In a real-world application this is often not possible. A solution for this problem is to use speech signals from a close-talking microphone and reverberate them artificially with multiple room impulse responses. This paper shows results on recognizers whose training data differ in size and percentage of reverberated signals in order to find the best combination for data sets with different degrees of reverberation. The average error rate on a close-talking and a distant-talking test set could thus be reduced by 29% relative.

1 Introduction

When developing speech-driven human-machine interfaces for hands-free control of devices in a living-room environment, like for television sets and VCRs, the microphones recording the user's utterances will be integrated into the device itself or distributed in the room. This leads to the problem that among other distortions the received signal is reverberated. In our work we used artificially reverberated training data to improve performance of speech recognition in reverberant rooms, as e.g. in [1, 2]. However, we tried to find a training set that is suitable for both reverberated and clean speech and, in general, for unknown target environments. Our research thus aims at ASR systems that are portable between different acoustic conditions. Other well-known methods for improving speech recognition performance on distant-talking data are environment-independent features (see an overview in [3, pp. 39-51]), sometimes with integrated normalization methods as in RASTA-PLP [4], or combining the signals from a microphone array [5]. These were not applied in our experiments.

---

* Our work was partially supported by the German Federal Ministry of Education and Research (grant no. 01 IMD 01 F) in the frame of the SmartWeb project. The responsibility for the contents of this study lies with the authors.
** Now with ATR, Kyoto, Japan.

V. Matoušek et al. (Eds.): TSD 2005, LNAI 3658, pp. 226–233, 2005.
© Springer-Verlag Berlin Heidelberg 2005

This paper is organized as follows: In Section 2 we present preliminary experiments with a reduced amount of training data from the EMBASSI corpus [6] allowing fast evaluation of different data and recognizer configurations. Based on the findings from these examinations we introduce recognizers with a large training set in Section 3. The data were taken from the VERBMOBIL corpus and allowed us to compare our results with earlier experiments on these data [7]. Section 4 summarizes the results.

2 Preliminary Experiments

2.1 Recognizer Specifications and Baseline System

As in a previous work, we used a baseline recognizer with only one hour of training data for fast evaluation of various setups where the training and test data were taken from the EMBASSI corpus [6]. This German speech collection was recorded in a room with a reverberation time of $T_{60} = 150\,\mathrm{ms}$ (i.e. the time span in which the reverberation decays by 60 dB). It consists of utterances of 20 speakers (10 male, 10 female) who read commands to a TV set and to a VCR, since the topic of EMBASSI was developing speech interfaces for these devices. A close-talking microphone (headset) and a linear array of 11 microphones were used for simultaneous recording. The center of the latter was either 1 meter or 2.5 meters away from the speaker (see Fig. 1). In each one of 10 sessions each speaker read 60 sentences which took approx. between 150 and 180 seconds. The size of the room was $5.8\,\mathrm{m} \times 5.9\,\mathrm{m} \times 3.1\,\mathrm{m}$, the center of the microphone array was at position $(2.0\,\mathrm{m}, 5.2\,\mathrm{m}, 1.4\,\mathrm{m})$. The speaker sat at position $(2.0\,\mathrm{m}, 4.2\,\mathrm{m}, 1.4\,\mathrm{m})$ or $(2.0\,\mathrm{m}, 2.7\,\mathrm{m}, 1.4\,\mathrm{m})$, respectively, i.e. the head was at about the same height as the microphones. The origin of the coordinate system in the room was the left corner behind the speaker.

The training data of the EMBASSI baseline system (EMB-base, see Table 1) consisted of the close-talking recordings of 6 male and 6 female speakers from two sessions (60 min of speech, 8315 words). One male and one female speaker formed the validation set (10 min, 1439 words), and one half of the test set consisted of the remaining three men and three women (30 min, 4184 words). The other half were the corresponding data of the central array microphone, which was 1 m away during one of the used sessions and 2.5 m during the other.

Our speech recognition system is based on semi-continuous HMMs. It models phones in a variable context dependent on their frequency of occurrence and thus forms the so-called polyphones. The HMMs for each polyphone have three to four states. The EMBASSI recognizers have a vocabulary size of 474 words and were trained with a 4-gram language model. For each 16 ms frame (10 ms overlap) 24 features were computed (signal energy, 11 MFCCs and the first derivatives of those 12 static features, approximated over 5 consecutive frames).

Before reverberating the training data artificially we trained a recognizer with EMBASSI data from a distant microphone (EMB-rev) in order to find out which results could maximally be reached when training and test environment were the same. Therefore we used the signals from the microphone from the center of the microphone array whose recordings were synchronously recorded with the close-talking training data. As two EMBASSI sessions were involved, half of the data were recorded at a distance of

Table 1. Data sets for the recognizers trained with EMBASSI data ("mic. dist." = microphone distance, "CT art. rev." = close-talking artificially reverberated)

recognizer	training		validation		test	
	mic. dist.	duration	mic. dist.	duration	mic. dist.	dur.
EMB-base (T_{60}: $\approx$ 0 ms)	close-talk	60 min	close-talk	10 min	close-talk 1 m 2.5 m	30 min 15 min 15 min
EMB-rev (T_{60}: 150 ms)	1 m 2.5 m	30 min 30 min	1 m 2.5 m	5 min 5 min	like EMB-base	
EMB-12 (T_{60}: 250, 400 ms)	close-talk (artif. rev.)	12·60= 720 min	close-talk (artif. rev.)	12·10= 120 min	like EMB-base	
EMB-2 (T_{60}: 0, 250, 400ms)	close-talk+ CT art. rev.	60 min 60 min	close-talk+ CT art. rev.	10 min 10 min	like EMB-base	

Table 2. Word accuracies for the EMBASSI recognizers (0-gram = no language model)

mic. dist.	lang. model	EMB-base	EMB-rev	EMB-12	EMB-2
close-talk	4-gram	94.3	87.5	91.7	95.5
close-talk	0-gram	70.0	40.0	57.7	71.4
1 m	4-gram	90.2	94.1	94.0	94.4
1 m	0-gram	52.4	66.2	61.9	63.0
2.5 m	4-gram	84.1	93.1	88.4	89.6
2.5 m	0-gram	37.5	63.2	52.4	55.3

1 m and the other half at 2.5 m distance (see Table 1). The situation for the validation data was similar. Only the test data were exactly the same as before.

Table 2 shows that, for distant talkers, the best results are achieved on the reverberated test data, i.e. for those acoustical environments that were present in the training data. For 1 m microphone distance the word accuracy was 94.1% (90.2% on EMB-base) and for 2.5 m distance it was 93.1% (84.1%). The close-talking signals, however, have disadvantages in this approach (87.5% vs. 94.3%). In the table we also added the results for the recognition without a language model in order to show how much the pure acoustic information contributed to the word accuracies. The good results when using the 4-gram model were achieved because the training data were not spontaneous, but read sentences.

Of course training a recognition system with reverberated speech is a simple way to improve the results on test data recorded with a large distance from speaker to microphone. This usually means, however, that the acoustical properties of the training data are the same as in the test data. In a real application the target environment is largely unknown before. Therefore, we investigate in the following to what extent artificially reverberated training data can match various test environments.

2.2 Training the System with Artificially Reverberated Data

If the goal is a recognizer which works robustly in many environments one might suggest that the training data should provide recordings that were made in a lot of different

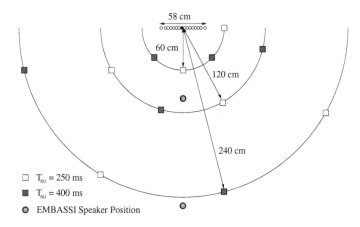

Fig. 1. Assumed speaker positions in the virtual recording rooms for artificially reverberated data; 12 room impulse responses from different positions and with two reverberation times (250 and 400 ms) were used. The circles mark the positions of the speaker in the real EMBASSI recording room

places. This would mean collecting speech data in many rooms with different impulse responses and place the microphone(s) in different angles and distances from the speakers who also have to be available in every location. Reverberating close-talking speech artificially with the help of pre-defined room impulse responses can reduce this effort.

The room impulse responses were measured in the room where also the EMBASSI corpus was recorded. However, the reverberation time was changed from $T_{60} = 150$ ms to $T_{60} = 250$ ms and to $T_{60} = 400$ ms by removing sound absorbing carpets and sound absorbing curtains from the room. 12 impulse responses were measured for loudspeaker positions on three semi-circles in front of the microphone array at distances 60 cm, 120 cm, and 240 cm. See Fig. 1 for the experimental setup. The close-talking training data of the baseline recognizer were convolved with each one of the impulse responses separately, i.e. 12 hours of reverberated data (EMB-12; cmp. Table 1) resulted from one hour of close-talking speech.

The results for the recognition experiments are summarized in Table 2. It can be noticed that the recognition performance for the reverberated data increased. Although the acoustical properties of the training data are different from those of the test data, especially for 1 m microphone distance similar results could be achieved as for matching training and testing conditions (94.0% vs. 94.1%). However, the recognition performance for the close-talking test data decreased. So we tested if a mixture of reverberated and clear training data can avoid this problem but still keep the recognition rates for the room microphones on their high level. Therefore we used as one part of the training set the entire training set of the baseline recognizer (see Table 1). The other part consisted of one twelfth of the artificially reverberated training files used in the EMB-12 recognizer, i.e. the new training set (EMB-2; see Table 1) was twice as big as for the baseline system and each room impulse response was present in $\frac{1}{24}$ of the data. Thus the ratio between close-talking and reverberated training data was 1:1. Other ratios are currently being examined.

The results for this approach in Table 2 show that the recognition could be enhanced for all three test sets, even for the close-talking recordings. This is very encouraging in view of a future application, but the question arose if the reason for this improvement was really (only) the reverberation of the training files. Note that the baseline recognizer had a very small training set of about one hour of speech data only, so it might be that the baseline training set (EMB-base) was simply too small for a robust estimation of the phone models. Which percentage of the improvement was the outcome of the sound quality and the size of the data set, resp., had to be estimated during further tests. Furthermore training and test data were both taken from the EMBASSI corpus up to now. The impulse responses for the artificial reverberation of the close-talking signals were measured in the same recording room. In the next section we therefore describe experiments with two other corpora for training and test.

3 Experiments with Verbmobil Training Data

In a next experiment, we study the recognition performance for a larger vocabulary and for longer reverberation time of the testing environment.

3.1 Training and Test Data

A widely used data collection for speech recognition in German-speaking countries is the German part of the VERBMOBIL corpus. We use a subset of this data consisting of about 27.5 hours of close-talking speech produced by 578 speakers (304 male, 274 female; cmp. [7]). The topic in the dialogues is appointment scheduling (spontaneous speech) involving a vocabulary of 6825 words. As test set, we used a subset of a currently unpublished corpus recorded at our faculty which will be denoted as "FAT" in the following. It was recorded in an office room of size 4.5 m × 4.3 m × 3.2 m with reverberation time $T_{60} = 300$ ms. 6 speakers (3 male, 3 female) read transliterations of VERBMOBIL dialogues. Thus the vocabulary of both speech collections was the same and the FAT data could easily serve as test data for the VERBMOBIL recognizers. The distant-talking microphone was placed at the position (2.0 m, 2.5 m, 1.4 m), the speaker position was (2.0 m, 1.5 m, 1.4 m), i.e. 1 m away from the distant-talking microphone. The origin of the coordinate system in the room was the left corner behind the speaker.

The training and validation data for the baseline VERBMOBIL recognizer (VM-base) were the same set as in [7]. As in the previous experiments, the recognizer was trained on mixtures of clean and artificially reverberated close-talking signals. The important difference, however, is that the sizes of training and validation set were not changed for the different acoustic conditions. Thus the changes in the results are only dependent of the degree of reverberation in the data, because the acoustic model of a specific phone gets the same amount of training data in all training processes, only the acoustic conditions change.

Concerning the training set, three different recognizers were set up (Table 3) comparable to those with the EMBASSI data:

- **VM-base:** This is the baseline VERBMOBIL recognizer as described in [7]. It was trained with close-talking recordings only (257,810 words, 11714 utterances).

- **VM-12:** All close-talking recordings were reverberated. The impulse responses were changed for each utterance for preventing that all utterances from the same speaker are convolved with the same impulse responses.
- **VM-2**: As for EMB-2 (Table 1) half of the training set consisted of close-talking signals and half of reverberated files. The 12 room impulse responses were equally distributed over the utterances.

The fact that only 48 utterances were in the original VERBMOBIL validation set was inconvenient for the test series as each one of the 12 room impulse responses was represented in the validation lists of VM-12 and VM-2 by very few files. Nevertheless the file lists were not changed in order to get results comparable with experiments in [7].

The recognizers were evaluated on four data sets (cmp. Table 3):

- the original VERBMOBIL test set (268 close-talking recordings, 4781 words, 30 min of speech) as defined in [7].
- the artificially reverberated VERBMOBIL test set: The original test set was convolved with the same 12 room impulse responses also used for the corresponding training data. The 268 files contain the 12 room impulse responses with equal proportions.
- the FAT close-talking set: The 1445 files contain 24738 words (vocabulary size: 865 words) and have a total duration of 150 min.
- the FAT room microphone set: These data were synchronously recorded with the close-talking data by a room microphone 1 m away from the speaker. This microphone was of the same type as those used for the EMBASSI corpus.

As the texts read in the FAT test data were transliterations of VERBMOBIL dialogues, all the utterances were in the training data of the language model. Therefore, the recognition results which are obtained for the FAT close-talking data using the 4-gram language model are better than for the (non-overlapping) VERBMOBIL close-talking test set (see Table 4). The test set perplexity of the FAT data was 87.7 while for the VERBMOBIL language model test data it was 151.5.

3.2 Results

Table 4 summarizes the results on the VERBMOBIL based recognizers. The word accuracy for the FAT close-talking test set is the highest for the VM-base recognizer (86.8% word accuracy using a 4-gram language model) and lowest for VM-12 where only reverberated data was in the training set (81.6%). VM-2 almost reaches the baseline result (85.5%). Regarding the FAT data recorded at 1 m distance in a room with $T_{60} = 300$ ms the close-talking recognizer VM-base shows least accuracy as expected (47.8%) and VM-12 the highest one (71.3%). Here VM-2 with 69.4% also nearly reaches the same value. Taking the average of the results on FAT close-talking data and distant-talking data the baseline word accuracy of 68.3% can be improved by 29.0% relative to a word accuracy of 77.5% on VM-2 (VM-12 reaches 76.5%). This result shows that artificially reverberated training data can help to improve the robustness of speech recognition in reverberant acoustic environments for mismatch of the room impulse responses for training and testing.

Table 3. Data sets for the recognizers trained with VERBMOBIL data ("mic. dist." = microphone distance, "CT art. rev." = close-talking artificially reverberated)

recognizer	training		validation		test	
	mic. dist.	dur.	mic. dist.	dur.	mic. dist.	dur.
VM-base (T_{60}: ≈ 0 ms)	close-talk	27 h	close-talk	7 min	close-talk CT art. rev. FAT CT FAT 1 m	30 min 30 min 150 min 150 min
VM-12 (T_{60}: 250, 400 ms)	close-talk (artif. rev.)	27 h	close-talk (artif. rev.)	7 min	*like VM-base*	
VM-2 (T_{60}: 0, 250, 400 ms)	close-talk+ CT art. rev.	13.5 h 13.5 h	close-talk+ CT art. rev.	3.5 min 3.5 min	*like VM-base*	

Table 4. Word accuracies for the VERBMOBIL recognizers (0-gram = no language model)

test set	lang. model	VM-base	VM-12	VM-2
VERBMOBIL close-talk	4-gram	80.1	72.1	77.9
VERBMOBIL close-talk	0-gram	51.4	37.4	49.1
VERBMOBIL art. rev.	4-gram	59.9	67.5	67.4
VERBMOBIL art. rev.	0-gram	28.5	39.8	37.6
FAT close-talk	4-gram	86.8	81.6	85.5
FAT close-talk	0-gram	49.4	38.3	46.5
FAT reverb.	4-gram	47.8	71.3	69.4
FAT reverb.	0-gram	12.5	32.3	28.8

4   Conclusions and Outlook

We tested artificially reverberated training data for improving the robustness of ASR against reverberation. For training, we used a small subset of the EMBASSI and the German VERBMOBIL corpus, respectively, using room impulse responses from environments with $T_{60} = 250$ ms and 400 ms reverberation time. For testing, we used the test set of the FAT corpus which contains synchronously recorded signals from a close-talking microphone and a distant-talking microphone at a distance of 1 m in a room with $T_{60} = 300$ ms reverberation time. The average word accuracy for both test subsets on a VERBMOBIL recognizer trained with close-talking data (VM-base) was 68.3%. Training with artificially reverberated data (VM-12) lead to an increase for reverberated data but to a decrease for close-talking data. Using half of both training sets in another recognizer (VM-2) did not only give the best average result (77.5%), but with merely moderate loss on the single subsets. Future experiments will include optimizing the relation between close-talking and distant-talking training data and testing other kinds of features like our MFCC variant with μ-law companded Mel spectrum coefficients [6].

References

1. Couvreur, L., Couvreur, C., Ris, C.: A Corpus-Based Approach for Robust ASR in Reverberant Environments. In Proc. of International Conference on Spoken Language Processing (ICSLP), volume 1, pages 397–400, Beijing, China, 2000.

2. Stahl, V., Fischer, A., Bippus, R.: Acoustic Synthesis of Training Data for Speech Recognition in Living Room Environments. In Proc. Int. Conf. Acoustics, Speech and Signal Processing (ICASSP), volume 1, pages 21–24, Salt Lake City, Utah, 2001.
3. Junqua, J.-C.: Robust Speech Recognition in Embedded Systems and PC Applications. Kluwer Academic Publishers, Boston, 2001.
4. Kingsbury, B.E.D., Morgan, N.: Recognizing Reverberant Speech with RASTA-PLP. In Proc. Int. Conf. Acoustics, Speech and Signal Processing (ICASSP), volume 2, pages 1259–1262, Munich, Germany, 1997.
5. Omologo, M., Svaizer, P., Matassoni, M.: Environmental conditions and acoustic transduction in hands-free speech recognition. Speech Communication, 25(1–3):75–95, 1998.
6. Haderlein, T., Stemmer, G., Nöth, E.: Speech Recognition with μ-Law Companded Features on Reverberated Signals. In V. Matoušek and P. Mautner, editors, Proc. 6th Int. Conf. on Text, Speech and Dialogue – TSD 2003, volume 2807 of Lecture Notes in Artificial Intelligence, pages 173–180, Berlin, 2003. Springer–Verlag.
7. Stemmer, G.: Modeling Variability in Speech Recognition. PhD thesis, Chair for Pattern Recognition, University of Erlangen-Nuremberg, Germany, 2005.

French–German Bilingual Acoustic Modeling for Embedded Voice Driven Applications

Jozef Ivanecký, Volker Fischer, and Siegfried Kunzmann

IBM AIM, European Voice Technology Development
Schönaicher-Str. 220, 71032 Böblingen, Germany
{ivanecky,vfischer,kunzmann}@de.ibm.com

Abstract. Multilingual access to information and services is a key requirement in any pervasive or ubiquitous computing environment. In this paper we describe our efforts towards multilingual speech recognition with a focus on applications that are designed to run on embedded devices, like e.g. a commercially available PDA. We give an overview on speech recognition techniques suited for the special requirements of the expected phonetic and acoustic environments and explore the ability to create multilingual acoustic models and applications that are able to run on embedded devices in real-time.

1 Introduction

Today, multilingual voice access to information is becoming more and more common in real applications. While multilingual ASR systems have reached a certain maturity in telephony ASR systems, where only weak CPU and memory usage constraints exist, the situation is completely different for systems supposed to run on small devices like PDAs, or mobile phones. In this case, both restrictive CPU and memory requirements, and the need to run in real-time still result in high error rates. Also, a very noisy acoustic channel with background noise of many different characteristics is an additional challenge for the creation of small acoustic models that are capable of simultaneously recognizing several languages.

Based on experiences from mono-lingual acoustic modeling and application design for embedded devices, we defined the following requirements for multilingual embedded systems:

- the size of a multilingual system should not be significantly larger than the size of a mono-lingual system,
- the phonology used for multilingual modeling should cover as many languages as possible, or at least it should seamlessly extend to languages not yet under consideration,
- digits recognition — which is of particular interest in many embedded applications — should not suffer too much from multilingual modeling.

As a first step towards these goals, in this paper we describe the construction of a bilingual French–German acoustic model for embedded devices. The remainder of the paper is organized as follows: In Section 2 we give a brief overview over the used common phone alphabet. In Section 3 we focus on the multi-language specific acoustic modeling parts. Section 4 describes the experiments and a brief summary is given in Section 5.

V. Matoušek et al. (Eds.): TSD 2005, LNAI 3658, pp. 234–240, 2005.

2 Common Phonetic Alphabets

The definition of a common phonetic alphabet for multilingual speech recognition has to deal with at least two conflicting goals: while on the one hand the phonetic inventory of each language should be covered as precise as possible in order to achieve high recognition accuracy, at the same time as many phones as possible should be shared across languages in order to efficiently utilize the training data and for the creation of reasonably small acoustic models.

Starting from available, disjoint phonetic alphabets for seven languages (Arabic, British English, French, German, Italian, (Brazilian) Portuguese, and Spanish) which are used within our monolingual speech recognition research activities we have designed two common phonetic alphabets of different level of details [6]. In a first step, language specific phone sets were simplified following available SAMPA transcription guidelines (see [8]) which affected each languages phone set to a different degree: While, for example the native French phone set remained unchanged, we gave up syllabic consonants for German, and at the same time introduced new diphthongs for British English. Then, language specific phones mapped to the same SAMPA symbol were merged into a common unit. This resulted in a common phonetic alphabet consisting of 121 phones (65 vowels, 56 consonants) for the seven languages. As can be seen in Table 1, this gave an overall reduction of 60 percent compared to the simplified language specific phonologies.

Table 1. Number for vowel and consonant phones for seven languages in the detailed common phone set. Languages are British English (En), French (Fr), German (Gr), Italian (It), Spanish (Es), Brazilian Portuguese (Pt), Arabic (Ar).

	Total	En	Fr	Gr	It	Es	Pt	Ar
vowels	65	20	17	23	14	10	20	14
consonants	56	24	19	26	32	30	22	29
Total	121	44	36	49	46	40	42	43

To further increase the overlap we also defined a less detailed common phonetic alphabet, cf. Table 2. We achieved this in three steps:

1. we dropped the distinction between stressed and unstressed vowels for Spanish, Italian, and Portuguese
2. we represented all long vowels as a sequence of two (identical) short vowels
3. we splitted diphthongs into their two vowel constituents.

In doing so, the average number of languages that contribute to the training data for each of the 76 phones (the sharing factor) increased from 2.28 to 2.53, and if Arabic is not considered, the sharing factor increased from 2.74 to 3.56.

While this more aggressive inventory reduction caused an increase in word error rate by about 7 percents (measured on an in-house database), if compared to the more detailed common phone alphabet, a benefit of the reduced phone inventory stems from the fact that additional languages with can be covered with less new phones as with

Table 2. Number of vowels and consonants for seven languages in the reduced common phone set.

	Total	En	Fr	Gr	It	Es	Pt	Ar
Vowels	31	13	15	17	7	5	12	11
Consonants	45	24	19	23	28	24	22	28
Total	76	37	34	40	35	29	34	39

the detailed inventory. The integration of eight additional languages (Czech, Japanese, Finnish, Greek, Dutch, Danish, Norwegian, and Swedish) required only 2 additional vowels and 12 consonants. The result makes us believe that the slight degradation in accuracy is tolerable and likely to be adjustable by improved acoustic modelling techniques.

Following the merging procedure outlined above, for our bilingual French–German acoustic model we ended up with 57 phones that are used for recognition of utterances from a general domain. However, since digit recognition is of particular importance in many applications for embedded devices, our language specific phonologies for embedded acoustic modeling were already enriched with some digit specific phones. In order to minimize the impact from using a common phone set on digit recognition, we decided to keep additional 59 digit specific phones separate for each language, which finally resulted in a set of 116 phones that are used in the bilingual model.

3   Speech Recognition

Multilingual acoustic modeling facilitates the development of speech recognizers for languages with only little available training data, and also allows reduced complexity of application development by creating acoustic models that can simultaneously recognize speech from several languages [7]. The use and combination of multilingual acoustic models has also proven advantageous for the recognition of accented speech produced by a wide variety of non-native speakers with different commands of the system's operating language [4].

Acoustic modeling for multilingual speech recognition to a large extend makes use of well established methods for (semi-)continuous Hidden-Markov-Model training. Methods that have been found of particular use in a multilingual setting include, but are not limited to, the use of multilingual seed HMMs, the use of language questions in phonetic decision tree growing, polyphone decision tree specialization for a better coverage of contexts from an unseen target language, and the determination of an appropriate model complexity by means of a Bayesian Information Criterion; see, for example, [7],[3] for an overview and further references.

Having now reached a certain maturity, the benefits of multilingual acoustic models are most evident in applications that require both robustness against foreign speakers and the recognition of foreign words. To see the same benefits also in embedded and mobile domain, the special needs have to be considered.

In the remainder of this section we will review the basic requirements imposed by the scenario under consideration and will describe how these are taken into account in the training of acoustic models as well as in the recognition phase.

The design of an embedded speech recognizer has to deal with only limited computational resources, both in terms of CPU power and memory capacity, that today's embedded devices can offer. While some applications may run entirely on the local device and therefore require a relatively compact acoustic model, others may defer parts of the recognition process to a recognition server, which requires compatibility of at least the client's and server's acoustic front–end.

The latter is ensured by the use of a standard acoustic front–end, that computes 13 Mel Frequency Cepstrum Coefficients (MFCC) every 15 milliseconds. Utterance based cepstral mean subtraction and C0 normalization are applied to compensate for the acoustic channel and the first and second order delta coefficients are computed to capture the temporal dynamics of the speech signal.

Recognizer training comprises the definition of a suitable HMM inventory and the determination of the HMM parameters. For that purpose, the training data is viterbi–aligned against its transcription in order to obtain an allophonic label for each feature vector. To bootstrap the initial multilingual system two monolingual systems had been used in the alignment step.

Context dependent non cross–word triphone HMMs are obtained from the leaves of a decision network [1] that is constructed by asking binary questions about the phonetic context P_i for each feature vector, $i = -1, \ldots, 1$. These questions are of the form:"Is the phone in position i in the subset S_j?", and the subsets are derived from meaningful phone classifications commonly used in speech analysis. Finally, the data at each leaf of the network is used in a k–means procedure to obtain initial output probabilities whose parameters are then refined by running a few iterations of the forward–backward algorithm.

The k–means procedure follows a simple rule of thumb and equally distributes a fixed number Gaussian mixture components across the HMM states. Usually, in a highly dynamic and heterogeneous environment, an increased total number of Gaussians can significantly improve the recognition accuracy. However, this is infeasible for applications that have to deal with a limited amount of memory, and therefore the determination of an appropriate acoustic model size is of particular importance.

The so created acoustic model can run with either IBM's large vocabulary telephony speech recognition engine, which employs a fast pre–selection of candidate words and an asynchronous stack search algorithm, or with a time–synchronous viterbi–decoder. The latter is the core of IBM's Embedded Speech Engine (ESE), which is designed for the use with a moderate vocabulary size and finite state grammars. The highly portable and scalable ESE can run on any suitable 32 bit general–purpose CPU; see [2] for an overview on design issues and performance.

4   Experiments

We used the procedure outlined in the previous section to generate a bilingual French–German acoustic model and to compare its recognition accuracy on different tasks to the respective monolingual models. For that purpose we used approx. 600.000 training utterances per language that were gathered in several in-car data collection efforts. Being primarily interested in application for embedded devices, we restricted the size of the bilingual acoustic model to that of the monolingual German model which uses roughly 800 triphone HMMs with a total of approx. 16.000 Gaussian mixture densities.

Our in-car speech recognition test scenario comprised both a digit recognition task and a radio command and control task. For the digit recognition task we run four different tests with an close digits grammar:

- German test set with German pronunciation only,
- German test set with mixed German and French pronunciation,
- French test set with French pronunciation only,
- French test set with mixed French and German pronunciation.

While experiments with only native pronunciations allow to measure the influence of multilingual modeling, we consider the experiments with mixed pronunciations as a step towards the development of true multilingual applications where grammars are shared across languages if possible. However, since only very few French–German homographs appear in the command and control grammars, in this case we experimented only with native pronunciations. Our automotive test set comprises 40 different speakers (20 male, 20 female), each of them recorded in 4 different driving conditions at 0 km/h (with engine off), 40 km/h, 80 km/h, and 110 km/h.

Digit recognition results averaged over all driving conditions are presented in Table 3. While a comparison with the mono-lingual baseline systems demonstrate the feasibility of our multilingual modeling approach, we faced a significant increase in word error rate when we allowed pronunciations from the second language. From the table is clear, that this is mainly caused by an increased number of insertions and substitutions. For German we found that most of these errors are due to the insertion of the word "un", which is French for "1". There is also an increased number of substitutions, but — different from our expectations — this problem was not caused by the confusion of the phonetically similar German digit 6 – "sechs" with the French digit 7 "sept".

Table 3. Word error rates for digit recognition with mono- and bilingual acoustic models.

	Del	Ins	Sub	total
German mono	0.46%	0.31%	2.16%	2.94%
German pr. only	0.47%	0.33%	2.30%	3.10%
German + French pr.	0.45%	0.63%	3.75%	4.83%
French mono	0.40%	1.57%	1.09%	3.06%
French pr. only	0.40%	2.18%	1.75%	4.32%
French + German pr.	0.39%	2.28%	2.30%	4.97%

For French we observed a larger decrease in accuracy when comparing the monolingual and the multilingual models. However, this is an expected result, since the French baseline system was specifically tuned for digit recognition and it uses many more Gaussians for digit phones than both the German and the bilingual model.

Results for the command and control test set are given in Table 4. The results are comparable to the digit test, and also show a larger increase in word error rate for the French system. We assumed that the main reason for the loss in accuracy is the system size of the bilingual model, which is equal to the German monolingual model.

Table 4. Word error rates for radio command and control phrases.

	Del	Ins	Sub	total
German mono	0.10%	0.10%	2.29%	2.49%
German + French	0.15%	0.15%	3.46%	3.75%
French mono	0.26%	0.53%	3.92%	4.71%
French + German	0.39%	2.16%	4.53%	7.08%

Table 5. Digits error rates obtained on the German test for different system size and close and open grammar.

System size	close		open	
	16k	24k	16k	24k
German mono	2.94%	–	3.52%	–
German pr. only	3.10%	2.93%	3.78%	3.56%
German + French pr.	4.83%	4.49%	6.31%	5.88%

In order to prove this assumption we therefore increased the number of Gaussians in the bilingual model by approx. 50 percent. Digit recognition results obtained with this model for both open and closed digit grammar are given in Table 5.

The achieved results confirm our assumption that multilingual speech recognition requires larger acoustic models. However, the size of the larger model with 24k Gaussians is already beyond the limit of todays commonly available embedded or mobile devices. Therefore, improved acoustic modeling still remains a need for future research.

5   Summary

In this paper we described various aspects of the development of a bilingual acoustic model for embedded devices. We explored the design of a common phonetic alphabet for up to 15 languages and described techniques for the training of highly noise robust acoustic models necessary for mobile as well as embedded devices. Experiments in bilingual French–German speech recognition demonstrated the feasibility of our approach, but at the same time unveiled the need for further research in acoustic modeling in order to create multilingual system of acceptable footprint without an unwanted decrease in accuracy.

References

1. Bahl, L., de Souza, P., Gopalakrishnan, P., Nahamoo, D., Picheny, M.: Context-dependent Vector Quantization for Continuous Speech Recognition. In Proc. of the IEEE Int. Conference on Acoustics, Speech, and Signal Processing, Minneapolis, 1993.
2. Beran, T., Bergl, V., Hampl, R., Krbec, P., Šedivý, J., Tydlitát, B., Vopička, J.: Embedded ViaVoice. In Proc. of TSD 2004, Brno, 2004.
3. Fischer, V., Gonzalez, J., Janke, E., Villani, M., Waast-Richard, C.: Towards Multilingual Acoustic Modeling for Large Vocabulary Speech Recognition. In Proc. of the IEEE Workshop on Multilingual Speech Communications, Kyoto, 2000.

4. Fischer, V., Janke, E., Kunzmann, S.: Likelihood Combination and Recognition Output Voting for the Decoding of Non-Native Speech with Multilingual HMMs. In Proc. of the 7th Int. Conference on Spoken Language Processing, Denver, 2002.
5. Fischer, V., Kunzmann, S.: Bayesian Information Criterion based Multi-style Training and Likelihood Combination for Robust Hands Free Speech Recognition in the Car. In Proc. of the IEEE Workshop on Handsfree Speech communication, Kyoto, 2001.
6. Kunzmann, S., Fischer, V., Gonzalez, J., Emam, O., Günther, C., Janke, E.: Multilingual Acoustic Models for Speech Recognition and Synthesis. In Proc. of the IEEE Int. Conf. on Acoustics, Speech, and Signal Processing, Montreal, 2004.
7. Schultz, T., Waibel, A.: Language Independent and Language Adaptive Acoustic Modeling for Speech Recognition, Speech Communications, Vol. 35, 2001.
8. Wells, C.J.: Computer Coded Phonemic Notation of Individual Languages of the European Community, Journal of the International Phonetic Association, Vol. 19, pp. 32-54, 1989.

Sinusoidal Modeling Using Wavelet Packet Transform Applied to the Analysis and Synthesis of Speech Signals

Kihong Kim[1], Jinkeun Hong[2], and Jongin Lim[1]

[1] Graduate School of Information Security, Korea University
1, 5-Ka, Anam-dong, Sungbuk-ku, Seoul, 136-701, South Korea
hong0612@hanmir.com, jilim@korea.ac.kr
[2] Division of Information and Communication, Cheonan University
115 Anse-dong, Cheonan-si, Chungnam, 330-740, South Korea
jkhong@cheonan.ac.kr

Abstract. The sinusoidal model has proven useful for representation and modification of speech and audio signal. One drawback, however, is that a sinusoidal model is typically derived using a fixed analysis frame size. It cannot guarantee an optimal spectral resolution to each sinusoidal parameter. In this paper, we propose a sinusoidal model using wavelet packet analysis, to obtain better frequency resolution at low frequencies and better time resolution at high frequencies and to estimate the sinusoidal parameters more accurately. Experiments show that the proposed model can achieve better performance than conventional model.

1 Introduction

The sinusoidal model has been widely used for speech and audio signal processing such as analysis/synthesis [1, 2], modification [3], coding [4], and enhancement [5]. This model assumes that most speech and audio signals can be well represented by many sinusoids with time-varying amplitudes, frequencies, and phases [1–5].

In the sinusoidal model, however, the analysis frame size is fixed to a size of about two times or more of the average pitch period [1–5]. Since each sinusoidal parameter has different frequencies, it cannot guarantee an optimal spectral resolution to each sinusoidal parameter. Another problem caused by fixed analysis frame size is difficulty in modeling noise-like components and time-localized transient event. And thus, these result in reconstruction artifact such as pre-echo distortion in synthetic signal [6–8]. There have been several different previous methods to solving the fixed-size analysis frame problem. One method is to use a parallel bank of constant-Q bandpass filters [9]. Then, one can perform sinusoidal model on each bandpass filter output. In this method, the amount of data storage and complexity increases linearly with the number of bandpass filters. Another method is adaptive windowing method in which the analysis frame size is varied based on the signal characteristics [7, 8].

In this paper, to obtain better frequency resolution at low frequencies and better time resolution at high frequencies and to estimate sinusoidal parameters more accurately, a sinusoidal model using a wavelet packet analysis is presented and its performance is evaluated against that of conventional model. This method applied a variable-size analysis frame to the subband signal analyzed by the wavelet packet analysis [10, 11].

V. Matoušek et al. (Eds.): TSD 2005, LNAI 3658, pp. 241–248, 2005.

That is, after decomposing an input speech signal into some subband signals using the wavelet packet transform, conventional sinusoidal models with different analysis frame size are applied to each subband signals, respectively. Lower frequency sinusoidal parameters are estimated with long analysis frame, which improves frequency resolution, and higher frequency parameters are estimated with short analysis frame, which improves time resolution. Experiments show that the proposed model can achieve better performance, in terms of spectral and phase characteristics and the synthetic speech quality, than conventional model.

The remainder of this paper is organized as follows. In the next section, a detailed description of the sinusoidal model is given. In section 3, a wavelet packet analysis and the proposed model are illustrated. Some experimental results are presented in section 4, and concluding remarks are provided in section 5.

2   Conventional Sinusoidal Model

The sinusoidal model represents a speech signal as a linear combination of sinusoids with time-varying amplitudes, frequencies, and phases. That is, the speech signal is represented as the sum of a finite number of corresponding sinusoidal parameters at the fundamental frequency and its harmonics during voiced speech regions, and is represented as numbers of corresponding sinusoidal parameters at peaks in the spectral domain during unvoiced speech regions [1–5]. In estimating the sinusoidal parameters, the peaks peaking method [1, 2] and analysis-by-synthesis/overlap-add (AbS/OLA) [3] is widely used, and the latter provides better estimation of the sinusoidal parameters than the peaks peaking method.

In the sinusoidal model, the input speech signal is given by

$$s(n) = \sum_{l=1}^{L} A_l cos(\omega_l n + \phi_l) \tag{1}$$

Where, L is the number of sinusoidal parameters, and A_l, ω_l, and ϕ_l represent the time-varying amplitude, frequency, and phase of each sine wave. As speech signal evolves from frame to frame, different sets of the above sinusoidal parameters are obtained.

This approach starts by taking the discrete Fourier transform (DFT) of overlapping frames of speech. Next, peak picking is applied to the magnitude spectrum of the DFT in order to obtain a list of frequencies and corresponding amplitudes at those frequencies. In the synthesis system, synthetic speech signal is synthesized with obtained sinusoidal parameters.

If the amplitudes, frequencies, and phases that are estimated for the kth frame are denoted by A_l, ω_l, and ϕ_l, then the synthetic speech signal $\tilde{s}^k(n)$ for that frame can be computed using as

$$\tilde{s}^k(n) = \sum_{l=1}^{L^k} A_l^k cos(\omega_l^k n + \phi_l^k) \tag{2}$$

Since the sinusoidal parameters will be time-varying, discontinuities at the frame boundaries will be introduced. To overcome this problem, overlap-add interpolation is used.

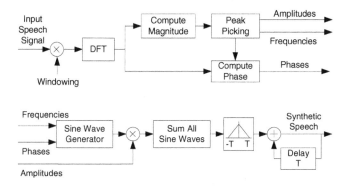

Fig. 1. Analysis (top) and synthesis system (bottom) of conventional sinusoidal model

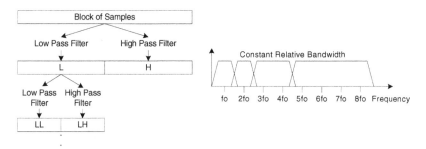

Fig. 2. Example of wavelet tree (left) and its subband decomposition (right)

3 Wavelet Packet and Proposed Sinusoidal Model

3.1 Wavelet Packet Analysis

Wavelet packet transform is a generalization of the wavelet transform that offers a rich set of decomposition structures [10, 11]. Wavelet packet transform was first proposed by Coifman et al. [10] for dealing with the non-stationarities of the data better than wavelet transform does.

Wavelet decomposition is achieved by iterative two channel perfect reconstruction filter bank operations over the low frequency band at each level. The frequency separation achieved by wavelet decomposition is depicted in Fig. 2 Wavelet packet decomposition, on the other hand, is achieved when filter bank is iterated over all frequency bands at each level. Fig. 3 shows the frequency separation achieved by wavelet packet decomposition. The final decomposition structure will be a subset of that full tree, chosen by the best basis selection algorithm.

3.2 Proposed Sinusoidal Model Using Wavelet Packet Analysis

In the conventional sinusoidal model, an analysis frame has fixed size and is about two times or more of an average pitch period [1–5]. This approach is not very effective in

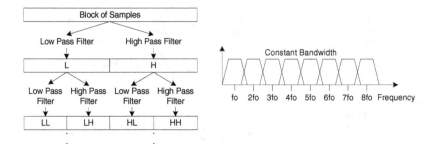

Fig. 3. Example of wavelet packet tree (left) and its subband decomposition (right)

terms of achieving an optimal spectral resolution to each sinusoidal parameter. Another problem is difficulty in modeling noise-like components and time-localized transient events. These result in pre-echo distortion in the synthetic signal [6–8].

In order to obtain better frequency resolution at low frequencies and better time resolution at high frequencies and to estimate sinusoidal parameters more accurately, we propose a sinusoidal model using a wavelet packet analysis in the conventional model. In the proposed sinusoidal model, first input speech signal is decomposed into some subband signals using a wavelet packet transform. Lower frequency parameters are calculated over a greater length of time and have higher frequency resolution. On the other hand, higher frequency sinusoidal parameters are estimated with high time resolution but poor frequency resolution.

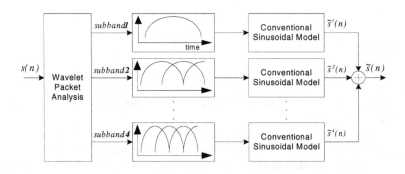

Fig. 4. Block diagram of proposed sinusoidal model using wavelet packet analysis

Fig. 4 shows a block diagram of the proposed sinusoidal model, and Fig. 5 shows the wavelet packet decomposition tree structure of proposed model. In this scheme, the input speech signal is decomposed into subband signals using a wavelet packet decom-position tree. These subband signals are then independently analyzed and synthesized with the conventional sinusoidal model.

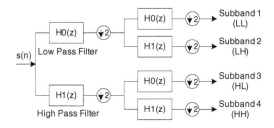

Fig. 5. Wavelet packet tree structure

4   Experimental Results

In this paper, we compared and analyzed the spectrum and phase of original and synthetic speech signal synthesized using the conventional and proposed sinusoidal model. The performance of the proposed model has been evaluated in terms of the perceptual evaluation of speech quality (PESQ) [12] test based on objective speech quality tests. Seventeen speech signals were sampled at 8KHz with 16 bits quantization per sample. In the conventional model, the analysis frame size is set to 20ms. For the wavelet packet analysis, we used a Daubechies filter with 10-tap. We decomposed input speech signals into 4 subbands using a wavelet packet transform. Ranging from the lowest to highest band, the subband sinusoidal model uses frame sizes of 40, 30, 20, and 10ms, respectively.

Fig. 6 shows the spectrum of the original and synthetic speech. (a) is the original speech signal, and (b) ~ (i) represent the synthetic signals using the conventional and the proposed model while sinusoids number is varied from 10 to 40. In this figure, we can see that the difference between original and synthetic speech signals increases according as sinusoids number decreases. And, the spectrum of the synthetic speech signals indicates that the proposed sinusoidal model achieves better performance than the conventional model.

The phase of the original and synthetic speech signals synthesized using conventional and proposed model is presented in Fig. 7. It is also demonstrated that the phase of the synthetic speech signals from the proposed model more accurately approximates that of the original signal.

Table 1. Result of PESQ test for the synthetic speech signals

Model	Sinusoids number				
	10	15	20	30	40
Conventional	MOS 3.05	MOS 3.05	MOS 3.30	MOS 3.53	MOS 3.65
Proposed	MOS 3.27	MOS 3.28	MOS 3.57	MOS 3.80	MOS 3.81

The result of the objective speech quality test, the PESQ test, is shown in Table 1. Simulation for comparison of synthetic speech quality shows that the proposed model

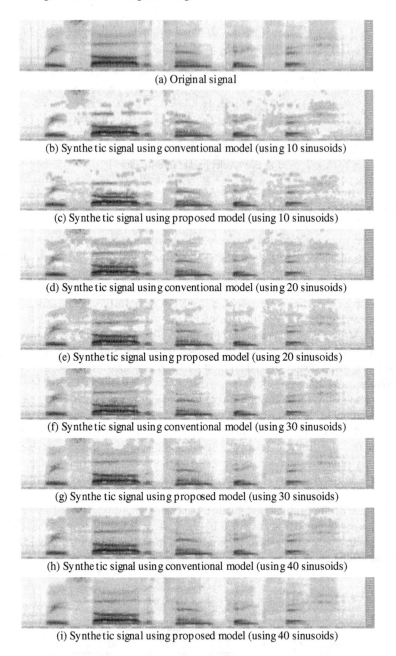

(a) Original signal

(b) Synthetic signal using conventional model (using 10 sinusoids)

(c) Synthetic signal using proposed model (using 10 sinusoids)

(d) Synthetic signal using conventional model (using 20 sinusoids)

(e) Synthetic signal using proposed model (using 20 sinusoids)

(f) Synthetic signal using conventional model (using 30 sinusoids)

(g) Synthetic signal using proposed model (using 30 sinusoids)

(h) Synthetic signal using conventional model (using 40 sinusoids)

(i) Synthetic signal using proposed model (using 40 sinusoids)

Fig. 6. Spectrum between original and synthetic speech signals using two analysis methods depending sinusoids number

improves mean opinion score (MOS) over $0.16 \sim 0.27$ compared with the conventional model.

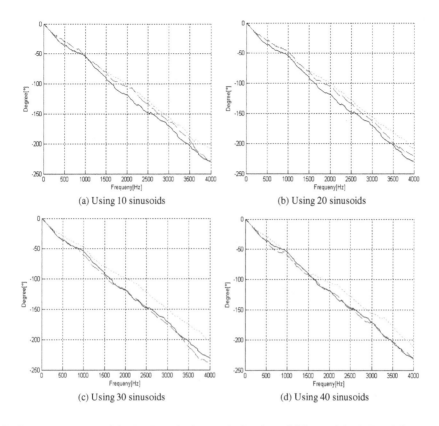

(a) Using 10 sinusoids

(b) Using 20 sinusoids

(c) Using 30 sinusoids

(d) Using 40 sinusoids

Fig. 7. Phase between original and synthetic speech signals (solid line: original, dotted line: conventional, dashed line: proposed)

5   Conclusions

In this paper, in order to solve the fixed-size analysis frame problem and to enhance performance of the parameters estimation in the conventional sinusoidal model, a sinusoidal model using a wavelet packet analysis is presented and evaluated against the performance of conventional model. In the proposed model, after decomposing an input speech signal into subband signals using the wavelet packet transform, conventional sinusoidal models with different analysis frame size a re applied to each subband signals respectively. Experiments showed that the proposed sinusoidal model achieved better performance in the spectral characteristics, phase characteristic, and synthetic speech quality than conventional model.

The proposed sinusoidal model provides natural speech signal decomposition and high quality output. The proposed model can be applied to many applications including text-to-speech (TTS) systems, audio signal processing, and enhancement.

References

1. McAulay, R.J., Quatieri, T.F.: Speech Analysis/Synthesis Based on Sinusoidal Representation. IEEE Trans. on ASSP, vol.34, pp.744-754, 1986.
2. Furui, S., Sondhi, M.M.: Advances in Speech Signal Processing, Dekker Inc., NY, 1992.
3. George, E.B., Smith, M.J.T.: Speech Analysis/Synthesis and Modification Using an Analysis-by-Syntehsis/Overlap-Add Sinusoidal Model. IEEE Trans. on ASSP, vol.5, pp.389-406, 1997.
4. Kleijn, W. B., Paliwal, K.K.: Speech Coding and Synthesis, Elsevier, 1995.
5. Quatieri, T.F., Daisewicz, R.G.: An Approach to Co-Channel Talker Interference Suppression Using a Sinusoidal Model for Speech. IEEE Trans. on ASSP, vol.38, pp.56-69, 1990.
6. Anderson, D.V.: Speech Analysis and Coding Using a Multi-Resolution Sinusoidal Transform. IEEE ICASSP, pp1037-1040, 1996.
7. Kim, K.H., Hwang, I.H.: A Multi-Resolution Sinusoidal Model Using Adaptive Analysis Frame. EURASIP EUSIPCO, pp.2267-2270, 2004.
8. Goodwin, M.: Multiresolution Sinusoidal Modeling Using Adaptive Segmentation. IEEE ICASSP, pp.1525-1528, 1998.
9. Goodwin, M., Vetterli, M.: Time-Frequency Models for Music Analysis, Transformation, and Synthesis. Time-Frequency Time-Scale Symposium, 1996..
10. Coifman, R., Meyer, Y., Quake, Y.S., Wickerhauser, V.: Signal Processing and Compression with Wavelet Packets. Numerical Algorithms Research Group, 1990.
11. Herley, C., Vetterli, M.: Orthogonal Time-Varying Filter Banks and Wavelet Packets. IEEE Trans. on. Signal Processing, vol.42, pp.2650-2663, 1994.
12. ITU-T Rec.: P.862, Perceptual Evaluation of Speech Quality (PESQ) an Objective Assessment of Narrowband Telephone Networks and Speech Code, 2002

Speaker Identification Based on Subtractive Clustering Algorithm with Estimating Number of Clusters*

Younjeong Lee[1], Ki Yong Lee[1], and Jaeyeol Rheem[2]

[1] School of Electronic Engineering, SoongSil University
Sangdo-dong, Dongjak-Ku, Seoul 156-743, Korea
{youn,klyee}@ssu.ac.kr
[2] School of Information and Technology, Korea University of Technology and Education
Byungcheon, Cheonan, 330-709, Korea
rheem@kut.ac.kr

Abstract. In this paper, we propose a new clustering algorithm that performs clustering the feature vectors for the speaker identification. Unlike typical clustering approaches, the proposed method does the clustering without the initial guesses of locations of the cluster centers and a priori information about the number of clusters. Cluster centers are obtained incrementally by adding one cluster center at a time through the subtractive clustering algorithm. The number of clusters is obtained by investigating the mutual relationship between clusters. The experimental results show the effectiveness of the proposed algorithm as compared with the conventional methods.

1 Introduction

Speaker identification is to select the best matching speaker from a speaker data-base given an unknown speaker's speech data. In speaker identification, clustering has been used for generating codebooks of speaker's identity. In the training phase, the speaker models are constructed by clustering the feature vectors in L separate clusters. In the test phase, the likelihood between an unknown speaker feature vectors and all speaker models is used for the speaker identification.

Clustering aims at partitioning given data sets into disjoint clusters. The best known clustering methods are the K-means and fuzzy c-means (FCM) algorithms. However, the K-means and FCM methods have two major problems encountered in clustering of real data [1, 2]. First, the improper initial guesses of cluster centers may degrade its performance. Second, the number of clusters cannot always be defined a priori. To cope with the difficulty of initial guesses of the cluster centers, the mountain clustering [3, 4] and the global K-means [5] methods are proposed on the assumption that the number of clusters is known. However, the computational load of the conventional methods is heavy when number of the data points is large.

To solve the above problems, in this paper, we propose a new clustering method based on subtractive clustering algorithm [6, 7] and mutual relationship of clusters

---

* This work was supported by the Korea Science and Engineering Foundation (KOSEF) through the Biometrics Engineering Research Center (BERC) at Yonsei University.

V. Matoušek et al. (Eds.): TSD 2005, LNAI 3658, pp. 249–256, 2005.

[8]. Firstly, cluster centers are obtained incrementally from adding one cluster center at a time through the subtractive clustering algorithm. Secondly, the estimation of the number of clusters is obtained from investigating the mutual relationship of a cluster with respect to all the other clusters. Mutual relationship is used to decide whether two clusters are statistically dependent. If two clusters are dependent, their mutual relationship is measured to be positive. Starting with one cluster, an optimal set of clusters can be found iteratively to apply the above procedure until at least one of the mutual relationships between clusters becomes positive.

2 Subtractive Clustering Algorithms with Estimating the Number of Clusters

2.1 Subtractive Clustering Algorithms for Estimating the Centers of Clusters

Most clustering algorithms such as K-means and FCM algorithm have the same purpose to minimize the total dissimilarity. Let the data set be $X = \{x(1), x(2), \cdots, x(N)\}$, $x(n) \in R^d$. To cluster X into L clusters, we find C_l , the center of l-th cluster, which minimizes the total dissimilarity objective function. Here, we use $S(x(n), C_l)$ to measure the similarity between $x(n)$ and C_l, and then the goal is to find the clusters which maximize the total similarity measure $J(C)$ with

$$J(C) = \sum_{l=1}^{L} \sum_{n=1}^{N} S(x(n), C_l)^r \tag{1}$$

where

$$S(x(n), C_l) = \exp\left(-\frac{\|x(n) - C_l\|^2}{\rho}\right).$$

$C = (C_1, \cdots, C_L)$ is the set of clusters and ρ is the variance of samples for normalization such as

$$\rho = \frac{1}{N} \sum_{n=1}^{N} \left\|x(n) - \bar{x}\right\|^2, \text{ where } \bar{x} = \frac{1}{N} \sum_{n=1}^{N} x(n). \tag{2}$$

In the similarity-based clustering method(SCM), the similarity relation $S(x(n) , C_l)$ given in Zadeh [4] is used and monotone increasing function γ is the value for normalization of parameter to determine the location of peaks in the objective function $J(C)$. Maximizing the total similarity measure is finding the peaks of the objective function. To find the peaks of data points, we can redefine eq. (1) to eq. (3) which represents the total similarity between data point $x(m)$ and the others:

$$\tilde{J}(x(m)) = \sum_{n=1}^{N} \exp\left(-\frac{\|x(n) - x(m)\|^2}{\rho}\right)^r, m = 1, \cdots, N \tag{3}$$

This function is closely related to the density shape of the data points in the neighborhood of $x(m)$. A large $\tilde{J}(x(m))$ means that the data point $x(m)$ is close to some cluster center and has many data points around it. Based on this fact, we can estimate the number of clusters by finding the cluster centers having the highest density from the given data distribution.

To estimate clusters, we consider the subtractive clustering algorithm. The subtractive clustering method considers each data point as a candidate cluster center. Given a data set $X = \{x(1), x(2), \cdots, x(N)\}$, $x(n) \in R^d$, the bounded total similarity function for the first cluster, $D_1(m)$, is defined for each data point $x(m)$ as a function of the Euclidean norm to all the other data points:

$$D_1(m) = \sum_{n=1}^{N} I(x(n), x(m)) \exp\left(-\frac{\|x(n) - x(m)\|^2}{\beta}\right) \quad \text{where } m = 1, \cdots, N \quad (4)$$

where α is a design parameter and $I(x, C)$ is defined by

$$I(x, C) = \begin{cases} 1 \text{ if } x \in B_c \\ 0 \text{ if } x \notin B_c \end{cases} \quad (5)$$

Here, B_c is the boundary of C cluster and can be obtained from using the sample variance ρ as

$$B_c = \kappa \cdot \rho \quad (6)$$

where κ represents the degree of boundary. Unlike the typical SCM algorithm, we don't need to measure the total similarity for all data points. To reduce further the computational load, we only compute the bounded total similarity for the data within a certain boundary instead of all data, because the data outside the boundary have little effect on the total similarity. Obviously one data point has high total similarity function when it is surrounded by many neighboring data. The first cluster center can be obtained from the data point with the highest value of the bounded total similarity function as

$$C_1 = x(m^*), \text{ where } m^* = \arg\max_m D_1(m). \quad (7)$$

Given the $(l-1)$-th cluster center, the bounded total similarity function for the l-th cluster center can be obtained from following formula:

$$D_l(m) = D_{l-1}(m) - I(x(n), C_{l-1})\left\{D_{l-1}(m^*)\exp\left(-\frac{\|x(n) - C_{l-1}\|^2}{\beta}\right)\right\} \quad (8)$$

where β is a design parameter. Then l-th cluster center is derived from

$$C_l = x(m^*), \text{ where } m^* = \arg\max_m D_l(m). \quad (9)$$

In order to avoid the selection of closely located cluster center, β is chosen to be greater than α. Since the l-th cluster center is obtained from the bounded total similarity function using the equations (8) and (9), the computational load of the proposed method is less than that of the global K-means algorithm.

2.2 Estimating the Number of Clusters

To investigate whether the number of clusters generated from the subtractive clustering is optimal, we measure the mutual relationship between clusters. Mutual relationship is used to measure how much the information is shared between two clusters. The mutual relationship between a cluster i and a cluster l can be defined as,

$$\varphi(i,l) = p(i,l) \log \frac{p(i,l)}{p(i)p(l)}, \quad i = 1, \cdots, l-1 \tag{10}$$

where $p(i)$ is the probability of the cluster i and $p(i,l)$ is the joint probability. In (10), the probability of cluster i, $p(i)$ and joint probability, $p(i,l)$ can be calculated respectively as,

$$p(i) = \frac{1}{N} \sum_{n=1}^{N} p(i \,|x\,(n)), \quad p(i,l) = \frac{1}{N} \sum_{n=1}^{N} p(i \,|x\,(n))\, p(l \,|x\,(n)) \tag{11}$$

where

$$p(i \,|x\,(n)) = \frac{\exp\left(-\frac{\|x(n)-C_i\|^2}{\alpha}\right)}{\sum_{k=1}^{l} \exp\left(-\frac{\|x(n)-C_k\|^2}{\alpha}\right)} \tag{12}$$

There are three possible values for $\varphi(i,l)$: negative, zero, and positive. If $\varphi(i,l)$ is zero, the cluster i and the cluster l are said to be statistically independent: $p(i,l) = p(i)p(l)$. If $\varphi(i,l)$ is positive, cluster i and cluster l are statistically dependent:$p(i,l) > p(i)p(l)$. If $\varphi(i,l)$ is negative, cluster i and cluster l can be regarded as much less dependent: $p(i,l) < p(i)p(l)$.

Therefore, when $\varphi(i,l)$ is positive, l-th cluster can be removed and then the optimal number of cluster is set as $L = l - 1$. Starting with a single cluster, the number of clusters can be obtained from adding clusters until at least one of $\varphi(i,l)$ becomes positive.

3   Speaker Identification

Speaker identification is to search the best matching speaker from a speaker database given an unknown speaker's speech data [9, 10]. In the training, a speaker model is created by clustering the training feature vectors into disjoint groups by any clustering algorithm. From a sequence of vectors

$$X_l = \left\{ x_l(n) \,\middle|\, l = \arg\max_{1 \leq k \leq L} S\,(x\,(n), \mu_k), n = 1, \cdots, N \right\}$$

in l-th region, it is obtained from the closest neighborhood sets of l-th cluster, μ_l, the Gaussian mixture density is defined by a weighted sum of M component densities as

$$p\,(x_l\,(n)\,|\lambda) = \sum_{i=1}^{M} \frac{p_{l,i}}{(2\pi)^{D/2}|\Sigma_{l,i}|^{1/2}} \exp\left\{-\frac{1}{2}\,(x_l(n)-\mu_{l,i})'\Sigma_{l,i}^{-1}\,(x_l(n)-\mu_{l,i})\right\} \tag{13}$$

where the mean vector is $\mu_{l,\,i}$ and variance matrix is $\Sigma_{l,\,i}$. The mixture weights satisfy the constraint that $\sum\limits_{l=1}^{L}\sum\limits_{i=1}^{M} p_{l,i} = 1$. Given $X = \{X_1, X_2, \cdots, X_L\}$, the complete GMM for speaker model is parameterized by the mean vectors, covariance matrices and mixture weights from all component densities. The notation collectively represents these parameters

$$\lambda = \{p_{l,\,i},\, \mu_{l,\,i},\, \Sigma_{l,\,i}\}, \qquad i = 1, \cdots, M \text{ and } l = 1, \cdots, L \qquad (14)$$

Then, the GMM likelihood can be written as

$$p\left(X \mid \lambda\right) = \prod_{n_1=1}^{N_1} p\left(x_1(n) \mid \lambda\right) \cdot \ \cdots \ \cdot \prod_{n_L=1}^{N_L} p\left(x_L(n) \mid \lambda\right) \qquad (15)$$

Parameter estimates can be obtained iteratively using EM algorithm. On each EM iteration, the weight, mean, and variance reestimation formulas are used which guarantee a monotonic increase in the model's likelihood value [9]. For speaker identification, each of S speakers is represented by robust GMM's λ_1, ..., λ_h, respectively. The objective of speaker identification is to find the speaker model which has the maximum a posteriori probability for a given feature sequence as

$$\hat{s} = \arg \max_{1 \le h \le S} \sum_{n=1}^{N} \log p\left(x\left(n\right) \mid \lambda_h\right) \qquad (16)$$

4   Experimental Results

To show effectiveness of the proposed method, we performed two experiments in which artificial data set and real speech data are used for the speaker identification.

Firstly, we used 2000 data set from a mixture of four Gaussian normal distributions with equal probability (case 1, $L = 4$) and a mixture of three Gaussian normal distributions with non-equal probability (case 2, $L = 3$) as

$$\text{Case1:} \begin{aligned} &0.25N\left[x \middle| \begin{pmatrix} 2.2 \\ 1.9 \end{pmatrix}, \begin{pmatrix} 0.07 & 0 \\ 0 & 0.02 \end{pmatrix}\right] + 0.25N\left[x \middle| \begin{pmatrix} 1.4 \\ 0.9 \end{pmatrix}, \begin{pmatrix} 0.07 & 0 \\ 0 & 0.02 \end{pmatrix}\right] \\ &+0.25N\left[x \middle| \begin{pmatrix} 2.4 \\ 1.2 \end{pmatrix}, \begin{pmatrix} 0.07 & 0 \\ 0 & 0.02 \end{pmatrix}\right] + 0.25N\left[x \middle| \begin{pmatrix} 1.3 \\ 2 \end{pmatrix}, \begin{pmatrix} 0.07 & 0 \\ 0 & 0.02 \end{pmatrix}\right] \end{aligned}$$

$$\text{Case2:} \begin{aligned} &0.1N\left[x \middle| \begin{pmatrix} 1.4 \\ 1.7 \end{pmatrix}, \begin{pmatrix} 0.04 & 0 \\ 0 & 0.02 \end{pmatrix}\right] + 0.3N\left[x \middle| \begin{pmatrix} 1.2 \\ 1.0 \end{pmatrix}, \begin{pmatrix} 0.06 & 0 \\ 0 & 0.02 \end{pmatrix}\right] \\ &+0.6N\left[x \middle| \begin{pmatrix} 2.5 \\ 1.2 \end{pmatrix}, \begin{pmatrix} 0.09 & 0 \\ 0 & 0.03 \end{pmatrix}\right] \end{aligned}$$

and the design parameters used were $\alpha = 0.1$, $\beta = 1.0$, and $\kappa = 2$.

For case 1, table 1(a) gives the experimental result of the proposed method obtained iteratively with starting from one cluster. Until 4th cluster is obtained, none of the mutual relationship between clusters has positive value. When 5th cluster is obtained, the

Table 1. The Process of the Proposed Method

(a)case 1				(b)case 2			
No. of Clusters(l)	Estimated l-th Cluster Center	i	$\varphi(i,l)$	No. of Clusters(l)	Estimated l-th Cluster Center	i	$\varphi(i,l)$
1	(2.1709,1.9278)	1	-	1	(2.5014,1.4009)	1	-
2	(2.4086,1.1962)	1	-0.0199	2	(1.2038,1.0024)	1	-0.0040
3	(1.2717,2.0062)	1	-0.0504	3	(1.3990,1.7041)	1	-0.0611
		2	-0.0191			2	-0.0572
4	(1.3825,0.868)	1	-0.0457	4	(2.4867,1.3978)	1	0.3310
		2	-0.0367			2	-0.0557
		3	-0.0342			3	-0.0256
5	(1.4136,1.2536)	1	-0.0453				
		2	-0.0343				
		3	-0.0344				
		4	0.0063				

Table 2. The Clustering error

(a)Case1				(b)Case2			
No. of Clusters	K-means	Global K-means	Proposed method	No. of Clusters	K-means	Global K-means	Proposed method
2	1708.33	752.28	810.03	2	1174.91	271.59	294.37
3	840.08	467.23	425.11	3*	333.24	210.13	206.19
4*	494.87	279.06	187.49	4	211.58	171.77	199.41
5	447.59	166.73	184.14	5	244.70	133.46	186.97
6	260.18	149.32	180.25	6	249.33	99.61	185.56

Table 3. Speaker identification Rates with M=1[%]

Algorithm	Number of Clusters (L)	Identification Rates
The K-means	8	96.27
(with fixed number of clusters)	16	98.21
The global K-means	17	98.02
The decreasing method based MMI	19	98.28
The proposed method	16	98.46

mutual relationship between 5th cluster and 4th cluster has positive value. Since 4th cluster and 5th cluster depend on each other, the 5th cluster is removed and finally the optimal number of clusters is obtained to be four. For case 2, table 1(b) gives the experimental result of the proposed method obtained iteratively with starting from one cluster. Until 3rd cluster is obtained, the mutual relationship between clusters has negative values. When 4th cluster is obtained, the mutual relationship between 4th cluster and 1st

cluster has positive value. Since 4th cluster and 1st cluster are dependent on each other, 4th cluster is removed and finally the optimal number of clusters is obtained to be three. Table 2 shows the clustering error as a function of the number of clusters.

$$E = \sum_{n=1}^{N} \|x(n) - C_{l_{\min}}\|^2, \text{ where } l_{\min} = \arg\min_{l} \|x(n) - C_l\|^2, l = 1, \cdots, L \quad (17)$$

Since the clustering errors of the K-means and the global K-means algorithms depend on the distance from all the data, it usually decreases as the number of clusters increases. The clustering error of the proposed method shows relatively small decrease after the optimum number of clusters. Clustering error of the original cluster is 177.4 at Case1, and 189.36 at Case2. In the optimum number of clusters, the proposed method shows the smallest clustering error comparing with the other approaches.

Secondly, we performed the speaker identification based on the proposed algorithm comparing with the K-means, the global K-means algorithm[4], and the decreasing method based on MMI(Maximum Mutual Information)[8]. We have used TIMIT database for its experiments. TIMIT contains 630 speakers (438 male and 192 female), each of them having uttered 10 sentences. 8 sentences were used for training and the other 2 sentences serve as test data. The speech was parameterized using 20 MFCCs – feature vector derived from 44 filter bank analysis. The analysis window size was 20ms with 10ms overlap. The results of the K-means algorithm are an average of 10 times executions with random initial positions and are used to the fixed number of clusters as 8 and 16. In case of the others, the number of clusters is estimated by mutual relationship. The method based MMI started from L=64. The experimental results are shown in table 3. The proposed method shows the highest performance as 98.46% with 16 clusters. Also, as measuring bounded similarity in the proposed method, the processing time for clustering reduced more than about 30% comparing with global K-means. It is clear from the experimental results that the proposed method does not need the initial guesses of locations of cluster centers and a priori information about the number of clusters, and the its performance is better than those of the K-means, the global K-means algorithms and the decreasing algorithm based MMI.

5   Conclusions

In this paper, a subtractive clustering algorithm with estimating the number of clusters is proposed for speaker identification. The proposed method removes the difficulty to decide initial guesses of the cluster centers and reduces the computation load. The number of clusters can be reasonably determined automatically by measuring the mutual relationship between clusters. The experimental results show the effectiveness of the proposed clustering algorithm.

References

1. Lozano, J.A., Pena, J.M. and Larranaga, P.: An empirical comparison of four initialization methods for the k-means algorithm,Pattern Recognition Letters, **20** (1999) 1027-1040

2. Gath and Geva, A.B. :Unsupervised optimal fuzzy clustering," IEEE Trans. Pattern and Machine Intelligence, **11(7)** (1989) 773-778
3. Ryager, R., Filev, D.P.: Approximate clustering via the mountain method, IEEE Trans on Systems, Man, and Cybernetics, **24** (1994) 1279-1284
4. Zadeh, L.A.: Similarity Relations and fuzzy Orderings, Information Science, **3** (1971) 177-200
5. Likas, A., Vlassis, N. and Verbeek, J.J.: The global k-means clustering algorithm, Pattern recognition, **36** (2003) 451-461
6. Chiu, S.L.: Fuzzy model identification based on cluster estimation, J. of Intelligent and Fuzzy sys., **2(3)** (1994) 267-278
7. Kothari, R., Pittas, D.: On finding the number of clusters, Pattern Recognition Letters, **20** (1999) 405-416
8. Yang, Z.R., Zwaliuski, M.: Mutual information theory for adaptive mixture model, IEEE Trans. Pattern and Machine Intelligence, **23(4)** (2001) 396-403
9. Lee, Y., Lee, J., Lee, K.Y.: Efficient Speaker Identification Based on Robust VQ-PCA, Springer, Lecture Note Computer Sciences, **2668** (2003) 631-638
10. Seo, C., Lee, K.Y. , Lee, J.: GMM based on local PCA for speaker identification, Electronic Letters, **37(24)** (2001) 1486-1488

On Modelling Glottal Stop
in Czech Text-to-Speech Synthesis*

Jindřich Matoušek and Jiří Kala

University of West Bohemia, Department of Cybernetics
Univerzitní 8, 306 14 Plzeň, Czech Republic
jmatouse@kky.zcu.cz, jkala@students.zcu.cz

Abstract. This paper deals with the modelling of glottal stop for the purposes of Czech text-to-speech synthesis. Phonetic features of glottal stop are discussed here and a phonetic transcription rule for inserting glottal stop into the sequences of Czech phones is proposed. Two approaches to glottal stop modelling are introduced in the paper. The first one uses glottal stop as a stand-alone phone. The second one models glottal stop as an allophone of a vowel. Both approaches are evaluated from the point of view of both the automatic segmentation of speech and the quality of the resulting synthetic speech. Better results are obtained when glottal stop is modelled as a stand-alone phone.

1 Introduction

Nowadays, concatenative synthesis is the most widely used approach to speech synthesis. This approach employs an acoustic unit inventory (AUI) which should comprise all relevant sounds of a language to be synthesized. Although diphones or triphones are the most often used units in the current speech synthesis systems, a system designer should always start with a phonetic inventory (i.e. with either phonemes or phones) of the given language. Such a phonetic inventory then constitutes a ground for more specific diphone or triphone inventories.

In our previous work we have designed ARTIC, a modern Czech concatenative text-to-speech (TTS) system (see e.g. [1]). It employs a carefully designed triphone AUI [1, 2]. In the first versions of our system we used a *phonemic inventory* of the Czech language as a ground for the triphone inventory. Later, the fundamental phonemic inventory was extended with the significant allophonic variants of some phonemes and thus it was replaced by a *phonetic inventory*, that incorporated 47 Czech phones (see SAMPA [3] for their notations).

Although the synthetic speech produced by our system sounded highly intelligibly, certain distortions were observed in some speech contexts, especially in words starting with a vowel. In natural speech, such contexts are characterized by the presence of so-called *glottal stop*. Since glottal stop is not usually considered as a phoneme in the Czech language (and its occurrence is often not mandatory), it was not included in our baseline phonetic inventory. However, in order to eliminate the distortions in the synthetic speech, an explicit glottal stop modelling and synthesis seems to be necessary.

---

* Support for this work was provided by GA ASCR, project No. 1ET101470416.

V. Matoušek et al. (Eds.): TSD 2005, LNAI 3658, pp. 257–264, 2005.

Two approaches to modelling glottal stop for the purposes of Czech TTS synthesis are introduced in this paper. The first one uses glottal stop as a *stand-alone phonetic unit*. The second one models glottal stop as an *allophone of a following vowel*, separating vowels with glottal stop from the vowels without glottal stop. In this paper, both approaches are evaluated from the point of view of both the automatic segmentation of speech and the quality of the resulting synthetic speech.

The paper is organized as follows. Section 2 briefly describes the phonetic features of glottal stop in the Czech language and discusses the automatic phonetic transcription of glottal stop. The Section 3 deals with the modelling of glottal stop in Czech synthetic speech. In Section 4 the results are presented. Finally, Section 5 concludes the paper by summarizing the main findings and outlines our future work.

2 Phonetic Features of Glottal Stop

From the point of view of Czech phoneticians [4], glottal stop (denoted as [?] in SAMPA [3]) is a glottal plosive that originates in vocal cords when a vowel or diphthong is articulated at the beginning of a word (especially after a silence, e.g. [?ahoj]) or inside a word at a morphological juncture (e.g. [na?opak]). When the articulation of a vowel in these contexts starts, vocals cords clamp tightly. Then, more audible separation of the vowel (or diphthong) from a preceding syllable is perceived. However, the point of view of Czech phoneticians is a little bit vague. Although glottal stop could distinguish the meaning of Czech words (e.g. *s uchem* [s?uxem] vs. *suchem* [suxem]), it is not common to consider it as a phoneme of the Czech language. Nevertheless, it could be considered as a stand-alone phone. On the other hand, as glottal stop could be viewed just as a beginning of a phonation, it can be defined as an allophone of the following vowel. In this paper, both conceptions are adopted and further described in Section 3.

As for the acoustic waveforms of glottal stop, it differs from context to context. In post-pausal contexts the acoustic waveform resembles the waveform of plosives. On the other hand, in intervocalic contexts it rather looks like a very transitional segment of speech. So, the contexts of glottal stop should be taken into account when modelling and synthesizing speech.

2.1 Phonetic Transcription of Glottal Stop

Obviously, there is a need of the automatic processing of the input text in text-to-speech synthesis tasks. The automatic conversion of the input text to its pronunciation (i.e. phonetic) form (so-called phonetic transcription) forms an important part of the text processing. As for the phonetic transcription of the Czech language, the phonetic transcription rules in the form of

$$A \rightarrow B \, / \, C\_D \tag{1}$$

(where letter sequence A with both left context C and right context D is transcribed as phone sequence B) were proposed to transcribe Czech texts in a fully automatic way [5].

If glottal stop is to be modelled in Czech text-to-speech synthesis, the set of phonetic transcription rules introduced in [5] should be extended with the rules describing the pronunciation of glottal stop. After a series of experiments (with respect to the observations of Czech phoneticians, e.g. in [4]) we proposed a phonetic transcription rule for inserting glottal stop into the sequence of Czech phones

$$\text{VOW} \rightarrow \text{?VOW} \; / \; \langle |, \text{PREF}- \rangle \; \_ \; , \tag{2}$$

where "VOW" stands for a vowel (or diphthong), "?" is a symbol for glottal stop, "PREF" is a prefix or a part of a compound word, and the symbol "$-$" marks the morphological juncture. The symbol "$|$" marks the word boundary. The text before the symbol "$\rightarrow$" describes the input text to be transcribed, the phones after "$\rightarrow$" express the result of the transcription. The symbol "$\_$" separates the left and right context of the input text. If various contexts are allowed (denoted by "$<$" and "$>$"), individual components are separated by a comma.

3   Modelling Glottal Stop

To be able to synthesize glottal stop in concatenative speech synthesis, glottal-stop-based units must be included in an acoustic unit inventory. In our previous work, we proposed a technique for the automatic construction of the acoustic unit inventories [1, 2]. Based on a carefully designed speech corpus [6], *statistical approach* (using three-state left-to-right single-density model-clustered crossword-triphone hidden Markov models, HMMs) was employed to create AUI of the Czech language in a fully automatic way. As a part of this approach, decision-tree-based clustering of similar triphone HMMs was utilized to define the set of basic speech units (i.e. clustered triphones) used later in speech synthesis. As a result, all the speech available in the corpus was segmented into these triphones. Then, the most suitable instance of all candidates of each triphone was selected off-line and used as a representative of the unit during synthesis. In this paper the process of AUI construction is extended with the modelling and segmentation of context-dependent glottal stop units.

Two approaches to modelling glottal stop have been proposed. Both approaches describe the glottal stop sounds in the context of the surroundings units, i.e. as the triphones. Hence, there is no need to explicitly differentiate between various acoustic waveforms of glottal stop as mentioned in Section 2, because triphones implicitly catch the context of the surrounding units. In the first approach the glottal stop is considered to be an independent phone of the Czech language (see Section 3.1 for more details). In the second approach the glottal stop is modelled as an allophone of a vowel (see Section 3.2).

The same corpus as described in [6] was used for the experiments with glottal stop modelling. The corpus was designed very carefully to contain phonetically balanced sentences. It comprises 5,000 sentences (about 13 hours of speech). Each sentence is described by linguistic and signal representations of speech. As for linguistics, both orthographic and phonetic transcriptions of each sentence are used. Speech signals are represented by their waveforms and their spectral properties are described by vectors of Mel Frequency Cepstral Coefficients (MFCCs) calculated using 20 ms windowed speech signal with 4 ms shift. In the current system 12 MFCCs plus normalized energy together with corresponding first, second and third differential coefficients (52 coefficients in total) are used.

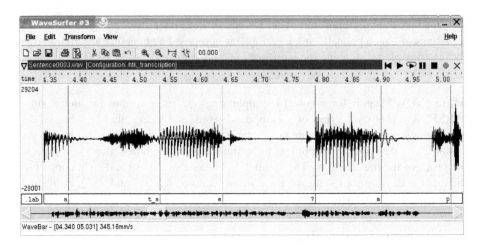

Fig. 1. An example of the delimitation of glottal stop represented as a stand-alone phone [?] in Czech synthetic speech.

3.1   Approach 1: Modelling Glottal Stop as a Stand-Alone Phone

In this approach (let's denote it APP1) the most straightforward modelling of glottal stop is performed. The phonetic inventory of Czech phones is extended with a single phone [?] that describes the glottal stop. The phonetic transcription rule (2) is employed to estimate the occurrences of glottal stop in Czech synthetic speech. The example of the phonetic transcription and the delimitation of glottal stop in the synthetic speech is shown in Fig. 1. The modelling and synthesis of glottal stop is the same as the modelling and synthesis of the other units in the statistical approach described above. The impact of glottal stop modelling both on the accuracy of segmentation of speech and on the quality of the resulting synthetic speech is described in Section 4.

3.2   Approach 2: Modelling Glottal Stop as an Allophone of a Vowel

Since it is sometimes hard to delimit glottal stop in the stream of continuous speech (especially in the intervocalic contexts), the alternative approach (APP2) to glottal stop modelling was proposed. In this approach glottal stop is not considered as a single phone but as an allophone of a corresponding vowel or diphthong. In fact, each vowel and diphthong is then represented by two different "phones" – vowel with glottal stop (e.g. [?a]) and vowel without glottal stop (e.g. [a]). Since there are 10 vowels and 3 diphthongs in Czech, there is a need to extend the phonetic inventory with 13 new "phones". If we use the phonetic transcription rule (2) to obtain glottal stop, a post-transcription is needed to convert glottal stops to corresponding vowel (or diphthong) units (see Fig. 2). Again, glottal stop units are then modelled and synthesized in the same way as the other units in the system. The impact of this approach on glottal stop modelling and synthesis is analyzed in Section 4.

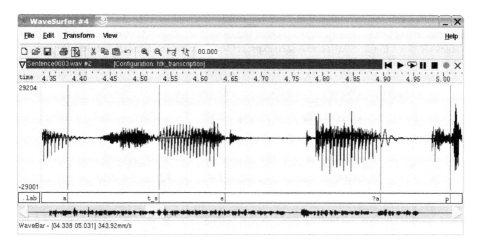

Fig. 2. An example of the delimitation of glottal stop represented as an allophone of a vowel ([a] in this case) in Czech synthetic speech.

4 Results

In this section the results of both approaches to glottal stop modelling are discussed. Since the quality of the resulting synthetic speech to a large extent depends on the quality of acoustic unit inventory and the quality of AUI is influenced by the accuracy the units are segmented with, the accuracy of the automatic segmentation of speech is evaluated in Section 4.1. The quality of the resulting synthetic speech is assessed in Section 4.2.

4.1 Segmentation Accuracy

To evaluate the segmentation accuracy of both approaches to glottal stop modelling described in Section 3, statistics of the deviation between the automatic and reference manual segmentation were computed (see Table 1). The reference segmentation consists of 50 sentences segmented by hand with no a priori information about the phone boundaries.

The segmentation accuracy is also often expressed as a percentage of automatically detected boundaries which lie within a tolerance region around the human labelled boundary. The tolerance region used to be chosen somewhat arbitrarily. We chose smaller (10 ms) and bigger (20 ms) regions.

Table 1 shows the evaluation of the automatic segmentation of speech. The segmentation accuracy of both approaches to glottal stop modelling is very similar. When comparing the segmentation of glottal stop (the stand-alone phone [?] in APP1 and the allophones of vowels in APP2), APP2 demonstrates better results. On the other hand, vowels were slightly better segmented in APP1. The total segmentation accuracy (when all phones were counted in) was slightly better in APP1 as well.

Table 1. The comparison of the segmentation accuracy. |MD| denotes the absolute mean deviation between the automatic and reference manual segmentation, |SD| is its standard deviation. Both values are given in ms. Acc10 and Acc20 express the segmentation accuracy in tolerance regions 10 and 20 ms.

Approach	Phone	|MD| [ms]	|SD| [ms]	Acc10 [%]	Acc20 [%]
	Glottal stop	8.63	8.32	69.12	95.71
APP1	Vowels	6.73	9.73	80.40	96.14
	All phones	6.60	9.16	82.29	95.71
	Glottal stop	7.40	7.80	82.29	92.62
APP2	Vowels	6.89	9.95	80.09	95.97
	All phones	6.70	9.28	82.20	95.37

4.2 Listening Tests

To evaluate the quality of the resulting synthetic speech generated using acoustic unit inventories based on both approaches to glottal stop modelling, two informal listening tests were carried out. Since glottal stop affects mainly the intelligibility of speech, the tested sentences were synthesized with neutral prosodic characteristics. 18 listeners participated in the tests.

The first test (TEST1) consisted of 18 specially designed sentences or collocations. Some contexts in these sentences could be pronounced with or without glottal stop. The presence or absence of glottal stop affects the meaning of sentences (e.g. *"Vypil asi dvě piva."* [vipil ?asi dvje piva] and *"Vypila si dvě piva."* [vipila si dvje piva] or *"Při boji za mír upadl"* [p\Qi boji za mi:r ?upadl=] and *"Při boji za Míru padl."* [p\Qi boji za mi:ru padl=]). Of course, 9 sentences were synthesized using APP1 and 9 sentences were synthesized using APP2. The sentence order was chosen randomly. Some sentences were synthesized with glottal stop present and the rest of sentences were synthesized with no glottal stop present. The listeners were given a single synthetic waveform for each sentence and two textual transcriptions which differed just by the presence/absence of glottal stop. The task of listeners was to choose such a transcription which best matches the synthetic waveform.

The aim of the second test (TEST2) was to compare two synthetic waveforms (generated using both approaches to glottal stop modelling) of the same sentence directly. The same 18 sentences as in TEST1 were utilized. Now, the task of listeners was to choose such a variant which sounded more intelligibly and more "fluently" for them. Again, to ensure the independence of the test, in 9 cases the first waveform in the pair of the waveforms was synthesized using APP1 and in 9 cases the first waveform was synthesized using APP2.

The results of both tests are shown in Fig. 3. TEST1 shows the correct mappings of the written sentences to the played synthetic waveform (in percentage). In TEST2 the listeners' evaluation of both approaches to glottal stop modelling is presented (in percentage). NO_PREF denotes cases when no preference was given. It can be seen that the listeners preferred modelling glottal stop as a stand-alone phone (APP1).

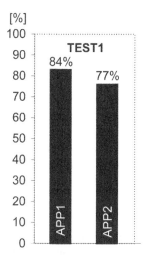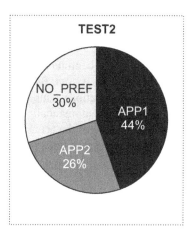

Fig. 3. The results of the listening tests.

To evaluate the contribution of explicit glottal stop modelling to the increase of the intelligibility of synthetic speech, another listening test was carried out. The previous version of our synthesizer with no explicit glottal stop modelling (AUI contained no glottal stop sounds) was compared to the APP1 version of glottal stop modelling. All listeners did prefer the synthetic speech with glottal stops.

5   Conclusion and Future Work

In this paper an explicit modelling of glottal stop for the purposes of Czech text-to-speech synthesis was described. Phonetic inventory of the Czech language was extended with glottal stop units. A phonetic transcription rule for inserting glottal stop to the sequence of Czech phones was also proposed. Two approaches to glottal stop modelling were proposed and examined as well. The first approach (APP1) models glottal stop as a stand-alone phone. The second approach considers glottal stop to be an allophone of a vowel. The results presented in Section 4 showed the superiority of the first approach (mainly from the point of view of the quality of the synthetic speech assessed by the listening tests).

Moreover, when comparing both approaches to glottal stop modelling from the systemic point of view, it is more convenient to employ the first approach (APP1) in speech synthesis tasks, because the phonetic inventory of Czech phones is extended just by a single phone. Beside the worse results presented in Section 4, there are also other drawbacks of the second approach (APP2):

- There is a need of more phone-sized units in the system (13 new "phones" should be added to the phonetic inventory of the Czech language).
- The occurrence of glottal stop in some contexts (e.g. in front of [O] or [o_u]) is very rare. So, a special care should be dedicated to sentence selection when recording the speech corpus for AUI creation in order to assure that such contexts will be present in the corpus.

- Due to separated modelling of vowels and diphthongs with/without glottal stop, some rare vowels (e.g. [O]) or diphthongs (e.g. [e_u]) could not have robust models resulting in less accurate segmentation of these units and less quality representatives in AUI.

In our next work we will continuously aim at improving the quality of the synthetic speech produced by our TTS system. Beside other aspects (e.g. enhanced prosody generation or dynamic unit selection) a substantial attention will be paid to the improvements in the quality of the automatically designed acoustic unit inventories. We will focus mainly on the increase of the accuracy of the automatic segmentation of speech and on defining the optimal set of units present in the acoustic unit inventory.

References

1. Matoušek, J., Romportl, J., Tihelka, D., Tychtl, Z.: Recent Improvements on ARTIC: Czech Text-to-Speech System. Proceedings of ICSLP 2004, vol. III. Jeju Island, Korea (2004) 1933–1936.
2. Matoušek, J., Tihelka, D., Psutka, J: Automatic Segmentation for Czech Concatenative Speech Synthesis Using Statistical Approach with Boundary-Specific Correction. Proceedings of Eurospeech 2003. Geneva (2003) 301–304.
3. Czech SAMPA. http://www.phon.ucl.ac.uk/home/sampa/czech-uni.htm.
4. Palková, Z.: Phonetics and Phonology of Czech (in Czech). Karolinum, Prague (1994).
5. Psutka, J.: Communication with Computer by Speech (in Czech). Academia, Prague (1995).
6. Matoušek, J., Psutka, J., Krůta, J.: On Building Speech Corpus for Concatenation-Based Speech Synthesis. Proceedings of Eurospeech2001, vol 3. Ålborg (2001) 2047–2050.

Analysis of the Suitability of Common Corpora for Emotional Speech Modeling in Standard Basque*

Eva Navas, Inmaculada Hernáez, Iker Luengo,
Jon Sánchez, and Ibon Saratxaga

Departamento de Electrónica y Telecomunicaciones Escuela Técnica Superior de Ingeniería
University of the Basque Country
Alameda Urquijo s/n, 48013 Bilbao, Spain
{eva,inma,ikerl,ion,ibon}@bips.bi.ehu.es
http://bips.bi.ehu.es

Abstract. This paper presents the analysis made to assess the suitability of neutral semantic corpora to study emotional speech. Two corpora have been used: one having neutral texts that were common to all emotions and the other having texts related to the emotion. Subjective and objective analysis have been performed. In the subjective test common corpus has achieved good recognition rates, although worse than those obtained with specific texts. In the objective analysis, differences among emotions are larger for common texts than for specific texts, indicating that in common corpus expression of emotions was more exaggerated. This is convenient for emotional speech synthesis, but no for emotion recognition. So, in this case, common corpus is suitable for the prosodic modeling of emotions to be used in speech synthesis, but for emotion recognition specific texts are more convenient.

1 Introduction

The ability to express emotions is a desirable feature in a high quality text to speech system. To achieve this feature, a deeper research of the prosodic characteristics of emotional speech is necessary and this cannot be done without a good emotional database. Different types of emotional speech databases can be distinguished according to the type of corpora selected [1]: there are databases of spontaneous speech, databases of elicited speech and databases of acted speech.

For the prosodic characterization of emotions, acted speech is usually selected, because the control of the recordings is better and they are easier to obtain. The design and acquisition of such a database requires a lot of effort because specific corpora have to be designed for each desired emotion and valid expressions of emotions must be recorded. It would be very interesting to know whether it is possible to appropriately express different emotions using always the same texts, because this would simplify the design of emotional databases of acted speech. This approach of using the same text to express different emotions has already been used [2][3][4], but no try to validate the

---

* This work has been partially funded by the Spanish Ministry of Science and Technology (TIC2003-08382-C05-03). Authors would also like to thank all the evaluators that took part in the subjective evaluation process.

V. Matoušek et al. (Eds.): TSD 2005, LNAI 3658, pp. 265–272, 2005.

naturalness of the expression has been described. The aim of this work is to study the acoustical correlates of emotion in a new database created for standard Basque [5] and to determine whether emotions are expressed in the same way no matter the relation of the text with the intended emotion.

2   Emotional Database

For the study of prosody of emotional speech for standard Basque a new database was designed and recorded. The database includes the following emotions: anger, disgust, fear, joy, sadness and surprise, that are considered the basic ones [6][7]. This set has been used in different studies related with speech, both for emotion recognition [8] and for emotion generation [9]. Neutral style has also been considered in common corpus, to be used as a reference.

For the study of the way of expressing emotion, two different text corpora have been designed.

– Common corpus: it consists of emotion independent texts, which are common for all the emotions, as well as for the neutral style. This common group of texts was phonetically balanced in order to achieve a phoneme distribution similar to the one that occurs in natural oral language. The texts have neutral semantic content. Trying to appropriately express emotion with a text that has not emotional content is difficult for the speaker, but it allows an easy comparison among styles. With this type of corpus, it is possible to use the standard approach of comparing parameters for the same sound sequence. Examples of emotional databases that use neutral texts are the Danish Emotional Database [10] and the Berlin corpus [11].
– Specific corpus: it includes texts semantically related to each emotion, and therefore, the texts are different for each of the emotions considered in the database. Neutral style was not considered in this part of the corpus. The use of texts semantically related to the emotion makes easier for the speaker to express that emotion naturally. But it makes difficult to compare the characteristics of different emotions and to phonetically balance the database. The collection of suitable texts to be recorded is also difficult. This is the approach used in many studies of emotional speech [12][2].

Emotion can be reliably identified in very short utterances [10], so isolated words seem to be suitable for this type of database. Both text corpora included isolated words and sentences of different complexity and syntactical structure. They were read by a professional dubbing actress. The recording was made using a laryngograph to capture also the glottal pulse signal. Speech and glottal pulse signals were sampled at 32 kHz, and quantified using 16 bit per sample.

The recording was made at a professional recording studio, during two days. The first day the texts related with the emotion were recorded, and the second day the common texts. Within a recording session, every emotion was recorded without interruption, to avoid the speaker loosing concentration. The speaker was allowed to rest between the recordings of texts corresponding to different emotions.

3   Subjective Evaluation of the Database

To prove the ability of the speaker to accurately simulate the emotions, a subjective test was prepared. The purpose of this test was to compare the recognition rates in both corpora and to check whether listeners could identify the intended emotion well above chance level, assessing this way the validity of the obtained data.

A forced choice test was designed, where users had to select one of the proposed emotions. The six emotions contained in the database and the neutral style were proposed to the listeners. To check the dependency on the semantic content of the signals and to determine whether the speaker had expressed emotion with the same level of accuracy in both corpora, sentences from both the common corpus and the specific corpus were selected. The test included 130 stimuli.

The subjects taking part in the experiment were selected among the students and staff of the Electronics and Telecommunication Department of the University of the Basque Country. A total of 15 participants (11 males and 4 females with ages varying from 20 to 36 years) took part in the experiments. All of them were native of Basque, or at least fluent in standard Basque. None of them reported speech or hearing problems.

The recognition rate obtained for each emotion is shown in Fig. 1. Results obtained for common and specific corpora are shown. The signals belonging to specific corpus are better identified, but it is difficult to determine to what extent this is due to the semantic content of the stimulus, which helps the listener to decide, or to the better expression of the emotion by the speaker. An analysis of variance (ANOVA) has showed that differences are no significant with a 99% confidence interval.

Disgust is the emotion that achieves the worst results. It has been confused mainly with the neutral style. This emotion has also been the most difficult to identify in other experiments made for different languages [12][13][14]. Recognition rates are similar in the common corpus and in the specific corpus for surprise, sadness and joy. Anger and fear get poorer results for the common corpus, but well above chance level. Therefore, the results of the subjective test performed on the common corpus are good enough to consider using the same texts to model all emotions.

4   Acoustic Analysis of the Database

Prosodic features are clearly related with emotion, but the nature of this relation has still to be determined. In this work, several acoustic parameters have been analyzed to know how the prosodic features change to express an emotion. Another important issue was to find out whether the speaker expressed emotions in the same way when reading texts with neutral emotional content or texts related with emotion.

4.1   Features Selected

For this study the prosodic features related with pitch and energy have been automatically measured for all the signals of the database and statistic measures have been calculated. The features used are: mean F0 value (Hz), F0 range (Hz), maximum positive slope in F0 curve (Hz/ms), root mean square energy (RMS) (dB), mean RMS in low band, from 0 to 2000 Hz (dB) and mean RMS in high band, from 2000 to 4000 Hz (dB).

Values have been studied independently for the common and specific corpora. In this study only long term prosodic information has been used, although temporal evolution of prosodic parameters may also be important to discriminate emotions.

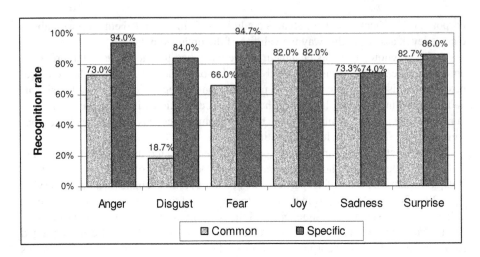

Fig. 1. Result of the subjective test, showing the recognition rate for each emotion separated by text type. Chance level is also displayed for comparison

4.2 Comparison of the Distributions of Parameters Between Both Corpora

To know whether the speaker had expressed the emotions in the same way when reading texts related with emotion and texts with neutral content, an ANOVA test has been applied to each parameter with a confidence interval of 99%. Results of this analysis are shown in Table 1, where a cell having the value "NO" indicates that differences between the distributions of this parameter in both corpora are not significant for the emotion considered. In other words, the speaker has used this parameter in the same way in both corpora. Therefore, the parameter that has been more consistently applied by the speaker has been the maximum positive slope of the pitch curve, because the differences are not significant for all the emotions. Besides, joy is the emotion that has been expressed more similarly in both corpora, because all the parameters studied have differences not significant between both corpora. Anger and surprise have been expressed in a different way in common and specific corpora, because most of the parameters have different distributions in both corpora.

An ANOVA analysis with a confidence interval of 95% was applied to the values of the parameters measured in both parts of the corpus, to determine whether differences among distributions were significant for different emotions. Results of this analysis for common corpus show that 79% of the differences of parameter distributions between pairs of emotions were significant, i.e., 79% of the cases are able to discriminate emotions in common corpus. The same analysis was applied to values measured in the specific corpus, and in this case less differences of parameter distribution between pairs of emotions were found significant (only 68% of the pairs were considered significant). This is probably due to the fact that the speaker overacted in the common corpus to distinguish emotions that could not be differentiated by the content. In the specific corpus, as semantics indicated what the intended emotion was, she acted more naturally with less exaggerated emotions.

Table 1. This table indicates whether the differences between the distributions of each studied parameter in the two corpora are significant with confidence interval 99%. NO in one cell indicates that distributions of the parameter of that column have not significant difference between both corpora for the emotion of that row

Emotion	Mean F0	F0 range	Max Slop	RMS	RMS 0-2	RMS 2-4
Anger			NO			
Disgust	NO	NO	NO			NO
Fear		NO	NO			
Joy	NO	NO	NO	NO	NO	NO
Sadness			NO	NO	NO	NO
Surprise			NO			

4.3   Analysis of Pitch Features

The values of pitch curve were obtained from data provided by the laryngograph, which gives the following three different synchronized signals, shown in Fig. 2:
- Speech signal (Sp).
- Glottal pulse signal (Lx): This signal is captured by the electrodes situated around the neck of the speaker. The local minima indicate the moments when the vocal cords close.
- Quasi-rectangular signal (Tx): This signal is created by the laryngograph processor using the information of Sp and Lx signals. It also serves to indicate the closure moments of the vocal cords.

F0 curve was calculated from the glottal closure curve (Lx) obtained with the laryngograph. The temporal resolution used was 1 ms. Mean values and their corresponding standard deviations for all the intonation related parameters, measured in the specific and common corpora, are shown in Table 2, separated by emotion. Sadness is the emotion with lower values in all the parameters measured. Surprise is the one with wider pitch range. With regard to F0 maximum positive slope, anger has the larger one in specific corpus and joy in common corpus. The emotion with higher mean pitch value is fear. The values of mean pitch and range corresponding to specific texts are lower than the ones corresponding to common texts for all the emotions.

4.4   Analysis of Power Features

For the analysis of the power features, the RMS of the signals was calculated. The spectral distribution of the energy has been considered important in previous studies about emotional speech for other languages [8], so the RMS energy of the 0-2 KHz band and that of the 2-4 KHz band have also been measured.

The values measured for the specific and common corpora are listed in Table 3. The emotions with more energy are anger and joy and sadness is the one with lower energy. The values measured in the specific part are in general, higher than the ones of common texts. This could be due to the fact that both parts of the database have been recorded in two different days, and no reference level was given to the speaker.

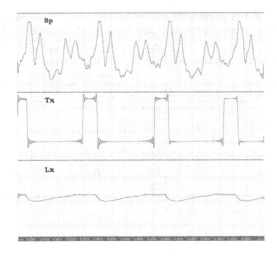

Fig. 2. Different signals recorded by the laryngograph: Sp is the speech signal, Tx a quasi rectangular signal that indicates the instants of glottal closure of the vocal chords and Lx is the glottal pulse curve

Table 2. Values of the pitch parameters measured in the specific corpus (*top rows*) and in the common corpus (*bottom rows*), separated by emotion. Mean value and standard deviation are shown in the form mean ± standard deviation

Emotion	Mean F0 (Hz)	Range F0 (Hz)	Max. Pos. Slope F0 (Hz/ms)
Anger	256.7 ± 51.9	282.5 ± 79.1	12.3 ± 5.3
Disgust	206.8 ± 33.7	201.4 ± 59.7	9.5 ± 3.9
Fear	322.2 ± 44.2	265.6 ± 104.6	5.5 ± 1.3
Joy	306.6 ± 32.1	320.0 ± 80.0	10.9 ± 4.4
Sadness	175.7 ± 21.1	144.0 ± 44.2	2.3 ± 0.7
Surprise	280.0 ± 33.9	371.8 ± 52.3	5.6 ± 1.3
Anger	370.8 ± 36.5	382.8 ± 73.9	11.6 ± 5.2
Disgust	217.8 ± 28.7	190.3 ± 53.4	8.8 ± 4.0
Fear	379.2 ± 36.3	302.2 ± 112.4	5.6 ± 1.5
Joy	314.1 ± 30.8	327.5 ± 87.9	12.3 ± 4.4
Sadness	212.6 ± 18.2	167.1 ± 56.1	2.4 ± 0.7
Surprise	339.0 ± 35.8	398.4 ± 61.8	5.4 ± 1.5

5   Conclusions

This work presents a study of the suitability of having a common text corpus to model different emotions. With this purpose, a common corpus has been recorded expressing six different emotions and neutral style. A specific text corpus, containing texts semantically related to the six emotions studied, has also been designed to compare the recognition rate and the expression of each emotion by the speaker.

Table 3. Values of the pitch parameters measured in the specific corpus (*top rows*) and in the common corpus (*bottom rows*). Mean value and standard deviation are shown in the form mean ± standard deviation

Emotion	RMS (dB)	RMS 0-2KHz (dB)	RMS 2-4 KHz (dB)
Anger	20.5 ± 1.5	20.0 ± 1.7	15.6 ± 1.8
Disgust	19.3 ± 2.1	19.0 ± 2.1	13.4 ± 2.9
Fear	19.8 ± 1.3	19.5 ± 1.3	14.0 ± 2.4
Joy	20.2 ± 1.3	19.6 ± 1.3	15.9 ± 1.7
Sadness	16.0 ± 2.1	15.8 ± 2.1	8.2 ± 2.7
Surprise	20.1 ± 1.6	19.7 ± 1.6	15.1 ± 1.9
Anger	19.3 ± 1.5	18.0 ± 1.8	16.6 ± 1.9
Disgust	18.4 ± 1.9	18.1 ± 1.9	13.3 ± 2.9
Fear	16.1 ± 1.6	15.7 ± 1.6	12.2 ± 2.3
Joy	19.8 ± 1.6	19.1 ± 1.8	15.6 ± 2.1
Sadness	16.4 ± 2.2	16.3 ± 2.2	8.5 ± 2.7
Surprise	16.7 ± 1.6	16.1 ± 1.6	13.3 ± 2.3

In the subjective test, signals from the common corpus have achieved worst results than the ones from specific corpus, but the values obtained were still good, except for disgust, an emotion that has also been difficult to identify in other languages. The subjective recognition rates are good enough to allow the use of a common text corpus for the study of different emotions.

In the objective analysis, common and specific corpora are different for all the prosodic parameters measured, except for the maximum positive slope of the pitch. Discrimination among emotions with the objective parameters measured is better in the common corpus (79% vs. 68%), probably because the speaker tried to exaggerate the characteristics of each emotion to distinguish them. Therefore, common corpus has provided a more stereotypical expression of emotions, which can be adequate for speech synthesis, but it is no so convenient for the training of models to be used in emotion recognition.

References

1. Campbell, N.: Databases of Emotional Speech. Proc. ISCA Tutorial and Research Workshop (ITRW) on Speech and Emotion. ISCA Archive (2000) 34-38
2. Montero, J. M., Gutiérrez-Arriola, J., Colás, J., Enríquez, E., Pardo, J. M.: Analysis and Modelling of Emotional Speech in Spanish. Proc. ICPhS 99. (1999) 957-960
3. Hozjan, V., Kacic, Z., Moreno, A., Bonafonte, A., Nogueiras, A.: Interface databases: Design and Collection of a Multilingual Emotional Speech Database. Proc. 3rd International Conference on Language Resources and Evaluation. (2000) 2019-2023
4. Seppánen T, Väyrynen E, Toivanen J.: Prosody-based classification of emotions in spoken Finnish. Proc. Eurospeech'2003, Vol. 1. (2003) 717-720
5. Alvarez, J.L.: The Future of Standard Basque. Uztaro, 11 (1994) 47-54

6. Scherrer, K.R.: Vocal Communication of Emotion: A Review of Research Paradigms. Speech Communication, Vol. 40. Elsevier, Amsterdam (2003) 227-256

7. Cowie, R., Cornelius, R.R.: Describing the Emotional States that Are Expressed in Speech. Speech Communication, Vol. 40(1,2). Elsevier, Amsterdam (2003) 2-32

8. Lay Nwe, T., Wei Foo, S., De Silva, L.: Speech Emotion Recognition Using Hidden Markov Models. Speech Communication, Vol. 41(4). Elsevier, Amsterdam (2003) 603-623

9. Boula de Mareüil, P., Célérier, P., Toen, J.: Generation of Emotions by a Morphing Technique in English, French and Spanish. Proc. Speech Prosody. Laboratoire Parole et Langage CNRS, Aix-en Provence (2002) 187-190

10. Enberg, I.S., Hansen, A.V., Andersen O., Dalsgaard, P.: Design, Recording and Verification of a Danish Emotional Speech Database. Proc. 5th European Conference on Speech Communication and Technology. (1997) 1695-1698

11. Paeschke, A., Sendlmeier, W.F.: Prosodic characteristics of Emotional Speech; Measurements of Fundamental Frequency Movements. Proc. ISCA Workshop on Speech and Emotion. ISCA Archive (2000) 75-80

12. Iida, A., Campbell, N., Higuchi, F., Yasumura, M.: A Corpus-based Speech Synthesis System with Emotion. Speech Communication, Vol. 40(1,2). Elsevier, Amsterdam (2003) 161-187

13. Burkhardt, F., Sendlmeier, W.F.: Verification of Acoustical Correlates of Emotional Speech using Formant-Synthesis. Proc. ISCA Workshop on Speech and Emotion. ISCA Archive (2000) 151-156

14. Iriondo, I., Guaus, R., Rodríguez, A., Lázaro, P., Montoya, N., Blanco, J.M., Bernardas, D., Oliver, J.M., Tena, D., Longhi, L.: Validation of an Acoustical Modelling of Emotional Expression in Spanish using Speech Synthesis Techniques. Proc. ISCA Workshop on Speech and Emotion. ISCA Archive (2000) 161-166

Discrete and Fluent Voice Dictation in Czech Language⋆

Jan Nouza

SpeechLab, Technical University of Liberec, Hálkova 6
461 17 Liberec 1, Czech Republic
jan.nouza@vslib.cz
http://itakura.kes.vslib.cz/kes/indexe.html

Abstract. This paper describes two prototypes of voice dictation systems developed for Czech language. The first one has been designed for discrete dictation with the lexicon that includes up to 1 million most frequent Czech words and word-forms. The other is capable of processing fluent speech and it can work with a 100,000-word lexicon in real time on recent high-end PCs. The former has been successfully tested by handicapped persons who cannot enter and edit texts by standard input devices (keyboard and mouse).

1 Introduction

In 2003 we introduced our concept of the first voice dictation system applicable for Czech [1]. The system was designed to operate with an extremely large vocabulary, which is necessary for highly inflective languages like the Slavic ones. Its discrete-speech version was capable of recognizing about a half of million words, the continuous-speech version operated with the vocabulary limited to some 20 thousand words if we wanted to keep the system's response below 2 seconds.

During the last two years both the systems have passed a significant improvement, namely with respect to the enhanced lexicon, now containing more words and multiple pronunciation variants. We focused also on improved language modeling, faster decoding algorithms and issues concerning practical usability. In this paper we describe the techniques that were applied in the most recent versions of the two dictation systems, we mention their new options as well as the remaining limits. In the final part we present the results achieved in several practical tests performed with discrete and fluent dictation in Czech.

2 Common Platform for Voice Dictation Systems

The discrete and the continuous voice dictation systems are based on the own speech recognition platform we have been developing for more than a decade. They share several basic modules, namely the signal processing part, the acoustic models of speech (and non-speech) units and also the core part of the decoder.

The input front-end includes the routines that control the sound-card and process an 8 kHz sampled signal from a microphone. Every 10 ms, a 25-ms long signal frame is

---

⋆ This work was supported by the Czech Grant Agency (GACR grant no. 102/05/0278).

V. Matoušek et al. (Eds.): TSD 2005, LNAI 3658, pp. 273–280, 2005.

parameterized to get 13 mel-frequency cepstral coefficients (MFCC) and their 1*st* and 2*nd* derivatives. The frame energy is also calculated but it is used only for detecting speech endpoints.

The decoding module works with a lexicon that has form of an alphabetically ordered list of words. Each item is represented by its text and phonetic form. The latter serves for constructing the acoustic model of the word by concatenating corresponding phoneme models. In the real-time implementation we employ three-state left-to-right HMMs of context-independent speech units supplemented by several models of noise. The HMMs have 64 to 100 gaussians per state and they have been trained on the database that consists of 42 hours of speech recorded by more than 400 speakers.

The lexicon and the language model have been built with the use of a large corpus of Czech texts (for details, see [2]). The size and the internal structure of the lexicons slightly differ for each of the two tasks. For discrete dictation, the standard vocabulary includes typically several hundreds of thousands words, while the continuous speech recognition system works with lexicons containing 45 to 100 thousands words, depending on the computer's speed. The former system is supported primarily by a unigram language model (LM), the latter needs a properly trained bigram model.

3   Discrete Dictation

The isolated-word dictation system has been designed as a tool that could really help people who cannot (e.g. handicapped users) or do not prefer (e.g. doctors) to input text through standard means, i.e. a keyboard and a mouse. Hence, the system has to offer not just the possibility to dictate words each after other, but also some options that are necessary for voice control of the system itself, for correcting possible recognition errors, for deciding between acoustically ambiguous items, like homophones, and, last but not least, for simple formatting operations. In the next sections we describe most of these techniques and algorithms.

3.1   Lexicon

The standard lexicon is denoted as Lex800K because it contains about 800,000 words, word-forms and multi-word phrases. It consists of several parts:

Standard Words. These are words that should appear within the dictated text. Their list has been compiled from a large corpus of newspaper, novel and professional texts. We included all those words that occurred in the corpus at least 3 times and successfully passed a Czech spell-checking program.

Punctuation Marks. This class includes the terms that are used to input punctuation marks, i.e. Czech equivalents of words "comma", "period", "question mark" or "new line". It should be noted that most of these words appear twice in the lexicon. For example, if a word "period" is uttered and recognized, the system must decide whether to type the word "period" or put a dot (".") to the text file. This situation is solved either by the system itself (utilizing the language model) or by the user who must choose which is more appropriate in the given context.

Control Commands. These include spoken commands, such as "start recognition", "stop recognition", "remove the last item", etc. Another set of commands allows the user to replace the originally recognized word by another acoustically similar (or even same) candidate that is shown in the candidate stack window. These commands have form of phrases, like "take the 1st (candidate)", "take the 2nd (candidate)", etc. All the control words or phrases must be chosen so that they are easily recognized and cannot be confused with the standard lexicon items.

Additional Phrases. To help the user in dictating some very frequent phrases that are usually uttered as single items, we extended the lexicon by several tens of word strings, like for example, "two thousand five", which will be automatically typed as "2005". Most of these strings represent numeral data, like dates, ordinal numbers, etc.

3.2 Lexicon Coding

Each lexicon item (either a word or a word string) is represented by its phonetic form. For most Czech words the pronunciation can be determined automatically using a set of transcription rules. For foreign or irregularly pronounced words we had to supply the proper transcription manually. Since the words are supposed to be uttered separately (with pauses between them) we have to take into account also the typical voicing onset in words with an initial vowel. This is solved by adding a special acoustic model at the beginning of these words. In similarly way, some words, namely mono-phonemic prepositions ("v", "s", "z", "k") need to be transcribed with a "schwa" following the consonant.

Internally, the lexicon is coded in form of a lexical tree, with prefix and suffix sharing. The prefix sharing is done in the common way from a lexicon that is alphabetically ordered. The suffix sharing involves the 20 most frequent inflection patterns, like the hard and soft pattern inflected adjectives, past tense verb patterns, etc [3]. Due to this coding strategy, an item in the 800K lexicon consumes in average only 1.11 tree arcs. In total, the whole 800K lexicon needs 881,568 arcs x 8 bytes, which is approximately 7 MB of memory. The size of the space necessary for the data driven search is given by the tree branching factor and by the beam pruning threshold. Experiments showed that the decoder for the largest 800K lexicon could conduct the search within a 16MB block of memory.

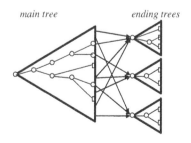

Fig. 1. Lexical tree with sub-trees sharing common endings

3.3   Language Model

Initial experiments showed that the word recognition strategy based only on the acoustic match produces too many errors in case of a lexicon whose size may go up to one million items. This is caused by the fact that the Czech lexical inventory includes a large portion of homophones (words that have the same pronunciation but different text form). Many other words (usually those derived from the same lemma) differ only in a single (final) phoneme, which is often pronounced with less care. To cope with this problem it was necessary to incorporate also some sort of language knowledge. This additional information has form of statistics about words and word-pair frequencies. The recent version of the system allows for combining scores from acoustic matching with word unigrams and bigrams.

To determine the most probable word w_t from lexicon L, given the acoustic vector sequence X, we search for the candidate whose acoustic and language scores maximize the equation:

$$w_t = \arg\max_{w \in L} \left[\log P(w_t|X) + \alpha \log P(w_t) + \beta \log P(w_t|w_{t-1}) \right] \qquad (1)$$

In Eq. 1, the first term represents the log probability of the corresponding word HMM, the second term, weighted by factor α, is log unigram probability and the last one, multiplied by factor β, is log (bigram) probability that word w_t follows the previously spoken w_{t-1}. This scheme is quite general and allows us to apply it in several different situations:

a) If only the unigram probabilities are available, factor β is set to 0. In our system this is the default case.
b) If the bigram probabilities are available for all lexicon items, factor α can be set to 0, because the bigram language model always outperforms the unigram one. Unfortunately, the bigram matrix for the whole 800K-word lexicon is too large to be computed and stored efficiently.
c) If only a part of the lexicon (usually the most frequent words) is supported by the bigrams, we still can use the unigrams and combine them with the bigrams where these are available. In this case the weighting factors α and β must be mutually balanced.

The optimal values of the two weighting factors for each of the three above mentioned cases have to be determined experimentally.

3.4   Practical Implementation

The implementation of this scheme is straightforward. First, the decoder computes the acoustic score $P(w|X)$ for all the words that survived the beam search. After that, for a selected number of the top candidates the score is complemented by unigram or birgam values. Even if only the unigrams are available, this simple scheme works surprisingly well. It gives the higher preference to the more frequent words, which helps namely in case of the homophones and the short conjunctions and prepositions.

The average word error rate (WER) is reduced by factor of 2-3 as demonstrated in the next section.

The layout of the prototype version of the dictation system (developed for the MS WinNT/XP) is shown in Fig. 2. We can see that the largest part of the application window is devoted to the dictated text. When a new word is uttered and recognized, it is added at the end of the previously input text. The last item in the text is always highlighted to indicate which part of the text can be edited by the special control commands mentioned in section 3.1 (e.g. "Remove the last", or "Take the 2nd", etc). In this way the user can replace the highlighted item by the more appropriate one from the list of the N best candidates provided by the system. This is important in situations when a word is misrecognized or when a homophone is to be replaced by another word.

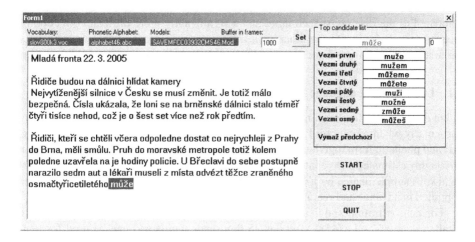

Fig. 2. A snapshot demonstrating the layout and the functions of the discrete dictation system. (The last entered word was recognized wrongly but the user can replace it by choosing the correct one from the ordered list of candidates that are displayed in the right part of the form.)

3.5   Evaluation Tests

The prototype has been tested by several tens of people on different computers. The words dictated in these sessions were automatically recorded and stored for later evaluation tests. Now, this database includes 4000 recordings that can be used in experiments to compare various system settings and recognition strategies. In Table 1 we present some of the most relevant results. These are quantified by WER values. We can observe that even the introduction of the simplest unigram model increased the performance in significant way. If we used also the bigrams (those available for the most frequent 140K words), the WER further reduced by almost 4 percent. All these tests were conducted with speaker-independent acoustic models. When speaker-adapted HMMs were employed we got another 1.4 percent improvement. More details about the speaker adaptation can be found in section [4].

Table 1. Summary of the most relevant results obtained in tests evaluating several different strategies in the discrete dictation system (4000 words dictated by 10 speakers, Lex800K)

	No Language model	Unigram model	Unigram and bigram model	After speaker adaptation
WER[%]	46.2	11.9	8.6	7.2

4   Continuous Dictation

Unlike the previous program tool, that can be already employed in practical tasks, the continuous-speech dictation system serves more for demonstration purposes rather than for practical usage at the moment. The main reason is the limited size of the vocabulary, which is still too small for serious work. The others are: a lower recognition rate compared to the discrete-speech input and a significantly more difficult correction of misrecognized words. On the other side, the system we describe below is apparently the first one that allows a Czech user to dictate whole sentences in a natural fluent way.

4.1   Lexicon and Language Model

In the discrete dictation task, modifications in the lexicon inventory make no problem, particularly when a unigram LM is used. Including a new word means just adding its text and phonetic form together with the word frequency (which is either known or can be roughly estimated). On contrary, the lexicon for continuous speech recognition must be always supplemented by a proper language model, usually bigrams. This has to be compiled in advance and recompiled whenever a new word is to be added.

For demonstration and evaluation purposes we have prepared two lexicons. The smaller, denoted as Lex45K, contains 45 thousands words and can be used for real-time dictation on computers running at least at 1.5 GHz. The second one, Lex92K, is (approximately) twice as large and can be used on the recent high-end PCs. The lexicons contain the most frequent Czech words that occured in the text corpus at least 500 times, or 150 times, respectivelly.

Each item in the lexicon is provided by one or more phonetic transcriptions. Multiple pronunciations have been added namely to the most frequent words. Usually, these words are short (monosyllabic and bisyllabic) and their pronunciation can vary in a considerable way depending on the speech context. In the Lex92K, almost 1.8 % of the lexicon items have more than one phonetic transcription.

The language model consists of bigrams estimated from a large corpus of mainly newspaper texts. A slightly modified version of the Witten-Bell method was used for smoothing the values [2]. They were packed to a special compressed format that can be efficiently read by the decoder. The compressed bigrams take 115 MB and 183 MB of memory for Lex45K and Lex92K, respectively.

4.2   Decoder for Continuous Speech

The system employs an optimized version of the time-synchronous Viterbi algorithm. The most probable word string W corresponding to the sequence of frame vectors

$(x(1), ...x(t), ...x(T))$ is determined from the equation:

$$W = (w_1, w_n, \ldots, w_N)$$
$$= \arg \max_{w_n \in L} \left[\sum_{n=1}^{N} \left(\log P \left(w_n | x \left(t_{n-1} + 1 \right) \ldots x \left(t_n \right) \right) + \beta \log P \left(w_n | w_{n-1} \right) \right) \right] (2)$$

where β is bigram weighting factor and t_n is end-time of word w_n. Again, the free parameter β must be determined experimentally on development data. To speed up the decoding procedure a double beam search is applied. One handles the initial parts of the words (one or two initial phonemes) that are common for large subsets of lexicon items, the other operating over the remaining parts of the individual words from the list of those that survived the first beam pruning. The recent version of the decoder generates only one best word sequence. On the other side, its optimized implementation allows for parallel (multi-thread) running of the acoustic processing part and the decoder. It means that the decoding process can start with just a short delay after a speech start point is identified.

4.3 Evaluation Tests

At present, the evaluation prototype of the continuous dictation system uses the same layout as shown in Fig. 1. A user can dictate either a whole sentence in one utterance or he/she can split it into shorter phrases. If the former option is chosen, the system is able to do a simple text formatting, i.e. capitalizing the initial letter of the first word and adding a period after the final word. On a PC with a Pentium 3.0 GHz HT processor, a spoken sentence is recognized no later than 1 to 2 seconds after the endpoint of the utterance (with the Lex92K). The actual delay depends on the sentence duration.

To evaluate the performance of the prototype we have asked two male speakers to dictate 200 sentences. These were taken from newspaper articles and from personal (quite informal) correspondence. In the first experiment the recognition was performed with speaker-independent acoustic models. Before the second experiment, the speakers recorded 100 sentences, which were used for adaptation of the HMMs. (The MAP+MLLR procedure was utilized in this stage [4].) The main results from both the experiments are summarized in Table 2. The results achieved in real-time dictation were compared to those of an off-line test, where the largest available lexicon (with 312,000 word entries) was used. We can observe that the size of the lexicon still plays a significant role, both with respect to the OOV (Out-of-Vocabulary) rate and consequently to the recognition rate. Unfortunately, the 312K lexicon requested approximately 4 times longer time to get the complete text transcription of the dictated sentences.

Table 2. Results obtained in continuous dictation tests with speaker-independent (SI) and speaker-adapted (SA) acoustic models and on-line as well as off-line processing

	WER (SI models) [%]	WER (SA models)[%]	OOV rate [%]
Real-time dictation (92K-word lexicon)	16.6	14.6	5.21
Off-line recognition (312K-word lexicon)	13.7	10.4	1.37

5   Conclusions and Further Work

Most likely, the systems described in this paper are the first ones designed for voice dictation in Czech. At the moment both are just prototypes used mainly for evaluation tasks and for orientation of the further research. However, we have been already working on incorporating the discrete dictation system in the recently developed voice-controlled PC platform that should serve primarily for handicapped people who cannot use keyboard and mouse. A commercial version of this platform named MyVoice has been available since March 2005 [1].

References

1. Nouza, J.: Voice Dictation into a PC: Recent Research State at TUL. In: Proc. of 6th International Workshop on Elektronics, Control, Measurment and Signals - ECMS 2003, June 2003, Liberec, Czech Republic, pp. 69-73.
2. Nejedlová, D., Nouza, J.: Building of a Vocabulary for the Automatic Voice-Dictation System. In: Text, Speech and Dialogue (TSD 2003), Springer-Verlag, Heidelberg, 2003, pp. 301-308.
3. Nouza, J., Nouza T.: A Voice Dictation System for a Million-Word Czech Vocabulary. In: Proc. Of Int. Conf. on Computing, Communications and Control Technologies (CCCT04), Austin, 2004.
4. Červa P., Nouza J.: Supervised and unsupervised speaker adaptation in large vocabulary continuous speech recognition of Czech. In: In: Text, Speech and Dialogue (TSD 2005), Springer-Verlag, Heidelberg, 2005
5. MyVoice - software for voice control of PC. Information available at http://www.fugasoft.cz/myvoice.htm

Unit Selection for Speech Synthesis Based on Acoustic Criteria

Soufiane Rouibia, Olivier Rosec, and Thierry Moudenc

France Telecom, R&D Division 2 avenue Pierre Marzin
22307 LANNION CEDEX, France
`{soufiane.rouibia,olivier.rosec,`
`thierry.moudenc}@francetelecom.com`

Abstract. This paper presents a new approach to unit selection for corpus-based speech synthesis, in which the units are selected according to acoustic criteria. In a training stage, an acoustic clustering is carried out using context dependent HMMs. In the synthesis stage, an acoustic target is generated and divided into segments corresponding to the required unit sequence. Then, the acoustic unit sequence that best matches the target is selected. Tests are carried out which show the relevance of the proposed method.

1 Introduction

Corpus-based approaches have become increasingly popular in the field of speech synthesis as they drastically improve the naturalness of synthetic speech. This technology relies on the concatenation of acoustic units selected from a large speech database. The selection process, which aims to find the unit sequence that best matches the synthesis context, is central in such approach. This process generally falls down to minimizing a given cost function through dynamic programming. Typically, such a function includes two kinds of costs: a target cost which reflects the suitability of a candidate unit to the synthesis context and a concatenation cost which measures how well units can be joined.

In recent years, numerous research efforts have focused on the definition of selection functions. Trainable statistical models have been proposed for the automatic preselection of units according to a set of symbolic targets [3], [6], [9]. However, the global optimization of a cost function remains difficult for two main reasons: on one hand, optimizing the combination of heterogeneous criteria is not straightforward [15], and on the other hand, defining a function that reflects audible mismatch between two units is very difficult [7], [8]. Thus, the main drawback of corpus-based techniques is the lack of acoustic control that one can have on the output speech. One way to improve a corpus-based synthesizer is to include a better acoustic control in the selection process. This has been made in the framework of Hidden Markov Model (HMM) synthesis [17], where a speech waveform is generated from a sequence of HMM parameters. However, while this technique provides a smooth acoustic target, the generation algorithm [16] produces a synthetic speech of low quality which lacks naturalness.

In this paper, we propose a new selection procedure. The HMM paradigm is used to build an acoustic target and a selection module has to determine the unit sequence that

V. Matoušek et al. (Eds.): TSD 2005, LNAI 3658, pp. 281–287, 2005.

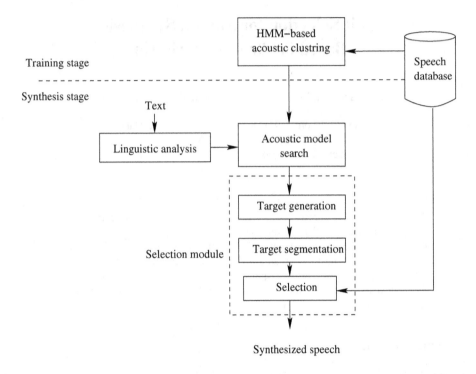

Fig. 1. System overview

best matches this acoustic target. The rest of the paper is organized as follows. Section 2 gives an overview of the proposed system. Section 3 and 4 respectively describe the learning and synthesis procedures. In section 5 synthesis results are presented while section 6 summarizes our major findings and outlines our future work.

2   System Overview

Fig. 1 gives a brief outline of the proposed method. In a training stage, the speech database is analyzed and the extracted spectral parameter vectors are used to estimate monophone HMMs. Then context dependent senone models are built through a clustering procedure based on decision trees. In the synthesis stage, according to the text to be synthesized, a sequence of context dependent senone models is determined and an acoustic target is generated from these HMM parameters using a smoothing algorithm [15]. This acoustic target is segmented into diphone-like units and then a selection module determines the diphone sequence that best matches this acoustic target. Finally, the selected units are concatenated and pitch smoothing is performed if necessary, using the TD-PSOLA algorithm [11].

3   Acoustic Clustering

In this section, a description of the acoustic clustering procedure is given in the case of the French language. For this purpose, a database dedicated to corpus-based speech synthesis is used, which contains about 7 hours of speech sampled at 16 kHz. The phonetic transcription as well as the phonetic segmentation associated to each sentence has been checked manually. The number of phonemes is 37 including three types of silence, namely beginning, ending and pause silences.

The speech database is first analysed in order to extract feature vectors comprising 12 MFCC (Mel Frequency Cepstrum Coefficients), energy, and the first and second derivatives of these parameters. This analysis is carried out using 20 ms frame duration with a uniform 5 ms frame step. These 39-dimensional vectors are then used in combination with phonetic labels to train a set of monophone HMMs. These HMMs are three state left-to-right models with no skip. For each state the observations are modeled by a single Gaussian distribution with a diagonal covariance matrix.

The obtained monophone models are then cloned to produce triphone models for every distinct triphones in the training data. The transition matrix remains tied across all the triphones of each phone. These triphone models are reestimated with the embedded training version of the Baum-Welch algorithm. For each set of triphones derived from the same base phone, corresponding states are clustered.

The decision trees that perform the clustering are then automatically constructed using the standard maximum likelihood tree growing procedure [5], [12]. The splits are made using a large list of questions which include linguistic information as immediate phonetic context, melodic marker and syllabic position of the phoneme. This acoustic clustering was implemented using the HTK software [10] which was modified in order to take into account the linguistic questions described above.

The two clustering parameters used to stop the tree growth are to ensure that each terminal node may address a minimum of 50 speech segments and a minimum increase in log-likelihood per split, done in such a way that there are approximately 8000 terminal nodes, which enables the best perceived quality on the training set.

4 Target Generation

4.1 Target Generation

In the synthesis part, the text to be synthesized is converted into a phoneme sequence. For each of these phonemes, the trees corresponding to each state are run through in order to locate the appropriate sequence of senone models.

Before generating an acoustic target, a duration must be assigned to each senone model. Numerous duration models have been proposed such as [3], [14]. In this paper, the model developed in [4] was used to predict phonemic duration. In order to assign a duration for each state i of a given phone model λ, one needs to evaluate the relative duration of this state $\overline{d}_i^{\lambda}$ given by the following relation:

$$\overline{d}_i^{\lambda} = \frac{1}{1 - a_{ii}^{\lambda}} \tag{1}$$

where a_{ii}^{λ} is the prior probability to remain in state i for model λ . Duration of state i of the considered model is then given by

$$\alpha_i^\lambda = \frac{\overline{d}_i^\lambda}{\sum_{i=1}^n \overline{d}_i^\lambda} \tag{2}$$

where n is the state number in the model λ. Duration of state i of the considered λ is given by

$$d_i^\lambda = \alpha_i^\lambda d \tag{3}$$

where d is the predicted phonemic duration value. Knowing d_i^λ, it is straightforward to determine the numbers of acoustic frames of the state i for the considered model λ .

Once the acoustic models associated to the senone sequence and the duration of each senone model have been determined, a sequence of acoustic target vectors containing 12 MFCC coefficients as well as energy is generated using the algorithm described in [16].

The obtained acoustic target can be used for any kind of synthesis units (e.g. diphones, half-phones, senones, syllables,...). The only operation to carry out is to segment the target according to the desired synthesis units. Fig. 2 illustrates the target segmentation in the context of diphone selection for the French word "BONJOUR" which means "good morning" in English. First, given the duration of each senone, the phone borders are found. Then the diphone borders are fixed at the center of each phone.

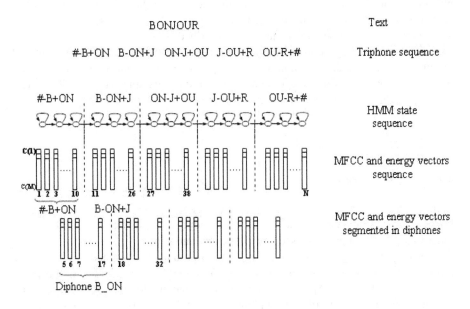

Fig. 2. Acoustic target generation for the word "bonjour"

4.2 Selection

This section describes the unit selection procedure for diphone units. As pointed out previously, the same methodology is possible for any kind of units. The basic principle is to compare, for each diphone to be synthesized, the instances of this diphone to the corresponding target segment by means of a Dynamic Time Warping (DTW) algorithm [13]. This algorithm, which is implemented using type I constraints, generates an alignment path without right angles and whose end-points are mutual comparisons of the initial and final frames. The global distance between both signals equals the average of the local distances in the alignment path multiplied by the ratio of the longest duration to the shortest duration. This global distance thus penalises relative differences in duration between the two compared signals. The selected instance is the one that minimizes this DTW distance.

5 Experiments and Results

The method proposed in this paper is tested on the speech database presented in section 3. A perceptual evaluation is carried out through a MOS (Mean Opinion Score) test in order to compare the proposed method against the unit selection procedure implemented in the France Telecom reference speech synthesis system (herein referred to as *FTR&D Reference*). Note that the implemented unit selection algorithm in the *FTR&D Reference* is mainly based on symbolic information such as linguistic ones and prosodic ones [2]. So the main comparison will concern essentially the use of acoustic information versus a large set of symbolic ones in the selection process. In the two cases, pitch and energy smoothing are applied when concatenating speech units. For that purpose, 20 phonetically balanced sentences are synthesized by both methods. The resulting 40 utterances are then evaluated by a group of 16 naïve listeners. Each listener is played the 40 utterances in a random order and is asked to rate the perceived speech quality on a 5 level scale, where 1 corresponds to "very poor", and 5 refers to "very good".

Table 1. Results of a MOS test considering the *FTR&D* selection algorithm vs. the proposed methods

Selection methods	MOS
FTR&D Reference method	3.53
Proposed method	3.09

Results presented in Table 1 globally show a preference for the *FTR&D Reference* method. Differences are noticed insofar as for 12 of the listeners clear preferences have emerged for 10 sentences. For these 12 listeners 7 of the test sentences are consistently preferred with *FTR&D Reference* method and 3 other test sentences are rated higher with the proposed acoustic method. For those particular utterances, a more careful inspection was carried out.

Among the utterances which received a lower score with our method, some concatenation problems occurred, which were essentially attributed to pitch discontinuities. For these samples, it was observed that the use of TD-PSOLA for pitch smoothing introduced a significant degradation of the synthetic speech quality. This result is not surprising as our method does not explicitly use pitch information in the selection process.

Conversely, when the *FTR&D Reference* method was given a lower score, this difference essentially comes from acoustic discontinuities at concatenation instants. To quantify these distortions, a measure similar to [7] is introduced:

$$D^2 = \sum_{i=1}^{n} \left[\frac{e_i - \mu_i^P}{\sigma_i^P} \right]^2 \tag{4}$$

where e is the difference between the n-dimensional MFCC parameter vector of the last frame of the first unit and the first frame of the second unit and μ^P and σ^P are respectively the mean vector and the diagonal covariance matrix of e for the concerned phoneme (P) where a concatenation is done. Fig. 3 shows the concatenation distortion observed on a sentence for which the proposed algorithm was preferred.

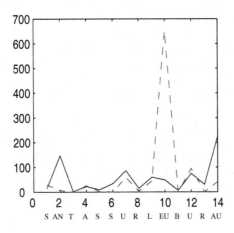

Fig. 3. Distortion distance at concatenation instants for a sentence synthesized by *FTR&D Reference* method (dashed line) and by the proposed method (continuous line)

6   Conclusion

In this paper, a new method was presented for unit selection based on a target acoustic criterion. Synthetic speech produced by this selection module was compared to the method currently used in France Telecom TTS system. The proposed method seems to offer a better acoustic control of the synthesized units even if pitch discontinuity were observed.

Future works will consist in taking into account the prosodic information explicitly, so as to generate more satisfying prosodic targets and to decrease pitch discontinuity.

Moreover, in order to speed up the selection process, the proposed method will be combined with a pre-selection module.

References

1. Black, A.W., Campbell, N.: Optimising Selection of Units from Speech Database for Concatenative Synthesis. Proc. Eurospeech, Madrid (1995) 581–584

2. Blouin, C., Rosec, O., Bagshaw, P.C., d'Alessandro C.: Concatenation Cost Calculation and Optimization for Unit Selection in TTS. IEEE Workshop on Speech Synthesis, Santa Monica CA, USA (2002)
3. Campbell, N., Isard, S.D.: Segment Durations in a Syllable Frame. Journal of Phonetics, 19 Special issue on Speech Synthesis (1991) 37–47
4. De Tournemire S.: Identification et Génération Automatique de Contours Prosodiques pour la Synthése Vocale à Partir du Texte en Français. PhD. Thesis, Ecole Nationale Supérieure des Télécommunication, Paris, (1998)
5. Donovan R.E.: Trainable Speech synthesis. PhD. Thesis, Cambridge University Engineering Department, (1996)
6. Donovan R.E. et al.: Current Status of the IBM Trainable Speech Synthesis System. Proc. 4th ESCA Tutorial and Research Workshop on Speech Synthesis, Scotland, UK, (2001)
7. Donovan R.E.: A new distance measure for costing spectral discontinuities in concatenative speech synthesisers. The 4th ISCA Tutorial and Research Workshop on Speech Synthesis, (2001)
8. Eide, E., Aron, A., Bakis, R., Cohen, P., Donovan, R., Hamza, W., Mathes, T., Picheny, M., Smith, M., Viswanathan, M.,: Recent Improvements to the IBM Trainable Speech Synthesis System. Proc ICASSP, Hong Kong, China, (2003)
9. Huang, X., Acero, A., Ju, Y., Liu, J., Meredith, S., Plumpe, M.: Recent Improvements on Microsoft's Trainable Text-To-Speech System - Whistler. Proc. ICASSP, Munich, Germany, (1997) 959–962
10. http://htk.eng.cam.ac.uk
11. Moulines, E., Charpentier, F.: Pitch-Synchronous Waveform Processing Techniques for Text-to-Speech Synthesis Using. Speech Communication, Vol. 9, (1990) 453–467
12. Odell J. J.: The Use of Context in Large Vocabulary Speech Recognition. PhD. Thesis, Queen's College, March, (1995)
13. Sakoe, H., Chiba, S.: A Dynamic Programming Algorithm Optimization for Spoken Word Recognition. In: IEEE Transactions on Acoustics, Speech and Signal Processing Vol. ASSP–26, N° 1, (1978) 43–49
14. Pierrehumbert, J.: The Phonology and Phonetics of English Intonation. PhD. Thesis, MIT, Boston, (1980)
15. Toda, T., Kawai, H., Tsuzaki, M.: Optimizing Sub-Cost Functions for Segment Selection Based on Perceptual Evaluations in Concatenative Speech Synthesis. Proc. ICASSP, Montreal, Quebec, Canada, (2004) 657–660
16. Tokuda K., Masuko T., Yamada T., Kobayashi, T., Imai, S.: An Algorithm for Speech Parameters Generation from Continuous Mixture HMMs with Dynamic Features. Proc. Eurospeech, (1995) 757–760
17. Tokuda, K., Zen, H., Black, A.: An HMM-based Speech Synthesis Applied to English. Proc. of IEEE Workshop on Speech Synthesis , Santa Monica, Sept. (2002)

Generative Model for Decoding
a Phoneme Recognizer Output

Mykola Sazhok

Int. Research/Training Center for IT and Systems, Kyjiv 03680 Ukraine
mykola@uasoiro.org.ua

Abstract. The paper presents a way to advance to a multi-level automatic speech understanding system implementation. Two levels are considered. On the first level a free (or relatively free) grammar phoneme recognition is applied and at the second level an output of the phonemic recognizer is automatically interpreted in a reasonable way. A Generative Model approach based model for phoneme recognizer output decoding is proposed. An experimental system is described.

1   Introduction

In accordance to the multi-level speech understanding system structure discussed in [1] an approach when continuous speech is firstly recognized as a phoneme sequence and then this phoneme sequence is recognized and understood as a word sequence and meaning (Fig. 1) appears constructive. Despite some criticism of this approach since the best method of speech signal understanding consists in its simultaneous recognizing and understanding, constructing such a multi-level system is a real possibility to distribute the research job between experts in acoustics, phonetics, linguistics and informatics.

Apparently, the multi-level speech understanding structure looks as if particularly corresponding for advancing a creation of dictation machines and spoken dialog systems for a series of highly inflected with relatively free word order languages, and Slavic ones are among them.

Obviously, the output of the Phoneme Recognizer level must imply a potential of its further processing. It means that a phoneme sequence produced by recognizer must be readable in sense of machine. This does not mean that it must be human-readable but the latter ability is by all means prominent. Besides, a machine, unlike a human, might intensively use other parameters the recognizer extracted from speech like phoneme length, amplitude etc.

Thus, the problem of the next by Phoneme Recognizer levels is to learn a machine to interpret an acquired phoneme sequence or to find a hidden phoneme sequence that is an actual transcription of the pronounced utterance. In terms of Generative Model [2], we must suggest a way to generate all possible phoneme sequences associated with the proper permissible sequences and to compare them with observation. This is exactly what is investigated in next two sections where appropriate models are justified and a training procedure is described.

How to attain the required phoneme recognition results and whether appropriate models and algorithms are available nowadays? Such a system is attainable due to sys-

V. Matoušek et al. (Eds.): TSD 2005, LNAI 3658, pp. 288–293, 2005.

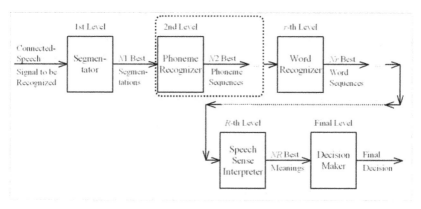

Fig. 1. Multilevel multi-decision Dictation/Translation Machine structure

tem parameters refinement and speaker individuality modeling by means of Speaker Voice Passport and we describe it in the experimental section.

2 Association Model Between a Phoneme Sequence Pronounced and the One Generated by the Phoneme Recognizer

We consider a recognizer output as a sequence of phoneme observations. Each phoneme observation associates phoneme name ö, duration d, energy E, likelihood g and may be more acoustic parameters the recognizer might extract from speech like pitch etc. We specify the machine readability of the recognizer output or the phoneme observation sequence as a possibility to generate its model by a phoneme transcription obtained from the pronounced text. Phoneme sequences associated with both observation and its generated model must match.

Let us consider an operator transforming a generated automatically by text phoneme sequence $(\varphi_1, \varphi_2, ..., \varphi_q)\, \varphi_k \in \Phi, 0 \leq k \leq q$ to all permissible sequence of phoneme observations of a given length l:

$$v^l(\varphi_1, \varphi_2, ..., \varphi_q) = \left(v^{l_1}(\varphi_1), v^{l_2}(\varphi_2), ..., v^{l_q}(\varphi_q)\right), \sum_{k=1}^{q} l_k = l, 0 \leq l_k \leq \bar{l}, \quad (1)$$

where $\bar{l}$ value means an upper length of the phoneme sequence replacing the phoneme φ_k and each $v^{l_k}(\varphi_k)$, $0 \leq k \leq q$, generates a subsequence of phoneme observations by a given phoneme φ_1 with length l_k :

$$v^{l_k}(\varphi_k) = \left(w_1^{l_k}(\varphi_k), w_2^{l_k}(\varphi_k), ..., w_{l_k}^{l_k}(\varphi_k)\right), \quad (2)$$

where model phoneme observation $w_s^{l_k}(\varphi_k)$, $0 \leq s \leq l_k$ follows from the associated with φ_k model, which structure will be considered later.

Equating l_k to 0 means the phoneme φ_k is substituted with zero-length phoneme sequence or dropped. To eliminate 2 running omissions the following restriction must be satisfied:

$$\exists k, \ 0 \le k \le q - 1 : \ l_k = 0 \ and \ l_{k+1} = 0. \tag{3}$$

To force a phoneme subsequence associated with $v^{l_k} (\varphi_k)$ taking out certain length $\underline{l} \le \bar{l}$ to contain the phoneme φ_k we require existence of one and only one $w_S^{l_k} (\varphi_k)$ associated with $\varphi_k, 0 \le S \le l_k$:

$$\forall l_k, \ \underline{l} \le l_k \le \bar{l} \ \exists ! S, \ 0 \le S \le l_k : \varphi_k \prec w_S^{l_k} (\varphi_k), \tag{4}$$

where $\prec$ is an association sign and state S is the terminal state of a model.

Thus, we introduce a model of the phoneme φ_k observation as an l_k-state generative model, $0 \le l_k \le \bar{l}$. Each state $s, 0 \le s \le l_k$, corresponds to a set of possible phonemes $\psi_{s,i}^k \in \Psi_s^k \in \Phi$ from the sequence with length l_k that substitutes φ_k. Hence, all sequences the k-th model generates may be interpreted as Descarte's product of sets Ψ_s^k by $s = \overline{1, l_k}$.

Proceeding from (4), $\Psi_S^k = \{\varphi_k\}$ for terminal state S of the k-th model.

Auxiliary input and output states are introduced to specify permissible transitions between states of adjacent models.

Acoustic parameters are described by their normal law distributions:

$$(A, \Sigma) = \left(\left(a^d, \sigma^d \right), \left(a^E, \sigma^E \right), \left(a^g, \sigma^g \right) \right),$$

where the distributions are specified for phoneme duration d, energy E and likelihood g.

The algorithm of hidden phoneme sequences decoding from speech output is similar to continuous speech recognition with grammar. It appears that a non-iterative algorithm to train the model might be derived.

3   Phoneme Observation Model Training

A proposed algorithm to learn phoneme observation model consists in extracting model prototypes from the found best trajectories on graph and updating final models by their prototypes. Configuration of links between nodes on the graph follows from (1)–(3).

Initially we assume each model prototype has a maximal number of states $\bar{l}$. Proceeding from (4) a terminal state S must be included and one of simplifications proposed is to assume S to a fixed state of the initial model prototype.

To catch a substitution of the phoneme with an empty phone sequence we insert an empty phoneme $\emptyset$ between phoneme observations and choose one of non-terminal state that is applicable to the empty phoneme.

In each graph node we compute an elementary likelihood that is a positive value when model and observation phoneme names coincide at the terminal state and zero otherwise. Therefore, from the human point of view the integral likelihood is proportional to number of common phonemes in the model transcription and in the phoneme recognizer output.

Note that an observation attained from phonemic recognizer is actually divided into two streams: phonetic and acoustic. As far considering initial prototypes we operate only with phoneme names a likelihood for acoustic stream is not available. So we just do collect acoustic data in prototypes. When updating final models by their prototypes the collected acoustic data is used to estimate their acoustic parameters distribution.

Analyzing a graph and likelihood one may conclude that normally multiple trajectories may have the best score (Fig. 2). It means that there exist a k-th model having $N_k > 1$

prototypes in context of one training sample and we keep all this prototypes assigning to them a probability equal to $1/N_k$. This value is accumulated in the respective model as well. After passing all training samples models are to be purged and merged to form a final set of models.

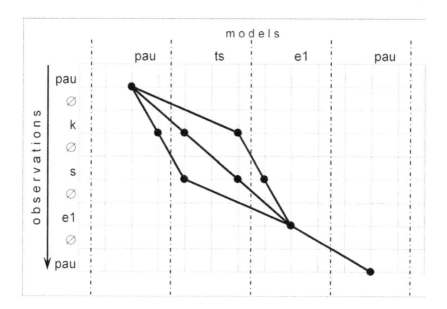

Fig. 2. Graph for phoneme observation models in a training sample. The recognizer output phoneme sequence is 'pau k s e1 pau', under conditions of pronounced word of 'pau ts e1 pau'. The best trajectories are shown. Following the trajectories the model prototypes are extracted. Note, acoustic data of observations is stored to build the global model

According to the graph illustration given in Fig. 2 we extract model prototypes with the following phonemic descriptions:

1:(PAU, k / pau, 4), 2:(PAU, k / pau, 5), 3:(pau, PAU / pau, 6); 4:(k / 1, ts, 7), 5:(k, s / 2, ts, 8), 6:(s / 3, ts, 9); 7:(s, E1 / 3, e1, 9), 8:(E1 / 4|5, e1, 9); 9:(PAU / 6|7|8, pau).

Here in brackets before the slash a phoneme sequence replacing a model phoneme is indicated. Each phoneme from the sequence is associated with the model state and a capitalized phoneme is associated with the terminal state. From the right of slash a model phoneme name and adjacent model prototypes instances, if applicable, are denoted. Additionally, a probability to each model prototype is assigned.

4   Experimental Training Setup

The experiment was divided into stages of (1) training and control sample preparation, (2) speaker voice file (passport) forming, (3) attaining phoneme recognition output and (4) performing the train procedure for the phoneme observation sequence decoder.

The text of training samples was formed from isolated words extracted from a dictionary of rated Ukrainian words taking into account each phoneme occurrence and acoustic variability. This work is based mainly on [3]. Thus, the training sample text contained 2113 words and total 16127 phonemes except a phoneme-pause. The alphabet contained 55 basic Ukrainian phonemes including both stressed and non-stressed versions of vowels, palatalized versions for all but two consonants and a phoneme-pause. Occurrences of each non-pause phoneme in the training text lied between 10 (palatalized 'sh' and 'zh') and 1001 non-stressed 'o'. No short pause model was provided as far the training sample includes only isolated words.

The control sample represented mostly top rated words and less phoneme variability. We just scanned a rate dictionary from the top and took words containing new triphones.

A speaker pronounced the entire training sample in each of three microphones having unlike acoustic characteristics. Acoustic models were trained and refined for each basic phoneme specifically taking into account its both acoustic variability and rate. Each phoneme model had three states and 1 to 6 Gaussian mixtures. So the speaker voice passport was formed.

A free-grammar phoneme recognition procedure was performed on total 11000 words from the control sample. Attained phoneme sequences exposed obvious resemblance with generated automatically by text transcriptions for pronounced words.

Before carrying out the train procedure for the phoneme observation sequence decoder the model parameters were adjusted: $\bar{l}$ and $\underline{l}$ were assigned to 3 and a model prototype terminal state S was fixed at 2 and empty phoneme applicable state is pre-assigned to 3. Permissible links are specified for each state by pairs (phoneme, state) indicating start node relatively to the current phone. For instance, (-1, 1) permits link to state 1 of the preceding phone.

Using the developed *Perl* module, all training samples were successfully passed and sets of 3000-5000 models were formed. The module for phoneme recognizer output decoding procedure is under construction.

5 Conclusion

The idea of machine-readable text has been investigated and a model proposed allows for converting phonetic recognizer output to valid phoneme sequences, theoretically, even in case they have no matching phonemes.

We dealt with only one best phoneme sequence of the phoneme recognizer output but actually $N \gg 1$ best recognition outputs might be considered. These procedures still take small time amount due to the free phoneme grammar used.

The future plans are to accomplish the global model training and a decoder procedure, to consider multiple decision phoneme recognizer output, to test the approach on continuous speech, to investigate fast speaker voice passport forming and to build models for speech recognition with no vocabulary restrictions.

References

1. Vintsiuk, T.: Multi-Level Multi-Decision Model for Automatic Speech Recognition and Understanding // International Summer School Neural Nets "E.R.Caianiello" 3rd Course "Speech Processing, Recognition and Artificial Neural Networks", 1998, Vietri sul Mare (SA) Italy, pp 341-344.
2. Vintsiuk, T.: Generative Phoneme-Threephone Model for ASR // In: Text, Speech, and Dialogue (4th Int. Conf. TSD 2001, Zelena Ruda, Czech Republic, Proceedings), Lecture Notes in Artificial Intelligence 2166 Subseries of Lecture Notes in Computer Science, Springer, 2001, pp. 201-207.
3. Vasylyeva, N.: Training Samples Forming for Automatic Speech Synthesis by Text. – Magister diploma work, Kyjiv 2003, 88 p.

Diction Based Prosody Modeling
in Table-to-Speech Synthesis

Dimitris Spiliotopoulos, Gerasimos Xydas, and Georgios Kouroupetroglou

University of Athens
Department of Informatics and Telecommunications
{dspiliot,gxydas,koupe}@di.uoa.gr

Abstract. Transferring a structure from the visual modality to the aural one presents a difficult challenge. In this work we are experimenting with prosody modeling for the synthesized speech representation of tabulated structures. This is achieved by analyzing naturally spoken descriptions of data tables and a following feedback by blind and sighted users. The derived prosodic phrase accent and pause break placement and values are examined in terms of successfully conveying semantically important visual information through prosody control in Table-to-Speech synthesis. Finally, the quality of the information provision of synthesized tables when utilizing the proposed prosody specification is studied against plain synthesis.

1 Introduction

Text material is primarily optimized for visual presentation by embedding several visual components. These range from simple "bold", "italic", or coloured letters directives to more complex ones such as those that define a spatial layout (tables, forms, etc.). Transferring a structure from the visual modality to aural is by no means an easy task. For example, tables are characterized by many qualitative and quantitative aspects that should be taken into consideration since successful vocalization is greatly affected by them. Most common approaches tend to linearize two-dimensional elements prior to their acoustic presentation. However, most of the semantic meaning of their enclosed text is implicit to the visual structure. This work is concerned with the vocalization of *data tables*, the most widely used two-dimensional structure in documents.

Data tables are categorized into *simple* and *complex*. Simple tables have up to one row and one column of header cells, while complex ones contain more than one level of logical row or column headers. This means that header and data cells can be expanded to encompass more than one row or column forming nested tables. Hence, complex tables can be thought of as three-dimensional structures [1], compared to the two-dimensional simple data tables. The third dimension of the semantic structure is embedded inside the two dimensional visual structure.

Complex visual structures bear a distinct association between the physical layout and the underlying logical structure [2]. Previous works show that appropriate mark-up can be used to assign logical structure to table cells [3] and suggest additional mark-up annotation to existing tables for adding context in order to improve navigation [4]. Other suggestions include automated approaches for retrieval of hierarchical data from

V. Matoušek et al. (Eds.): TSD 2005, LNAI 3658, pp. 294–301, 2005.

HTML tables [5] or transforming tables into a linear, easily readable form by screen readers [6]. The semantic structure of HTML tables can be used to aid their navigation and browsing [7]. However, since the problem is addressed on the visual level, the major handicap of the linearized transformation approach to the actual spoken form remains.

Previous studies focusing on the speech representation show that one-dimensional elements such as bold and italic letters, gain their acoustic representation by the use of prosody control [8][9], while others deal with the acoustic representation of linear visual components using synthesized speech [10].

In [11], a script-based open platform for rendering meta-information to speech using a combination of prosody modifications and non-speech audio sounds has been presented. However, the exploitation of synthetic speech prosody parameterization necessitates the utilization of the human natural spoken rendition for tables. Our motivation is to examine and model the natural speech specification of table meta-information by analyzing spoken paradigms from human readers in order to aid speech synthesis.

Using the acquired analyzed speech data from the most preferred human spoken renditions [12], we derived a prosody model concerning phrase accents and pause breaks. In the following sections we present the resulted prosody specification as well as the psychoacoustic experiments on the corresponding speech-synthesized data tables.

2   Requirements for Human Spoken Rendition of Tables

Recent research shows that advanced *browsing* techniques may be used to create table linearization that analyses the implicit structural information contained in tables so that it is conveyed to text (and consequently to speech) by navigation of the data cells [1]. It is obvious that complex data tables are much more complicated to browse since they may have multiple levels of structures in a hierarchical manner. Pure linear as well as intelligent navigation for the tables are accounted for in this work. Intelligent navigation is a process that takes place before the actual synthesis and, for the case of simple tables, results in header-data cell pair linearization while, for the case of complex tables, a decomposition revealing the respective sub-tables takes place.

Natural spoken rendition required human subjects as readers of data tables. Selecting appropriate sample tables for rendering to natural speech required several factors to be taken into consideration. Table wellformedness is ensured through certain compliance to W3C table specification [13] and W3C WAI recommendations [14]. In this work, only pure *data tables* are considered, that is tables used solely to convey information comprising of pure data of certain relationship, not used for page layout and without any visual enhancements or styles applied. Moreover, for human spoken rendition the so-called *genuine tables* [15], that is tables where the two dimensional grid is semantically significant are considered.

3   The Prosody Model Specification

The human spoken table rendition feedback from the listeners has led to the design of an initial specification for prosodic modeling of simple and complex table structures for synthetic speech. For prosody markup, the ToBI annotation model [16] conventions

Table 1. Simple and complex table (linear browsing) phrase accent specification

position	tone	conditions (simple table)	conditions (complex table)
Header cell	L-	row-final	row-final
Header cell	H-	not-row-final	not-row-final
Data cell	H-	row-penultimate	row-initial AND row-is-nested-table-final
Data cell	L-	not-row-penultimate	(row-initial AND row-is-not-nested-table-final) OR row-final

Table 2. Simple and complex table (intelligent browsing) phrase accent specification

position	tone	conditions
Header cell	L-	not-part-of-pair
Header cell	H-	row-final
Data cell	L-	(none)

Table 3. Simple table (linear) pause breaks

position	ms	multiplier
Cell	600	x1.00
Row	900	x1.50

Table 4. Simple table (intel.) pause breaks

position	ms	multiplier
header cell	200	x1.00
data cell	500	x2.50
Row	750	x3.75

were used as a means of qualitative analysis. Rules pertaining to phrase accent and boundary tone assignment (L- describing the fall in pitch at the end of spoken data cells, H- describing the rise in pitch) were constructed according to the experimental data. Moreover, pause break parameters were set up according to the preferred natural language rendition adjusted by the listeners' proposed modifications.

Linear browsing was modeled as shown in Table 1, the phrase accent model specification describing position and type of phrase accent tone according to conditions that apply for either simple or complex table. Table 2 shows the respective specification derived for intelligent browsing of simple and complex tables. An obvious observation is the simplicity of the model for intelligent browsing as a result of semantic resolution prior to vocalization.

Pause breaks have been assigned at the end of cells and rows as absolute values in milliseconds, calculated as multiples of the shortest pause selected according to the experimental data analysis.

Tables 3 and 4 show the actual values and multiplier factors for linear and intelligent browsing for simple tables, while tables 5 and 6 the respective data for complex tables.

4 Experiments

We carried out a set of psychoacoustic experiments using a group of 10 experienced listeners, 21-24 years old. They were asked to take part in a formal listening to known and unseen synthesized spoken tables. We used the DEMOSTHeNES Document-to-

Table 5. Complex table (linear) pause breaks

position	ms	mult.
header row	750	x2.50
data row	750	x2.50
Table header cell	300	x1.00
Nested table header cell	600	x2.00
Data cell	525	x1.75

Table 6. Complex table (intel.) pause breaks

position	ms	mult.
Nested table header cell	750	x3.75
header cell	200	x1.00
data cell	750	x3.75
row	1250	x6.25

Audio platform [11] to host the derived prosody specification by the means of two auditory scripts for the simple and the complex table respectively. Table de-compilation to logical layer was followed by the application of the above mentioned prosodic phrase accent and pause break parameters. The selected tables were rendered using both plain speech synthesis (without parameterization) and enhanced one (with prosody model parameterization) by the newly acquired parameterization in order to experiment with the proposed Table-to-Speech approach.

The aim of the first experiment was a comparative subjective analysis of plain and enhanced speech synthesis renditions of already known example tables (as introduced in [12]) in order to measure the impact of the new prosodic adjustment model. The second experiment involved unseen test tables that were used to determine the competence of the prosodic model measured by the resulting understanding of table data, as well as subjective listener input for each rendition described by the model. The tables that were selected for this experiment were similar to the reference simple and complex tables described in the literature. The text data in both tables were provided in Greek, which is the native language of all listeners.

The subjects listened to the synthesized tables in random order and were asked to assert their understanding of the data in the range of 1 (lowest) to 5 (highest). The results have shown that the parameterization has led to significant increase in their understanding of the table data semantic structure (Fig. 1).

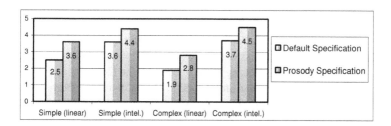

Fig. 1. Side-by-side comparison of prosodic model against default specification

The second part of this included synthesized spoken formats of unseen Tables 7 and 8 much larger than the initial experiment ones. The simple table linear spoken format included repeats of the header row, a usual practice for larger tables that contain several rows of data. The translation of the content to English is provided by italicized text in square brackets.

Table 7. The larger simple data table contains one header row and eight data rows

Πρόγραμμα μεταδόσεων αθλημάτων από το ραδιόφωνο.
[Radio-transmitted sports schedule].

Ημέρα [Day]	Άθλημα [Sport]	Έναρξη [Start time]	Λήξη [End time]
Δευτέρα [Monday]	Στίβος [Athletics]	11.00	18.00
Τρίτη [Tuesday]	Τένις [Tennis]	20.00	23.00
Τετάρτη [Wednesday]	Στίβος [Athletics]	09.00	18.00
Πέμπτη [Thursday]	Γυμναστική [Gymnastics]	16.00	21.00
Παρασκευή [Friday]	Πόλο [Water polo]	12.00	15.00
Σάββατο [Saturday]	Γυμναστική [Gymnastics]	16.00	18.00
Σάββατο [Saturday]	Ποδόσφαιρο [Football]	21.00	23.00
Κυριακή [Sunday]	Στίβος [Athletics]	09.00	12.00

During the second experiment, the subjects were asked to listen to each synthesized rendition and answer carefully selected key questions (asked beforehand and chosen in random order) designed to retrieve data from the tables. The listeners were asked to look for specific information and expected to recognize nested tables, data spanning several rows or columns, etc, in order to answer. Moreover at the end of each session they were asked to provide subjective opinion for overall impression on the quality of rendition, the listening effort required to understand each table, and their acceptance.

Figure 2 shows overall impression (5 = excellent, 1 = bad) of synthesized speech rendering of tables as well as listening effort needed by the listeners in order to answer the key questions (5 = no meaning understood with any feasible effort, 1 = no effort required). It is worth mentioning that half of the listeners were unhappy with linear rendition of simple table while 8 out of 10 were unable to understand the linear rendition of the complex table. This shows that, for linear navigation, prosody control fails to replace semantic structure when that is completely lost, less so for simpler tables where some of it may be retained.

It is obvious that linear reading of complex tables really failed to render the semantic relationship of the data understandable, which was the case for the natural speech rendition during the initial experiments as well. However, the prosody model worked successfully for the other cases, the result being improvement in acoustic representation as well as reduced effort.

Table 8. The complex data table contains three nested sub-tables

Πόλεις και ο καιρός τους τις επόμενες μέρες.
[*Cities and their weather for the following days*]

	Δευτέρα [*Monday*]	Τρίτη [*Tuesday*]	Τετάρτη [*Wednesday*]	Πέμπτη [*Thursday*]	Παρασκευή [*Friday*]
Αθήνα [***Athens***]					
Θερμοκρασία [*Temperature*]	23	24	26	22	18
Άνεμος [*Wind*]	Βορειοδυτικός [*Northwest*]	Δυτικός [*West*]	Νοτιοδυτικός [*Southwest*]	Βορειοδυτικός [*Northwest*]	Βόρειος [*North*]
Θεσσαλονίκη [***Salonika***]					
Θερμοκρασία [*Temperature*]	16	17	20	16	13
Άνεμος [*Wind*]	Βόρειος [*North*]	Βόρειος [*North*]	Δυτικός [*West*]	Βόρειος [*North*]	Βορειοδυτικός [*Northwest*]
Πάτρα [***Patra***]					
Θερμοκρασία [*Temperature*]	19	22	23	20	19
Άνεμος [*Wind*]	Βορειοδυτικός [*Northwest*]	Δυτικός [*West*]	Νότιος [*South*]	Νοτιοδυτικός [*Southwest*]	Νοτιοδυτικός [*Southwest*]

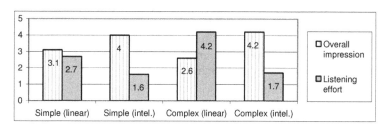

Fig. 2. Overall impression (higher=better) and listening effort (higher=worse)

As an overall assessment of the results from these experiments, it can be deducted that the prosodic model provided a promising approach to modeling visual structures and to identify potential implementation issues in Table-to-Speech synthesis from real speech derived data. Navigation manner makes a strong impact on the final result and for that it should be pursued. Furthermore, it is concluded that by careful prosody modeling, a degree of semantic structure essence is retained in the resulting synthesized tables, thus making the content easier for the listener to comprehend. Finally, there is strong indication of several structural elements (e.g. rows, header-data cell pairs) that contain semantic importance for data understanding, and can be used by the synthesis system.

5   Conclusions

We presented an experimental study of vocalizing data tables. A set of prosodic parameters was derived by natural speech data that were analyzed in terms of phrase accent tones and pauses, clearly illustrating consistency against cell content and visual structure. The deducted specification formed the basis for a prosody model presented in this work that was used for automated rendering through synthetic speech. Experienced listeners through a formal acoustical assessment examined the generated utterances in cases of simple and complex tables. It was shown that such prosody modeling approach can successfully lead to improved understanding of synthesized speech rendition of tables, eventually conveying semantically important visual information to speech by prosody control.

Direct comparison of the prosody model aided synthetic speech against the default parameters used by a TtS system revealed the fact that certain semantic information can be carried from the visual structure to the spoken output through the use of phrase accent and pause break parameters.

It is concluded that further investigation should be granted to this area, especially in terms of determining which prosodic features have the most significant role in conveying semantic content. Furthermore the positive results encourage further analysis on the real speech data including additional parameters such as speech rate and duration.

Acknowledgments

The work described in this paper has been partially supported by the HERACLITUS project of the Operational Programme for Education and Initial Vocational Training (EPEAEK) of the Greek Ministry of Education under the 3rd European Community Support Framework for Greece. Special thanks to M. Platakis, O. Kostakis, P. Kollias, G. Marinakis, P. Karra, E. Kouvarakis, and L. Perellis for their participation in the psychoacoustic experiments described in this work.

References

1. Pontelli, E., Xiong, W., Gupta, G., Karshmer, A: A Domain Specific Language Framework for Non-visual Browsing of Complex HTML Structures. Proc. ACM Conf. Assistive Technologies - ASSETS 2000, 180-187, (2000).
2. Ramel, J-Y., Crucianou M., Vincent, N., Faure, C: Detection, Extraction and Representation of Tables. Proc. 7th Int. Conf. Document Analysis and Recognition - ICDAR 2003, 374-378, (2003).
3. Hurst, M., Douglas, S.: Layout & Language: Preliminary Experiments in Assigning Logical Structure to Table Cells. Proc. 4th Int. Conf. Document Analysis and Recognition - ICDAR 2003, 1043-1047, (1997).
4. Filepp, R., Challenger, J., Rosu, D.: Improving the Accessibility of Aurally Rendered HTML Tables. Proc. ACM Conf. on Assistive Technologies - ASSETS 2002, 9-16, (2002).
5. Lim, S., Ng, Y.: An Automated Approach for Retrieving Hierarchical Data from HTML Tables. Proc. 8th ACM Int. Conf. Information and Knowledge Management - CIKM 1999, 466-474, (1999).

6. Yesilada, Y., Stevens, R., Goble, C., Hussein, S.: Rendering Tables in Audio: The Interaction of Structure and Reading Styles. Proc. ACM Conf. Assistive Technologies - ASSETS 2004, 16-23, (2004).

7. Pontelli, E., Gillan, D., Xiong, W., Saad, E., Gupta, G., Karshmer, A.: Navigation of HTML Tables, Frames, and XML Fragments. Proc. ACM Conf. on Assistive Technologies - ASSETS 2002, 25-32, (2002).

8. Xydas, G., Argyropoulos, V., Karakosta, T., Kouroupetroglou, G.: An Experimental Approach in Recognizing Synthesized Auditory Components in a Non-Visual Interaction with Documents. Proc. Human-Computer Interaction - HCII 2005, to appear, (2005).

9. Xydas, G., Spiliotopoulos D., Kouroupetroglou, G.: Modeling Emphatic Events from Non-Speech Aware Documents in Speech Based User Interfaces. Proc. Human-Computer Interaction - HCII 2003, Theory and Practice, 2, 806-810, (2003).

10. Raman, T.: An Audio View of (LA)TEX Documents, TUGboat, Proc. 1992 Annual Meeting, 13, 3, 372-379, (1992).

11. Xydas, G., & Kouroupetrolgou, G.: Text-to-Speech Scripting Interface for Appropriate Vocalisation of E-Texts. Proc. 7th European Conf. Speech Communication and Technology - EUROSPEECH 2001, 2247-2250, (2001).

12. Spiliotopoulos D., Xydas, G., Kouroupetroglou, G., and Argyropoulos, V.: "Experimentation on Spoken Format of Tables in Auditory User Interfaces". Universal Access in HCI, Proc. HCI International 2005: The 11th International Conference on Human-Computer Interaction (HCII-2005), 22-27 July, 2005, Las Vegas, USA, to appear.

13. Raggett, D., Le Hors, A., Jacobs, I.: Tables, HTML 4.01 Specification, W3C Recommendation, http://www.w3.org/TR/REC-html40, (1999).

14. Chisholm, W., Vanderheiden, G., Jacobs, I.: Web Content Accessibility Guidelines 1.0, W3C Recommendation, 5 May 1999, http://www.w3.org/TR/WAI-WEBCONTENT/, (1999).

15. Penn, G., Hu, J., Luo, H., McDonald, R.: Flexible Web Document Analysis for Delivery to Narrow-Bandwidth Devices, Proc. 6th Int. Conf. on Document Analysis and Recognition - ICDAR 2001, 1074-1078, (2001)

16. Silverman, K., Beckman, M., Pitrelli, J., Ostendorf, M., Wightman, C., Price, P., Pierrehumbert, J., & Hirschberg, J.: ToBI: A Standard for Labeling English Prosody. Proc. Int. Conf. Spoken Language Processing - ICSLP-92, 2, 867-870, (1992).

Phoneme Based Acoustics Keyword Spotting in Informal Continuous Speech*

Igor Szöke, Petr Schwarz, Pavel Matějka, Lukáš Burget,
Martin Karafiát, and Jan Černocký

Faculty of Information Technology, Brno University of Technology, Czech Republic
szoke@fit.vutbr.cz

Abstract. This paper describes several ways of acoustic keywords spotting (KWS), based on Gaussian mixture model (GMM) hidden Markov models (HMM) and phoneme posterior probabilities from FeatureNet. Context-independent and dependent phoneme models are used in the GMM/HMM system. The systems were trained and evaluated on informal continuous speech. We used different complexities of KWS recognition network and different types of phoneme models. We study the impact of these parameters on the accuracy and computational complexity, an conclude that phoneme posteriors outperform conventional GMM/HMM system.

1 Introduction

Acoustic keyword spotting (KWS) systems are widely used for the detection of selected words in speech utterances. Searching for various words or terms is needed in applications such as spoken document retrieval or information retrieval. An advantage of acoustic keyword spotting is in the possibility to spot out-of-vocabulary words, which are dropped in LVCSR systems. The paper deals with comparison of different KWS systems and their evaluation on informal continuous speech (recordings of meetings) within AMI project.

The paper first discusses training and testing data sets. Metrics of evaluation are defined later. The configuration of the GMM/HMM and the FeatureNet phoneme posterior estimator is discussed next. Description of several types of recognition networks of acoustic KWS system follows. Results are discussed and conclusions are drawn at the end of the paper.

A modern acoustic keyword spotter was proposed in [4] and it is based on maximum likelihood approach [1]. General KWS network using phoneme models is shown in Figure 1. Parts denoted A and C are filler models (phoneme loop) which model non-keyword parts of utterance. Part B is linear model for given keyword. Part D is a background model (phoneme loop) which models the same part of the utterance as the keyword model. The confidence L_R of detected keyword is computed as likelihood

---

* This work was partially supported by EC project Augmented Multi-party Interaction (AMI), No. 506811 and Grant Agency of Czech Republic under project No. 102/05/0278. Jan Černocký was supported by post-doctoral grant of Grant Agency of Czech Republic No. GA102/02/D108.

V. Matoušek et al. (Eds.): TSD 2005, LNAI 3658, pp. 302–309, 2005.

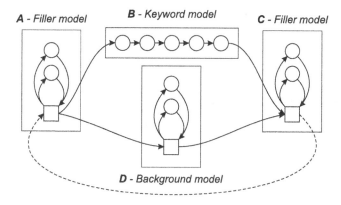

A - Filler model   **B** - Keyword model   **C** - Filler model

D - Background model

Fig. 1. General model of keyword spotting network.

ratio $L_R = L_{ABC}/L_{ADC}$, where L_{ADC} is likelihood of the best path through the model not containing the keyword and L_{ABC} is likelihood of a path through this same model containing the keyword.

2   The Data and Evaluation

Our keyword system was tested on a large database of informal continuous speech of ICSI meetings [3] (sampled at 16 kHz). Attention was paid to the definition of fair division of data into training/development/test parts with non-overlapping speakers. It was actually necessary to work on speaker turns rather than whole meetings, as they contain many overlapping speakers. We have balanced the ratio of native/nonnative speakers, balanced the ratio of European/Asiatic speakers and moved speakers with small portion of speech or keywords to the training set. The training/development/test parts division is 41.3, 18.7 and 17.2 hours of speech respectively. Development part is used for phoneme insertion penalty tuning.

In the definition of keyword set, we have selected the most frequently occurring words (each of them has more than 95 occurrences in each of the sets) but checked, that the phonetic form of a keyword is not a subset of another word nor of word transition. The percentage of such cases was evaluated for all candidates and words with high number of such cases were removed.

The final list consists of 17 keywords: *actually, different, doing, first, interesting, little, meeting, people, probably, problem, question, something, stuff, system, talking, those, using.*

Our experiments are evaluated using *Figure-of-Merit* (FOM) [4], which is the average of correct detections per 1, 2, ... 10 false alarms per hour. We can approximately interpret it as the accuracy of KWS provided that there are 5 false alarms per hour.

Realtime coefficient (computational cost) was measured for some experiments. That was done at one computer with Intel P4 2.5 GHz HT processor. Computational cost experiment was run on 0.67 h of test set which equals to 2405 s. There was no other load on test computer. The *RT* coefficient means ratio between *total time spent by CPU* and *total time of utterances*.

$$RT = \frac{T_{CPU}}{T_{utterances}} \tag{1}$$

3   Acoustic Keyword Spotting System

Presented KWS system is based on that described in [4], but we did some simplifications to run our system on-line. The after-keyword filler model C is not used. Background model D and front filler model A are grouped – they are the same phoneme loops. An example of our recognition network (for context-independent phonemes) is shown in Figure 2. The network has two parts: *keyword models* and *filler and background model*. Each keyword model contains concatenated phoneme models, we allow also for pronunciation variants. After a token goes through the keyword model to the end node, corresponding token is taken from phoneme loop (node F). Then likelihood ratio of these two is computed. Background and filler model contains no language model.

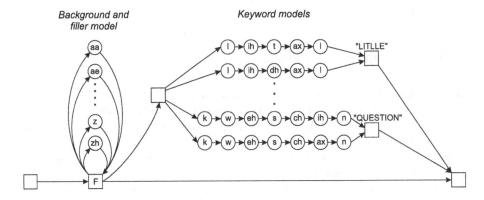

Fig. 2. Keywords spotting network using context-independent phonemes.

3.1   GMM/HMM System

Gaussian mixture model hidden Markov model based system is trained on 10 h long subset of the training set (denoted as **ICSI10h**). Raw data was parameterized using 13 Mel-frequency cepstral coefficients with Δ and $\Delta\Delta$. Two different sets of models were trained. Context-independent phonemes (*phonemes*, 43 units) and context-dependent phonemes (*triphones*, 77659 units). Standard training technique for GMM/HMM based on HTK was used.

Another set of experiments were done using triphone models trained on conversational telephone speech (*CTS*) database. CTS database contains about 277 hours of speech (mainly from the the Switchboard database), see Table 1. Raw data was parameterized using 13 perceptual linear prediction (*PLP*) coefficients [2] with Δ and $\Delta\Delta$. Parameters were normalized by cepstral mean and variance normalization. Models trained

Table 1. Definition of training set of CTS database.

Database	Time
Switchboard 1	248.52 h
Switchboard 2 - Cellular	15.27 h
Call Home English	13.93 h
Sum	277.72 h

on CTS database are denoted as **CTS277h-noad**. ICSI database was down-sampled to 8 kHz and PLP parameterized in the same way as CTS database. Then the *CTS277h-noad* models were adapted using MAP adaptation on full ICSI train set (adapted models are denoted as **CTS277h-adap**).

3.2   LCRC FeatureNet System

Another approach to get acoustics keyword spotting is to use our LCRC FeatureNet phoneme recognizer [5]. It is a hybrid system based on Neural Networks (NN) and Viterbi decoder without any language model. An unconventional feature extraction technique based on long temporal context is used: The temporal context of critical band spectral densities is split into left and right context (*LCRC*). This allows for more precise modelling of the whole trajectory while limiting the size of the model (number of weights in the NN). Both parts are processed by DCT to de-correlate and reduce dimensionality. The feature vector which is feed to NN is created by concatenation of vectors over all filter bank energies. Two NNs are trained to produce the phoneme posterior probabilities for both context parts. Third NN functions as a merger and produces final set of posterior probabilities. We use 3-state models and the NN produces 3 posteriors for the beginning, the center and the end of a phoneme.

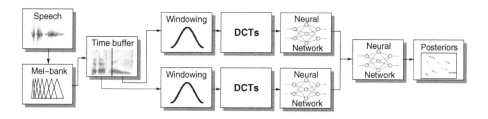

Fig. 3. Phoneme recognizer with split temporal context.

The LCRC FeatureNet system is trained on the same 10 h long subset of the training set as GMM/HMM system (denoted as **LCRC10h**) and on full training set 41.3 h (denoted as **LCRC40h**). System produces posteriori probability only for context-independent phoneme set (*phonemes*, 43 units).

Posteriori Probability Transformation. Logarithmized histogram of distribution of linear posteriori probability is plotted in Figure 4. Two maxima at 0 and 1 are caused

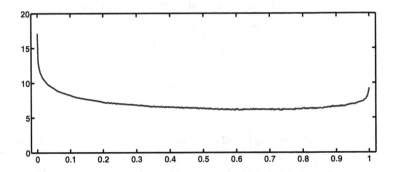

Fig. 4. Logarithmized histogram of linear posteriori probability distribution.

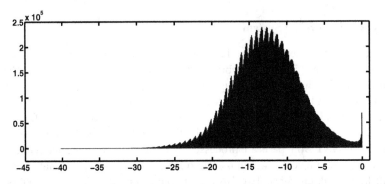

Fig. 5. Histogram of logarithmized posteriori probability.

by the fact that NN is always too sure that a phoneme is or is not present (it is trained to discriminate). For the decoding, it is useful to "soften" these maxima.

The posterior probabilities are logarithmized. Logarithm function has ability to "increase resolution" close to 0, so the probabilities will not be so concentrated there. We can see the histogram of logarithmized posterior probabilities in Figure 5. The distribution of log-probabilities is nearly gaussian. But there is still one peak close to 0, which is caused by the value of linear probabilities around 1.

We design a posterior transformation to soften out both maxima. The transformation function (so-called *PostTrans*) contains two logarithms:

$$PostTrans_{(I,L,R)}(P) = \begin{cases} \log_L(\frac{P}{I}), & P < I \\ \log_R(\frac{P}{1-I}), & P \geq I \end{cases} \tag{2}$$

where L, R and I are constants. We experimentally tuned the constants to $I = 0.1$, $L = 50$ and $R = 1.1$. A new *LCRC40h* system with posteriori transformation $PostTrans_{(0.1,50,1.1)}$ is denoted as **LCRC40hPostTrans**.

3.3 Recognition Networks

Experiments were done with the following KWS recognition networks. All recognition networks contain no language model.

- A network consisting of phonemes (denoted as **CI**, Figure 2).
- A network consisting of reduced set of triphones (denoted as **CDred**). Background and filler model of *CDRed* network contains only triphones which appears in keyword models. No context sensitive links are used (eg. triphone A-B+C has a link to triphone D-E+F) in *CDred* network.
- A network consisting of reduced set of triphones and phonemes (denoted as **CI&CDred**). It is *CDRed* network with added phonemes to the filler and background model.
- A network consisting of full set of triphones (denoted as **CD**, Figure 6). Links among triphones in *CD* network are context sensitive (eg. there is link between triphones A-B+C and B-C+D but not between A-B+C and D-E+F). The first and the last phoneme of keyword is expanded to all context possibilities in triphone networks (*CDred*, *CI&CDred* and *CD*). *CD* network was also optimized using algorithm for finite state automaton minimization (denoted as **CDopt**).

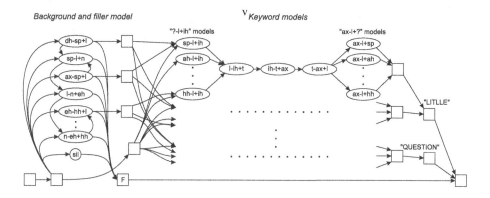

Fig. 6. Keyword spotting network using full set of triphones.

4   Results

Results of GMM/HMM based acoustic keyword spotting system are listed in Table 2. The *ICSI10h* experiment set shows, that using full set of triphones (*CD* network) gives the best FOM. Disadvantage of this approach is huge network size and slow decoding. *CDred* is a good compromise between speed and accuracy. Comparison between *CTS277h-noad* and *CTS277h-adap* with *CDred* network shows 3% improvement caused by adaptation of models. Network optimization has important impact on the speed. The system is about $8\times$ faster. The best GM/HMM based keyword spotting system which we have is the *CTS277h-adap* using *CDopt* network with 63.66% FOM.

The results of LCRC FeatureNet based acoustic keyword spotting system are listed in Table 3. All the LCRC FeatureNet systems work with *CI* network. This makes the decoding (the posteriors can be pre-computed) very fast – the realtime coefficient is 0.021. The best LCRC FeatureNet based keyword spotting system is the one using posteriori transformation function *LCRC40hPostTrans* with 64.46% FOM. The ROC curves are ploted in Figure 7.

Table 2. The results of different acoustic keyword spotting systems based on GM/HMM.

Model	Network	#HITs	#FAs	#KWs	FOM	Realtime coefficient	Net size nodes, links
ICSI10h	CI	3142	2877867	3289	**47.77**	0.51	264, 339
ICSI10h	CDred	3177	2774259	3289	**57.15**	1.07	4375, 8461
ICSI10h	CI&CDred	3164	2904486	3289	**57.52**	1.50	4417, 8545
ICSI10h	CD	3173	2914897	3289	**61.88**	56.62	102k,3508k
CTS277h-noad	CDred	3189	2752492	3289	**56.39**	–	7637, 14742
CTS277h-adap	CDred	3159	2927968	3289	**59.39**	–	7637, 14742
CTS277h-adap	CD	3147	3032251	3289	**63.66**	73.03	119k, 4256k
CTS277h-adap	CDopt	3147	3032251	3289	**63.66**	8.50	28k, 83k

Table 3. The results of different acoustic keyword spotting systems based on LCRC FeatureNet.

Model	Network	#HITs	#FAs	#KWs	FOM	Realtime coefficient	Net size nodes, links
LCRC10h	CI	3145	3065025	3289	**61.39**	0.021	263, 337
LCRC40h	CI	3153	3062984	3289	**62.46**	0.021	263, 337
LCRC40hPostTrans	CI	3148	3031465	3289	**64.46**	0.021	263, 337

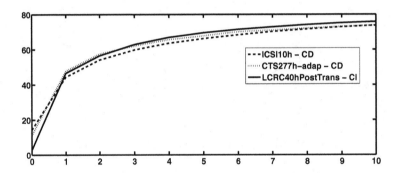

Fig. 7. ROC curves of three best systems. X-axis is the number of FAs per hour, Y-axis is the percentage of detected keywords.

5   Conclusion

The paper deals with a comparison of different KWS systems and their evaluation on informal continuous speech (recordings of meeting). We measured the accuracy of GMM/HMM based and FeatureNet based systems. *Figure-of-merit* scoring method was used to compare the performance of systems. The test data-set (about 17 h of speech and 17 searched keywords) was designed for statistically reliable results.

The best system using Gaussian mixtures hidden Markov models approach is triphone models trained on 277.72 h of narrow-band conversational telephone speech corpus adapted to target ICSI database. FOM of the system is 63.66%. Triphone system trained on 10 h of wide-band ICSI database has reached 61.88% FOM. The best LCRC

FeatureNet system was trained on 41.3 h of ICSI database. It generates phoneme posteriori probabilities which are transformed using proposed function. FOM of the LCRC FeatureNet system is 64.46% and outperform conventional GMM/HMM system. The system uses *CI* network in comparison to *CDopt* network for the best GMM/HMM system, which makes it simple and fast.

References

1. Bahl, L.R., Jelinek, F., Mercer, R.L.: A maximum likelihood approach to continuous speech recognition. In IEEE Trans. Pattern Analysis and Machine Inteligence, PAMI-5(2).
2. Hermansky, H.: Perceptual linear predictive (PLP) analysis for the speech. In Journal of the Acoustical Society of America, 1990. JASA-90, pages 1738–1752, 1990.
3. Janin, A., Baron, D., Edwards, J., Ellis, D., Gelbart, D., Morgan, N., Peskin, B., Pfau, T., Shriberg, E., Stolcke, A., Wooters, C.: The ICSI meeting corpus. In International Conference on Acoustics, Speech, and Signal Processing, 2003. ICASSP-03, Hong Kong, April 2003.
4. Rohlicek, J.R., Russell, W., Roukos, S., Gish, H.: Continuous hidden markov modeling for speaker-independent word spotting. In International Conference on Acoustics, Speech, and Signal Processing, 1989. ICASSP-89, volume 1, Glasgow, UK, May 1989.
5. Schwarz, P., Matějka, P., Černocký, J.: Towards lower error rates in phoneme recognition. In Proc. TSD 2004, number ISBN 87-90834-09-7, pages 465–472, Brno, Czech Republic, September 2004.

Explicit Duration Modelling in HMM/ANN Hybrids

László Tóth and András Kocsor

Research Group on Artificial Intelligence
H-6720 Szeged, Aradi vértanúk tere 1., Hungary
{tothl,kocsor}@inf.u-szeged.hu

Abstract. In some languages like Finnish or Hungarian phone duration is a very important distinctive acoustic cue. The conventional HMM speech recognition framework, however, is known to poorly model the duration information. In this paper we compare different duration models within the framework of HMM/ANN hybrids. The tests are performed with two different hybrid models, the conventional one and the "averaging hybrid" recently proposed. Independent of the model configuration, we report that the usual exponential duration model has no detectable advantage over using no duration model at all. Similarly, applying the same fixed value for all state transition probabilities, as is usual with HMM/ANN systems, is found to have no influence on the performance. However, the practical trick of imposing a minimum duration on the phones turns out to be very useful. The key part of the paper is the introduction of the gamma distribution duration model, which proves clearly superior to the exponential one, yielding a 12-20% relative improvement in the word error rate, thus justifying the use of sophisticated duration models in speech recognition.

1 Introduction

In some languages like Finnish or Hungarian phone durations may be the only clue in discriminating certain words. Good duration modelling can therefore be an important issue. The conventional HMM speech recognition framework however does not really make use of the duration information. Though the state transition probabilities can be regarded as a geometric duration model, this model is not that effective. First, the geometric distribution is a very poor approximation of real phone durations. Second, several authors have reported that the state transition values have practically no influence on the recognition scores [2]. In this paper we examine the issue of duration modeling within the framework of HMM/ANN hybrids. Two types of hybrid models will be tested: the conventional one known from the literature, and a novel one recently proposed. In both cases we seek to answer two questions. First, we want to either prove or refute the common view that the geometric duration model is wholly ineffective. Second, we would like to know whether the replacement of the geometric model with a more sophisticated gamma distribution can improve the performance of the two hybrids.

2 A Segment-Based View of HMM/ANN Hybrids

This paper deals with the kind of HMM models where the usual Gaussian mixture component is replaced by artificial neural network (ANN) estimates. We will refer to

V. Matoušek et al. (Eds.): TSD 2005, LNAI 3658, pp. 310–317, 2005.

such models as "HMM/ANN hybrids". And, as a special case, the term "conventional HMM/ANN hybrid" here will mean the model proposed by Bourlard et al. [1]. The basic idea behind the latter is very simple: in a standard HMM, we replace the state-conditional emission likelihood estimates $\hat{P}(x_t|q_k)$ by ANN-based posterior estimates $\hat{P}(q_k|x_t)$ divided by the state priors $P(q_k)$. According to Bayes' rule, this quotient will be proportional to the state-conditional likelihood within a scaling factor $P(x_t)$, but this factor does not influence the optimization, so the resulting system should behave like a conventional HMM.

In the following we will adopt a more general approach of the ANN-based hybrid models, where we prefer to interpret the decoding process as a search over phonetic segmentations rather than state sequences. This may be done because HMM/ANN hybrids do not use 3-state models, but have only one state per phone, so states directly correspond to phones and any state sequence naturally corresponds to a segmentation (and vice-versa). Because of this, instead of thinking in state sequences, the subsequences where the model remains in the same state can be thought of as phonetic segments; and the whole state sequence can be interpreted as a series of segments. This scheme is more general that the traditional one and will allow us to introduce a new type of hybrid model that we will call the "averaging hybrid" model. Moreover, the explicit duration models we are going to discuss can be more readily explained within this framework. However, we will also see that the conventional HMM/ANN hybrid is just a special case of this representation.

Let us now examine how the hybrid model evaluates a supposed segment. Let $X = x_1, ..., x_T$ denote the observation sequence, $U = u_1, ..., u_N$ a sequence of phonetic units over a phone set $\{q_1, ..., q_M\}$, and $S = s_0, ..., s_N$ a segmentation (given as $N+1$ segment boundary time indices).

First of all, as is usual with HMMs, we separate the acoustic and language models. Mathematically this means that we model $P(X|U)P(U)^{\alpha_L}$ instead of $P(U|X)$. The prior probability of a phone sequence, $P(U)$, is produced by the language model, and α_L is a weighting factor that is found useful in practice [4]. Here we are going to focus on the acoustic model $P(X|U)$. This factor is approximated by examining all possible state sequences or, in our jargon, segmentations S. That is,

$$P(X|U) = \sum_S P(X, S|U) \approx \max_S P(X, S|U). \tag{1}$$

Next $P(X, S|U)$ is decomposed into segment-level scores. In our general model this decomposition takes the form

$$P(X, S|U) \approx \prod_{i=1}^{N} \frac{P(u_i|x_{s_{i-1}}^{s_i-1})^{\alpha_U} \cdot P(S_i|x_{s_{i-1}}^{s_i-1})^{\alpha_S} \cdot I}{P(u_i)}, \tag{2}$$

where $x_{s_{i-1}}^{s_i-1} = x_{s_{i-1}}, ..., x_{s_i-1}$ denotes the observation subsequence belonging to the ith segment, and $P(u_i)$ is the prior probability of phoneme u_i. $P(S_i|x_{s_{i-1}}^{s_i-1})$ can be interpreted as the probability that $x_{s_{i-1}}^{s_i-1}$ is a correct phonetic segment. The α exponents were introduced based on experience with a similar weighting factor for the language model. I is a phone insertion penalty that can be used to balance the phone insertions and deletions; again, such a factor is known to be useful in language modeling [4].

Let us examine the two main components of Eq. (2). The first, $P(u_i|x_{s_{i-1}}^{s_i-1})$, which will be referred to as P_U later on, represents the fact that each phonetic unit u_i has to be identified from $x_{s_{i-1}}^{s_i-1} = x_{s_{i-1}}, ..., x_{s_i-1}$, the signal segment mapped to it. This segment-based posterior probability can be approximated by the formula:

$$P(u_i = q_k|x_{s_{i-1}}^{s_i-1}) \approx \frac{\frac{1}{P(u_i=q_k)^{d(i)-1}} \prod_{j=s_{i-1}}^{s_i-1} \hat{P}(u_i = q_k|x_j)}{\sum_{r=1}^{M} \left[\frac{1}{P(u_i=q_r)^{d(i)-1}} \prod_{j=s_{i-1}}^{s_i-1} \hat{P}(u_i = q_r|x_j) \right]}, \quad (3)$$

where $\hat{P}(u_i = q_r|x_j)$ are the frame-based posterior estimates and $d(i) = s_i - s_{i-1}$ is just a compact notation for the length of the segment.

In classifier combination theory Eq. (3) is known as the *product rule* and is used for obtaining an estimate of the class posteriors from the estimate of $d(i)$ independent classifiers [8]. Note that the role of the denominator is simply to normalize the estimates of the different phone classes so that they add up to one. It would not be required if the frames were truly independent. But, in fact, both theoretical arguments and experimental findings show that the frames are far from being independent. In [9] it was demonstrated that we obtain more reasonable estimates if we normalize the values and do not rely on the unrealistic independence assumption.

Alternatively, we could use the *averaging rule* of classifier combination theory:

$$P(u_i = q_k|x_{s_{i-1}}^{s_i-1}) \approx \frac{\sum_{j=s_{i-1}}^{s_i-1} \hat{P}(u_i = q_k|x_j)}{d(i)}. \quad (4)$$

Note that in this case the estimates belonging to the various classes always add up to one, ensuring that the estimates form a correct probability distribution.

Now let us turn our attention to the other component, $P(S_i|x_{s_{i-1}}^{s_i-1})$. Its role is to compute the probability that the given segment indeed corresponds to a phone, and hence to guide the model towards finding the correct segmentation of the signal. Duration models are possible candidates because the duration information is implicitly present in $x_{s_{i-1}}^{s_i-1}$. The next section is devoted to a detailed discussion of some of the duration models that are available. Here we present an alternative, and a rather unusual interpretation of this component. This approach makes use of the frame-based posterior estimates to construct an approximation for $P(S_i|x_{s_{i-1}}^{s_i-1})$. It is based on the idea that a disagreement of the frame-based experts is likely to refer to a phonetically inhomogenious segment. Hence, it is reasonable to look for a formula that expresses the coherence of the frame-based scores. In [9] we proposed to use the expression

$$P(S_i|x_{s_{i-1}}^{s_i-1}) \approx \sum_{k=1}^{M} P(u_i = q_k|x_{s_{i-1}}^{s_i-1}) \quad (5)$$

for this purpose, where the $P(u_i = q_k|x_{s_{i-1}}^{s_i-1})$ values are obtained from the product rule (Eq. (3)). One can argue that the larger the disagreement between the frame-based experts, the smaller the value is for this formula. Hence, it may be interpreted as a measure of incoherence of the frame-based posteriors and can be used as an estimate for $P(S_i|x_{s_{i-1}}^{s_i-1})$. From now on we will refer to this approximation for $P(S_i|x_{s_{i-1}}^{s_i-1})$ as P_S.

Note that the incoherence of the frame-based estimates and the duration of the segment are quite different pieces of information, so it seems reasonable to make use both of them. In the experiments we will incorporate both P_S and duration models P_D in the model configurations, and they will be combined in the form $P_S^{\alpha_S} P_D^{\alpha_D}$.

3   Duration Models

No Duration Model. It has been observed by several researchers and reported in the literature that the values of the state transition probabilities have practically no effect on the recognition result [2]. Thus it is theoretically possible not to use a duration model at all. The results obtained this way can serve as a baseline for comparing the effect of the various duration models.

Exponential (Geometric) Duration Model. Hidden Markov models incorporate an implicit duration model coded by the self-transition probabilities of the states. If the self-transition probability of a state q is denoted by a_{qq}, then the probability that the models stays in state q for d steps (the duration of d frames) is $P_D(d) = (1 - a_{qq})a_{qq}^{d-1}$. This corresponds to a discrete geometric distribution, or an exponential one if we think in term of a continuous distribution. The great advantage of this exponential duration model is that it can be calculated recursively, that is $P_D(d) = P_D(d-1) \cdot a_{qq}$, so it nicely fits the dynamic programming framework of HMMs. However, in practice the duration of phones does not follow an exponential distribution. The example in Fig. 1 clearly demonstrates this fact.

The proper values for a_{qq} can be found quite easily. We only need one piece of data for this, namely the average duration for the model to stay in state q. In our one-state model the states q directly correspond to phones, so this average duration can be estimated as the mean of the phone durations over a manually segmented speech corpus. From M_q, the empirical mean of the data a_{qq} can be estimated by $a_{qq} = (M_q - 1)/M_q$ or $a_{qq} = exp(-1/M_q)$, depending on whether we are using a discrete geometric or a continuous exponential distribution.

Shared Exponential Duration Model. While in conventional HMM systems the state transition probabilities are estimated as part of the expectation maximization training procedure, in HMM/ANN systems it is common practice to use the same fixed value for all state transition probabilities [3]. It may be interpreted as if all phones had the same shared duration model. In our experiments the shared parameter value was set to 0.7.

Exponential Duration Model with Minimum Duration Restriction. If we compare the data histogram and the exponential curve fit over it in Fig. 1, we see that the largest mismatch is with small durations. A relatively simple remedy for this is to impose a minimal duration on the phones during the decoding process. For the duration model this corresponds to zeroing out the first couple of values (see Fig. 1). It is also interesting to observe that, in a 3-state model, phones are implicitly constrained to have at least 3 frames (if skipping states is forbidden). Restricting the minimal duration to 3 frames in a 1-state model will have a similar effect. Actually, in the experiments we set this value to 4 rather than 3 because this yielded slightly better results.

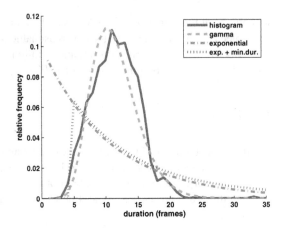

Fig. 1. Fitting a duration histogram by various pdfs.

Gamma Distribution Duration Model. Quite evidently, the exponential duration model gives a very poor approximation of the real distribution, even with a minimum duration restriction. It is natural, then, to look for another type of distribution that is only slightly more complicated, but fits the data much better. One possibility is to use the gamma distribution for this purpose. Mathematically it has the form [12]:

$$P_D(d) = \frac{(d/\beta)^{\gamma-1}e^{-d/\beta}}{\beta\Gamma(\gamma)},\qquad(6)$$

where γ is the shape parameter, β is the scale parameter, and Γ is the gamma function. The method of moments estimators of the gamma distribution are $\gamma = M_q^2/V_q$ and $\beta = V_q/M_q$, where M_q and V_q are the empirical mean and variation of the data [12].

A purely practical issue is that the gamma function cannot be computed directly but requires numerical approximations. Note, however, that it does not influence the shape of the curve but simply acts as a normalizing constant. Realizing this, we replaced it by a third parameter whose value is estimated by minimizing the mean square error between the histogram of durations and the approximation given by $P_D(d)$.

Fig. 1 shows that a gamma distribution indeed fits the data much better than an exponential distribution. The price to be paid for this is that the former cannot be computed recursively, so the usual dynamic programming decoding scheme has to be modified. This brings some additional complexity to the decoding process. Fortunately, this extra burden is manageable, because the other components (P_U and P_S) can still be computed recursively, and evaluating $P_D(d)$ for different d values is not cpu demanding. The reader should see [7] and [6] for more on how the conventional HMM or HMM/ANN structure has to be modified to incorporate explicit duration models in them.

4 Experimental Results

Database. All the results presented here were obtained using the MTBA Hungarian Telephone Speech Database [10]. This is the first Hungarian speech corpus that is publicly available and has a reasonably large size. The most important data block of the corpus contains recorded sentences that were read out loud by 500 speakers. These sentences are relatively long (40-50 phones per sentence), and were selected in such a way that together all the most frequent phone connections of Hungarian occur in them. The recordings were made via mobile and line phones, and the speakers were chosen so that their distribution corresponded to the age and gender distribution of the Hungarian population. All the sentences were manually segmented and labelled at the phone level. A set of 58 phonetic symbols was used for this purpose, but after fusing certain rarely occurring allophones, we worked with only 52 phone classes in the experiments.

For training purposes 1367 sentences were selected from the corpus. The test results described here are isolated word recognition tests performed on another block of the database that contained city names. All the 500 city names (each pronounced by a different caller) were different. From the 500 recordings only 431 were employed in the tests as the rest contained significant non-stationary noise or were misread by the caller. The language model used was a simple pronunciation dictionary that contained one phonetic transcript for each word and assumed that each of them had equal priors.

Preprocessing. For acoustic preprocessing we applied the Hvite module of the well-known Hidden Markov Model Toolkit (HTK) [11]. We used the most popular preprocessor configuration, that is we extracted 13 MFCC coefficients along with the corresponding delta and delta-delta values, thus obtaining the usual 39-element feature vector [11]. For recognition we used our own HMM/ANN decoder implementation, which was earlier found to have a performance similar to that of the standard HTK recognizer.

Model Configurations. The neural net used in the system contained 150 sigmoidal hidden neurons and a softmax output layer. Training was performed by conventional backpropagation. The net was trained by making use of the manual segmentation of the database, that is no embedded training was applied here (although a Viterbi-like embedded training scheme is known to be applicable to hybrid models [1]).

Two different model configurations were examined in the experiments. In our shorthand notation, the formula evaluated for each segment is

$$\frac{P_U^{\alpha_U} \cdot P_S^{\alpha_S} \cdot P_D^{\alpha_D} \cdot I}{P(u_i)}. \tag{7}$$

In the first model configuration P_U is calculated using the product rule (Eq. (3)), P_S is obtained from Eq. (5), and the duration model P_D and insertion penalty I will be varied from experiment to experiment. Both the α_U and α_S exponents will be set to 1. Notice that in this case P_S is the same as the denominator of P_U so they cancel out. Moreover, with the $P(u_i)$ in the denominator the exponent of $P(u_i)$ will become $d(i)$, the number of frames in the segment. So in practical terms what is left is the product of the frame-based probabilities, with one division by the class priors per frame. This means that this configuration is equivalent to the conventional HMM/ANN model – apart from, of course, the duration component that we are going to experiment with.

In the second configuration P_U is calculated using the averaging rule (Eq. (4)), P_S is obtained from Eq. (5), and the duration model P_D and insertion penalty I will again be varied. α_U will be set to 1, but α_S in this case will be set to 0.1, which was found to be optimal earlier [9]. We will refer to this configuration as the averaging hybrid model.

Table 1. Word error rates for various exponential model settings.

Duration Model	Model Configuration	
	Conventional	Averaging
No duration model	18.10%	34.11%
No dur. model, min.dur=4	6.04%	12.06%
Shared exponential	15.32%	10.21%
Shared exp., min.dur=4	6.96%	5.10%
Exponential	13.00%	10.21%
Exponential, min.dur=4	7.20%	9.28%

Table 2. Word error rates (WER) after fine-tuning α_D and I.

Duration Model	Conventional Hybrid			Averaging Hybrid		
	α_D	I	WER	α_D	I	WER
No duration model	–	1.5117	**5.80%**	–	0.2542	**4.87%**
Shared exp. dur. mod.	0.2667	2.0360	**5.80%**	0.9343	0.8061	**4.87%**
Exponential dur. mod.	0.3406	3.8044	**5.80%**	0.5603	1.0981	**4.87%**
Gamma duration model	0.3823	3.3117	**5.10%**	0.3069	0.4158	**3.94%**

5   Results and Discussion

In the first series of experiments we were interested in finding out how the minimum duration restriction and/or sharing a common exponential base influences the performance of the exponential duration model. In these experiments the α_D exponent and the insertion penalty I were always set to 1. Table 1 summarizes the results. From the scores it is quite apparent that the minimum duration constraint significantly improves the recognition performance (not to mention that it also dramatically decreases the run time). As regards the other question, it was surprising to see that both exponential models can be detrimental to the recognition score, and the model using the same fixed value performed better than the phone-specifically tuned one. But this was probably due to an improper choice of α_D and I (the averaging hybrid turned out to be especially sensitive to these). So the optimization of these parameters was a reasonable next step.

In the second set of experiments the weight factor α_D and insertion penalty I were fine-tuned (with the minimum duration restriction always being turned on). The optimal parameter values were found by a global optimization algorithm called SNOBFIT [5]. The resulting values along with the recognition scores are shown in Table 2. The results apparently underpin the belief that the exponential duration model brings no advantage over using no duration model at all (and, according to Table 1, with an improperly chosen exponent it can be even detrimental!). Furthermore, the practice of using one shared exponential base value instead of phone-specific ones also proved reasonable, as these models did not differ in performance. These findings seem independent of the model configuration used – conventional or averaging. In both cases only the gamma duration model was better than not applying a duration model at all. It achieved a 12-20% relative improvement in the word error rate, depending on the system configuration.

6   Conclusions

This paper investigated the feasibility of applying sophisticated duration models – in our case the gamma distribution within the framework of HMM/ANN hybrids. In addition, we were also curious to see whether the exponential duration model is indeed ineffective. Two kinds of hybrid model configurations were examined in the test, the conventional one and the recently proposed "averaging hybrid". Independent of the configuration used, we found that the exponential duration model had no detectable influence on the recognition performance. Hence the practice of replacing the phone-based self-transition probabilities by a quasi-ad hoc constant is indeed harmless – as this simplified exponential duration model is just as ineffective as the original one. On the contrary, we found that imposing a minimum duration constraint on the phonetic segments not only speeds up the decoding process, but also significantly improves the results. The other thing that yielded an improvement was the gamma duration model. Thus, altogether we are justified in saying that the exponential duration model inherent to HMM is a really poor one, and that replacing it with just a slightly more complicated model can certainly bring a modest improvement to the error rate.

Finally, let us remark that we did not discuss the differences between the conventional and the averaging hybrids because we were more interested in the duration models. But the scores clearly show the superiority of the averaging hybrid – at least, on this corpus. Moreover, during the experiments we found that the averaging model is much more tunable so, hopefully, with the introduction of new components it can be more easily improved. This is the direction we plan to take in the near future.

References

1. Bourlard, H. A., Morgan, N.: Connectionist Speech Recognition – A Hybrid Approach. Kluwer Academic (1994)
2. Bourlard, H., Hermansky, H., Morgan, N.: Towards Increasing Speech Recognition Error Rates. Speech Communication, Vol. 18., pp. 205-231, 1996.
3. Hagen, A., Morris, A.: Recent advances in the multi-stream HMM/ANN hybrid approach to noise robust ASR. Computer Speech and Language, Vol. 19., pp. 3-30. 2005.
4. Huang, X. D., Acero, A., Hon, H-W.: Spoken Language Processing. Prentice Hall, 2001.
5. Huyer, W., Neumaier, A.: SNOBFIT - Stable Noisy Optimization by Branch and Fit. Submitted for Publication
6. Morris, A. C., Payne, S., Bourlard, H.: Low Cost Duration Modelling for Noise Robust Speech Recognition. Proc. ICSLP' 2002, pp. 1025-1028.
7. Pylkönnen, J., Kurimo, M.: Duration Modeling Techniques for Continuous Speech Recognition. Proc. ICSLP' 2004, pp. 385-388.
8. Tax, D. M. J., van Breukelen, M., Duin, R. P. W., Kittler, J.: Combining multiple classifiers by averaging or by multiplying? Pattern Recognition Vol. 33., pp. 1475-1485, 2000.
9. Tóth, L., Kocsor, A.: Lessons from a Segment-Based Interpretation of HMM/ANN Hybrids. Submitted to Speech Communication
10. Vicsi, K, Tóth, L., Kocsor, A., Csirik, J.: MTBA – A Hungarian Telephone Speech Database. Híradástechnika, Vol. LVII, No. 8 (2002) 35- 43 (in Hungarian)
11. Young, S. et al.: The HMM Toolkit (HTK) – software and manual. http://htk.eng.cam.ac.uk
12. NIST/SEMATECH e-Handbook of Stat. Methods, http://www.itl.nist.gov/div898/handbook/

Mapping the Speech Signal onto Electromagnetic Articulography Trajectories Using Support Vector Regression

Asterios Toutios and Konstantinos Margaritis

Parallel and Distributed Processing Laboratory, Department of Applied Informatics
University of Macedonia, Thessaloniki, Greece
{toutios,kmarg}@uom.gr

Abstract. We report work on the mapping between the speech signal and articulatory trajectories from the MOCHA database. Contrasting previous works that used Neural Networks for the same task, we employ Support Vector Regression as our main tool, and Principal Component Analysis as an auxiliary one. Our results are comparable, even though, due to training time considerations we use only a small portion of the available data.

1   Introduction

The acoustic-to-articulatory mapping [1, 2], also termed acoustic-to-articulatory inversion of speech, is a special speech processing related problem that has attracted the attention of several researchers for many years now. It refers to the estimation of articulatory (speech production related) information using solely the speech signal as an input source. A succesful solution could find numerous applications, such as helping individuals with speech and hearing disorders by providing visual feedback, very low bit-rate speech coding and the possibility of improved automatic speech recognition.

In the past, the articulatory features used in such a context were mostly inferred by the corresponding acoustic data using vocal-tract models, synthesis models, or linguisting rules. But recent technologies have made it possible to record actual articulator movements in parallel with speech acoustics in a minimally invasive way. This "real" human data is arguably preferable to older techniques, where additional complications may be imposed by intrinsic flaws of the models themselves.

One of the forementioned technologies is the Electromagnetic Misdagittal Articulography (EMMA) or Electromagnetic Articulography (EMA). Roughly speaking, for the aquisition of EMA data, sensor coils are attached to the human subject, on specific places on the lips, the teeth, the jaw, and the soft palate (velum). Then the human subject wears a special helmet that produces an alternating magnetic field that records the position of the coils at end points of small fixed-size time intervals. The outcomes are trajectories that illustrate the movement of the coils. Usually, there are two trajectories for each coil, one for the movement in the front-back direction of the head, and one for the top-bottom direction.

In this paper we follow Richmond's work [1], who proposed a quite succesful mapping of the speech signal to EMA data, using Neural Networks (Multilayer Perceprtons and Mixture Density Networks). We study an alternative –Machine Learning– approach

V. Matoušek et al. (Eds.): TSD 2005, LNAI 3658, pp. 318–325, 2005.

using Support Vector Regression, a more recent and very promising method. We also employ, as part of our experimentation, the techinque of Principal Component Analysis, as a means to account for the interrelationships among the EMA trajectories. We use the same dataset as Richmond (though we finally arrive at a significantly smaller training set), namely the fsew0 speaker data from the MOCHA dabase.

2 The MOCHA Database

The MOCHA (Multi-Channel Articulatory) [3] database is evolving in a purpose built studio at the Edinburgh Speech Production Facility at Queen Margaret University College.

During speech, four data streams are recorded concurrently straight to a computer: the acoustic waveform, sampled at 16kHz with 16 bit precision, together with laryngograph, electropalatograph and electromagnetic articulograph data. The articulatory channels include EMA sensors directly attached to the upper and lower lips, lower incisor (jaw), tongue tip (5-10mm from the tip), tongue blade (approximately 2-3cm posterior to the tongue tip sensor), tongue dorsum (approximately 2-3cm posterior from the tongue blade sensor), and soft palate. Two channels for every sensor are recorded at 500Hz: the positioning on the x-axis (front-back direction) and on the y-axis (top-bottom direction).

The speakers are recorded reading a set of 460 British TIMIT sentences. These short sentences are designed to provide phonetically diverse material and capture with good coverage the connected speech processes in English. All waveforms are labelled at the phonemic level.

The final release of the MOCHA database will feature up to 40 speakers with a variety of regional accents. At the time of writing this paper two speakers are available. For the experiments herein, the acoustic waveform and EMA data, as well as the phonemic labels for the fsew0 speaker, a female speaker with a Southern English accent, are used.

3 Support Vector Regression

The ϵ-SVR algorithm [4] is a generalization of the better known Support Vector Classification algorithm [5] to the regression case. Given n training vectors $\mathbf{x_i}$ and a vector $y \in R^n$ such that $y_i \in R$, we want to find an estimate for the fuction $y = f(\mathbf{x})$ which is optimal from a Structural Risk Minimization viewpoint. According to ϵ-SVR, this estimate is:

$$f(\mathbf{x}) = \sum_{i=1}^{n}(a_i^* - a_i)k(\mathbf{x_i}, \mathbf{x}) + b, \qquad (1)$$

where the coefficients a_i and a_i^* are the solution of the quadratic problem

maximize

$$W(\mathbf{a}, \mathbf{a}^*) = -\epsilon\sum_{i=1}^{n}(a_i^* + a_i) + \sum_{i=1}^{n}(a_i^* - a_i)y_i - \frac{1}{2}\sum_{i,j=1}^{n}(a_i^* - a_i)(a_j^* - a_j)k(\mathbf{x_i x_j})$$

subject to $0 \leq a_i, a_i^* \leq C, i = 1, \ldots, n$, and $\sum_{i=1}^{n}(a_i^* - a_i) = 0.$ \qquad (2)

$C > 0$ and $\epsilon \geq 0$ are parameters chosen by the user. The "penalty parameter" C may be as high as infinity, while usual values for ϵ are 0.1 or 0.001.

The "kernel" $k(x_i x_j)$ is a special function which serves to convert the data into a higher-dimensional space in order to account for non-linearities in the estimate function. A commonly used kernel is the Radial Basis Function (RBF) kernel:

$$k(\mathbf{x}, \mathbf{y}) = \exp(-\gamma \parallel \mathbf{x} - \mathbf{y} \parallel^2), \tag{3}$$

where the γ parameter is selected by the user.

4   Principal Component Analysis

PCA [2] is a transform that chooses a new coordinate system for a data set such that the greatest variance by any projection of the data set comes to lie on the first axis, the second greatest variance on the second axis, and so on. The new axes are called the *principal components*. PCA is commonly used used for reducing dimensionality in a data set while retaining those characteristics of the dataset that contribute most to its variance by eliminating the later principal components.

The direction $\mathbf{w}_1$ of the first principal component is defined by

$$\mathbf{w}_1 = \arg \max_{\|w\|=1} E\{(\mathbf{w}^T\mathbf{x})^2\} \tag{4}$$

where $\mathbf{w}_1$ is of the same dimension as the data vectors $\mathbf{x}$. Having determined the direction of the first $k - 1$ principal components, the direction of the kth component is:

$$\mathbf{w_k} = \arg \max_{\|w\|=1} E\{\mathbf{w}^T(\mathbf{x} - \sum_{i=1}^{k-1} \mathbf{w}_i\mathbf{w}_i^T\mathbf{x})^2\}. \tag{5}$$

In practice, the computation of the $\mathbf{w}_i$ can be simply accomplished using the sample covariance matrix $E\{\mathbf{x}\mathbf{x}^T\} = \mathbf{C}$. The $\mathbf{w}_i$ are then the eigenvectors of $\mathbf{C}$ that correspond to the largest eigenvalues of $\mathbf{C}$.

5   Data Processing

The MOCHA database includes 460 utterances of the fsew0 speaker. In order to render these data into input-output pairs suitable for function estimation, we process them as follows.

First, based on the label files we omit silent parts from the beginning and end of the utterances. During silent stretches the articulators may possibly take any configuration, something that could pose serious difficulties to our task.

Next, we perform a standard Mel Frequency Spectral Analysis [6] on the acoustic signal with the VOICEBOX Toolkit [7], using a window of 16ms (256 points) with a shift of 5ms. We use 30 filterbanks and calculate the first 13 Mel Frequency Cepstral Coefficients. Then, we normalize them in order have zero mean and unity standard deviation.

In order to account for the dynamic properties of the speech signal and cope with the temporal extent of our problem, we just use a commonplace in the speech processing field *spatial metaphor for time*. That is, we construct input vectors spanning over a large number of acoustic frames. Based on some previous small-scale experiments of ours, we construct input vectors consisting of the MFCCs of 17 frames: the frame in question, plus the 8 previous ones, plus the 8 next ones.

The steps taken to process the EMA data are similar to those described by Richmond. First, the EMA data are resampled to match the frameshift of the acoustic coefficients (5ms). At the same time, they are smoothed, using a moving average window of 40ms so that recording noise is eliminated (after all, it is known that EMA trajectories vary relatively slowly with time).

The mean values of the EMA trajectories calculated for every utterance vary considerably during the recording process. There are two kinds of variation: rapid changes, due to the phonemic content of each utterance, and slowly moving trends, mainly due to the fact that te subject's articulation adapts in certain ways during the recording session. It is beneficial to remove from the EMA data the second type of variation, while keeping the first. Thus, we calculate the means, low-pass filter them, and subtract those filtered means from the EMA data. (See Figure 1 for an explanation).

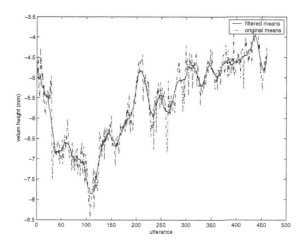

Fig. 1. Mean values of the "velum height" (v_y) channel across the utterances in the recording session. The dashed line shows the real means and the solid line their filtered version which is actually used for normalization.

Finally, we scale the EMA data by four times their standard deviation (across the whole corpus), so that they roughly lie in the interval $(-1, 1)$, something crucial for SVR training.

Thus, we end up with training examples with a 221-dimensional (17×13) real-valued vector as input and a 14-dimensional real-valued vector as output. We split our data into two big halves: the even-numbered utterances constitute a "big training set", and the odd-numbered ones a "big test set". Each one has more than 100.000 examples.

But, since SVR training is a relatively slow process, using the whole "big training set" for training would merely be out of the question. We would like a reduced training set, that is somehow "representative" of the whole corpus. Knowing (from the label files) the phoneme that each of our "big training set" examples corresponds to, we randomly select 200 examples "belonging" to every phoneme. With 44 phonemes in the database, we end up with 8800 training examples.

Finally, for our test set, we simply use 10 utterances spanning across our whole "big test set".

6   SVR Training and Results

The ϵ-SVR algorithm, as described, works for only one output. It does not work "as is" for multiple outputs. Thus, we have to split our problem into 14 distinct (and assumably independent) function estimation problems, considering each time a different EMA trajectory as output.

We use the RBF kernel with $\gamma = 0.0045$ and select $C = 1$, $\epsilon = 0.1$, based on heuristics found in [8], employing the LibSVM software [9] for our experiments. We, finally, virtually "combine" the 14 estimators into one "system".

For evaluating the performance of our system we use two measures. The first one is the RMS error which is an indication of the overall "distance" between two trajectories. It is calculated as:

$$E_{RMS} = \sqrt{\frac{1}{N} \sum_{i=1}^{N} (o_i - t_i)^2} \tag{6}$$

where N is the number of input-output vector pairs, in the test set, o_i is the estimated value for the articulator channel output, and t_i is the real value. The values are rescaled back to the original domain measurement in millimeters.

The second measure is the correlation score, which is an indication of similarity of shape and synchrony of two trajectories. It is calculated by dividing their covariance by the product of their variances:

$$r = \frac{\sum_i (o_i - \bar{o})(t_i - \bar{t})}{\sqrt{\sum_i (o_i - \bar{o})^2 \sum_i (t_i - \bar{t})^2}} \tag{7}$$

where $\bar{o}$ and $\bar{t}$ are the mean channel value for the estimated and real articulator position respectively.

The results of this first experiment are presented in Table 1 and Figure 2.

As a second experiment, and as an attempt to account for the interrelationships between the EMA trajectories we add PCA to the previous experimental context. We know that some pairs of trajectories are highly correlated. By PCA, we move to a new output space where the new trajectories are uncorrelated among each other.

Most of the times PCA is used for data reduction, by "cutting off" components that correspond to small eigenvalues. This is not our case. We just want to render our data into an uncorrelated form, so we keep all 14 Principal Components. We perform SVR, with the exact same parameters as previously, in this new output space and then, at testing, revert back to our original one. Table 2 shows the results of this experiment.

Table 1. Performance of the System of Estimators. (First experiment, without PCA).

Articulator	RMS Error (mm)	Correlation
lower incisor x	1.054	0.479
lower incisor y	1.217	0.807
upper lip x	0.999	0.565
upper lip y	1.327	0.548
lower lip x	1.403	0.499
lower lip y	2.375	0.803
tongue tip x	2.534	0.806
tongue tip y	2.750	0.809
tongue body x	2.339	0.788
tongue body y	2.248	0.814
tongue dorsum x	2.262	0.743
tongue dorsum y	2.573	0.671
velum x	0.455	0.690
velum y	0.397	0.726

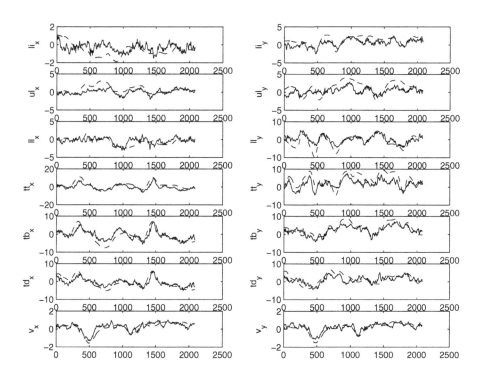

Fig. 2. Real (dashed lines) and estimated (solid lines) articulatory trajectories of fsew0 uttering the phrase "Clear pronunciation is appreciated.". The first column is the projection of the articulator's movement on the x axis and the second on the y axis. From top to bottom: lower incisor (jaw), upper lip, lower lip, tongue tip, tongue dorsum, tongue blade and velum.

Table 2. Performance of the System of Estimators (Second Experiment, with PCA).

Articulator	RMS Error (mm)	Correlation
lower incisor x	1.053	0.481
lower incisor y	1.200	0.812
upper lip x	1.006	0.559
upper lip y	1.327	0.548
lower lip x	1.329	0.550
lower lip y	2.363	0.805
tongue tip x	2.556	0.802
tongue tip y	2.766	0.807
tongue body x	2.353	0.785
tongue body y	2.226	0.818
tongue dorsum x	2.271	0.740
tongue dorsum y	2.557	0.675
velum x	0.452	0.693
velum y	0.399	0.723

7   Conclusion

We applied Support Vector Regression to the task of mapping the acoustic speech signal onto EMA trajectories. Our results were comparable to those found in the literature, even though we used a (selected by a rather ad-hoc procedure) small subset of the data available to us. We extended our method by employing Principal Component Analysis, in order to account for the interrelationships inherent among the trajectories, with a slight increase in performance.

In order to improve further our results we should try to better exploit the vast amount of data in the MOCHA database. This may be done in one of two ways, the first one being to use more training data. Training time is always an issue, but recent findings in the machine learning field, such as Cross-Training [10], seem quite promising in the direction of speeding up things. One second way is to use a more formal way, perhaps by applying a clustering technique to our input space, in order to select training examples.

Finally, PCA lead to only a slight increase in performance. We expected better. It may be the case that other data transformations, such as Independent Component Analysis [11], should also be considered.

References

1. Richmond, K.: Estimating Articulatory Parameters from the Speech Signal. PhD thesis, The Center for Speech Technology Research, Edinburgh, (2002).
2. Carreira-Perpiñán, M.A.: Continuous Latent Variable Models for Dimensionality Reduction and Sequential Data Reconstruction. PhD thesis, University of Sheffield, UK (2001)
3. Wrench, A.A., Hardcastle, W.J.: A multichannel articulatory database and its application for automatic speech recognition. In: 5th Seminar on Speech Production: Models and Data, Kloster Seeon, Bavaria (2000) 305–308
4. Smola, A., Schölkopf, B.: A tutorial on support vector regression. Statistics and Computing 14 (2004) 199–222

5. Vapnik, V.: Statistical Learning Theory. Wiley, New York (1998)
6. Davis, S.B., Mermelstein, P.: Comparison of parametric representations for monosyllabic word recognition in continuously spoken sentences. In Waibel, A., Lee, K.F., eds.: Readings in speech recognition. Morgan Kaufmann Publishers Inc. (1990) 65–74
7. Brooks, M.: (The VOICEBOX toolkit) Software vailable at http://www.ee.ic.ac.uk/hp/staff/dmb/voicebox/voicebox.html.
8. Weston, J., Gretton, A., Elisseeff, A.: SVM practical session (how to get good results without cheating). (Machine Learning Summer School 2003, Tuebingen, Germany.)
9. Chang, C.C., Lin, C.J.: LIBSVM: a library for support vector machines. (2001) Software available at http://www.csie.ntu.edu.tw/~cjlin/libsvm.
10. Bakir, G., Bottou, L., Weston, J.: Breaking SVM complexity with cross training. In: 18th Annual Conference on Neural Information Processing Systems, NIPS-2004. (2004)
11. Hyvärinen, A., Oja, E.: Independent component analysis: Algorithms and applications. Neural Networks 13 (2000) 411–430

Automatic Transcription of Numerals in Inflectional Languages*

Jan Zelinka, Jakub Kanis, and Luděk Müller

University of West Bohemia, Department of Cybernetics
Univerzitní 8, 306 14 Plzeň, Czech Republic
{zelinka,kanis,muller}@kky.zcu.cz

Abstract. In this paper we describe the part of the text preprocessing module in our text-to-speech synthesis system which converts numerals written as figures into a readable full-length form, which could be processed by a phonetic transcription module. The numerals conversion is a significant issue in inflectional language as Czech, Russian or Slovak because morphological and semantic information is necessary to make the conversion unambiguous. In the paper three part-of-speech tagging methods are compared. Furthermore, a method reducing the tagset to increase the numerals conversion accuracy is presented in the paper.

1 Introduction

Text-to-speech (TTS) synthesis is a challenging task especially when miscellaneous texts as SMSs, emails, articles or another complex text has to be read. Even if the text which has to be processed has relatively a simple form the text preprocessing module is an indispensable part of the TTS system. One of the most important problems is how to process acronyms, numerals, abbreviation, and other parts of text which are not written in their full text format. The set of letter-to-sound rules or another simple phonetic transcription system cannot cope with them because the phonetic transcription does not deal with morphology, syntax, and meaning. The text preprocessing module exploits the necessary morphological information and converts the text into the form which could be processed by the phonetic transcription module [1]. In this work we have concentrated on the correct numerals pronunciation. The described part of the text preprocessing module is going to be applied in the Czech TTS system [2]. Figure 1 shows the scheme of the Czech TTS system.

There are a lot of numerals written as figures in a conventional text. Conversion of this text to their textual version in languages like English is not a big issue. However, in languages as Czech, Polish, Russian or Slovak the numerals to words conversion is not so trivial task. Word declension is the reason why the figures conversion is not unambiguous. In spite of we restrict the problem to the ordinal numerals in this article, the described method can be used for other numeral types. The applicability of the method on every inflectional language was one of our most important aims.

---

* Support for this work was provided by the Ministry of Education of the Czech Republic (MŠMT LC536).

V. Matoušek et al. (Eds.): TSD 2005, LNAI 3658, pp. 326–333, 2005.

There are miscellaneous types of numerals in a text: cardinal numerals, ordinal numerals, nominal numerals, roman numerals, fractions, ratios, percentage, time (hour, minute, second), date (day, month), year, telephone number, address (post number, street number ...), decimal number etc. There are specific problems with each mentioned numeral type. Therefore, the detection and classification of the numeral type is an important issue of text processing.

There are two forms of Czech ordinal numerals written as figures. The first form is a sequence of figures finished by a period. The second form is a sequence of figures finished by a dash and a suffix part. We consider only the first form because it is much frequent although the second form is admissible too and common in other languages.

To detect the ordinal number by finding its accompanying period is an easy task, only in the end of a sentence, which is also finished by a period, this approach fails because the numeral in the end of sentence can be also the cardinal numeral. To distinguish the cardinal numeral from the ordinal one in the end of sentence, one needs to deal with the meaning of the sentence, generally.

Also several of other numeral types can have the first ordinal numerals form. The most important one is a date. The day and month in a date are often written as two ordinal numerals. Unfortunately, their grammatical cases are different from the grammatical case of ordinal numerals written in formally identical form as the given date. However, we have to remark that the occurrence of ordinal numerals sequence in the text is very improbable.

Our approach of changing numerals to words is based on the presumption that the morphological tag of a numeral is sufficient information to convert the numerals into words exactly and unambiguously. Czech morphological tags surely fulfill this presumption. Another problem is that the tag contains much other information irrelevant to our task. Thus, reducing tagset may contribute to the numerals conversion accuracy.

This section has introduced the general numerals conversion problem. The training and test data are described in Section 2. Section 3 deals with the task how to obtain the necessary morphological information. Section 4 is devoted to the tagset reduction problem. Section 5 describes conversion of tagged numerals. The next section depicts the experiments and evaluations of the presented method.

2 Used Corpus and Czech Morphological System

We used the Prague Dependency Treebank (PDT) 1.0 to create our training, development, test, and evaluation test data. The whole PDT has a three-level structure [3]. The first level is morphological, the second analytical, and the last one is a tecto-grammatical level. We exploit only the full morphological annotation, i.e. the lowest level of PDT. Moreover, only the part-of-speech (POS) tagging is of our interest. The morphological tag is a combination of labels of individual morphological categories.

The PDT morphological tag is a string of 15 characters [4]. The characters represent the following morphological categories: part of speech, detailed part of speech, gender, number, case, possessor's gender, possessor's number, person, tense, degree of comparison, negation, voice, reserve 1, reserve 2, and variant/style.

In PDT 1.0 29,561 sentences (469,652 tokens) are reserved as the training data (for training a tagger), 8,244 (129,574 tokens) sentences are reserved as development test data, and 8,046 (124,957 tokens) sentences are reserved as evaluation test data. For the development tests and the evaluation tests we selected only sentences that included at least one ordinal numeral because other sentences are not relevant to our task.

3 Tagging

First, we need to assign a correct morphological tag to each numeral. Since not only this part of the text preprocessing module uses the morphologically processed text, all words are tagged. Only the percentage of the correctly tagged numerals instead of usual tagging accuracy is used as the tagger quality measure because it better characterizes the success of numerals classification. The PDT 1.0 does not explicitly contain any information to compute the numerals conversion accuracy but the percentage of correctly tagged numerals is the lower estimation of this accuracy.

We suppose that the end of each sentence is correctly detected. The ends were determined by hand in the training and the test data but during operation of our TTS system this detection is provided by an algorithm based on artificial neural network. The algorithm is described and evaluated in [5].

Before tagging we have replaced each numeral in the training and test text with a special symbol. This operation merges numerals into meaningful categories but above all it prevents perceiving a numerals unseen in the training data as an out-of-vocabulary word. This increases the tagging accuracy, and especially the numerals tagging accuracy. This fact indicates that similar replacing could be applied in other tasks. After tagging the special symbol is converted back into the original numeral.

Three types of taggers were investigated. The first tagger is the Hidden Markov Model (HMM) tagger. The HMM tagger uses a sentence generating model which is a stochastic discrete system with final number of states. We used trigram based HMM tagger. The most probably sequence of tags are computed trough the Viterbi algorithm. A lexicon based morphological analyzer was applied before HMM tagging to help the tagger to reduce the number of all possible tags.

The second tagger we have used was the transformation based tagger (TBT). TBT is constructed by means of transformation based error driven learning. In this tagger an ordered set of rules is applied to the initial tag. The learning process together with other details is described in [6]. We have used the free transformation based learning toolkit – fnTBL for construction of the TBT. The link devoted to the fnTBL is in [7]. Details are shown in [8] and [9].

The third tagger is the memory based tagger (MBT). The tagger takes advantage of the training set of examples and uses the IGTrees to compress the memory demands [10]. The MBT (we have used free available MBT 2.0) is constructed by force of supervised, inductive learning from examples [10].

Besides the accuracy another practical aim is low computation time and memory demands. These requirements are crucial in real-time text preprocessing especially when a TTS system is implemented in a mobile phone or in another small device like PDA. The TBT satisfies the both requirements under the condition that it is not enormously overtrained. The time demands of the HMM tagger may be reduced by much more sophisticated morphological analyzer than the morphological analyzer based on lexicon.

4   Tagset Reduction

Unfortunately, there are a lot of specific tagging problems owing to a high number of morphological categories which are included in a tag. It complicates the tagger training. A high percentage of occurring out-of-vocabulary words is another complication of tagging in inflectional language. Both phenomena decrease the accuracy much more than languages such as English. The paper [11] compares part-of-speech (POS) tagging of English with POS tagging of inflectional languages.

The whole morphological tag of a numeral contains also information which is not necessary for correct numeral conversion. Omitting the redundant information makes the tagging more robust and consequently increases the tagging accuracy.

This omitting is implemented as a tagset reduction. The tagset is a set of all tags. The tagset reduction may depend on the numeral paradigm. The optimal tagset reduction should keep the information necessary for numerals conversion whilst maximizes the tagging accuracy.

The easiest and straightforward tagset reduction method is to lower the length of each tag by omitting tag characters which represent irrelevant morphological categories. We keep only characters which represent the detailed part of speech, gender, number, and case. The same reduction is accomplished for the other tags (i.e. other than numeral tags).

The second designed way of tagset reduction is merging all such numeral tags whose numerals have the same form after the conversion. This merging depends on the numeral paradigm. The numeral paradigm can be determined from the number which the numeral represents. This second way of tagset reduction reduces only the numeral tags and could be applied with or without using the first tagset reduction method.

In Section 6 the contribution of both tagset reduction methods is verified on the test data. However, we should be conscious of the fact that the methods lead only to a suboptimal tagset reduction.

5   Tagged Numerals Conversion

While the numeral is correctly tagged, it can be converted independently of its context. Numerals form an open set and hence its number is potentially infinite and the usage of a dictionary is not practicable owing to its infinite size for the conversion.

We cope with this problem in the following way. Because the text form of each Czech numeral is assembled from elementary numeral words, the number of possible elements is usually very small. The elements are simply given by the decimal number system. Therefore, first we decompose the input numeral into a list of its elements and then let tag each element separately. This dramatically decreases the required size of the dictionary because the dictionary now contains only the elements and its conversion. The example below illustrates the process of the decomposition.

English: 328/JJ → 300/JJ 20/JJ 8/JJ → three hundred twenty eighth
Czech: 328/rFS1 → 300/ rFS1 20/ rFS1 8/ rFS1 → třístá dvacátá osmá

In Czech the numbers can be alternatively expressed in two different ways if the last two figures formed a number higher or equal to 21 and which is indivisible by 10.

21. / rFS1 → dvacátá první × jednadvacátá

The second way is often used in spontaneous speech. This has to be respect in language models for speech recognition but in our case of TTS we need to obtain rather an unambiguous result. That is why we have chosen only one alternative. The first one was chosen because it seems to be simpler and more regular then the second one.

Every numeral belongs to its paradigm, which rules the mode of its declension. The declension of ordinal numerals is the same as the declension of adjectives. There are only two paradigms for the Czech ordinal numerals (mladý, jarní). These paradigms determine two modes of tags merging. Numerals, their word transcriptions (lemmas) and corresponding paradigms are shown in the Table 1.

Table 1. Table of number elements and its word equivalents.

Numeral	Lemma	Paradigm
0.	nultý	mladý
1.	první	jarní
2.	druhý	mladý
...	...	...
9.	devátý	mladý
10.	desátý	mladý
...	...	...

After the decomposition each numeral is converted according to its tag into a sequence of words with usage of the dictionary and the set of derivation rules. The dictionary has the form of Table 1 and includes all numerals which appear after the decomposition, its lemma, and its paradigm. Subsequently, the set of derivation rules is used to convert the lemma into the proper form according to all morphological categories (e.g. grammatical case) given by the tag. The derivation rules are of the following form: If the tag is T and the paradigm is P, then the string A which is the end of the lemma is replaced by the string B. Formally:

$$T, P \rightarrow -A, B.$$

Because the number of rules is small, the set of rules had been written by a human expert. Consequently, if the tag is correct, the resultant conversion of the numeral accompanied by its tag is exact and unambiguous.

6   Experiments and Results

All three tagging methods mentioned above were tested without the tagset reduction, with the first presented reduction method, and with the combination of the both described reduction methods. Each tested tagset reduction does not reduce the information needful for the numeral conversion. The tagset reduction was performed before either tagging or after tagging and then the results of these two approaches were compared. Our both tagset reduction methods permit the both techniques.

In the first experiment the substitution of each numeral by a special symbol (see Section 3) and the first method of tag reducing was considered. The results in the first and the second columns were obtained without the substitution while the third and the fourth one were obtained with using it. Furthermore, the first and the third columns are for the methods which do not provide the tag character omitting, whilst the second and the fourth columns include the results obtained by characters omitting.

Table 2. The results of the first experiment.

Tagger	Accuracy 1 [%]	Accuracy 2 [%]	Accuracy 3 [%]	Accuracy 4 [%]
HMM	70.43	69.65	73.54	74.71
TBT	46.30	46.30	15.17	66.14
MBT	51.33	52.11	57.59	58.37

In the second table the results of the experiment which tries to evaluate the second proposed tagset reduction are presented. The first column is computed without the tagset reduction whereas the second column was obtained using the second tagset reduction method. The first tagset reduction method and numerals replacing were always used.

Table 3. The results of the second experiment.

Tagger	Accuracy 1 [%]	Accuracy 2 [%]
HMM	89.11	80,16
TBT	79.38	76.26
MBT	78.60	73.15

The best tagging for the numerals conversion is the one which leads to the highest tagger accuracy. This is the case of the HMM tagger. The first tagset reduction represents only omitting the irrelevant characters. The second tagset reduction increases accuracy too but we found that more beneficial approach is to carry out it after the tagging. Than the resulting accuracy computed on the evaluation test data for the winning HMM tagger exceeded 90 %:

$$Accuracy = 90.48\%.$$

The last experiment was done to demonstrate the text preprocessing module ability to convert numerals in common or even in much less common sentences. The results are represented as a screen-shot taken from our text preprocessing demonstration program.

7   Conclusion and Future Work

The experiment results show that the presented automatic numeral conversion method is applicable in TTS systems. The method could be painlessly used for any inflectional

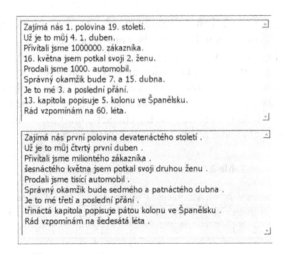

Fig. 1. A screen-shot from the text preprocessing demonstration program.

language. The method efficiency primarily depends on precision of the used tagger. Therefore, in the future we will try to apply a more accurate tagging method and simultaneously we will try to find a method which can be applied in text preprocessing system for small devices like mobile phone.

Nowadays, we are extending the system to process all numeral type conversion. Moreover, this method could processe not only numerals. In the future, we want to equip the system with text preprocessing for acronyms conversion, missing diacritics insertion or typos correction. Our next aim is also developing text processing module for our Slovak TTS system [12].

References

1. Van den Bosh, A.: Automatic Phonetic Transcription of Words Based on Sparse Data. In: Workshop Notes of the ECML/MLnet Workshop on Empirical Learning of Natural Language Processing Tasks, Prague, Czech Republic (1997), 61-70.
2. Matoušek, J., and Psutka: ARTIC: a New Czech Text-to-Speech System Using Statistical Approach to Speech Segment Database Construction. In: Proceedings of ICSLP2000, vol. IV. Beijing (2000), 612-615.
3. Böhmová, A., Hajič, J., Hajičová, E., Hladká, B.: The Prague Dependency Treebank: Three-Level Annotation Scenario. In: A. Abeillé, editor, Treebanks: Building and Using Syntactically Annotated Corpora. Kluwer Academic Publishers (2001).
4. Hana, J., Hanová, H., Hajič, J., Hladká B., Jeřábek, E.: Manual for Morphological Annotation - Instructions for Annotators. -In: CKL Technical Report TR-2002-14, Charles University, Czech Republic (2002).
5. Romportl J., Tihelka D., Matoušek J.: Sentence Boundary Detection in Czech TTS System Using Neural Networks. In: Proceedings of the Seventh International Symposium on Signal Processing and its Applications. Paris, France, (2003), 247-250.
6. Brill, E.: Transformation-Based Error-Driven Learning and Natural Language Processing: A Case Study in Part-of-Speech Tagging. In: Computational Linguistics (1995), 247-250.

7. Florian, R.: http://nlp.cs.jhu.edu/ rflorian/fntbl.
8. Florian, G., Ngai.: Transformation-Based Learning in the fast lane. In: Proceedings of North America ACL-2001, (2001).
9. Florian, R., Ngai, G.: Fast Transformation-Based Learning Toolkit. Technical Report.
10. Daelemans, W., Zavrel, J., Berck, P., Gillis, S.: A Memory-Based Part of Speech Tagger-Generator. In: Proceedings of the 4th Workshop on Very Large Corpora, (1996).
11. Hajič, J.: Morphological Tagging: Data vs. Dictionaries. In: Proceedings of the 6th Applied Natural Language Processing and the 1st NAACL Conference, Seattle, Washington, (2000), 94-101.
12. Matoušek J., Tihelka D.: Slovak Text-to-Speech Synthesis in ARTIC System. In: Proceedings of 7th International Conference on Text, Speech and Dialogue, TSD 2004. Springer-Verlag, Berlin (2004) , 155-162.

Experimental Evaluation of Tree-Based Algorithms for Intonational Breaks Representation

Panagiotis Zervas[1], Gerasimos Xydas[2], Nikolaos Fakotakis[1],
George Kokkinakis[1], and Georgios Kouroupetroglou[2]

[1] Electrical and Computer Engineering Dept., University of Patras, Greece
{pzervas,fakotaki,gkokkin}@wcl.ee.upatras.gr
[2] Department of Informatics and Telecommunications, University of Athens, Greece
{gxydas,koupe}@di.uoa.gr

Abstract. The prosodic specification of an utterance to be spoken by a Text-to-Speech synthesis system can be devised in break indices, pitch accents and boundary tones. In particular, the identification of break indices formulates the intonational phrase breaks that affect all the forthcoming prosody-related procedures. In the present paper we use tree-structured predictors, and specifically the commonly used in similar tasks CART and the introduced C4.5 one, to cope with the task of break placement in the presence of shallow textual features. We have utilized two 500-utterance prosodic corpora offered by two Greek universities in order to compare the machine learning approaches and to argue on the robustness they offer for Greek break modeling. The evaluation of the resulted models revealed that both approaches were positively compared with similar works published for other languages, while the C4.5 method accuracy scaled from 1% to 2,7% better than CART.

1 Introduction

In speech communication, intonational phrases (IP) are separated by breaks in the form of pauses in speech. Accurate prediction of IP breaks in Text-to-Speech (TtS) synthesis heavily affects utterances structure and thus alters their understandability. As IP breaks divide utterances into meaningful 'chunks' of information [1], variation in phrasing can change the meaning listeners assign to utterances of a given sentence. For example, the interpretation of a sentence like "I will come because I was told so." (in Greek "Ta 'erTo epiD'i mu to 'ipan") will vary, depending upon whether it is uttered as one phrase or two. Situations where phrase breaks are missing when necessary or added in wrong places make the synthetic speech sound unnatural and boring.

In the past, the prediction of intonational boundaries for text-to-speech systems that handle unrestricted text was conducted using simple phrasing algorithms [2] based on orthographic indicators, keywords or part-of-speech spotting, and simple timing information. Research on the location of IP breaks was predicated on the relationship of prosodic and syntactic structures. Rule-based approaches [3] applied to this particular task were most successful in applications where syntactic and semantic information was available during the generation process. A weakness of this particular approach is that even if accurate syntactic and semantic information could be obtained automatically

V. Matoušek et al. (Eds.): TSD 2005, LNAI 3658, pp. 334–341, 2005.

and in real time for TtS, such hand-crafted rule systems are extremely difficult to build and maintain.

In addition, the relationship between prosody and syntax is not fully understood, though it is generally accepted that there is such a relationship. No current proposal integrating such information into the phrase assigned process has been shown to work well, even from hand-corrected labeled input. Some general proposals have been made which assume the availability of even more sophisticated syntactic and semantic information to be employed in IP breaks prediction [4].

In the field of IP break prediction, attention has been given by researchers in derivation of phrasing rules for text-to-speech systems from large labeled corpora [5]; most recently, attempts have been made to use self-organizing procedures to compute phrasing rules automatically from such corpora. The primary learning techniques currently being used include Hidden Markov models [6], neural networks [7], classification and regression trees (CART) [8], transformational rule-based learning (TRBL) [9] and Bayesian techniques [10].

The most commonly used feature set in such training frameworks for IP break prediction include part-of-speech (POS), pitch accent, syntactic structure, duration, length of the current sentence, number of words and syllables from the last break, etc. From the above POS has been proved to be an effective and easy to derive feature.

In this work, we inspect on the performance of tree-structured predictors for IP breaks placement. Along with the commonly used CART approach, we introduce a C4.5 classifier to evaluate over a rapid extracted shallow textual feature set. The experiments were carried out by utilizing two speech corpora in the Greek language provided by the University of Patras (Artificial Intelligence Group) and the University of Athens (Speech Group).

2   Data Resources

For the analysis of the proposed approaches experiments were conducted with the exploitation of two prosodic annotated datasets. The first one featured prosodical phenomena encountered in a generic textual environment while the other was derived from a museum domain text corpus. Professional speakers uttered both corpora in Athenian dialect. Both corpora were annotated to the full ToBI specification and checked for their consistency.

2.1   Corpora Description

The generic corpus consists of 5.500 words, distributed in 500 paragraphs, each one of which may be a single word utterance, a short sentence, a long sentence, or a sequence of sentences. For the corpora creation we used newspaper articles, paragraphs of literature and sentences constructed and annotated by a professional linguist. The corpus was recorded under the instructions of the linguist, in order to capture the most frequent intonational phenomena of the Greek language.

The museum domain corpus includes exhibits' descriptions from a museum guided tour. It consisted of 5484 words, distributed in 516 utterances. Half of the corpus contains grammatically restricted texts, while the remaining half is unrestricted text [8].

As the original corpus included enriched linguistic information provided by a Natural Language Generator, the corpus was recorded appropriately in order to capture a big variety of emphatic events, for example by the introduction of new or old mentioned information to the visitor.

2.2   Shallow Features

In order to predict the juncture class of an IP, textual features were incorporated. Apart from POS, researchers have stressed the important role of syntactic and morphological information for several languages. Taking into account that in real-time IP break prediction tasks, fully syntactic parsing would be time-consuming and would produce many syntactic trees, as well as that in several languages, including MG, syntactic tools are not freely available, a syntactic feature labeling each word with the syntactical chunk which belongs in a sentence was introduced [10]. The phrase boundary detector [12], or chunker, is based on very limited linguistic resources, i.e. a small keyword lexicon containing some 450 keywords (articles, pronouns, auxiliary verbs, adverbs, prepositions etc.) and a suffix lexicon of 300 of the most common word suffixes in MG. In the first stage the boundaries of non-embedded, intra-sentential noun (NP), prepositional (PP), verb (VP) and adverbial phrases (ADP) are detected via multi-pass parsing. Smaller phrases are formed in the first passes, while later passes form more complex structures. In the second stage the head-word of every noun phrase is identified and the phrase inherits its grammatical properties.

2.3   Task and Feature Definition

For the purpose of IP breaks prediction within TtS, it is common to flatten the prosodic hierarchy, hence a word juncture is considered to be a break or a non break.

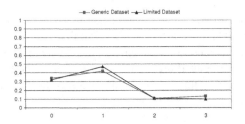

Fig. 1. IP breaks distribution in corpora

In an effort to deviate from that, we considered word junctures of the whole IP break marks proposed by ToBI transcription. Therefore our phrase break label files contain break indices ranging from 0 to 3 (b0, b1, b2 and b3), describing the strength of the juncture between each two lexical items; where b0 is representing that cliticization has merged two lexical items into a prosodic word while b3 is indicating a maximal, or fully-marked, intonational phrase boundary.

Our task was the derivation and application of a common set of shallow textual features extracted rapidly from text for both corpora and the application to the decision tree classifiers for IP breaks placement. Previous works have shown the optimized performance of both models using their full feature set [10], [8] in predicting prosodic phrase breaks, pitch accents and endtones.

Eventually, in order to facilitate the evaluation of the IP break prediction models, we adapted both databases according to the following feature vector:

– *pos:* the part of speech of the word. Values: verb (V), noun (N), adjective (ADJ), adverb (ADV) and a function word (FW) class holding non-content word pos types. For our experiments, the POS of the words in a window of -2,+1 words was employed.

– *chunk:* a syntactic feature that has been successfully applied to intonational phrase break detection [10]. These information is considered as shallow syntactic information, it is unambiguous and can be extracted rapidly [13]. In this work we introduce some combinational features extracted from syntactic chunking and information provided by punctuation. These features are described below:

   • *parent_chunk:* a binary indicator showing whether a word belongs to a different syntactic chunk than its previous one. A window of -1,+1, around the word, was utilized.

   • *chunk_break:* the distance in words from the beginning of the next syntactic chunk or of a major punctuation break.

   • *neigh_chunk:* a binary indicator that shows whether a word belongs to the same syntactic chunk with its next one. A window of -1,+1, around the word, was utilized.

– *word_in:* feeds the classifier with the information of words position from previous major punctuation break.

– *word_out:* presents the number of words until a major punctuation break.

– *syll_num:* the number of syllables in the present word. The values of this feature ranges from 1 to 5 where the last class (5) includes any polysyllabic words with 5 or more syllables. The latter group contains all the low frequency classes of word syllables.

– *syll_str_strct:* indicates the index of the syllable that holds the lexical stress in the word. The values for the Greek language are final, penultimate, antepenultimate and none. The above features were applied to the word level.

3   Phrase Break Prediction Schema

The present study provides an insight into the prosodic parameter classification experiments conducted into ToBI annotated corpora for IP break prediction. The windowed data described above was firstly applied to a decision tree inducer (CART) [13]. Furthermore, C4.5 [14] algorithm was employed. Decision trees have been among the first successful machine learning algorithms applied to IP break and pitch accent prediction for TtS. The three basic elements that a decision tree is composed of are:

– a decision node specifying a test feature.

– an edge or a branch corresponding to the one of the possible attribute values which means one of the test attribute outcomes.

– a leaf which is also named an answer node contains the class to which the object belongs.

In decision trees two major phases should be ensured; the phase of tree building on a given training set, and the classification. In order to classify a new instance, we start by the root of the decision tree, then we test the attribute specified by this node. The result of this test allows the tree branch relative to move down to the attribute value of the given instance. This process will be repeated until a leaf is encountered. The instance is then classified in the same class as the one characterizing the reached leaf. Several algorithms have been developed in order to ensure the construction of decision trees and its use for the classification task.

3.1 Classification and Regression Trees (CART)

The Regression trees, induced by the CART method, are a statistical approach for predicting data from a set of feature vectors. In particular, a CART uses a binary decision tree to model a conditional distribution. CART contains yes/no questions regarding the features and provides either the probability distribution or a mean and standard deviation.

CART analysis consists of four basic steps. Initially a tree is built by means of recursive splitting of nodes. All resulting nodes are assigned with a predicted class, based on the distribution of classes in the learning dataset which would occur in that node and the decision cost matrix. In each node a predicted class assigned whether or not that node is subsequently split into child nodes. The next step consists of stopping the tree building process. At this point a "maximal" tree has been produced, which probably greatly overfits the information contained within the learning dataset. The resulted "maximal" tree is "pruned", which results in the creation of a sequence of simpler trees, through the cutting of increasingly important nodes. Optimal tree selection of the resulted simpler trees is the fourth step, during which the tree fitting the information in the learning dataset, but does not overfit the information, is selected among the sequence of pruned trees.

3.2 C4.5 Algorithm

C4.5 is an improvement of the ID3 [14] algorithm being able to handle numerical data. The first task for C4.5 is to decide which of the non-target variable is the best to split the instances. Then, every possible split is tried. The value of potential splits in C4.5 is calculated from a criterion called information ratio. Information ratio suggests an estimate of how probable split on a variable will lead the decision to a leaf containing the fewer errors or has low disorder. The concept of low disorder means that the node contains instances with one major target variable.

Calculation of information ratio is realized for all the variables and the 'winner' variable is the one with the largest information ratio and is chosen as the split variable. The tree will grow in a similar method. For each child node of the root node, the decision tree algorithm examines all the remaining attributes to find candidate for splitting. If the field takes on only one value, it is eliminated from consideration since there is no way it can be used to make a split. The best split for each of the remaining attributes is determined. When all cases in a node are of the same type, then the node is a leaf node.

C4.5 uses a method called pruning to avoid overfitting. There are two types of pruning applied in the C4.5 procedure: pre-pruning and post-pruning. Post-pruning refers to the building of a complete tree and pruning it afterwards, making the tree less complex and also probably more general by replacing a subtree with a leaf or with the most common branch. When this is done, the leaf will correspond to several classes but the label will be the most common class in the leaf. Post-pruning is affected by a parameter called confidence interval. The application of lower confidence results more drastic pruning. For our models we applied a confidence value of 25 %. Pre-pruning concerns the decision about when to stop developing subtrees during the tree building process. For example specifying the minimum number of observations in a leaf we can determine the size of the tree. A minimum number of 2 was utilized in our model. We have to also point out that in our case we applied post-pruning only while pre-pruning application showed any difference to the models resulted tree. After a tree is constructed, the C4.5 rule induction program can be used to produce a set of equivalent rules. The rules are formed by writing a rule for each path in the tree and then eliminating any unnecessary antecedents and rules.

4   Evaluation

The performance of the proposed approaches with the induction of the suggested features was measured by the utilization of f-measure metric per each IP break class, as they have been explained in Section 2. Results were obtained using the 10-fold cross validation method [15]. Defining f-measure (FM), is the harmonic mean of precision and recall, calculated as:

$$1/\left(\alpha\frac{1}{P} + (1-\alpha)\frac{1}{R}\right) \tag{1}$$

α is a factor determining the weighting of precision and recall. The value of $\alpha = 0.5$ has been used for the current evaluation for equal weighting of precision and recall.

4.1   Results

In an attempt to evaluate the IP break models we calculated the total accuracy, kappa statistic, mean average error (MAE) and root mean square error (RMSE).

Table 1. Total accuracy of the IP break models

Methods	Generic	Museum
CART	83.79%	87.71%
C4.5	86.02%	88.62%

All resulted models revealed a kappa statistic higher than 0.75 which is generally regarded as a good statistic correlation. Accuracy of the models is tabulated in Table 1. We can see that in all cases C4.5 performed better than CART especially in the case of generic dataset.

It is clear that MAE values for all models are close to the corresponding RMSE values giving us the insight that there were not test cases in which the prediction error was significantly greater than the average prediction error.

A detailed observation of the prediction of each class presented by each model, the following can be derived. In Figure 2 the f-measure for each IP break class is depicted for the generic dataset. For these models, classification for the IP break cases with the highest occurrence in the dataset along with class b3, performed better.

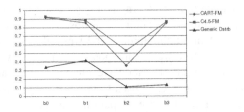

Fig. 2. F-measure for generic domain models

As regards b3 the high f-measure is a result of the fact that this class has low correlation with the other. C4.5 performed better than CART especially in the prediction of the b2 category. Non-breaks were predicted with an f-measure higher than 0.9 for both models.

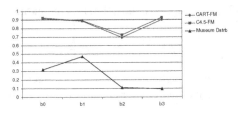

Fig. 3. F-measure for museum domain models

The next step of our exertion was the evaluation of the models derived from the museum domain dataset. F-measure of those models is illustrated in Figure 3. For this domain, both approaches performed sufficiently well with C4.5 performing slightly better almost in every category. For the prediction of non-breaks, both approaches achieved a score of f-measure more than 91% while the lowest was the prediction of b2 class with CART with an f-measure of 0.7.

5   Conclusions

We constructed IP break prediction models with the utilization of decision trees and the induction of shallow textual features. Specifically, we trained CART and C4.5 decision trees with a generic and a museum domain corpus. Both algorithms performed equally well in the prediction of all classes. As expected, museum domain models gave higher prediction scores for all IP break classes as breaks are described by simpler "rules" due to the limitation of the domain. C4.5 performed slightly better than CART in all models. Furthermore, museum domain models showed high prediction accuracy for both approaches with C4.5 having the highest score.

The shallow textual feature set used in these experiments showed an improvement in the prediction of IP break prediction classes of b1, b2 and b3, especially in the case of the generic dataset, compared to the feature set used in earlier works by the two Universities [10], [8]. Further improvements in the tree-structured predictors can be achieved by the introduction of more delicate linguistic features as has been inspected on [16] for the CART approach.

References

1. Bolinger, D.: Intonation and its Uses: Melody in Grammar and Discourse, London, UK, Edward Arnold, 1989.
2. Anderson, M., Pierrehumbert, J., Liberman, M.: Synthesis by rule of English intonation patterns", ICASSP, pp. 281-284, 1984.
3. Prieto, P., Hirschberg, J.: Training Intonational Phrasing Rules Automatically for English and Spanish text-to-speech, Speech Communication, 18, ps. 281-290, 1996.
4. Bachenco, J., Fitzpatrick, E.: A Computational grammar of Discourse-Neutral Prosodic Phrasing in English, Computational Linguistics 16(3), 155-170, 1990.
5. Ostendorf, M., Veilleux, N.: A hierarchical stochastic model for automatic prediction of prosodic boundary location, Computational Linguistics, 20(1), 1989.
6. Taylor, P., Black, A.W.: Assigning Phrase Breaks from Part-of-Speech Sequences, Computer Speech and Language 12:99-117, 1998.
7. Muller, A. F., Zimmermann, H. G., and Neuneier, R.: Robust Generation of Symbolic Prosody by a Neural Classifier Based on Autoassociators, ICASSP-96, 1285-1288, 1996.
8. Xydas, G., Spiliotopoulos, D. and Kouroupetroglou, G.: "Modeling Prosodic Structures in Linguistically Enriched Environments", in "Text, Speech and Dialogue", Lecture Notes in Artificial. Intelligence. (LNAI), Springer-Verlag Berlin Heidelberg, Vol 3206, pp. 521-528, 2004.
9. Fordyce, C., S., Osterdorf, M.: Prosody Prediction for Speech Synthesis Using Transformational Rule-Based Learning, ICSLP-98, 682-685, 1998.
10. Zervas, P., Maragoudakis, M.: Fakotakis, N., Kokkinakis, G., Bayesian Induction of intonational phrase breaks, EUROSPEECH, Geneva, Switzerland, Sept. 1-4, 2003, pp. 113-116, 2003.
11. Silverman, K., Beckman, M., Pitrelli, J., Ostendorf, M., Wightman, C., Price, P., Pierrehumbert, J., Hirschberg, J.: ToBI: A standard for labeling English prosody,. ICSLP, pp. 867-870, 1992.
12. Stamatatos, E., Fakotakis, N. and Kokkinakis, G.: A Practical Chunker for Unrestricted Text, 2nd Int. Conf. of Natural Language Processing, pp. 139-150, 2000.
13. Breiman, L., Friedman, J.H., Olshen, R. A., Stone C. J.: Classification and Regression Trees, Belmont, CA: Wadsworth International Group, 1984.
14. Quinlan, J.R.: C4.5: Programs for Machine Learning, San Francisco: Morgan Kaufmann Publishers, 1993.
15. Stone, M.: Cross-validation choice and assessment of statistical predictions, Journal of the Royal Statistical Society, 36, 111-147, 1974.
16. Xydas G., Spiliotopoulos D., Kouroupetroglou G.: "Modeling Improved Prosody Generation from High-Level Linguistically Annotated Corpora", in IEICE Transactions of Information and Systems, 2005 (to appear).

Compact Representation of Speech Using 2-D Cepstrum – An Application to Slovak Digits Recognition*

Roman Jarina, Michal Kuba, and Martin Paralic

Department of Telecommunications, University of Zilina
Univerzitna 1, 010 26 Zilina, Slovakia
{jarina,kuba,paralic}@fel.utc.sk

Abstract. HMM speech recogniser with a small number of acoustic observations based on 2-D cepstrum (TDC) is proposed. TDC represents both static and dynamic features of speech implicitly in matrix form. It is shown that TDC analysis enables a compact representation of speech signals. Thus a great advantage of the proposed model is a massive reduction of speech features used for recognition what lessens computational and memory requirements, so it may be favourable for limited-power ASR applications. Experiments on isolated Slovak digits recognition task show that the method gives comparable results as the conventional MFCC approach. For speech degraded by additive white noise, it reaches better performance than the MFCC method.

1 Introduction

A majority of the state-of-the-art ASR systems [1] models a speech signal as the first-order Markov process. In such model, only neighbouring states depend on each other, and past history, except of the neighbour previous state is ignored. Although this simplification enables much easier computation, it represents rather inaccurate modelling since speech perception is conditional on much longer time period. The conventional way of including temporal information into the speech feature is to augment the short-time spectral features with their time derivatives known as delta features. Hence the 39-dimensional feature vector may consist of 13 MFCCs, 13 delta (or velocity) and 13 delta-delta (or acceleration) coefficients. The feature vectors are computed on frame-by-frame basis with the frame shift of about 10 ms. In such case the one second long utterance is represented by almost 4,000 parameters.

Since consequent feature vectors are highly correlated in time, such parameterisation is not optimal from either statistical or perceptual point of view. A great redundancy in the speech features makes further processing computationally much more costly.

Nowadays, since there is an increasing demand after voice-enabled services and applications for hand-held terminals such as PDAs or mobile phones, power-saving requirements become an important aspect in ASR system design. One of the way is to lessen the amount of speech parameters by finding more efficient and compact representation of speech patterns to speed-up a classification process.

* This research was supported by Science and Technology Assistance Agency under the contract No. APVT-20-044102 and by a Marie Curie European Reintegration Grant within the 6th European Community Framework Programme.

V. Matoušek et al. (Eds.): TSD 2005, LNAI 3658, pp. 342–347, 2005.

An alternative way to traditional 1-D cepstrum analysis of speech signal is Two-Dimensional Cepstrum (TDC) analysis. TDC represents both static and dynamic features of speech signal implicitly in matrix form. One dimension of the TDC matrix represents cepstrum and the second dimension indicates the temporal variations (so called modulation spectrum) of each cepstral coefficient. Each acoustic observation, which is formed from TDC features, will incorporate information from several hundreds milliseconds of speech what is in accordance with the time interval of the short-time memory of human perception. TDC computed via 2-D Discrete Cosine Transform (DCT) produces almost uncorrelated set of coefficients in both quefrency and modulation frequency dimensions. We hypothesise that if TDC is applied, much smaller number of observations is necessary in HMM based recogniser.

The paper is organized as follows. First, TDC analysis procedure is briefly explained and previous works are reviewed. In the following section, experiments with TDC-HMM recogniser on isolated digits recognition task in Slovak language are described. We evaluated recognition rate as a function of redundancy in the observation space. The redundancy in TDC-based speech features is affected by changing a block shift during TDC analysis. That means the greater block shift the smaller number of TDC matrices is used for parametrisation. Experiments with noisy speech recognition are also performed. Results are compared with a conventional ASR system based on MFCC and delta features.

2 Two-Dimensional Cepstrum Analysis

TDC, which was introduced by Ariki [2], represents both static and dynamic features of speech signal implicitly in matrix form. The TDC matrix $C(u, v)$ is obtained by applying a 2-D DCT to a block of consecutive log spectral vectors. Since 2-D DCT can be decomposed into two 1-D DCTs, the TDC matrix can also be obtained by applying 1-D DCT to a block of L successive MFCC speech vectors $c(u)$ along time axis

$$C(u, v) = \sum_{t=0}^{L-1} c_t(u) . \cos \left[\frac{\pi(2t + 1)v}{2L} \right] \qquad (1)$$

Dimension u represents quefrency and dimension v represents the modulation spectrum. Between column index v and modulation frequency θ in Hz is the relation as follows

$$\theta = v . f_s / (L . N) = v / T \qquad (2)$$

where f_s is the sampling rate, L is the number of frames in the analysis block, N is the length of the frame, and T is the total duration of the analysis block in seconds. The first row of the matrix with index $u = 0$ represents temporal variations of short time energy. The first column with index $v = 0$ contains the average or steady-state value of the MFCCs within analysis block. Any stationary or slow moving channel distortion presented in the speech signal will be compressed into this zeroth column. By removing this column from the TDC feature set, these channel effects will be removed from the speech features. This has the same effect as Cepstral Mean Substraction (CMS) method [3].

Pai [4] and Lin et al. [5] used only one TDC matrix for each word, while Milner [6] used a 2-D cepstrum for each frame. Although the first word-level approach significantly reduces number of features and also solves the time alignment problems, it is impractical to be applied to European languages because of great variability in word durations. The second frame-level approach outperforms the conventional MFCC approach for noisy speech recognition [3] but the number of coefficients remains almost the same as in MFCC representation. Our proposed approach can be seen as a trade-off between these two approaches. The proposed TDC analysis works on sub-word or block level. Thus one speech pattern (e.g. word) is represented by only a small number of TDC matrices.

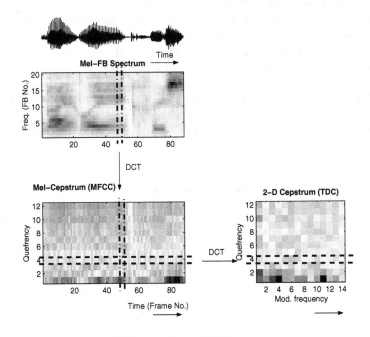

Fig. 1. Procedure of TDC analysis

2.1 Selection of TDC Parameters

Two questions have to be answered for a successful application of TDC to ASR front-end: number of spectral vectors for TDC matrix computation; and a speech feature selection from TDC matrix.

The time duration of the block of consequent frames (or spectral vectors), used for TDC analysis, must be large enough to include the temporal characteristics of time-varying spectral features, on the other hand it is limited by statistical properties of the signal and by the length of the speech unit being recognized. It is also useful if the duration of the blocks meets perceptual cues. Human auditory system is most sensitive to modulation frequencies around 4 Hz that reflects the syllabic rate of speech [7]. Thus human hearing in perception of modulated signals acts as a band-pass filter with the length of the impulse response of minimally 150-250 ms what is the length of 15-20 frames.

Since the components of TDC matrix are not equally important for speech recognition, only small sub-set of TDC coefficients may be selected as speech features. Results of speech recognition experiments have shown that the components of the modulation spectrum below 1 Hz and above 16 Hz have only minor role in both human perception and ASR [3, 7]. Milner [8] experimentaly investigated the effect of both the duration of the analysis block and the number of columns in TDC matrix on the recognition performance. For both isolated and connected digit recognition tasks, Milner reported the best recognition performance if 11 frames were used for TDC matrix computation and only the TDC coefficients from the first three or four columns were selected. Note the zeroth column was skipped. The modulation frequency is allocated to each column according to Eq. 2.

3   Experiment

We design the continuous density left-right HMM with a reduced number of acoustical observations represented by TDC features. The model is evaluated on Slovak isolated digit recognition task. Speech database consists of 12 Slovak words (digits 0-9, digits 1 and 2 are spelled-out as both "jeden" and "jedna", and "dva" and "dve" respectively) uttered by 61 speakers. Details about the speech database are summarised in Table 1. The ASR system is designed as speaker-independent. We used different non-overlapping sub-set of the database uttered by different group of speakers for training and testing. One HMM was created for each class.

Table 1. Train and test speech database

Recognition task	Isolated Slovak digits
Number of speakers	61 (40 for training + 21 for testing)
A/D conversion	f_s = 8 kHz, resolution = 8 bits/sample, telephone quality
Number of records	4 records per word per speaker, 12 words , 2928 records in total

First, the signal is pre-emphasised by the 1st-order FIR filter with k=0.97. The sliding 30 ms long window with the 20 ms shift is used for signal analysis. For each frame 23 mel-FBE are computed. DCT is applied on a block of 12 consequent 9-D MFCC vectors to get TDC matrix. The first 4 columns were selected as speech features. Note the 0th row ($u = 0$) and 0th column ($v = 0$) of the TDC matrix are skipped. Thus 36 TDC coefficients selected from one TDC matrix represent one acoustic observation for HMM.

Preliminary experiences with TDC analysis and proposed HMM were already published in [9]. The continuous output probabilities for each state of HMM are modelled by PDFs with 4 multivariate Gaussians defined by the mean vectors and the spherical covariance matrices [9]. Here experiments with various TDC analysis block shifts are shown. The length of the block is 12 frames as mentioned above and shift of the block varies from 2 frames up to its whole length. Thus number of observations per second decreases from 25 down to 4 when the TDC analysis blocks don't overlap. The number of states in HMM N_{stat} is set according to the number of observations N_{obs} most likely expected for a given word but it is limited to the number of phonemes N_{phon} in the word:

$$N_{stat} = \begin{cases} N_{obs}, & N_{obs} \leq N_{phon} \\ N_{phon}, & N_{obs} > N_{phon} \end{cases} \tag{3}$$

The longest Slovak digits (e.g. "jeden", "sedem") consist of five phonemes thus such words are described by HMMs with up to 5 states.

The models are trained on clean speech only but they are tested on both clean speech and speech with additive white noise. The results are shown in Table 2 and Figures 2.a and 2.b.

The results are compared with the conventional MFCC approach. In this case a signal is analysed with the same time resolution. For each 20ms frame, 12 MFCCs together with 12 delta and 12 delta-delta coefficients are extracted. Coefficient $c(0)$ is not used.

Table 2. Dependence of the number of speech features and recognition performance on TDC analysis block shift. The analysis block duration is 12 spectral frames. Performance of TDC analysis is compared with the conventional MFCC approach

Block shift		Block overlap [%]	Normalized No. of features pre second	Recognition rate [%]	
[Frames]	[ms]			Clean Speech	Noisy speech SNR = 10dB
2	40	83.3	900	95.5	59.3
4	80	66.7	450	94.6	57.4
6	120	50.0	300	93.8	53.8
8	160	33.3	225	92.0	44.7
10	200	16.7	180	92.3	44.3
12	240	0.0	150	89.8	43.7
12 MFCC + 12 Δ + 12 Δ^2			50x36 = 1800	93.7	47.9

From the results shown in Figure 2.b, it is seen that the performance of the TDC analysis with 50 % block overlap is comparable with the conventional 1-D MFCC approach. TDC with greater block overlaps (block-shift up to 6 frames or up to 50 % of its length) even gives higher recognition score, mainly for noise-degraded speech as seen from Figure 2.a. However the most notable advantage of the proposed method is a massive reduction of speech features used for recognition. As it can be seen from Table 2, in the case of the TDC analysis with 50 % block overlap, six times less features is used in contrast with the conventional MFCC method.

4   Conslusion

It is shown that 2-D cepstrum (TDC) analysis enables a compact representation of speech signals. We proposed TDC-HMM speech recogniser with a small number of

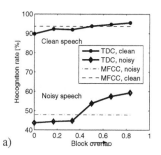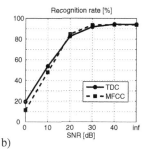

Fig. 2. a) Recognition performance for various TDC analysis block overlaps (see Table 2); b) Recognition performance of noisy speech for TDC analysis with 50% block overlap

acoustic observations. The experiments on isolated Slovak digits recognition task show that the method gives comparable results as the conventional MFCC approach. For speech degraded by additive white noise, the proposed method reaches better performance than the MFCC method. A great advantage of the proposed model is a massive reduction of speech features used for recognition what lessens computational and memory requirements. Hence the proposed method is favourable for limited-power ASR applications.

References

1. OShaugnessy, D.: Interacting with computer by voice: Automatic Speech Recognition and Synthesis. Proceedings of the IEEE, Vol. 91, No. 9 (2003) 1272-1305
2. Ariki, Y., Mizuta, S., Nagata, M., Sakai, T.: Spoken-Word Recognition Using Dynamic Features Analysed by Two-Dimensional Cepstrum, Proceedings of IEE, Vol. 136, Pt.I, No.2, April (1989) 133-140
3. Kanedera, N., Hermansky, H., Arai, T.: Desired characteristics of modulation spectrum for robust automatic speech recognition. In: Proc. of ICASSP98, Seatle, USA (1998) 613-616
4. Pai, H.-F., Wang, H.-C.: A Study of the Two-Dimensional Cepstrum Approach for Speech Recognition, Computer Speech and Language, Vol. 6 (1992) 361-375
5. Lin, C.-T., Nein, H.-W., Hwu, J.-Y.: GA-Based Noisy Speech Recognition Using Two-Dimensional Cepstrum, IEEE Trans. on Speech and Audio Processing, Vol. 8., No. 6., Nov (2000) 664-675
6. Milner, B.P., Vaseghi, S-V.: Speech modelling using cepstral-time feature matrices and Hidden Markov Models. In: Proc. of ICASSP94, Adelaide Australia (1994) 601-604
7. Kanedera, N., Arai, T., Hermansky, H., Misha, P.: On the importance of various modulation frequencies for speech recognition. In: Proc. of Eurospeech97, Rhodos, Greece (1997) 1079-1082
8. Milner, B.: Cepstral-Time Matrices and LDA for Improved Connected digit and Sub-word Recognition Accuracy. In: Proc. of Eurospeech97, Vol.1, Rhodos Greece, (1997) 405-408
9. Jarina, R., Kuba, M.: Speech Recognition Using Hidden Markov Model with Low Redundancy in the Observation Space, Komunikacie Vol. 6, No. 4 (2004) 17-21

An Alternative Way of Semantic Interpretation

Miloslav Konopík and Roman Mouček

University of West Bohemia, Department of Computer Science
Univerzitní 22, CZ - 306 14 Plzeň, Czech Republic
{konopik,moucek}@kiv.zcu.cz

Abstract. In this work we deal with interpretation methods of speech utterances. We describe the basics of interpretation theory as well as a classic approach to interpretation. After that we suggest an alternative method based on modern knowledge in artificial intelligence. We describe the main points of that methodology; show its advantages, drawbacks and successfulness in selected restricted domain.

1 Introduction

Semantic interpretation is an essential part of natural language understanding process, however it is being omitted in many systems. An interpretation process has to be present in every system, which takes new information from its environment. The dialog systems cannot skip it completely so they frequently integrate it implicitly in another module. E.g. many dialog systems don't have stand alone semantic interpretation module but the dialog manager module holds its function. This approach leads inevitably to the degradation of understanding quality. Having system with high level of (speech, scene ...) understanding, it is necessary to cope with interpretation.

Actually, what does the interpretation mean? We can simply imagine it as an interface between the system knowledge base and its environment. In linguistic context we call it semantic interpretation (abbr. SI). SI has to use the same cognitive actions as a man would to understand the utterance. The better the semantic interpretation will be the more clever the system we will get. "More clever" in this context means that the system is more similar to a human. Then an ideal human-to-computer dialog wouldn't be recognized from human-to-human dialog. Such a system would pass the Turing test. This is of course only the Utopia. Given all current knowledge about the interpretation we cannot achieve such a good interpretation in an unrestricted domain [3]. However we are able to enclose such ideal interpretation in narrowly restricted domains.

We describe the reasoning part (called the semantic interpretation module or the Lint in this paper) of language understanding process in this work. No syntactic or semantic parsing is discussed.

In the following sections we briefly describe the SI method, which uses the first order predicate calculus. We show its weak points and then we suggest an alternative method.

2 Theoretical Background

2.1 Theory of Compositionality

The main assumption made about semantic interpretation is that it is a compositional process. This means that the meaning of a constituent is derived solely from its sub-

V. Matoušek et al. (Eds.): TSD 2005, LNAI 3658, pp. 348–355, 2005.

constituents [1]. We use this theory because of its attractive properties. The main advantage is that we can build interpretation of an utterance incrementally from its subphrases. Then the inference rules are much simpler and can deal with problems at separated levels. One of the formalisms of theory of compositionality is based on lambda calculus (chapter 9 in [1]).

We introduce the following notation to simplify referring to constituents in an utterance. We refer to the part of an utterance, which can be interpreted independently of the remaining utterance, as an UFO (utterance field object) [5]. In other words the UFO is an sub-constituent. The generalized form of the UFO is called a concept. A concept is according to Merriam-Webster dictionary "an abstract or generic idea generalized from particular instance". This description perfectly suits the way how we use the word concept.

Example: We want to interpret the utterance "I want to travel to Prague at six o'clock" (Fig. 1).

Fig. 1. The decomposition of user's utterance

In Fig. 1 UFO1 is the instance of a concept, e.g. called CDestination, UFO2 corresponds to CDepartureTime and UFO3 to CTravel.

The compositional models tend to make the database of inference rules easier to extend and maintain. But this theory also introduces many problems. For instance a classic problem arises from quantified sentences or from the presence of idioms.

2.2   Semantic Interpretation

The SI works with information gathered from speech data. It has to set new information into the current knowledge model (called the belief model) and to check its relevance to the current context.

First the interpretation transforms the utterance from its logical form (provided by syntactic and semantic analysis) to a knowledge representation structure (see 4.2). Then the reasoning is executed. During this process the system has to use default knowledge (to add obvious but not mentioned information, e.g. that Prague is in Czech Republic). According to the theory of compositionality the knowledge from sub-constituents is linked together by the superior constituent. At last but not at least the history of dialog (the dialog context) has to be used.

There are two cases of extending the current knowledge model by new information. The first one is the monotonous extension. Such a extension doesn't have any conflict with the existing model. The second case violates the monotonous extension and introduces a conflict. Such a conflict cannot be solved by deleting or overwriting existing knowledge because such a action would break the derivation chain. It is necessary to overlay the old knowledge with this new knowledge and gradually propagate the change upward to the rest of the belief model.

2.3 Belief Model

The belief model contains the current knowledge model. It includes all relevant facts gathered so far in the dialog progress and the relations between them. Besides that, it contains rules on how to infer new knowledge and rules used to fill in implicitly assumed knowledge (called default knowledge, see section 2.2). The next important goal is to maintain a coherent knowledge model. It means such model, from which contradicting information cannot be derived.

The belief model cooperates with the interpretation module very closely. The interpretation uses rules and knowledge stored in the belief model to derive new information. The result of the interpretation is also saved here.

2.4 Anchoring

Every new piece of information has to be anchored in the belief model. The process of anchoring means to find a correct position in the belief model. It is very easy for complete sentences (e.g. "I want to leave at six o'clock"), but much harder for elliptical sentences (e.g. "at six o'clock"). Does that elliptical utterance belong to the departure time or to the arrival time? An elliptical utterance occurs especially as a reaction to some question. Prediction from the dialog manager has to be used to anchor such utterances.

3 FOPC Systems

3.1 Brief Description

Interpretation systems based on first order predicate calculus (FOPC) use propositional resolution to derive new knowledge. Hence there is no need to develop the inferential algorithm. FOPC systems almost always use pure declarative representation of knowledge. One representative of these systems is the SIL language from SUNDIAL project ([2], [5]). The core of the inference mechanism used in this system is based on paths matching and on attempts to meet predicate constraints. It uses the forward procedure to infer all possible inferences. Regardless of details this methodology stores relation between facts in knowledge base in a nice and clear declarative way (it is said what constraints have to be met but not how to meet them). Everything sounds nice up to this point, but the following section will show problems introduced by this approach.

3.2 Weak Points

To make this system work properly, rules need to be "equilibrated". There must not be multiple rules (multiple means to contain the same relation and to derive the same knowledge; overspecified system) because it can cause inference to be nondeterministic or to be trapped inside an infinite loop. Also if any part of a rule is missing, the system will not give any interpretation (underspecified system). It seems to be easy to create a system, which meets this restriction. But the more complicated the system is the harder it is to keep these restrictions. And it is very hard to find such "bad" rules because there is no clue to lead you. The debugging of FOPC systems is a very complex process.

During the development of the rules the developer also suffers from the incompleteness of the declarative languages. No matter how powerful the declarative language is used, some predicates are always missing. The developer is forced to use either the procedural techniques built within the language itself or some external language. When substituting missing predicates it is always necessary to ensure that bounding and unbounding variables (e.g. in PROLOG) work and it is sometimes a really complicated task.

4   Lint

Lint = <u>L</u>INGVO <u>int</u>erpretation module.

4.1   Overview

We have listed some drawbacks of a pure (or mainly) declarative approach in the previous section. The pure procedural approach has its disadvantages too. Although it is very effective solving specific inference task (section 13.1 in [1]) it is highly dependent on that task and it cannot be transferred to another problem. Such systems are also hard to analyze because of the lack of formality. The complicated systems are not mostly clearly arranged.

To avoid drawbacks and profit from advantages of both approaches we develop a declarative-procedural interpretation system based mainly on principles of the SIL language. We store the procedural inference rules in a declarative structure. The knowledge is represented by a concept dependency structure. Each concept represented as a Java class is treated as an autonomous agent. Every agent (= concept) reacts to a stimulant by activating its rules. The stimulant is a notification about a change of any sub-constituent, which the agent is dependent on. The position in the knowledge structure is stored declaratively as well as the concept dependency. On the other hand, the rules are written in Java code, but they can use many services of declarative structure (e.g. notify somebody about a change, overlay knowledge, recall the history and others).

Our system incorporates the automatic anchoring algorithm. The system accepts predictions from the dialog manager and tries to anchor the knowledge in the structure. We describe the anchoring algorithm in detail further.

4.2   Knowledge Representation

As we mentioned before, the knowledge representation is a hybrid combination of declarative and procedural technique built on SIL language basis. The knowledge model is stored within concepts and their structure. Every concept is embedded in one object (= class).

Every concept is described declaratively by its parent concept (except the root concept), children concepts (the sub-constituents) and inheritance from another concept.

Procedural description of a concept is stored within the concept body. The body is a set of procedures reacting to particular stimuli.

When we look more closely at the knowledge representation structure we find that two main separated structures can be distinguished. The first one is the concept dependency. The concept is dependent on its every part (e.g. the number is part of a vehicle therefore the vehicle is dependent on that number). It can be also dependent on another concept, which is not part of it (relative clauses, references, etc.). The second structure is the inheritance hierarchy. Every concept can inherit some properties from exactly one other concept. More formally:

Definition 1 (Concept). *Let $\mathcal{C}$ be a set of concepts. The concept $C \in \mathcal{C}$ is an ordered four-tuple $C = (P, D, O, R)$, where :*

- *$P \in \mathcal{C} \cup \emptyset$ is the parent concept (in inheritance hierarchy)*
- *$D = \{c_1, c_2, ..., c_n\} \cup \emptyset$ is a set of sub-constituents (concepts on which the C is dependent)*
- *$O \in \mathcal{C} \cup \emptyset \wedge type(C) = type(O)$ overlayed concept from dialog history (non-monotonous extension of the belief model).*
- *$R = \{r_1, r_2, ..., r_n\}$ set of rules reacting to stimuli.*

Definition 2 (The Root).

- *$\exists_1 C_0 = (\emptyset, D, O, R)$ – root of inheritance hierarchy*
- *$\exists C_{task} = \{C_{task_i} : \forall C_j = (P, D, O, R) : C_{task_i} \notin D\}$ – "roots" of dependency structure (does not occur in any list of dependent concepts).*

We call the root of dependency structure the task concept. The task concept is specific for current task (e.g. to find particular connection in public city transport).

Axiom 1 (Dependency structures) *the concept dependency structure is a directed graph.*

Axiom 2 (Inheritance hierarchy) *the inheritance hierarchy is a tree.*

When we compare this representation with the SIL language (we assume that there is used logic language with procedural elements (complete language) for SIL language implementation) we can state that they have the same express power, because the structure of SILdef-concepts can be transformed to a directed graph.

4.3 System Architecture

The interpretation is done in the following steps:

1. The input stream containing identified UFOs in user's utterance is read. Every isolated UFO is saved in the unanchored list.
2. A new world (world = representation of one utterance) is created and the anchoring procedure is executed. After this step the new world is filled either with new knowledge or with a reference to old knowledge.
3. The inferential algorithm is initialized (the message queue is filled with newly created concepts) and the interpretation is started. When the message queue is empty the maximal interpretation has been reached.

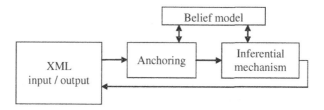

Fig. 2. Interpretation module architecture

4. The task dependent result of interpretation is saved to the task frame. It is another autonomous action of an agent/concept reacting to stimulus "to write task dependent information".
5. Finally the difference of the new task frame from the previous one is written to the output stream.

We will deal with more details of particular problems in the following two sections.

4.4   Anchoring

As we mentioned before, the Lint system is able to perform automatic anchoring. We now briefly describe the anchoring process.

The dependency structure is searched during the anchoring and the most likely anchoring is selected. The goal of anchoring is to find the correct concept on which the anchored knowledge can be dependent (an empty concept can be created during this process).

When a new unanchored UFO arrives, the anchoring algorithm is executed in several steps:

1. The structure is searched and the list of compatible anchoring points (anchoring point = the concept on which can be this unanchored UFO dependent) is found.
2. For every anchoring point the path from that point to the root* is created (* root = root of dependency structure, the task concept). Paths are stored in the anchoring path list.
3. When the prediction from the dialog manager is available, the path containing the prediction is selected to be tried first.
4. Every path hypothesis is examined by interpretation process. If the path leads the belief model to an inconsistent state, it is rejected. The most probable anchoring is accepted. (If it cannot be determined, which anchoring is more probable, the first one is taken and warning report is announced).

4.5   Inferential Algorithm

The inferential algorithm is based on message processing and concepts reactions to stimuli. To explain this in the simplest possible way, we can say that the concept is informed when some of the concepts, on which it depends, have changed. When it happens, the informed concept reacts and possibly changes its data (data derived from concepts, on which it is dependent). This change can trigger the action of informing the dependent concepts. The information about the change is gradually propagated through the dependent concepts to the task concept (the "root").

We can say, that the complexity of this algorithm is $O(n) = \log_k(n) * l$, where $k = \frac{\sum_i(|D_i|)}{|C|}$ and l is the number of passings through the loop (which can be in badly designed system the infinity).

A non-monotonous change in the belief model is solved in following way. The old concept is overlaid and the concept, which is dependent on this overlaid concept, is informed about the change. The change is then propagated through the structure towards the task concept.

5   System Evaluation

We evaluated our interpretation system (the reasoning part, not the parsing) on the public transport domain within a city information dialog system. The rules in Lint system were manually written and were extracted from 70 sentences. The Lint system was tested on 30 similar sentences (but they were not seen during training) from 5 dialogs. We are now working on a larger training and testing set. The sentences were in Czech language and have the following form: "I want to go to Kosutka, when does it leave?". The correct syntactic and semantic parsing was presented to the Lint system input. We compared the result of the Lint output with a manmade interpretation, which is considered the correct one (see in table 1). The interpretation was classified as a complete one when there were no differences between manmade interpretation and the computer interpretation. The partial interpretation means that there were some parts of the final knowledge representation missing. The failed interpretation means that the system derived incorrect data or made empty interpretation of the sentence carrying nonempty information.

Table 1. The system evaluation

	Count	Percentage
Complete interpretation	25	83,3 %
Partial interpretation	3	10 %
Failed interpretation	2	6,7 %
Overall count of utterances	30	100 %

6   Conclusion

In this article we present an alternative approach to semantic interpretation. This approach is not limited for speech tasks only, but it is usable for any kind of task when the knowledge of the whole is derivable from its parts. The theory of semantic interpretation was shortened in this article. For more details see references.

The main advantages of our system are the high level of modularity and reusability (you may take existing concept (or even a set of concepts stored in a package) and modify it by inheriting from it), high speed of development and good possibility for debugging. On the contrary, the declarative system stores its rules in more natural way and has good mathematical background.

References

1. Allen J.: Natural Language Understanding – 2nd edition. The Benjamin Cummings Publishing Company, Inc., 1994.
2. Youd N., McGlashan S.: Semantic Interpretation in Dialogue. SCS Research Report, Logica Cambridge Ltd., Cambridge, 1996
3. Mouček R.: Semantics in Dialogue Systems. PhD. Thesis, University of West Bohemia, Plzeň, 2004
4. Konopík M.: Natural language recognition methods – design and implementation of semantic interpretation module (in Czech). Thesis, University of West Bohemia, Plzeň, 2003
5. Ocelíková J.: Processing of semantics of spontaneous utterances within human-computer dialog (in Czech). PhD. Thesis, Univ. of West Bohemia, Plzeň, 1998

Robust Rule-Based Method
for Automatic Break Assignment
in Russian Texts

Ilya Oparin[1,2]

[1] St.Petersburg State University, Dept. of Phonetics
199034, Universitetskaya nab. 11, St.Petersburg, Russia
[2] Speech Technology Center
196084, ul. Krasutskogo 4, St.Petersburg, Russia
ilya@speechpro.com
http://www.speechpro.com

Abstract. In this paper a new rule-based approach to break assignment for the Russian language is discussed. It is a flexible and robust method of segmentation of texts in Russian in prosodic units. We implemented it in the recent "Orator" text-to-speech (TTS) system. The model was developed to use for the inflective languages as an alternative both for statistic and for strict rule-based algorithms. It is designed in such a way that all potentially tunable context dependencies are brought up to the interface grammar and can be easily modified by linguists. The algorithm we developed performs well on different kinds of texts due to this simple and intuitive grammar built upon an elaborate mechanism of morpho-grammatical analysis. Juncture correct rate varies between more than 98% for simple literary texts and 85% for raw transcripts of spontaneous speech.

1 Introduction

Correct prosodic breaks detection is very important for various linguistic applications. Prosody often has to be predicted from the text which is processed. TTS systems is a perfect example showing how important the quality of the break assignment may be. Breaks specify not only physical pauses (both filled and unfilled) but also the segmentation in prosodic phrases. This segmentation can be viewed as the basis of naturalness of synthesized speech, thus being crucial for any TTS system. Moreover, the information on breaks positioning for a given input text is used by a number of other standard modules of a TTS system, such as the pitch behavior or the transcription one.

There is a number of algorithms for break assignment created so far. At first, rule-based models were developed [2], [5], [11]. They were designed by linguists and contained detailed sets of rules for making decisions on segmentation. These systems lacked flexibility since the set of rules appeared to be a kind of a closed module that can not be easily subjected to modification. Stochastic approaches were introduced later on and different probabilistic techniques have been dominating the field since then [4], [10]. Probabilistic algorithms, though generally disregarding linguistic knowledge, performed well and appeared easy to create and modify (i.e. train). However, there is no

V. Matoušek et al. (Eds.): TSD 2005, LNAI 3658, pp. 356–363, 2005.

extensive annotated corpora for Russian yet, which is crucial to train a statistical model. Building of such corpora is a difficult and time-consuming task itself. Thus, we considered it natural to revert to the idea of the use of linguistic knowledge in algorithms for break assignment. At the same time, we paid special attention to avoiding major drawbacks of the earlier rule-based methods. We did it by introducing a simple and intuitive interface grammar, easy subject to modifications of any kind.

Most rule-based models take account of syntax to find positions of possible breaks. As the algorithm deals with a text, it is natural to predict prosodic phrasing from the syntactic information. Despite there is no one-to-one correspondence between prosodic and syntactic boundaries [1], [7], syntax is the main source of information used to perform automatic segmentation of a text into prosodic units for rule-based systems. For Russian the rate of correspondence between prosodic and syntactic boundaries was shown to be quite high: the level of 85% was reported [6]. We generally followed this approach but restricted it more to account of contextual dependencies in order to maintain the simplicity and flexibility of the model.

2   Basic Principles of Segmentation

The algorithm of break assignment we present in this paper is based on the use of syntactic-contextual information. It does not require text parsing which is very important due to a number of reasons. Firstly, it is not obvious whether a type of a parser with a satisfying ratio between precision and computational costs can be found. Secondly, parsers for the Russian language are just being constructed at present and all existing ones can be regarded more as demo versions[1]. We claim there are no parsers for Russian one can use to get good performance of an automatic break assignment system. However, it is possible to dispense with full syntactic analysis because there is considerable redundancy between events, predicting places of prosodic boundaries [12]. We confine ourselves to the use of the context in order to find bound groups in a sentence. The context analysis we introduce here take account of part-of-speech (POS) and grammatical information about all the words in an input text. The complicated construct of the automatic morpho-grammatical analysis constitutes the base of a very simple interface grammar.

The model presented in this paper is integrated in the recent concatenative triphone "Orator" TTS system for the Russian language, developed at Speech Technology Center (http://www.speechpro.com/). The break assignment module consists of four main sub-modules:

- Morpho-grammatical analysis,
- Punctuation analysis,
- Basic context analysis,
- Interface grammar.

2.1   Morpho-grammatical Analysis

The POS tagging as well as the grammatical analysis is based on the use of a large morpho-grammatical dictionary. The dictionary is based on ideas of Zaliznyak [13],

---

[1] E.g. http://www.phil.pu.ru/depts/12/AGFL/eng/index.htm

widely accepted for the Russian language, and some of the practical solutions proposed by Zharkov et al. [14]. It covers 1.3 million of wordforms and was shown to perform well for different kinds of texts [8].

The module of morpho-grammatical analysis assigns every word from an input text all possible POS markers with relevant grammatical information. In the simplest case a word has got only one possible POS marker with a corresponding set of values for grammatical categories. Nevertheless, usually there is more than one possible variant, mostly due to the high inflective power of the Russian language. In order to detect the correct variant special algorithms of homography disambiguation are used. Those, being auxiliary for break assignment, are not introduced in the interface grammar and the detailed coverage is out of scope in this paper.

2.2   Punctuation

Punctuation plays the greatest role for break detection in Russian texts. The marks of outer punctuation which serve as the end-of-sentence markers always correspond to prosodic boundaries. In most cases the inner punctuation denote breaks as well. We created a set of special rules for those cases when an inner punctuation sign does not indicate the presence of a prosodic boundary. The number of such rules is quite small and the whole set can be kept as closed for further changes. That is why it is not brought up to the interface grammar.

Punctuation information makes the task of break assignment a great deal simpler. The average number of words per an inner punctuation sign (or punctuation marks per sentence) varies greatly for different texts [9] but the punctuation always gives a kind of a pre-segmentation of an arbitrary text. Then the phrase-length factor, as another one playing a great role in the automatic break assignment [12], is used in order to make an assumption whether further context analysis should be performed.

2.3   Basic Context Analysis

Basic context analysis is not brought up to the interface grammar. It includes description of those situations which are well-established and unambiguous. For instance, a preposition in Russian is always bound to the right neighbor if the latter is a noun. Suchlike rules do not presuppose any variations and thus can be kept out-of-reach when dealing with more subtle and non-obvious context dependencies.

2.4   Interface Grammar

In order to find those breaks which are not inferred from the punctuation marks, we designed a special contextual interface grammar. It performs as an intermediate between a linguist and the core of the model. Such a mechanism allows us to tune the whole system in a very efficient and, which is very important, intuitive way.

This interface grammar detects intonationally unbreakable sequences of words in an input text. The basis of the grammar is a definition of POS sequences, augmented with so-called affixes, expressing relevant grammatical information. We call these sequences contextual groups. This notion differs from the common notion of syntactical groups (for example, both coordinating and subordinating relations are possible within a group). The group we use is rather a contextual unit but not a syntactical one. Each group is described by a rule. When running the break assignment module we search for rules matching different word sequences. There are more than 200 rules in the grammar we used for "Orator" TTS to define possibly bound groups.

Groups can nest and intersect. Matching word sequences from an input text with rules in the grammar provide us with only a pre-segmentation of the text. An additional lap is needed to get the final segmentation which is obtaied by computing and assigning weights for each potential boundary. Boundaries of groups with the larger number of members gain larger weight: quite naturally, if a linguist introduces a long group and a segment of an input text matched (i.e. the whole combination of affixes matched, not only POS), such a group is more likely to be prosodically integral. Another main factor is break strength. If several nested groups start with the same word, the boundary before this word gains more weight in proportion to the number of groups starting with this word. A boundary after a word that several nesting groups end at is treated in the same fashion. The final decision is taken according to the weights assigned to different potential boundaries.

By means of the affixes we can describe grammatical agreement between any pair of members in a rule or state the grammatical values explicitly. Then, if those coincide with the actual properties of a string of words from an input text, the rule is considered matched. Basic set operations, such as union, logical "or" and negation, can be performed on affixes. For example, some word sequence in a text will be matched with the rule

$PRON(case=nom, gender=2, person=2) + V + PREP(accord=4) + N$

in case first word in this sequence is a pronoun in the nominative case, gender and person of which concides with those of the verb as a second word; at the same time preposition at the third position agree with the noun in the fourth position.

POS markers and affixes we use are as follows:

- POS markers: *V* (verb), *I* (infinitive), *N* (noun), *PRON* (pronoun), *NUM* (numeral), *FULL_ADJ* (full adjective), *SHORT_ADJ* (short adjective), *FULL_PART* (full participle), *ADV* (adverb), *CONJ* (conjunction), *PREP* (preposition), *COMP* (comparative), *INT* (interjection);
- Main Affixes: *animation, case, gender, number, person, tense, voice*;
- Additional Affixes: *accord* (grammatical agreement in different pre-defined sets of affixes), *addinfo* (addition information, e.g. that the verb is copulative), *lemma* (to introduce a certain wordform in a rule when it is unavoidable[2].

Such an unsophisticated design allows us to keep the grammar simple both conceptually and technically. It is very easy for a linguist to create new rules (or modify existing ones) to enlarge the grammar in order to describe those unhandled situations which appear in training corpora. After a rule is created conceptually it is a matter of seconds to formalize it using the syntax of the grammar. Adding new rules or modifying the existing ones do not call for the re-compilation of the whole system. After having made changes to the grammar a linguist can immediately start checking the influence of the rule introduced. We would also like to note that the translation of the grammar,

---

[2] This affix is used extremely rarely due to the nature of the grammar.

carried out at the start of session, as well as matching rules from the grammar with input sequences of words, is performed in a fast and efficient way.

3   Robustness Experiments

One of our main aims was to evaluate the robustness of the interface grammar we propose in this paper. The performance of the whole algorithm for various kinds of texts had already been evaluated. We used different small corpora of literary texts [9] and transcripts of spontaneous speech (the INTAS corpus [3]). The transcripts of spontaneous speech were prepared for further reading, i.e. contained punctuation that was posed by a linguist according to the Russian grammar. The results appeared at a high level, proving validity of the approach [9]. A summary is presented in Table 1.

The commonly accepted method of evaluation is used, taking account of juncture-correct rate (JC), break-correct rate (BC), juncture insertions (JI) and juncture deletions (JD) [4], [1]. Juncture is between each pair of words (the number of junctures thus corresponds to the number of whitespaces in all the sentences in a corpus). The BC rate shows the percentage of breaks in the test corpus that were predicted by the algorithm. The JC rate accounts for junctures of the same value (break or non-break) in a test and a reference corpora. JI or JD account for the wrong break insertion or, vice versa, break omission in a reference corpus. Hesitation pauses as well as speech disfluencies of any kind were not taken into account at this stage. We did not aim to model those phenomena, which, however, pertain to the directions of future research.

Table 1. Break assignment results for different corpora with account for punctuation

Corpus type	JC (%)	BC (%)	JI (%)	JD (%)
Literary corpus 1	98.1	94.3	0.9	1.0
Literary corpus 2	94.1	87.9	2.9	3.0
INTAS spontaneous speech corpus	92.0	78.1	4.1	3.9

In this paper we present the results for evaluation of a different kind. We found it interesting to perform the evaluation on the same corpora using the same evaluatio techniques, but with all inner punctuation marks deleted. Thus we totally discharge the punctuation module that generally gives the most stable and unambiguous pre-segmentation.

In case the analysis is performed on transcripts of raw spontaneous speech, the system is obviously set in the most difficult conditions possible. The results obtained in this case allow for the general evaluation of the lowest boundary of the algorithm performance.

We also get the information on contribution of inner punctuation to the prosodic segmentation of Russian texts when carrying out the break assignment tests on such punctuation-free corpora.

4   Results

Since we were mostly interested in evaluating the performance in the worst possible conditions, we firstly present the results for the raw spontaneous speech in details in

Table 2. The same evaluation was performed on two corpora of literary texts (corresponding tables for the same corpora with the account of punctuation and the description of the evaluation methods can be found in [9]). The summary results are given in Table 3.

Table 2. Results of break assignment for the INTAS spontaneous speech corpus without account for punctuation

Speaker ID	JC (%)	BC (%)	JI (%)	JD (%)
1	85.5	60.7	4.9	9.6
2	86.6	66.7	3.1	10.3
3	80.7	50.4	5.8	13.5
4	87.8	60.0	4.6	7.6
5	83.9	70.3	3.8	12.3
6	86.7	61.6	3.5	9.8
7	87.7	57.5	4.0	8.3
8	82.6	58.7	3.5	13.9
9	79.6	53.7	7.8	12.8
10	84.3	54.5	4.9	10.8
Overall	85.2	58.9	4.6	10.2

Table 3. Break assignment results for different corpora without account for punctuation

Corpus type	JC (%)	BC (%)	JI (%)	JD (%)
Literary corpus 1	89.3	53.6	2.6	8.1
Literary corpus 2	84.8	59.8	6.2	9.0
INTAS spontaneous speech corpus	85.2	58.9	4.6	10.2

As expected, when compared to the results with the inner punctuation included, the performance of the algorithm in terms of comparative JC and BC rates changes greatly.

The gaps between BC-values for different corpora reduce astonishingly from 16.5% to 6.2% between the first and the third results. Moreover, the BC-rate for the INTAS corpus appears higher than for the linguistically simplest one. Together with the fact that the latter still outperforms the former in terms of the JC-rate, this seems rather odd at a first glance. However, quite a natural explanation can be proposed. Corpus 1 is generally characterized by a small number of breaks to set due to the inherent peculiarities of constituent texts. In such a situation the cost of insertion errors appears to be much higher and the BC-rate drops faster. Even a small value of juncture-insertions turns out to be very costly due to the small number of breaks in general. At the same time the JC-rate is not as strongly influenced by the insertion errors and behave more stably.

The JC-rate for the INTAS corpus turned out higher than for the literary corpus 2. The latter is generally characterized by very long compound sentences with sophisticated linguistic structures. Thus, the inner punctuation marks play a prominent role for the segmentation of this text, defining most of the breaks. As a sequence, the loss of information on segmentation obtained from the inner punctuation marks highly influence the JC-rate.

5   Conclusions

The performance of the algorithm of break assignment presented in this paper has been evaluated both on raw and punctuationally annotated corpora. It was shown that though the performance depends on the peculiarities of an input text it stays at an acceptable level for all of them and outperforms other break assignment models developed earlier for the Russian language [6]. The algorithm was successfully implemented in the recently developed "Orator" TTS system considered state-of-art for Russian at present.

The results for the corpora without the inner punctuation turned out to be much lower than those for the punctuationally complete versions. This is in fact inevitable due to the great importance of the punctuation for break assignment algorithms of any kinds. Nevertheless, the results show that even in the worst possible case of analyzing transcripts of the raw spontaneous speech, the context analysis still does the job of prosodic segmentation. It indicates the robustness of the whole system which was one of the initial tasks to prove.

We paid special attention to keep the whole mechanism flexible and easy-to-modify. Absence of those qualities is generally the main drawback of rule-based systems. We presume the interface grammar, aimed to serve as a very simple and intuitive connector between a linguist and the core of the model, secure sufficient flexibility.

The approach was developed for the Russian language but we assume it can be used for other inflective languages. The interface grammar is designed to carry out the context analysis which is based on taking account of grammatical features of inflected wordforms. It allows detecting contextually bound groups, within which the occurrence of a prosodic boundary is highly improbable. Thus, in order to extend the approach to another inflected language, a new set of rules should be made for the grammar, which, in turn, can also be adopted to this language (new POS markers and affixes added or, vice versa, removed). The main difficulty lies in the demand for the performing of a high quality POS tagging and a grammatical annotation of an input text at earlier stages of the analysis.

References

1. Atterer, M.: Assigning Prosodic Structure for Speech Synthesis: A Rule-based Approach. In: Proceedings of Prosody 2002. Aix-en-Provence (2002) 147–150
2. Bachenko, J., Fitzpatrick, E.: A Computational Grammar of Discourse-Neutral Prosodic Phrasing in English. In: Computational Linguistics. 16 (1993) 157–167
3. Bondarko, L.V., Volskaya, N.B., Tananaiko, S.O., Vasilieva, L.A.: Phonetic Properties of Russian Spontaneous Speech. In: Proceedings of the 15th ICPhS. Barcelona, Spain (2003) 2973–2976
4. Black, A.W. Taylor, P.: Assigning phrase breaks from part-of-speech sequences. In: Proceedings of Eurospeech 1997. Rhodes, Greece (1997) 995–998.
5. Gee, J.P., Grosjean, F.: Performance Structures: A Psycholinguistic and Linguistic Appraisal. In: Cognitive Psychology, 15 (1998) 411–458
6. Krivnova, O.F.: Perceptual and semantic meaning of prosodic boundaries in a coherent text. In: Problemy Fonetiki. Moscow, Russia (1995) 228–238. In Russian.
7. Monaghan, A.I.C.: Rhythm and stress shift. In: Computer Speech and Language. 4 (1990) 71–78

8. Oparin, I., Talanov, A.: Stem-Based Approach to Pronunciation Vocabulary Construction and Language Modeling of Russian. Submitted to Eurospeech 2005. Lisbon, Portugal (2005)
9. Oparin, I.: Flexible Rule-Based Breaks Assignment for Russian. Submitted to Eurospeech 2005. Lisbon, Portugal (2005)
10. Sanders, E.: Using Probabilistic Methods to Predict Phrase Boundaries for a Text-to-Speech System. Phd thesis, University of Nijmegen, the Netherlands (1995)
11. Traber, C.: Syntactic Processing and Prosody Control in the SVOX TTS System for German. In: Proceedings of Eurospeech 1993. Berlin, Germany (1993) 2099–2102
12. Wang, M., Hirschberg, J.: Automatic Classification of Intonational Phrase Boundaries., In: Computer Speech and Language, 6 (1992).
13. Zaliznyak, A.A.: Grammatical Dictionary of the Russian Language. Moscow, Russia (1977). In Russian.
14. Zharkov, I.V., Slobodanuk, S.L. and Svetozarova, N.D.: Automatic Accent-Intonational Transcriber of a Russian Text. Bochum-St.Petersburg (1994). In Russian.

Introduction of Improved UWB
Speaker Verification System⋆

Aleš Padrta and Jan Vaněk

University of West Bohemia, Department of Cybernetics
Univerzitní 8, 306 14 Plzeň, Czech Republic
{apadrta,vanekyj}@kky.zcu.cz

Abstract. In this paper, the improvements of the speaker verification system, which is used at Department of Cybernetics at University of West Bohemia, are introduced. The paper summarizes our actual pieces of knowledge in the acoustic modeling domain, in the domain of the model creation and in the domain of score normalization based on the universal background models. The constituent components of the state-of-art verification system were modified or replaced by virtue of the actual pieces of knowledge. A set of experiments was performed to evaluate and compare the performance of the improved verification system and the baseline verification system based on HTK-toolkit. The results prove that the improved verification system outperforms the baseline system in both of the reviewed criterions – the equal error rate and the time consumption.

1   Introduction

The speaker recognition task is being solved for several years at the Department of Cybernetics. Many experiments with the constituent components of the verification system were performed since that time. At first, the module designed for acoustic modeling [1] was tested. Then, the module, which ensures the training of the model [2] was investigated. Finally, the main verification module, which evaluates the correspondence of the test data and the target speaker model [3], was tested. The constituent components were based on techniques, which were originally designed for the speech recognition [4][5] and they were modified for the speaker verification purposes.

The components, which are borrowed from the speech recognition systems, cannot be further modified, because all meaningful possible modification has been already done. Thus, we have to propose the alternative modules, which are designed primary for speaker recognition. This allows a better adaptation of the modules to the speaker recognition task and further improve the performance of the speaker recognition system.

This paper introduces the components, which are primary designed for the speaker recognition task. The baseline verification system based on HTK and the improved verification system based on new components are introduced in Section 2. The experiments

---

⋆ The work was supported by the Ministry of Education of the Czech Republic, project No. MSM 235200004, and by the Grant Agency of the Czech Republic, project No. 102/05/0278.

V. Matoušek et al. (Eds.): TSD 2005, LNAI 3658, pp. 364–370, 2005.

are described in Section 3 and their results are discussed in Section 4. Finally, a conclusion is given in Section 5.

2 Description of Verification Systems

2.1 Feature Vectors, Acoustic Modelling

The acoustic modeling module has to extract suitable speaker characteristics, which allow us to distinguish the individual speakers. These characteristics are further used for the model training and the following verification. Both tested speaker verification systems are based on the short-time spectral characteristics. A non-speech events detector is used in both systems, but they differ in the detector working domain.

Baseline System. The baseline features are computed by the HTK-Toolbox. The features are standard Mel-Frequency Cepstral Coeficients (MFCC) augmented by delta and acceleration coefficients. A preemphasis coefficient is 0.97. The length (resp. an overlap) of a Hamming window is 25 (resp. 15) millisecond. A Mel-frequency filter bank contains 25 triangular filters. Then, 13 cepstral coefficients, including zero-th (log-energy) coefficient, are computed. 13 delta and 13 acceleration coefficients are added. The final dimension of the feature vector is 39. A voice activity detector [4] removes non-speech segments from input wave files, i.e. it works in the time domain.

Improved System. The schema of the signal processing module is showed in Figure 1. It is a modified version of MFCC extended by a voice activity detector. An input speech signal is preemphasised with the coefficient 0.97. The Hamming window has 25 millisecond length and 15 millisecond overlap. A power spectrum is computed by FFT. 25 triangular band filters are set up linearly in the mel-scale between 200 and 4000 Hz. The logarithms of band-filters outputs are decorrelated by the discrete cosinus transformation (DCT). The computed cepstrum has 20 coefficients without the zero-th (log-energy) coefficient which is discarded. A time sequence of the each coefficient is smoothed by a 11 frames long Blackman window. Then the delta coefficients are added. The final dimension of the feature vector is 40. A downsampling with factor 3 is applied to the final features for the reduction amount of data. At the end, frames, which were marked as non-speech event, are removed. The non-speech event detector estimates the noise level and the speech level independently in each band. If the estimated speech level is lower than the estimated noise level then the actual feature vector is marked as non-speech event and is discarded.

2.2 Speaker Models

The speaker model, created by the model-training module, has to represent the training data exactly. Next, a good ability of data generalization is desired, because the training set is limited. The short-time spectral characteristics are usually modeled by Gaussian mixture model (GMM) [6]. The baseline system and the improved system are based on GMM, but they differ in the model training techniques.

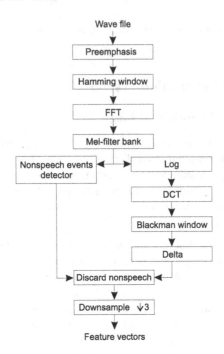

Fig. 1. Schema of acoustic modeling for improved system.

Gaussian Mixture Model. A Gaussian mixture density of a feature vector o given the parameters λ is a weighted sum of M component densities, and is given by the equation

$$p(o|\lambda) = \sum_{i=1}^{M} c_i p_i(o), \tag{1}$$

where o is an N-dimensional random vector, $p_i(o)$, $i = 1, \ldots, M$, are the component densities, and c_i, $i = 1, \ldots, M$, are the mixture weights. Each component density is an N-variate Gaussian function of the form

$$p_i(o) = \frac{1}{(2\pi)^{N/2}|\Sigma_i|^{1/2}} \exp\left\{(o - \mu_i)'\Sigma_i^{-1}(o - \mu_i)\right\} \tag{2}$$

with the mean vector μ_i and the covariance matrix Σ_i. The mixture weights satisfy the constraint

$$\sum_{i=1}^{M} c_i = 1. \tag{3}$$

The complete Gaussian mixture density model is parameterized by the mean vectors, the covariance matrices, and the mixture weights from all component densities. These parameters are collectively represented by the notation

$$\lambda = \{c_i, \mu_i, \Sigma_i\}, \quad i = 1, \ldots, M. \tag{4}$$

Baseline System. The baseline system used the HTK-toolbox for GMM training. This HTK-toolbox was originally designed for the training of Hidden Markov models (HMM). It can be used for GMM training, because an one-state self-loop continuous density HMM (Figure 2) is equivalent to a GMM. As mentioned above, the HTK-toolbox was designed for the speech recognition and its training procedure (Expectation-Maximization algorithm) is optimized for this purpose. The model created by this optimized EM algorithm differs from the model created by the standard EM algorithm.

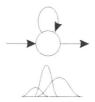

Fig. 2. One-state self-loop CDHMM: Schema of HMM and appropriate output probability density modeled by GMM.

Improved System. We desire a robust model training procedure, which is able to create the model from a relative small amount of the training data, and a high precision of the model as well. First condition is fulfilled by the Distance-based (DB) algorithm [7], but its precision is not quite accurate due to the interpretation of the clusters as the mixtures of GMM. Thus, the model created by the DB algorithm was used as the initial condition for the standard EM algorithm. The combination of the DB algorithm and the EM algorithm results in a stable, fast, and precious training procedure even for a small amount of the train data [2].

2.3   Verification Algorithm

The verification algorithm is the same for the baseline verification system and the improved verification system. The goal of the speaker verification systems is to determine whether a given utterance is produced by the claimed speaker or not. This is performed by comparing a score, which reflects the agreement between the given utterance and the model of the claimed speaker, with an a priori given threshold. In verification systems based on GMM the simplest score is the likelihood of the utterance given the model of the claimed speaker.

Assume that there is a group of J reference speakers and that each speaker is represented by a Gaussian mixture model. We denote the model of the j-th speaker as ρ_j, $j = 1, \ldots, J$. Further suppose that a test utterance O consists of I feature vectors o_i, $i = 1, \ldots, I$. The score reflecting the agreement between the feature vector o_i and the speaker j is then represented by the likelihood $p(o_i | \rho_j)$ and is computed according to the formula (1).

However, such a score is very sensitive to variations in text, speaking behavior, and recording conditions, especially in the utterances of impostors. The sensitivity causes wide variations in scores, and makes the task of the threshold determination a very difficult one. In order to overcome this sensitivity, the use of the normalized score based on a background model has been proposed [6]. The score is then determined as the normalized log likelihood $\bar{p}(o_i|\rho_j, \Lambda)$,

$$\bar{p}(o_i|\rho_j, \Lambda) = \log(p(o_i|\rho_j)) - \log(p(o_i|\Lambda)), \tag{5}$$

where $p(o_i|\Lambda)$ is the likelihood of the background model computed again using the formula (1).

3   Experimental Setup

3.1   Speech Data

Both verification system were tested on three different databases. An overview of the databases and their properties is given in Table 1. A detail description follows.

Table 1. Overview of the databases used for tests.

	UWB_S01	YOHO	KING
Number of speakers	100	138	51
Number of models	100	552	51
Number of test data	100	5,520	51
Number of trials	10,000	16,560	2,601

A part of the UWB_S01 corpus [8] was used in our experiments. It consists of speech of 100 speakers (64 male and 36 female). In our experiments, 40 sentences per speaker were used from close-talking microphone. Further, the utterances were downsampled to 8 kHz and divided into two parts: 20 utterances of each speaker were used for the training of the GMMs of the reference speakers, and one other utterance of each speaker was used for the tests. Further, 2 other utterances of each speaker were reserved for the training of the background model for the first half of speakers (the speakers with the indexes 1-50). Each model was verified with each test utterance, i.e. the total number of the performed trials was $100 \cdot 100 = 10,000$.

The recordings from the corpus YOHO [9] were used for the next test of the verification systems. It consists of a speech of 138 speakers. The training data were recorded in 4 sessions and each was modeled independently, i.e. $138 \cdot 4 = 552$ models were created. The test data were recorded in 10 sessions, each of them was tested independently. 5 other sentences from each train session for the speakers 1-69 were reserved for the background model training. Each model was verified with all target speaker sessions and 20 impostor sessions, which were randomly chosen. It means, $552 \cdot 10 + 552 \cdot 20 = 16,560$ trials were performed.

Third testing database was the KING[10] database. Only a part of the recordings, acquired via the narrow-band microphone, was used in our experiments. The utterances were divided into two parts: 5 utterances of each speaker were used for the training of the GMMs of the reference speakers and one other utterance of each speaker was used for the tests. Further, one other utterance of each speaker was reserved for the training of the background model for the first half of speakers (the speakers with the indexes 1-25). Each model was verified with each test utterance, i.e. the total number of the performed trials was $51 \cdot 51 = 2,601$.

3.2 Description of Experiments

The tests of the performance and the time consumption were measured for the baseline verification system and for the improved verification system. Both criteria were tested on the three above specified databases. The performance of the systems was measured by the equal error rate (EER). The measured time represents the duration of all steps, which are necessary to evaluate all of the specified trials: the acoustic modeling of the train data, the test data, and the background model data; the training of the speaker models and the background model; the verification procedure.

The number of the mixtures was set to 32 for all speaker models and to 256 for the background models. These settings were common for all performed experiments. The training procedures are described in Section 2.2. The number of re-estimations was set to 9 in case of the baseline verification system and to 16 in case of the improved verification system [2].

4 Experimental Results

In Table 2, the performance of both systems are presented for the above mentioned databases. The first column identifies the name of the database, second column contains EER values of the baseline verification system and the last column contains the results of the improved verification system. It can be seen from Table 2 that the improved verification system outperforms the baseline system in all tested databases.

Table 2. Overview of the EER for various databases for both systems.

Corpus	HTK-based baseline System	Improved System
UWB_S01	1.00%	0.97%
YOHO	1.83%	1.72%
KING	16.20%	13.46%

The time consumed in the experiments is presented in Table 3. The structure of the table is the same as in case of Table 2, but the duration of the tests is showed instead of the EER values. The time data are in hh:mm format. We can say after the inspection of the results in Table 3 that the improved verification system needs significantly less time to perform the speaker verification than the baseline verification system based on the HTK-toolbox. The time savings are mainly in the model training module [2].

5 Conclusion

In this paper, an improved verification system was introduced. This system consists of the modules primary designed for the speaker recognition, i.e. it does not use modified components, which were originally designed for speech recognition. At first, the

Table 3. Overview of the consumed time for various databases for both systems.

Corpus	HTK-based baseline System	Improved System
UWB_S01	9:19	0:17
YOHO	23:17	1:08
KING	6:17	0:16

acoustic modeling module, which incorporates the non-speech events detector, was presented. Then, a model training module, which is capable of a fast model creation even from a relative small amount of the training data, was described. The proposed improved verification system was compared with our baseline verification system based on the HTK-toolbox. Three databases were used to evaluate the performance of both systems. The results show that the improved system need less time to perform the verification than the baseline system. Furthermore, the performance of the improved system is better than the performance of the baseline system. It can be said, that the proposed system based on the new modules outperforms of the baseline system.

References

1. Vaněk, J., Padrta, A.: Optimization of features for robust speaker recognition, In Speech processing. Prague : Academy of Sciences of the Czech Republic, 2004. pp. 140-147. ISBN 80-86269-11-6.
2. Vaněk, J., Padrta, A., Radová, V.: An algorithm for speaker model training, Eurospeech 2005, Lisabon, 2005 (submitted)
3. Padrta, A., Radová, V.: On the background model construction for speaker verification using GMM, TSD 2004 - Text, speech and dialogue, Berlin: Springer, 2004. pp. 425-432. ISBN 3-540-23049-1. ISSN 0302-9743.
4. Prcín, M., Müller, L., Šmídl, L.: Statistical Based Speech/Non-speech Detector with Heuristic Feature Set. SCI 2002 – World Multiconference on Systemics, Cybernetics and Informatics Orlando FL-USA (2002), pp. 264–269
5. S. Young, et al.: The HTK book , Cambridge, 1995.
6. Reynolds, D. A.: Speaker identification and verification using Gaussian mixture speaker models. Speech Communication **17** (1995) 91–108
7. Zilca, R. D., Bistricz, Y., "Distance-Based Gaussian Mixture Model for Speaker Recognition over the Telephone", ISCLP 2000, pp. 1001-1003, 2000
8. Radová, V., Psutka, J.: UWB_S01 Corpus – A Czech Read-Speech Corpus. Proc. ICSLP 2000 Beijing China (2000) 732–735
9. Campbell, J. P.: Testing with the YOHO CD-ROM voice verification corpus, ICASSP 1995, 1995
10. Campbell Jr., J. P., Reynolds, D. A.: Corpora for the Evaluation of Speaker Recognition Systems, ICASSP 1999, 1999

Formal Prosodic Structures
and Their Application in NLP[*]

Jan Romportl and Jindřich Matoušek

University of West Bohemia, Department of Cybernetics
Univerzitní 8, 306 14 Plzeň, Czech Republic
{rompi,jmatouse}@kky.zcu.cz

Abstract. A formal prosody description framework is introduced together with its relation to language semantics and NLP. The framework incorporates deep prosodic structures based on a generative grammar of abstract prosodic functionally involved units. This grammar creates for each sentence a structure of immediate prosodic constituents in the form of a tree. A speech corpus manually annotated by such prosodic structures is presented and its quantitative characteristics are discussed.

1 Introduction

Each sentence (i.e. utterance as an abstract concept) offers various levels of abstraction of its description. These levels mostly hierarchically cover the broad scale ranging from an acoustic and phonetic/orthographic description to a semantic and logical analysis. Suprasegmental features of speech (i.e. prosody), however, do not fit into this linear ordering – rather they parallelly interconnect the acoustic level with semantics and pragmatics in mutual interaction, which is particularly nontrivial.

Since even the transformation of a sentence from one level of a language description to a neighbouring one is noncanonical (once we have a phonetic representation of a sentence, we cannot *precisely* recall its original acoustic form, nor we often can exactly disambiguate its meaning unless we concern its context or even human "knowledge-about-world"). Generally, the closer (in terms of the aforementioned scale) two description levels are, the easier the transition from one to another is (yet still noncanonical). Obviously this is the reason for adopting such a stratificational language description – a transition from the acoustic form of a sentence directly to its semantic or logical representation (omitting the intermediate levels) is almost impossible (more formal analysis of this phenomenon from the cognitive point of view using the Alternative Set Theory is in [1]).

We propose a formal theory for the description of prosodic phenomena interaction with other levels of the language system – its aim is to "bridge" the gap on the theoretical field between suprasegmental acoustic speech features and semantics, while still being suitable for NLP purposes, such as TTS (text-to-speech) or ASR (automatic speech recognition) tasks. This framework involves description of sentences by abstract

[*] This research was supported by Grant Agency of Czech Republic, project No. GAČR 102/05/0278.

prosodic structures (in the form of trees generated by a special prosodic phrase grammar) and linkage of these structures both to the surface realization of prosodic phenomena (specially F0, intensity, duration) and the deep semantic structure (tectogrammatics).

The current stage of the research involves partial implementation of a TTS prosody model based on this concept (see [2]), development of specially annotated corpora and appropriate prosodic grammar parser, which is crucially needed for the full implementation of the TTS prosody model.

2   Prosodic Structures

Let us suppose each sentence can be fully semantically – in the scope of linguistics (e.g. not logic, paralinguistics or whatsoever) – described by a tectogrammatical representation (tree structure, similar to surface syntactic structure, see [5]) which takes into account various contextual "inter-sentence" links and dependencies (e.g. topic-focus articulation).

A sentence (concerning only its surface representation) can often have more different tectogrammatical representations, especially in the case it is in a written form and without further context. This semantic ambiguity is caused by homonymy principally bound to the syntax and can be eliminated either by the sentence context analysis or by the suprasegmental acoustic means (prosody).

A frequent and well known example is: "I saw an airplane flying to Chicago." One can utter this sentence with many distinct intonations, yet each will eventually be understood in one of two ways corresponding to two different readings (e.g. interpretations, tectogrammatical structures) of the sentence. This supports the assumption there are two levels of prosody – the surface level (actual realization of intonation and timing using F0, intensity and duration modulations) and the underlying deep level, which is one of the constitutive components of the sentence meaning.

We propose the framework where the structures of this underlying prosody level consist of the following abstract entities (non-terminal symbols for a generative grammar are parenthesised):

Prosodic sentence (PS)
Prosodic sentence is a prosodic manifestation of a sentence as a syntactically consistent unit, yet it can also be unfinished or grammatically incorrect.
Prosodic clause (PC)
Prosodic clause is such a linear unit of a prosodic sentence which is delimited by pauses.
Prosodic phrase (PP)
Prosodic phrase is such a segment of speech where a certain intonation scheme is realized continuously. A single prosodic clause often contains more prosodic phrases.
Prosodeme (P0), (Px)
Prosodeme is an abstract unit established in a certain communication function within the language system. We have postulated that any single prosodic phrase consists of two prosodemes: so called "null prosodeme" and "functionally involved prosodeme" (where (Px) stands for a type of the prosodeme chosen from the list shown below),

depending on the communication function the speaker intends the sentence to have. In the present research we distinguish the following prosodemes (for the Czech language; other languages may need some modifications):

P0 – null prosodeme; P1 – prosodeme terminating satisfactorily (P1-1 no indication; P1-2 indicating emphasis; P1-3 indicating imperative; P1-4 indicating interjection; P1-5 indicating wish; P1-6 specific); P2 – prosodeme terminating unsatisfactorily (P2-1 no indication; P2-2 indicating emphasis; P2-3 indicating "wh-" question; P2-4 indicating emphasised "wh-" question; P2-5 specific); P3 – prosodeme nonterminating (P3-1 no indication; P3-2 indicating emphasis; P3-3 specific)

Prosodic word (PW)

Prosodic word (sometimes also called phonemic word) is a group of words subordinated to one word accent (stress). Languages with a non-fixed stress position would need a stress position indicator too.

Semantic accent (SA)

By this term we call such a prosodic word attribute, which indicates the word is emphasised (using acoustic means) by a speaker.

2.1 Prosodic Grammar

The well formed prosodic structures (trees) are determined by the generative prosodic phrase grammar. This grammar uses two more terminal symbols ("$" and "#") which stand for pauses differing in their length. The symbol (w_i) stands for a concrete word from a lexicon and $\emptyset$ means an empty terminal symbol. The rules should be understood this way: $(PC) \longrightarrow (PP)\{1+\} \#\{1\}$ means that the symbol (PC) (prosodic clause) generates one or more (PP) symbols (prosodic phrases) followed by one $\#$ symbol (pause).

$$(S) \longrightarrow (PC)\{1+\} \$\{1\} \tag{1}$$

$$(PC) \longrightarrow (PP)\{1+\} \#\{1\} \tag{2}$$

$$(PP) \longrightarrow (P0)\{1\} (Px)\{1\} \tag{3}$$

$$(P0) \longrightarrow \emptyset \tag{4}$$

$$(P0) \longrightarrow (PW)\{1+\} \tag{5}$$

$$(P0) \longrightarrow (SA)\{1\} (PW)\{1+\} \tag{6}$$

$$(Px) \longrightarrow (PW)\{1\} \tag{7}$$

$$(Px) \longrightarrow (SA)\{1\} (PW)\{2+\} \tag{8}$$

$$(PW) \longrightarrow (w_i)\{1+\} \tag{9}$$

The grammar can be transformed into the Chomsky's normal form, yet the "intuitive" form shown above is more explanatory. The rule (1) rewrites a sentence into one or more prosodic clauses followed by an inter-sentence pause. The rule (2) analogically rewrites a prosodic clause into prosodic phrases followed by an inter-clause (intra-sentence respectively) pause.

The important rule (3) represents the structure of a prosodic phrase: a prosodic phrase consists of two prosodemes – a "null" prosodeme and a "functionally involved" prosodeme. The "null" prosodeme can either be empty or consist of any number of prosodic words – according to the rules (4) and (5) – or it comprises a semantic accent at the beginning, followed by at least one prosodic word, as it is in the rule (6) used for a specific "wh-" question intonation.

The rules (7) and (8) represent the structure of a "functionally involved" prosodeme: it either consists of a single prosodic word (common case with automated "unmarked" position of an intonation centre at the end of a sentence), or it starts with a semantic accent followed by at least two prosodic words (this is a "marked" scheme reflecting the topic-focus articulation).

The relation between semantic distinctions and prosodic features can be seen on the following examples. The question: "Why are you so sad?" can easily have the answer: "They stole our car." (in Czech: "Ukradli nám auto.") Such a situation is represented by this structure:

$$((_S) (_{PC}) (_{PP}) (_{P0}) \text{ ukradli nám}) (_{P1-1}) \text{ auto})))) $$

On the contrary, if one asks: "Did they steal your motorbike again?", the reply can be: "CAR it is, what they stole." (in Czech, more flexibly: "AUTO nám ukradli.").

$$((_S) (_{PC}) (_{PP}) (_{P0}) \emptyset) (_{P1-1}) (SA) \text{ auto nám ukradli})))) $$

Another example demonstrates different prosodic structures of the "same" (on the surface level, not in the tectogrammatics) sentence even without changing the word order:

$$((_S) (_{PC}) (_{PP}) (_{P0}) \text{ I saw}) (_{P3-1}) \text{ an airplane})) (_{PP}) (_{P0}) \text{ flying}) (_{P1-1}) \text{ to Chicago})))) $$

$$((_S) (_{PC}) (_{PP}) (_{P0}) \text{ I saw}) (_{P1-1}) (SA) \text{ an airplane flying to Chicago})))) $$

2.2   Prosody-Semantics Relation

Now let us suppose we have a sentence S with its one and only one corresponding tectogrammatical structure T_S (possible homonymy is thus disambiguated). Let $\mathcal{P}_S$ be a set of all conceivable prosodic structures of the sentence S without considering T_S. Then T_S determines a subset $\mathcal{P}_{TS} \subseteq \mathcal{P}_S$ of the prosodic structures "allowed" for this particular T_S, i.e. the given semantic interpretation. The different structures from $\mathcal{P}_{TS}$ may perhaps slightly vary in the deployment of prosodic phrases or other units, but only to the extent not contradictory to the given T_S. The relation between prosodic structures from $\mathcal{P}_{TS}$ and the appropriate surface prosodic forms of the uttered sentence S (i.e. F0, intensity and segmental duration) is crucial for prosody modelling in TTS systems and is analysed in [2].

The opposite process (e.g. suitable for ASR and natural language understanding) assumes we have an uttered sentence S_u with a particular (measurable) surface prosodic features (intonation, etc.) i_{S_u}. The sentence S_u can be assigned with a set $\mathcal{T}_S$ of all its possible tectogrammatical representations. Each element $T_S^j \in \mathcal{T}_S$ (j-th possible tectogrammatic structure, i.e. j-th meaning) determines its own $\mathcal{P}_{TS}^j$ as it is described above. The surface prosody i_{S_u} is assigned (theoretically using an appropriate classifier) with a set $\mathcal{P}_i$ of all its possible deep prosodic interpretations (i.e. homonymous tree prosodic structures – having the same allowed surface form, again see [2]). As a result we obtain a set of *correct* semantic interpretations of the uttered sentence S_u: it is a subset $\mathcal{T}_C \subseteq \mathcal{T}_S$ of T_S^j such that

$$\forall T_S^j \in \mathcal{T}_S : T_S^j \in \mathcal{T}_C \Leftrightarrow \left(\exists p : p \in \mathcal{P}_{TS}^j \land p \in \mathcal{P}_i \right) \tag{10}$$

Informally: T_S^j is a correct semantic interpretation of S_u provided that at least one prosodic structure determined by T_S^j is also allowed by (or is "underlying" of) the surface prosody i_{S_u}. In case the set $\mathcal{T}_C$ has more than one element the meaning of the uttered sentence cannot be fully disambiguated through prosody itself and thus perhaps further context of the sentence must be taken into account to prune the set $\mathcal{T}_S$. However, the aforementioned relations well capture the mutual functioning of prosody, semantics and deliberate acting of a speaker.

3   Prosodic Data

Since this paper does not deal with the relation between the prosodic structures and the surface prosodic form (concrete F0, intensity and duration), we leave the question of gathering such data open. The issue of generating the surface prosody from the prosodic structures for the sake of a TTS system is discussed in the article [2].

If there is to be a prosodic parser suitable for TTS systems (i.e. the parser producing correct prosodic structures for input sentences, perhaps with partially or fully unknown tectogrammatic structures), one must employ suitable training and testing data of adequate amount.

3.1   Prosodic Corpus Annotations

We have chosen 3 most frequent radio news announcers from the *Czech TV & Radio Broadcast News Corpus* recorded at the Department of Cybernetics, University of West Bohemia in Pilsen (see [3], [4]) and arranged a project of manual prosodic annotation of their speech (with additional constraints and criteria approx. 1,500 sentences altogether have been selected from the total of 16,483). Since this was the first attempt to employ the presented prosodic theory for a real corpus, the amount of data was relatively small and such was also the number of annotators involved. Another drawback is the fact the corpus consists in crushing majority only of declarative sentences.

The first stage of the corpus processing involved three annotators – each annotating one speaker. The second stage is still in progress and involves independent re-annotating of all three speakers (each by an annotator other than the one in the first stage) which allows assignment of the inter-annotator consensus. We do not expect this consensus to be much high because the process of the prosodic annotating often requires subjective judgement, rather we expect each annotator profiles himself/herself with a specific style of "prosody understanding" and we presuppose this style to be more or less constant even among various speaker annotations.

During the annotation process each annotator has available a waveform of all uttered sentences together with their transcriptions and F0, filtered F0 and intensity curves. Moreover, there is a manual and a set of pre-annotated examples at disposal to set up a general standard for the annotation and precedents for arguable or ambiguous cases.

The F0 curve was extracted from the waveforms using the RAPT algorithm [6] implemented in the *Snack* toolkit [7]. Despite being very robust, this algorithm is also susceptible to doubling and halving errors. It has been shown [8] the estimated pitch having been exposed to halving and doubling obeys the lognormal tied mixture (LTM) probabilistic distribution with 3 parameters

$$
\begin{aligned}
\log(\hat{F}_0) &\sim LTM\left(\mu, \sigma, \lambda_1, \lambda_2, \lambda_3\right) = \\
&= \lambda_1 \cdot \mathcal{N}\left(\mu - \log(2), \sigma^2\right) + \lambda_2 \cdot \mathcal{N}\left(\mu, \sigma^2\right) + \\
&\quad + \lambda_3 \cdot \mathcal{N}\left(\mu + \log(2), \sigma^2\right)
\end{aligned}
\tag{11}
$$

and the constraint $\sum_{i=1}^{3} \lambda_i = 1$. The parameters λ_i can be estimated by the Expectation-Maximisation (EM) algorithm. As the parameters are set up it is basically possible to exclude such pitch values that are more probable to be halved or doubled than correct.

Since the LTM fitted F0 curve still incorporates microprosody features irrelevant to the suprasegmental scope of the prosodic structures, it is purposeful to exclude them by modelling (filtering respectively) each voiced region by a piecewise linear function with nodes $\{x_k, g(x_k)\}_{k=0}^{K}$:

$$
g(x) = \sum_{k=1}^{K} \left(a_k x + b_k\right) \mathbf{I}_{[x_{k-1} < x \le x_k]}
\tag{12}
$$

The nodes are placed so as to minimise the functional

$$
MSE\left(\{x_k, g(x_k)\}_{k=0}^{K}\right) = \frac{1}{T} \sum_{t=1}^{T} \left(F_0(t) - g(t)\right)^2
\tag{13}
$$

The details on F0 extraction for the prosodic corpus together with a description of the whole *Czech TV & Radio Broadcast News Corpus* and links to the relevant literature are in [3].

In the prosodic corpus the utterances of grouped into "turns" which are annotated at once to ensure proper context and semantic link-up necessary for topic-focus and semantic accent assignment. The annotators perceptually evaluate the prosodic structures of the utterances with the aid of knowing the semantics, contextual bindings and graphical representation of the surface prosodic features (i.e. F0 and intensity).

For example the prosodic phrase boundaries are often perceptually ambiguous and hard to capture, thus the annotators are instructed to link them with the places of the major discontinuities of filtered F0 (except for those covering unvoiced consonants). Deciding whether a word bears the semantic accent is also supported by visual evaluation of the F0 slope changes – a major F0 semantic accent change should not be followed by any significant F0 discontinuity till the end of the prosodic phrase (i.e. the first discontinuity following the semantic accent is the prosodic phrase boundary) and it is also accompanied by the intensity change and does not obey the rhythmical layout of the prosodic phrase boundaries.

3.2   Quantitative Characteristics

	#PS	#PC/#PS	#PP/#PC	#SA/#PP	P1-1	P1-2	P2-1
Speaker 1	847	1.90	1.78	0.34	29.37 %	0.08 %	0.10 %
Speaker 2	410	1.17	4.86	0.23	17.00 %	0.11 %	0.10 %

	P2-3	P3-1	P3-2	P3-3	av.l.P0	av.l.Px
Speaker 1	0.10 %	66.55 %	3.66 %	0.14 %	2.25 w.	1.55 w.
Speaker 2	0.10 %	82.13 %	0.45 %	0.11 %	1.02 w.	1.27 w.

The table shows some of the relevant quantitative characteristics of the corpus and compares them between two annotators: the absolute number of sentences; the number of clauses relatively to the number of sentences; the number of phrases relatively to the number of clauses; the number of semantic accents relatively to the number of phrases; percentual occurrences of prosodemes; the average number of words in the "null" and "functionally involved" prosodemes.

Apparently the number of prosodic clauses (i.e. speech pauses) realized by the Speaker 1 (and annotated by the Annotator 1) is significantly higher than by the Speaker 2 (and the Annotator 2). This means the Speaker's 2 clauses are longer and thus composed of more prosodic phrases. However, such a difference between the speakers' ratios of the prosodic phrases (1.78 and 4.86) probably means the Annotator 2 had a higher tendency to place prosodic phrase boundaries. The integral consequence of this phenomenon is the Speaker's 2 relatively smaller number of the P1 prosodemes and higher number of the P3 prosodemes (due to the relatively higher number of non-terminating phrases).

Concerning the Speaker's 1 higher relative number of the semantic accents and thus shorter "functionally involved" prosodemes (if a Px prosodeme is longer than one word, it is necessarily linked with a semantic accent) we can perhaps assume there occurs a specific surface prosodic phenomenon in the speech which was treated as a semantic accent within a single phrase by the Annotator 1 and as a different structure of a clause (i.e. an inserted phrase boundary) by the Annotator 2 (the speech of the Speaker 2 was perhaps less emphasised). However, obviously only the independent re-annotation can contribute any firm conclusion and show whether this was the difference between speakers or annotators (or both).

4   Conclusion

Our previous research has proved the prosody model introduced in [2] is able to generate very natural prosody if supplied with adequate analysis of the deep prosodic structure of a sentences to be synthesised. A statistical parser capable of providing such an analysis has demanded the framework of the deep prosodic structures to be revisited and more suitable prosodic structure corpus to be created.

The concept of prosodic structures presented in the Section 2 of this paper formally explicates the relations between prosody and semantics and is also suitable for TTS and ASR systems. The initial project of a specific prosodic corpus creation has shown to be sufficient for the first experiments with a statistical prosodic parser necessary for our TTS prosody model. However, the future work will involve more consistent and extensive prosodic corpus (covering also a wider range of sentence modalities) annotated both in terms of prosody and semantics, chosen from such text and recorded such a way that it is also suitable for TTS speech unit retrieval combined with a unit selection method of synthesis.

References

1. Romportl, J.: Text to Prosody Generation for Speech Synthesis Purposes. University of West Bohemia in Pilsen, Pilsen (2004).
2. Romportl, J., Matoušek, J., Tihelka, D.: Advanced Prosody Modelling. Proceedings of TSD 2004. Brno (2004) 441-447.
3. Kolář, J., Romportl, J., Psutka, J.: Czech Speech and Prosody Database Both for ASR and TTS Purposes. Proceedings of Eurospeech 2003, Vol. 2. Geneve (2003) 1577-1580.
4. Psutka, J., Radová, V., Müller, L., Matoušek, J., Ircing, P., Graff, D.: Large Broadcast News and Read Speech Corpora of Spoken Czech. Proceedings of Eurospeech 2001. Aalborg (2001) 2067-2070.
5. Sgall, P., Hajičová, E., Panevová, J.: The Meaning of the Sentence in Its Semantic and Pragmatic Aspects. Reider, Dordrecht (1986).
6. Talkin, D.: A Robust Algorithm for Pitch Tracking (RAPT). In Speech Coding and Synthesis, pp. 495-518. Elsevier Science, Amsterdam (1995).
7. Sjölander, K.: The Snack Sound Toolkit <http://www.speech.kth.se/snack/>.
8. Sönmez, K., Heck, L., Weintraub, M., Shriberg E.: A Lognormal Tied Mixture Model of Pitch for Prosody-Based Speaker Recognition. In Speech Coding and Synthesis, pp. 495-518. Elsevier Science, Amsterdam (1995).

The VoiceTRAN Speech-to-Speech Communicator*

Jerneja Žganec Gros[1], France Mihelič[2], Tomaž Erjavec[3], and Špela Vintar[2]

[1] Alpineon d.o.o., Ulica Iga Grudna 15
SI-1000 Ljubljana, Slovenia
jerneja@alpineon.com
http://www.alpineon.com
[2] University of Ljubljana
SI-1000 Ljubljana, Slovenia
france.mihelic@fe.uni-lj.si
spela.vintar@guest.arnes.si
[3] Jožef Stefan Insitute, Jamova 39
SI-1000 Ljubljana, Slovenia
tomaz.erjavec@ijs.si

Abstract. The paper presents the design concept of the VoiceTRAN Communicator that integrates speech recognition, machine translation and text-to-speech synthesis using the DARPA Galaxy architecture. The aim of the project is to build a robust speech-to-speech translation communicator able to translate simple domain-specific sentences in the Slovenian-English language pair. The project represents a joint collaboration between several Slovenian research organizations that are active in human language technologies. We provide an overview of the task, describe the system architecture and individual servers. Further we describe the language resources that will be used and developed within the project. We conclude the paper with plans for evaluation of the VoiceTRAN Communicator.

1 Introduction

Automatic speech-to-speech (STS) translation systems aim to facilitate communication among people who speak in different languages [1], [2], [3]. Their goal is to generate a speech signal in the target language that conveys the linguistic information contained in the speech signal from the source language.

There are, however, major open research issues that challenge the deployment of natural and unconstrained speech-to-speech translation systems, even for very restricted application domains, due to the fact that state-of-the-art automatic speech recognition and machine translation systems are far from perfect. Additionally, in comparison to translating written text, conversational spoken messages are often conveyed with imperfect syntax and casual spontaneous speech. In practice, when building demonstration systems, STS systems are typically implemented by imposing strong constraints on the application domain and the type and structure of possible utterances, i.e. both in the range and in the scope of the user input allowed at any point of the interaction. Consequently, this compromises the flexibility and naturalness of using the system.

---

* The authors of the paper thank the Slovenian Ministry of Defense and the Slovenian Ministry of Higher Education, Science and Technology for co-funding the project.

V. Matoušek et al. (Eds.): TSD 2005, LNAI 3658, pp. 379–384, 2005.

The VoiceTRAN Communicator is being built within a national Slovenian research project involving 5 partners: Alpineon, the University of Ljubljana (Faculty of Electrical Engineering, Faculty of Arts and Faculty of Social Studies), the Jožef Stefan Institute, and Amebis as a subcontractor.

The project is cofunded by the Slovenian Ministry of Defense. The aim of the project is to build a robust speech-to-speech translation communicator, similar to Phraselator [4] or Speechalator [5], able to translate simple sentences in a Slovenian-English language pair.

The application domain is limited to common application scenarios that occur in peace-keeping operations on foreign missions when the users of the system have to communicate with the local population. More complex phrases can be entered via keyboard using a graphical user interface.

2 System Architecture

The VoiceTRAN Communicator uses the DARPA Galaxy Communicator architecture [6]. The Galaxy Communicator open source architecture was chosen to provide inter-module communication support as its plug-and-play approach allows interoperability of commercial software and research software components.

The VoiceTRAN Communicator consists of the Hub and five servers: audio server, graphic user interface, speech recognizer, machine translator and speech synthesizer (Fig. 1).

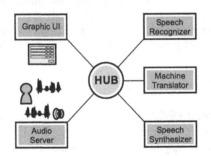

Fig. 1. The VoiceTRAN system architecture.

There are two ways of porting modules into the Galaxy architecture: the first is to alter its code so that it can be incorporated into the Galaxy architecture; the second is to create a wrapper or a capsule for the existing module, the capsule then behaves as a Galaxy server. We have opted for the second option since we want to be able to test commercial modules as well. Minimal changes to the existing modules were required, mainly those regarding input/output processing.

A particular session is initiated by a user either through interaction with a graphical user interface (typed input) or the microphone. The VoiceTRAN Communicator servers capture spoken or typed input from the user, and return the servers' responses with synthetic speech, graphics, and text. The server modules are described in more detail in the next subsections.

2.1   Audio Server

The audio server connects to the microphone input and speaker output terminals on the host computer and performs recoding user input and playing prompts or synthesized speech. Input speech captured by the audio server is automatically recorded to files for later system training.

2.2   Speech Recognizer

The speech recognition server receives the input audio stream from the audio server and provides at its output a ranked list of candidate sentences, the N-best hypotheses list that can include part-of-speech information generated by the language model.

The speech recognition server used in VoiceTRAN is based on the Hidden Markov Model Recognizer developed by the University of Ljubljana [7]. It will be upgraded to perform large vocabulary speaker (in)dependent speech recognition on a wider application domain. A bigram or a back-off class-based trigram language model will be used. Given a limited amount of training data the parameters in the models will be carefully chosen in order to achieve maximum performance.

Further in the project we want to test other speech recognition approaches with an emphasis on robustness, processing time, footprint and memory requirements.

Since the final goal of the project is a stand-alone speech communicator used by a specific user, the speech recognizer can be additionally trained and adapted to the user of the device in order to achieve higher recognition accuracy at least in one language.

A common speech recognizer output typically has no information on sentence boundaries, punctuation and capitalization. Therefore, additional postprocessing in terms of punctuation and capitalization will be performed on the N-best hypotheses list before it is passed to the machine translator. The inclusion of a prosodic module will be investigated in order to link the source language to the target language, but also to enhance speech recognition proper.

2.3   Machine Translator

The machine translator (MT) converts text strings from a source language into text strings in the target language. Its task is difficult since the results of the speech recognizer convey spontaneous speech patterns and are often erroneous or ill-formed.

A postprocessing algorithm inserts basic punctuation and capitalization information before passing the target sentence to the speech synthesizer. The output string can also convey lexical stress information in order reduce disambiguation efforts during text-to-speech synthesis.

A multi-engine based approach will be used in the early phase of the project that makes it possible to exploit strengths and weaknesses of different MT technologies and to choose the most appropiate engine or combination of engines for the given task. Four different translation engines will be applied in the system. We will combine TM (translation memories), SMT (statistical machine translation), EBMT (example-based machine translation) and RBMT (rule-based machine translation) methods. A simple approach to select the best translation from all the outputs will be applied.

A bilingual aligned domain-specific corpus will be used to build the TM and train the EBMT and the SMT phrase translation models. In SMT an interlingua approach, similar to the one described in [3] will be investigated and promissing directions pointed out in [8] will be pursued.

The Presis translation system will be used as our baseline system [9]. It is a commercial conventional rule-based translation system that is constantly being optimized and upgraded. It will be adapted to the application domain by upgrading the lexicon. Based on stored rules, Presis parses each sentence in the source language into grammatical components, such as subject, verb, object and predicate and attributes the relevant semantic categories. Then it uses built-in rules for converting these basic components into the target language, performs regrouping and generates the output sentence in the target language.

2.4 Speech Synthesizer

The last part in a speech-to-speech translation task is the conversion of the translated utterance into its spoken equivalent. The input target text sentence is equipped with lexical stress information at possible ambiguous words.

The AlpSynth unit-selection text-to-speech system is used for this purpose [10]. It performs grapheme-to-phoneme conversion based on rules and a look-up dictionary and rule-based prosody modeling. It will be further upgraded within the project towards better naturalness of the resulting synthetic speech. Domain-specific adaptations will include new pronunciation lexica and the construction of a speech corpus of frequently used in-domain phrases. Other commercial off-the-shelf products will be tested as well.

We will also explore how to pass a richer structure from the machine translator to the speech synthesizer. An input structure containing information on POS and lexical stress information resolves many ambiguities and can result in more accurate prosody prediction.

2.5 Graphical User Interface

In addition to the speech user interface, the VoiceTRAN Communicator provides a simple interactive user-friendly graphical user interface where input text in the source language can also be entered via a keyboard.

Recognized sentences in the source language along with their translated counterparts in the target language are displayed.

A push-to-talk button is provided to signal an input voice activity, a replay button serves to start a replay of the synthesized translated utterance. The translation direction can be changed by pressing the translation direction button.

3 Language Resources

For building the speech components of the VoiceTRAN system, existing speech corpora will be used [11]. The language model will be trained on a domain-specific text corpus that is being collected and annotated within the project. The AlpSynth pronunci-ation lexicon [10] will be used for both speech recognition and text-to-speech synthesis. Speech synthesis will be based on the AlpSynth speech corpus. It will be expanded by the most frequent in-domain utterances. For developing the initial machine translation component, the dictionary of military terminology and various existing aligned parallel corpora will be used [12].

3.1 Data Collection Efforts

The VoiceTRAN team will participate in the annotation of an in-domain large Slove-nian monolingual text corpus that is being collected at the Faculty of Social Studies, University of Ljubljana. This corpus will be used for training the language model in the speech recognizer, as well as for inducing relevant multiword units (collocations, phrases and terms) for the domain.

Within VoiceTRAN, an aligned bilingual in-domain corpus is also being collected. It will consist of general and scenario-specific in-domain sentences. The compilation of such corpora involves selecting and obtaining the digital original of the bi-texts, recoding to XML TEI P4, sentence alignment, word-level syntactic tagging and lem-matisation [13]. Such pre-processed corpora are then used to induce bi-lingual single word and phrase lexica for the MT component, or as direct inputs for SMT and EBMT systems. They will also serve for additional training of the speech recognizer language model.

4 Planned Evaluation

Evaluation efforts within the VoiceTRAN project will serve for two purposes: to eval-uate whether we have improved the system by introducing improvement of individual components of the system; and to test the system acceptancy by potential users in field tests.

We intend to perform end-to-end translation quality tests both on manually tran-scribed and automatic speech recognition input. Human graders will asses the end-to-end translation performance evaluating how much of the user input information has been conveyed to the target language and also how well formed the target sentences are. Back-translation evaluation experiments involving paraphrases will be considered, as well.

We will also perform individual component tests in order to select the most ap-propriate methods for each application server. Speech recognition will be evaluated by computing standard word error rates (WER). For the machine translation component subjective evaluation tests in terms of fluency and adequacy are planned, as well as ob-jective evaluation tests [14], having in mind that objective evaluation methods evaluate the translation quality in terms of the capacity of the system to mimick the reference text.

5 Conclusion

The VoiceTRAN project provides an attempt to build a robust speech-to-speech trans-lation communicator able to translate simple domain-specific sentences in a Slovenian-

English language pair. The concept of the VoiceTRAN Communicator implementation is discussed in the paper. The chosen system architecture allows for testing a variety of server modules.

References

1. Lavie, A., Waibel, A., Levin, L., Finke, M., Gates, D., Gavalda, M., Zeppenfeld, T., Zhan, P.: Janus-III: Speech-to-Speech Translation in Multiple Languages. In Proceedings of the ICASSP, Munich, Germany (1997) (99-102)
2. Wahlster, W.: Verbmobil: Foundation of Speech-to-Speech translation. Springer Verlag (2000)
3. Lavie, A., Metze, F., Cattoni, R., Costantin, E.,, Burger, S., Gates, D., Langley, C., Laskowski, K., Levin, L., Peterson, K., Schultz, T., Waibel A., Wallace, D., McDonough, J., Soltau, H., Lazzari, G., Mana, N., Pianesi, F., Pianta, E., Besacier, L., Blanchon, H., Vaufreydaz, D., Taddei, L.: A Multi-Perspective Evaluation of the NESPOLE! Speech-to-Speech Translation System. In Proceedings of the ACL 2002 workshop on Speech-to-speech Translation: Algorithms and Systems, Philadelphia, PA (2002)
4. Sarich, A.: Phraselator, one-way speech translation system. (2001) Available at http://www.sarich.com/translator/
5. Waibel, A., Badran, A., Black, A. W., Frederking, R., Gates, D., Lavie, A., Levin, L., Lenzo, K., Mayfield Tomokyo, L., Reichert, J., Schultz, T., Wallace, D., Woscsyna, M., Zhang, J. Speechalator: Two-Way Speech-to-Speech Translation on a Consumer PDA. In Proceedings of the Eurospeech, Geneva, Switzerland. (2003) pp. 369-372
6. Seneff, S., Hurley, E., Lau, R., Pao, C., Schmid, P., Zue, V.: Galaxy-II: A Reference Architecture for Conversational System Development. In Proceedings of the ICSLP, Sydney, Australia (1998) pp. 931-934
7. Dobrišek, S.: Analysis and Recognition of Phrases in Speech Signals. PhD Thesis, University of Ljubljana, Slovenia. (2001)
8. Ney, H.: The Statistical Approach to Spoken Language Translation. In Proceedings of the International Workshop on Spoken Language Translation, Kyoto, Japan (2004) pp. XV-XVI
9. Romih, M., Holozan, P.: Slovensko-angleški prevajalni sistem (A Slovene-English Translation System). In Proceedings of the 3rd Language Technologies Conference, Ljubljana, Slovenia (2002) p. 167
10. Žganec Gros, J., Mihelič, A., Žganec, M., Pavešić, N., Mihelič, F., Cvetko Orešnik, V.: Alp-Synth corpus-driven Slovenian text-to-speech synthesis : designing the speech corpus. In Proceedings of the joint conferences CTS+CIS, Rijeka, Croatia (2004), pp. 107-110
11. Mihelič, F., Gros, J., Dobrišek, S., Žibert, J., Pavešić, N.: Spoken language resources at LUKS of the University of Ljubljana. International Journal on Speech Technologies, Vol. 6. No. 3 (2003) pp. 221-232
12. Erjavec, T.: The IJS-ELAN Slovene-English parallel corpus. International Journal on Corpus Linguistics, Vol. 7 No. 1 (2002) pp. 1-20
13. Erjavec, T., Džeroski, S.: Machine Learning of Language Structure: Lemmatising Unknown Slovene Words. Applied Artificial Intelligence, Vol. 18, No. 1 (2004) pp. 17-41
14. MT Evaluation Kit. NIST MT Evaluation Kit Version 11a. (2002) Available at http://www.nist.gov/speech/tests/mt.

Cluster Analysis of Railway Directory Inquire Dialogs*

Mikhail Alexandrov[1,2], Emilio Sanchis Arnal[2], and Paolo Rosso[2]

[1] National Polytechnic Institute, Mexico
dyner1950@mail.ru
[2] Polytechnic University of Valencia, Spain
{esanchis,prosso}@dsic.upv.es

Abstract. Cluster analysis of dialogs with transport directory service allows revealing the typical scenarios of dialogs, which is useful for designing automatic dialog systems. We show how to parameterize dialogs and how to control the process of clustering. The parameters include both data of transport service and features of passenger s behavior. Control of clustering consists in manipulating the parameter s weights and checking stability of the results. This technique resembles Makagonov s approach to the analysis of dweller s complaints to city administration. We shortly describe B. Stein s new MajorClust method and demonstrate its work on real person-to-person dialogs provided by Spanish railway service.

1 Introduction

In the recent years, much effort has been devoted to development of automatic dialog systems. This topic is well represented at the conferences related with Dialog Processing [6]. One of the first phases in the design of such systems consists in definition of the dialog domain, as well as the different types of dialogs to be conducted. The type of dialog depends on the information requested (which is reflected in lexical and semantic restrictions of the task), the type of user (novice or expert), etc. Usually this analysis is performed manually basing on a set of real person-to-person dialogs. Then the obtained classification is used to define the behavior of the dialog manager or to acquire a corpus of dialogs by using the Wizard of Oz technique [5].

In this paper, we consider another technique consisting in:
- manual parameterization of dialog set;
- filtering selected parameters;
- objective clustering.

These steps correspond to the approach developed by Makagonov [3] for the analysis of letters and complaints of Moscow dwellers directed to Moscow city administration.

The set of parameters is supposed to reflect both the specificity of a given public service and some features of a passenger. We show how to make correct scaling for quantitative or qualitative parameters of a dialog. Analysis of the parameter s distribution allows detecting and eliminating non-informative parameters. Clustering is applied both to dialogs themselves and to their parameters.

---

* Work done under partial support of the Government of Valencia, Mexican Government (CONACyT), R2D2 CICYT (TIC2003-07158-C04-03), and ICT EU-India (ALA/95/23/2003/077-054).

V. Matoušek et al. (Eds.): TSD 2005, LNAI 3658, pp. 385–392, 2005.

The procedure of clustering uses the MajorClust method recently developed by Stein et al. [7]. This method was selected because it proved to be more adequate to data and problem settings than other methods. We briefly describe it below.

In the experiments we used examples related with Spanish railway directory inquires, obtained in the framework of Basurde projects [1].

2   Parametrization

2.1   Examples of Dialogs and Their Parameterization

The final purpose of dialog parameterization is to present all acts of dialogs in the form of the numerical matrix "objects/parameters", where the objects are dialogs themselves and the parameters are characteristics reflecting both railway service and passenger behavior. Such a matrix allows calculating the distance (similarity) between objects, which is the input data for any method of cluster analysis.

Table 1 shows the difficulties of parameterization (the records are translated from Spanish into English). Here *US* stands for a user and *DI* for a directory inquire service. This example concerns the train departure from Barcelona to the other destinations both near the Barcelona and in other provinces of Spain. Such limited dialogs constitute approximately 25% of total number of dialogs, other dialogs being 2 to 5 times longer. This dialog gives an impression on the difficulties of dialog parameterization.

Table 1. Example of real dialog between passengers and directory inquires

DI: Renfe, good day US: Yes, good day DI: Yes, well. US: OK, could you inform me about the trains that go from here, from Barcelona to Valladolid? DI: What day it will be? US: The next Thursday. DI: Let us to see. \<PAUSE\> on Thursday is off the one at thirteen, which come at twenty	two hours to Valladolid US: Are there any more? DI: No, on Thursday only this one, eh? US: Nothing more, say me, please. DI: Exactly. US: \<CONTINUALLY\> before the Wednesday or Thursday. DI: The train will be exactly at evening, on Thursday or Friday it is off. US: Thank you, bye

One can note the following three features of such dialogs: many aspects concerning the trip are not reflected in a specific dialog; many characteristics are diffuse; and much information is presented in a hidden form. To take into account these circumstances, we use nominal scales with the value "indifference" and interval scales, respectively. All parameters are normalized to the interval [0, 1]. The parameters we initially introduced are presented below:

1. **City weight** (*City*). This parameter reflects the economic importance of the city. Its possible values are 0.75, 0.5, 0.25, 0, reflecting large, middle, small, and local cities, respectively. The value 1 is reserved.

2. **Complexity** (*Cx*). In our case, this binary parameter reflects the necessity of transfer.

3. **Urgency and definiteness** (*U/D*). This numerical parameter is introduced to reflect the profile of passenger rather then the railway service. Its possible values are 1, 0.5, and 0: urgent departure at the same day, departure at a certain day during a week or month, and the indifference to the day of departure.

4. **Round trip** (*T/F*). It is a binary parameter with obvious values 1 and 0.

5. **Time of departure** (*T*). This parameter is presented in the form of three nominal scales with two binary values 1 and 0 for each of them: indifference to time (*Ti*), leaving in the morning or in the day (*Tm*), leaving in the evening or at night (*Te*).

6. **Time of departure on return** (*F*). This parameter is similar to the previous one.

7. **Sleeping car** (*Car*). It is a binary parameter.

8. **Discounts** (*Ds*). It is a binary parameter meaning whether or not a passenger discussed his/her possible discount with directory inquire service.

9. **Knowledge** (*Kn*). This parameter reflects any a priori information a passenger possesses about railway service. Values 1 and 0.5 mean the passenger wants to check up or refers to any previous information, respectively; otherwise, we use 0.

10. **Length of talking** (*Tk*). This parameter can serve as an indicator of question complexity or the passenger s competence. It has five numerical values from 1 to 0 with step 0.25, which correspond to non-uniform scale of question-answer numbers.

11. **Politeness** (*Pl*). We introduced formal rules for evaluation of this characteristic. Value 1 means that the passenger uses "you" in the polite form (Spanish distinguishes two degrees of polite treatment, reflected in different forms of "you" and verbal conjugation), "please" , and apologetic style (reflected in the use of subjunctive forms in Spanish). Value 0.5 means a passenger uses "you" in polite form or in normal familiar form together with subjunctive forms; otherwise, we use 0.

Given these parameters, our example can be presented in a parameterized form, as shown in Table 2. Here *Ti-Tm-Te* and *Fi-Fm-Fe* are nominal scales for qualitative parameters (5) and (6).

Table 2. Parametrized example

City	Cx	U/D	T/F	Ti-Tm-Te	Fi-Fm-Fe	Car	Kn	Ds	Tk	Pl
0.25	0	0.5	0	0 0 1	1 0 0	0	0	0	0	0.5

2.2 Parameter Filtering

The clustering procedure requires that the introduced parameters be filtered in order to reduce the influence of any strong dominant processes and any sources of possible noise. The former can hide the real structure we want to reveal and the latter can disfigure it. For this, all parameters are divided into the following three groups [3]:

- Parameters from the first group have a significant value for almost all objects;
- Parameters from the second group have a significant value for a small fraction of the total number of objects;

- Parameters from the third group have a significant value for more than, say, 30% of the total number of objects.

By a significant value of a parameter, we generally mean a value larger than 50% of the maximum value for this parameter. By almost all objects or a small fraction of all objects, we mean 90% 95% and 5% 10% of the total number of objects, respectively.

From the point of view of the system, the parameters in the first group reflect the processes in a system of higher level in comparison with the one under consideration. The parameters in second group reflect the processes in a subsystem [3]. On the current level of data consideration, the mentioned groups of parameters should be eliminated.

This conclusion is supported by cluster analysis. From the point of view of cluster analysis, the first group of parameters is oriented to the uniform object set, i.e. to one cluster, whereas the second group of parameters is oriented to very granulated object set, at least 10 clusters or more [4]. The first situation is not interesting at all, and the second one is too detailed for reflecting the structure as a whole. Therefore, cluster analysis approach also confirms the necessity of eliminating of both groups of parameters.

To apply these results to our data set, we calculated the average value for each parameter; see Table 3.

Table 3. Average value of each parameter for 100 dialogs, in percents

City	Cx	U/D	T/F	To-Tm-Te	Fi-Fm-Fe	Car	Kn	Ds	Tk	Pl
37	7	44.5	35	32 32 36	80 9 11	18	4	9	31	40

Since the maximum value of each parameter is equal to 1, we can easily select the parameters of the second group: Cx, Fm, Fe, Kn, Ds. For all these parameters, the number of significant values is less or equal to 10%. As for the first group, we decided to eliminate the parameter Fi, because its value is very close to the boundary value of 90% and from the other hand, this parameter is not interesting for interpretation: it means the indifference to the time of departure from the point of destination.

3   Clustering

3.1   Method of Clustering

For a moment, there are dozens of methods and their modifications in cluster analysis, which can satisfy practically all necessities of users. The most popular ones are K-means, oriented on the structures of spherical form, and Nearest Neighbor (NN), oriented on the extended structures of chain form [2]. In our work, we use the MajorClust method, recently developed by Stein et al. [7], which has the following advantages over the mentioned two:

- MajorClust distributes objects to clusters in such a way that the similarity of an object to the assigned cluster exceeds its similarity to any other cluster. This natural criterion provides the grouping of objects, which better corresponds to the users intuitive representation. Neither K-means nor NN methods possess such optimization property: they do not evaluate the similarity between clusters.

- MajorClust determines the number of clusters automatically and in all cases tends to reduce this number. K-means requires the number of cluster to be given, and NN does not determine this number at all: cutting of the dendrite is performed by the user.

MajorClust has been successfully used with various data sets and demonstrated very good results [8]. The main disadvantage of MajorClust is its runtime. However, in case of sparse matrix of relations this disadvantage is not essential. In our problem, we are faced just with this case because of zero values of the majority of dialog parameters.

3.2 Distance Matrices and Manipulations with Them

In our clustering procedure, we used two distance matrices: objects/objects (cities/cities) and parameters/parameters. To construct such matrices, we define the distance measure and apply it to the source objects/parameters matrix. It is well known that:
- Cosine measure is used if the proportion between object s coordinates is important, but not their specific values. This is the case when the coordinates have the same meaning.
- Euclidean measure is used when the contribution of each coordinate to object's properties is important. This is the case when the coordinates have different meaning.

Therefore, we used the cosine measure to evaluate the distance between parameters whose coordinates were cities, and Euclidean measure to evaluate the distance between objects (cities) whose coordinates were parameters.

During clustering procedure we changed the distance matrix:
- To emphasize the role of certain objects (cities) while clustering parameters or certain parameters while clustering objects;
- To reveal stronger but less numerous clusters;
- To determine the stable number of clusters.

The first goal is reached by weighting the coordinates of objects or parameters, respectively. The second goal is achieved by eliminating weak connections between objects. At in the last case we vary the connections between objects and observe the changes of number of clusters.

4 Experiments

4.1 Experimental Data

The data we used in the experiments were a corpus of 100 person-to-person dialogs of Spanish railway information service. The short characteristic of the corpus (length of talking, volume of lexis) is described in [1]. The data were analyzed in detail in [5] for constructing artificial dialogs.

4.2 Clustering Parameters

Here in all experiments we used the cosine measure with the admissible level of connections not less than 0.7. In the first experiment all objects (cities) had no any privileges. In the second one the more important cities, that is the large and middle cities (see above) obtained the weight 5. It was the minimum weight, which allowed revealing new result.

Experiment 1. Two parameters *City Weight* and *Length of Talking* were joined to one cluster and the others remained the independent ones.

Experiment 2. Three parameters *City Weight, Urgency and Definiteness* and *Length of Talking* were joined to one cluster and the other parameters remained independent.

These results can be easily explained: the larger the city, the more possibilities to get it, the longer discussion a passenger needs. The urgency of trip is usually related with large cities: usually the trip to the small cities is completed without any hurry.

4.3   Clustering Objects (Dialogs)

Here in all experiments, we use Euclidean measure with the admissible level of connections not less than 0.5 of the maximum. In the first experiment, all parameters were equal. In the second experiment, we wanted to emphasize the properties of passengers. For this, we assigned the weight 2 to the parameters *Urgency and Definiteness*, *Length of Talking* and *Politeness*. This weight was the minimum one to obtain the significant differences with the first experiment. Parameters presented in nominal scales were weighted by the coefficient 0.33 that is inverse value to the number of scales. Cluster descriptions are presented below.

Experiment 1.

Cluster 1 (10 objects). The large and middle cities, no urgent trips (only 10%), round trips, night trips (70%-90%), sleeping cars, enough long talking.

Cluster 2 (25 objects). No urgent trips (only 8%), round trips, a few number of night trips (25%), no sleeping cars.

Cluster 3 (8 objects). Small cities (75%), undefined day of departure, one-way trips, night trips (90%), sleeping cars.

Cluster 4 (57 objects). Small or local cities (75%), one-way trips, no sleeping cars, short talking (80%).

Experiment 2.

Cluster 1 (31 objects). No urgent trips, no night trips (only 20%), only ordinary politeness.

Cluster 2 (44 objects). Urgent trips or defined days of trips (95%), advanced level of politeness (85%).

Cluster 3 (12 objects). Only small and middle cities, no urgent trips, one-way trips (75%), short talking (85%), the highest level of politeness.

Cluster 4 (13 objects). Only small and local cities, undefined days of trip, one-way trips (75%), no night trips (only 15%), short talking (75%), advanced level of politeness.

Some of the clusters were expected (e.g. the cluster 4 in both experiments) and the others need to be analyzed more closely. In all cases in comparison with manual classification where only costs and time-table were considered, our experiments gave the additional information [5]. Table 4 presents some examples of clustered objects.

Table 4. Examples of objects from cluster 3 in the experiment 2

City	U/D	T/F	Ti	Tm	Te	Car	Tk	Pl	Name of City
0.25	0.5	0	1	0	0	0	0.25	1	Girona
0.5	0.5	0	0	1	0	0	0.25	1	Alicante

5 Conclusions

Results. The quality of automatic dialog systems used in public transport service crucially depends on the scenarios of dialogs. These scenarios may be determined by means of clustering in the space of parameters defined by an expert. We have shown (a) how to parameterize the records of dialog and to solve the problems of incompleteness and diffuseness of the source data; (b) how to accomplish the clustering procedure providing stability of results and their usefulness for a user. We have tested the MajorClust method for this and recommend using it for such type of problems. The obtained results were judged by experts as interesting and useful for determining the main themes of dialogs and the profile of passengers related with these themes. This information can be used to the design of scenarios for an acquisition of dialogs person-to-machine by means of the Wizard of Oz technique.

Future Work. In the future, we plan to consider more extensively the problems of Knowledge Discovery and to use both geographic information and the other parameters related with transport service.

References

1. Bonafonte, A., et. al.: Desarrollo de un sistema de dialogo oral en dominios restringidos. In: I Jornadas en Tecnologia de Habla, Sevilla, Spain, 2000
2. Hartigan, J.: Clustering Algorithms. Wiley, 1975.
3. Makagonov, P.: Evaluating the performance of city government: an analysis of letters by citizens to the Mayor by means of the Expert Assistent System. Automatic Control and Computer Sciences, Allerton Press, N-Y, vol. 31, N_3, 1997, pp. 11-19

4. Makagonov, P., Alexandrov, M., Sboychakov, K.: A toolkit for development of the domain-oriented dictionaries for structuring document flows. In: Data Analysis, Classification, and Related Method, Springer, series "Studies in classification, data analysis, and knowledge organization", 2000, pp. 83-88

5. Sanchis, E., Garcia, F., Galiano, I., Segarra E.: Applying dialog constraints to the understanding process in a dialog system. In: Proc. of TSD-02 (Text, Speech, Dialog), Springer, LNAI, N_2248, 2002, pp. 389-395

6. Sojka, P., et. al. (Eds.): Proceedings of Conf. Text, Speech, Dialog. Springer, LNAI, N_3206, 2004

7. Stein, B., Eissen, S. M. Document Categorization with MajorClust. In: Proc. 12th Workshop on Information Technology and Systems, Tech. Univ. of Barcelona, Spain, 2002, 6 pp.

8. Stein, B., Eissen, S. M. Automatic Document Categorization: Interpreting the Performance of Clustering Algorithms. In: Proc. 26th German Conference on Artificial Intelligence (KI-2003), Springer, LNCS, N_2821, 2003, pp. 254-266

A Framework for Rapid Multimodal Application Design

Pavel Cenek[1], Miroslav Melichar[2], and Martin Rajman[2]

[1] Masaryk University, Faculty of Informatics, Laboratory of Speech and Dialogue
60200 Brno, Czech Republic
xcenek@fi.muni.cz
[2] École Polytechnique Fédérale de Lausanne (EPFL)
Artificial Intelligence Laboratory (LIA)
CH-1015 Lausanne, Switzerland
{miroslav.melichar,martin.rajman}@epfl.ch

Abstract. The aim of the work described in this paper is to extend the EPFL dialogue platform with multimodal capabilities. Based on our experience with the EPFL Rapid Dialogue Prototyping Methodology (RDPM), we formulate precise design principles that provide the necessary frame to use the RDPM to rapidly create an efficient multimodal interface for a given application. We analyze the consequences of the proposed design principles on the generic GUI and architecture required for the system.

1 Introduction

Spoken dialogue systems can be viewed as an example of an advanced application of spoken language technology. Dialogue systems represent an interface between the user and a computer-based application that allows for interaction with the application in a more or less natural manner. Although limited spoken communication with computers is now a reality, not only in laboratories, but also in commercial products, several problems still remain to be solved.

One significant problem is the fact that there does not yet exist a really generic operational approach for dialogue design; each application requires the development of a specific model. To address this problem, the authors of [1, 2] proposed an efficient Rapid Dialogue Prototyping Methodology (RDPM) and implemented a software platform (hereafter referred to as the *EPFL dialogue platform*) that allows the concrete design of dialogue systems with a very short development cycle.

Another problem that prevents spoken dialogue systems from broader use is the limited performance and reliability of current speech recognition and natural language understanding technologies. One of the research directions foreseen to overcome these limitations is the use of multimodal dialogue systems that exploit (besides speech) other interaction channels for the communication with the user.

Within this perspective, the aim of the work described in this paper is to extend the EPFL dialogue platform with multimodal capabilities. Notice that the original RDPM has already been tested in several unimodal (voice-only) dialogue systems, among which the InfoVox system[1] (an interactive vocal system for providing information about

---

[1] InfoVox: Interactive Voice Servers for Advanced Computer Telephony Applications, funded by Swiss national CTI 4247.1 grant.

V. Matoušek et al. (Eds.): TSD 2005, LNAI 3658, pp. 393–403, 2005.

restaurants) or the Inspire system[2] [3–5] (a dialogue system for the vocal control of domestic devices within a SmartHome environment). The multimodal features of the new version of RDPM are currently tested in the Archivus system [6] that aims at providing the users with an intuitive way to access recorded and annotated meeting data.

The rest of this contribution is organized as follows: Sect. 2 provides a brief overview of the standard speech-only RDPM. Sect. 3 first discusses the extensions needed to include the multimodal capabilities; it introduces the notion of multimodal generic dialogue node (Sect. 3.1) and it presents the associated design goals and principles (Sect. 3.2), a generic GUI layout (Sect. 3.3) and some details about the proposed system architecture (Sect. 3.4). Finally, Sect. 4 provides the conclusions and some future works.

2   Rapid Dialogue Prototyping Methodology

Dialogue prototyping represents a significant part in the development process of spoken dialogue systems. The Rapid Dialogue Prototyping Methodology [1, 2] allows the production of dialogue models specific for a given application in a short time. In outline, the RDPM divides the design into the following steps: (1) producing a task model for the targeted application; (2) deriving an initial dialogue model from the obtained task model; (3) carrying out a series of Wizard-of-Oz experiments to iteratively improve the initial dialogue model.

The RDPM focuses on frame-based dialogue systems [7], i.e. dialogue systems following the slot-filling paradigm. Although there exist more advanced dialogue system paradigms [8], they usually lack robustness and therefore are difficult to use in real-life applications with short design cycles. Frame-based dialogue systems seem to be a good compromise for practical dialogue systems, especially in the case where they are combined with robust natural language processing techniques.

The general idea behind the RDPM is to build upon the hypothesis that a large class of applications potentially interesting for the setup of interactive user-machine interfaces can be generically modeled in the following way: the general purpose of the application is to allow the users to select, within a potentially large set of targets, the one (or the ones) that best corresponds to the needs (search criteria) that are progressively expressed by the users during their interaction with the system. Notice that this generic application model, although simple, is in fact quite powerful as it covers important classes of interactive systems such as information retrieval systems (in which case the targets are data items to be retrieved with respect to the information needs expressed by the users) and interactive control systems, such as Smart Home control systems (in which case the targets correspond to the various actions that the system can perform on behalf of the users).

Within this framework, we further make the assumption that the available targets can be individually described by sets of specific attribute:value pairs, and the goal of the interactive, dialogue based interface is then to provide the guidance that is required for the users to express the search criteria (i.e. the correct attribute:value

---

[2] Inspire: INfotainment management with SPeech Interaction via REmote microphones and telephone interfaces, IST-2001-32746.

pairs) leading to the selection of the desired targets. In the rest of this contribution, the descriptive `attribute:value` pairs will also be referred to as (depending on the context) the *constraints* or *semantic pairs*.

2.1 The Task Model

The definition of the valid constraints (e.g. the list of available attributes and attribute combinations, as well as the possible associated values) will generically be called hereafter the *task model* (or the *data model* in the specific case of information retrieval systems). The cumulated set of constraints acquired by the system at any given time during the interaction will be referred to as the *current (search) frame* and the subset of targets matching the current search frame will be called the *current solution space* or (*search space*).

In the simple but frequent case where all the targets can be homogeneously described by a unique set of attributes, the task model simply corresponds to the schema of the relational database, the entries of which are the individual targets. An example of such a situation is given in Fig. 1, where the entries of the database correspond to annotated transcription of dialogue utterances recorded during a meeting. These types of targets are used in the Archivus system.

Date			Person		Topic	DialogAct	Transcription
Year	Month	Day	FirstN	FamilyN			
			...				...
2004	April	7	David	P.	sport	request	"Buy a new bike."
2004	April	30	Susan	A.	furniture	question	"What colour?"
			...				...

Fig. 1. An example of dialogue targets

2.2 The Dialogue Model

The dialogue model defines the types of interactions that are possible between the system and the user. In the RDPM, a dialogue model consists of two main parts: (1) the application-dependent declarative specification of so called *Generic Dialogue Nodes* (GDNs) and (2) the application-independent local and global dialogue flow management strategies. While the GDNs must be defined by the designer of a particular application, the dialogue strategies have been implemented as a part of the EPFL dialogue platform and they are generally not intended to be modified by application designers.

Generic Dialogue Nodes. There is a GDN associated with each of the attributes defined in the task model. The role of the GDN is to perform the interaction with the user that is required to obtain a valid value for attribute. Different types of interactions are possible according to the nature of the values being sought:

1. *Simple GDNs* allow the user to directly specify a value for the associated attribute. Such GDNs are useful when the number of possible choices for the value is small. Example: selecting a day of the week or a device the user wants to operate.

2. *List Processing GDNs* allow the user to browse through a list of values and select one of them using the number identifying its position in the list. This GDN is particularly useful in the case of a large number of possible values for an attribute or when the values are linguistically complex. Reducing the interaction vocabulary to numerals adds robustness to the speech recognition component, potentially substantially improving its recognition rate. Example: a list processing GDN for selecting from a list of movies or names.

In addition to the GDNs associated with some attribute in the task model, the system also contains *Internal GDNs* that are invoked by the dialogue manager in specific dialogue situations, such as at the beginning of the dialogue or when the user over-specified a request.

To realize the interaction for which it is responsible, each GDN contains two main types of components: prompts and grammars. The prompts are the messages uttered by the GDN during the interaction. The role of the grammars is to make the connection between the surface forms appearing in the natural language utterances produced by the user and their semantic content expressed in the form of `attribute:value` pairs compatible with the task model. The grammars might also be used as a language model for the speech recognition engine to improve the quality of the recognition.

Dialogue Strategies.   The term *dialogue strategy* refers here to the decision of the dialogue manager about the next step in the dialogue. The RDPM dialogue management handles dialogue strategies at two levels: local and global.

The purpose of the *local strategies* is to handle problems related with the interaction within a particular GDN. The goal of these strategies is to guide the user towards providing some information for the attributes. When local strategies are applied, the control remains at the GDN level. The local strategies are carried out by the local dialogue manager which is a part of the GDN. Situations managed by the local strategies typically include: (1) requests for help; (2) no input provided; (3) reestablishing the dialogue context; (4) speech recognition failures(No match); (5) request for prompt repetitions; (6) suspend/resume/start over dialogue, etc.

As soon as the user provides a value compatible with the attribute associated with current GDN, control is handed back to the global dialogue manager where the *global strategies* are encoded. The purpose of these strategies is to process the newly populated attributes and to progress in the dialogue process towards its goals by selecting the next GDN that should be activated. The global strategies include: (1) a confirmation strategy; (2) a strategy for dealing with incoherencies; (3) a dialogue dead-end management strategy; (4) a dialogue termination strategy and (5) a branching strategy (selection of the next GDN).

For more information on local and global dialogue strategies, see [1].

2.3   Wizard-of-Oz Experiments

Wizard-of-Oz (WOz) Experiments [9] are an integral part of the RDPM. Their main role is to allow (in early steps of the design) the acquisition of experimental data about the behaviour of the users when interacting with the system. Not yet implemented functionalities that are in fact simulated by the hidden human operator called the Wizard. In the experiments, the Wizard uses a Wizard's Control Interface (WCI) to fulfil his task. The interface required for a given WOz experiment is generated automatically from the task and dialogue models.

The WCI consists of a set of modules which are inserted to appropriate places in the dialogue system. Their role is to redirect the dialogue system data flows to the Wizard's control station. At the control station, the incoming data is visualized so that the Wizard can check or modify it, or even create new pieces of data if necessary. Once the Wizard is satisfied with the acquired data, it is sent back to the dialogue system where the dialogue processing can continue.

Currently, the WCI allows the simulation or supervision of the following modules: automatic speech recognition, natural language understanding, and (re)starting or stopping the entire system. If needed, other modules can easily be developed and integrated.

3   Extending the RDPM to Multimodal Applications

As already mentioned, the aim of the work described in this paper is to extend the currently unimodal (voice-only) EPFL dialogue platform with multimodal capabilities. We believe that adding multimodality to a vocal dialogue system increases user satisfaction and/or the task achievement ratio. In addition, we might also observe interesting, unexpected user behaviour due to the increased complexity of the multimodal system.

Creating a multimodal system is a complex task. One of the challenges is to cope with the problems of fusion and fission of modalities. The term *multimodal fusion* is generally understood as the process of combining the inputs coming from different channels into one abstract message that is then processed by the dialogue manager (often called the *interaction manager* in multimodal systems). Analogically, the term *multimodal fission* refers to the process of communicating to the user an abstract message (issued by the interaction manager) through some combination of the available output channels.

The fission techniques are usually thought of as of practical nature. In this perspective, user preferences have been observed and practical guidelines have been proposed [10], e.g. the fact that speech and graphic outputs need to be coordinated and unnecessary redundancy between the two channels should be avoided (the speech should convey a short version of the main message while the details might be displayed on the screen).

The *multimodal fusion* is usually more complex to cope with. Indeed, since the fusion may happen at several levels in the system, there exist several different ways of understanding this term.

- At the lowest level, we can think of fusing *multiple coordinated streams* of information generated by the user, not necessarily consciously. For example, speech processing can be combined with lip reading (image processing) in order to improve the accuracy of speech recognition. This type of multimodal fusion is not discussed in this paper.
- Fusion can also take place at a higher level when, for example, some information that is loosely related to the ongoing communication act provides a useful context

for interpretation of the user's message. An example is the use of user's location (e.g. in front of a lamp) to process a vocal utterance such as "Switch *this* on!". We plan to focus on this type of fusion after the first set of experiments has been performed, provided that we have experimental evidence that this is a sufficiently frequent phenomenon in our applicative context.

- Another type of fusion happens when Each modality provides different semantic pairs that simply need to be combined together. An example: if "What Susan said about this?" (semantic pair `speaker:Susan`) is said together with a click on the topic "sofa" visualized on the screen (`topic:sofa`), the resulting semantic pair set {`speaker:Susan`, `topic:sofa`} is simply produced. This type of modality fusion has already been implemented in our system by means of applying simple time stamp related rules during the fusion process.
- The user voluntarily selects one of the available communication modalities (e.g. speech, mouse, or keyboard) for performing a task with the system. The different modalities can be then understood as *alternative communication interfaces* to the system. As the user is often allowed to use different modality for each subtask of a compound task, this type of modality switching might also be considered as a specific kind of fusion. However, we do not consider modality switching to be a true modality fusion since the fusion actually happens only at the discourse level (i.e. at the level of the combination of the outcomes of single subtasks).

Notice that the classical example "Put this there" can be solved at the level of the NLU (by disambiguating the deictic references "this" and "there" with the help of the pointing modality) or at the level of semantic pairs (by the temporal alignment of the semantic pairs – {`action:move`, `object:this`, `location:there`}; {`pointingTo:objectX`, `pointingTo:PlaceY`}).

3.1 Multimodal GDNs

Multimodal GDNs (hereafter referred as mGDNs) are GDNs as described in Sect. 2.2, but extended with additional elements required for multimodal interaction. These additional (or modified) elements include:

- grammars for written and spoken natural language input;
- a set of multimodal prompts to guide the user;
- the information about the graphical representation (layout) of the mGDN;
- a definition of the role of each GUI element.

All of the elements must be specified in a declarative specification language in order to allow automatic derivation of the dialogue model and the associated multimodal dialogue-driven interface from the task model.

3.2 Design Goals and Principles

In order to be able to fulfil our goal to extend the EPFL dialogue platform with multimodal capabilities, we define the following design principles:

1. Similarly to the standard RDPM, *the elementary building blocks of our multimodal interface are mGDNs*. Again, there are several types of mGDNs, each type encapsulating a particular kind of interaction and providing various graphical layouts (see

(a) Selecting a movie from a list   (b) Selecting a meeting participant

Fig. 2. GDN graphical representations (layouts)

Fig. 2). This allows the rapid building of multimodal dialogue systems exploiting existing building blocks.

2. *The mGDNs represent the only interaction channel with the system.* In other words, all inputs/outputs going to/coming from the system must be managed by some mGDN. The underlying design implication is that every active piece of the graphical user interface must be connected to some mGDN.

3. *Every mGDN is fully multimodal,* i.e. every mGDN systematically gives the users the possibility to communicate using all the defined modalities. It ensures that users can communicate in the way that is most comfortable for them and can switch between modalities if they find that communication using one of them is not yielding the expected results.

4. *At any time, only one single mGDN is in focus (i.e. operational) in the interface.* This very important principle strongly contributes to the overall feasibility of our objectives by narrowing the interpretation context for the multimodal fusion, as explained hereafter. It is important to notice that, even if only one mGDN can be in focus, several mGDNs can be active, i.e. ready to process the input provided to the mGDN in focus. This functionality is needed for the support of the mixed initiative.

5. *Only a limited number of modalities are taken into account* during system design. In our experiments, we will focus on three active input modalities, namely voice, pointing (either using a mouse or a touch screen) and text (keyboard), one passive input modality, namely emotion recognition (by face analysis) and three output modalities (graphics, sound and text).

The aim of the above postulated design principles is to narrow the problem of modality fusion which is usually believed to be difficult to solve in the general case. In particular, in our approach, the multimodal fusion is handled at the level of individual mGDNs, and this is possible because only one mGDN is in focus at any given time to process the user's inputs. In addition, each mGDN is aware of its role (what subtask should be solved by using it), of its graphical layout, speech input grammars etc., which makes it possible to foresee the structure of the multimodal input and fuse it correctly.

3.3   GUI

In general, the dialogues covered by the RDPM consist of two phases: (1) eliciting from the user the constraints that are needed to identify a small set of solutions that can then be presented to them and (2) giving the user the possibility to browse the current solution set in order to select the right solution. With respect to this dialogue structure and the above mentioned design principles, we propose the general GUI structure that is depicted in Fig. 3.

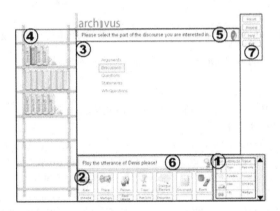

Fig. 3. The proposed general GUI structure (demonstrated on the multimodal system Archivus [6] for browsing a database of recorded meetings)

The screen is divided into four main areas, each occupied by an mGDN. The area (4) serves for visualization of the solution space and should highlight the solutions that meet the current constraints defined by the user. The user should have the possibility to issue commands that switch between various visualization modes, rearrange the solution space or allow browsing the solution space. (3) is the area used by all the mGDNs (except the internal ones). Notice however that, in accordance with the above mentioned design principles, only the mGDN in focus is visualized here. The possibility to explicitly switch between various constraint selection mGDNs is under the responsibility of a special mGDN called *Criteria Selection* that occupies the area (2). Area (1) is reserved for the *history mGDN* that serves for browsing and modifying the history of the interaction (e.g. changing or deleting an acquired semantic pair). The system prompt component (5), the text input component (6) and the control buttons (7) are special parts of the user interface shared by all mGDNs.

3.4   The Proposed Architecture

A multimodal dialogue system is a considerably complex software consisting of a relatively high number of modules. Each module requires different data sources for its initialization and information from different sources to produce its outputs. It is also often the case that the modules are created by various authors and were originally targeted for different kinds of applications. In addition, the number and types of modules in multimodal dialogue systems are not fixed and there is no consensus on what are exactly the responsibilities of every single module.

This implies that a very flexible architecture is required that allows for a simple modification or addition of new modules. In the ideal case, the system should represent a complete development environment that supports all phases of the development cycle. It should also come with modules for immediate use (e.g. modules for speech recognition, synthesis, dialogue management) to allow researchers to focus on the functionality they are interested in.

Frameworks that might be considered as satisfying the above criteria are the Galaxy-II [11] and the Open Agent Architecture [12]. However, we see as a drawback the fact that they are both too general and do not impose any predefined communication paradigm on the dialogue system. Also the distributed nature of these frameworks makes the debugging of the targeted system more difficult.

For all there reasons, we have chosen another approach to module composition. Each module is implemented as a simple Java class and the communication with other modules is simply realized by methods calls using well-defined interfaces. The exact configuration of the system is declaratively defined in a configuration file. When the system is launched, a special module called *the application builder* creates instances of all modules (each of them is identified by a name) and interconnects them as described in the configuration file. Since the initialization of each module is unique (as far as the resources and start-up parameters are concerned), there is a configuration file associated with each module which is used by the module for its initialization.

The selected approach leads to a system that is very flexible and simply configurable and allows a simple module development and debugging (modules are objects in the Java language with well defined interfaces). In the same time, the possibility of some distributed processing is still fully open. On the local system, any module performing real operations can be replaced by a proxy that forwards the method calls to another computer and receives results from it. From the point of view of the rest of the system, this process remains fully transparent.

The most complex case is the situation where a graphical module needs to be displayed on a remote machine(s). A possible solution to this problem is to rely on the standard VNC protocol. This choice makes the distribution extremely simple, but the price to pay is a higher network bandwidth consumption.

Since WOz experiments are an important part of the RDPM, we should be able to supervise the functionality of certain module or even substitute them by the Wizard (human operator) using the graphical user interface that is used during the dialogue. This can be easily archived by inserting the graphical WOz module as a proxy of the module that we want to supervise. An example: if the goal is to supervise the quality of the speech recognition, the graphical module is plugged in between the SRE and the NLU. Then the recognized utterance is displayed to the Wizard who is able to modify it, if necessary. Similarly the Wizard can check the semantic pairs resulting from the NLU module.

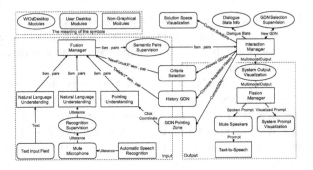

Fig. 4. Proposed module composition and the main data flow

The proposed module composition is depicted in Fig. 4. The *Interaction Manager* controls two groups of modules: the input and output modules. The role of the *Fusion Manager* is to combine the semantic pairs from the different input sources (modalities).

The *Text Input Field* module (area (6) in Fig. 3) allows the user to type in some text that is consequently translated by the *NLU* into semantic pairs. The same happens with the text produced by the *ASR*. Note that the *ASR* might be disabled using the *Mute Microphone* GUI module and the *ASR* result might be corrected by Wizard's *Recognition Supervision* module. Possible values for the mGDN in focus are displayed in the *GDN Pointing Zone* (area (3) in Fig. 3). Mouse clicks are translated into semantic pairs by the *Pointing Understanding* module. The graphical modules *History* and *Criteria Selection* mGDNs (areas (1) and (2) in Fig. 3) work in a similar fashion except that they display only one GDN. Semantic pairs resulting from the fusion process are supervised by the Wizard in the *Semantic Pair Supervision* module and are then sent to the *Interaction Manager*.

The *Interaction Manager* processes the semantic pairs and selects the next GDN to be in focus (the decision can be modified by the Wizard in the *GDN Selection Supervision*). The dialogue state information is then updated, the *Solution Space Visualization* is modified and the multimodal output is issued by the *Interaction Manager*. The output is sent by the *Fission Manager* to the *System Prompt Visualization* module that displays it on the screen and sends it to the *Text-to-Speech* module which gives vocal feedback to the user.

Each of the modules in the system can be sensitive to the global state of the dialogue (e.g. the GDN in focus, the list of active GDNs) through dynamic selection of its resources (e.g. using appropriate GDN dependent grammars). The information about the dialogue state can be obtained by reading the information published by the interaction manager.

4   Conclusion

The approach described in this contribution is believed to be generic enough to provide rapid prototyping techniques for a large class of multimodal dialogue systems. The main idea behind the approach is that problems that are difficult to solve in general can be reduced to solvable instances by a specific design of the multimodal interface relying on a precise set of the associated interaction principles.

Although our approach has already been partially tested in several prototypes, we are now faced with the need for building a complete multimodal system, as only the process of building and testing such a complete system makes it possible to identify the potentially problematic parts in our methodology and to improve the underlying theory.

An important fraction of the work now lies in testing with real users, trying to understand what they really want, like, and do not like, and identifying how one can respond to that. Only a complete system reveals the real extent of the various problems encountered in human-machine interaction and allows us to focus on the most critical ones. Therefore we are currently building the first version of a multimodal system prototype, the Archivus system [6].

References

1. Bui, T.H., Rajman, M., Melichar, M.: Rapid dialogue prototyping methodology. In: Proc. of TSD 2004, Brno, Czech Republic, Springer-Verlag (2004) 579–586
2. Rajman, M., Bui, T.H., Rajman, A., Seydoux, F., Trutnev, A., Quarteroni, S.: Assessing the usability of a dialogue management system designed in the framework of a rapid dialogue prototyping methodology. Acta Acustica united with Acustica, the journal of the European Acoustics Association (EAA) **90** (2004) 1096–1111
3. Möller, S., Krebber, J., Raake, A., Smeele, P., Rajman, M., Melichar, M., Pallotta, V., Tsakou, G., Kladis, B., Vovos, A., Hoonhout, J., Schuchardt, D., Fakotakis, N., Ganchev, T., Potamitis, I.: INSPIRE: Evaluation of a Smart-Home System for Infotainment Management and Device Control. In: International Conference on Language Resources and Evaluation (LREC). Volume 5., Lisbon, Portugal (2004)
4. Krebber, J., Möller, S., Pegam, R., Raake, A., Melichar, M., Rajman, M.: Wizard of Oz tests for a Dialogue System for Smart Homes. In: Proceedings of the 30th German Convention on Acoustics (DAGA) together with the 7th Congrès Francais d'Acoustique (CFA), Strasbourg, France (2003)
5. Boland, H., Hoonhout, J., van Schijndel, C., Krebber, J., Melichar, M., Schuchardt, D., Baesekow, H., Pegam, R., Möller, S., Rajman, M., Smeele, P.: Turn on the lights: investigating the Inspire voice controlled smart home system (2004)
6. Lisowska, A., Rajman, M., Bui, T.H.: Archivus: A system for accessing the content of recorded multimodal meetings. In: Proc. of the MLMI'04, Switzerland (2004)
7. McTear, M.F.: Spoken dialogue technology: Enabling the conversational user interface. ACM Computing Surveys **34** (2002) 90–169
8. Pallotta, V.: Computational dialogue models. MDM research project deliverable, Faculty of Computer and Communication Sciences, Swiss Federal Institute of Technology, EPFL IC-ISIM LITH, IN-F Ecublens, 1015 Lausanne (CH) (2003)
9. Dahlbäck, N., Jönsson, A., Ahrenberg, L.: Wizard of oz studies: Why and how. In: Proc. of International Workshop on Intelligent User Interfaces, Orlando, FL (1993)
10. Bohus, D., Rudnicky, A.: Larri: A language-based maintenance and repair assistant. In: Spoken Multimodal Human-Computer Dialogue in Mobile Environments. Volume 28 of Text, Speech and Language Technology. Springer (2005) 203–218
11. Seneff, S., Hurley, E., Lau, R., Pao, C., Schmid, P., Zue, V.: Galaxy-II: A reference architecture for conversational system development. In: Proc. ICSLP'98. (1998)
12. Martin, D.L., Cheyer, A., Moran, D.B.: The open agent architecture: A framework for building distributed software systems. Applied Artificial Intelligence **13** (1999)

Language-Independent Communication Using Icons on a PDA*

Siska Fitrianie and Leon J.M. Rothkrantz

Man-Machine-Interaction, Delft University of Technology
Mekelweg 4 2628CD Delft, The Netherlands
{s.fitrianie,l.j.m.rothkrantz}@ewi.tudelft.nl

Abstract. As language is fundamental to human activities, proficiency in other languages becomes important. Besides for developing abilities for communication, the knowledge is also a tool for a survival. With the introduction of computerized mobile devices, i.e. PDAs, new opportunities for communicating in other language arose. This paper describes a new communication paradigm that is language independent using icon language on a PDA. Users can create iconic messages as realization of their concepts or ideas in mind. The proof of concept tool is able to interpret and convert the messages to (natural language) text and speech in different languages. To provide faster interactions in next icon selection, the tool has icon prediction. Our user test results confirmed that using provided icons our target users could express their concepts and ideas solely using a spatial arrangement of icons.

1 Introduction

Humans communicate to share facts, feelings, and ideas among each other. The dream of being able to understand and communicate in any language has not yet been satisfied. However, there do exist signs and symbols (icons), which are understood universally. It is supported by the fact that on one hand while interacting with the environment and with others, humans form internal mental models and representation of themselves, the outside world and of things which they are interacting [19]. On the other hand, an icon is understood as a representation of a concept, i.e. an object, an action, or a relation. An icon serves a function as communication means by virtue of a resemblance between the icon and the object or the movement it stands for.

Icons also offer a direct method for conversion to other modalities. According to [6], an icon can be interpreted by its perceivable form (syntax), by the relation between its form and what it means (semantics), and by its use (pragmatics). By this way, icons also form a language, where each sentence is formed by a spatial arrangement of icons [7]. The meaning of individual icons can represent a word or a phrase, which is created according to the metaphors appropriate for the context of this type of languages. Since icons are representations of models or concepts, with which humans are actually interacting, we expect this language is easy to learn. Once a set of iconic representations

---

* The research reported here is part of the Interactive Collaborative Information Systems (ICIS) project, supported by the Dutch Ministry of Economic Affairs, grant nr: BSIK03024.

V. Matoušek et al. (Eds.): TSD 2005, LNAI 3658, pp. 404–411, 2005.

is established, increased usages can lead to more stylized and ultimately abstract representation, as has occurred in the evolution of writing systems, e.g. the Chinese fonts [9].

As icons offer a potential across language barriers [19], the icon language can also offer a potential as an independent human natural language like Esperanto. Thereby, any interaction using this type of languages opens opportunities for the development of different applications in different languages and domains. One might think of those where verbal communication is not possible, for example a communicator media to help people with speech disability.

Nowadays, icons are used in almost every Graphical-User-Interface-based computer software. Besides a direct manipulation on the icons allows us to have a faster interaction, as pictorial signs, they can be recognized quickly and committed to memory with surprising persistence [12]. Therefore, icons can evoke a readiness to responds for a fast exchange of information and a fast action as a result [17]. A research showed that direct manipulation with a pointer has better time performance than form filling with Soft Input Panels or handwriting recognition [15].

Despites its popularity as a personal information manager, the user interaction options for a Personal Digital Assistant (PDA) are quite limited. Like a traditional workstation, interaction with a PDA can be realized by a pointing device on a sized external keyboard. Most PDAs only contain a few physical buttons and a few of them have a small-sized keyboard. Recent researches have been done in adding multimodal capabilities to a PDA, such as a multimodal life-like character [20], fusing speech and pen input [10], speech recognition and synthesis [8], etc. However, for optimal speech recognition, the environment in which the technology is used should be the same as the training environment of the system [5], whereas PDAs are often used in various environments under various conditions. The result is misrecognition of commands, which is frustrating to the user. Since the current technology makes speech input less suitable for mobile activities, we aimed at a natural interaction style that is based on the strength of GUI. With regard to the applicability of icons as communication means and also as a natural interaction style, in this project, we developed an iconic interface that applied as a communication tool for travelers on a PDA.

2   Related Work

Icons have been used as early as the middle ages complex iconic systems such as the heraldic coats of arms, astrological signs, and the communication system of ancient Egyptian. In modern society, icons are familiar from the everyday context of living to the packaging for the latest products, for example: door signs, road signs, electronic goods manual, etc. In the computer world, they have role as a small graphical representation of a program, resource, state, option or window.

Recent researches have been done in developing computer-based iconic communication, for example: the Hotel Booking System that allows communication on a restricted domain [18], CD-Icon: a pure person-to-person communication system [2], Sanyog: a communication device for disable people in India [1], and the Elephant's memory: a computer iconic environment that allows the user to build a visual message by combining symbols from its vocabulary [14]. Most of these iconic communication systems are too complex to learn or a language-specific system. A deep research has been done by [16] on designing an iconic communication system to allow people communicate with each other when they share no common language. The system is based on the notion of simplified speech by reducing a significant complexity, such as: it has no inflection, no number, gender, or tense markers, no article and no linear order. This is possible because it was designed as a visual language in contrast to written languages, where sequencing and ordering is critical.

The icon language proposed in this paper is used to represent concepts or ideas. It was designed particularly suitable for language-independent contexts. The use of PDAs created new constraints and requirements for user interaction and the interface. Therefore, besides adopting the language simplicity principle of [16], our developed tool was designed also for a mobile use of context.

3   Corpus-Based Natural Language Processing

Icon language is a visual language where each visual sentence is a spatial arrangement of icons. Figure 1 shows two example iconic messages. This language is based upon a vocabulary of icons where each icon has a unique or multiple meanings [7]. Individual icons provide only a portion of the semantics of an iconic sentence. The meaning of individual icons with more than just one icon can still be represented by the same set of icons, but it turns out to be very difficult to determine the sentence meaning. It is due to the only thing that can be automatically derived from the semantics of the icons in an iconic sentence is a fixed word or phrase belonging to these icons. For example: "not", "speak", and "the Netherlands". The meaning of an iconic sentence cannot be understood without a global semantic analysis of the sentence. This meaning is derived as a result of the combination of these icons. It is unlikely that constructing an iconic message with one to one matching of icons to words would be appropriate. Humans, on the other hands, have innate ability to see the structure underlying a string of symbols. They are equipped with a number of innate rules that determine the possible shapes of human languages.

We conducted an experiment to have more insight of how humans express their concepts or ideas using this type of message [11]. It involved eight participants and one as a pilot. The participants were asked to form iconic sentences that represented six natural language sentences using a given set of icons. We compared the results by analyzing a large number of iconic message corpora. Although to represent a natural

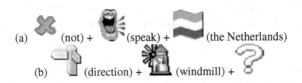

Fig. 1. Two examples of icon strings: (a) I do not speak Dutch and (b) Do you know the direction to a windmill

language sentence may use different set of icon string, the results from both studies showed a similarity. All participants tended to use icons to represent important key-words of a message. Based on this study, we developed grammar rules using Backus Naur Form. We used English as the base-language to define these rules. The terminal symbol of the grammar is a lexicon of allowable vocabulary icons. This vocabulary was grouped into its word class, such as: nouns, pronouns, proper-nouns, verbs, adjective, adverbs, prepositions, and quantifier. The grouping was done based on the metaphor represented by each icon, for example: These terminal symbols were combined into

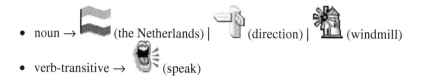

- noun → (the Netherlands) | (direction) | (windmill)
- verb-transitive → (speak)

phrases as nonterminal symbols, such as Sentence, Noun Phrase, Verb Phrase, Preposi-tional Phrase and Negation Sentence. Two iconic messages in figure 1 above result the following grammar rules:

```
Noun-Phrase  →  noun | noun Noun-Phrase
Verb-Phrase  →  verb-transitive Noun-Phrase
Sentence  →  Noun-Phrase question-sign | Verb-Phrase
Negation-Sentence  →  negation Sentence
```

A parser takes an icon string and extracts each icon against the grammar rules. If the icon string is syntactically correct, the parser creates seven slots of a natural language sentence: a prefix slot for question words; a subject slot; an infix slot for a to-be or an auxiliary and a negation ("not"); a verb slot; an object slot; a preposition slot; and a suffix slot for a question mark, an exclamation mark, or an archaic word ("please"). A slot may be empty or contain more than one word. The arrangement of the seven slots depends on a sentence type. The corpus (b) in figure 1 results the seven slots depicted in table 1(a).

We developed a rule based-module to construct a complete sentence from the syn-tax analysis result. The rules specify conversion of an iconic sentence into a natural lan-guage sentence based on the semantic context of the iconic sentence. They derive the meanings associated with iconic sentences from the meaning associated with the indi-vidual icons forming the sentence. Based on the corpora (b) in figure 1, table 1(b) shows the results of some rules, such as: a rule for adding a subject, a rule for adding a verb, a rule for adding an article, a rule for adding an auxiliary, and a rule for adding a prepo-sition. We developed these rules using a corpus based approach. Table 1(c) shows the sentence composition from the resulted slots.

4   N-Grams Icon Prediction

To generate a smoother dialog in communication and due to the high number of pre-sented icons, an icon prediction could help users to reduce the number of look up pro-

Table 1. An example of an icon string conversion into seven slots (a), a contruction of a complete sentence (b), and composing a natural language sentence (c)

| (a) Syntax analysis result: | ```Prefix   = [empty]
Subject   = [empty]
Infix   = [empty]
Verb   = [empty]
Object   = [noun ("direction")]
Preposition = [noun ("windmill")]
Suffix   = [sign ("?")]``` |
|---|---|
| (b) Sentence construction result: | ```Prefix   = [empty]
Subject   = [pronoun ("you")]
Infix   = [auxiliary ("do")]
Verb   = [verb-transitive ("know")]
Object   = [article ("the")] +
              [noun ("direction")]
Preposition = [preposition ("to")] +
              [article ("a")] + [noun ("windmill")]
Suffix   = [sign ("?")]``` |
| (c) Sentence composition result: | ```Infix+Subject+Verb+Object+Preposition+Suffix```
Do you know the direction to a windmill? |

cesses that are necessary to generate an icon string. Besides improving the input speed, the prediction also improves the quality of syntax. It predicts which icons are most likely to follow a given segment of an icon string. For this purpose, a word prediction technique was adapted. It operates by generating a list of suggestions for possible icons after the first icon is selected. The predictor only considers those next icons that can create a grammatically correct sentence. When a user selects one of the suggestions, it is automatically inserted into the string. Otherwise, the user can continue to input icons until the intended string appears.

The probability of an icon string is estimated with the use of the following Bayes rule as the product of conditional probabilities:

$$P(s) = P(w_1, w_2, \ldots, w_n) = \prod_{i=1}^{N} P(w_i | w_1, \ldots, w_{i-1}) = \prod_{i=1}^{N} P(w_i | h_i)$$

where h_i is the previous segment of an icon string when prediction w_i ($=$ icon$_i$). Estimating terms of the form of $P(w|h)$ is done by assuming some generative probabilistic model using estimating conditional probabilities of n-grams type features. The n-grams language modeling aims at computing the frequency of an icon (uni-gram), icon-pairs (bigram), proposing the most likelihood icon by knowing the previous ones (trigram), and proposing the most likelihood for the entire sentence (n-gram). As the approach needs a large amount data to compute the multi-grams model, our tool collects it from user selections during the interaction.

5   A Language Tool for Travelers

Our iconic communication tool was designed to play as a foreign language phrase book for travelers. A user can select a sequence of icons as a realization of his/her concepts

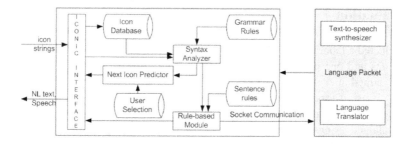

Fig. 2. The architecture of our iconic communication tool on a PDA

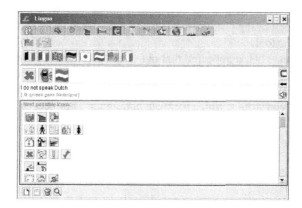

Fig. 3. The interface of our iconic communication tool on a PDA

or ideas. Besides supporting a fast interaction by converting the message into natural language, the tool also can be combined with any language translator. It also provides a speech synthesizer to read aloud the resulted translations with correct pronunciations. Figure 2 shows the architecture of our developed tool.

Figure 3 shows the current version of our language tool. On the interface, icons are grouped based on their concept. Besides supporting a compact interface, this grouping is a powerful way to hint where an icon can be found because the meaning of icons almost exists in the context of other icons [13]. The next-icon predictor ranks and groups the next possible icons based on their concept. A user can select any icon from the menu or from the prediction window. Any changing on the input, the resulted text will be refreshed. The interface was designed to cope with the mobile users who cannot devote fully attention to operate the system.

Through a socket network, the tool is able to create a communication environment by TCP/IP connections. The socket allows the interface to communicate to other language tool (i.e. a text-to-speech synthesizer and a language translator) or to other applications if applicable (e.g. a web application or other communication system). These language tools and applications can be produced by third parties. For an experiment purpose, we used CMU's Flite [3] for reading aloud the resulted text.

6   Evaluation

We conducted a laboratory test using the Thinking Aloud method [4]. It involved eight participants and one pilot. They were selected from different linguistics background. This test aimed at evaluating whether or not users capable to express their concepts in mind solely using a spatial arrangement of icons. The test also addressed usability issues on interacting with the communication tool. Each participant performed five tasks that were explained using cartoon-like stories. A story described a situation for travelers in which the participants should have used the tool to communicate with others. The participants were asked to create iconic messages based on the story and think aloud. There were no incorrect answers, except if a participant did not perform a task at all. All activities were recorded on a tape and all user interactions were logged for analyses purposes. At the end of the test, the participants were asked to fill their satisfaction on interacting with the tool.

From the results [11], it appeared that our target users could compose iconic messages for every given task. They understood that they could select an icon string to represent important keywords of their message. However, we also found that users tried to generate some icon strings, which were out of domain. They needed time to adapt the interface and rethink to find another relevant concept to represent their message using only the given set of icons.

7   Conclusion

An experimental iconic communication tool has been developed, applied on a language tool for travelers. The developed tool was designed to be language independent with the use of icons and the connection to a socket network to communicate with other digital language aids or other applications. Thereby, it opens opportunities for the development of other application in different languages and domains.

NLP has provided a method to interpret and convert iconic messages to natural language texts/speech. We solved the problems of ambiguity and missing information that resulted by this type of messages. The BNF grammar has been used to select sentences which are grammatical correct. We also developed rules to create more natural sentences. N-grams language model was used to predict the next likelihood icon given a segment of icons. Our experimental results showed that an icon interface could serve as communication mediator. However, future work is still necessary to analyze more corpora of iconic messages. Furthermore, a field study is also necessary to gather data about how people use and experience the iconic interface in real situations to cover more user requirements in mobile context use.

References

1. Basu A., Sankar S., Chakraborty K., Bhattarcharya S., Choudhury M, Patel R.: Vernacula Education and Communication Tool for the People with Multiple Disabilities, Development by Design Conference, Bangalore (2002)

2. Beardon C.: CD-Icon, an Iconic Language-Based on Conceptual Dependency, Intelligent Tutoring Media, (1992), 3(4)

3. Black A.W., Lenzo A.K.: Flite, a Small, Fast Speech Synthesis Engine, System Documentation Edition 1.2, for Flite version 1.2, USA (2003)

4. Boren T., Ramey J.: Thinking Aloud, Reconciling Theory and Practice, IEEE Transactions on Professional Communication, (2000), 43-3

5. Bousquet-Vernhettes C., Privat R., Vigouroux N.: Error Handling in Spoken Dialogue Systems, Toward Corrective Dialogue, Proc. Of ISCA'03, USA (2003)

6. Chandler D.: Semiotics, the Basic, Routledge (2001)

7. Chang S.K., Polese G., Orefice S., Tucci M.: A Methodology and Interactive Environment for Iconic Language Design, International Journal of Human Computer Studies, (1994), 41: 683-716

8. Comerford L., Frank D., Gopalakrishnan P., Gopnanth R., Sedivy J.: The IBM Personal Speech Assistant, Proc. of the ICASSP 2001, USA (2001)

9. Corballis M.C.: Did language Evolve from Manual Gestures?, 3rd Conference of The Evolution of Language'00, France (2000)

10. Dusan S., Gadbois G.J., Flanagan J.: Multimodal Interaction on PDA's integrating Speech and Pen Inputs, Proc of. EUROSPEECH'03, Switzerland (2003)

11. Fitrianie S.: An Icon-Based Communication Tool on a PDA, Postgraduate Thesis, Eindhoven University of Technology, the Netherlands (2004)

12. Frutiger A.: Sign and Symbols, Their Design and Meaning, New York: van Nostrand Reinholt (1989)

13. Horton W.: The Icon Book, New York, John Wiley (1994)

14. Housz T.I.: The Elephant's Memory (1994-1996)

15. Kjeldskov J., Kolbe N.: Interaction Design for Handheld Computers, Proc. of the 5th APCHI'02, Science Press, China (2002)

16. Leemans N.E.M.P.: VIL, A Visual Inter Lingua, Doctoral Dissertation, Worcester Polytechnic Institute, USA (2001)

17. Littlejohn S.W.: Theories of human communication, 5th Edition, Wadsworth (1996)

18. Mealing S., Yazdabi M.: Communicating Through Pictures, Department of Computer Science, University of Exeter, England (1992)

19. Perlovsky L.I.: Emotions, Learning and Control, Proc. of International Symposium: Intelligent Control, Intelligent Systems and Semiotics, Cambridge, MA (1999), 131-137

20. Wahlster W., Rethinger N., Blocher A.: SmartKom, Multimodal Communication with a Life-Like Character, Proc. Of EUROSPEECH'01, Denmark (2001)

Software Tutors for Dialogue Systems

Jaakko Hakulinen, Markku Turunen, and Esa-Pekka Salonen

Department of Computer Sciences
University of Tampere, Finland
{jaakko.hakulinen,markku.turunen,esa-pekka.salonen}@cs.uta.fi

Abstract. We have used text, graphics and non-speech audio to tutor new users in a spoken dialogue system. The guidance is given by a software tutor, a software component that interactively tutors the user. Four different variations of tutoring were implemented and experiences were collected from user tests in order to gain insights into these tutoring concepts. Real-time visualization of speech interaction with comic book style balloons and structured guidance were received well while various other methods received mixed acceptance.

1 Introduction

While speech is a natural way of human to human interaction, speech interfaces may become inherently easy to use only when computers understand speech like a human being. Such ultimate speech systems are not possible with today's technology and therefore guidance is needed [3]. Currently speech interfaces lack the fluency and unlimited language of human interaction. Only when users know what each system understands speech applications can be successful services.

Providing on-line help is challenging in speech interfaces. Embedded assistance on the other hand is common and is realized as hint type guidance, expanding system prompts and system initiated dialogue [9]. Many speech application use traditional manuals as well, commonly in the form of web pages.

One option for initial user guidance is a software tutor. A tutor provides guidance within the actual software application, monitors user actions and is capable of providing help in appropriate context and according to users' needs [1]. There are some studies of tutorials in the context of speech interfaces. Kamm et al. [4] studied a tutorial that was not connected to an application but showed in a web page how an example task can be carried out. Consistently higher user satisfaction ratings were found in the tutored group compared to embedded assistance only. We have found an actual software tutor in speech interfaces to be effective as well. Tutoring was delivered in between system prompts and enabled users to learn a speech interface with significantly fewer problems than with a web manual [2].

Incorporating text and graphics has potential benefits of tutoring in a speech interface. Separate tutoring modality widens communication channel and tutoring can happen simultaneously and in synchrony with the system actions [6]. Graphics can also stay on screen as long as needed. Graphical presentations can be very powerful, for example, Terken and te Riele [8] conclude that in their study the graphical part of a multimodal interface gave users a mental model of the interface. While graphics are

V. Matoušek et al. (Eds.): TSD 2005, LNAI 3658, pp. 412–419, 2005.

not usually available when speech interface is used, the initial learning often happens in a situation where this is not the case, for example, web pages and Java applets can be available.

In order to effectively guide users to speech interfaces one must understand what the users need to learn. We have identified the following topics: 1) Interaction style; when and how to speak and turn taking. 2) The error prone nature of speech recognition. 3) System functionality. 4) Language models i.e. what kind of inputs the system understands.

In particular, tutoring must consider recognition errors. If a tutor can detect an error, it should provide guidance that helps users identify the error situation and correct it. One option is to visualize the recognition results and thus help the users to detect errors. A tutor can also give explicit instructions for the user to say something and monitor speech recognition results to make sure that the user can give inputs successfully.

In this paper we introduce a set of graphical software tutors that provide guidance to the users of a speech-based timetable system. The tutors use graphics and audio notifications. They are connected to the telephone-based timetable system to visualize the system and monitor users' actions. The next chapter describes the tutors and our experiences with them. The experiences and findings are discussed in the end.

2   Four Multimodal Tutoring Implementations

The tutors teach how to use Bussimies, a telephone service for bus timetables. Bussimies has grammars of around 1500 words with word spotting. Users can express themselves reasonably freely, but they need to know what questions Bussimies can answer, and what concepts, like bus lines and destinations, it knows. Interaction style is mixed-initiative; users can ask questions freely, but when errors occur the system can take initiative.

The four tutor versions share the same four part structure: an initial instruction set, a guided hands-on exercise, a second set of instructions and a free experimentation. Initial instructions introduce Bussimies, explain speech recognition and show some example inputs. During the hands-on exercise a user gives a call to Bussimies and gives it some inputs by following tutor's instructions. The second set of instructions contains more guidance on valid inputs and a summary. Free experimentation with Bussimies is possible in the end.

During the hands-on exercise and free experimentation tutors the speech recognition results and systems outputs are visualized. Context sensitive help is given in error situations. Users control the tutor with *Continue* and *Back* buttons.

During the iterative development of the tutors 19 people participated in user tests. All users tested each of the four versions. Observation, questionnaires and discussions were used to collect opinions and findings to guide the development.

The differences between the four tutors are mostly in the visual representations of the Bussimies system. Next, the four variations are discussed with findings from the user tests.

2.1   Balloon Tutor

The balloon tutor, as seen in Figure 1, visualizes the spoken interaction with balloons similar to those in comic books. New balloons scroll into screen from right and when more space is needed, the leftmost balloon is removed. The user and system balloons have slightly different shapes. The primary motivation for using balloons is to show the users the results of speech recognition and thus help them to notice speech recognition errors. The visualization of system output should help the users with speech synthesis. Comprehension of speech synthesis often improves after listening to it for a few minutes. During this period, seeing the same information as text can help. Balloons also leave a short term dialogue history visible on screen.

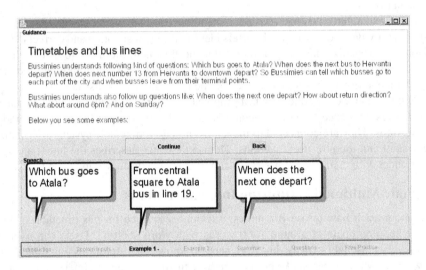

Fig. 1. Balloon tutor

Balloons are an efficient visualization of a dialogue since people are familiar with the concept from comics and associate balloons with speech. Dialogue turns are also naturally visualized.

In the user tests, the balloon tutor was received very well. Mostly people liked the tutor because of its simplicity; the balloons were considered easy to understand and follow. The idea was familiar and the movement from right to left provided the feeling of an advancing dialog. The timing of the balloons that appeared slightly before Bussimies started speaking also seemed effective. The visualization matched the flow of the spoken dialogue very well.

The users were able to follow the performance of speech recognition using the balloons. In error situations they knew what had happened and some of those who had problems with recognition, reported that they used this information to adjust their way of speaking to get better results. The fact that they could see how Bussimies had recognized their speech was often reported to be the best feature of the tutoring.

The only negative comments on balloons concerned the animation; some participants found the movement a bit confusing.

2.2   Form Tutor

The form tutor, as seen in Figure 2, visualizes a form that Bussimies uses in dialogue management. In addition, another form shows users' input as form items. Speech recognition results and system outputs are visualized as separate balloons. The idea is that revealing the systems internal representation of the queries provides the users with an accurate mental model of the system. This model should tell what kind of questions the system understands.

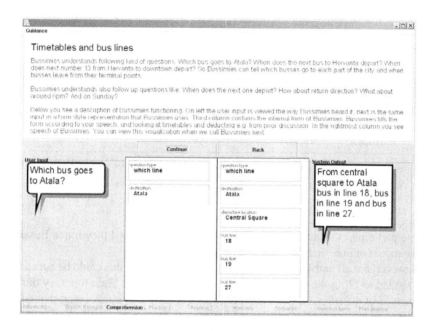

Fig. 2. Form tutor

The form tutor was favored by some participants because it provided a way to see how Bussimies understands the user inputs. However, many of the participants found the forms useless and irrelevant. They were also considered complicated and technical. One participant wrote: "[The form] Clarifies the understanding [...], but on the other hand requires a terrible amount of concentration."

2.3 Interactive GUI Tutor

The interactive GUI tutor has a graphical user interface (GUI) that users can construct queries with. As seen in Figure 3, the resulting natural language queries are shown to the users in balloons. The tutor formulates the queries into a phrasing that Bussimies accepts. The balloons also provide the visualization of dialogue. One of the strengths of GUI is that the possibilities and limitations of the system can be seen from the interface. In the case of Bussimies, the users can see from the GUI what kind of queries can be made with speech.

The participants liked the interactive GUI tutor because it allowed them to do things themselves. The interactive GUI tutor also best communicated the features of Bussimies

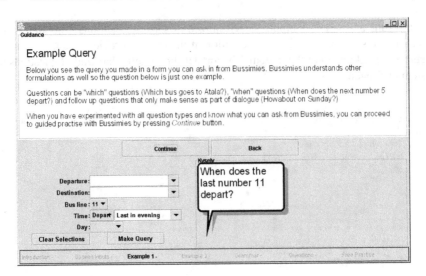

Fig. 3. GUI tutor

to some participants. Many commented that after using the GUI they found Bussimies to have more features than they previously thought.

However, not all participants found the GUI useful. Partly this could be because the users tended to fill in the whole GUI form once and proceed. Therefore they did only see one type of question. Only a small proportion of the participants experimented with the GUI to find out the possibilities and features of Bussimies. The lack of interest in the GUI may be because the GUI was not available when the users freely experimented with Bussimies. The design of the GUI did not clearly suggest all the possibilities either.

2.4 Animated Tutor

The animated tutor, as seen in Figure 4, has two animated features: on the left side the system components of Bussimies are visualized and on the right a human like character does the tutoring. There are visualization icons for speech input, speech output, database and a form to visualize dialogue management. The icons are animated when the corresponding system component is active. The visualization was supposed to show the users what the system is doing at any given time.

The motivation behind using a human like character is "persona effect"; users find interface with an anthropomorphic character more helpful, credible and entertaining [5]. The character in the tutor was animated so that it pointed and looked at the icons. Additionally, the character randomly rotated its head and torso a little bit all the time. These idle-time acts [7] are supposed to tell the users that the character is "alive" and the system is responsive.

The participants who preferred the animated tutor referred to the character in a way compatible with the persona effect, e.g.: "[It] felt like there was somebody helping." However, the character received negative comments from the majority of the participants; it was considered foolish and annoying. Opinions on the visual design seemed

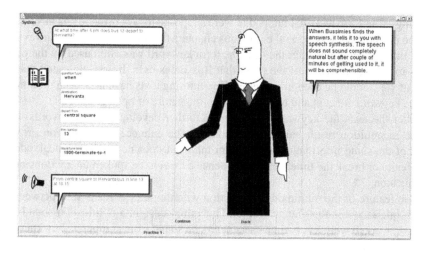

Fig. 4. Animated tutor

important to the acceptance of this tutor. A feature like this should be optional and easy to get rid of if one finds it useless or annoying.

The visualizations icons were in general considered helpful. However, the initial versions that consisted of abstract visualizations of speech recognition and synthesis were considered unnecessarily complex and even scary. Simplified versions seen in figure 4 were accepted by the participants. The complex layout of the animated tutor was also found problematic as there was information on both sides of the screen. The users did not always know where to look at.

3 Discussion

The concept of graphical tutoring was received well in the user tests. Most users reported that they learned to use Bussimies with the tutors. Each participant selected a favorite tutor; balloon tutor was selected 5 times, form tutor 6, the interactive GUI tutor 6 and the animated tutor 2 times.

The interaction style tends to be the most challenging topic to teach using traditional manuals. The tutors taught this to the participants successfully. All users learnt when and how to speak. If they had problems during the tutoring, the tutors detected it and appropriate guidance was given. Additionally, the balloons enabled the users to notice problems themselves.

The real-time visualization of interaction was valued by the participants and it was often selected as the best feature of the tutoring. The participants understood well the error-prone nature of speech recognition and words like "mishear" were used to describe this. The visualization of recognition results gave the users a possibility to learn what kind of mistakes the system makes, how it behaves when errors happen, and how one should speak to avoid errors.

To some participants the guidance failed to explain the rather open nature of grammars and the word spotting. They thought that the given examples were the only valid phrasings. The form and GUI tutors that were supposed to best provide this information had the problems discussed in the previous chapters that turned many users away from them. In the discussions after the tests the term keyword was often used by the participants to refer to the parts of the input that Bussimies uses. It was suggested that this point of view could be used in the tutors. The tutoring texts have now been modified to use the keyword concept and to better convey the nature of open grammars.

After the tests the keyword concept was further developed: the keywords in the speech recognition result balloons are bolded. The enhanced visualization provides much of the same information as the form tutor but does not look technical, add the complexity or break the timely correspondence between the spoken interaction and the visualization.

One feature of the multimodal interaction with the tutor is focus shift between the speech interface and the graphical tutor. Our initial design, a notification sound from the tutor, worked well. Every time users heard the sound from computer, they knew that there was something to look at on screen.

A theory that rose from the experience is the required correspondence between the spoken interaction and the visualization in the tutor. The moving balloons as well as the animated icons successfully match the dialogue flow. The form did not have much correspondence to the dialogue flow and the GUI breaks down the speech interaction even more.

4   Conclusions

We have built four versions of graphical tutoring for a speech interface. From users tests we gained insight on this tutoring concept. In general the multimodal tutoring worked well. Several improvements for the current tutoring concepts were found but the foundation is firm.

The big challenge with tutoring in speech interfaces is speech recognition errors. The users must not get stuck in the tutoring process due to errors and appropriate guidance must be given to sort out the problems. The visualization of recognition results and context sensitive guidance help users to understand what is going on and to effective adjust to the speech interface when necessary.

The best feature in the tutors was the real-time visualization of the dialogue with balloons. It helped users to notice speech recognition errors and provided an effective view on how the system sees the dialogue. The timely correspondence between the visualization and the dialogue was received favorably.

Already in the tested form, the multimodal software tutoring of speech applications was found a viable concept. It can teach novice users the interaction style and functionality of a speech interface in matter of minutes.

References

1. García, F.: CACTUS: Automated Tutorial Course Generation for Software Applications. Proceedings of Intelligent User Interfaces 2000 (IUI'2000). (2000) 113–120
2. Hakulinen, J., Turunen, M., Salonen, E-P. and Räihä, K-J.: Tutor Design for Speech-Based Interfaces. Proceedings of DIS2004. (2004) 155–164

3. Heisterkamp, P.: "Do not attempt to light with match!": Some thoughts on progress and research goals in Spoken Dialog Systems. Proceedings of Eurospeech 2003. (2003) 2897–2900

4. Kamm, C., Litman, D. and Walker, M.A.: From Novice to Expert: The Effect of Tutorials on User Expertise with Spoken Dialogue Systems. Proceedings of the International Conference on Spoken Language Processing, (ICSLP98). (1998) 1211-1214

5. Lester, J. C., Converse, S. A., Kahler, S. E., Barlow, S. T., Stone, B. A. and Bhogal, R. S.: The Persona Effect: Affective Impact of Animated Pedagogical Agents. Proceedings of CHI 97. (1997) 359–366

6. Nakatami, L.H., Egan, D.E., Ruedisueli, L.W., Hawley, P.M. and Lewart, D.K.: TNT: A Talking Tutor 'N' Trainer for Teaching the Use of Interactive Computer Systems. Proceedings of CHI'86 (1986) 29–34

7. Rist, T., André, E., Müller, J.: Adding Animated Presentation Agents to the Interface. Proceedings of the 2nd international conference on Intelligent User Interfaces. (1997) 79–86

8. Terken, J., te Riele, S.: Supporting the Contruction of a User Model in Speech-only Interfaces by Adding Multimodality. Proceedings Eurospeech 2001 Scandinavia (2001) 2177–2180

9. Yankelovich, N.: How Do Users Know What to Say? Interactions, 3, 6 (1996) 32–43

Questions in Estonian Information Dialogues:
Form and Functions*

Tiit Hennoste[1,2], Olga Gerassimenko[2], Riina Kasterpalu[2], Mare Koit[2],
Andriela Rääbis[2], Krista Strandson[2], and Maret Valdisoo[2]

[1] University of Helsinki, P.O. Box 9
00014 Helsinki, Finland
{tiit.hennoste}@helsinki.fi
http://www.helsinki.fi/university/
[2] University of Tartu, J. Liivi 2
50409 Tartu, Estonia
{tiit.hennoste,gerro,riina.kasterpalu,mare.koit,
andriela.raabis,krista.strandson,maret}@ut.ee
http://www.cl.ut.ee

Abstract. Questions have been analyzed in Estonian information dialogues with the purpose of finding out the linguistic features that can be used in automatic recognition of various types of questions. Information questions (i.e. the questions that are used for requesting information) and questions that initiate solving communication problems are considered. The study shows which types of questions (wh-question, open and closed yes/no question, question that offers answer, alternative question) are preferred in both cases. The results can be implemented in a dialogue system which performs the role of information provider and interacts with a user in Estonian.

1 Introduction

There are many spoken dialogue systems (DS) which interact with a user in a natural language, e.g. flight reservation systems worked out in USA, flight and train schedule systems developed in Europe, the Verbmobil meeting agreement system in Germany, a help desk and bus schedule system developed within the Interact project in Finland [8].

Our goal is to build a DS which gives information in Estonian and follows norms and rules of human-human communication. The main part of a conversation with such a DS is formed by questions and answers. An analysis of actual dialogues is needed in order to find out the ways of using questions by humans and their formal features depending on language and culture which can be used for the automatic recognition of questions in a DS.

Our analysis is based on the Estonian Dialogue Corpus which includes about 600 spoken human-human dialogues, among them 328 information dialogues (http://www.cs.ut.ee/~koit/Dialoog/EDiC)[6]. For this paper, a subcorpus consisting of 101 calls for information (asking phone numbers, addresses etc.), calls to travel agencies, shops and outpatients' departments has been analyzed.

---

* This work is supported by Estonian Science Foundation (grant No 5685).

V. Matoušek et al. (Eds.): TSD 2005, LNAI 3658, pp. 420–427, 2005.

2   Questions as Dialogue Acts

2.1   Types of Questions

Dialogue acts that are used for requesting information form certain act group which is differently classified in different typologies. For example, DAMSL [1] considers questions and information requests which produce an obligation of the hearer to give information as one subgroup (Info-request) and acts that influence partner's future non-communicative actions as another (Influencing-Addressee-Future-Action).

In our typology of dialogue acts, questions are determined as the utterances which have a specific form in Estonian: questioning words, a specific word order and/or intonation [7]. There are five types of questions in our typology:
- questions that expect giving information: wh-question and open yes/no question
- questions that expect agreement/refusal: closed yes/no question and question that offers answer
- questions that expect the choice of an alternative: alternative question.

Open and closed yes/no questions have similar form but they expect different reactions from the partner. A closed question expects the answer yes or no (*Are you open in winter? – Yes.*) while an open question expects giving information (e.g. by asking the question *Is there a bus that arrives to Tallinn after 8?* the client intends to learn the departure times of buses). Closed yes/no questions and questions that offer answer are both questions that expect yes/no answers. Their difference lies in the presuppositions of the speaker. Asking a question that offers answer the speaker has an explicit opinion, hypothesis, and he is expecting a confirmation by the partner. No such presuppositions exist in case of a closed yes/no question.

2.2   Using Questions in Different Dialogue Acts

According to our typology, the following dialogue acts can be represented as questions (cf. [5]):
- conversation rituals which are used at the beginning and end of conversations (*how are you? – how are you?*)
- topic changes which are used for transition from one topic to another
- solving communication problems (repair initiation, contact control, adjusting the conditions of answer)
- request for information
- questions asked from oneself: rhetorical questions, solving communication problems by oneself (*What more did I want to tell you?*).

Our analysis has given the following results. First, questions that are used in conversation rituals build certain formulas which can be given as lists (*kuidas läheb? / how are you?*). Our analyzed subcorpus did not contain formulas in the form of questions. Secondly, our subcorpus did not contain questions asked from oneself. Thirdly, one way to change a topic is to ask a question with a single topic change function (*what more do you want to know?*). On the other hand, a topic can be changed with a question the main function of which is to get information, and the topic change is only an additional function (*by the way, do you make travel insurances?*). Our subcorpus did not contain separate utterances for topic change.

Therefore, the most important questions are (1) information questions, and (2) questions for solving communication problems. In the following sections, our main attention is dedicated to these questions.

2.3 Information Questions and Questions for Solving Communication Problems

Our dialogue act typology is based on the conversatsional analysis (CA) approach. First, dialogue acts are divided into two groups – adjacency pair (AP) acts where the first act requires certain second act (e.g. question requires an answer) and non-AP acts (e.g. acknowledgement). Questions and answers both belong to AP acts.

Secondly, different communication problems can occur in a conversation (linguistic errors, non-hearing, misunderstanding, etc.). Solving communication problems is differently understood and modelled by different researchers [1], [2], [3]. Our typology includes special problem solving acts. Problem solving is a universal mechanism which is used in case of different problems regarding text, its meaning, and conversation. The speaker can solve these problems himself using a non-AP repair act. On the other hand, problems can be solved in co-operation. In the last case, the speaker indicates a problem by asking a question, and the partner who has caused the problem performs a repair.

We have three types of acts indicating communication problems in our typology: adjusting the conditions of answer, contact control, and repair. Three kinds of repair initiations have been differentiated: clarification, reformulation, and misunderstanding [4].

Clarification is an act where the speaker repeats an utterance, phrase or word of the partner more or less exactly in order to explain it (*did you say so?*).

Reformulation is an act where the speaker gives his own interpretation (hypothesis, paraphrase, generalization, conclusion) of a previous utterance. Its purpose is to get the confirmation by the partner (*did you think so?*).

Misunderstanding is an act where the speaker reports that he did not hear or did not understand the previous information, or the information contradicts with his knowledge and beliefs, and therefore must be checked. The are two kinds of misunderstandings: (a) the speaker only indicates that there was a problem, or (b) he localises the problem exactly.

Adjusting the conditions of answer is an act whereby the information provider intends to get additional information needed for answering.

Contact control is a specific act in telephone conversations. Its function is to check whether the conversation channel does function. In our dialogues, the word *hallo* is typically used, seldom a question (*do you hear me?*).

In this paper, we will investigate how various linguistic means help recognise the question types. Secondly, we will compare information questions with the questions that indicate communication problems and initiate solving them.

3 Grammatical Features of Questions in Estonian Dialogues

There are many different possibilities to form questions in Estonian. The Table 1 summarizes the usage of questions in our subcorpus.

Table 1. Types of questions in the analyzed dialogues

Question type	Number	%
Wh-question	230	36
Question offering answer	177	28
Open yes/no question	110	17
Closed yes/no question	81	13
Alternative question	18	3
Ambiguous	20	3
Total	636	100

Wh-questions are mostly (93%) expressed by a sentence which begins with a wh-word[1] (*ja mis teie nimi on. / and what is your name?*). Few of wh-questions are expressed by a phrase or a wh-word (Client/C: *ma olen huvitatud reisist Londonisse / I'm interested in a trip to London.* Information provider/P: *Millal / When?*), a non-finished sentence which expects the partner to finish it (C: *mhmh (1.0) ja 'ruutmeetreid oli / uhuh (1.0) and square meters were... –* P: *no seal on 'kümme ruutmeetrit, väike. / there are ten square meters, small*).

Alternative questions are mostly (83%) expressed by a sentence that includes conjunction *või /or/*.

There are three special formulations that are statistically rare. First, an alternative question can be expressed as a phrase. Secondly, alternatives can be represented without the conjunction *või /or/*. Thirdly, alternatives are sometimes represented in separate utterances. In such case, the first sentence is a closed yes/no question. Then a pause follows which indicates that the hearer does not want to answer and after that the speaker reformulates the question by offering an alternative which begins with *or* in the next utterance (P: */.../ se=programm on väga pikk, kas ma loen selle kõik 'ette teile. /this program is very long, shall I read it to you/ (0.5) või (.) või=te=huvitab=teid=nüd 'hind. /or or are you interested in the price/*).

Three types of questions cause more problems: open and closed yes/no questions and questions that offer answer. The Table 2 demonstrates that similar linguistic means are used in open and closed yes/no questions.

(a) Most of these questions begin with a question-particle *kas/whether* which is not translated (*kas ta tuli? /did she come?/*)

(b) sometimes a sentence/phrase ends with a question-particle *või, vä* /literally: or/ (*ta tuli või? /did she come, then?/*)

(c) sometimes both particles are used (*kas ta tuli või? /did she come, then?/*).

These three variants give 75% of closed and 72% of open yes/no questions. The fourth, most frequent variant is to formulate a question like an assertion but the word order is inverted.

Some linguistic features can be used in order to differentiate closed and open yes/no questions. Open yes/no question can include (a) pronouns *mingi, mingisugune /any, a, mõni/some* indicating indefiniteness (*kas 'Baierimaale läheb ka mõni reis / are there*

---

[1] Transcription of CA s used in the examples.

Table 2. Form of closed and open yes/no questions and questions that offer answer

Form	Closed yes/no (%)	Open yes/no (%)	Offering answer (%)
kas /whether	59	55	2
või/vä / or	9	11	7
kas + või/vä / whether + or	7	6	-
word order	12	5	2
ega /nor	5	6	0.5
sentence+intonation	6	10	17
phrase+intonation	-	-	32
jah/yes	-	-	16
et (+ siis /või /ühesõnaga) that (+then/or/in a word)	-	-	10
eks/eksju/eksole / eh/is it not true	-	-	4
siis / then	-	2	3
other (ambiguous)	2	4	6.5

any trips go to Bavaria); (b) a plural partitive, frequently used with a word *mingi/ any (kas mingeid 'soodustusi ka on / do you have any price discounts)*. 31% of open yes/no questions include these features. Still, a part of yes/no questions remains problematic, and the interpretations of the speaker and the hearer can be different. There are two possible misinterpretations: a closed yes/no question is interpreted as an open yes/no, and vice versa. The first misinterpretation does not cause problems – there are no dialogues in our subcorpus where the hearer indicated that the information was redundant. In the second case, when giving information was expected instead the yes/no answer three possibilities exist to continue the conversation:

(a) a long pause follows which indicates that providing information was expected, and the speaker gives the information (C: *ja on seal ka mingisuguseid 'sporditegemise võimalusi./ are there some possibilities to do sport there / P: ikka on./ yes there are / (1.0) / 'palli mängida saab ja 'piljardit siis=ja 'keeglit=ja /.../ one can play ball, snooker and bowling*)

(b) the client gives the turn back using a particle (*mhmh/uhuh, ahah/oh, aa/oh, jaa/yes*, with a raising intonation). A new question of the client is expected after the answer. If a particle that gives back the turn comes instead then the partner interprets his/her previous turn as non-sufficient or non-suitable and will adjust it

(c) the client asks an adjusting question in order to get the missing information.

Various linguistic means are used in questions that offer answer. 49% of these questions are formulated by a declarative sentence or a phrase with specific questioning intonation (*kõik 'kokku, koos 'maksudega. / all together, including taxes*). Certain particles at the beginning of an utterance (*et/that, sis/siis / then*), at the end (*jah /yes, eks/eksju/eksole /eh, sis/siis / then*) or their combinations can indicate an hypothesis. The most frequent ones are *jah/yes: ma õõ 'annan teile te- Tartu 'numbri jah?/ I'll give you the Tartu number yes* (16%), *et/that* (10% together with other particles) and *või/vä*

/or (7%). As mentioned above, some of linguistic means used in forming of these questions are distinct from means used for questions of two previous types: *et/that, jah/yes, eks/eh*, phrases with questioning intonation. Their only similarity can be the questioning particle *või/vä /or* at the end of an utterance. At the same time, the question that offers answer clearly prefers the single questioning particle *või/vä /or*, and uses seldom the particle kas/whether (or the combination *kas+vä (whether+or)*.

The second important difference between the question types is in preferring of a sentence, a phrase or a single word. 95% of wh-questions, closed and open yes/no questions are formulated as full sentences. Alternative questions use full sentences in 78% of cases. In case of the question that offers answer, phrases and single words are preferred (66%).

4   Dialogue Acts Performed by Different Questions

Our analysis has shown that wh-question, closed and open yes/no question are used mostly for construction of information sequences – the main line of dialogue. Only few questions of these types are used to initiate solving of communication problems. The use of information questions depends on information needs. Different question types are preferred at different stages of conversation. It is typical (70%) that a new topic or subtopic is started with a wh-question or an open yes/no-question. A closed yes/no question is used in 10% and an alternative question in 3% of cases. Request is used in 16% of cases (cf. [6]).

Most questions that offer answer (144 questions, or 81%) are used for repair initiation. Different repair initiations are represented differently. Clarification is formed as a question that offers answer in all cases. Reformulation, similarly, is formed as a question that offers answer; a wh-question is used in one case.

The detailed analysis of these questions has given the following results. Clarification (72 cases) is mostly (55%) formed as a phrase with questioning intonation. The second more frequent form is the particle *jah/yes* (20%). Another forms occur less. Reformulation (34 cases) is formed in more various ways: a phrase with questioning intonation (28%), using a particle *et/that* (22%), using *jah/yes* (11%). Therefore, the main formulations are similar in both groups. The difference lies only in the meaning of an utterance.

Misunderstanding (18 cases) is mostly expressed by a wh-question. The questioning word *kuidas/how* is used in 39% of cases. This word can be used both for indicating non-hearing, surprise (translation: *what?*), and adjusting facts (*how?*).

Alternative questions can be classified in their own way. 47% of questions were adjustments to the conditions of answer and 53% were information questions in our subcorpus. Adjusting to the conditions of answer (55 cases) is formulated as a wh-question in 60% of cases.

The second important difference is that information questions are mostly formed as full sentences while repair initiations are mostly phrases or single words. 79% of clarifications are phrases or words. Reformulation and misunderstanding is formed by a full sentence in half of cases. Adjusting the conditions of answer prefers full sentences (71%).

5   Conclusion

We have analyzed questions in Estonian information dialogues. First, we analyzed linguistic means of questions formulation. Wh-questions can mostly be recognised on the basis of a questioning word and alternative questions on the basis of the word *või/or*. Yes/no questions remain problematic. The form of a yes/no question does not give sufficient information to determine whether the question is closed or open. If the answerer gives information instead of the answer yes then there are no problems in actual conversation. If the answerer interprets an open yes/no question as a closed one and does not give information then a repair sequence follows where missing information is asked for. Therefore, the reasonable solution for a DS would be to give information in suspicious cases.

The questions that offer answer can be recognised on the basis of intonation and particles that are rarely used in another question types (*et/that, jah/yes, eks/eh* etc.). They are preferably formed by phrases and single words while the other questions mostly are formed by full sentences.

We can conclude that the form of questions gives sufficient information in order to determine whether a question is an information question or it is used for solving a communication problem. Wh-question, open and closed yes/no question are used mostly as information questions. The usage of alternative questions can be divided into two parts. Questions that offer answer are repair initiations in 3/4 of cases and information questions in the remaining cases.

Similarly, the question types can be differentiated on the basis of the usage of full or incomplete sentences. Information questions almost always are formed by full sentences. Repair initiations are different. Clarification is formed mostly by phrases. Reformulation and misunderstanding use full sentences in half of the cases and phrases in the remaining cases. Full sentences are preferred in adjustments of the conditions of answer.

A simple program has been implemented which answers questions in Estonian (http://www.dialoogid.ee/reisiagent/). A user types in his/her question about the departure time of a flight from Tallinn Airport as a written text or phrase and gets an answer in the form of text or speech.

References

1. Allen, J., Core, M.: Draft of DAMSL: Dialog Act Markup in Several Layers (1997) http://www.cs.rochester.edu/research/cisd/resources/damsl/RevisedManual/RevisedManual.html (last visited May 30, 2005)
2. Allwood, J., Ahlsen, E., Björnberg, M., Nivre, J.: Social activity and communication act-related coding. In: Jens Allwood (ed.): Gothenburg Papers in Theoretical Linguistics **85**. Dialog Coding – Function and Grammar. Göteborg Coding Schemas. University of Göteborg (2001) 1–28
3. Bunt, H.: Dynamic Interpretation and Dialogue Theory. In: Taylor, M.M., Neel,F., Bouwhuis, D.G. (eds.): The Structure of Multimodal Dialogue II. John Benjamins Publishing Company, Phiadelphia Amsterdam (1999) 139–166

4. Gerassimenko, O. Hennoste, T., Koit, M., Rääbis, A.: Other-Initiated Self-Repairs in Estonian Information Dialogues: Solving Communication Problems in Cooperation. In: Strube, M., Sidner, C. (eds.): Proceedings of the 5th SIGdial Workshop on Discourse and Dialogue, Cambridge (2004) 39–42

5. Gerassimenko, O., Hennoste, T., Koit, M., Rääbis, A., Strandson, K., Valdisoo, M., Vutt, E.: Annotated Dialogue Corpus as a Language Resource: An Experience of Building the Estonian Dialogue Corpus. In: The First Baltic Conference: Human Language Technologies. The Baltic Perspective. Riga, Latvia (2004) 150–155

6. Hennoste, T., Gerassimenko, O., Kasterpalu, R., Koit, M., Rääbis, A., Strandson, K., Valdisoo, M.: Information-Sharing and Correction in Estonian Information Dialogues: Corpus Analysis. In: Langemets, M., Penjam, P. (ed.): Proceedings of the Second Baltic Conference on Human Language Technologies. Tallinn (2005) 249–254

7. Hennoste, T., Koit, M., Rääbis, A., Strandson, K., Valdisoo, M., Vutt, E.: Directives in Estonian Information Dialogues. In: Matousek, V., Mautner, P. (eds.): Text, Speech and Dialogue. Proceedings of the 6th International Conference, TSD 2003, Lecture Notes in Computer Science, Vol. 2807. Springer-Verlag, Berlin Heidelberg New York (2003) 406–411

8. McTear, M.F.: Spoken Dialogue Technology. Toward the Conversational User Interface. Springer-Verlag, Berlin Heidelberg New York (2004)

Reducing Question Answering Input Data
Using Named Entity Recognition*

Elisa Noguera, Antonio Toral, Fernando Llopis, and Rafael Muñoz

Grupo de investigación en Procesamiento del Lenguaje Natural y Sistemas de Información
Departamento de Lenguajes y Sistemas Informáticos
University of Alicante, Spain
{elisa,atoral,llopis,rafael}@dlsi.ua.es

Abstract. In a previous paper we proved that Named Entity Recognition plays an important role to improve Question Answering by both increasing the quality of the data and by reducing its quantity. Here we present a more in-depth discussion, studying several ways in which NER can be applied in order to produce a maximum data reduction. We achieve a 60% reduction without significant data loss and a 92.5% with a reasonable implication in data quality.

1 Introduction

Question Answering (QA) is a task of Natural Language Processing (NLP) whose aim is to obtain specific answers to user questions. Its main problem is that it is computationally expensive. Thus, it is important to reduce the data QA needs to process.

A common approach is to apply Information Retrieval (IR) [1] or Passage Retrieval (PR) [2] as a preprocess. These systems return a sorted list of the most relevant documents or passages respectively and have the advantadge that their computational cost is quite low. Then, QA is applied only to the relevant documents obtained, due to the fact that in these documents the probability of finding the answer is greater that in the non relevant ones.

An innovative proposal to reduce even more the data consist of applying also Named Entity Recognition (NER). Most of the times, the answer to a QA query fits with an entity category (i.e. person, location, etc), thus we can obtain the category of the QA answer and look for entities of that category in the documents using NER. In this proposal, from the relevant documents that IR returns, only the documents in which at least an entity that belongs to the same category as the answer category is found are considered. This proved to be a good approach as it achieved a significant reduction of data.

Following this line of research, we now discuss several ways in which we could apply NER to achieve a greater data reduction. Different evaluations were carried out considering different ways of applying NER. These provide different data reduction ratios having also different implications to data quality.

---

* This research has been partially funded by the Spanish Government under project CICyT number TIC2003-07158-C04-01 and under project PROFIT number FIT-340100-2004-14 and by the Valencia Government under project number GV04B-268.

V. Matoušek et al. (Eds.): TSD 2005, LNAI 3658, pp. 428–434, 2005.

This paper is structured as follows. The next section provides background information about IR/PR, QA and NER. Section 3 presents the architecture and experiments carried out. The fourth section presents the evaluation results and finally, section five outlines conclusions and future work.

2   Background

2.1   Information Retrieval and Passage Retrieval

Information Retrieval is the task that consist of finding the relevant documents from a collection of these to user queries. Returning the whole relevant documents, like this approach does, implies several restrictions. For these to be overcomed, a new paradigm called Passage Retrieval emerged. This new conceptualization studies the appearance of query terms in contiguous fragments of the documents (also called passages) and thus provides a set of advantages:
- Values the proximity of appearance of query words
- Determine which part of each document is the most relevant
- It avoids normalization problems when applying the similarity measure

PR systems are classified according to the way the passages are built. A commonly accepted classification is the one defined by Callan [3], which classifies PR systems in:
- Discourse based model use the structural properties of documents in order to delimite the passages. These properties may be paragraphs, sections, text marks, etc.
- Semantic model defines the passages according to the semantic relations that can be established in the different fragments of the documents.
- Window model splits the documents in fixed length passages. Usually the basic units of the passages are bytes or words.

Similarity between documents and queries is calculated as in classical IR systems. Different measures may be applied, being the most common cosine [4], pivoted cosine [5], okapi [6] and prosit [7].

2.2   Question Answering

Question Answering may be defined as the task that tries to locate concrete answers in collections of text to questions considering an open domain. This task is very useful for the users of these systems do not need to know all the document or fragment to obtain a specific answer.

Because of the importance of these systems, there is a growing interest in the scientific community. For example, in the TREC[8] and CLEF[9] conferences there is now a specific track that deals with this task.

QA needs linguistic information to carry out its task. Therefore, several language analysis should be applied, mainly lexical, morphologic, syntactic and semantic. On the other hand, QA systems usually have a time constraint that makes impossible to apply these computationally expensive analysis to big collections of documents. Thus, a common way to overcome this limitation is to apply IR to the whole collection and QA only to a limited set of relevant documents that IR returns.

2.3 Named Entity Recognition

As defined in the MUC conferences [10], NER is the task that consist of identifying and categorizing entity names which can include also temporal and/or numerical expressions. It was originally considered a subtask of the NLP Information Extraction task, but nowadays there exists a wide consensus that NER can play an important role for other NLP tasks.

Like in other NLP tasks, NER has been treated in two manners [11]. One is based in knowledge while the other uses a supervised learning algorithm. Regarding resources, the first uses gazetteers and rules whereas the later needs an annotated corpus. Most research is done nowadays in the learning approach, but we should bear in mind that the knowledge based has some advantages. It can obtain better results for restricted domains without much effort, it is capable of detecting complex entities as rules can be tailored accurately and finally, it can be easily adapted to deal with different kinds of entities.

3 Method

3.1 System Architecture

The architecture used is detailed in a previous work [12] and thus here it will be just briefly outlined. The system is made up of two modules. Their description follow.

– IR-n [13] is an IR system that belongs to the PR approach. It uses the okapi method as the similarity measure. As other IR systems, it has two modules, one performs indexing tasks while the other retrieves passages. The first is used as a preprocess to speed up the system whereas the later carries out the main task, that is, returns relevant passages to a given query.

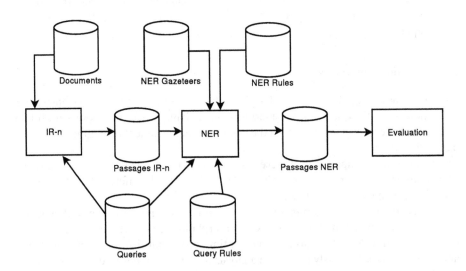

Fig. 1. System architecture

– DRAMNERI [14] is a knowledge based Named Entity Recognition system that uses rules and gazetteers in order to identify and classify named entities. This is done sequentially by applying several modules which perform different tasks: tokenization, sentence partition, named entity identification and finally named entity classification. Although not being part of this NER system, an answer type recognition is utilized in it. This analyses the query and provides the answer entity type. By doing so, the NER is called to detect only the entities of this type in the documents.

3.2 Experiments

Our objective by doing these experiments was to determine the maximum data reduction that the application of NER can achieve. We considered several approaches that had different consequences to the system effectiveness.

We have carried out several experiments whose description follows. For all of them, we considered 8 as the passage size, and 10 as the number of passages, because we concluded in a previous study [12] that these are the optimum values.

Experiment 1. In this experiment we compare the result of applying PR and PR when applying NER to its output (PR-NER). Thus, the number of output passages is different, as PR-NER returns from the PR passages the subset of passages where at least a classified entity is found.

In our previous work we took into account the whole question collection. However, we think that it is more meaningful to take into account only the questions for which the answer belongs to an entity class. Thus, we repeated the experiment for these questions, so that we can compare the result with the other experiments carried out for this study.

Experiment 2. In this experiment we compare PR and PR-NER with the same number of passages. For doing that, we obtained the first 10 passages for PR and the first 10 passages for PR-NER (PR-NER-Whole).

Then, we tried to minimize the output data returned by PR-NER while keeping the same number of passages. On one hand, we filtered all the sentences in which there was no classified entity (PR-NER-Sentences). On the other hand, we just returned the classified entities (PR-NER-Entities).

4 Evaluation

In this section we present the collection used. Then, we check if the entity type detected as the corresponding to the answer is the correct one. Later on, the evaluation measure is outlined and finally, the evaluation results of our system are presented.

4.1 Collection

We have used the Spanish collection which was used at QA CLEF 2004. The document collection is the EFE1994, which is made up of 215,738 documents in Spanish (509

Mb). We have used also the collection of queries that was used at the QA track (Spanish) in CLEF-2004. It has 200 queries. We have chosen this collection because of its large size, which thus, provides realistic results.

4.2 Answering Entity Type Detection

Regarding our answer type recognition, we classified correctly 150 out of 200 queries. From the remaining 50 queries, 46 were not classified, and 4 were classified into an incorrect entity type. Therefore the recall is 75% and the precision 97.4%.

The experiments have been applied to the 154 questions that we find an entity type for the answer. Because we did a previous experiment [12] taking into account the whole question collection (200 questions), we repeated it only for the 154 that we consider here, so that we can compare the results of both experiments. For the 46 non classified NER would return all the input passages.

4.3 Evaluation Measure

We use the Mean Reciprocal Rank (MRR) [8] to evaluate our system. The value assigned to each question is the inverse value of the first passage in which the answer is found or zero if the answer is not found. The final value is the average of the values for all the questions. This is obtained with the following formula:

$$MRR = (\sum_{i=1}^{Q} 1/far(i))/Q \tag{1}$$

Where
Q is the number of queries,
$far(i)$ refers to the position of the first passage in which the correct answer is found to the query i,
$1/far(i)$ will be zero if the answer is not found in any passage.

4.4 Results

Experiment 1. Applying NER to the output of PR produces a greater MRR (0.23 versus 0.21) and moreover decreases the output number of passages in a 33%.

Table 1. Results of Experiment 1

System	MRR	output reduction
PR	0.21	
PR-NER	0.23	33%

Experiment 2. First, we evaluated the passages that PR returns (as a baseline like it is done for the first experiment). Then, we evaluated PR-NER returning the same number of passages (PR-NER-Whole). Obviously, the data reduction is null. The increase of MRR is greater than for the first experiment, 0.24 versus 0.23.

Secondly, we evaluated the same passages returning the sentences in which there is at least a classified entity (PR-NER-Sentences). This resulted in a minimal MRR loss and in a significant output data reduction (60%).

Finally, we just returned the classified entities (PR-NER-Entities). This had an important impact in the MRR but proved to reduce drastically the amount of output data (92,5%).

Table 2. Results of Experiment 2

System	MRR	output reduction
PR	0.21	
PR-NER-Whole	0.24	0%
PR-NER-Sentences	0.2	60%
PR-NER-Entities	0.16	92.5%

5   Conclusions and Future Work

General conclusions are positive. We have showed that NER systems applied to QA tasks substantially decrease the amount of data the later has to process. As it has been proved by our experiments, NER can provide different ratios of output data reduction, with different implications to the data efficiency. Depending on the purpose of the QA system, we may use the approach that best suits us.

We consider two possible lines of future research. First, to apply hybrid NER, so that we would benefit from the advantages of both the learning and the knowledgde based approaches. Secondly, to focus in the answer extraction stage of QA, taking advantage of the fact that we have marked the entities which we know are of the same type of the answer. This could lead to more efficient QA systems.

References

1. Lancaster, F.W.: Information Retrieval Systems: Characteristics, Testing and Evaluation. John Wiley and Sons, New York (1979)
2. Kaskziel, M., Zobel, J.: Passage retrieval revisited. In: Proceedings of the 20th annual International ACM Philadelphia SIGIR. (1997) 178–185
3. Callan, J.: Passage-level evidence in document retrieval. In: Proceedings of the 17th annual conference on Research and Development in Information Retrieval, London, UK, Springer Verlag (1994) 302–310
4. Salton, G.: Automatic text processing: The transformation, analysis, and retrieval of information by computer. (1989)
5. Singhal, A., Buckley, C., Mitra, M.: Pivoted document length normalization. In: Proceedings of the 19th Annual International ACM SIGIR Conference on Research and Developement in Information Retrieval, Experimental Studies. (1996) 21–29

6. Roberston, S., Walker, S., Beaulieu, M.: Okapi at trec-7. In: Seventh Text RETrieval Conference, volume 500-242, National Institute of Standard and Technology. Gaithersburg, USA (1998) 253–264

7. Amati, G., Van Rijsbergen, C.J.: Probabilistic models of information retrieval based on measuring the divergence from randomness. ACM TOIS **20** (2002) 357–389

8. TREC-10: Tenth Text RETrieval Conference. In: Tenth Text REtrieval Conference. Volume 500-250 of NIST Special Publication., Gaithersburg, USA, National Institute of Standards and Technology (2002)

9. CLEF: Workshop of cross-language evaluation forum (clef 2003). In: Workshop of Cross-Language Evaluation Forum (CLEF 2003). Lecture notes in Computer Science, Trondheim, Nordway, Springer-Verlag (2003)

10. Chinchor, N.: Overview of muc-7. In: Proceedings of the Seventh Message Understanding Conference (MUC-7). (1998)

11. Borthwick, A.: A Maximum Entropy Approach to Named Entity Recognition. PhD thesis, New York University (1999)

12. Toral, A., Noguera, E., Llopis, F., Muñoz, R.: Improving question answering using named entity recognition. In: Proceedings of the 10th NLDB congress. Lecture notes in Computer Science, Alicante, Spain, Springer-Verlag (2005)

13. Llopis, F.: IR-n: Un Sistema de Recuperación de Información Basado en Pasajes. PhD thesis, University of Alicante (2003)

14. Toral, A.: DRAMNERI: a free knowledge based tool to Named Entity Recognition. In: Proceedings of the 1st Free Software Technologies Conference. (2005) Accepted.

Annotating Structural Constraints in Discourse Corpora

Claudia Sassen[1] and Peter Kühnlein[2]

[1] Universität Dortmund, Institut für Deutsche Sprache und Literatur
D-44221 Dortmund, Germany
[2] Universität Bielefeld, Fakultät für Linguistik und Literaturwissenschaft
D-33615 Bielefeld, Germany

Abstract. An enriched corpus annotation lies at the core of this paper. We will argue for an annotation that builds upon the tagging of moves and is thus meant as addendum to existing annotations. To this end, we will propose some way of marking up the fulfilment and violation of constraints by an XML-annotation which thereby allows to predict where rhetorical relations might occur: only if all constraints are fulfilled between two discourse units a rhetorical relation can obtain between them. As a starting point, two constraints will be explained and annotated which play an important role in discourse, namely Polanyi's *Right Frontier Constraint* and a constraint we will term *Semantic Compatibility Constraint*. Our approach acknowledges and supports Asher's and Lascarides' principle *Maximise Discourse Coherence* [1].

1   Fundamentals

Corpus-based projects such as TRAINS and MATE target at dialogue games or post-Searlean speech acts. By annotating moves, they reveal dependencies that exist between discourse units. One of their essential interests is the description of sequences of utterance types. The drawback of corpus annotations like these lies in the fact that they are explanatorily poor. Relations simply become overt in the form of regularities, but neither *is* their occurrence explained nor *can* it be explained in this framework. In addition, a descriptive annotation like this does not elucidate why sequences of other types may lead to a clash. We will argue for an enriched annotation of corpora which goes beyond the tagging of moves and is meant to complement existing annotations. We will set out our proposal for an enriched annotation by introducing Polanyi's structural *Right Frontier Constraint* (RFC) [3], a well-formedness condition located at the interface of semantics and pragmatics. Apart from the RFC, we will introduce a constraint we call *Semantic Compatibility Constraint* (SCC). For an overview of various non-structural types of constraints see [5].

2   Annotating Constraints

2.1   Adhering to the Right Frontier Constraint

The RFC defines anaphoric availability through pronouns in discourse: a new discourse constituent β can by pronominal anaphora attach only to the last utterance α or any

V. Matoušek et al. (Eds.): TSD 2005, LNAI 3658, pp. 435–442, 2005.

discourse constituent which dominates α. α and all constituents dominating α are said to be at the right frontier of the discourse. Figure (1) represents the structure of the following discourse from [1] in which the RFC applies:

(1) a. Max had a great evening yesterday.
     b. He had a great meal.
     c. He ate salmon.
     d. He devoured lots of cheese.
     e. He then won a dancing competition.

Utterances (b) and (e) form a narration that elaborates (a). Utterance (b), in turn, is elaborated by the narration formed by (c) and (d).

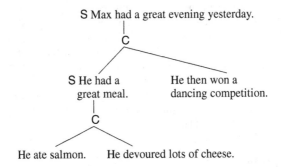

Fig. 1. Tree diagram with an expansion tree (Polanyi-type tree) representing Example (1)

Livia Polanyi was the first to integrate the RFC into a formal model which she terms *Linguistic Discourse Model* (LDM). Ever since, the RFC has become part of many other discourse theories. Before embarking upon an enriched annotation of rhetorical relations, we will sketch Polanyi's LDM, as a rough understanding of her model marks a good starting point for our annotation proposal. According to Polanyi, a discourse is composed of *discourse constituent units* (DCUs), which can either be recursively embedded or constitute atomic utterances (called DUs) [3]. Applied in discourse parsing, this assumption leads to trees, Polanyi-type trees as they are called, which assign each discourse a structural description on a left-to-right and sentence-by-sentence base. These taken together with the RFC allow to make predictions which discourse units are available as attachment points and which are not ([3]). The coordination and subordination of the trees' nodes (see Figure (1)) is the result of the rhetorical relations, or discourse relations, that obtain. As defined by the LDM, no DU can immediately be subordinate to the discourse node, but DCUs can. The Polanyi-type tree can be recognised from the content models of the elements `discourse` and DCU. It may come along in several different flavours of embedding. A DTD as licensed by the LDM has been enriched in such a way that the constraints can be determined that hold or are violated between the DUs or DCUs in question.

```
<!ELEMENT document (discourse,constraints)>
<!ELEMENT discourse (DCU+)>
<!ELEMENT DCU ((DU+|DCU+)+)>
<!ELEMENT DU (#PCDATA)>
<!ATTLIST DCU id ID #IMPLIED
              idref IDREF #IMPLIED>
<!ATTLIST DU  id ID #IMPLIED
              idref IDREF #IMPLIED>
<!ELEMENT constraints (constraint)*>
<!ELEMENT constraint EMPTY>
<!ATTLIST constraint type (RFC|CSC|SCC) #REQUIRED
                     fulfilled (yes|no) #REQUIRED
                     source IDREF  #REQUIRED
                     target IDREF  #IMPLIED>
```

The element document, which breaks down into the two nodes discourse and constraints, functions as root of the enriched DTD. Each DCU and DU has been assigned an ID and IDREF attribute to unequivocally mark how the utterances are related to each other in the tree. The element constraints consists of the element constraint, whose content model is empty. However, it has a list of attributes. The attributes make statements about the type of constraint, whether the constraint is fulfilled and to which DCUs or DUs it refers. An annotation of the document instance would look like this:

```
<?xml version="1.0" standalone="no"?>
<!DOCTYPE document SYSTEM "rfc.dtd">
<document>
<discourse>
  <DCU id="DCU_1">
    <DU id="DU_1"> Max had a great evening yesterday. </DU>
      <DCU id="DCU_2" idref="DCU_1">
      <DU id="DU_2.1" idref="DCU_2"> He had a great meal.</DU>
      <DCU id="DCU_3" idref="DCU_2">
        <DU id="DU_3.1" idref="DCU_3"> He ate salmon.</DU>
        <DU id="DU_3.2" idref="DCU_3"> He devoured lots of cheese.</DU>
      </DCU>
      <DU id="DU_2.2" idref="DCU_2"> He then won a dancing
      competition.
      </DU>
    </DCU>
  </DCU>
</discourse>
<constraints>
<constraint type="RFC" fulfilled="yes"  source="DU_2.1" target="DU_1"/>
<constraint type="RFC" fulfilled="yes"  source="DU_3.1" target="DU_2.1"/>
<constraint type="RFC" fulfilled="yes"  source="DU_3.2" target="DU_3.1"/>
<constraint type="RFC" fulfilled="yes"  source="DU_2.2" target="DU_1"/>
</constraints>
</document>
```

Some notes on construction may guide navigation within the XML-document instance: its skeletal structure consists of the XML-declaration along with the discourse displayed in Example (1), hence the element document and its embedded element discourse. Furthermore, each utterance was assigned its DCU together with a labelled DU tag. Finally, the constraints element was added along with its attribute list.

The list of constraint annotations has to be read as follows: as far as the RFC is concerned, all anaphoric pronouns in the discourse were identified. In a next step, it was determined how the pronouns can be related to their specific antecedents. For example in what was labelled as DU_2.1 (*He had a great meal*), *he* relates to the antecedent *Max* in DU_1 (*Max had a great evening yesterday*). When DU_2.1 was uttered, *Max* was located at the right frontier of the discourse. This conforms with an RFC fulfillment. In DU_3.2 (*He devoured lots of cheese*), *he* relates to the *he* of DU_3.1 (*He ate salmon*). Considering the tree's hierarchical structure, *he* might as well relate to the *he* in DU_2.1 (*He had a great meal*).

This sort of an enriched annotation puts us in the position to predict where rhetorical relations might occur: only if all constraints are fulfilled between two discourse units a rhetorical relation can obtain between them. This method acknowledges Asher's and Lascarides' principle of *Maximise Discourse Coherence*. They suggest that a discourse interpretation is the most convincing under the following conditions:

- the interpretation assigns the largest number of rhetorical relations to a given piece of text;
- it allows for the largest number of anaphoric relations to be resolved;
- it displays the highest degree of gradable rhetorical relations.

Asher and Lascarides took great care in axiomatising their rhetorical relations. They rely for instance on relations between events on the semantic side and utterances on the discourse-structural side. To employ constraints that only hold between discourse-structural units in order to predict the presence of rhetorical relations would complement such an enterprise.

2.2   Exemplifying RFC-Violations and Annotating the SCC

In this section, the annotation of an RFC-violation will be illustrated. In addition, an example will be given of how constraints can be used to anticipate an utterance failing to rhetorically relate to a discourse. Reconsider the discourse

(2)   a. Max had a great evening yesterday.
      b. He had a great meal.
      c. He ate salmon.
      d. He devoured lots of cheese.
      e. He then won a dancing competition.

Attaching Utterance (f) *It was a beautiful pink* to the discourse results in a strange outcome. Intuitively and in accordance with the RFC, the addition of Utterance (f) results in a reduced acceptability. The pronoun *it* apparently cannot refer to the *dancing competition* in *He then won a dancing competition* because *dancing competition* is not specified for colours. However, Utterance (e) is at the right frontier of the discourse and thus offers an attachment point for the pronoun *it*. The other possible attachment point would be the C-node on the superordinate level which corresponds to Utterance (a) *Max had a great evening yesterday*. However, neither utterance does offer an adequate antecedent for pronominal reference. They fail to fulfill semantic restrictions for which we suggest the term *Semantic Compatibility Constraint* (SCC) under which we also subsume the requirement of gender and number agreement. The SCC can be spelled out in terms of [1]. Within the framework of SDRT, it is assumed that a (structured) discourse can be interpreted only if a compositional semantic interpretation is derivable. This is exactly what lies behind the SCC: a new constituent can be attached to a discourse (constituent) unit only if it does not render the compositional semantic interpretation impossible. More precisely, in terms of dynamic semantics, the formulation can be given as follows.

Let $\{\langle \mathcal{M}_1, f_1 \rangle, \ldots, \langle \mathcal{M}_n, f_n \rangle\}$ be the output set of model-assignment pairs of D(C)U α. Then a new constitutent β can attach to α only if there is some non-empty set $\{\langle \mathcal{M}_m, f_m \rangle\}$ such that

$$\{\langle \mathcal{M}_1, f_1 \rangle, \ldots, \langle \mathcal{M}_n, f_n \rangle\} \supseteq \{\langle \mathcal{M}_m, f_m \rangle\} \tag{1}$$

with $\langle \mathcal{M}_m, f_m \rangle \in [\![\beta]\!](\{\langle \mathcal{M}_1, f_1 \rangle, \ldots, \langle \mathcal{M}_n, f_n \rangle\})$ where the double square brackets map an expression onto its semantics. Following the standard view of dynamic semantics, e.g. [2], a formula, or logical form (LF) of an expression, can be viewed as a filter over input model-assignment pairs. The SCC then claims that a new constitutent can only be attached to a discourse (constituent) unit if it does not filter away all input model-assignment pairs, i.e. if it does not end up in a null interpretation.

Consider Example (1) again: a sufficiently rich LF for the discourse contains the information that *evening* and *dancing competition* are specified as being abstract, hence colourless, objects. While the RFC does not prohibit the attachment of *It was a beautiful pink* to the corresponding DUs/DCUs, the SCC blocks the attachment. This is because the result of filtering the output model-assignment pairs of the attachment point would result in an empty set of model-assignment pairs, which is ruled out.

The formulation of the SCC is sufficiently general to capture the attachment to nodes at any level of a Polanyi-type tree. Given the compositionality of dynamic semantics and the SCC, it is always possible to derive a pair of sets of model-assignment pairs as an interpretation for the respective node. A proof for this claim could be given by induction, but limitations in space do not allow for this here.

As may have become obvious from the structures above, the SCC already forms part of the list of constraints in the enriched DTD. We will exemplify its annotation along with the RFC-violation. To supply a parallel annotation of more than one constraint that does or does not hold between the same D(C)Us, constraints have not been assigned attribute status, but instead element status. The order of the constraint annotation is not restricted. Here, they were sorted by type and occurrence.

Rendering an RFC-violation in XML is helpful because it permits to treat the violation by the ID/IDREF, source and target-attributes, as illustrated here:

```
<?xml version="1.0" standalone="no"?>
<!DOCTYPE document SYSTEM "rfc.dtd">
<document>
<discourse>
  <DCU id="DCU_1">
    <DU id="DU_1"> Max had a great evening yesterday. </DU>
    <DCU id="DCU_2" idref="DCU_1">
      <DU id="DU_2.1" idref="DCU_2"> He had a great meal.</DU>
      <DCU id="DCU_3" idref="DCU_2">
        <DU id="DU_3.1" idref="DCU_3"> He ate salmon.</DU>
        <DU id="DU_3.2" idref="DCU_3"> He devoured lots of cheese.</DU>
      </DCU>
      <DU id="DU_2.2" idref="DCU_2"> He then won a dancing
      competition.
      </DU>
    </DCU>
  </DCU>
```

```
<DCU id="DCU_4">
  <DU id="DU_4"> It was a beautiful pink. </DU>
</DCU>
</discourse>
<constraints>
<constraint type="RFC" fulfilled="yes" source="DU_2.1" target="DU_1"/>
<constraint type="RFC" fulfilled="yes" source="DU_3.1" target="DU_2.1"/>
<constraint type="RFC" fulfilled="yes" source="DU_3.2" target="DU_3.1"/>
<constraint type="RFC" fulfilled="yes" source="DU_2.2" target="DU_1"/>
<constraint type="RFC" fulfilled="no"  source="DU_4" target="DU_3.1"/>
<constraint type="RFC" fulfilled="yes" source="DU_4" target="DU_2.2"/>
<constraint type="RFC" fulfilled="yes" source="DU_4" target="DU_1"/>

<constraint type="SCC" fulfilled="yes" source="DU_2.1" target="DU_1"/>
<constraint type="SCC" fulfilled="yes" source="DU_3.1" target="DU_2.1"/>
<constraint type="SCC" fulfilled="yes" source="DU_3.2" target="DU_3.1"/>
<constraint type="SCC" fulfilled="yes" source="DU_2.2" target="DU_1"/>
<constraint type="SCC" fulfilled="yes" source="DU_4" target="DU_3.1"/>
<constraint type="SCC" fulfilled="no"  source="DU_4" target="DU_2.2"/>
<constraint type="SCC" fulfilled="no"  source="DU_4" target="DU_1"/>
</constraints>
</document>
```

To explain the violation as caused by Utterance (f): DCU/DU_4 (*It was a beautiful pink*) is part of the discourse, but obviously does not relate to anything. After some insight it becomes obvious that the *it* of DU_4 refers to *salmon* in DU_3.1 (*He ate salmon*). This would result in semantic compatibility (hence SCC fulfilled), but the RFC is not fulfilled, thus the attribute fulfilled was assigned the value no. According to the RFC, *it* may refer to DU_2.2/Utterance (e) (*He then won a dancing competition*) without producing a clash and also to DU_1 (*Max had a great evening yesterday*), as those are located at the right frontier. However, DU_4 relating to these DUs is blocked by way of SCC-violation which can be read off from the last three entries relating the same units as the corresponding entries in the RFC-list. But matters are complementary here: whenever the RFC would be fulfilled, the SCC is not and vice versa. Only in the first four cases, neither the RFC nor the SCC is violated.

Given the amount of information in the XML-document instance, the question might arise whether an annotation of constraint fulfilment is a redundant task and a waste of time. It does have an important plus: the explicit annotation of constraints explains why an utterance is or is not in the right place (RFC) and why it may or may not come to semantic clashes in some places (SCC).

Adding utterances like *It was a beautiful pink* to the discourse about Max's evening is strikingly odd because there is no rhetorical relation that would explain how the utterance has to be linked to its preceding utterances: the constraint violations allow to predict where no rhetorical relations occur. *It was a latin-dance contest* does on the other hand attach perfectly to *He later won a dancing competition* in that RFC and SCC are fulfilled. According to the RFC, the antecedent may be any (pro)noun that is located at the right frontier of the discourse. The alternative *Max had a great evening*, which is also at the right frontier, does not qualify as an antecedent because the SCC is not fulfilled.

Annotations exist that, following Dialogue Games Theory (DGT), describe relations between successive utterances. They describe what type of utterance follows another utterance, as exemplified by answers following questions. But, just like DGT, they offer no option to determine whether an answer is semantically compatible with its preceding question. Within the framework of this paper, it is not only possible to capture structural (RFC) and semantical (SCC) properties of discourse. The regular patterns which determine that e.g. an answer is subsequent to a question can themselves be conceptualised as constraints: corresponding types for rhetorical relations might be added to the DTD as values for the `type`-attribute of the element `constraint`.

3 Prospect

Up to now, it was tacitly assumed that every sentence contains a (unique) antecedent for a (unique) anaphoric expression. Of course, this is not necessarily the case. Consider the following short discourse:

(3) a. Pia owns a pig and a piano.
     b. She feeds it regularly.

It is clear that *she* in (3b) co-refers with *Pia* in (3a); it is also quite clear that *it* in (3b) does not co-refer with *piano* in (3a). This is enforced by the SCC. And from both this fact and the assumption that *it* should refer anyway, it follows that it should co-refer with *pig*. But it is immediately patent that this co-reference cannot yet be expressed in the XML-annotation.

The annotation spelled out so far allows for an analysis on the sentence (or utterance) level only. What Example (3) reveals is that a more fine-grained analysis is needed. And there is also an indication of which kind of problems will be encountered. One kind of problem is already indicated by the possible value CSC in the `type`-attribute list of `constraint`. This is an allusion to the *Coordinate Structure Constraint* formulated by [4]. We expect the difficulties which are discussed there and others: while *it* can be excluded from co-referring with *piano* in Example (3), given the SCC, it must be postulated either that nothing like the RFC holds on the subsentential level or that the RFC blocks the anaphoric relation between *it* and *pig*. It has to be tested whether there are strong intuitions in such a case (a study of this kind is currently carried out and a large-scale investigation via internet is in preparation). If it really should be proven that the RFC still holds, either constraint would have to be reconceived as working on that level of granularity. This would also imply a reconception of the grammars that put the RFC at work on an utterance or sentence level. If it was proven that the RFC does not hold on that level of granularity, but the SCC does (which is obvious), the consequence would be that both constraints would have to be annotated on different levels.

But already as it stands, an annotation of constraint violations has the advantage of marking at which point in a discourse exceptions occur and where alternative interpretations are feasible.

References

1. Asher, N. and Lascarides, A.: Logics of Discourse. Cambridge University Press (2003)
2. Benthem, J. van: Exploring Logical Dynamics. CSLI & FoLLI, Studies in Logic, Language and Information (1996)

3. Polanyi, L.: A formal model of the structure of discourse. Journal of Pragmatics, **12** (1988) 601–38
4. Ross, R. J.: Infinite Syntax!. Ablex (1986)
5. Webber, B. L.: Computational Perspectives on Discourse and Dialogue. In D. Schiffrin, D. Tannen, and H. Hamilton (Eds.), The Handbook of Discourse Analysis. Blackwell Publishers (2001)

A Passage Retrieval System
for Multilingual Question Answering *

José Manuel Gómez Soriano[1], Manuel Montes y Gómez[2],
Emilio Sanchis Arnal[1], and Paolo Rosso[1]

[1] Departamento de Sistemas Informáticos y Computación
Universidad Politécnica de Valencia, Spain
{jogomez,esanchis,prosso}@dsic.upv.es
[2] Laboratorio de Tecnologías del Lenguaje
Coordinación de Ciencias Computacionales
Instituto Nacional de Astrofísica, Óptica y Electrónica (INAOE), Mexico
mmontesg@inaoep.mx

Abstract. In this paper we present a new method to improve the coverage of Passage Retrieval (PR) systems when these systems are employed for the Question Answering (QA) tasks. The ranking of passages obtained by the PR system is rearranged to emphasize those passages with more probability to contain the answer. The new ranking is based on finding the n-gram structures of the question that are presented in the passage, and the weight of the passages increases when they contain longer n-grams structures of the question. The results we present show that the application of this method improves notably the coverage of the classical PR system based on the Space Vectorial Model.

1 Introduction

A QA system is an application that allows a user to question in natural language a non-structured document collection in order to look for the correct answer.

Recently, at the Cross-Language Evaluation Forum (CLEF)[1] which is a reference workshop to evaluate IR/QA systems operating on European languages, the task of multilingual QA has been incorporated. For this task, a QA system must be capable to accept questions in several languages and to search for the answers in a set of multilingual document collections.

In the multilingual QA task, it is very interesting the use of methodologies of document (or passage) retrieval as independent as possible of the language. This is the case of some pattern matching approaches, in which it is not necessary the use of a-priori knowledge of the languages.

Document or passage retrieval is typically used as the first step in current question answering systems [1]. In most of the QA systems, classical PR systems are used [2–5].

---

* We would like to thank CONACyT for partially supporting this work under the grant 43990A-1 as well as R2D2 CICYT (TIC2003-07158-C04-03) and ICT EU-India (ALA/95/23/2003/077-054) research projects.

[1] http://clef.iei.pi.cnr.it/

V. Matoušek et al. (Eds.): TSD 2005, LNAI 3658, pp. 443–450, 2005.
© Springer-Verlag Berlin Heidelberg 2005

The main problem that these QA systems have is due to the fact they use PR systems which are adaptations of classical document retrieval systems instead of being oriented to the specific problematic of QA. These systems use the question keywords to find relevant passages. For instance, if the question is *Who is the President of Mexico?*, these systems return those passages which contain the words *President* and *Mexico*.

In [6, 7] it is shown that standard IR engines often fail to find the answer in the documents (or passages) when the question is presented with natural language questions. In [8] is presented a study of the performance of a QA system using just the top 20 passages showing that these passages contain the answer for only 54% of the question set [9].

Other PR approaches are based on Natural Language Processing (NLP) [9–12]. These approaches have the disadvantage to be very difficult to be adapted to other languages or to multilingual tasks.

The strategy of [13–15] is to search the obviousness of the answer in the Web. They run the user question into a Web search engine (usually Google[2]) with the expectation to get a passage containing the same expression of the question or a similar one. They suppose that due to the high redundancy[3] of the Web, the answer will be written in several different ways including the same form of the question.

To increase the possibility to find relevant passages they make reformulations of the question, i.e., they move or delete terms to search other structures with the same question terms. For instance, if we move the verb of the question *Who is the President of Mexico?* and we delete the question term *Who*, we can produce the query *the President of Mexico is*. Thanks to the redundancy, we might find a passage with the structure *the President of Mexico is **Vicente Fox***. [14] makes the reformulations carrying out a Part Of Speech analysis of the question and moving o deleting terms of specific morphosyntactic categories. Whereas [13] makes the reformulations doing certain assumptions about the verb position and the prepositional phrases boundaries on the question. The problem of these systems is that all the possible reformulations of the question are not taken into account.

With the methods used by [14] and [13] it would be very costly to realize all the possible reformulations since every reformulation must be searched by the search engine.

Our QA-oriented PR system makes better use of the redundancy bearing in mind all the possible reformulations of the question efficiently running the search engine with just one question as it will be described in detail in the next section.

Our system has the advantage to be language independent because it is based on processing the question and the passages without using any knowledge about the lexicon and the syntax of the corresponding language. In a language with not many differences between the question and the answer sentences, our system should work very well.

This paper presents our PR system for QA. In Sect.2, we describe the general architecture of the system. In Sect.3 we discuss the results which were obtained using the Spanish CLEF questions and corpus, whereas in the last section we draw conclusions and future works.

---

[2] www.google.com

[3] Certain repetition of the information contained in the collection of documents or Web, which allows, in spite of the loss of a part of this one, to reconstruct its content

2 System Architecture

The architecture of our PR system is shown in Fig.1.

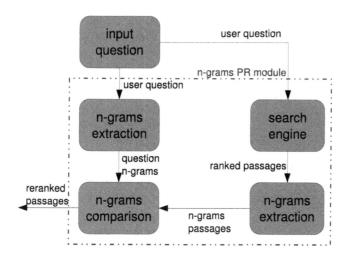

Fig. 1. Main diagram of the PR system

Given an user question, it will be transferred to the *search engine* and *n-grams extraction* modules. Passages with the relevant terms (no stopwords) are found by the *search engine* using the classical IR system. Sets of unigrams, bigrams, ..., n-grams are extracted from the extended passages and from the user question. In both cases, n will be the number of question terms.

With the n-gram sets of the passages and the user question we will make a comparison in order to obtain the weight of each passage. The weight of a passage is related to the greater n-gram structure of the question which can be found in the passage itself. The weight of a passage will be longer if the passage contains greater n-gram structures of the question. This weight will be calculated using (1).

$$Sim(d, q) = \frac{\sum\limits_{j=1}^{n} \sum\limits_{\forall x \in Q_j} h(x, D_j)}{\sum\limits_{j=1}^{n} \sum\limits_{\forall x \in Q_j} h(x, Q_j)} , \qquad (1)$$

where $Sim(d, q)$ is a function which measures the similarity of the set of n-grams of the question q with the set of n-grams of the passage d. Q_j is a set of j-grams that are generated from the question q and D_j is the set of j-grams of the passage d to compare with. That is, Q_1 will contain the question unigrams whereas D_1 will contain the passage unigrams, Q_2 and D_2 will contain the question and passage bigrams respectively, and so on until Q_n and D_n.

The result of (1) is equal to 1 if the longest n-gram of the question is in the set of passage n-grams.

For instance, if we ask *"Who is the President of Mexico?"* the system could retrieve two passages: one with the expression *"...**Vicente Fox** is the President of Mexico..."*, and the other one with the expression *"...**José Luis Rodríguez Zapatero** is the President of Spain..."*. Of course, the first passage must have more importance because it contains the 5-gram *"is the President of Mexico"*, whereas the second passage only contains the 4-gram *"is the President of"*, since the *"is the President of Spain"* 5-gram is not in the original question.

The function $h(x, D_j)$ measures the relevance of the j-gram x with respect to the set of passage j-grams, whereas the function $h(x, Q_j)$ is a factor of normalization. The function $h(x, D_j)$ is defined by (2).

$$h(x, D_j) = \begin{cases} 1 & \text{if } x \in D_j \\ 0 & \text{otherwise} \end{cases}. \tag{2}$$

That is, (2) returns 1 if the j-gram x belongs to the set of passage j-grams and 0 otherwise. In this way, the denominator function $h(x, Q_j)$ returns always 1 since the j-gram x always is in the set of j-grams Q_j and, therefore, the (1) can be simplified as:

$$Sim(d, q) = \frac{\sum_{j=1}^{n} \sum_{\forall x \in Q_j} h(x, D_j)}{\sum_{j=1}^{n} j}. \tag{3}$$

The (3) has the disadvantage that it gives the same weight to all question terms, no matter if they are relevant words or not. Therefore, if we find the *"the President of Mexico"* 4-gram, it would have the same weight than *"is the President of"*. In spite of that, this approximation improves the results considerably with respect to the classical vectorial model.

Of course, it would be interesting to give more weight to those n-grams which contain more relevant words. For this purpose, we would have to redefine (2) as:

$$h(x, D_j) = \begin{cases} \sum_{k=1}^{|x|} w_k & \text{if } x \in D_j \\ 0 & \text{otherwise} \end{cases}. \tag{4}$$

where $w_1, w_2, ..., w_{|x|}$ are the associated weights of the terms of the j-gram x. The associated weights should give an incentive to those terms which do not appear much in the document collection. Moreover, the weights should also discriminate the terms against those (e.g. stopwords) which often occur in the document collection. The next function was used in the experiments in order to assign a weight to a term:

$$w_k = 1 - \frac{\log(n_k)}{1 + \log(N)}. \tag{5}$$

where n_k is the number of passages in which the associated term to the weight w_k appears and N is the number of system passages. We make the assumption that stopwords occur in every passage (i.e., n_k takes the value of N). For instance, if the term appears once in the passage collection, its weight will be equal to 1 (the greatest weight). Whereas if it is a stopword its weight will be the lowest.

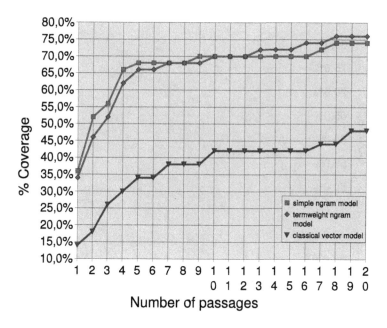

Fig. 2. Correct answers versus consulted passages

3   Preliminary Results

The experiments detailed in this paper will be evaluated using a metric know as coverage (for more details see [7]).

Let Q be the question set, D the passage collection, $A_{D,q}$ the subset of D containing correct answers to $q \in Q$, and $R_{D,q,n}$ be the top n ranked documents in D retrieved by the search engine given a question q.

The *coverage* of the search engine for a question set Q and a document collection D at rank n is defined as:

$$coverage(Q, D, n) \equiv \frac{|\{q \in Q | R_{D,q,n} \cap A_{D,q} \neq \emptyset\}|}{|Q|} \qquad (6)$$

Coverage gives the proportion of the question set for which a correct answer can be found within the top n documents retrieved for each question.

Some experiments were carried out on the CLEF Spanish corpus which is composed of documents of the *Agencia EFE (1994/1995)*. The 200 questions which we used are those of the 2003 Spanish QA task.

Due to the fact that whether the answers were included in the passages or not had to be manually verified, for the prelimnary experiments we only analyzed the first 50 questions of the corpus. In the Fig. 2 is possible to appreciate the substantial improvement of our two models with respect to classical vector model.

This figure shows that the percentage of found answers increases as the number of considered passages does. The 75% of answers is found by both the *simple ngram model*

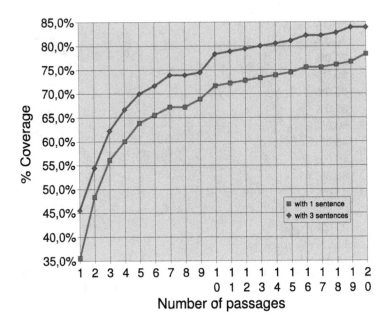

Fig. 3. Correct answers found in passages of 1 and 3 sentences

(2) and the *termweight ngram model* (4). We can appreciate that the *termweight ngram model* is lightly better when the number of observed passages is higher whereas the *simple ngram model* works better when the number of passages is smaller. This is because the *simple ngram model* returns, in the first passages, the n-grams which contain most of the words of the question. Therefore, it is more likely that these passages could contain the longest n-grams. As the *simple ngram model* does not prioritize any word, when we increase the number of passages, we start to find passages with smaller n-gram structures. Moreover, the shortest n-grams could be composed by words which are not necessarily relevants. On the other hand, the *termweight ngram model* has a smaller coverage in the first passages because it prioritizes more the weight of the terms than the n-gram structures which contain little relevant terms. In fact, the last model could provide relevant passages (with respect to the question) which do not necessarily contain the correct answer. The *termweight ngram model* improves in the final part due to the number of relevants longer structures decreases and the weight of the terms becomes more important.

In order to study the importance of redundancy and the coverage which our system could obtain, the 200 questions corpus was used. Fig. 3 shows the results which were obtained with the *termweight ngram model* for passages of 1 and 3 sentences.

In this figure we can apreciate that the coverage with passages of 3 sentences is higher than passages of 1 sentence (about 85% for the first 20 passages). This is due to the fact that often the answer is in the previous or following sentence.

Another important characteristic of our system is the redundancy of the correct answers which is about **7** (whith passages of 3 sentences) and **5.5** (when only one sentece is in the passage). There results make our system suitable for those answer extraction methods based on redundancy [3–5, 13, 14, 16, 17].

4   Conclusions and Future Work

The n-grams comparison method which allowed us to obtain passages that contain the answer worked very well with the CLEF Spanish corpus, giving a very good coverage with a high redundancy (i.e., the correct answer was found more than once in the returned passages). Moreover, our system, does not make use any linguistic information and it is language independent. Therefore, we suppose it should allow to tackle the problem of the Multilingual QA since it will be able to distinguish what translations are better considering their n-gram structure in the corpus and it will discriminate the bad translations that are very unlikely that they appear. Our further interest is to proof the above assumption using as input several automatic translations and merging the returned passages. Those passages obtained with bad translations will have less weight than those which correspond to the correct ones.

As future work it would be necessary to see if this behavior stays for other corpora (e.g. the TREC[4] English corpus and the CLEF transcripted dialogue corpus), as well as other languages. In addition, we would be interesed in incorporating our system to a Multiligual QA system, to implement the modules of question analysis and extract the answer.

References

1. Corrada-Emmanuel, A., Croft, B., Murdock, V.: Answer passage retrieval for question answering. Technical Report, Center for Intelligent Information Retrieval (2003)
2. Magnini, B., Negri, M., Prevete, R., Tanev, H.: Multilingual question/answering: the DIOGENE system. In: The 10th Text REtrieval Conference. (2001)
3. Aunimo, L., Kuuskoski, R., Makkonen, J.: Cross-language question answering at the university of helsinki. In: Workshop of the Cross-Lingual Evaluation Forum (CLEF 2004), Bath, UK (2004)
4. Vicedo, J.L., Izquierdo, R., Llopis, F., Muñoz, R.: Question answering in spanish. In: Workshop of the Cross-Lingual Evaluation Forum (CLEF 2003), Trondheim, Norway (2003)
5. Neumann, G., Sacaleanu, B.: Experiments on robust nl question interpretation and multilayered document annotation for a cross-language question/answering system. In: Workshop of the Cross-Lingual Evaluation Forum (CLEF 2004), Bath, UK (2004)
6. Hovy, E., Gerber, L., Hermjakob, U., Junk, M., Lin, C.: Question answering in webclopedia. In: The Ninth Text REtrieval Conference. (2000)
7. Roberts, I., Gaizauskas, R.J.: Data-intensive question answering. In: ECIR. Volume 2997 of Lecture Notes in Computer Science., Springer (2004)
8. Gaizauskas, R., Greenwood, M.A., Hepple, M., Roberts, I., Saggion, H., Sargaison, M.: The university of sheffield's trec 2003 q&a experiments. In: The 12th Text REtrieval Conference. (2003)
9. Greenwood, M.A.: Using pertainyms to improve passage retrieval for questions requesting information about a location. In: SIGIR. (2004)

---

[4] Text REtrieval Conference (http://trec.nist.gov/)

10. Ahn, R., Alex, B., Bos, J., Dalmas, T., Leidner, J.L., Smillie, M.B.: Cross-lingual question answering with qed. In: Workshop of the Cross-Lingual Evaluation Forum (CLEF 2004), Bath, UK (2004)

11. Hess, M.: The 1996 international conference on tools with artificial intelligence (tai'96). In: SIGIR. (1996)

12. Liu, X., Croft, W.: Passage retrieval based on language models (2002)

13. Del-Castillo-Escobedo, A., y Gómez, M.M., Villaseñor-Pineda, L.: Qa on the web: a preliminary study for spanish language. In: Proceedings of the Fifth Mexican International Conference in Computer Science (ENC'04), Colima, México (2004)

14. Brill, E., Lin, J., Banko, M., Dumais, S.T., Ng, A.Y.: Data-intensive question answering. In: The 10th Text REtrieval Conference. (2001)

15. Buchholz, S.: Using grammatical relations, answer frequencies and the world wide web for trec question answering. In: The 10th Text REtrieval Conference. (2001)

16. Brill, E., Dumais, S., Banko, M.: An analysis of the askmsr question-answering system (2002)

17. Costa, L.: First ealuation of esfinge - a question answering system for portuguese. In: Workshop of the Cross-Lingual Evaluation Forum (CLEF 2004), Bath, UK (2004)

Error Analysis of Dialogue Act Classification

Nick Webb, Mark Hepple, and Yorick Wilks

Natural Language Processing Group
Department of Computer Science
University of Sheffield, UK
{n.webb,m.hepple,y.wilks}@dcs.shef.ac.uk

Abstract. We are interested in the area of Dialogue Act (DA) tagging. Identifying the dialogue acts of utterances is recognised as an important step towards understanding the content and nature of what speakers say. We have built a simple dialogue act classifier based on purely *intra-utterance* features – principally word n-gram cue phrases. Although such a classifier performs surprisingly well, rivalling scores obtained using far more sophisticated language modelling techniques for the corpus we address, we want to understand further the issues raised by this approach. We have performed an error analysis of the output of our classifier, with a view to casting light both on the system's performance, and on the DA classification scheme itself.

1 Introduction

In the area of spoken language dialogue systems, the ability to assign user input with a functional tag which represents the communicative intentions behind each utterance – the utterance's *dialogue act* – is acknowledged to be a useful first step in dialogue processing. Such tagging can assist the semantic interpretation of user utterances, and can help an automated system in producing an appropriate response. In common with the work of Samuels *et al.* [1], we have automatically detected word n-grams in a corpus that might serve as useful cue phrases, potential indicators of dialogue acts. The method we chose for selecting such phrases is based on their *predictivity*. The predictivity of cue phrases can be exploited directly in a simple model of dialogue act classification that employs only intra-utterance features, that is, makes no use of the relationship between utterances, such as preceding DA labels.

Having built such a classifier [2], we were surprised that the results we obtain rival the best results achieved on our target corpus, in work by Stolcke *et al.* [3], who use a far more complex approach involving Hidden Markov modelling (HMM), that addresses both the sequencing of words *within* utterances and the sequencing of dialogue acts *over* utterances. In order that we might better understand the performance of our classifier, we decided to perform a simple error analysis - looking at which of the categories in our corpus are most consistently tagged correctly, and which are not. In Section 2 of this paper, we present previous work in DA modelling. A brief overview of our previous classification experiments is presented in Section 3. In Section 4 we outline the error analysis performed using this classifier, and in the light of this, an experiment in collapsing some of the target categories for the corpus is reported in Section 5. We end with some discussion and an outline of intended further work.

V. Matoušek et al. (Eds.): TSD 2005, LNAI 3658, pp. 451–458, 2005.

2   Related Work

One approach utilised for dialogue act tagging is that of n-gram language modelling, exploiting principally ideas drawn from the area of speech recognition. For example, Reithinger and Klesen [4] have applied such an approach to the VERBMOBIL corpus, which provides only a rather limited amount of training data, and report a tagging accuracy of 74.7%. Stolcke *et al.* [3] apply a somewhat more complicated HMM method to the SWITCHBOARD corpus, one which addresses both the sequencing of words *within* utterances and the sequencing of dialogue acts *over* utterances. They use a single split of the data for their experiments, with 198k utterances for training and 4k utterances for testing, achieving a DA tagging accuracy of 71% on word transcripts. These performance differences, with a higher tagging accuracy score for the VERBMOBIL corpus despite significantly less training data, can be seen to reflect the differential difficulty of tagging for the two corpora.

A second approach that has been applied to dialogue act modelling, by Samuel *et al.* [5], uses transformation-based learning over a number of utterance features, including utterance length, speaker turn and the dialogue act tags of adjacent utterances. They achieved an average score of 75.12% tagging accuracy over the VERBMOBIL corpus. One significant aspect of this work, that is of particular relevance here, has addressed the automatic identification of word sequences that might serve as useful dialogue act cues. A number of statistical criteria are applied to identify potentially useful word n-grams which are then supplied to the transformation-based learning method to be treated as 'features'.

Dialogue Act	% of corpus	% accuracy	Dialogue Act	% of corpus	% accuracy
statement-non-opinion	36%	92%	action-directive	0.4%	25%
acknowledge	19%	97%	collaborative completion	0.4%	0%
statement-opinion	13%	26%	repeat-phrase	0.3%	0%
agree-accept	5%	31%	open-question	0.3%	67%
abandoned	5%	55%	rhetorical-questions	0.2%	0%
appreciation	2%	86%	hold before answer	0.2%	33%
yes-no-question	2%	51%	reject	0.2%	0%
non-verbal	2%	100%	negative non-no answers	0.1%	14%
yes answers	1%	0%	signal-non-understanding	0.1%	0%
conventional-closing	1%	47%	other answers	0.1%	0%
uninterpretable	1%	55%	conventional-opening	0.1%	50%
wh-question	1%	46%	or-clause	0.1%	0%
no answers	1%	5%	dispreferred answers	0.1%	0%
response acknowledgement	1%	0%	3rd-party-talk	0.1%	0%
hedge	1%	64%	offers, options commits	0.1%	0%
declarative yes-no-question	1%	3%	self-talk	0.1%	0%
other	1%	0%	downplayer	0.1%	0%
backchannel in question form	1%	19%	maybeaccept-par	< 0.1%	0%
quotation	0.5%	0%	tag-question	< 0.1%	0%
summarisereformulate	0.5%	0%	declarative wh-question	< 0.1%	0%
affirmative non-yes answers	0.4%	0%	apology	< 0.1%	50%

Fig. 1. SWITCHBOARD dialogue acts, by occurrence and tagging accuracy

3   Simple DA Classification

In Webb *et al.* [2], we describe our simple approach to DA classification, based solely on intra-utterance features, together with our evaluation experiments. A key aspect of our approach is the selection of word n-grams to use as cue phrases in tagging. Samuel

et al. [1] investigate a series of different statistical criteria for use in automatically selecting cue phrases. We use a criterion of *predictivity*, described below, which is one
that Samuel *et al.* do not consider.

3.1   Experimental Corpus

For our experiments, we used the SWITCHBOARD data set of 1,155 annotated conversations, which together comprise in the region 205k utterances. The dialogue act types
for this set can be seen in Jurafsky *et al.* [6]. The corpus is annotated using an elaboration of the DAMSL tag set [7], involving 50 major classes, together with a number
of diacritic marks, which combine to generate 220 distinct labels. Jurafsky *et al.* [6]
propose a clustering of the 220 tags into 42 larger classes and it is this clustered set
used both in the experiments of Stolcke *et al.* [3], and those reported here. The 42 DA
classes can be seen in Figure 1. We used 198k utterances for training and 4k for testing,
with pre-processing to remove all punctuation and case information, in common with
Stolcke *et al.* [3] in order that we might compare figures. Some of the corpus mark-up,
such as filler information described in the paper by Meteer [8], was also removed.

Our experiments use a cross-validation approach, with results being averaged over
10 runs. For our data, the test set is much less than a tenth of the overall data, so a standard ten-fold approach does not apply. Instead, we randomly select dialogues out of the
overall data to create ten subsets of around 4k utterances for use as test sets. In each
case, the corresponding training set was the overall data minus that subset. In addition
to cross-validated results, we also report the single highest score from the ten runs performed for each experimental case. We have done this to facilitate comparison with the
results of Stolcke *et al.* [3].

3.2   Cue Phrase Selection

For our experiments, the word n-grams used as cue phrases during classification are
computed from the training data. All word n-grams of length 1 – 4 within the data are
considered as candidates. The phrases chosen as cue phrases are selected principally
using a criterion of *predictivity*, which is the extent to which the presence of a certain
n-gram in an utterance is predictive of it having a certain dialogue act category. For
an n-gram n and dialogue act d, this corresponds to the conditional probability:
$P(d \mid n)$, a value which can be straightforwardly computed. Specifically, we compute all
n-grams in the training data of length 1–4, counting their occurrences in the utterances
of each DA category and in total, from which the above conditional probability for
each n-gram and dialogue act can be computed. For each n-gram, we are interested
in its *maximal* predictivity, i.e. the highest predictivity value found for it with any DA
category. This set of n-grams is then reduced by applying thresholds of predictivity
and occurrence, i.e. eliminating any n-gram whose maximal predictivity is below some
minimum requirement, or whose maximal number of occurrences with any category
falls below a threshold value.

3.3   Using Cue Phrases in Classification

The selected cue phrases are used directly in classifying previously unseen utterances
in the following manner. To classify an utterance, we identify all the cue phrases it contains, and determine which has the highest predictivity of some dialogue act category,

and then that category is assigned. If multiple cue phrases share the same maximal predictivity, but predict different categories, the category indicated by the phrase with the *highest* frequency count is assigned. If no cue phrases are present, then a default tag is assigned, corresponding to the most frequent tag within the training corpus.

3.4   Experimental Cases

In our previous work [2] we performed five different experiments using a variety of simple methods for pre-processing the data. Our best reported figures on the 202k utterance corpus are a cross-validated score of 69.09%, with a single high score of 71.29%, which compares well with the (non-cross-validated) 71% reported in Stolcke *et al.* [3].

In each experiment, there are two important variables used to select n-grams as potential cue phrases - the frequency of occurrence of each n-gram, and how predictive an n-gram is of some dialogue act. In more recent work [9], we have shown that we can select these scores automatically, using a validation set separate from our test data, without suffering a significant decrease in tagging performance. During these experiments, we observed some dialogue act categories that seemed to be most easily confused - where utterances of one category are consistently incorrectly tagged as being of a second category. The focus of this paper is to perform an explicit error analysis to determine empirically which categories are most confused by our classification method. By further inspection of the errors, perhaps there are issues within our model which can be adjusted to attain better performance, or perhaps we have reached the limit possible given only intra-utterance classification models, and the resulting ambiguities can be solved only with reference to dialogue context.

Dialogue Act Name	count	% accuracy
statement-opinion	469	26%
Incorrectly tagged as:	*count*	*% error*
appreciation	4	0.9%
abandoned	13	2.8%
yes-no-question	1	0.2%
hedge	1	0.2%
acknowledge	2	0.4%
conventional-closing	1	0.2%
statement-non-opinion	315	67.2%
acknowledge-accept	11	2.3%
wh-question	1	0.2%

Fig. 2. Single category error analysis

4   Error Analysis

Taking our best performing DA model from Webb *et al.* [2], we performed an error analysis, calculating the accuracy of recognition for each dialogue act in the corpus. The results of a single, non-cross-validated run, using a test set of 3279 utterances and a training set of some 198k utterances, can be seen in Figure 1. There are some interesting points to note here. We can see that 'statements-non-opinion' score very highly 92% recognition accuracy), but that 'statements-opinion' score far lower (26%). What could be worrying, for automatic dialogue systems, is the low recognition rate for important categories such as 'yes-answers' (0%) and 'no-answers' (5%). Some of these low scores can be attributed to sparse amounts of training data for specific dialogue acts - given their low frequency of occurrence in the SWITCHBOARD corpus. Others can be easily explained in terms of the lexicalisations which realise the utterances. We will look at this in more detail later.

Alone, these figures do not necessarily help us identify areas of the classification mechanism on which we should focus for improvement. For each occurrence of a dialogue act which we tagged incorrectly, we noted which tag was used in error. For example, the tag 'statement-opinion' occurs 469 times in the chosen test data, of which we correctly tagged 120, or 26%. Of the incorrect tags assigned to 'statement-opinion' utterances, the scores for tagging with other DAs can be seen in Figure 2, along with the proportional scores calculated by dividing the number of times an incorrect tag is used for a specific category, by the number of times the correct category occurs in the corpus. It seems clear that the significant score here is the number of times that a 'statement-opinion' utterance is tagged as a 'statement-non-opinion'. We determined that this proportional score is one useful discriminator for selecting interesting, regularly confused DA tags. We chose to look at only those tags where 50% or more of the proportion of errors to total occurrences are tagged as a single incorrect category.

An equally important factor is the number of occurrences of the DA tag in question. It makes sense in the first instance to concentrate on those DAs whose count was significant - i.e. those where correcting errors in classification would have a statistically significant effect on classifier performance. We chose to concentrate on those DAs whose occurrence in the test data is higher than 40 - the equivalent to an effective 1% gain in classifier performance, if all instances are tagged correctly. Interestingly, there are only two instances where both criteria of significant count and significant proportional errors are fulfilled. The first of these is as already mentioned, the case of 'statement-opinion' being incorrectly tagged as 'statement-non-opinion'. The second is the case of 'agree-accept' being tagged as 'acknowledge' (there are 228 instances of 'agree-accept' in the test data, of which 70 were tagged correctly; of the 158 errors, 140 were tagged as 'acknowledge', 61.4% of all instances). We shall examine both cases in turn.

For the confusion regarding 'statement-opinion', we first look at the tagging guidelines for the SWITCHBOARD corpus, laid out in Jurafsky et al. [6]. They themselves are unable to ascertain if the distinction between the categories is fruitful. Having trained separate tri-gram models on the two sets, Stolcke *et al.* claim these tri-gram models look somewhat distinct, and yet found that this distinction was very hard to make by human labellers. Jurafsky *et al.* report that this distinction accounted for a large proportion of their inter-labeller disagreements. They provide 'clue' phrases, which may be present in a 'statement-opinion' utterance. These include: *'I think'; 'I believe; 'It seems'* and *'It's my opinion that'*. Looking at the n-grams created from the entire corpus, we can start to identify some potential problems. 'I think' is a common n-gram, occurring more than 6250 times. However, while some 63% of those occur in utterances tagged with 'statement-opinion', there is still a large margin of error. 31% of the remaining n-grams occur in 'statement-non-opinion' utterances. This position is much the same with 'it seems' (472 total instances, 307 as 'statement-opinion' (65%), 144 as 'statement-non-opinion' (31%). In these cases, although the 'clue phrases' are clearly indicative of 'statement-opinion', if some other, more highly predictive n-gram is present, it's possible that the presence of such clues will be ignored. It is even worse with respect to 'I believe', which occurs 190 times in total, but where 88 (46%) of those predict 'statement-opinion', 91 (48%) occur in 'statement-non-opinion' utterances. The only one of Jurafsky's examples to fare well is 'it's my opinion that', but as this occurs only once in the entire corpus, is of limited use. This investigation bears out the argument that labellers had extreme difficultly in differentiating between these two categories. There is then a substantial argument here that if this is a hard category for human labellers to separate, perhaps there should not be two, distinct categories.

The second problem category, where 'agree-accept' can often be tagged as 'acknowledge', is more straightforward to understand. By looking at a sample of the utterances coded in each category, we can see that, as might be expected, they have substantially similar lexicalisations. Both are represented often by 'yeah', 'yes' and 'right'. According to the labellers manual [6], there are several contextual issues which may help to disambiguate the two. This raises an important point. Since this far we have concerned ourselves only with intra-utterance features, we are unable to disambiguate some of the categories at this stage. We hope that higher level processes, perhaps powered by machine learning alorithms, may enable to us to leverage the context of surrounding utterances in our classification. We speculate that a machine learning approach, using context, might do better at disambiguating between 'agreement-accept' and 'acknowledge', but not do significantly better for 'statement-opinion' and 'statement-non-opinion'.

5   Merging Categories

As we have shown, the categories 'statement-opinion' and 'statement-non-opinion' are often confused. This split of the STATEMENT category is one that Jurafsky et al. created for the SWITCHBOARD corpus, as there is no such distinction made in the DAMSL [7] coding schema from which the annotation set for the SWITCHBOARD corpus is derived. In order to test the performance of a system where such a distinction was not made, we created a version of the corpus where all instances of both 'statement-opinion' and 'statement-non-opinion' were *replaced* by the single category 'statement'. The results from the error-analysis would seem to indicate that there should be an almost 10% improvement in our classification accuracy. In previous work, we reported a best cross-validated score of 69.09% (with a high score of 71.29%) [2]. After repeating the cross-validation experiment on the new corpus, we achieve a score of 76.73%, with a high of 78.58%, in both cases a gain of over 7%.

Another possible solution to this problem is to use the phrases suggested by Jurafsky *et al.*, and their variants, to create a distinct set of utterances, all of which *should* be labelled at 'statement-opinion'. This would correct the error indicated in Figure 3. Alternatively, when we merge the 'statement-opinion' and 'statement-non-opinion' utterances into a single category, we propose a separate indicator of whether an utterance

`Speaker A: DA="statement-non-opinion":` **but I also believe that the earth is a kind of a self-regulating system**

Fig. 3. An example utterance incorrectly labelled

contains a lexical indicator of opinion. This would make annotation easier, in that when clear evidence of opinion was identified, this information could be added to the basic 'statement' annotation.

6 Discussion and Future Work

The task of labelling spoken, conversational data is clearly complex. Our error analysis has shown that some categories are difficult for humans and machines to separate. Perhaps this can be turned into a mechanism whereby we can have some automatic measure of the efficiency of coding schemes. One possible limitation of our error analysis is the question of whether the problems faced are specific to our classification approach. If the problems we report are common across a range of tagging approaches, this presents a stronger argument for merging categories. Stolcke *et al.* and Jurafsky *et al.* both indicate difficulties with the categories we identify as problematic.

We have shown that a simple dialogue act tagger can be created that uses solely intra-utterance cues for classification. This approach performs surprisingly well given its simplicity. However, in order to improve the performance of our classifier still further, it is clear that we need to make use of features outside of the individual utterance - such as DA sequence information. Clearly one next step is to pass these results to some machine learning algorithm, to exploit inter-utterance relationships. In the first instance, Transformation-Based Learning (TBL) will be investigated, but the attractiveness of this approach to previous researchers [5] was due in part to the tolerance of TBL to a potentially large number of features. We will use our classification method to pass as a single feature our suggested category for each utterance, without the need to represent the large set of word n-grams in the learning algorithm's feature set. If this proves successful we can use a far larger set of possible machine learning approaches to advance our classification performance.

References

1. Samuel, K., Carberry, S., Vijay-Shanker, K.: Automatically selecting useful phrases for dialogue act tagging. In: Proceedings of the Fourth Conference of the Pacific Association for Computational Linguistics, Waterloo, Ontario, Canada. (1999)
2. Webb, N., Hepple, M., Wilks, Y.: Dialogue Act Classification Based on Intra-Utterance Features. In: Proceedings of the AAAI Workshop on Spoken Language Understanding. (2005)
3. Stolcke, A., Ries, K., Coccaro, N., Shriberg, E., Bates, R., Jurafsky, D., Taylor, P., Martin, R., Ess-Dykema, C.V., Meteer, M.: Dialogue act modeling for automatic tagging and recognition of conversational speech. In: Computational Linguistics 26(3), 339–373. (2000)
4. Reithinger, N., Klesen, M.: Dialogue act classification using language models. In: Proceedings of EuroSpeech-97. (1997)

5. Samuel, K., Carberry, S., Vijay-Shanker, K.: Dialogue act tagging with transformation-based learning. In: Proceedings of the 36th Annual Meeting of the Association for Computational Linguistics and 17th International Conference on Computational Linguistics, Montreal (1998)
6. Jurafsky, D., Bates, R., Coccaro, N., Martin, R., Meteer, M., Ries, K., Shriberg, E., Stolcke, A., Taylor, P., Ess-Dykema, C.V.: Switchboad discourse language modeling project final report. Research Note 30, Center for Language and Speech Processing, Johns Hopkins University, Baltimore (1998)
7. Core, M.G., Allen, J.: Coding dialogs with the DAMSL annotation scheme. In: AAAI Fall Symposium on Communicative Action in Humans and Machines, MIT, Cambridge, MA (1997)
8. Meteer, M.: Dysfluency annotation stylebook for the switchboard corpus. Working paper, Linguistic Data Consortium (1995)
9. Webb, N., Hepple, M., Wilks, Y.: Empirical determination of thresholds for optimal dialogue act classification. In: Proceedings of the Ninth Workshop on the Semantics and Pragmatics of Dialogue. (2005)

Author Index

Lecture Notes in Artificial Intelligence (LNAI)

Vol. 3446: T. Ishida, L. Gasser, H. Nakashima (Eds.), Massively Multi-Agent Systems I. XI, 349 pages. 2005.

Vol. 3445: G. Chollet, A. Esposito, M. Faundez-Zanuy, M. Marinaro (Eds.), Nonlinear Speech Modeling and Applications. XIII, 433 pages. 2005.

Vol. 3438: H. Christiansen, P.R. Skadhauge, J. Villadsen (Eds.), Constraint Solving and Language Processing. VIII, 205 pages. 2005.

Vol. 3430: S. Tsumoto, T. Yamaguchi, M. Numao, H. Motoda (Eds.), Active Mining. XII, 349 pages. 2005.

Vol. 3419: B. Faltings, A. Petcu, F. Fages, F. Rossi (Eds.), Constraint Satisfaction and Constraint Logic Programming. X, 217 pages. 2005.

Vol. 3416: M. Böhlen, J. Gamper, W. Polasek, M.A. Wimmer (Eds.), E-Government: Towards Electronic Democracy. XIII, 311 pages. 2005.

Vol. 3415: P. Davidsson, B. Logan, K. Takadama (Eds.), Multi-Agent and Multi-Agent-Based Simulation. X, 265 pages. 2005.

Vol. 3403: B. Ganter, R. Godin (Eds.), Formal Concept Analysis. XI, 419 pages. 2005.

Vol. 3398: D.-K. Baik (Ed.), Systems Modeling and Simulation: Theory and Applications. XIV, 733 pages. 2005.

Vol. 3397: T.G. Kim (Ed.), Artificial Intelligence and Simulation. XV, 711 pages. 2005.

Vol. 3396: R.M. van Eijk, M.-P. Huget, F. Dignum (Eds.), Agent Communication. X, 261 pages. 2005.

Vol. 3394: D. Kudenko, D. Kazakov, E. Alonso (Eds.), Adaptive Agents and Multi-Agent Systems II. VIII, 313 pages. 2005.

Vol. 3392: D. Seipel, M. Hanus, U. Geske, O. Bartenstein (Eds.), Applications of Declarative Programming and Knowledge Management. X, 309 pages. 2005.

Vol. 3374: D. Weyns, H. V.D. Parunak, F. Michel (Eds.), Environments for Multi-Agent Systems. X, 279 pages. 2005.

Vol. 3371: M.W. Barley, N. Kasabov (Eds.), Intelligent Agents and Multi-Agent Systems. X, 329 pages. 2005.

Vol. 3369: V. R. Benjamins, P. Casanovas, J. Breuker, A. Gangemi (Eds.), Law and the Semantic Web. XII, 249 pages. 2005.

Vol. 3366: I. Rahwan, P. Moraitis, C. Reed (Eds.), Argumentation in Multi-Agent Systems. XII, 263 pages. 2005.

Vol. 3359: G. Grieser, Y. Tanaka (Eds.), Intuitive Human Interfaces for Organizing and Accessing Intellectual Assets. XIV, 257 pages. 2005.

Vol. 3346: R.H. Bordini, M. Dastani, J. Dix, A.E.F. Seghrouchni (Eds.), Programming Multi-Agent Systems. XIV, 249 pages. 2005.

Vol. 3345: Y. Cai (Ed.), Ambient Intelligence for Scientific Discovery. XII, 311 pages. 2005.

Vol. 3343: C. Freksa, M. Knauff, B. Krieg-Brückner, B. Nebel, T. Barkowsky (Eds.), Spatial Cognition IV. XIII, 519 pages. 2005.

Vol. 3339: G.I. Webb, X. Yu (Eds.), AI 2004: Advances in Artificial Intelligence. XXII, 1272 pages. 2004.

Vol. 3336: D. Karagiannis, U. Reimer (Eds.), Practical Aspects of Knowledge Management. X, 523 pages. 2004.

Vol. 3327: Y. Shi, W. Xu, Z, Chen (Eds.), Data Mining and Knowledge Management. XIII, 263 pages. 2005.

Vol. 3315: C. Lemaître, C.A. Reyes, J.A. González (Eds.), Advances in Artificial Intelligence – IBERAMIA 2004. XX, 987 pages. 2004.

Vol. 3303: J.A. López, E. Benfenati, W. Dubitzky (Eds.), Knowledge Exploration in Life Science Informatics. X, 249 pages. 2004.

Vol. 3301: G. Kern-Isberner, W. Rödder, F. Kulmann (Eds.), Conditionals, Information, and Inference. XII, 219 pages. 2005.

Vol. 3276: D. Nardi, M. Riedmiller, C. Sammut, J. Santos-Victor (Eds.), RoboCup 2004: Robot Soccer World Cup VIII. XVIII, 678 pages. 2005.

Vol. 3275: P. Perner (Ed.), Advances in Data Mining. VIII, 173 pages. 2004.

Vol. 3265: R.E. Frederking, K.B. Taylor (Eds.), Machine Translation: From Real Users to Research. XI, 392 pages. 2004.

Vol. 3264: G. Paliouras, Y. Sakakibara (Eds.), Grammatical Inference: Algorithms and Applications. XI, 291 pages. 2004.

Vol. 3259: J. Dix, J. Leite (Eds.), Computational Logic in Multi-Agent Systems. XII, 251 pages. 2004.

Vol. 3257: E. Motta, N.R. Shadbolt, A. Stutt, N. Gibbins (Eds.), Engineering Knowledge in the Age of the Semantic Web. XVII, 517 pages. 2004.

Vol. 3249: B. Buchberger, J.A. Campbell (Eds.), Artificial Intelligence and Symbolic Computation. X, 285 pages. 2004.

Vol. 3248: K.-Y. Su, J. Tsujii, J.-H. Lee, O.Y. Kwong (Eds.), Natural Language Processing – IJCNLP 2004. XVIII, 817 pages. 2005.

Vol. 3245: E. Suzuki, S. Arikawa (Eds.), Discovery Science. XIV, 430 pages. 2004.

Vol. 3244: S. Ben-David, J. Case, A. Maruoka (Eds.), Algorithmic Learning Theory. XIV, 505 pages. 2004.

Vol. 3238: S. Biundo, T. Frühwirth, G. Palm (Eds.), KI 2004: Advances in Artificial Intelligence. XI, 467 pages. 2004.

Vol. 3230: J.L. Vicedo, P. Martínez-Barco, R. Muñoz, M. Saiz Noeda (Eds.), Advances in Natural Language Processing. XII, 488 pages. 2004.

Vol. 3229: J.J. Alferes, J. Leite (Eds.), Logics in Artificial Intelligence. XIV, 744 pages. 2004.

Vol. 3228: M.G. Hinchey, J.L. Rash, W.F. Truszkowski, C.A. Rouff (Eds.), Formal Approaches to Agent-Based Systems. VIII, 290 pages. 2004.

Vol. 3215: M.G.. Negoita, R.J. Howlett, L.C. Jain (Eds.), Knowledge-Based Intelligent Information and Engineering Systems, Part III. LVII, 906 pages. 2004.

Vol. 3214: M.G.. Negoita, R.J. Howlett, L.C. Jain (Eds.), Knowledge-Based Intelligent Information and Engineering Systems, Part II. LVIII, 1302 pages. 2004.

Vol. 3213: M.G.. Negoita, R.J. Howlett, L.C. Jain (Eds.), Knowledge-Based Intelligent Information and Engineering Systems, Part I. LVIII, 1280 pages. 2004.

Printed in the United States
By Bookmasters